First Nations Cultural Heritage and Law

Law and Society Series
W. Wesley Pue, General Editor

The Law and Society Series explores law as a socially embedded phenomenon. It is premised on the understanding that the conventional division of law from society creates false dichotomies in thinking, scholarship, educational practice, and social life. Books in the series treat law and society as mutually constitutive and seek to bridge scholarship emerging from interdisciplinary engagement of law with disciplines such as politics, social theory, history, political economy, and gender studies. A list of other titles in this series appears at the end of this book.

First Nations Cultural Heritage and Law is the first of two volumes. The second volume is *Protection of First Nations Cultural Heritage: Laws, Policy, and Reform,* edited by Catherine Bell and Robert K. Paterson. Both are in the Law and Society series.

Edited by Catherine Bell and Val Napoleon

First Nations Cultural Heritage and Law

Case Studies, Voices, and Perspectives

UBCPress · Vancouver · Toronto

20 19 18 17 16 15 14 13 12 11 10 09 08   5 4 3 2 1

Printed in Canada on ancient-forest-free paper (100 percent post-consumer recycled) that is processed chlorine- and acid-free, with vegetable-based inks.

Library and Archives Canada Cataloguing in Publication

First Nations cultural heritage and law: case studies, voices, and perspectives / edited by Catherine Bell and Val Napoleon.

(Law and society series, 1496-4953)
Includes bibliographical references and index.
ISBN 978-0-7748-1461-4

1. Cultural property – Protection – Canada – Case studies. 2. Cultural property – Protection – Law and legislation – Canada. 3. Indians of North America – Legal status, laws, etc. – Canada. 4. Indians of North America – Land tenure – Canada. 5. Indians of North America – Material culture – Canada. 6. Native peoples – Material culture – Canada. I. Bell, Catherine Edith, 1961- II. Napoleon, Val, 1956- III. Series: Law and society series (Vancouver, B.C.)

E78.C2F47 2008   971.004'97   C2008-901790-0

Canadä

UBC Press gratefully acknowledges the financial support for our publishing program of the Government of Canada through the Book Publishing Industry Development Program (BPIDP), and of the Canada Council for the Arts, and the British Columbia Arts Council.

This book has been published with the help of a grant from the Canadian Federation for the Humanities and Social Sciences, through the Aid to Scholarly Publications Programme, using funds provided by the Social Sciences and Humanities Research Council of Canada.

UBC Press
The University of British Columbia
2029 West Mall
Vancouver, BC V6T 1Z2
604-822-5959 / Fax: 604-822-6083
www.ubcpress.ca

Contents

Preface: Respect for Elder Knowledge / vii
Eric McLay and Lea Joe interviewing Luschiim, Arvid Charlie
Dorothy First Rider, in consultation with Frank Weasel Head

Acknowledgments / xi

Introduction, Methodology, and Thematic Overview / 1
Catherine Bell and Val Napoleon

Part 1: Our Voices, Our Culture

1 Recovering from Colonization: Perspectives of Community Members on Protection and Repatriation of Kwakwa̱ka̱'wakw Cultural Heritage / 33
Catherine Bell, Heather Raven, and Heather McCuaig, in consultation with Andrea Sanborn, the U'mista Cultural Society, and the 'Na̱mgis Nation

2 The Law Is Opened: The Constitutional Role of Tangible and Intangible Property in Gitanyow / 92
Richard Overstall, in consultation with Val Napoleon and Katie Ludwig

3 Northwest Coast *Adawx* Study / 114
Susan Marsden

4 *'A'lhut tu tet Sul'hweentst* [Respecting the Ancestors]: Understanding Hul'qumi'num Heritage Laws and Concerns for the Protection of Archaeological Heritage / 150
Eric McLay, Kelly Bannister, Lea Joe, Brian Thom, and George Nicholas

5 Repatriation and Heritage Protection: Reflections on the Kainai Experience / 203
Catherine Bell, Graham Statt, and the Mookakin Cultural Society

6 *Poomaksin:* Skinnipiikani-Nitsiitapii Law, Transfers, and Making Relatives: Practices and Principles for Cultural Protection, Repatriation, Redress, and Heritage Law Making with Canada / 258
Brian Noble, in consultation with Reg Crowshoe and in discussion with the Knut-sum-atak Society

7 Protection and Repatriation of Ktunaxa/Kinbasket Cultural Resources: Perspectives of Community Members / 312
Catherine Bell and Heather McCuaig, in consultation with the Ktunaxa/Kinbasket Tribal Council and the Ktunaxa/Kinbasket Traditional Elders Working Group

Part 2: Experiences across the Nation

8 First Nations Cultural Heritage: A Selected Survey of Issues and Initiatives / 367
Catherine Bell, Graham Statt, Michael Solowan, Allyson Jeffs, and Emily Snyder

Part 3: Reflections on Selected Themes

9 Canadian Aboriginal Languages and the Protection of Cultural Heritage / 417
Marianne Ignace and Ron Ignace

10 Canada's Policy of Cultural Colonization: Indian Residential Schools and the *Indian Act* / 442
Dale Cunningham, Allyson Jeffs, and Michael Solowan

11 Owning as Belonging/Owning as Property: The Crisis of Power and Respect in First Nations Heritage Transactions with Canada / 465
Brian Noble

Concluding Thoughts and Unanswered Questions / 489
Val Napoleon

Appendix: Standard Question Set / 491

Contributors / 493

Index / 501

Preface: Respect for Elder Knowledge

Eric McLay and Lea Joe interviewing Luschiim, Arvid Charlie

Dorothy First Rider, in consultation with Frank Weasel Head

Throughout this project we have struggled with the issue of how to properly respect and acknowledge the expertise of elders. As we progressed through various stages of our work, it became apparent that elder knowledge is not well understood within academic institutions, nor is elder expertise properly compensated through funding mechanisms available to support academic research. Of critical concern is the implied hierarchy of knowledge associated with elders and other community experts through their treatment as "human subjects" and "informants" rather than as equals who bring knowledge that is different from, but equally important as, that offered by academic researchers.

Elder expertise may vary among First Nations, and elders are not experts in all areas. For this reason, and to ensure accuracy and to avoid exploitation, many First Nations have research protocols that are designed to provide assistance to outside researchers and to ensure that they speak to the right people, or a proper representative sample of the community, depending on the nature of the research question. Not all participants in this research are elders. However, all elders participating share in common a process of life-long learning, a willingness only to speak to matters within their knowledge (or to indicate where they are uncertain), and a respect within their communities for the knowledge that they have acquired not because of their age but because of their experiences and the teachings that have been passed on to them.

Part of the dilemma of compensation, as seen through the eyes of academic institutions, is the delicate balance between coercion and exploitation. Within the academic world, strict rules govern research involving human participants. Although honoraria are often paid, it is a woefully inadequate recognition of the expertise being shared. However, ethical rules governing academic work assume significant compensation may coerce people into participation and thus call into question the voluntariness of their consent. As we elaborate in the introduction and methodology section of this volume, research programs that provide direct community benefit and that enable First Nations input into interpretation of data and dissemination of results help alleviate some of these concerns.

The issues raised here are best understood in the words of the elders themselves and those who work closely with them. We ask you to keep the following remarks in mind as you read the contributions to this volume.

Acknowledging the Importance of Elders and Listening to Their Knowledge Today

From an interview conducted by Eric McLay and Leah Joe with Luschiim, Arvid Charlie, a Hul'qumi'num elder and member of the Cowichan Tribes, on 26 January 2006, in Ladysmith, British Columbia.

What is important about the elders? Well, as you know, up to now, we have been oral, meaning everything has been passed on orally. So, our knowledgeable elders are not only volumes of books, they're a whole library of knowledge. That's why the elders are important. To be listened to. They're *st'utulnamut – knowledgeable, totally knowledgeable.* We can compare them to a whole library. Some of them are several libraries put together. As you know, one library is kind of hard to have everything in there. So together, the elders are our whole libraries.

Sharing the teachings is important, but it's also important to know what teachings you can share. I've had a difficult time, because in my home – meaning my dad's and mom's side, they each have grandparents and great-grandparents – my home gets large quickly. Our teachings there – you teach or share your family teachings to your children, grandchildren, great-grandchildren. In today's world, I'm asked to go outside that.

I have great difficulty doing that. And I still do. But then when I look back and listen to my mom, her grandmother, Tth'ulxwmiyel [traditional name], Mary Victor from Hwlummi [Hul'qumi'num place name for Lummi], was put in the rez [residential] school back in the late 1800s. For some, they were left there all their growing life and lost their language and their teachings at that time. From then on, our teachings and language have been eroded. And not all families are fortunate enough to have somebody that carried that. That's how I was able to open, myself, the door to share the teachings. I'm still trying to keep that door open. Meaning that I'm having difficulty sharing, but when I'm called upon in the longhouse, school, or wherever somebody comes along for a visit, I have to try keeping that door open.

One of the ways that's done by our elders, I'm starting to practise that way, I guess I have always practised that way, when I hand somebody some teachings, I'll give a limited amount and see how they handle it and handle themselves. If they don't practise it, I won't share that much more with them. Some of the teachings that elders have shared with me, one really important one, it was thirty years before that one person shared more with me – an extension or continuation of that teaching. I was observed for that long on how I would handle myself and how I would use it. When he was satisfied that I would be using it the right way, he has been handing me this for the last twenty, twenty-five years. He's been adding to that one.

I think I'll go back to my opening remarks there and I'll add more to it. In the modern world, we can go to the library and books and study what we need to be knowledgeable about. Our oral history is such that we carry our knowledge and history with us in every one of those elders there.

Huy ts'eep q'a [Thank you]

Consultant Status for Elders

These remarks are offered by Dorothy First Rider, a member of the Motoki Society and Blood Tribe who works closely with the elders, in consultation with Frank Weasel Head, an elder of the Blood Tribe.

The elders have passed down the history and the teachings of the Blood Tribe from one generation to the next through oral transmission because the Blood Tribe has an oral language and not a written language. The elders since time immemorial have been the keepers of the history of the tribe and are responsible for the teachings of the traditions from generation to generation. Valiant attempts have recently been made to create a Blackfoot dictionary using the English orthography. However, in many cases there is no equivalent English for a Blackfoot concept. Problems with the English orthography have also proved that the Blood Tribe needs to continue relying on the oral teachings of the elders. Without a written language, the elders will continue to be the experts on various topics, ranging from Blood history, to proper alienation of artifacts, to entitlement and rationale for repatriation, among many others.

Unfortunately, the role of elders has not been recognized as equal to [that of] anthropologists, sociologists, archaeologists and other academics who have gained the status of experts in Blackfoot history and experiences. This is because the world of academics has a list of criteria that they take into consideration before a researcher is considered to be an expert on a certain "subject." Some of the criteria used for measuring expertise include graduate and postgraduate degrees and experience researching and studying human subjects utilizing recognized social science methodologies such as participatory research methods and qualitative and/or quantitative methodology.

What is not understood by the world of academics is that elders throughout the course of their lives receive the same levels of education in order to attain the status of learned elders. Within the Blood Tribe social structure, in order for an elder to reach the status of a learned elder and to be recognized as a learned elder, he or she will undergo traditional teachings from other elders from birth to grave. This is the true meaning of lifelong learning. These earlier years of teaching are equivalent to kindergarten. Those who continue to display interest may proceed to abide by elder teachings, attend Blood sacred ceremonies, and/or be involved on a peripheral basis only. This level is similar to that occupied by those taking general studies at university while working towards a degree. At some point the individual may make a decision to pledge to be the sole caretaker of a specific bundle, much as one decides on a specific discipline upon completion of general studies. An individual may choose to further his or her education by taking on additional bundles with other societies, much as one proceeds to graduate studies. After years of personal sacrifice and commitment, a person reaches the final level of recognition as a learned elder based upon lifelong learning, and this is similar to those who attain their doctorate.

Elders use their own form of participatory methodology to gain knowledge and to attain status. Upon acquiring this status, they are responsible for teaching the next group of upcoming elders. The Blood Tribe recognizes those individuals who have attained these teachings as learned elders not based upon their age, but based upon their experience and their understanding and knowledge of what they have been taught by elders before them. Learning the teachings of Blood elders is a lifelong process, and the transfer of bundles from one to another is a very expensive process. Individuals sacrifice personal belongings, material goods, and currency to take on such a responsibility to care for the knowledge and the bundles entrusted. They too make financial and personal sacrifices, like those who pursue an academic career.

Unfortunately, that is where the similarities end. Academics gain their teachings and receive their information from their "primitive" human subjects. Academics then go on to publish their research and are considered to be the "experts" in a particular field or a particular subject while learned elders are merely regarded as a resource.

Only in the last decade have elders begun to understand the unequal treatment of their levels of expertise as compared to the levels of expertise attained by academics who tapped into the knowledge base of elders. Elders spend hours of their time and endure the interruption of their personal schedules in order to give freely to those who go on to become renowned experts. The time has come for elders, as experts in their field, to be compensated adequately for the time they spend with external researchers – teaching them and sharing information and experiences – at the same level as professional consultants who get paid by the hour or by the day. The exploitation of elders by external researchers is no longer acceptable.

Acknowledgments

The initial idea for research leading to publication of this and its companion volume *(Protection of First Nations Cultural Heritage: Laws, Policy, and Reform)* emerged from a smaller research project conducted by Sonja Tanner-Kaplash and Associates and sponsored by the U'mista Cultural Society, First Peoples' Cultural Foundation, and the First Nations Confederacy of Cultural Education Centres. It would not have come about without the dedication of the late Linda Manz of Alert Bay (executive director of the U'mista Cultural Centre, 1992-2001), the late Lawrence Ambers (band manager of the 'Namgis Nation), and Chief Bill Cranmer ('Namgis Nation). The final design and its implementation was developed in collaboration with the U'mista Cultural Society, 'Namgis Nation, Gitanyow Hereditary Chiefs, Ganeda (Frog Clan) House of Luuxhon, Ktunaxa/Kinbasket Tribal Council, Oldman River Cultural Centre (Piikani Nation), Mookakin Cultural Society (Kainai Nation), and Hul'qumi'num Treaty Group. We owe a continuing debt of thanks to these partners for their support and active participation in this research. We also thank the First Peoples' Cultural Foundation and Hamatla Treaty Society for providing letters of support for funding applications, and we regret that Hamatla and the Nedo'at Hereditary Chiefs were unable to remain partners throughout the entire duration of the project.

We are grateful for the financial assistance received from the University of Alberta (Social Sciences Research Operation Grant), the Social Sciences and Humanities Research Council, and contributions from each of our First Nations partners. Robert K. Paterson (University of British Columbia) and Heather Raven (Nakasheohow, of the University of Victoria) also provided invaluable help in the initial stages of the research program. We also wish to acknowledge UBC Press and, in particular, Wes Pue (Law and Society Series) and Randy Schmidt for their encouragement and special accommodations that were made to ensure the meaningful participation of First Nations partners in the publication process.

Case studies contained in this volume are a rich source of information concerning protection, repatriation, and control of First Nations cultural heritage in Canada. We thank Heather McCuaig for helping to develop the case study methodologies, providing tools for communities to conduct this research, and for transcribing and coding case study data. We also thank the many community members involved in coordinating case studies, co-authoring reports, reviewing case studies, gathering data, transcribing, and translating. Of particular significance are the oral contributions and oral authorship of many elders, ceremonialists, and other community members who agreed to share information with us. Your knowledge and experience enables us not only to facilitate respect for, and greater understanding of, concerns relating to protection and repatriation but also demonstrates the importance of recognizing and respecting unique features of every First Nation's culture and the limits of external law reform. We acknowledge the contributions of the following people for each study contained in this volume.

1 *Hul'qumi'num Treaty Group:* We respectfully acknowledge the following elders and community members who shared their time, knowledge, ideas, and concerns: Ronald Alphonse, Amelia Bob (Cowichan Tribes), Joey Caro (Cowichan Tribes; HTG Research Director), Arvid Charlie (Cowichan Tribes), Simon Charlie (Cowichan Tribes), Roy Edwards (Chemainus First Nation), Florence Elliott (Cowichan Tribes), George Harris (Chemainus First Nation), Irene Harris (Chemainus First Nation), Sylvia Harris (Chemainus First Nation), Florence James (Penelakut Tribe), Bernard Joe (Cowichan Tribes), Mabel Mitchell (Chemainus First Nation), Ross Modeste (Cowichan Tribes), Sally Norris (Lyackson First Nation), Ray Peter (Cowichan Tribes), Ruby Peter (Cowichan Tribes), Edward Seymour (Chemainus First Nation), William (Charles) Seymour Jr. (Cowichan Tribes), August Sylvester (Penelakut Tribe), Richard Thomas (Lyackson First Nation), and Abner Thorne (Halalt First Nation). We also thank the Hul'qumi'num Board of Directors and team of researchers: Eric McLay, Brian Thom and Lea Joe (HTG), Kelly Bannister (University of Victoria), and George Nicholas (Simon Fraser University). Special thanks to Edna Thomas, Mabel Mitchell, and Arvid Charlie for editing and the translation of Hul'qumi'num words, and to Robert Morales, Joey Caro, and Arvid Charlie for transcriptions of interviews.
2 *Ktunaxa/Kinbasket Tribal Council:* We respectfully acknowledge and honour the following Ktunaxa elders and community members who shared their time, knowledge, ideas, and concerns: Violet Birdstone, Georgina Clarricoates, Diana Cote, Pat Gravelle, Troy Hunter, Allan Hunter, Christopher Horsethief, Wilfred Jacobs, John Nicholas, Nelson Phillip, Joe Pierre, Lucille Shovar, Margaret Teneese, Robert Williams, and Anonymous. We thank Heather Raven and Heather McCuaig for

work on the initial drafts and Laura McCoy for overseeing the case studies and conducting the interviews. We also thank Laura McCoy, Violet Birdstone, and Margaret Teneese for their assistance in designing questions for this study and reviewing drafts, as well as elders and members of the Ktunaxa/Kinbasket Traditional Elders Working Group for reviewing final versions of this study.

3 *The Ganeda House of Luuxhon and Gitanyow Hereditary Chiefs:* We respectfully acknowledge and honour the following members of the House of Luuxhon and other Gitanyow and Gitksan Houses authorized to speak about social institutions and legal process who shared their time, knowledge, ideas, and concerns with us: Godfrey Good (Gwinu), Robert Good (Sindihl), Ray Jones (Niis Noolh), the late Guy Morgan (Luuxhon), Don Russell (Luuxhon), Herb Russell (Ts'iiwa'), and Victoria Russell (Amsisa'ytxw). We thank Richard Overstall, Katie Ludwig, and Val Napoleon for their work designing this study; Richard Overstall for writing the study; and Katie Ludwig for interviewing, translating, and transcribing. We are also grateful for the assistance of the Gitanyow Hereditary Chiefs in administering the project and the feedback received from Glen Williams and Darlene Russell of that office.

4 *Mookakin Cultural Society:* We respectfully acknowledge and honour the following elders and spiritual leaders of the Horn Society and members of the Kainai Nation who shared their time, knowledge, ideas, and concerns with us, including Narcisse Blood, Adam Delaney, Francis First Charger, Martin Heavy Head, Mary Louise Oka, and Frank Weasel Head. We also thank Graham Statt for his work on initial drafts of the study; Dorothy First Rider and Annabel Crop Eared Wolf for coordinating this project; and Dennis First Rider, Dorothy First Rider, Shannon First Rider, Andrew Blackwater, and Louise Smith for helping with interviews, transcription, and translation. Special thanks to Annabel Crop Eared Wolf, Dorothy First Rider, Gerald Conaty, Adam Delaney, Martin Heavy Head, Mary Louise Oka, Frank Weasel Head, and members of the Mookakin Cultural Society Board of Directors for reviewing and commenting on final versions of this study. We also wish to thank Jack Ives for providing information on Alberta's repatriation legislation.

5 *Oldman River Cultural Centre:* We acknowledge the Brave Dog Society for supporting this research and providing protocols for its proper conduct. We respectfully acknowledge and honour the following elders, spiritual leaders, and members of the Piikani Nation, most of whom hold, or previously held, transferred rights, bundles, membership in societies, dances, songs, designs, games, piercing, fire and smudge tendering, and other specified ceremonial rights: Deborah Bad Eagle, Robert Bad Eagle, Sidney Bad Eagle, Mills Big Bull, Ricky Prairie Chicken, Geoff Crow Eagle, Anita Crowshoe, Heather Crowshoe-Hirsch, Reg Crowshoe, Rose

Crowshoe, Elizabeth Gallant, George Gallant, Kathleen Grant, Bryan Jackson, Sheena Jackson, Doris Many Guns, Gordon Many Guns, Herman Many Guns, Allan Pard, Pat Provost, Dexter Smith Jr., Dylan Starlight, and Naomi Windy Boy. Special thanks to Reg Crowshoe for organizing and conducting discussion circles and commenting on the case study. We thank Brian Noble for authoring the report and conducting discussion circles and Maria Crowshoe and Naomi Windy Boy for administration and transcription.

6 *U'mista Cultural Society:* We acknowledge and honour the following elders and Kwakwa̱ka̱'wakw community members who shared their time, knowledge, ideas, and concerns: Basil Ambers (Kwakiutl), Ethel Alfred ('Na̱mgis), Andrea Cranmer ('Na̱mgis), Bill Cranmer (Chief of 'Na̱mgis), Vera Newman, Christine Joseph (Tlowitsis), Peggy Svanik ('Na̱mgis), Emma Tamlin ('Na̱mgis), Spruce Wamiss (Quatsino), and William Wasden Jr. ('Na̱mgis). We also thank Andrea Sanborn (executive director of the U'mista Cultural Centre and member of the Ma'a̱mtaglia Nation) for coordinating this study, providing copies to participants and U'mista Board members for comment, and consulting on final versions; Juanita Pasco (former employee of U'mista); Stan Ashcroft and John Pritchard for sharing their knowledge about the specific claim against the federal government concerning harms flowing from the anti-potlatch laws and Guy Buchholtzer for sharing his work on repatriating linguistic material and the Kwakwa̱ka̱'wakw Centre for Language and Culture in Community (KCLCC). We also thank Barbara Cranmer for conducting interviews and focus groups, securing necessary research approvals, and preparing initial transcripts; Vera Newman for translations; and Lawrence Ambers for overseeing the project on behalf of the 'Na̱mgis.

7 We thank Susan Marsden, author of the "Northwest Coast *Adawx* Study." We respectfully acknowledge and honour the Gitksan and Tsimshian chiefs and matriarchs, whose powerful memories have preserved a record of thousands of years of Northwest Coast history, and especially the chiefs and matriarchs who told the *adawx* quoted in the Marsden report: the late Gitksan chiefs and matriarchs; John Brown, Kwiiyeehl, of the Gisgahaast Clan, Kispiox Tribe; Maggie Good, Xamlaxyeltxw of the Ganeda Clan, Gitanyow Tribe; Solomon Marsden, Xamlaxyeltxw, of the Ganeda Clan, Gitanyow Tribe (son and successor of Maggie Good); Stanley Williams, Gwisgyen, Gisk̲'ahaast Clan, Gitwingax Tribe; James Morrison, Txawok, of the Laxgibuu Clan, Gitanyow Tribe; Fred Johnson, Lelt, Ganhada Clan, Gitwingax Tribe; Martha Brown, Xhliyamlaxha, of the Laxgibuu Clan, Kispiox Tribe; Harriet Hudson, of the Kitselas Tribe; and the current chief, Art Mathews, Tenimgyet, of the Laxgibuu Clan, Gitwingax Tribe.

Research leading to publication has been conducted over a period of six years and would not have been possible without the help of many dedicated research assistants from various disciplines and universities. For work on the first volume, from the University of Alberta faculties of law, anthropology, and native studies, we thank Nduka Ahanonu, Adrienne Belch, Julia Buck, Clayton Cunningham, Esther de Vos, Nonnie Jackson, Allyson Jeffs, Clayton Leonard, Lisa Lehane, Robyn Mitchell, Heather McCuaig, Erin McGregor, Michael Sinclair, Brock Roe, Michael Solowan, Graham Statt, and Erin McGregor. We also thank Stephanie Gabel (University of Victoria) and Sarah Cooper, Maureen Keough, and Britt Vegsund (Dalhousie). Special thanks to Clayton Leonard for developing our website and to Kim Cordeiro, Gregg Dearborn, Clayton Leonard, Michael Sinclair, and Michael Solowan for maintaining it. We also thank Emily Snyder and Sheryl Savard for their assistance with final edits to the manuscript. As well, thanks to Jane for driving us to, and recording, our critical planning meetings in Alberta and British Columbia.

We acknowledge the authors of chapters in this volume who dedicated themselves to a truly collaborative research process. We are also grateful to many other First Nations and non-aboriginal organizations and individuals who helped us identify issues and commented on drafts of work posted on our website, including our survey report on issues and recent initiatives across Canada. You helped strengthen our conviction about the importance of our work and the need to raise awareness about issues of reform. Thank you also to Elder Jerry Wood for providing guidance and helping to facilitate the work in progress symposium attended by authors and First Nations partners.

As usual, we are indebted to Kim Cordeiro for the endless hours she devoted to this manuscript and for her grace under pressure. This book would not have been possible without her dedication and hard work. Finally, we wish to express our love and gratitude to our partners Wil Lawson and Darren Lesperance for their hugs and humour throughout the course of this research.

First Nations Cultural Heritage and Law

Introduction, Methodology, and Thematic Overview

Catherine Bell and Val Napoleon

Rationale and Content of Research

The last decade has witnessed an increased demand by indigenous peoples around the world for protection, repatriation, and control of cultural heritage in accordance with their laws and protocols, internal structures, and priorities.[1] The desire for increased control is inextricably linked to relationships with the land and is concerned with continuity, revival, and preservation of languages, spirituality, values, beliefs, and practices that help form a people's cultural and political identity.[2] In Canada, this has been acknowledged in modern land claims and treaty processes, negotiated agreements with government and private institutions, amendments to heritage conservation laws, policy initiatives, and, in Alberta, provincial repatriation legislation. However, rights of ownership, protection, and control enforceable in Canadian courts are also regulated by federal, provincial, and territorial legislation enacted prior to recognition and judicial consideration of unique aboriginal constitutional rights. Although some change has occurred in the administration of Canadian law and policy, particularly in northern Canada, and throughout Canada in the context of archaeological sites and ancestral remains, most heritage conservation and cultural property legislation is outdated and fails to expressly address the unique legal and moral rights and interests of the aboriginal peoples of Canada.

In its brief consideration of "Arts and Heritage," the Royal Commission on Aboriginal Peoples (RCAP) emphasized the importance of protecting aboriginal cultural heritage in the process of decolonization. It recommended that federal, provincial, and territorial governments work in collaboration with aboriginal organizations to review legislation affecting cultural heritage.[3] Before the RCAP, Canada engaged in some consultation concerning the creation of federal archaeological legislation. At the time of writing, research on federal legislation was also being conducted by Parks Canada. To be more responsive to aboriginal interests, British Columbia has also consulted on potential changes to its heritage conservation legislation.[4] Recent decisions of the Supreme Court of Canada have also generated new consultation policies within governments regarding developments affecting aboriginal interests in land. However, since the RCAP, national federal research initiatives have largely concerned intangible heritage. For example, Canada has consulted and commissioned research on the opportunities and limits of protecting indigenous knowledge within the existing intellectual property regime independent of, and in cooperation with, initiatives of the World Intellectual Property Organization. More recently, Canadian Heritage produced a series of discussion papers and hosted regional workshops to discuss issues relating to indigenous knowledge, language, and intellectual property.[5] Subject to these and a few other exceptions (including research in response to particular claims), little research and consultation has been conducted in Canada concerning aboriginal peoples' perspectives on Canadian cultural heritage law. These perspectives include questions regarding (1) the extent to which diverse cultural institutions, processes, priorities, and perspectives can (or cannot) be partnered and respected within Canadian law and (2) the benefits and detriments of engaging in heritage law reform within a pluralist democracy and Canadian legal system in which the rights and interests of the broader Canadian public must also be taken into consideration.[6] *First Nations Cultural Heritage and Law* is the first of two volumes arising from a research program commenced in June 2000 to explore these issues through collaboration, consultation, and academic analysis.[7] The research program was developed by Catherine Bell (principal researcher and coordinator) in response to concerns raised at First Nations conferences and by the first Protection and Repatriation Project sponsored by the U'mista Cultural Society (U'mista), the First Nations Confederacy of Cultural Education Centres, and the First Peoples' Cultural Foundation. U'mista initiated research because of the problems it encountered while seeking return of the Charles J. Nowell button and bead blanket exported for sale at Sotheby's in New York.

The broad objectives of the initial repatriation research were to draft a position paper on the need for protective legislation for items of spiritual, cultural, and historic importance to First Nations and to recommend strategies for action towards achieving this objective as well as preservation, maintenance, and protection.[8] Upon receipt of the preliminary strategy, education, and policy reports from Sonja Tanner-Kaplash and Associates, it became apparent that more detailed research and diverse expertise was required to explore the legal environment in Canada and the wide array of legal issues raised. As the primary concern for U'mista at the time was to address problems First Nations encounter in preventing exports of cultural items, the first project shifted its emphasis to examine in greater detail how the *Cultural Property Export and Import Act* might better serve the needs of First Nations.[9]

Some of the results of that work are discussed in the second volume. Catherine Bell undertook to seek more funding for a broader research program to be informed by First Nations experiences and shaped in consultation with U'mista, the 'Namgis Nation, and other First Nations partners.

Developed in collaboration with First Nations partners in British Columbia and Alberta and scholars in law, anthropology, and archaeology, our research is informed in part by community case studies. Our community partners are the Ktunaxa/Kinbasket Tribal Council (KKTC); the Mookakin Cultural Society (Mookakin) of the Kainai Nation (also known as the Blood Tribe, Kainai); the Oldman River Cultural Centre (in discussion with the Knut-sum-atak, or Brave Dog Society) of the Piikani (Peigan Nation, Piikani); the Frog Clan (Gitksan) House of Luuxhon (Luuxhon) and Gitanyow Hereditary Chiefs; the U'mista Cultural Society and 'Namgis Nation (home to the U'mista Cultural Centre); and the Hul'qumi'num Treaty Group (HTG). The broad objectives of the research are to: (1) provide First Nations participants with the opportunity to identify, define, and articulate their own concepts of property and law and their experiences relating to protection, repatriation, and control of their cultural heritage; (2) facilitate greater understanding and respect for diverse First Nations cultures, perspectives, and experiences; (3) create reflective case study reports with the potential for diverse uses and means of dissemination; (4) assist First Nations partners to collect data and to develop practical resources on cultural heritage issues that are of concern to their communities; (5) disseminate information about the operation, impact, and limits of the existing Canadian legal regime as it applies to First Nations cultural heritage; and (6) critically analyze domestic law within a broad international, social, political, and legal context. It is also intended that information gathered be used by our First Nations partners to develop strategies to address their cultural protection priorities.

Through case studies, this first volume identifies (1) a range of protection and repatriation issues faced by our First Nations partners and (2) strategies within and external to Western legal frameworks that may be used to address concerns raised. The case studies represent a range of participant understandings of, and experiences with, cultural heritage, legislation, repatriation and protection, and indigenous laws and processes concerning belonging, responsibility, and control. The case studies are organized thematically around data derived primarily from discussion circles and interviews with elders, ceremonialists, spiritual leaders, community members engaged in conservation, repatriation, and heritage protection activities, and others considered by their respective communities to be knowledgeable in cultural matters. An exception is Susan Marsden's "Northwest Coast *Adawx* Study," which draws on the formal oral histories of the Gitksan and Tsimshian peoples. Marsden's methodology did not include a case study; it derives from her extensive archival work and direct experience with the

Gitksan and Wet'suwet'en testimonies that were part of the landmark *Delgamuukw* aboriginal title case.[10] We decided that, given the widespread concern with oral histories generally and the expectations created by *Delgamuukw*, we should include this careful and critical chapter. Also included is a chapter that surveys selected repatriation and protection experiences across the country, including feedback generated from the project's website.[11] The case studies do not represent a generalized First Nations perspective. Indeed, all participants have emphasized the uniqueness of every First Nation in Canada and the need for more extensive consultation on these issues.

Some chapters also reflect more deeply on two themes arising from the case studies – the role played by residential schools and discriminatory government policy in loss of cultural knowledge and the centrality of language to cultural preservation. Brian Noble's chapter offers a segue into the analytical chapters in the second volume by (1) exploring what he identifies as a crisis in power and respect in Western law and property practices and (2) contrasting concepts of property, owning, and belonging within First Nations and Canadian legal contexts. All of the chapters begin to consider existing and potential legal responses to issues raised, the benefits and detriments of finding solutions in Canadian law, and other strategies for change.

In the second volume, *Protection of First Nations Cultural Heritage: Laws, Policies, and Reform*, legislation affecting tangible and intangible cultural heritage is considered along with issues of law and policy reform. Its chapters are informed by a range of sources in addition to the case studies, including developments in domestic common law, international law, and policy; literature reviews; contemporary and emerging ethical principles and policies in archaeology, anthropology, museum administration, and other relevant disciplines; and legal initiatives in other jurisdictions with colonial legal histories. Reflections on the revitalization of First Nations legal orders and laws, strategies for change outside the Western legal tradition, and critical commentary on the problems of using external legal mechanisms as a means to empower First Nations communities are also important features of the second volume. We hope that, together, both volumes will generate an awareness of challenges faced by our First Nations partners and provide helpful information to other indigenous peoples within and outside of Canada. We also hope the volumes will form a platform for much needed intercultural dialogue on issues of law reform.

Inherent Contradictions: Design, Terminology, Organization, and the Trickster

When discussing the role law might play in protecting First Nations autonomy and cultural heritage, understandably, several participants were not familiar with legal barriers to their heritage protection goals and questioned the utility of Canadian law reform. Basically, their experiences with legislation directed at First Nations people (such as the *Indian Act*)[12] were of oppression, and they saw a failure in the enforcement of general laws intended to protect heritage resources. Many desired to enforce, restore, or enact their own laws concerning cultural property protection. Francis First Charger echoes the concerns of some participants when he cautions, "We are beginning to move to the direction of the white man's ways ... Once we start doing that, then we are undermining our own ways."[13] However, greater First Nations control may require changing some features of the existing legal environment and restructuring relationships between First Nations, Canadian governments, and public institutions. Thus, despite reservations, the Mookakin Cultural Society and respected Kainai elders participated in developing Alberta's repatriation legislation, and the Hul'qumi'num call not only for respect for customary laws concerning their archaeological heritage but also for the reform and enactment of Canadian legislation. Other participants familiar with the inadequacies of legislation in specific areas, such as intellectual property and cultural export, also address the need for change. These examples demonstrate a tension running through our work. On the one hand, some participants do not want to engage Canadian law unless necessary, preferring instead to rely on indigenous laws; on the other hand, some participants also understand that statutory reform may be necessary to achieve First Nations cultural heritage goals. All call for mutual respect and cooperation.

As both volumes illustrate, cultural heritage issues are fundamentally about how societies understand their place in the world according to their cultural horizons. How we understand ourselves as peoples, and the institutions we build, are founded on our cosmologies and ontologies. The challenging work undertaken by the people involved in the case studies was to describe the constructs and meaning of their cultural heritage so that they may be appreciated by people from other cultures. For example, ownership is not a universal construct; rather, ownership sets out a particular relationship in our culturally constructed world. Brian Noble demonstrates this very clearly in his study of the Piikani. By describing ownership as belonging, he creates a different understanding of a Piikani relationship in a Piikani-constructed world.

This is similar to ideas of the sacred and the law. Ultimately, what is sacred and what is law is entirely bounded by culture. Law or the sacred is only law or sacred in the society that created it. For instance, law created by Gitksan peoples is not law for Cree peoples. If we are to understand these cultural constructs, we must situate them within the culture that created them and that gives them meaning: and, throughout this process, we must be aware of our own blinders and judgments. Basically, if we can see our own cultural scaffolding, including our ideas of the sacred, and understand how it forms us, then we have a better chance of understanding the scaffolding and the sacred in other cultures. So it is not a matter of trying to explain the sacred in other cultures but, rather, of developing an appreciation of how the sacred (or law) is created and how it makes sense inside that other culture. This is one of the overarching lessons of this research project.

Case study participants were also reluctant to speak about cultural heritage in language and discrete categories familiar to Western legal thought (*e.g.*, tangible, intangible, moveable, immovable, land, object, intellectual, and material). It appears that the problem lies not with the answers given, but with the questions being asked. In order for research to be both manageable in scope and congruent with the Canadian legal system, subject areas and questions were developed in consultation with First Nations partners.[14] The University of Alberta's ethics policy for conducting research with human participants also required prior approval of areas for questioning and intellectual categories for research. However, as Susan Marsden points out, despite the involvement of First Nations partners in designing the research questions, "[t]here is ... an inherent contradiction in the design of this project, namely that the issues were predefined in a non-aboriginal context."[15]

The very terms "culture," "property," and "ownership" are Western legal, social, economic, and political constructs that are imposed on First Nations. Given the consistent use of these terms in the literature, the dynamics of cultural interaction, and First Nations participation in the market economy, it is not surprising that most participants in this research now use and understand Western property terminology. However, to varying degrees and within specific contexts these terms are still incomprehensible (*i.e.*, no equivalent concept in First Nations languages), inappropriate (*i.e.*, disrespectful of First Nations concepts), or inadequate (*i.e.*, too narrow). Nevertheless, they continue to be used, though with qualification and explanation, in order to simplify communication and to give meaning to participant experience within a multicultural and legal pluralistic world.

The challenge of finding appropriate terminology is most pronounced in the discussion of defining "cultural property." For example, in his chapter, Richard Overstall explains how this concept "obscures Gitxsan law":

> [T]he concept of "cultural property" obscures Gitxsan law; that is, through its implicit assumption that a part of an indigenous legal culture can be carved out and separate from the rest of that culture. While this may be a valid approach to Canadian legal analysis – for example, looking at the obligations of museums to return certain artifacts or remains – it obscures the significance of objects, images, words, and inventions under indigenous law. Besides being possessions in their own right, many of the objects, and particularly the images, words, and music they contain, have a critical

> constitutional role in the indigenous law. Perhaps this would be less of a concern if there was a general familiarity with the indigenous legal system being considered, but this level of understanding has yet to be achieved.[16]

Similarly, from the *Poomaksin* chapter we learn that intangible "property" is also integrated and inalienable, one element from another. For example, "the transferred song for a teepee design; cannot be separated from the transferred bundle for that design nor can it be separated from the design itself" – a point echoed by Francis First Charger in the Kainai study.[17] To the Gitksan and Tsimshian, "[t]he term 'property' implies separation: this thing that I own is outside of me, is controlled by me, and can be taken from me. There is no equivalent concept in Gitksan and Tsimshian thought."[18] Moreover, "there is no separation between people and the cultural 'things' collectively called heritage, nor is there a separation between people and the world they inhabit."[19] Whenever possible, context-specific terminology is preferable. For example, as Reg Crowshoe explains, the term "Nitsiitapii property" is far more appropriate than is the term "cultural property" or even the very word "culture." He adds, "I would say there is our Nitsiitapii properties, whether it's cultural property or not, the word 'culture' is a white man's problem, not ours."[20] A similar disdain for the word "property" is acknowledged by Andrea Cranmer, who notes that the term is not used in the Big House or by the "well-versed cultural people in the community."[21] The term "cultural heritage" is preferred.[22]

After much deliberation, we decided to use the phrase "cultural heritage," rather than "cultural property," in the titles of our books because it has meaning in a range of legal and extralegal contexts.[23] It is broad enough to cover differing cultural understandings and the subject matter in both volumes while being succinct enough to be used in a book title. It is also consistent with most of the participants' perspectives. However, we use this phrase with a sharp awareness of its limitations, including how, within a Western legal context, more specific language may be required and importance is given to protection of rights characterized as proprietary in nature. Some authors continue to use the term "property" for this reason as well as in order to be clear in their references to particular laws and legal instruments.

Although we seek to communicate information in a manner that respects First Nations perspectives, we also seek to present our research in a way that is accessible to indigenous and non-indigenous readers and that has meaning in Canadian legal and policy contexts. The difficulties are evident not only in our choice of terminology but also in how we have organized the material in the two volumes. Since one of the objectives of publishing the case studies is to portray a wide array of individual First Nations experiences and perspectives, the studies include extensive quotations. However, they were edited for publication, and more detailed versions of some are on the project website. The case study reports are published independently so that the information shared is not obscured or lost in the legal academic analysis contained in the second volume. In that volume, the chapters are organized along more conventional lines, according to the expertise of the academics involved: repatriation and trade in First Nations material culture, heritage sites and ancestral remains, intangible heritage, human rights, and First Nations legal orders and law. These chapters respond to those in this volume mainly through the topics examined and the use of examples from the case studies to illustrate points raised.

There is also a more fundamental question of whether Canadian law can help further First Nations goals without continuing the colonization of indigenous ways of knowing and being. As experienced in the administration of the *Native American Graves Protection and Repatriation Act*[24] in the United States, the administration of rules intended to benefit indigenous peoples can give rise to unanticipated effects. Given this, it is important to consider both the benefits and detriments of using Canadian law as a tool to address what is, in essence, a question of "respectful treatment of native cultures and indigenous forms of self-expression within mass societies."[25] We also struggle to reconcile the belief that First Nations should be able to exercise jurisdiction over aspects of their own cultural heritage with consideration of the interests of the broader Canadian public. Several participants recognized this dual approach and the need to build respectful coexistence. However, the practical realities of the economic, legal, and political landscape in Canada – combined with (1) the vital role cultural heritage has in survival of a people, (2) the consistent refusal by governments to recognize First Nations jurisdiction over intellectual property and heritage resources located off reserve lands, and (3) the cost, time, and complexity of negotiating jurisdiction over the range of areas raised in this research – all serve to bring us back to thinking about Canadian legislation and policy reform.

To remind us of the contradictions, tensions, and limitations in our work, Val Napoleon introduces the intellectual instrument of the Trickster into both volumes. The Trickster "is a central figure in the myth worlds of many hunting and gathering societies. A divine figure, but deeply flawed and very human, the *Trickster* is found in myth cycles from the Americas, Africa, Australia, and Siberia ... The *Trickster* symbolizes the frailty and human qualities of the gods and their closeness to humans. These stand in pointed contrast to the omnipotent, all-knowing but distant deities that are central to the pantheons of state religions and their powerful ecclesiastical hierarchies."[26] It is our hope that the Trickster will enable us to see contradictions and perhaps even to intellectually straddle cognitive dissonance in order to move our thinking along.

In indigenous societies, the Tricktser is not simply a literary device (as it often is in Western society, where literature is, at least conceptually, separate from politics, law, and economics); rather, it is an intellectual device that provides a way of seeing and thinking that does not separate politics, law, and economics from the fabric of the whole. As such, the Trickster is both a teacher and challenger of norms, be they legal, political, or social. This is why the Trickster is a part of these volumes. The critical work of the Trickster lies in the discomfort s/he creates. It is in our discomfort that we see things that we are not used to seeing and think what we are not used to thinking. Consequently, we urge the reader to stay with any discomfort that these volumes may create.

Methodology

First Nations participation, at all stages of the research program, has been an important aspect of this project. This has involved three key components: participation in research program design and preparation of funding applications; participation in case study research, design, development and authorship; and comment on, or authorship of, academic essays that draw on case studies and other sources. In particular, the case study methodology was informed by the following principles: production of practical and tangible benefits for First Nations partners; creation of reflective texts with the potential for diverse uses and broad dissemination; compliance with First Nations laws and protocols; active and meaningful participation by First Nations partners in design and development of research questions and outcomes; and regular communication throughout.[27] Research progressed in three stages over a period of six years: conceptualization and preliminary consultations, data collection, and, finally, analysis and publication.

Academic research has been "applied" to First Nations for many years. Research has been an integral part of the colonization that placed First Nations communities in the petri dish as research objects. Geared to primarily non-indigenous audiences, the standard premise was that research *on* aboriginal peoples was of universal benefit and so direct local impacts need not be considered. In contrast, the collaborative approach to research that we have adopted is consistent (to the extent possible within the constraints imposed by universities and funding agencies) with what, in the social sciences, is generally referred to as participatory action research (PAR).[28] Multidisciplinary influences have characterized this research method as a "systematic inquiry that is collective, collaborative, self-reflective, critical and undertaken by participants in the inquiry."[29] Ortun Zubert-Skerritt outlines four themes in this methodology: "empowerment of participants; collaboration through participation; acquisition of knowledge; and social change."[30] Gough continues, "When defined as a goal of research with collaboration of those involved, PAR can be used to assist in the reappropriation of cultural knowledge" by providing "the opportunity to reflect, maintain, and advance First Nation cultural values."[31] Critical questions that must be addressed in this methodology are: Whose research is it? Who owns it? Whose intentions does it serve? Who will benefit from it? Who has designed its questions and framed its scope? Who will carry it out? Who will write it up? How will the results be disseminated?[32]

At the beginning of our research project we planned and developed our strategy, organized the research team, created an international bibliography on cultural heritage law, established First Nations partnerships, drafted the case study proposals and grant applications, and commenced the preliminary research. With funding provided by the University of Alberta, Catherine Bell and Heather Raven (Nakasheohow) visited First Nations communities in British Columbia and Alberta that had expressed concerns about cultural heritage or were engaged in repatriation and protection initiatives. Local meetings were held with cultural heritage staff, elders, society members, band councillors, and other representatives responsible for overseeing cultural research in their communities. Topics discussed included research goals (broad and community specific) and outcomes; phases and time lines; short-term community benefits and long-term benefits of research and publication; community research protocols and authorization processes; the role of the case studies; community resources for the project; budgets (for equipment and interviewers, translators, interpreters, and other participants); research experience and training materials; culturally appropriate methods to gather and record information and consents; selection of participants; disposition of data on completion of research; copyright, data ownership, and anticipated published outcomes; and potential risks of participation. Subject areas for the interview questions and processes involving human participants were also discussed, with the understanding that questions could change to reflect local heritage protection priorities, practical community information needs, and differing cultural understandings.[33] Questions selected served as a general guide to structure dialogue and allowed for more narrative responses and elaboration of topics that participants thought most relevant to the broad subject areas.

Following the preliminary meetings, Catherine Bell and Robert K. Paterson prepared a detailed research proposal that was provided to all First Nations partners for comment prior to submission for funding to the Social Sciences and Humanities Research Council of Canada (SSHRC). In-kind and other funding commitments by First Nations partners helped support the research and were included in the application. Upon notification of SSHRC funding, each partner was contacted to confirm continued interest and again invited to modify case study questions to suit particular research interests and methodologies. Mookakin, KKTC, and U'mista made minor modifications to their original question sets to accommodate the range and expertise of people interviewed and specific initiatives in their communities, including language protection initiatives and enactment of repatriation legislation. For the Luuxhon study, a unique set of questions relating to intangible possessions and laws about oral history were designed in an attempt to avoid "the imposition of Western state constructs of property and ownership."[34]

It was at this later point that the HTG joined the research program because, while the Hamatla Treaty Society continued to support the project, it had to withdraw due to unexpected developments in treaty negotiations. The HTG developed a unique question set to address three specific objectives of its study: to articulate Hul'qumi'num customary laws relating to historically significant places, artifacts, and human remains; examine current problems relating to respect and enforcement of Hul'qumi'num customary laws; and explore how the legal environment might be changed.

The primary methods for gathering case study data were individual interviews and facilitated discussion circles. Where interviews were conducted in the First Nation's language, community members were hired as translators and transcribers. Community case study coordinators and interviewers, or academics with existing relationships with the First Nation, conducted the interviews and facilitated the discussions. A training workbook was prepared and reviewed with all interviewers to ensure consistency of data collection and reporting, and compliance with university ethics requirements. Nevertheless, some transcripts were reformatted and tapes were compared to transcripts, which were provided to the research team to ensure accuracy. While most case studies engaged between fifteen and twenty-five participants, the design for the Luuxhon and Kainai studies involved fewer people. With Luuxhon, only Luuxhon members or those closely related persons have the authority to speak on behalf of the House. Similarly, for the Kainai, only members of the Horn Society (recognized among the Blood Tribe for its spiritual leadership in the Sundance) and members of the Mookakin Cultural Society (established to promote and preserve the spiritual doctrine of the Blood Tribe and engage in repatriation activities on behalf of the tribe) were interviewed.

The Blood Tribe, KKTC, and U'mista had files and archival materials that were reviewed to help formulate questions and give context to information gathered. The HTG study drew on materials and experiences related to litigation and treaty negotiation. Electronic and printed community materials and some academic papers were also consulted in several of the case studies.

Data analysis began with Catherine Bell and her assistants reading a subset of interview transcripts from various communities to identify key words, phrases, and themes contained within them. The case study authors also read all transcript data relating to their case studies in order to identify themes and to organize individual participant responses. Where a large number of interviews were conducted, special software (Nudist 6) was used to code and organize transcript data according to the themes identified. The first drafts of the case study reports contained extensive quotes from transcripts.

These drafts were provided to the originating communities and the authors of the second volume, and, upon approval, most were posted to our project website. One of the objectives of the initial drafts was to organize as much of the transcript data as possible for use at the community level and to include enough information in each study report to ensure that its evolution, purpose, and methodology were properly understood. As some of the original reports were quite lengthy and repetitive in places, they were edited for publication. The common methodology descriptions were removed and summarized in this introduction.

In our original vision, interviews and discussions were to be audio-visually recorded. Our hope was to produce audiotapes for each community archive derived from their specific case studies and an edited video of all case study interviews that might be used for educational or other purposes. However, few participants felt comfortable with video recordings. Consequently, we did not obtain sufficient footage to achieve this latter goal. Although some participants interviewed want their information kept in local archives so that maximum control over use can be maintained, others have given permission for transcript data and tapes to be donated to a public archive to be determined in consultation with our First Nations partners.

Important questions in collaborative work are: Who will write it up? And how will authorship be acknowledged? This project was built upon preexisting relationships between academics and members of participant First Nations organizations. Thus, early in the process, the First Nation decided who would write up the case study. In all the case studies, the expertise of the case study authors and community coordinators, combined with the knowledge of local protocols, built a foundation of trust and helped to ensure that appropriate community members were consulted. Authors for the academic chapters in the two volumes were approached to participate according to their areas of expertise.[35] Biographies of these people, plus the general area of research they intended to explore, were provided to First Nations partners in our initial meetings. First Nations partners were also advised of changes in the research team. Community partner representatives and these researchers later met to discuss draft papers.

A more complicated question is how to acknowledge authorship in a manner that respects oral traditions and reflects a truly collaborative process. The Kainai study addresses this issue by including Mookakin as an author. In other studies, this is dealt with by specifying that the studies were developed in consultation with a specific First Nation individual or organization. For practical reasons, it became difficult to name all people who made oral contributions to this project as authors. However, if requested, we would have been prepared to do this despite the challenges it would have created for publishing and making standard contract arrangements for authors' copies, copyright, and allocation of royalties. In the end, we decided that all participants who chose to be identified would be included in the acknowledgments; First Nations partner organizations or designated individuals from partner communities would hold joint copyright to case studies with the authors named (to the exclusion of the publisher); every community would receive not only transcripts and tapes originating from their community but also free published volumes issuing from the research; and royalties would be donated to a First Nation organization in Canada.

Drafts of all transcripts and case studies were provided to participants and other authorities within the community for review and comment on the use and analysis of transcript information. While an effort was made to maintain the actual words used and the natural flow of thoughts, excerpts from transcripts have been lightly edited using ellipses and square brackets, where necessary, to clarify meaning. Authors attended meetings to review the case studies when requested. In the community review processes, no suggestions were made to change meaning or use of data, even when disagreement over points of view were raised. However, passages identifying people by name or circumstance were removed from some studies. Subject to this exception, all comments from First Nations partners and participants pertained to the control of information (discussed further below), accuracy of the transcript, typographical errors, and, if interviews were conducted in languages other than English, matters of translation, spelling, conceptual understanding, and proper use.

During the data-gathering phase, we created a project website and contacted all First Nations cultural education centres, tribal councils, treaty organizations, and other First Nations governments and organizations in Canada about our work.[36] We invited these groups to participate in the research by using outcomes posted on the website (such as case studies, bibliographies, and background reports prepared for our research) and to contribute their own thoughts through electronic submissions. A few electronic submissions were received from the United Sates, Nova Scotia, Ontario, Yukon, British Columbia, Manitoba, and Saskatchewan. Catherine Bell, Robert K. Paterson, and other research team members also participated in various international and national conferences and workshops at the invitation of First Nations and government officials in British Columbia, Saskatchewan, Quebec, Ontario, New Zealand, and the United States. We also received suggestions from people who visited our website and were involved in protection and repatriation initiatives discussed in our survey chapter. Information and feedback gathered from these processes is incorporated into the survey chapter in Part 2 and chapters in the second volume.

One response identified what was perceived to be an application of Canadian law to First Nations spiritual matters. Although when explained fully, it was understood that this was not our intent, this response underscores the importance of addressing issues of First Nations jurisdiction and recognizing the diversity of First Nations perspectives on matters of external law reform. If reform occurs, it is also important to explore the possibility of optional legislative frameworks and how to incorporate different positions within them.

In the final stages of our research program, we completed wide-ranging literature and case reviews and prepared the academic chapters for the two volumes. In a working group session with representatives from our First Nations partners we shared preliminary drafts and disseminated them for comment. We prepared a thematic review of the case studies and distributed it. We offered the complete manuscript to elders' councils and other local authorities for review. At this time, we also submitted it to the publisher for review.

Challenges in Meeting Our Objectives

We have already elaborated one of the biggest challenges in our work – communicating through using terminology that respectfully incorporates First Nations understandings and is cognizable to the non-indigenous legal world. Many other challenges have arisen in our attempt to work in true partnership and collaboration. These challenges include reconciling academic independence and meaningful First Nations participation, working within university and funding policies, and managing limited resources and complex approval processes within First Nations communities. It is beyond the scope of this introductory chapter to elaborate on all of the challenges we have faced. Our purpose in sharing these is not to discourage collaborative research but, rather, to illustrate the commitment required and the importance of encouraging academic institutions, publishers, and funding agencies to negotiate new approaches to research and products of research that increase indigenous control of indigenous information. Our methodology is not perfect and will not work in all partnerships, but we hope it will generate some helpful lessons. In the end, each partnership must be negotiated independently to meet the needs of the parties involved.

There is often an assumption in mainstream academic research that objective truth can be discerned through impartial analysis of a range of data. Given this, credibility in academia means that conclusions are not influenced by the research subjects who may or may not agree with the interpretation of data gathered from or about them. However, in order to decolonize research methodologies we must ensure that First Nations communities and researchers participate in the interpretation of data derived from their communities or lands. For most First Nations groups, this includes not only those participating in interviews and discussions but also local or regional authorities charged with the task of overseeing any research initiatives that relate to the group.

For this project, the rights of the interview and discussion participants were governed by standard ethical procedures that allowed them, at any time, to withdraw information provided. Similar principles were applied to First Nation authorities charged with approving the case studies. To avoid potential problems, for example where a participant might wish his or her information included in the research but the appropriate First Nation authority did not, participants were advised of the approval processes that affected them and of how the proposed disagreements would be resolved. Participants were already aware of, and supported, these internal authorization processes. Although critics may argue that this could have influenced the information shared, First Nations internal research protocols must be respected. Further, such criticism assumes that a First Nations authority might try to dictate what should be said or attempt to revise the reports to meet political goals – an assumption that proved false in our experience and, in fact, ran contrary to the intent of First Nation protocols applied to this work.

Ultimately, we decided that all project participants and, where appropriate, First Nations authorities would be given copies of their own transcripts and case studies for comment and, as requested or required by local research protocols, drafts of all chapters produced for publication in the two volumes. In the event of disagreement about the use and interpretation of data on the part of an approving authority, we agreed that the authors would not use the information in dispute but that different points of view on interpretation of the data would be clearly articulated. All authors were asked to agree to this process before case study data was given to them. We also agreed to make it clear in the introduction to both volumes that case studies represent perspectives of the participating community members but that other chapters that draw on case studies and other sources of information reflect the opinions of the authors and not necessarily those of all communities engaged in the project. First Nations partners also retained the right to withdraw use of portions or all of the case studies. In our experience, there has been a willingness of all involved to respect academic independence. All chapters were eventually discussed at a workshop with representatives from First Nations partners and/or were circulated for comment. None of our partners identified areas of significant disagreement or chose to withdraw; rather, a wide range of voices is heard because of the time spent defining expectations, the independent publication of case studies, and the diversity of opinions offered in these volumes.

Two issues that arose in the initial and final phases of our research demonstrate the challenges of complying with community protocols and addressing the consequences of this within an academic and publishing environment. While it is important to obtain band council approval for research conducted in some communities, band councils are often not the appropriate entity to oversee and approve all forms of research. For example, the KKTC research protocol requires that research requests be reviewed by the Elders

Group, the Ktunaxa Treaty Council, and the KKTC. The latter two bodies provide comments and advice, but the authority to approve or deny research remains with the Elders Group. Our research revealed that this process may need to be modified slightly depending on the length and nature of the publication (*e.g.*, not all members of an elders group may be able to read lengthy documents in English and summaries may be required). Complying with internal processes can also be time consuming and cause a delay in the publication of outcomes. Depending on the length, sensitivity, and complexity of a manuscript and the methods of communication preferred by First Nations partners, several meetings may be required. This can cause problems in complying with granting agency timelines for expenditure of funds as well as recognition of academic work within institutions that evaluate performance on the basis of annual publications. It also requires publishers to exercise flexibility in the review process and to acknowledge the importance of including First Nations processes in academic refereeing procedures.

Identifying the appropriate authority is more complex when official research protocols have not been developed. For example, among the Gitanyow, cultural information and entitlements belong to the House groups. Given this, the proper authority to share and approve information is not the Office of the Gitanyow Hereditary Chiefs but, rather, the hereditary chief, Luuxhon, on behalf of the Luuxhon House members. Similarly, among the Piikani, only people with properly transferred rights to leadership and communal ceremonials have the authority to discuss matters raised in that study. It is therefore necessary to appreciate the appropriate authority structures within a First Nation group before preliminary consultations can even commence. The issue can be further complicated by changes in local government or internal conflicts between authority structures. Further, typical ethical procedures require written consents from participants or, where justified, recorded verbal consents. The latter is usually provided through reading and recording a script and having consent recorded on tape. Under Piikani protocol, the fact that the Brave Dog Society bundle holders hosted a circle discussion and agreed to be recorded indicates approval to use the information given.

Another example illustrates some of the challenges of trying to conduct collaborative research that respects First Nations communication processes and interests in controlling accurate and respectful use of their cultural information. In a typical publishing contract, copyright is assigned to the publisher or retained by authors and editors with the publisher. In our study, we wanted First Nations partners to have greater control over issues of reproduction and royalties associated with copyright. Consequently, we decided that the copyrights to the case studies would be held jointly by the author, the editors of the first volume, and the appropriate First Nation partner. Therefore, it was necessary to identify an individual or entity recognized in

Canadian law. For example, the House of Luuxhon is an entity recognized within the Gitksan legal order but not within the Canadian legal order. Finally, we needed to find a publisher willing to surrender copyright to the case studies in this fashion and to donate royalties to an organization of our choice.

Our approach to information control had to be reconciled with rules of funding agencies and universities with respect to ownership of data derived from research during the course of employment. It was our view that First Nations partners and participants should, to the extent possible, control use of transcripts and tapes issuing from their communities. We dealt with this in three ways: we required that (1) all tapes and transcripts used by case study authors be returned to the research coordinator and kept at the University of Alberta unless participants agreed otherwise; (2) ethics procedures approved by affected universities include the right of individual participants to determine disposition of data, including data retained by the researcher and the provision of copies to partner organizations; and (3), where necessary, in order to enable us to adopt this approach, other opinions on relevant contractual provisions be sought. We also advised participants and partners that any item deposited in a public archive would be clearly marked by us as intended for research and educational purposes only but that we could not guarantee this use restriction.

The subjects of copyright and publication also demonstrate the challenge of trying to communicate within a different cultural and linguistic context. For example, in preliminary meetings it was clear that Mookakin had an interest in ensuring that information gathered would be used in a respectful way that would promote the preservation of Blackfoot culture. Although interest was expressed in copyright, the concept of copyright is not capable of addressing the responsibilities of individuals towards use of information and the understanding that "ownership" of information rests with the Creator. In the final stages of research it also became apparent that "publication" did not have the same meaning for the case study author and one of the partner representatives. This misunderstanding gave rise to the impression that original goals had changed. Coupled with concerns over the ability to reuse words in their original form (an important issue in oral cultures) and the nature of copyright protection, these problems resulted in several meetings concerning publication of the Kainai study. It was ultimately decided that Mookakin would hold copyright to the study and that the lead author would continue to work with Mookakin as desired on legislative reform. It was also agreed that publication for an audience wider than the Blood Tribe was important to ensure that voices of knowledgeable community members – not just the sometimes inaccurate and misleading voices of academics – would be heard on matters of cultural heritage.

Happily, through creative thinking, good will, commitment, and cooperation on the part of the affected universities, First Nations partners and participants, authors, SSHRC, and UBC Press, we were able to overcome many of the challenges we faced. However, these challenges point (1) to a need for more time and resources to develop and implement collaborative research initiatives and (2) to the importance of a flexible regime to accommodate methodologies committed to increasing indigenous participation in, and control over, the products of research.

Part 1: Our Voices, Our Culture

Case studies produced in this volume cover a wide range of topics. Although each has a different emphasis, certain themes emerge. What follows is a thematic introduction to the case studies and the subject areas discussed in the academic chapters in the two volumes. We adopt this approach to highlight connections between the two volumes as well as to introduce the content of the first volume.

General Observations

A meta-theme running throughout is the need to restructure relations (some more than others) in a manner that acknowledges and respects unique First Nations identities and is consistent with First Nations values, beliefs, laws, and practices. Such a paradigm shift involves acknowledging past injustices as well as embracing a dynamic concept of cultural heritage by supporting cultural continuity and revitalization both in word and deed. Though implicit in any discussion of First Nations cultural heritage, several case studies explicitly address the damaging effects of colonialism, the notorious residential school system, and, in particular, the *Indian Act*, which sought to destroy indigenous culture through, among other things, bans on the potlatch and Sundance ceremonies. In the words of Diana Cote:

> [T]he *Indian Act* took our culture away and as a result of that we are in the situation that we're in right now, which is we have unhealthy members in our community. We have lost our culture. We have sad families because it took that ability to be a family away. So it's probably the worst thing that ever happened to the First Nations people in Canada.[37]

Just as important as correcting past injustices is the need to support and enhance cultural expression among present and future generations. The message in this volume is that, while colonialism endeavored to destroy First Nations cultures, these cultures have survived by the sheer strength of resolve among their peoples. All community participants interviewed are committed to revitalizing their cultures and restoring that which Western society sought to colonize. Protection and repatriation of both tangible and intangible cultural heritage is viewed as important for revival and continuity of cultural knowledge, practices, laws, and, ultimately, cultural awareness, identity, and self-esteem among the peoples.

In advocating for respect and understanding of First Nations identities, laws, practices, and protocols, some participants expressed frustration over the many hurdles encountered, which took the form of biases and prejudices inherent in the Western worldview. A fundamental point expressed by many is the need to recognize the distinctiveness of First Nations cultures. There is also concern that First Nations laws, which many feel should govern matters of cultural heritage, are not given equal standing in Canadian law and negotiations and that, instead, they are constantly adapting to conform to Western legal concepts and values. In the courts, Western academic credentials are privileged over indigenous credentials. Experiences shared also demonstrate that similar challenges may arise in repatriation negotiations with some institutions wherein Western institutional knowledge is considered to be more accurate than First Nations knowledge. Bias towards documentation may also undermine protection for sacred sites. As Arvid Charlie, Luschiim, explains, in keeping with Hul'qumi'num traditions, there are few written records of things sacred to the people. This can result in the erroneous conclusion that the Hul'qumi'num simply don't have sacred areas.[38]

Participants also speak about relationships of belonging and responsibility to material culture, which can have individual, familial, and communal aspects. As Gloria Cranmer Webster explains, the Kwakwa̲ka̲'wakw "concept of ownership differs from that of other people in that while an object may leave our communities, its history and the right to own it remain with the person who inherited it."[39] Similarly, participants in the Ktunaxa study argue that, based upon their cultural connection to a cultural item and irrespective of how an item was removed from the Ktunaxa territories, the Ktunaxa Nation may maintain a superior claim to the item over non-Ktunaxa citizens. Moreover, as the authors of the Kainai chapter note:

> [T]he concept of communal property and the responsibilities that arise from individual relationships with spiritual objects extend to many forms of spiritual inheritance, whether involving land, objects, or intangible information, and this makes it difficult to use the term "ownership" in any context relating to cultural heritage. Rather, individuals acquire rights and responsibilities of use through clearly defined transfer processes.[40]

The Luuxhon report describes House relationships to tangible and intangible possessions, noting that, while it is the House chief who holds these items, the chief does not have a personal property right in the possessions *per se*; rather, the chief has the responsibility to hold and protect the House's tangible and intangible property in trust on behalf of the House members.

Several participants are frustrated by how their relationships to cultural heritage are viewed by non-indigenous people. For example, participants are critical of non-aboriginals who romanticize the communal aspects of "ownership" among First Nations and wrongly assume that there are no family or individual entitlements and responsibilities. For some First Nations, strict transfer protocols regulate the passing on of rights and responsibilities of possession and use of everything from ceremonial bundles, names, songs, dances, and knowledge to hunting and gathering territories and sacred sites. Only those who possess the proper entitlement may make a transfer, and failure to follow protocol results in an illegal transfer. It is on this basis that some seek repatriation of cultural items, noting the irrelevance of deeds of title and receipts of payment according to their indigenous laws.

The effects of colonialism – epidemics, dwindling resources, cultural interactions, Christian conversion, and the *Indian Act* – have resulted in adaptation and undermining of indigenous laws (this is not to suggest that indigenous laws were unchanging). For example, the U'mista report relates how the borrowing and singing of family songs by non-family members is common today, although permission is sought and original ownership acknowledged. The KKTC report notes that the need to educate members and reverse cultural loss has resulted in the acknowledgment of a communal interest in items to which families of origin have primary entitlement.

Repatriation and Trade in Material Culture

Rationales for repatriation vary and are rarely offered in isolation, but some are emphasized more than others. For example, repatriation efforts of the Blood Tribe are explained as part of a broader struggle for recognition of religious and cultural freedoms. However, this emphasis on sacred and ceremonial objects does not reflect a lack of interest among the Blood for repatriation of other material culture. In contrast, participants in the U'mista and KKTC studies make it clear that ceremonial use, although important, is not the primary rationale for repatriation efforts in their communities. For the House of Luuxhon, possession and control of the use of images on certain items may be of greater significance than repatriation of the object itself.

Cultural continuity is a common refrain in discussing repatriation goals. Cultural knowledge of the objects, not only the objects themselves, is important. For example, Vi Birdstone explains that, when "cultural items were sold and placed in museums, we lost a lot of our traditional cultural knowledge."[41] She elaborates, pointing out that knowledge is "placed ... far away, where most of our people will never get to and never see. And our children will never see them. So, they don't have a connection to the culture and that's, that's severed."[42] For her, the return of representative samples of material, such as duck decoys and baskets, is important because of the knowledge they represent. Participants in the U'mista study agree and also frame repatriation as a means of redress for injustices brought about by the potlatch ban. Repatriated cultural items are building blocks that may be used to restore and strengthen the cultures that colonialism endeavoured to destroy.

Participants express mixed emotions concerning museums. Several express gratitude to museums for preserving their material culture, and some note that such measures would not have been necessary had their culture not been taken from them in the first place. Until full repatriation is achieved, and regardless of whether repatriation is pursued, a common sentiment is that museums and First Nations need to work as equal partners in caring for, displaying, and interpreting cultural items. An example of this is the partnership between the Mookakin Foundation and the Glenbow Museum for the use and, ultimately, full repatriation of ceremonial items, as well as co-management or complete Kainai control over specific uses and treatments of other material, depending on its nature, that the Glenbow continues to hold. There are many other examples of positive partnerships between museums and First Nations.

The case studies also indicate that relations between museums and First Nations have substantially improved and that a new ethic of collaboration has been adopted in Canada. Positive relations hinge on respect, mutual understanding, open communication, and compromise. First Nations have been working hard with museum personnel and museums have been developing responsive programs and policies. However, there are still barriers to overcome. For example, the Piikani report notes that *how* museums return items is just as important as *that* they return them.[43] Too much emphasis on documentation and independently verifiable sources may be viewed as evidencing a lack of respect for community experts and oral traditions. The discretionary nature and diversity of museum repatriation policies, the scope of items eligible for return, and the conditions imposed on the return of non-ceremonial items are other examples given to illustrate how museums have more power in negotiations than do First Nations groups. The Kainai and U'mista chapters note that underlying sources of fear, museum mandates, and issues of legal liability may affect "the tone of negotiations, direct the actions of the parties involved, or alter the spirit of communication surrounding repatriation discussions."[44] However, these concerns are not as dominant in contemporary Canadian negotiations.

Funding is always a concern. Costs associated with locating items and negotiating and facilitating their return are significant. Some participants discuss how the cost of constructing and operating museum-like facilities and training staff may also place repatriation beyond the realm of possibility for many First Nations and be viewed as inappropriate costs for certain materials by others. International repatriations add additional costs to, and difficulty in, locating items, as do private repatriations. This, of course, assumes that the private collectors actually agree to sell, since there are no laws requiring them to part with the items. Like domestic repatriations, international repatriations may also generate unique challenges, such as laws that forbid repatriation and positions that regard collections as part of the heritage of humankind, wherein preservation in museums ensures maximum access. Specific concerns include poor communication and lack of notification; the necessity of purchasing, and the significantly inflated prices of, cultural items that a First Nation is fortunate to discover but are intended for export; and lack of sufficient funding to make such purchases.

Repatriation of Ancestral Remains

Repatriation of ancestral remains is a theme common to the Hul'qumi'num, KKTC, and Kainai case studies. All describe it as an emotionally charged issue. While protocols surrounding the care for ancestors vary among these groups, there is a common sentiment that human remains and the land surrounding them are to be left undisturbed. Respect for one's ancestors is the value that grounds the requirement for following proper protocols when handling ancestral remains. Respect is also what makes repatriation a necessity.

It should come as no surprise that participants who discuss ancestral remains consider the storage and mistreatment of remains as contrary to concepts of human dignity and respect for the dead. Some call for equal rights so that First Nations remains will be treated with the same degree of respect afforded to non-aboriginal remains – nothing more, nothing less. This should apply equally to museums that store human remains in drawers and private citizens who showcase human skulls as candle holders. As Chris Horsethief explains:

> I don't care who has them or where they came from. I don't care if they came out of a National Park. If they're human remains and you know where they came from ... then they have to be returned ... Somebody has got to come forward and say this is a basic human right ... Our people are in boxes. They're labelled with numbers.[45]

Many museums and other institutions are sensitive to the concerns of First Nations and are willing to repatriate human remains, but problems remain. For example, internal laws prevent the Blood Tribe from viewing or hand-ling remains. At the other end of the spectrum, Hul'qumi'num participants discuss their customary laws regarding the inherited right to care for the dead. Similarly, a Ktunaxa participant explains that certain individuals hold specialized knowledge concerning protocol that must also be followed. Both the HTG and KKTC chapters address the issue of funerary material and insist that such items cannot be separated from the remains and must also be repatriated. There are also fears that interfering with the dead can have spiritual and physical repercussions in the here and now. However, most participants do not speak specifically to this issue.

More generally, as with repatriation of material culture, resources and community readiness to receive repatriated remains are common concerns. Escorting remains home and reburial according to First Nations protocol is costly. Who should pay is the subject of discussion in both the institutional and the private-sector (*i.e.*, land developer, collector) contexts.

Heritage Sites

A strong and intimate connection to the land is a theme common in all of the case studies. So strong is that connection that, when asked what sites need to be protected, a common answer is "all of them." Many participants struggle with the notion that only specific sites can be earmarked for special protection because many areas hold aspects of their history and identity and are considered vital for the continuation of cultural practices and knowledge. An exception is the HTG report, which focuses on burial grounds: "In fact, the subject of burials so dominated the discussions of heritage issues, that if other site types were mentioned during the interviews, it was usually only as an indirect reference to their importance as burial locations."[46] When asked, other First Nations partners concur that burial grounds are particularly important, along with sacred sites, and are most in need of special consideration and protection.

Serious concerns are expressed over the lack of respect given to First Nations cultural heritage and burial sites by the general public, government officials, developers, and some archaeologists. The HTG report, in particular, places significant emphasis on this point. The Hul'qumi'num people express a strong conviction that their ancestors and ancestral places must be respected, but they perceive that their heritage is "not publicly valued in British Columbia."[47] The message is that First Nations burial grounds should receive the same respect as do non-aboriginal cemeteries.

Failure to enforce heritage protection legislation is cited as evidence of the low value placed on First Nations cultural sites and burial grounds. The perception is that lack of public, and therefore political, will is what lies behind this inactivity. Private interests are seen to continually supersede First Nations protection efforts, and development is the trump card against which First Nations have little recourse. For example, some Hul'qumi'num elders are convinced that the roots of this disrespect may be found in colonialism and the continued public disdain for aboriginal title claims to Hul'qumi'num territory.

Knowledge of indigenous legal orders and law, protocols, sincerity, and spiritual connection are prerequisites for proper site protection and, according to some interviewees, may only be found within the First Nations. Some participants explain that unfettered access to ceremonial places, traditional hunting and gathering territories, and rights of removal are also needed both on private lands and in parks. Moreover, First Nations must have a role in interpreting cultural sites, receive proper external acknowledgment of their connection to the land, and have the power to restrict access to sacred places.

Participants who spoke to the utility of heritage protection legislation emphasize the inadequacy of existing laws and, in particular, lack of enforcement. When sites are disturbed, notification to affected First Nations is not always given. In general, the impression is that First Nations are only given a minor consultative role in heritage management. Moreover, sacred sites are not easily protected by conventional legal approaches because site identification may conflict with confidentiality requirements, and identification increases the risk of exploitation.

Language as the Core

Given the oral nature of First Nations cultures, it is not surprising that language is identified for the primary role it plays in shaping First Nations peoples' identities, culture, history, and connection to their land. According to William Wasden Jr., "It's what makes us Kwakwa̱ka̱'wakw. The name says it all: Kwak'wala-speaking people. And I don't know what we are going to call ourselves after if we don't, if we're not speaking our language."[48] Without the language one's history is lost. As John Brown, Kwiiyeehl of the Gisgahaast (Fireweed) Clan of the Kispiox Tribe of the Gitksan, explains:

> It was customary to transmit the *adawx* so that they may be preserved. A group that could not tell their *adawx* would be ridiculed with the remark, "What is your *adawx*?" And if you could not give it you were laughed at. What is your grandmother's name? And where is your crest? How do you know of your past, where have you lived? You have no grandfather. You cannot speak to me because I have one. You have no ancestral home. You are like a wild animal, you have no abode. *Niiye'e* and *adawx*, grandfather and history are practically the same thing.[49]

Without that oral record, identification of traditional territories and ownership rights are jeopardized. Transmission of traditional knowledge, rights, and entitlements is also stymied by one's inability to understand and speak the language. Language revitalization is identified as a prerequisite for all other aspects of cultural continuity and restoration. For example, the central role of songs in ceremonial practice and transfer protocol is premised on an understanding of the language. Elizabeth Gallant explains this interrelationship:

> [T]hat's what's so important, when they can understand the language and sing the songs. The spirits that come to us do not understand English, they don't sing in English: but they do understand Blackfoot language and songs, and that's why it's so important that Blackfoot be learned. That's when we can.go back to our way of life and our religion. And this is how they [children] will learn as they grow, and will know our way of life.[50]

Given the central role language plays in First Nations cultures, increasing the number of language speakers is a primary concern, as is the need to transmit and record cultural knowledge before knowledgeable elders pass on. Participants agree that it is important that all members of the community receive language training and education; however, the studies note a particular emphasis on training youths.

Cultural Appropriation and Copyright

Questions fashioned in consultation with First Nations partners concerned with the issue of cultural appropriation and copyright focus much of the discussion on proper use of, and entitlement to, songs, names, designs, and crest images. Examples of appropriation take various forms, such as improper access to sacred information or songs and unauthorized taking, use, modification, reproduction, or recording contrary to the indigenous laws of the First Nation in question. For example, Troy Hunter notes:

> A good example of that is the use of the word *"Nipika."* That's our word for, like, [the] Creator. And there's companies that use that word ...[T]o me it's no different than if we were to call the casino that we just opened up, say, the "Holy Mary Jesus Christ Casino" or something like that.[51]

Although many First Nations have their own laws concerning proper use and control of names, words, and other intangible heritage, such laws are usually orally based. A difficult question for many is whether some laws need to be written down in order for them to be recognized and clearly communicated outside the community. Even then, Canadian law may not offer the type of protection sought.

While commercial enterprises are frequent offenders, appropriation by academics is also a serious concern. Further, the Canadian intellectual property regime fails to address First Nations concepts and law pertaining to ownership and control of intangible cultural heritage. Rather than assisting in protection, copyright law is seen by some participants to facilitate cultural appropriation by non-aboriginals and even, ultimately, to restrict the ability of First Nations to practise their own culture. This sometimes arises from misunderstanding of copyright law.

Strategies for Repatriation and Protection

The case studies stand for the proposition that First Nations partners want greater control over their culture, in all its manifestations, for the simple reason that it is theirs and that they are best equipped to care for and protect it. Some participants explain that they are tired of adapting to non-indigenous structures and having the government dictate their culture to them. As Allan Hunter elaborates, some participants want jurisdiction over their cultural heritage as well as the ability to enact laws where First Nations laws do not exist and to have those laws fully recognized:

> Right off the bat, Ktunaxa law, we need to create our own laws, and then have them recognized by other governments and have them incorporate it into their laws. Something like that. [B]ut rather than changing their laws and looking at their laws and how we want their laws to fit us, we need to create our own laws.[52]

In addition to freeing themselves from government control, some participants also comment on the need to free themselves from reliance on outside "experts" and to reclaim faith and trust in their own communities to protect their culture. There is a recognition that dependency on Western ways is undermining their own ways. As Andrea Cranmer explains:

> Action needs to be taken, enough asking, enough of having people com[ing] and telling us what they think we should do, non-native people and linguists and you name it. We don't need that. We know what we need to do. We need to put our trust into our own people [so] that we can do the job of saving our language, of teaching our children, of preserving our history, of keeping the U'mista Cultural Centre open, because it's important. And we don't need people coming in to tell us that. And what really irritates me is that we pay them such big dollars to do that. It's so silly.[53]

Increasingly, First Nations are controlling research by assuming the role of researcher and implementing research protocols and codes of conduct. Formal written protocols are discussed in the Kainai, U'mista, and KKTC studies. Central to these protocols is a concern for parity between researchers and the First Nation, and the assurance that the latter will benefit from the research. Guidelines must allow First Nations to act as gatekeepers: they must be allowed to control the use of their knowledge and to correct misunderstandings and misrepresentations of their culture.

Building positive relationships with museum and government personnel, the scientific community, resource developers, and others, and educating them in First Nations law and practices, are essential steps towards protection and repatriation. Ideally, these will be lasting relationships built on collaborative negotiation, equality, and moral responsibility; however, some participants acknowledge that power imbalances may sometimes prevent the achievement of this goal. The general consensus of those who speak to the issue is that existing Canadian law is ineffective. Reluctance by some participants to rely on Western law reform to address these problems is caused, in part, by the tendency of Western law to ignore distinctions among First Nations cultures and a perception that legislation will impose inflexible rules that hamper relationship building. Acceptance of legislative reform hinges on First Nations having an active role in its creation and implementation rather than simply, in the name of "consultation," receiving a copy of the draft law prior to first reading. For those participants who emphasize the importance of respecting First Nations laws, successful legislative proposals will be those that validate, enable, and enforce First Nations laws. In essence, what is called for is an intercultural dialogue between First Nations law and Canadian law.

Repatriation, cultural revitalization, and heritage protection are costly. Participants are unanimous in their call for more resources to assist with protection and repatriation efforts. They speak about the significant costs associated with location, negotiation, and return of cultural items and remains. In their view, these costs are properly borne by, or at least contributed to by, the government that forced them to hand over their cultural items, the institutions that acquired and benefited from their removal, and the developers and other private parties who have uncovered First Nations ancestors and disturbed cultural sites in their exploitation of the land. A similar sentiment is shared with respect to funding for language training. First Nations communities would not be incurring great cost to save their language if not for the assimilative policies of the federal government.

Acknowledgments

The authors gratefully acknowledge the research assistance of Michael Solowan and Erin McGregor in preparing a thematic overview of the case study data.

Notes

1 In 1995, United Nations Special Rapporteur Dr. Erica Irene Daes proposed a definition of heritage for the purpose of developing international principles and guidelines for the protection of indigenous heritage. See Commission on Human Rights, Sub-Commission on Prevention of Discrimination and Protection of Minorities, *Final Report of the Special Rapporteur:*

Protection of the Heritage of Indigenous Peoples, UNESCOOR, 47d Sess., UN Doc. E/CN/.4/Sub.2/1995/26 (1995). First Nations cultural heritage includes land, language, objects, and knowledge pertaining to a particular First Nation or its territory. Marie Battiste and Sákéj (James Youngblood) Henderson explain in *Protecting Indigenous Knowledge and Heritage* (Saskatoon: Purich Publishing, 2000) at 65 that indigenous understandings of cultural heritage are not restricted to historical manifestations of knowledge or material heritage and are best understood as that which "belongs to the distinct identity of a people." This definition is consistent with the range of issues and understandings of "cultural property" raised by participants in the research leading to this volume. The struggle to find appropriate terminology that respects First Nations understandings and has meaning within a Canadian legal context is addressed in further detail below and in most of the chapters in this volume.

2 See *e.g.* Miriam Clavir, *Preserving What Is Valued: Museums, Conservation, and First Nations* (Vancouver: UBC Press, 2002); Tamara Bray, ed., *The Future of the Past: Archaeologists, Native Americans, and Repatriation* (New York: Garland Publishing, 2001); Marie Battiste and J. Sákéj Henderson, *Protecting Indigenous Knowledge and Heritage* (Saskatoon: Purich Publishing, 2000); Terri Janke, *Our Culture: Our Future – Report on Australian Indigenous Cultural and Intellectual Property Rights* (Sydney: Australian Institute of Aboriginal and Torres Strait Islanders and the Torres Strait Commission, 1998); and Bruce Ziff and Pratima Rao, eds., *Borrowed Power: Essays on Cultural Appropriation* (New Brunswick, NJ: Rutgers University Press, 1997).

3 Canada, *Report of the Royal Commission on Aboriginal Peoples: Gathering Strength,* vol. 3 (Ottawa: Supply and Services Canada, 1996) at 599-601.

4 *Proposed Act Respecting the Protection of Archaeological Heritage in Canada* (Communications Canada, 19 December 1990). The proposed federal legislation was never enacted for a variety of reasons, including concerns raised by aboriginal organizations about insufficient consultation and failure to include aboriginal ownership of archaeological resources. Again issues concerning First Nations ownership and jurisdiction resulted in disagreement in the BC review. In the end, a section was included in the amended legislation to enable agreements between First Nations and the province concerning cultural preservation and protection of sites and objects. See *Heritage Conservation Act,* R.S.B.C. 1996, c. 87. For further discussion see Catherine Bell, "Aboriginal Claims to Cultural Property in Canada: A Comparative Analysis for the Repatriation Debate" (1992) 17 Am. Indian L. Review 457 at 495-97; Catherine Bell and Robert K. Paterson, "Aboriginal Rights to Cultural Property in Canada" (1999) 8:1 Int'l J. of Cult. Prop. 167 at 187 and 192-93.

5 See *e.g.* Simon Brascoupé and Howard Mann, *A Community Guide to Protecting Indigenous Knowledge* (Ottawa: Research and Analysis Directorate, Department of Indian Affairs and Northern Development, 2001). See also discussion papers prepared for *Traditions: National Gatherings on Indigenous Knowledge* (2005), online: Canadian Heritage <http://www.traditions.gc.ca/ docs/docs_disc_e.cfm>.

6 A few books have been published in Canada that critically assess the extent to which the rights, needs, and interests of indigenous peoples are addressed through Canadian courts, domestic and international heritage laws, and law reform. See *e.g.* Michael L. Ross, *First Nations Sacred Sites in Canada's Courts* (Vancouver: UBC Press, 2005); Rosemary Coombe, *The Cultural Life of Intellectual Properties: Authorship, Appropriation and the Law* (Durham, NC: Duke University Press, 1998). Battiste and Henderson, and Ziff and Rao, *supra* note 2, also discuss Canada's legal regime within a broader discussion of international law and the experiences of indigenous peoples. In 1992, the Canadian Museums Association and Assembly of First Nations also released a report that considered input from museums and First Nations organizations and made recommendations relating to improving relations between museums and First Peoples, including recommendations for repatriation. See Assembly of First Nations and Canadian Museums Association, *Turning the Page: Forging New Relationships between Museums and First Peoples,* 3d ed. (Ottawa: Canadian Museums Association, 1994). There are many books, articles, and reports on indigenous cultural heritage issues and several that critically assess the application and reform of international laws and domestic laws in the United States and Australia. See *e.g.* Michael Brown, *Who*

Owns Native Culture? (Cambridge, MA: Harvard University Press, 2003), which also contains a list of sources on "Indigenous Cultural Rights" at 299; and Terri Janke, *supra* note 2. Of these, Terri Janke's work is framed by consultations and collaboration with indigenous peoples and organizations in Australia. A bibliography of some of the sources used in this work can be found on the project website, *infra* note 11.

7 The second volume is also published by UBC Press. See Catherine Bell and Robert K. Paterson, eds., *Protection of First Nations Cultural Heritage: Laws, Policy, and Reform* (Vancouver: UBC Press, 2008).

8 The aboriginal peoples in Canada include Indian, Inuit, and Métis peoples. Our research is concerned with Indian Nations, also referred to in Canada as First Nations. Sonja Tanner-Kaplash and Associates Inc. was hired to conduct the initial research and Catherine Bell was retained as an advisor to U'mista and the research team, which included Val Napoleon, co-editor of this volume, Dr. Eldon Yellow Horn, and Brenda Beck.

9 R.S.C. 1985, c. 51.

10 *Delgamuukw v. British Columbia,* [1997] 3 S.C.R. 1183.

11 See <http://www.law.ualberta.ca/research/aboriginalculturalheritage>. This website contains, among other things, more detailed community versions of case studies and background research documents, including a review of Canadian legislation, workshop proceedings, and original case study proposals. The Hamatla Treaty Society and Nedo'at Hereditary Chiefs were also original partners in this study but had to withdraw as a result of other unexpected priorities that arose in their communities.

12 R.S.C. 1985, c. I-5. Earlier versions expressly ban cultural practices such as the Sundance and potlatch. See Dale Cunningham, Allyson Jeffs, and Michael Solowan, "Canada's Policy of Cultural Colonization: Indian Residential Schools and the *Indian Act,*" c. 10, this volume at 442.

13 Catherine Bell, Graham Statt, and the Mookakin Cultural Society, "Repatriation and Heritage Protection: Reflections on the Kainai Experience," this volume at 209.

14 See appendix at page 491 of this volume.

15 Susan Marsden, "Northwest Coast *Adawx* Study," this volume at 114.

16 Richard Overstall, in consultation with Val Napoleon and Katie Ludwig, "The Law Is Opened: The Constitutional Role of Tangible and Intangible Property in Gitanyow," this volume at 93.

17 Brian Noble, in consultation with Reg Crowshoe and in discussion with the Knut-sum-atak Society, "*Poomaksin:* Skinnipiikani-Nitsiitapii Law, Transfers, and Making Relatives: Practices and Principles for Cultural Protection, Repatriation, Redress, and Heritage Law Making with Canada," this volume at 272; *supra* note 13 at 229-30.

18 *Supra* note 15.

19 *Ibid.* at 114-15.

20 Noble, *supra* note 17 at 291: "Nitsiitapii: 'real people' is a term designating how Blackfoot recognize themselves by their socio-cultural practices, laws, and relationships with the Creator," this volume at 259.

21 Catherine Bell *et al.*, in consultation with Andrea Sanborn, the U'mista Cultural Society, and the 'Na̲mgis Nation, "Recovering from Colonization: Perspectives of Community Members on Protection and Repatriation of Kwakwa̲ka̲'wakw Cultural Heritage," this volume at 39.

22 *Ibid.* For further discussions of issues of terminology, see Lyndel V. Prott and Patrick J. O'Keefe, "'Cultural Heritage' or 'Cultural Property?'" (1992) 1:2 Int'l J. Cult. Prop. 307.

23 See *e.g. supra* notes 1 and 2.

24 25 U.S.C.A. ss. 3001-3013 (West Supp. 2000).

25 Brown, *supra* note 6 at 10. Focusing on controversies concerning sacred sites and intangible expressions of indigenous heritage, Brown emphasizes that this goal is best advanced through approaches that acknowledge the "inherently relational nature of the problem," including "judicious modification of intellectual property law, development of workable policies for protection of cultural privacy, and reliance on the moral resources of civil society." For discussion of potential negative effects of law reform and NAGPRA, see *e.g.* Brown at 213; the Kainai case study, *supra* note 13 at 220-23 and 225 (Frank Weasel Head). This issue is also

discussed in several chapters in the second volume, Catherine Bell and Robert K. Paterson, eds., *Protection of First Nations Cultural Heritage: Laws, Policy, and Reform* (Vancouver: UBC Press, 2008).
26 Richard Lee and Richard Daly, eds., *The Cambridge Encyclopedia of Hunters and Gatherers* (Cambridge: Cambridge University Press, 1999) at 4-5.
27 Particulars relating to modification of case study methodologies are discussed in the relevant studies in this volume.
28 See *e.g.* Linda Smith, *Decolonizing Methodologies* (New York: Zed Books, 1999).
29 R. Rappoport, "Three Dilemmas in Action Research" 23:6 Human Relations at 499 as cited in James McKernan, *Curriculum Action Research: A Handbook of Methods and Practices for the Reflective Practitioner* (London: Kogan, 1991) at 4.
30 Ortrun Zubert-Skerritt, "Improving Learning and Teaching through Action Learning and Action Research" (Paper presented to the HERDSA Conference, 1992, University of Queensland) [unpublished] at 2, cited in Meagan Gough, *Repatriation as Reflection of Stó:lô Cultural Values: Tset Tháyeltxwem Te lálém S'olh etawtxw (We Are Building a House of Respect)* (MA Thesis, Department of Sociology and Anthropology, Carleton University, 2004) [unpublished] at 2.
31 Gough, *ibid.* at 30.
32 *Supra* note 28 at 10, cited in Gough, *ibid.* at 14.
33 *Supra* note 14.
34 *Supra* note 16 at 95.
35 Unfortunately, indigenous legal scholar June McCue (University of British Columbia) had to withdraw. We acknowledge and appreciate her contributions to the earlier phases of this research program. Kelly Russ (Haida lawyer and member of the Canadian Human Rights Commission) participated in our research symposium but was unable to contribute to the publication.
36 *Supra* note 11.
37 Catherine Bell and Heather McCuaig, in consultation with the Ktunaxa/Kinbasket Tribal Council and Ktunaxa/Kinbasket Traditional Elders Working Group, "Protection and Repatriation of Ktunaxa/Kinbasket Cultural Resources: Perspectives of Community Members," this volume at 354.
38 Eric McLay *et al.*, "*'A'lhut tu tet Sul'hweentst* [Respecting the Ancestors]: Understanding Hul'qumi'num Heritage Laws and Concerns for Protection of Archaeological Heritage," this volume at 151.
39 Gloria Cranmer Webster, "The Potlatch Collection Repatriation" (1995) Special Issue U.B.C. L. Rev. 137 at 141, as cited in *supra* note 21 at 70-71.
40 *Supra* note 13 at 225.
41 *Supra* note 37 at 316-17.
42 *Ibid.*
43 This is also emphasized in the HTG and KKTC chapters in relation to the return and internment of ancestral remains.
44 *Supra* note 13 at 233.
45 *Supra* note 37 at 350.
46 *Supra* note 38 at 157.
47 *Ibid.* at 173.
48 *Supra* note 21 at 43.
49 *Supra* note 15 at 115.
50 *Supra* note 17 at 273.
51 *Supra* note 37 at 328.
52 *Ibid.* at 357.
53 *Supra* note 21 at 61-62.

Part 1: Our Voices, Our Culture

In the land that is now Virginia, the Monacan Trickster is the Great Rabbit Chief known as Bobtail. This Trickster is a "moral trope designed to teach the normative ideal, mores, and morals through reverse psychology."[1] He is international and contemporary – irreverently showing up in the Supreme Court of Canada[2] and in obscure editorial discussions about the aggressive actions of Israelis and Palestinians.[3] Bobtail gets a kick out of the cosmopolitan Tricksters and has been doing some travelling himself around the beautiful lands now called Alberta and British Columbia.

And Bobtail is reading and listening. There's a lot of interesting stuff happening, especially about cultural heritage and aboriginal peoples. This involves law and tradition. Bobtail considers: "Tradition can be the dead faith of living people, or the living faith of dead people. If Indigenous traditions are not regarded as useful in tackling contemporary concerns and recognized as applying in current circumstances, then they are nothing but the dead faith of living people."[4] Bobtail picks up another book: "Tradition means giving votes to the most obscure of all classes, our ancestors. It is the democracy of the dead. Tradition refuses to submit to the small and arrogant oligarchy of those who merely happen to be walking about."[5] And another: "[I]f our people, institutions, and ideologies have relevance beyond our boundaries, this marks the living faith of our ancestors – the living traditions of dead people."[6]

Hmmm. Dead faith. Democracy of the dead. Living traditions of dead people. Bobtail suspects that this has something to do with him, too, but he just can't quite pin it down. Bobtail wonders how these questions apply to the current cultural heritage dialogue. These are exactly the kind of questions that give Bobtail a big headache. Why do things have to get so complicated and uncomfortable?

Hmmm ... Lately, Bobtail just can't shake the suspicion that somebody is getting him back and is having a good laugh on him. Weget? Clown? Or maybe Wisakedjak has returned?

Val Napoleon

Notes

1 Jay Hansford C. Vest, "Braves or Brave Hawks at UNCP: A Philosophical Review of a 'Native' Mascot" (Paper presented to the Mid-Atlantic Conference on the Scholarship of Diversity, Roanoke, Virginia, 2005), online: University of North Carolina at Pembroke <http://www.uncp.edu/relations/bulletin/v6/16/jay_vest.doc> at 2.

2 John Borrows, *Recovering Canada: The Resurgence of Indigenous Law* (Toronto: University of Toronto Press, 2002) at 57.

3 Mary Lynne Hill, "Trickster's Mask: Representations of Aggressive Actions of the Israelis and Palestinians in Editorial Coverage" (2003) 2:2 Trickster's Way, online: Trickster's Way <http://www.trinity.edu/org/tricksters/TrixWay/current/Vol%202/Vol_2/Mhill.htm> and <http://www.trinity.edu/org/tricksters/trixway/current/Vol%202/Vol2_2/mhill.pdf>.

4 Borrows, *supra* note 2 at 147.

5 G.K. Chesterton, *Collected Works* (San Francisco: Ignatius Press, 1986) vol. 1 at 251, quoted in H. Patrick Glenn, *Legal Traditions of the World, Sustainable Diversity in Law,* 2d ed. (Oxford: Oxford University Press, 2004) at 5, n. 13.

6 Borrows, *supra* note 2 at 147.

1

Recovering from Colonization: Perspectives of Community Members on Protection and Repatriation of Kwakwaka'wakw Cultural Heritage

Catherine Bell, Heather Raven, and Heather McCuaig, in consultation with Andrea Sanborn, the U'mista Cultural Society, and the 'Namgis Nation

> I hope that some day before I leave this world that I see a lot of – all our stuff come back. 'Cause I hear we got things all over the world. And why did we lose it? What really happened? Why was the government against us? ... [was] it just to kill our souls? To kill us? Maybe that was one way of getting rid of us. And why was it against the law to have a potlatch? And it's so, it's so beautiful, especially when you celebrate the birth of a baby, when you're giving names to your child when it grows up, and when [a] woman becomes a woman and the young man steps into his father's shoes. And that they did such a beautiful job on doing that. You know, why on earth was it against the law?
>
> — Emma Tamilin[1]

Loss of cultural items, knowledge, and language arising from government-sanctioned discriminatory laws and policies, and the importance of recovering from that loss to Kwakwaka'wakw (Kwakiutl) survival, is a fundamental theme in this case study. Anger, grief, shock, confusion, and frustration are some of the feelings expressed by participants as they reflect on efforts undertaken by the U'mista Cultural Society (U'mista), the 'Namgis Nation, and the broader Kwakwaka'wakw community to repatriate material culture, revive cultural practices, and reclaim the knowledge, values, laws, principles, and beliefs associated with them. Yet equally strong are feelings of optimism, hope, happiness, pride, confidence, and satisfaction as participants recall the potlatch ceremony and discuss the positive effects that repatriation of cultural objects and information and the revival of the Kwak'wala language can have on the cultural life of the community. The importance of repatriating material culture surrendered and sold as a consequence of anti-potlatch laws is linked to community well-being and healing through the revival of traditions and the acknowledgment of injustices suffered at the hands of the Canadian government. The value of potlatch items lies not only in the "tangible evidence" they provide of Kwakwa̲ka̲'wakw history but also, and more significantly, "in the intangible aspects of the culture they symbolize and the cultural knowledge and norms they represent."[2]

Although participants offer broad definitions of cultural property, the emphasis in this case study is on material culture, stories, and songs; the importance of reviving the potlatch system; and how the potlatch system has operated as a means for understanding laws, values, rights, and responsibilities in relation to the tangible and intangible cultural heritage of the Kwakwa̲ka̲'wakw. Equally important to the retention of cultural knowledge, identity, and traditions is the survival and protection of the Kwak'wala language. For this reason, U'mista also chose to include specific questions concerning language use and preservation. However, the emphasis in this study is not intended to suggest that protection of traditional lands, cultural sites, and other aspects of Kwakwa̲ka̲'wakw cultural heritage are less important to the Kwakwa̲ka̲'wakw than is the protection of language.

We begin this study with a brief introduction to the Kwakwa̲ka̲'wakw, the 'Na̲mgis Nation, and U'mista. This is followed by a description of case study methodology and a thematic presentation of information gathered primarily through a focus group involving U'mista board members and interviews with Kwakwa̲ka̲'wakw elders, U'mista employees, and others who are assisting U'mista with specific protection and repatriation initiatives. We define cultural property and explore priorities for protection, then offer a discussion of language retention and revival. Next, we address three broad themes: the potlatch, establishing "ownership" or belonging, and repatriation. We place particular emphasis on the role of the potlatch in sustaining and recovering Kwakwa̲ka̲'wakw cultural knowledge and traditions. This is followed by discussions about the rationale for repatriation, ownership issues that arise in repatriation claims, the role of museums, the repatriation of information and language material, and the authenticity and appropriation of art. We conclude with reflections on the role of Canadian law and government in addressing some of the issues raised. As one of the goals of the case study methodology is to accurately portray the views of a range of individuals selected by U'mista to participate in this research, the study includes extensive quotations from transcripts.[3] However, it is not intended to represent a generalized Kwakwa̲ka̲'wakw or 'Na̲mgis perspective.

The People and Their Territory

Kwakwa̲ka̲'wakw refers to the people who speak Kwak'wala in the northwestern regions of British Columbia. They have also been known as the

Kwakkewlths (by the federal government) and the Kwakiutl (by anthropologists).[4] Traditional Kwakwa̱ka̱'wakw territory extends from Comox to the north end of Vancouver Island and the adjacent mainland inlets from Smith Inlet south to Toba Inlet. Consisting of a number of tribes with separate names and creation stories, Kwakwa̱ka̱'wakw communities include Kwagu'ł (Fort Rupert), 'Na̱mgis (Alert Bay), Da̱'naxda'x̱w (New Vancouver), Dzawada̱'enu̱xw (Kincome Village), Ḵwikwa̱sutinux̱ (Gilford Island), Gwawa'enux̱w (Hopetown), G̱usgimukw (Quatsino), Gwat'sinux̱w (Winter Harbour), Tłatła̱siḵwa̱la (Hope Island), Weḵa'yi (Cape Mudge), and the Wiweḵ'a̱m (Campbell River). Other tribes no longer inhabiting their original territories include the Mama̱liliḵa̱la (Village Island), Ławit'sis (Turnour Island), Ma'a̱mtagila (Estekin), 'Nak'waxda'x̱w (Blunden Harbour), and Gwa'sa̱la (Smiths Inlet). Some of the original tribes have disappeared, including the A̱'wa̱'etła̱la (Knight Inlet), the Na̱ka̱mgla̱lisa̱la of Hope Island, and the Yutlinux̱ of the Cox and Lanz islands.[5]

The main village site of the 'Na̱mgis is at Alert Bay, on Cormorant Island, which is located off the northeast coast of Vancouver Island. The name 'Na̱mgis comes from the 'Na̱mx̱xelagiyu, who was a halibut-like monster. After a great flood, 'Na̱mx̱xelagiyu swam ashore near the mouth of the Nimpkish River. Once on land, he became a man named 'Namukusto'lis. Needing shelter, he wanted to build a house at Xwa̱lkw , which is located at the mouth of the Nimpkish River. However, he could not lift the beams by himself. He saw a large bird perched on a nearby rock and wished that it could help him. Being a supernatural creature, a Thunderbird, the bird knew about 'Namukusto'lis' wish without being asked. Thunderbird agreed to help build the house and revealed his human face underneath his bird face. Thunderbird used his talons to lift the beams into place. After the work was completed, Thunderbird removed his bird skin and became human. He threw his bird skin into the air and it flew away. As the bird skin flew away, he said, "You will only cause thunder and lightening [sic] when one of the Chiefs of the 'Na̱mgis dies."[6]

After the establishment of Xwa̱lkw, the 'Na̱mgis occupied the entire watershed of the Nimpkish River, Malcolm Island, and Cormorant Island, and they regularly travelled to Knight Inlet and Kincome Inlet on the mainland of British Columbia. Xwa̱lkw was the major 'Na̱mgis village until most of the people moved to 'Ya̱lis (Alert Bay), beginning in the 1870s. 'Ya̱lis had long been a place that the 'Na̱mgis used for various purposes. In 1870, two entrepreneurs, Spenser and Huson, constructed a saltery at 'Ya̱lis and attempted to induce the 'Na̱mgis to move from Xwa̱lkw and their other permanent settlements. The banning of the potlatch and removal of children to residential schools caused the decline of outlying villages as parents moved closer to Alert Bay to be closer to their children in the residential school. Although the 'Na̱mgis have eight separate reserves in their former territory, today most members live in Alert Bay.

As the U'mista Cultural Centre is located on the 'Namgis reserve in Alert Bay, the 'Namgis Nation has been actively involved in supporting cultural research and other initiatives undertaken by U'mista. For example, the 'Namgis have partnered with U'mista to conduct research on language retention and renewal, the creation of the Kwakwaka'akw Centre for Language and Culture in Community (KCLCC), initiatives concerning the protection and repatriation of cultural property, and, along with the other Kwakwaka'wakw nations, it is supporting U'mista in a specific claim against the federal government concerning harms suffered as a result of the anti-potlatch laws. Members of the 'Namgis Nation, along with other Kwakwaka'wakw, serve on the board for U'mista, volunteer as instructors in language and cultural education programs offered by U'mista, and participate in a variety of research programs designed to document and preserve Kwakwaka'wakw culture. The 'Namgis are also engaged in the British Columbia treaty process and are negotiating increased protection and control of cultural resources, including lands and natural resources, as part of that process.

U'Mista Cultural Society

The U'mista Cultural Society was established in 1974 and is governed by a board of ten directors composed of members from any tribe of the Kwakwaka'wakw.[7] The broad mandate of U'mista is to "ensure the survival of all aspects of cultural heritage of the Kwakwaka'wakw."[8] It "exists to serve both the Kwakwaka'wakw and non-native population as a whole by the dissemination of cultural, historical, and artistic information about the Kwakwaka'wakw regionally, provincially, nationally, and internationally."[9] Kwakwaka'wakw elders provide an "invaluable" role in research conducted by U'mista, including collections interpretation and advising on traditional potlatch protocol and other aspects of Kwakwaka'wakw culture.

One of the initial objectives of the society was to build a facility in Kwakwaka'wakw territory to exhibit potlatch items "illegally confiscated in 1922 by Indian Agent William Halliday" after the Village Island potlatch and "returned from the Canadian Museum of Civilization [then the National Museum of Man] and the Royal Ontario Museum in 1979 and 1988 respectively."[10] "Repatriation of all the illegally confiscated regalia is a continuing commitment that the Society has had from its inception."[11] The name of the society reflects this purpose. The term *"u'mista"* is derived from a historical practice of the Kwakwaka'wakw. In earlier times, people were sometimes taken captive during raids. They were most often returned to their homes through the payment of a ransom to their captors or by a retaliatory raiding party. On returning home, they were said to have u'mista.[12] The modern equivalent of u'mista is the recovery and return of artifacts, records, and other items that have been held captive in museums and personal collections outside of Kwakwaka'wakw territory. Since 1980, the permanent display at

U'mista has contained items in the Potlatch Collection, which was recovered, or *u'mista,* from museums and private collections in Canada and the United States. Other permanent exhibits include "description of the traditional ethnobiology of the Kwakwa̱ka̱'wakw and origin stories of the Kwakwa̱ka̱'wakw villages, as well as historical and contemporary Kwakwa̱ka̱'wakw pieces."[13]

Although repatriation of the Village Island potlatch items continues to be an important part of U'mista operations, the objectives of the society have evolved over the years to reflect the role of U'mista in the revival of Kwakwa̱ka̱'wakw culture and the Kwak'wala language. Some of the more specific objectives of U'mista are to:

1. Collect, preserve, and exhibit native artifacts of cultural, artistic, and historical value to the Kwakwa̱ka̱'wakw;
2. Promote and foster carving, dancing, ceremonials, and other cultural, artistic activities engaged in by the Kwakwa̱ka̱'wakw;
3. Collect, record, and make available information and records relating to the language and history of the Kwakwa̱ka̱'wakw;
4. Promote, build, and maintain facilities for carrying out the above aims; and
5. Recover from other institutions and individuals artifacts and records of cultural, artistic, and historical value to the Kwakwa̱ka̱'wakw.[14]

Pursuant to these objectives, U'mista has engaged in a number of initiatives inside and outside the community, invoking the legal system where necessary. In addition to maintaining and displaying the Potlatch Collection, U'mista is actively engaged in law reform activity and has initiated a specific claim, with the support of all Kwakwa̱ka̱'wakw tribes, to seek compensation for the harm suffered as a consequence of the anti-potlatch laws.[15] This claim was submitted to the Specific Claims Branch of the Department of Indian and Northern Affairs in 1998. A detailed description of this claim is offered further on in this chapter.

Other U'mista initiatives include gathering tapes, photographs, books, slides, and any other information available to facilitate its role as an information and resource centre on Kwakwa̱ka̱'wakw culture; recording and documenting elder knowledge; conducting genealogical research; working with Kwakwa̱ka̱'wakw and other interested individuals to develop language retention programs; promoting retention of language and culture through cultural activities in the community and support for Kwakwa̱ka̱'wakw artists; upgrading and funding facilities, including the Big House, in which potlatches and other community events are held; and creating resources that will enable non-Kwakwa̱ka̱'wakw to obtain accurate information and to learn more about Kwakwa̱ka̱'wakw culture. U'mista is also involved in supporting the education and training of individuals of Kwakwaka'wakw descent and in economic development through tourism in Alert Bay.

Case Study Methodology

Participation in this study was supported by resolutions of the U'mista board and was approved by the chief and council of the 'Namgis Nation. As research was conducted on the 'Namgis Reserve, the methodology also complied with *'Namgis Guidelines for Visiting Researchers*.[16] The guidelines are intended to "ensure clarity and fairness" in the relationship between the researcher, his/her supporting institutions and funding sources, and the band.[17] Before research commences, researchers must submit a curriculum vitae, references, and a written proposal for assessment by band staff and cultural advisors and approval by the chief in council. Research must "be of benefit to the Band, both in its intent and its outcome," comply with "professional standards and ethics," and ensure that the "interests of the Band" and "the confidentiality of informants be protected with respect to the dissemination of original research data to any third party."[18] Upon approval, a contract may be required that generally stipulates that all original tapes and notes "remain with or be provided to the Band," that "copies of the original research data not be disseminated to any third party (person or institution) without prior knowledge and consent of the Band," and that "the Band be consulted prior to the publication or public presentation" of research outcomes.[19] Issues of copyright and restrictions the band may wish to place on interpretations and dissemination of research data must also be discussed before the proposal is submitted.

Data for the study was gathered primarily through interviews, focus groups, and a review of files in the U'mista office dealing with repatriation of culturally and historically significant items and artifacts. Information about the first Potlatch Collection repatriation is also drawn from published sources, including articles written by Gloria Cranmer Webster, U'mista's first director and curator. Participants spoke mainly in English but also used Kwak'wala words. A list of potential interview and focus group participants was developed by Andrea Sanborn and Barb Cranmer. These include people who have memories of, or whose families participated in, the Village Island (Cranmer) and other potlatch ceremonies before the ban: six Kwakwaka'wakw elders and others with significant knowledge and expertise who live in Alert Bay; the executive director and collections manager for U'mista; a lawyer and anthropologist working on the specific claim; and an anthropologist working on language matters for U'mista. Five U'mista board members from the 'Namgis, Ławit'sis, Dzawada'enuxw, and Kwagu'ł nations also participated in a focus group discussion.

With the exception of those asked of Guy Buchholtzer, Stan Ashcroft ('Namgis legal counsel), and John Pritchard (specific claim researcher), the standard question set was used as a general guide for interviews and focus groups. Additional questions relating to the role of Canadian museums and the challenges of repatriation were asked of those with experience in these areas. Guy Buchholtzer was asked to describe his work on the language repatriation project for the KCLCC, and Stan Ashcroft and John Pritchard were asked questions concerning the specific claim and the role of law in protecting cultural heritage. The interviews and focus group were guided by cultural interpretations of the questions asked and the interest and importance that participants placed on particular topics.

Definition and Protection of Cultural Property

Individual and focus group interviews with Kwakwa̱ka̱'wakw participants began with an introduction to the project and examples of how we were using the phrase "cultural property." Participants were asked what the term "cultural property" meant to them. William Wasden Jr. suggested that the term "is a little bit more precise to families because the family makes up the community, but the community doesn't own everything. The families are the ones in control of it."[20] Andrea Cranmer notes that the term "cultural property" is not used in the Big House or by the "well-versed cultural people in the community" and that she feels more comfortable with the phrase "cultural heritage" to describe what the Kwakwa̱ka̱'wakw "own as a people."[21]

In response to these questions, participants set out a wide number of tangible and intangible items, such as the land, medicines, songs, history, values, and language. Participants do not make divisions among kinds of property, and they connected property with values and things given by the Creator to be used by the Kwakwa̱ka̱'wakw. A mask might have particular songs, dances, land use, or rights, names, and families associated with it. All are seen as part of a whole. The mask has little to no meaning or value if it is separated from the other elements of its whole being. The Western practice of dividing property into distinct classes does not fit with the view of property being "a whole existence." Responding to the question, "What does cultural property mean to you," Andrea Sanborn replies: "[C]ultural property, to me, is anything about us, for us, given to us by our Creator and is ... to be used by all of us with respect."[22] Nevertheless, the concept of "property" as rights and responsibilities adhering to a particular group or individual is consistent with participant views on the meaning of property:

> Okay, my whole existence as Andrea is cultural property. It's who I am. It's all the traditions of the Kwakwa̱ka̱'wakw that belong to me and belong to our people. It's the language, the Kwak'wala language and, most importantly, our values we have as a people, *maya'x̱ala,* which means respect or treating someone good or something good. It's protecting all our songs and

dances and history. It's protecting our land because all the land base comes out of our creation stories in this area. That's cultural property. So those are the things. It's family passing on family values and the history of each family and all the treasures they own culturally. (Andrea Cranmer)

The language is the most important I think, 'cause without the language, we wouldn't have any culture at all. So, yep, the songs, the songs are cultural property ... specifically to families. And that's pretty sacred and important to people. And the masks, masks go along with the songs. Not everybody has the right to certain masks and dances. So that's cultural property in my eyes. The land, I think that the land is real cultural property, specifically to families. I think we've drifted away from the ownership and our land title. Our people used to – we lived off the land and our people controlled these areas and monitored them and guarded them. (William Wasden Jr., part 2)

[C]ultural property, to me, is what everybody has said, but I'll go into the food, things that we eat, the fish, clams, whatever, even the bears. It seems to be harder and harder to go and pick the natural things and that, to me, is really important.[23] (Peggy Svanvik)

The areas of priority for protection identified by Kwakwa̱ka̱'wakw participants reflect the broad concept of cultural property adopted and the importance of the potlatch ceremony and language in the survival of Kwakwa̱ka̱'wakw cultural practices and identity.

It's really important to keep giving the history [of] what [the] potlatch is supposed to do. It's supposed to give an example, a record – the history of each of those dances and the names that go with it – in front of our people because they are there to witness the property that belongs to the family.[24] (Vera Newman)

The potlatch ceremony and all that it represents – marriage, births, deaths, etc., the Kwak'wala language and the cultural ... and creation stories – those are all the kind of things that I think should be protected here. Property and intellectual knowledge, anything that is derived through the potlatch ceremony, should be protected ... They should be protected because they are our culture. It is who we are and that's why it should be protected. (Andrea Sanborn)

When asked if it is important to "protect our ways that we practise in our Big House," Ethel Alfred replied that all customs, including regalia, language, songs, and dance, are gifts from the Creator that must be protected so that they will not "disappear" and so that "white people won't touch it" or "come around and boss what belongs to us."[25] This includes the skills relearned by artists and the contemporary potlatch regalia created by them. All participants expressed a common fear of further cultural loss. It is important to reclaim cultural knowledge and pass it on to younger generations before the old people die. When asked, "Is it all right in your heart to call it cultural property?" Ethel Alfred replied:

> It's terrible what they did to our people. It completely destroyed our customs in all areas, not just when they took the masks. Our people learned themselves to be great artists. Nobody taught them how. It was their natural ability. They learned it while they were growing up, by holding a strong heart and listening to our old people when the old people instructed them on what to create. That's why it's so important for us to protect our culture now, our regalia, and all the customs of our people. That's the way of our people ... That's why it is so important for us to protect it, so we will never lose it again. It really destroyed the people, what they did. (Ethel Alfred)

Kwakwa̱ka̱'wakw participants are confident the community will take the necessary steps to ensure that the culture will survive. This confidence is inherent in their discussions of strategies and community responsibility. They can rely on their resilience and perseverance to find solutions to the problems they are facing:

> [Y]ou know, as Kwakwa̱ka̱'wakw people, all the Kwak'wala-speaking people are survivors of the flood, and the ancestors that survived the flood were all chosen by the Creator. They were sent messages that it was coming, so they prepared. So we are all chosen people [whose purpose is] to carry out these sacred things and to continue on. So that's why I think we're okay with where we're at culturally, because the Creator already had it in place that we were going to be survivors and survive this thing – the flood – and that we're here for a reason and we're still here today. No matter what, all the different types of catastrophes that have happened to us, our people are still here. Even all the epidemics and that, you know, the germ warfare that was put on our people, we still survived it, and the Creator wants us here for a reason. So these, you know, these cultural properties that we talk about are all part of a – all these things are gifts given to us by our Creator for a reason. (William Wasden Jr., part 2)

In considering protection priorities, Juanita Pasco, a former employee of the U'mista Cultural Centre, explains that the current focus of the society is repatriation of material culture such as blankets, masks, and rattles because Canada's system of export controls "isn't really working."[26] She also draws attention to the fact that "Canadian copyright law doesn't really take into consideration First Nations customs and what they consider ownership of songs." Bill Cranmer, chief of the 'Na̲mgis, shares those concerns and also identifies language protection and revival as a priority.[27]

Spruce Wamiss expresses concern about people taking items from burial grounds, and he wishes they could somehow be returned: "[I]t would be awesome if there was a way to protect our burial grounds wherever they are."[28] Participants also feel it is important to protect the land and its resources, particularly forests and seas, as they are a source of traditional foods and medicines. William Wasden Jr. explains that rights to certain harvesting areas are also considered family property:

> I'm just thinking about my great grandfather [who] owned a trapline, and he also had a halibut kind of fishing ground that was given to him through dowry through my great grandmother ... [O]ur people of old weren't stingy, and they allowed other people to access the resources when they needed it and stuff. And there was certain families that were in control of certain areas, and it all ties back to the origin story, where the first ancestor came down. That's the reason they are the owners of it. They were the first ones there and the first ones to occupy it and re-populate it after the flood. (William Wasden Jr., part 2)

In his opinion, protecting the land is a top priority, and the 'Na̲mgis should not have to participate in a treaty process to prove that it is theirs; rather, the government should have to prove that it is not theirs because "the writing is everywhere. The paintings are on the cliffs ... the petroglyphs are all over the land [and] there's old fish weirs and middens everywhere." It is also important that the treaty process discuss hereditary chieftainships because "those are the original landowners, keepers, land keepers and owners of the territories." Different chiefs had responsibility over the management of different resources, such as sockeye and eulachon, "to ensure that these resources were going to survive into the next season or cycle of return." These are obligations of the people and "are heavy roles that come along with the different cultural properties."

Language Retention and Renewal

As U'mista is currently engaged in several initiatives concerning language retention and protection, we chose to ask participants specific questions about this issue. Kwakwa̲ka̲'wakw participants were asked whether it is important to protect Kwak'wala, why it is important, and what challenges the community faces in protecting this and other forms of cultural property. All participants spoke passionately about the centrality of language to the continuity and survival of Kwakwa̲ka̲'wakw cultural practices and identity.

It is, according to Andrea Cranmer, "the thread that puts it all together." "When you lose language" Spruce Wamiss adds, "[Kwakwaka'wakw] culture is gone, Indian names are gone, songs are gone." According to Bill Cranmer, knowledge is also lost without language because, without it, "you are not going to be able to look into the oral traditions." William Wasden Jr. sums it up this way:

> I just say that our language is so important. It's what makes us Kwakwaka'wakw. The name says it all: Kwak'wala-speaking people. And I don't know what we are going to call ourselves after if we don't, if we're not speaking our language. So we got to get on it. So many good elders have passed away. Just look at Uncle Glen and Uncle Charlie Williams. [Y]ou know, that's so sad, how we just lost two key players in our culture, just like that, and we didn't think that was going to happen. So there's so much we gotta grasp, and [it's] time to get serious about our language. (William Wasden Jr., part 2)

Protection of the Kwak'wala language and the potlatch ceremony are inextricably linked. Potlatches are conducted in the Kwak'wala language. This practice ensures that the language is preserved and that it continues to evolve. It also requires the Kwakwaka'wakw to learn their language if they want to fully participate in their culture.

> It's most important because if we don't have our language, we don't have a culture. Because our language has all the meaning of our culture in it. And you know, when you are in the *guwkzdi* [Big House] it's so – means so much more. When it's spoke[n] in your language, it means so much more. I understand my language, so I understand when the chiefs speak Kwak'wala, especially wonderful speakers like Charlie Williams. He could speak our old Kwak'wala. There's a few of them left, you know, and it means so much more when it's in our language. It tells us who we are. We're not Haida. We're not Nuu-chah-nulth. We are Kwakwaka'wakw and we have our own language and it separates us from anything else. And it's really, really important; it's probably the most important of our properties, is our language. (Vera Newman)

Some participants speak about how difficult it was to maintain their language after they were punished for using it in the residential schools. The suppression of Kwak'wala is linked not only to undermining the survival of Kwakwaka'wakw culture but also to separating the people from their land.

> That's why it is so terrible that our newer generation don't seem to know anything because they went as far as not allowing us to speak our language

> because they wouldn't allow us to practise our customs ... Like when I was in school and when I was caught speaking our language with my friends by the matron, I had to write out five hundred times, "I must speak English." I had to do it after school, before we had supper. The reason I never lost our language is because my friends and I used to sneak in the corners to speak our language together. That's how I never lost our language. I was only eleven years old when our culture was taken away. (Ethel Alfred)

Andrea Cranmer agrees that one of the challenges to language revival and retention is to overcome the impact of the residential schools: "Generations of people have been influenced to say that Kwak'wala is not important anymore, and they really believe it now." Consequently, not everyone in the community has the same "mind set or the passion behind saving the language." An overriding theme is the urgent need to increase the number of language speakers before elders die. This can best be accomplished by community and family members taking responsibility for learning and using the language. Participants acknowledge the importance of language education through community programs and the schools but emphasize that both adults and youth must be educated and use the language outside of the classroom. Andrea Cranmer notes that one of the challenges is the absence of teaching material in Kwak'wala and the need for Kwakwa̱ka̱'wakw to write their own books. Although he agrees that language retention and revival is dependant on initiatives within the community, Bill Cranmer adds that the federal government should also enact a law for the protection of aboriginal languages. Common sentiments are reflected in the follow passage:

> And if we keep stalling and we keep sitting back, we are going to lose it. And we have to find a way to try and save as much as we can and teach as much as we can. Because I know that there are many different teachers that we have out there [who are] supposed to be teaching Kwak'wala and they can't even speak it. And then I ask them, "[W]ell, what are you using? What are you using to teach our children? Tape recorders?" And I don't understand sometimes that they don't use, they don't use us, the elders that can speak Kwak'wala, in the teaching system. And it's pretty sad because some of our children, they speak Kwak'wala but it doesn't sound the same. So I believe it's very, very important.[29] (Christine Joseph)

Although some participants stated they did not expect to be compensated for teaching the language, Basil Ambers thinks it is important that those teaching Kwak'wala be recognized by the school system and paid properly.[30] Language teachers are "underpaid" and "cut back." Money is also needed so that community members can develop creative programs rather than having to rely on outside consultants. However, Spruce Wamiss does not feel that community members should expect payment. To him, the only payment that is needed is "to see more and more of [the] young people learn to speak the language properly." This means developing a written and recorded curriculum for the schools, and resources are needed for such projects. Peggy Svanvik also agrees with Spruce but says, "if we are going to pay people to teach our language, they should be paid a decent wage."

Participants offered a number of creative strategies for teaching the language in a way that would appeal to the youth and make it fun for all members of the community to learn. One important strategy involved the singing of traditional songs. William Wasden Jr. tells of a CD recording of traditional songs he and a friend sang and recorded at a fundraiser for the Łaxwe'gila canoe gathering. Remembering how he laughed when Moody picked him up once with "our Łaxwe'gila blaring in his car," he suggests that "CDs are an awesome learning tool." Basil Ambers and several others also suggest using tools that children like to play with, such as video games and TV. It is important to "[m]ove with the times" and "take the technology and use it to your advantage." However, all participants recognize that learning the language also requires hard work and personal commitment on the part of those wishing to learn. Several discuss the importance of First Nations control over education and of having immersion programs that students can begin at an early age. Whatever strategy is adopted in the schools, Christine Joseph emphasizes the importance of working with elders.

In 2000-1, U'mista commissioned a report entitled *Review of* Kwakwa̱ka̱'wakw *Language Retention and Renewal*, which was a review of Kwak'wala language usage in the 'Na̱mgis Nation.[31] The report was a product of extensive consultation among U'mista, the Nimpkish School Board, tribal school staff, and community members. The core finding of the study on language use was that, "without immediate community-wide changes and additional language programming, Kwak'wala will become extinct. The community probably has no more than a decade to reverse this decline."[32] An important outcome of the review of language usage was Dr. Guy Buchholtzer's idea to establish the Kwakwa̱ka̱'wakw Centre for Language and Culture in Community. The main purpose of the project is to "bring together community members to full exposure of the *Kwak'wala* language, and to facilitate re-immersion."[33] The idea includes gathering all information produced in any language about the Kwakwa̱ka̱'wakw language in a centralized place easily accessible to the community. Grants have been obtained from private and public funding sources to begin the process of cultural information and language material repatriation. In addition to his work on language repatriation, Buchholtzer has assisted U'mista in its attempt to repatriate work conducted by a linguist. U'mista annual reports describe how the linguist maintains that the work he did with Kwak'wala speakers in compiling a Kwak'wala database (computerized interactive dictionary) is his property and that he is not required to share the information with the 'Namgis Nation until he is satisfied with it.[34] Language repatriation is also a matter that should be discussed at the current treaty negotiations among the 'Namgis Nation, Canada, and British Columbia.

U'mista is engaged in a number of other language programs dependent on project-based funding. For example, it has secured funding for a "series of introductory level interactive media (CD-ROM) language lessons and developed the digital materials for the first of those lessons."[35] U'mista continues to work on this project as well as on the comprehensive computerized talking dictionary. U'mista has also produced educational videos and "digitally video-taped seventy hours of interviews with elders on language, history and culture of the Kwakwaka'wakw."[36] Other projects included developing the Kwak'wala alphabet, language books and tapes, and the translation of Anglican hymns into Kwak'wala. The centre also offers beginning Kwak'wala classes. U'mista has been working with Kwakwaka'wakw school districts, bands, and tribal councils on these and other initiatives. It identifies the major problem as being lack of funds. Other challenges it has identified include lack of in-depth curricula, insufficient support inside and outside the community, lack of a common writing system/orthography, and a need for more qualified teachers.[37]

The Potlatch

Importance of the Potlatch

The potlatch is of fundamental importance to the Kwakwaka'wakw. "Potlatch" is a term used to describe ceremonies that mark significant events, such as marriages, naming of children, memorials to the dead, raising of totem poles, and transfers of rights and privileges. As part of the ceremony, these events are validated before witnesses by the giving of gifts of property. Feasting, speeches, storytelling, dancing, and singing are also an integral part of the potlatch. Potlatches were the foundation of Kwakwaka'wakw economic, political, social, spiritual, and legal systems and the means for transferring cultural knowledge to future generations. They also promoted values such as humility, generosity, responsibility, and respect. Potlatches were the "essence of Kwakwaka'wakw culture":[38]

> The literal word "potlatch" means "to give," so our people had really strict laws around the ceremonies and around the potlatch. And in the old days ... it was about competition within tribes and who had the most status and who had the most power and things like that. And you showed that through the treasures you gained, and the treasures you gained [were] from your wife ... Treasures that would come through marriage would be the songs,

the dances, the names, high-ranking names, names for your babies, names for the children, property, rights to go to hunt in certain places, rights to go and trap furs in certain places. And in the old days you married someone of your status. And in our culture, what is really unique is that the more you gave away as a chief, the higher your status went. So it wasn't about – even though it was like a competition with other people within your tribe, chief[-] wise, there was still this place of humbleness, because the more you gave away, the higher you became. And you could say anything you wanted to whoever you wanted because you gained such status within your tribe. Also what comes with the potlatch and with being a chief, it's not about boasting and being arrogant. It's about looking after and embracing. [I]t was about looking after your people. A chief would look after his people, provide shelter, food, make sure the tribe [was] running well ... And as a witness, your responsibility was to pay attention so that you can see all the treasures and all the names and all the things that the chief's doing. And the reason for a potlatch was very important. Naming his children was one big thing. Passing on his chieftainship, passing on privileges and rights, passing on songs and dances, weddings, memorials. All those are very important things in a person's life, and our people had a structure in place for that. And that was through the potlatch system. So it was very important. (Andrea Cranmer)

The reality of the thing is that the chief that's throwing the potlatch, that's his way of choosing his successor for his family. He usually picks his oldest son to become the *hamat'sa* and that's his way of making sure that he's passing on the rights to the rest of his family. And like, he's supposed to end off, if he's done everything right and he's thrown the four potlatches he's supposed to throw, he's supposed to have nothing left. He's supposed to have no rights left, and all his rights are supposed to have gone to his oldest boy. You know, it's up to the oldest boy to make his name right. You know, he's got to throw four potlatches and start the process of passing the rights on – songs, dances, and names, and stuff like that. (Basil Ambers)

Modern potlatches continue to be integral to Kwakwa̲ka̲'wakw culture and serve many of these same functions, sometimes in a modified form. However, not everyone in the community is aware of, or endorses, the values, beliefs, and principles that the potlatch represents. Thus, strategies for protection of Kwakwa̲ka̲'wakw culture discussed by participants later in this report include the need to educate community members in their own traditions. Repatriation of potlatch items and acquisition of as much material as possible relating to Kwakwa̲ka̲'wakw history and culture is pivotal to achieving this goal.

Significant financial and human resources are expended in preparation to host a potlatch. The old people need to be consulted to ensure that proper protocols are followed and that accurate family information is shared. New dances and songs may need to be composed, money and gifts need to be gathered, and meals must be prepared:

> And whenever they showed the cedar bark ceremony, when it comes in through the front door, you have to distribute a bit of money to the people. My uncle Sam Charlie held [the] right to that ceremony in Village Island. And my mother, being his sister, always supported him financially ... That's the best way to be is to stand as one, as a family, to help out in any way you can when one of the family members have to practise our customs. Some of us still practise that custom today because potlatches are such a tremendous undertaking, even today, financially. It's an incredible custom [t]hat our people have. It takes months to prepare for a potlatch. What I remember seeing was incredible, enormous wealth being distributed. What our people did when they started to have money, silver coins, they melted it down to make jewellery to be distributed. All our relatives helped prepare, the people that do silver jewellery start doing it to help out. And they all come with their different talents to help out. (Ethel Alfred)

> Well, one of the responsibilities dad had was to save his money. He had to – he always used to say that, in the Big House, you want to talk, put your money where your mouth is. And maybe, in everyday language, that's what my dad used to say 'cause it's very costly to carry on our culture. It's very time-consuming and, and one of his, one of our responsibilities, as a family, is to stand up and back up our chief, whether it be food preparation, regalia-making, the carvers to carve, or what's needed to be sewn. (Vera Newman)

> We went through thirty, forty years where people didn't even have an Indian blanket anymore. When they first started to teach how to Indian dance, people used bath towels because there's no more regalia at that time. So that's part of the responsibility that granny had to have as the grandmother of our family. She made blankets for all of us grandchildren who were interested. (Vera Newman)

Potlatches are held in the Big House, where there are strict protocols surrounding activity. Vera Newman explains that "if you fell while walking in the Big House 'cause you're being clumsy and not paying attention to what's going on, then your family has to, what they call *digita* [to make it right]; they have to pay money to wipe away the shame of what just happened." Money also had to be distributed for other transgressions of protocol, such as allowing animals in the Big House or allowing kids to run freely; also, dancers had to pay for any mistakes or clumsiness on their part.[39] However, these protocols are not followed as strictly today as they used to be. "Rules" ranged from ceremonial protocol about matters such as who could be on the dance floor and when and what jewellery a person could wear to laws about who could exercise certain intangible property rights, such as the performance of a dance or song:

> I remember those black-faced *hamat'sas*, they were so scary [A *hamat'sa* is a young man becoming possessed by the man-eating spirit Baxbakwalanuksiwe' who through rituals, song, and dance is purified and tamed, which brings him back to his human state. This is the most important ceremony in the potlatch ceremony. It is a rite of passage]. My uncle was one of them, uncle Alfred, and I – oh, God, when I used to walk into the Big House. I see them sitting there and all they do is watch the crowd, and boy, if you made a mistake, they would just get up and they would hit each other with their sticks and yell ... and jump around and, oh, my God. I asked my mom, "What are they doing, anyway?" and she said, "They are very angry. Something happened in here that shouldn't have happened. So somebody's gonna have to pay for it." Everything was serious in those days, hey. And it's something that I don't see anymore. Sometimes I wish they could bring it back so they can scare the kids that are running around in the Big House today, because we're not allowed to. (Emma Tamilin)

> And my older brother, Alec, was the attendant for the *hamat'sa* and he tripped on a rope that was holding the dance screen up. He fell and he left right away to go get money at our village. They had to have a washing ceremony right there. (Ethel Alfred)

> [T]he Nułamała [the enforcer, or keeper of order, in the potlatch ceremony], he was the second most important guy in the potlatch. He was the keeper of the rules. If he came in – like he could come in anytime – he didn't just come in to act the fool. Like, he came in sometimes all dressed in black, and he looked around. I got caught once in Turnour Island, Umbas gave me a, a chocolate bar, and I was chewing the chocolate bar. You're never supposed to eat before the chiefs, no matter if it's your food or not. Well, I got caught eating this chocolate bar and they put a stake in by the fire and tied me up to the stake with a stick in my mouth, you know. And Umbas had to bail me out. That's just an indication of how strict the rules were. (Basil Ambers)

Historically, the potlatch served (and continues to serve) as a means of sharing and verifying Kwakwa̲ka̲'wakw history. It serves to remind participants about their family histories and the connection to their lands. Masks are danced and songs are shared to tell of family origins and significant historical events:

> [T]he chiefs that invite, whether they are hereditary or potlatching chiefs, invite the various nations that are able to attend and the ones that they want to witness – to come and witness this family's business, that they're taking care of, whether it's commemorating death or marriage, or transferring ... names, or putting up a totem pole. They're inviting the people to publicly show them whether it's just through songs, or song and dance, relaying their history through, you know, song and dance. [A]nd that's what it is. And the speaker gets up and tells the history. So what the host is doing is sharing that family's history with the people that have come to witness and, in the end, paying them according[ ] ... to what ... their standing is. [Giving them] gifts, so that they will remember that forever ... and ... be able to repeat the story. And that's why the speaker in the Big House is so key, because he is the one who relates the stories of the dances, relates the name that's associated with the dance, [tells] who is assuming the dance and where it comes from. And always, with everything that is done, the speaker is retelling the history that goes along with these specific ceremonies and different activities that are going on. (William Wasden Jr., part 2)

Drama, magic, and theatrics are also an important part of the potlatch ceremony, whatever its particular purpose. Ethel Alfred and Emma Tamilin share the same vivid memory of the brilliance of some of the dramas performed:

> I'm sitting up there with my mother and this woman came out. And she – there was a man behind her with this knife, with this big sword ... All of a sudden, this woman – and they were singing and she was walking, she went around the Big House, I think, probably four times, and, all of a sudden, this man went and chopped her head off. And her head fell on the floor, and the man behind her picked it up. The head and the blood was running down, it was running down his arm. I didn't know what to think. I just about started – I just about screamed. My mother had to put her hand on my mouth so I wouldn't say anything. She said, "You better keep very quiet. This is really, really serious." Yeah, but that poor woman, you know, all I could see, all this blood. And they picked up her head, and they put it on these boxes in the corner of the Big House. And the eyes was moving, the eyes were moving like, you know, they were just moving, you know, and the blood was running down. And, oh, my God, I kept saying to my mother, "How come that woman was killed? How come that man killed that woman?" The fourth day, they came out again ... and the woman was singing and here come[s] the man behind her with this head, her head, in his hand. [He] put it back on her shoulder. How did they do this? This was pure magic. (Emma Tamilin)

The potlatch also operates as an educational and legal system. For example, through the potlatch ceremony, entitlements to songs, dances, masks, and regalia are demonstrated and transferred before witnesses. It is also a forum for the public resolution of disputes:

> We have our own laws through the potlatch ceremony. It includes the protocols for the use and ownership of the materials, whether it be songs, dances, stories, names, this sort of thing ... [Y]ou have to be part of the Kwakwa̱ka̱'wakw to want to understand what the potlatch ceremony means. And if you want to save your cultural property and intellectual knowledge, you have to want to learn the language to do that ... I, again, I only refer to the potlatch ceremony as being the law. Anything that is conducted, any ceremonies that are conducted and information given to the people, that is the law. If, if a song is being identified as being passed down from a chief to his son, or from whomever, and it's done in a potlatch ceremony, that's the law. (Andrea Sanborn)

> And that was in Gilford Island, and Tom Patch had a big potlatch in Gilford Island, and that's when I saw the breaking of the copper ... I guess what happened was Bill, Billy Matilpi, angered Tom Patch in some ways, and that's when the breaking of the copper came in. And they – that's how they used to solve a lot of the problems, by breaking the copper. My grandfather says after it was broken, when it finished, you don't talk about it anymore. (Emma Tamilin)

The potlatch may also connect participants to the spirit world and function as a place of healing and spiritual awakening. For example, William Wasden Jr. explains that some ceremonies, such as the cedar ring ceremony, could only be carried out by certain tribes and people within those tribes. He emphasizes that ceremonies and accompanying songs, stories, and regalia were "very sacred and guarded stuff and [that] they were handed to deserving people." Christine Joseph speaks to the healing nature of the potlatch, offering a story about how, despite crippling arthritis, her grandmother would "brighten" up as if "she had no more pains" and "would just dance" in the Big House. Below, Andrea Cranmer elaborates on the spiritual and healing functions of the potlatch:

> [I]n the potlatch, there is the *t'seḵa* ceremonies, which is the red cedarbark dances. And our people would go and fast in the woods; and the supernatural beings would be around, our people believed, in the wintertime. So when they were out there, those beings would come to them and they would get possessed by the different spirits and then would be brought back into the Big House. And those are how the dancers – that's how they got their spirit to do the dance that they do. So not only was the system in place, but the spiritual connection was there also, which is a very important

> part of who you are as a people ... I would say that it makes your body, spirit, and mind strong, being connected. And you go to the land, you know, so you cover all the bases. Again, you'd go to the land, you'd go in the water, all those important connections, then you'd go back into the Big House. So it all goes full circle ...
>
> It embraces all your emotions, and because of the process of the potlatch, you always start with the mourning songs. And the mourning songs are about – they are cry songs that you sing ... when your family loved ones have crossed over to the spirit world. So you go through the emotions of crying and letting go the spirit so that they can go walk with grace to the Creator. And all the emotions are present at a potlatch. There's crying. There's happiness and joy because a chief is seeing his family come together to prepare for the potlatch and sees his grandchildren or great-grandchildren dancing ... The potlatch brings a lot of the spirituality, and it brings a lot of the emotional part of who we are. And it's the basis of cultural, the cultural well-being of this community, the potlatch. That's where I feel, in 2003, that we can still go, and, yes, I may not agree with so and so politically, but we can still go to the Big House and let go of our differences so we can sit and witness what's going on in the Big House. I believe that's ... the place that still has honour and respect to a certain degree, whereas when you go anywhere else in your community or anywhere else in the world, well, you don't see that all the time. But at least we still have that in our Big House. (Andrea Cranmer)

The potlatch also serves an important function in bringing the community and families together, providing a space for the participants to step outside of their current activities and put aside their disagreements with each other:

> [E]verybody gets together with all their relatives and interacts, and there's a lot of hugging and stuff going on. And I think the reason – the real reason, you know, on a spiritual level – is the oneness of people coming together. And we all know that when we go to the Big House that we're supposed to have one spirit and we leave all our worldly B.S. behind, outside of the Big House, and that when we go in there, we change ourselves and we become spiritual and we carry ourselves with dignity and pride in that House. And we should carry it on outside, but you know that doesn't happen. (William Wasden Jr., part 2)

> It's very important. It gives you a sense of belonging. It gives you a sense of pride and humbleness and a feeling of belonging to a tribe. See, once we are in the Big House, there is nobody out there that's starving because everybody gets fed while they are in the Big House. That's just a little example

of taking care of, of the chief that is hosting the potlatch. They feed you right there. (Vera Newman)

The Banning of the Potlatch

In 1884, amendments to the federal *Indian Act*[40] were introduced, enacting the first legislation prohibiting the potlatch ceremony.[41] This legislation was later revised in 1895[42] because its vague wording made it difficult to enforce.[43] The legislation was aimed at expediting the assimilation of First Nations in Canada. The primary proponents of the ban were missionaries and government officials intent on civilizing the Indians. However, people continued to potlatch and ignored the laws. Subsequent amendments were made in 1918 to make celebration of the potlatch a summary conviction offence.[44] Prior to this, John Pritchard (specific claim researcher for U'mista) explains that, although it was an indictable offence, it was difficult to "find a judge anywhere in the province" who would send a person to jail "for what nobody considered to be a crime." He also points out that "convictions routinely resulted in suspended sentences."[45] The prohibition remained in place until 1951.[46]

The actions of Duncan Campbell Scott (deputy superintendent general of Indian affairs), Indian Agent Halliday, and Sergeant Angerman were instrumental in bringing about the 1884 and 1918 amendments. John Pritchard suggests that Scott and Halliday "induced government to pass the (1884) amendment on the basis of incomplete and faulty information." They knew that the potlatch was not the "deprived, barbarous custom that [it] was made out to be by the missionaries and the Indian agent." Following the amendment, Scott "struck a deal with the people of the Kwakiutl agency that, in exchange for [the agency] going along with certain parts of the prohibition, a full-scale investigation would be carried out on the [potlatch] custom because the [Kwakwa̱ka̱'wakw] people were convinced [that] if the government knew really what was going on, it would ease up or back off." Although Scott had "information in hand that the potlatch was not what it was made out to be," he "effectively suppressed the information and broke the agreement."

Stan Ashcroft ('Na̱mgis legal counsel) speaks to evidence that indicates that "Halliday and Sergeant Angerman effectively concocted a scheme to ... break the potlatch" through the 1918 amendments, with full understanding of its significance to the economic, cultural, and social life of the Kwakwa̱ka̱'wakw.[47] John Pritchard argues that the intent of the amendment was to "jolt the community and terrorize them" into giving up the potlatch ceremony. Indian agents were instructed to "observe carefully the comings and goings of people." The following passages describe the scheme they concocted and the illegal nature of their actions:

> Halliday had amendments made to the *Indian Act* which provided that the conviction could be by way of summary conviction. What that meant is it didn't have to go to a judge. It could go to a magistrate, which happened to be Halliday. So what happened then, of course, is the people go before Halliday, he convicts them, sentences them to prison. But he and Angerman concocted a scheme whereby the individuals and the various bands and chiefs are offered, essentially, an ultimatum. If you turn over your potlatch artifacts and regalia, not only of those persons who have been charged and/or convicted, but all the other, the other potlatch regalia and artifacts, we won't put these people in jail and we will be lenient in terms of any other prosecutions. In the future, in fact, we won't prosecute if you agree to this. So, effectively, it was coercion. It was duress. It resulted in the giving up of a huge amount of regalia and artifacts, portions of which have only recently been returned. (Stan Ashcroft)

> [O]ne of the most odious features of this is that people who are not present at the potlatch at Village Island and who may have not been subject to prosecution, were essentially coerced into giving up their material to keep people out of jail. So that, in itself, that kind of collective punishment is utterly inappropriate. In addition to which, although the *Act* had specified that people could not engage in ceremonies at which dances were given and songs were given, it neglected to prohibit the possession of regalia. So ... they were perfectly entitled to possess that material, whether they had been at a potlatch or not. (John Pritchard)

John Pritchard explains that, following a large potlatch held at Village Island in 1921, forty-five people were charged. Offences included making speeches, dancing, arranging articles to be given away, and carrying gifts to recipients. Gloria Cranmer Webster describes the potlatch and the trial that ensued:

> Three or four hundred people came from several villages to witness the ceremony. Unfortunately for the potlatch givers, the missionaries had been partially successful in their efforts, as several people who attended the potlatch became police informers. They gave the names of forty-five people, most of whom were the highest-ranking chiefs and their wives, who had performed such criminal acts as singing, dancing, making speeches, and giving and receiving gifts. The trial took place in April of 1922, with Indian Agent William Halliday, who had laid the charges, acting as magistrate. The interpreter was a woman who had become a Christian. When the magistrate asked each of the accused, "How do you plead, guilty or not guilty?" she translated the question into our language as, "He wants to know, were you there?" Everyone, of course, replied, "Yes."[48] (Gloria Cranmer Webster)

Twenty men and women were sent to Oakalla Prison. First offenders were to serve sentences of two months, while second offenders were to serve three months. The rest received suspended sentences after agreeing to give up their potlatch items to Indian Agent William Halliday.[49] According to Stan Ashcroft, "[U]pon receiving these artifacts and regalia [Halliday] did two things. One, he sold a number of them to Mr. Heye of the, what is now known as the American Museum of American Indian[50] [sic], and even Duncan Scott himself has said that was improper. And second, the coppers that were supposed to be paid for never were." After being inventoried and crated, most items were sent to Ottawa, where they were divided up between the Victoria Memorial Museum in Ottawa (renamed the National Museum of Man and known today as the Canadian Museum of Civilizatión) and the Royal Ontario Museum in Toronto. Some objects were set aside for the personal collection of Duncan Campbell Scott, who was at that time the superintendent of Indian affairs. New York collector George Heye purchased thirty-three items from Halliday before the material even left Alert Bay for Ottawa. These were shipped to the National Museum of the American Indian/Heye Foundation in New York.[51]

The Kwakwa̲ka̲'wakw are a resourceful people and, following the Village Island potlatch, the potlatch continued in modified forms. During the oral evidence given at the Indian Claims Commission Inquiry in February of 2003, several witnesses spoke of the elaborate ways that potlatches had to be hidden. For example, no potlatches were held in Alert Bay, even though the main village site had been the scene of most potlatches prior to the ban; instead, they were held in the winter and in outlying areas where the police boat could not travel due to ice. In addition, rather than hold potlatches, chiefs would often have to go door-to-door telling of the naming of their children and presenting gifts.[52] Although prosecutions continued following the Cranmer potlatch, "white officials lost their desire to enforce the law" and "no one was sent to jail":[53]

> I was sitting on a Japanese orange box, those little wooden boxes, when the police arrived and stood at the doorway. Chief Harry Mountain made light. He was looking at the singers, saying, "more, more, more," trying to lead the police to believing that they were having a play potlatch. He was joking around. I got so scared. I slid off my little box when I saw the police standing there; I thought for sure I'd be put in jail. Chief Harry Mountain and Bob Harris just started clowning around. We got so terrified of the police. (Ethel Alfred)

Harms Flowing from the Ban

Every Kwakwa̲ka̲'wakw settlement has a story about its creation. Most families know their histories or are attempting to rediscover them. These stories and histories are kept vibrant by their retelling in the Big House at potlatches, by being retold to younger family members, by being recorded, and by being added to as new events occur. These stories are a living connection to the ancestors and to the future of the Kwakwa̱ka̱'wakw. The events surrounding the banning of the potlatch and the aftermath of the Village Island potlatch have been incorporated into family histories so that the Kwakwa̱ka̱'wakw do not forget the lessons learned in those dark and trying times.

The following account illustrates the traumatic effect that the forfeiture of regalia and imprisonment had on Amos Dawson and his family. It also shows that some Kwakwa̱ka̱'wakw were able to persevere in practising the potlatch, despite the ban and the likelihood that they would be imprisoned and have to forfeit their regalia if caught. Emma Tamilin recalls how she only learned about her grandfather's imprisonment when she was about ten years old:

> I was in a Big House in Gilford Island. There was a big potlatch going on there and I was sitting with my mother and Mr. Todd, and two RCMP officers walked into the Big House and scared the heck out of my poor mother. Anyhow, she started to cry and I looked at her, "What are you so afraid of? It's only our Indian agent. He's not here to harm us." And she kept saying, "We're going to go back to jail. We're going to go back to jail." And I says, "What do you mean, we're gonna go back to jail?" And I says, "What is going on here anyway Mom?" And she said, "When you go back to Alert Bay you go and see your grandmother, she'll tell you everything." And so when I came back I went to see my granny, and I asked her what happened in 1922. Well, she said: "Your grandfather went to jail. I remember the day those people walked into our house ... Halliday, Angerman, and Mrs. Cook walked in." Mrs. Cook said to my grandfather, "Dawson," she said, "this has to stop. You've been going to potlatches and I hear you have been doing a lot of things that [are] against the law. And if you don't stop this you're going to go to jail. But if you forfeit your masks and your regalias you won't go to jail." And he said, "I promise you [I] won't." And she says, "Do you promise never to attend a potlatch anymore?" And I guess he looked at my grandmother and ... he said to my grandmother: "If that's what they want I will never do it again. I will never attend another potlatch as long as I live." Anyhow, they lied to him. He lost everything and went to jail anyway. And that was the beginning of the end for my grandfather, 'cause once he came back from Oakalla my grandmother said he was never the same. He just lost his spirit. He couldn't do anything. What he wanted to do when he came home was to have a feast to fix what happened to him 'cause that's what we do when something bad happens: we fix it. So anyhow ... that's what happened. And I guess he just slowly died inside [so] that he lost his spirit. My grandmother said [that] he still put his suit on every Sunday and went to church, like he was afraid not to. He went to church every Sunday,

> but he was not the same. My grandmother said he just lost everything, like he had no will to live anymore. So, and I wonder, you know – God, you know – I wonder why was this happening to our people? I can't fathom what they went through because it must have really, really hurt him, and I think his pride was cut in half or whatever ... And I guess my Grandfather Spruce, he just fought and he didn't care what they said. And he said, "They can't hurt me anymore, anyways. I don't care what they do to me but I'm going to have another potlatch." And he did. And I wonder why my grandfather [Amos Dawson] wasn't strong enough to fight them. But I guess maybe he was hurt so bad that he didn't want to fight anymore. (Emma Tamilin)

Kwakwaka'wakw individuals like Amos Dawson paid a very high price for their participation in the Village Island potlatch. Dan Cranmer, the giver of the Village Island potlatch, predeceased this interview process, but his widow, Agnes Cranmer, talked to John Pritchard in an interview he conducted as part of his research for the specific claim on the harms stemming from the potlatch prohibition. Dan Cranmer apparently suffered much grief and guilt about his part in holding the potlatch:

> We did, as I say, talk in a preliminary way to Dan Cranmer's widow, who talked about the effect that the process had on him. How for the rest of his life he grieved about the anguish he thought he had caused to fellow members of the community by [their] having to go to jail, by seeing the effects of everything on the language, economy, on the social system. And, wrongly, he took on the burden himself, thinking had he not held that potlatch this calamity would have not happened to his community; and that had a grievous effect on him for the rest of his life. (John Pritchard)

Participants share other accounts of the shame felt over the treatment of noble women in the community and the trauma that they suffered:

> I can imagine the shame they felt by going to jail. For Pete's sake, the women went to jail. Like Mit'sa said, that's what really bothered him ... [T]he noble ladies feeding the pigs. And then they hosed them, with cold water too, just in case they had lice. He said it was, it was awful, it was an awful thing to see. He said he cried. Him and my grandfather were watching this, and he said, "You know, Emma, you don't even know what we went through." (Emma Tamilin)

> I'll never forget Watis, when she used to cry down the beach here. And she said they shamed her. They cut her hair. They undressed her in front of everybody. She used to cry about that. And it's true, what Basil said, we never ever talk about the ones that held us up, that never stopped to continue to teach us these different things. (Christine Joseph)

Fear and trauma characterized the relationship of the Kwakwa̲ka̲'wakw to the "white man" during this time. Parents and grandparents were afraid to teach the language and culture to their children and grandchildren because they knew the consequences they would have to endure:

> Our grandparents were afraid to teach us for fear of the implications that they felt we would have to endure, such as beatings like they got at residential school, humiliation, and even jail sentences. I remember asking my mother about this when I heard her singing in Kwak'wala and how beautiful that I thought those songs were, even not knowing what they were about. But she would never teach them to us or tell us about them because she was afraid of what would happen to us if we talked about it in public. It was not until I came to work at the U'mista and discovered that one of the masks in the Potlatch Collection has my grandfather's name on it that I then came to understand why my grandfather at times seemed to me to be in another place. I think I can now understand how he was torn between religion and culture – taking up religion in fear of using the culture and what using it could/might bring to us.[54] (Andrea Sanborn)

> [Vera Newman] talked about growing up in Alert Bay in the large houses that they were in and having the fear once of being arrested. Fear was embedded in people such that when the women were in the houses and white people of whatever description came to the door, whether they be salesmen or schoolteachers or whatever, the women would flee to the back of the house and children would be told to go to the door and say nobody is home. And that effectively characterized the relations with the outside community. It was fear and trauma.[55] (John Pritchard)

In addition to personal guilt, fear, and trauma, the Kwakwa̲ka̲'wakw endured other harms from the banning of the potlatch and the events flowing from the Village Island potlatch. Some people totally rejected Kwakwa̲ka̲'wakw practices and culture and took up the culture, religion, and practices of the settlers. Their withdrawal from the traditional practices produced gaps in the overall knowledge of Kwakwa̲ka̲'wakw culture that, to this day, have not been filled. Stan Ashcroft succinctly assesses the impact of the potlatch ban: "we say that the bringing in of the potlatch laws was designed to and did have the effect of destroying the potlatch, which was, of course, the fundamental social and economic basis of the culture." The Crown's banning of the potlatch through the creation of this law effectively functioned as a tool of forced assimilation. According to Ethel Alfred, it was part of a campaign to make the Kwakwa̲ka̲'wakw "disappear."

As the Kwakwa̲ka̲'wakw struggle to reclaim their laws and culture, the gaps caused by the aftermath of the potlatch ban continue to be problematic.

Some generations do not know their laws and traditions, so they are unable to pass them on to the members of their families who want to properly respect them. And, most unfortunately, some of the elders died without passing on their knowledge:

> I guess one of the things that's challenging is we're living in a time now, in 2003, where a lot of family members that are in their fifties and late sixties, they grew up in a time where they weren't paying attention to what was going on with our potlatch system. So now they have younger generations wanting to learn and some of them don't, just don't know, they just don't know what the system is. They don't know names. They don't know songs, dances. And that's the scary part ... [W]hen my granny, Agnes Cranmer, lived to be eighty-seven, eighty-eight, there was a whole set of them, all these older people that were still alive and sharing all the things that go with culture. Not just singing, not just dancing, but everything that went. [W]'eve lost a lot of old people that are knowledgeable and that's the scary part. And the challenge is, where do we go now, to preserve, with the present-day old people, what we have. (Andrea Cranmer)

> Because of being so young when they took away the masks, I have forgotten what masks belonged to certain families [and were] used during the peace dance and the Red Cedar Bark Ceremony. That's why it's of the utmost importance for us to be concerned to protect our customs so that the government will never take it away from us again. Because when you think of what the government did to us, it was devastating what they did. They went on an out-and-out campaign to work towards making our people disappear. That's why it [is] right for us to worry about it, because when you think of what they did to us, it's really amazing: they just wanted us to be like a white man. (Ethel Alfred)

Loss of language and, thus, a loss of culture also flowed from the ban. School-aged children were forced to speak English in residential schools for eight months each year, and this made it difficult for younger people to learn how to speak their language fluently. Since the potlatch and most Big House ceremonies were conducted in Kwak'wala, young people, unless they were determined to pay the costs of retaining their language, could not fully participate. As Ethel Alfred explains in the following passages, the residential school system also caused people to be ashamed of their culture. She recounts how, for a time, she was "brainwashed" and did not want to continue with her cultural practices:

> I didn't complete what I said earlier about my older sister losing her oldest child. My dad did something right away. I was the one that knew where

> my dad kept his money, and he asked me to get some. My mom trusted me. I said to my dad, "Dad, it's not good what you are doing." 'Cause I got really, got confused and brainwashed while I was in the girls' school. I didn't like to practise our customs anymore. I told my dad that we were gong to end up with no money if [he] continue[d] to practise our customs. "Don't speak that way," my dad said to me. He said, "Your older sister's heart would be just broken if we didn't do anything for her." They gave a potlatch right away. (Ethel Alfred)

In an ironic twist, after the ban came into force, carvers continued to produce masks and other items; however, since they could not be used in the Big House, they were sold to non-aboriginal collectors and tourists:

> And what I can't understand today is that they would purchase masks now from our carvers when they are the ones that stopped us from practising our customs. It puzzles me when I think about it, why they would want to touch our sacred objects, our sacred pieces, when we weren't allowed to continue to use them. (Ethel Alfred)

Revival of Kwakwa̱ka̱'wakw Culture

A consistent theme in all interviews is that the potlatch must remain a central institution, although the reasons given for this vary. For some, it is because the potlatch is a spiritual and healing practice that gives strength to the participants. Equally important is the role the potlatch plays in educating community members about history and affirming relationships of belonging. Songs, dances, names, and associated regalia have their own histories, and these histories identify entitlements:

> [T]here's always a purpose for a potlatch. A speaker is there, along with the chief and the chief's family, to reinforce ownership of the chief's property ... who owns the songs, who owns the dances, how they got them, who they will be passed on to. That's how the potlatch ceremony works and [is] relevant to carrying on culture. [I]f somebody wants to challenge a statement, it should be done right ... during that ceremony ... and it will be settled at the ceremony. (Andrea Sanborn)

The potlatch also has a role in reviving traditional governance and management of land rights:

> I'm just saying we need to redefine what 'Na̱mgis people are and who are our hereditary chiefs and who the, you know, the potlatching chiefs are and establish our own traditional government again to get things rolling. And, in that way, we can find out who, what families lived in certain territories 'cause we all didn't live together at certain times. We travelled

around and had different camps and stuff; and people, their cultural property was their specific territories for doing things and they controlled it, guarded and protected it, you know, and made sure it was reusable in the next seasons and stuff. (William Wasden Jr., part 2)

Revival is not just a matter of bringing back the potlatch and traditional dances, songs, and ceremonies; it is also a matter of reviving the language, values, beliefs, teachings, and principles that go with them:

I think that songs, you know, are a crucial part of our ceremonies. Without the songs, we wouldn't dance. However, I believe that one of the challenges we have is that the beliefs and values have to go together with the teaching of the songs and the protection of the songs. That just 'cause a young person is learning how to sing songs, it doesn't give them the right to be in any public forum to be singing inappropriate[ly] or out of turn, kind of thing. So I believe that older members and wise people and knowledgeable people need to be present during the sharing of these songs so that the beliefs and values go along with what they are doing, and it's not just something cool to do. (Andrea Cranmer)

Of particular concern to Spruce Wamiss is the fact that social services continues to remove children from the community. Once they are taken, they are "lost in the system." Those he knows "lost their language. They lost their culture. They lost touch with their families." Many come home and want to reunite with their families, and it is "very hard for them to learn anything," especially the language and the culture. He compares this to the impact of the residential schools: "We lost our culture. We lost our language. We lost touch with our families and that's the same way social services is doing it. Take them out, take [them] away from the community, and they get lost in the system."

Participants know what must be done in order to best accomplish the revival and continuance of Kwakwaka'wakw culture: they must trust their own people to take the lead in protecting and preserving their culture and laws. Community research and education play a vital role in this process, as does the child's ability to learn "old ways" from parents and grandparents.[56] Although participants feel it is important to work with youth, it is equally important to work with adults and to provide them with an opportunity to learn:

Action needs to be taken, enough asking, enough of having people come and telling us what they think we should do, non-native people and linguists, and you name it. We don't need that. We know what we need to do. We need to put our trust into our own people that we can do the job of saving our language, of teaching our children, of preserving our history, of

> keeping the U'mista Cultural Centre open, because it's important. And we don't need people coming in to tell us that. And what really irritates me is that we pay them such big dollars to do that. It's so silly. And the other thing, we need a college. We need a First Nations college that teaches history, that teaches language, that teaches the beliefs and values ... going back to the land ... going on the canoes, going to the rivers, bathing in the rivers. We need a cultural university in this community because we are educating our young people. They get singing. They get dancing. They get Kwak'wala once in a while. They have community members go in and share their story about legends and all those kinds of things. But the adults aren't getting it. The adults don't have the opportunity to learn. And I'm only fortunate because I grew up in a family of potlatch people. Since I could walk, I knew what the Big House was, while not everyone my age had that opportunity. And we need to get everyone my age and give them that opportunity and give them that choice. (Andrea Cranmer)

> I guess, for me, one of the most important [things] is research from our own people and learning our own songs. And thank God there was our old people [who] recorded things way back and we are able to now access it, to research it, like the Łaxwe'gila CD. And if it wasn't for Dan Cranmer, we would have not – we would have lost the 'Namgis songs that belong to our people. And I'm really grateful to the young men that kept it alive, like Wa, because of his research. (Vera Newman)

As we discuss below, the repatriation of potlatch material that had been surrendered and confiscated after the Village Island potlatch is an important part of cultural revival. It is crucial to helping to address harms caused by the potlatch ban and to acknowledging those who suffered as a consequence. The Kwakwaka'wakw do not seek the return of potlatch items so that the originals can be used in the potlatch ceremony; rather, they seek them so that they may learn from them, so that they may transmit and preserve the cultural knowledge that those items represent. The histories, dances, and songs associated with these items are infused with cultural significance. Thus, the repatriation of potlatch items and the information concerning them provides a "basis for rebuilding and strengthening" Kwakwaka'wakw culture.[57]

Ownership and Belonging

Kwakwaka'wakw Traditions around Belonging

Entitlements to, and responsibility for, dances and associated songs performed at potlatches have individual, family, and community dimensions. Dances and associated prerogatives can be held by men and women and are transferred from generation to generation. Some songs and dances are intended for men and others for women. It is also customary for a woman to transfer property to her husband on marriage. Transfers within and among families occur at potlatch ceremonies marking death, marriage, and important family events. The following passages illustrate these points:

> Talking about my grandfather's dance, what House he came from, who he danced it for, and it belongs to our family. Because dad only had one son, it went to my dad first after my grandfather, then it went to his son, his only son. And then, when my brother became a *hamat'sa* for my dad, the old people from the Mamalilikala – Jimmy Sewid, Jumbo Bell – put it on me, not my granny. [T]hose guys, the chiefs of Village Island people at that time, [put it on me] to be a caretaker for it with the understanding that it would always remain in our family. You can't give it away like we do other property in an Indian wedding and that. It stays in the Dick line, my dad's family line. I took the time to tape my grandmother who was the mother of the grandfather of the young lady who was having an Indian wedding this weekend at the potlatch in Alert Bay. And what we did, what I did as being a member of the Alfred family ... I went through my tapes, through my books, to think about what we could transfer to the husband because that is what we do. "You," my granny said, "the worst thing you could do as a family is to have an Indian wedding and your daughter doesn't bring anything, you come empty-handed." Whether it be a name, a dance, a song, you know, you had to transfer something because it means that you are upholding your daughter or granddaughter in our way. (Vera Newman)

> The groom's parents have to approach your family to request a marriage to be arranged between their son and you. So I can become a wife, they turn over a sum of money to the bride's family. I guess it could be looked at as an engagement ring. Granny Axu got grandpa Moses to give three hundred dollars to have a hold on me. [M]y uncle Sam Charlie didn't think it was enough. So granny just put her hands inside her petticoat and gave some more to grandpa. Then my uncle felt the money was enough. They transferred a copper to my husband's family. Then my husband's family was asked, "Does the copper stay with us?" So all the money that was transferred was given back to keep the copper, and the money went back to my father-in-law. And the copper was to validate the event. That was the way [of] the custom of our Indian marriage at that time. It was very different in the olden days. (Ethel Alfred)

Songs and dances are also composed for specific reasons, to acknowledge specific events and to relate family histories. Just as there were skilled carvers in the community, so there were skilled composers who composed songs for individuals and families. New songs and dances continue to be composed today:

> I've heard the majority of our elders say that every new dancer had their own new song ... either composed for them or it comes to them through their fasting and dreaming and stuff. So this is part of our ceremonies ... I went to a really awesome singing conference in Kincome, and one of my uncles said to me up there, "If you don't have new songs, then the dances ... everything will remain the same. Our culture will never move forward. Only the faces will change." ... [E]verybody had their own songs in the old days. And those songs sang and talked about that person, specifically, and it was really personal. You know, it was something individual and sacred, and it lifted people up about who they were ... I just thought that was really powerful that, you know, in your lifetime, that if you're part of the system, you'll have your own song to kind of carry you and you'll feel good about yourself and proud. When you hear your song, you know your spirit is lifted and you dance and feel good. (William Wasden Jr., part 2)

Family lineage groups have their own creation stories, which trace their ancestry to a supernatural being. Crests, names, songs, dances, and masks may represent, or derive from, that supernatural origin. The traditional concept of "belonging" associated with masks, dances, stories, and songs does not anticipate wrongful appropriation but, rather, common knowledge and compliance with Kwakwa̱ka̱'wakw protocols on use and responsibility. Relationships of "belonging" were traditionally demonstrated through performance and verified when witnessed by the community. Songs, dances, and masks were an integral part of family identity. Andrea Cranmer explains that "it was the elders, the ladies, like the grannies, that were the record keepers of the language, or names, or songs and dances." Although the chief and other men speak and take on important roles at the potlatch, it is the "grannies and the knowledgeable ladies of that family that guide the male in what he is doing":

> The other one that I'm familiar with is my grandmother, the Speck side of my family, is Numa̱s, the butterfly, how we got the creation story. That belongs to the family that my grandmother comes from, Ławit'sis, Turnour Island ... [M]ost creation stories all started ... from the great flood, from the bible. That blew me away when I found out. Numa̱s was an old, old man with a neck ring on. He was sitting on top of a mountain. He could see something flying towards him, way off. He was holding his hand ... on top of his forehead, looking up, and here it was a butterfly, and [it] came straight for him and sat on his head. And to this day, when the Tlowitsis people potlatch,

Numa̱s will walk in and come visit us; and if he gives a cedar ring, that means we have to continue on and he goes back out. My dad talks about Granny Ada crying every time Numa̱s came to visit because of the connection of who we are. She was a Ławit'sis; that's this person from Turnour Island. (Vera Newman)

[L]aw and order in the Big House was very, very important, very strict. And our leaders, the hereditary chiefs, they were taught at an early age, and everybody knew who their songs ... belonged to, who their dances belonged to. And there was law and order. And if you *udzag̱ali* [mishap in Big House] or *digita* [to make it right] somebody else's, long time ago, they would stop you and correct you on that part. We don't do that anymore. A lot of our own songs, even our own dances, [are] gone because of what happened to our elders. (Christine Joseph)

Stories, dances, and songs may require regalia to be properly performed. Regalia is transferred to, and held by, an individual as part of a family's "treasures." Ceremonial masks are intended to be danced and transferred among family members, along with the songs and dances that go with them. Dances, songs, and masks are viewed as part of an integrated whole. Repatriated items belong to the originating family by virtue of the fact that they were held by a family member who is now deceased and unable to transfer it to another family member. These items were lost as a result of confiscation, forced surrender, or sales (sometimes for a token payment).

Dynamic Traditions

Despite the cultural and societal changes experienced by the Kwakwa̱ka̱'wakw, the potlatch continues to play a vital role in their ability to acquire and learn about their traditions and rights to ceremonial dances, songs, masks, and other potlatch regalia. However, some families and individuals converted to Christianity and totally withdrew from any potlatch-like activities. Others died without passing on their knowledge. As composers died, confusion and disagreements arose. These situations led to disagreements about belonging and usage that are still being worked out. They also resulted in the emergence of new traditions and a form of community property that enabled a wider section of the community to use family property. The example that almost all participants referred to involves the practice of borrowing and singing other people's songs. The tension between retaining older values, fulfilling responsibilities, and adapting to contemporary circumstances underscores the comments of many participants as they discuss the potlatch. Given the gaps in cultural memory caused by the anti-potlatch laws and other forms of assimilation, it is not surprising that disagreements arise in the process of rebuilding. And, of course, original Kwakwaka'wakw laws had no way of anticipating the problems that would arise with contact and the suppression of the potlatch.

However, seeking permission and acknowledging original entitlements is still an important part of Kwakwaka'wakw culture. If a mask is borrowed from a family member so that it may be danced, permission is necessary. Also, it must be kept safe, and "you return it and make sure it's returned to the person you borrowed it from."[58] Similarly, if the owner is known, using songs without gaining permission from the appropriate family or individual is viewed as a form of wrongful appropriation and disrespect. If a song is borrowed, its origins and owner should be acknowledged when it is performed:

> And because we've lost a lot, we just sometimes ... borrow each other's in the Big House. But we don't use those songs just as they are. You have to ask the person who it belongs to before you can sing it. Especially with our masks and dances. If I was to use Basil's dance, one of his dances, I don't just go on the floor and use it. I have to ask permission from him ... And if I used his dance, he'd come after me right away. (Spruce Wamiss)

> I know there's a lot of problems with families breaking special laws now, you know, because I don't think a lot of them know where it came from ... [Y]ou know, like we have different crests ... Well, everybody uses other people's crests now. Like, you know, it used to belong to one family. Now everybody is entitled to use it ... and that's the way it looks to me now. (Emma Tamilin)

> Everything that we do in this world comes from the Big House. We say that all our laws that govern our lives come from the Big House. Everything we do in this world comes from the Big House. But we don't really do that. We don't really protect a lot of those things ... [o]ur family has the butterfly. It's now being used by other people, you know, and it's sad. There's nothing really we can do to protect that. Your relatives, my relatives, have asked me to do something about it, but what can I do about it? There's nothing I can do about it. I can't even go to anybody in the Big House to say, "Look, that should not be used by other families. That belongs to our family. That's our right." I've been told, "Why don't you potlatch to try to straighten it out?" Other people have tried to potlatch, and it really never has, it's never come to anything because there's no rules regarding that ... [T]here's people that potlatch that don't really have a right potlatching but we don't have anything to stop that. I know that the system is changing ... but that's fine. There's nothing wrong with that. It's the ones that don't have the right that get in there that bothers me ... And I don't see anything wrong with other, other families using other songs and stuff like that because we almost lost that. We're now getting a rebirth in that, where we have young people

> like Wa creating songs and stuff like that ... What do we got to be scared of? The only thing that we've got to be scared of really is loss of our culture. (Basil Ambers)

Generosity and giving of oneself is a fundamental tenet of Kwakw<u>a</u>k<u>a</u>'wakw society, demonstrated not only through gift giving at potlatches but also through the generosity of individuals who share their family songs. At the same time, entitlements to songs, dances, and potlatch regalia come with responsibilities. The delicate balance between generosity and responsibility is revealed in the following passages:

> I think ... the example I'd like to give again ... [is] Elsie, when a lot of young people learned her mother's sacred chant, you know, *Yelak̲'wala* [sacred chant] for the *h<u>a</u>ms<u>a</u>mł* [cannibal bird mask]. I think things would have been different if there was acknowledgment [of] where the song had came from and if they had gone to get permission, there would have been a different route taken on that. But she did things publicly in the Big House, played a tape of her mother and father singing this sacred song, and she told the people: "[T]his is my mother's song and I would appreciate it if people would stop just getting up and singing it freely." So, I thought that was powerful, and people may [have] thought, "gee, she's rowdy" or whatever. This goes back to cultural property, and this was a sacred chant, and it had to have been in their family for a long time, a gift from the Creator to their family in order to carry out their ceremony. So, of course, they need to protect it. So, to me, she had to make a serious stand because that was her obligation, on behalf of her mother's song. So, to me, like a lot of people, like back to the Num<u>a</u>s, their obligation is to protect that mask. There's a lot of big history that goes along with each piece and each mask and ... there's a lengthy story and a lengthy spirituality that came with it and teaching and lessons. (William Wasden Jr., part 2)

> We got ten, ten top values, I guess, or ten commandments of the Kwakw<u>a</u>k<u>a</u>'wakw [that] came through my granny, and a lot of them paralleled ... what Uncle Glen had to say. And one of them was to give of oneself; and to give of oneself to your family and friends because that's what our culture is based on, is giving, and not just giving gifts at potlatches but to give of yourself to help somebody if you know they need help. To give of yourself and to be, to be a total asset to your community and to help your community to make your community and people proud of you. (William Wasden Jr., part 2)

Economic pressures, the commercial art market, the process of cultural revival, lack of knowledge, and other factors have resulted in disagreement over proper use. For example, some artists have used images that, under traditional protocol, should only be used by a particular family or tribe. William Wasden Jr. also suggests that new guidelines and rules, or at least "common respect," are needed to address these problems:

> But when there's outside parties, like with non-native people, copying our styles and ... these things are our right and our privilege, and these have been handed down to us, and what we do with it is our, ultimately our personal choice. But I don't agree with other tribes that don't know anything about what they are producing, imitating and copying our style. And I know they feel the same about us because I've heard that when our people carve x*wi xwi* masks, that the Salish people are very offended by that, or even when we dance it. We have stories [of] how it has come down to us and to me. I've seen many other First Nations groups carving in our style the *ha̱msa̱mł,* and that's our most sacred mask, and it offends me. So maybe we just have to establish some kind of guidelines and rules around that or some common respect. I think it's just out of the knowledge about it. You know, our own people need to be educated about ... what these things represent. There's a lot of cultural people out there and cultural carvers, and then there's carvers who are seriously in the commercial market – you know what I mean – that they're just banging things out to make a living. And I'm not condemning that, you know. People need to make a living in this day and age, and a lot of our industry has collapsed on us. Now there's not too [many] places to turn to. But I think that there are other ways of getting around selling very sacred pieces. (William Wasden Jr., part 2)

The commercial art market has also induced individuals to sell items that, under traditional protocols, they do not have the right to sell outside of the family or that have come to be recognized by the community as cultural treasures. As Juanita Pasco explains, the problem is exacerbated by Canada's export control system. This is one of several problems identified with Canadian export laws, which are discussed later in this study:

> Some of the challenges are, say, for instance, people selling things that they don't have the rights to sell; and when things are done through cultural properties, they don't really demand a paper trail. I don't think they ask for enough assurances that whoever is selling it has the right to sell it. We get things that we purchase from them, and there's no history behind it, who owned it, and how did they get it. And I think that's important, that they should have to prove ownership of it. (Juanita Pasco)

Reflecting on this problem and safeguards that might be taken to ensure that material culture is returned to the appropriate community, Juanita Pasco also suggests that museums have no legal or moral right to place conditions on return; however, she also suggests that returning the Village Island potlatch items to family members who, for economic reasons, might be pressured to sell to dealers, would not have been a good idea. The community, affected families, and elders agreed that "the pieces were too fragile to go back to individual families." Two facilities were created in Cape Mudge and Alert Bay. It was "up to the families to decide where the pieces went."

A common theme among participants is that removal of important items from the community can be avoided if both outsiders and community members increase their respect for and understanding of Kwakwa̱ka̱'wakw culture. More steps need to be taken within the community to educate people about traditional laws and the significance of cultural property to retention of cultural knowledge and practices on the part of the broader Kwakwa̱ka̱'wakw community.

Repatriation

In the early 1960s, repatriation efforts began. With the assistance of Professor Michael Jackson (Faculty of Law, University of British Columbia), representatives of the Kwakwa̱ka̱'wakw community began negotiations with the National Museum of Man (formerly the Victoria Memorial Museum and now the Canadian Museum of Civilization). In 1975, the museum agreed to repatriate the Village Island potlatch items in its collection on the sole condition that a museum be built to house them. The Kwakiutl Museum opened in 1979 in Cape Mudge, and in 1980 the U'mista Cultural Centre was opened in Alert Bay.[59] However, negotiations with the Royal Ontario Museum (ROM) were not as smooth. The ROM asserted that its claim to legal ownership was "as strong as anyone else's"; sought compensation for expenses such as "curatorial care, conservation, [and] insurance"; and wanted a "co-operative travelling exhibit," with some of the collection, or contemporary replacement pieces, to remain at the ROM.[60] It was not until 1988, after the intervention of the minister of Indian affairs, that the potlatch items were taken out of the ROM collection and returned to U'mista.[61] An Order-in-Council was also passed, affirming the transfer of title of the collection to U'mista.[62]

Around that time, the Museum of the American Indian/Heye Foundation became the National Museum of the American Indian (NMAI) and part of the Smithsonian Institution. This turn of events resulted in a change of museum staff, and negotiations went much more smoothly than they had previously. Prior to this, efforts to deal with the Museum of the American Indian were unsuccessful, partly due to a fear that repatriation to the Kwakwa̱ka̱'wakw would open the door to many more claims:

[W]hen I went to New York we went to the fourth floor ... We were allowed to see the stuff that was all hidden in vaults ... and we had to, we had to go up to the fourth floor, and they were all open for us and I was looking at all the stuff that was in there. My God, there was hundreds of items. And I asked the curator, "Why don't you give it back to us?" And she says, "Because, for one thing, if we give it back to you people, we'd have to give everybody's back." "Yeah, but ours was stolen," I said, "Our stuff was stolen. So I think it's about time you returned it, don't you think so?" ... [A]nyhow I, that's all I said. I didn't want to, I didn't want to get into a fight with her. It's not her fault, like, you know, 'cause this happened ... just about a hundred years ago now. (Emma Tamilin)

In the United States, in the late 1980s, the relationships between museums and First Nations were changing. A new federal law was being negotiated to provide for repatriation, ownership, and control rights over Native American "cultural items" to federally recognized Indian tribes.[63] Although the NMAI and Canadian First Nations do not fall within the scope of the legislation that was eventually enacted, the NMAI developed its own repatriation policy in the spirit of that legislation, which was even broader in scope.[64] In addition to human remains, funerary objects, communally owned material, and ceremonial and religious items, the NMAI policy also contemplates the return of illegally acquired material. Although the policy anticipates that claimants will be Native American groups or Hawaiian organizations, claims have not been limited to these groups and may be made by "descendants and those that can demonstrate cultural affiliation to the materials."[65] Pursuant to negotiations under this policy, nine items were returned to Alert Bay in 1994. In July of 2000, the NMAI agreed to return another sixteen pieces.[66] The return of these items was celebrated on 23 November 2002.

Unlike the repatriation claims of some First Nations, those of the Kwakwa̲ka̲'wakw with regard to potlatch items are not so much linked to the assertion of communal rights or to violation of traditional laws concerning belonging, possession, and control as to rectification of injustices suffered as a consequence of the potlatch ban and its disruption to the continuity of Kwakwa̲ka̲'wakw culture. Nor do they assert that actual, original use is necessary for the performance of spiritual ceremonies. Although the potlatch ceremony is central to the spiritual life of the community, masks and other potlatch regalia continue to be created by Kwakwa̲ka̲'wakw artists. As Gloria Cranmer Webster explains:

Most demands for repatriation are based on the argument that the treasures are vital to the spiritual health of native communities. This was not the basis in our case. We did not need our masks returned so that we could use

> them. In fact, most of them are in extremely fragile condition, due to years of neglect in the museums which housed them. Our goal in having our treasures come home was to rectify a terrible injustice that is part of our history. The objects used in contemporary potlatches have been and continue to be created by our artists. Some of the masks are replicas of earlier ones, several of which are from the Potlatch Collection. Our concept of ownership differs from that of other people in that, while an object may leave our communities, its history and the right to own it remain with the person who inherited it.[67]

However, as transfer of ownership was considered to be an important step in rectifying past injustices, U'mista was not prepared to accept the potlatch items on long-term loan. The same position has been taken with respect to potlatch items not yet returned. According to Andrea Sanborn: "It's important to have it returned because it belongs to our people. They, the institutions, can keep replicas. The originals have to come back."

Many participants spoke about the experiences of their relatives and of how the repatriation of their regalia is one way to acknowledge that suffering and to help the family and community heal. As Emma Tamilin explains, "[i]t's just part of healing, 'cause we all need to be healed because of what happened in 1922 it affected all of us." Basil Ambers emphasizes that it is also important to acknowledge "old-timers" as "heroes" and to respect those who are still in the community and who suffered, or whose immediate family members suffered. He suggests that U'mista could still do more in this regard.

Lack of emphasis on their original use in spiritual ceremonies does not mean that the spiritual nature of repatriated materials is ignored or that their return is unimportant to the spiritual and emotional well-being of the community:

> Because if we believe in spirituality, the spirit[s] of those masks, the spirits in those masks that are all over the world ... they must be really sad and lonely. Like, if you think about it in that [way], and it's probably lost, they're probably lost, wondering, "[W]here am I?" And, "[I]t's time for me to go home now." And I believe when the masks, like the ones from New York, they came and they bridged that gap with our people and we got our stuff back. Now I believe that the spirits can rest now. They can go home now, and the essence of them can go now and the masks can stay with us to remind us of that time when our people went through so much hardship. (Andrea Cranmer)

Participants also speak of the importance of repatriating items in order to rebuild ceremonies, values, beliefs, and knowledge. All participants emphasized that the importance of repatriating potlatch items also lies in the cultural knowledge that they represent. As William Wasden Jr. explains (part 2 of interview): "There's a lot of big history that goes along with each piece and each mask, and ... there's a lengthy story and a lengthy spirituality that came with it, and teaching and lessons. And you know that a lot of pieces in our ceremonies represent things and are giving us teachings and tools to function better."

Participants, including those who are members of families that have had potlatch items returned, agree that it is important to keep them safe and accessible so that future generations can learn from them, despite the fact that, under Kwakwa̱ka̱'wakw law, they belong to specific families. For this reason, the requirement that they be housed in a museum-like facility is not considered to be an unreasonable request, particularly given that the facility is located on Kwakwa̱ka̱'wakw territory and controlled by Kwakwa̱ka̱'wakw. Participant opinions confirm Clavir's observation (below) that proper care of the items validates their importance to the family and community.[68] Vera Newman's words reflect a common sentiment:

> I'm so proud of U'mista because we have our own members that are board members, our own people. There's no non-native administrator telling us how to do things. It's our people that are the board members of our cultural centre, and I believe that's where our family treasures are stored and it's really important for us to know it's in a safe place. So I have a great deal of respect and appreciation for the cultural centre. (Vera Newman)

However, Basil Ambers cautions that it is important not to lose sight of the fact that families are the true owners of the potlatch material.

Access to potlatch items on the part of entitled family members is crucial. However, circumstances can arise in which it is important to use a particular item that is too fragile. Quoting Juanita Pasco, Miriam Clavir explains how U'mista accommodates this need:

> In the preceding case, the use of the objects at the potlatch was facilitated by staff at the U'mista Cultural Centre, where the family had chosen to house the objects. As museum-like storage in Alert Bay was the family's choice, and as the family was concerned about the objects' well-being, in this instance standard conservation practice integrated well with First Nations' need for use of the object at the potlatch. In fact one could say that following standard conservation practice validated the importance of these older pieces for their family of origin because it signified that the family took good care of the pieces. The collections manager at U'mista brought the objects over to the Big House for the potlatch: "I brought them in, and told them how to handle things, just a little: 'This is how you do it, you

> know, you use two hands. Don't hold two objects' – and just went over the basics with them. They were all excited. They wanted to use the little white gloves – but I didn't have any!"[69]

U'mista also purchases contemporary objects to loan to families to use in potlatch ceremonies and, when requested, stores personal regalia that is still in use.[70]

A challenge in repatriation involves divergent views on "ownership." Concepts of ownership and belonging vary among First Nations and between First Nations and Canadian institutions. For these reasons, repatriation negotiations in Canada have tended to be resolved according to moral and ethical grounds rather than according to which concepts and laws of ownership and belonging prevail. Nevertheless, it is still necessary for First Nations communities to establish prior cultural connection and "ownership" of the items they want returned. Sometimes it is possible to find written information to verify community understandings or entitlement. However, conflict between written documents in the hands of museums and oral traditions in the hands of the First Nations community can result in protracted, expensive, and complicated negotiations. Sometimes items are clearly marked. For example, Emma Tamilin explains that it was not uncommon for people to carve their names inside of masks. However, at other times the objects are so old and worn that it is impossible to identify the original owner:

> A lot of the problem is establishing, or having the records to establish, the rightful ownership because there were no written – there wasn't a written language for Kwak'wala in the early days and anything that was written was ... second-hand information, which can easily be misconstrued or whatever, misinterpreted, by those that are writing them ... So I think that's, that's a big problem, establishing the ownership without written information. (Andrea Sanborn)

Once ownership is established, negotiations can be further complicated by disagreements in the community and legal barriers that prevent a museum from deaccessioning objects without imposing conditions with respect to preservation and public access. This may mean that a First Nation must first obtain funds to create and operate a museum-like facility in their community. For example, a condition for repatriating the Potlatch Collection from the National Museum of Man and the ROM was that U'mista build a museum and follow museum conservation procedures. Exceptions have been made with respect to the loan and return of sacred and ceremonial items necessary for the practice of ceremonial and religious traditions.[71] As Gloria Cranmer Webster explains:

> This condition, unfortunately, resulted in long delays as there was disagreement about where such a building should be located. Eventually it was decided that two museums would be built, one in Cape Mudge and the other in Alert Bay, with the collection to be divided between the two. Another problem emerged. Halliday had prepared a list of the objects for the Victoria Memorial Museum [later the National Museum of Man and then the Canadian Museum of Civilization]. The document was quite inaccurate according to our own research on ownership of the individual pieces, so that reaching an agreement on the division of [the] collection took some time.[72]

All participants see a role for elders, family members, and the community in resolving disagreements and ascertaining rights to Kwakwa̲ka̲'wakw material culture. Juanita Pasco describes the approach that she used when conducting repatriation research with U'mista: "[I talk to] the older people first and then, if there aren't any that can help me, then I work my way down the line to the knowledgeable people that I know." Bill Cranmer also emphasizes the importance of consultation:

> I think the safeguards would have to involve open discussions with – take, for instance, the Kwakwa̲ka̲'wakw. We, our territories, stretch right from northern Vancouver Island to the Campbell River, and so it would have to involve discussions with everybody within that, that area. I think we have already experienced that with the return of some of the collection to the Kwakiutl Museum in Cape Mudge, where some of the families that lived in this area wanted their pieces returned to the U'mista so that they would see these pieces here on a daily basis if need be. It's a matter of talking to everybody and making sure that what the families want is what actually happens. (Bill Cranmer, part 1)

Although the Kwakwa̲ka̲'wakw are best suited to deal with healing the harms caused by the potlatch ban, participants agree that there is a role for Canadian institutions in restoring the potlatch to its central place. Participants expressed an appreciation for the role museums have played in protecting cultural items and as repositories of cultural information. U'mista has now assumed this role for the Kwakwa̲ka̲'wakw community it serves. Participants also note that it is important for museums to continue to return regalia and other items significant to Kwakwa̲ka̲'wakw culture. Museums have responsibilities to the community with respect to Kwakwa̲ka̲'wakw items and the information that they retain. This includes sharing information, consulting with regard to proper use and display, and limiting access to information not intended to be shared with the public. As Bill Cranmer emphasizes, "[T]he reason that they have these [potlatch] pieces and information in their collection is because of the circumstances our people found themselves in as a result of different government policies." Their responsibilities to First Nations should be viewed in this light.

Participants who are engaged in negotiations for potlatch items and cultural information relayed positive attitudes towards Canadian and American museums that understood the harm suffered by the banning of the potlatch and the importance of returning potlatch items for community healing and cultural revival. U'mista's success in building positive relationships and repatriating cultural items and information is attributed to a number of factors, including having a facility that meets museum standards, common interest in preserving cultural items and information for future generations, properly trained staff, and a credible reputation within the museum community. As part of the repatriation process, U'mista also conducts its own research and engages in constructive publicity to raise awareness about the importance of repatriating the items requested. Successful relationships are also attributed to the efforts and understanding of individuals who are working for museums and are helping to initiate change, such as Peter MacNair, a former curator in the ethnology department of the Royal British Columbia Museum (RBCM).

Participants also identified several challenges to successful repatriation negotiations. The recovery and repatriation of confiscated regalia costs a significant amount of money. Although many museums will provide lists of materials within their collections, these lists are not always accurate and site visits are required both for the identification of items and for the negotiation of their return. Once found, a missing item may have to be purchased from the present possessor and then be shipped, catalogued, cleaned, and restored before it can be placed on display. Money is also required to build an appropriate facility and for the ongoing maintenance of the display and research space. These costs are one reason why the 'Na̲mgis and U'mista have initiated a specific claim against the federal government:

> The difficulty with the specific claims policy is that it only can provide monetary compensation. Nevertheless, what we are seeking is monetary compensation for the harm that was done to the community or the communities by the taking away of the potlatch and compensation for those articles that were seized and which were never paid for and, in particular, we are talking about the coppers. What we have sought from the federal Crown, and will be seeking, is monies in order for there to be repatriation of any remaining items that were, were seized or surrendered, the proper housing and maintenance of those items, the proper museum facilities for them to be properly presented, proper storage, and all of the administration and the costs that go along with that. (Stan Ashcroft)

In 2004, the University of British Columbia's Museum of Anthropology returned, on long-term loan, three masks that were believed to be part of the Village Island Potlatch Collection. Another item recently returned to U'mista on long-term loan is the Transformation Mask held by the British Museum. The RCMP officer who carried out the 1921 arrests sold it under his wife's name.[73] Originally part of the collection of the National Museum of the American Indian, in 1936 it was transferred to the Cranmore Ethnographical Museum in Chislehurst, Kent, England, and from there to its current location.[74] Repatriating from the British Museum has proven to be the most difficult task yet. The museum initially refused U'mista's request for the mask's return, citing legislative barriers.[75] According to museum director, Dr. Robert Anderson, to turn over the mask would be illegal: "I would, in fact, be breaking British law."[76]

U'mista's usual approach to repatriation is to avoid the assertion of legal rights, emphasize moral obligations, and avoid using the media to put pressure on negotiating parties. Rather, the media is used constructively to celebrate returns and to build understanding about the importance of the repatriation of cultural items. However, initial difficulties encountered with regard to the British Museum repatriation resulted in the adoption of different strategies. Particularly frustrating was the fact that the Transformation Mask was not even on display:

> They told us that the gallery that was housing it was under construction and all the pieces were packed away and would be for at least three years. Since that time, I've talked to people that know about the situation. People from England, people from the Netherlands have told me that they have gone specifically to see that piece and it is not on display. And they don't know if it will ever be on display, and I'm sure it's because of the controversy around it now ... [t]hey'd just as soon leave [it] in the back room somewhere and not allow people to have access. Although they have said it is the museum law for them to have it so that anybody who wants to study it, anybody with any interest in it, will be able to go at any time and study it, and yet it's not even on display ... It's pretty hard to go and study something that's in a box. (Andrea Sanborn)

As a result of media interest, public pressure, changes in personnel at the British Museum, and U'mista's increased experience with negotiating, an agreement to return the Transformation Mask on loan was finally reached – eight years after the first request was made. This return was largely due to the efforts of Jonathan King, a keeper at the British Museum's Department of Africa, Oceania, and the Americas. He supported the request that the mask be returned to the U'mista Cultural Centre.[77]

U'mista purchases and seeks the repatriation of various items of cultural, historic, or artistic value that are currently in the hands of museums or private collectors. Of particular concern is the export of Kwakwa̲ka̲'wakw cultural items outside of Canada. Whenever possible, U'mista has attempted to prevent export and to negotiate the donation and/or purchase of such property. Because of various problems encountered in this process, in 1999 U'mista initiated a review of the impact of federal import and export law on First Nations.

Given the passing of elders and the impact of acculturation on retention of cultural knowledge, it is important that items be returned along with the information that is associated with them. Also, sometimes associated information is inaccurate; because of this, the community needs to review it:

> In the meantime, it's very important to keep that link between language and objects in any kind of action we are undertaking now outside to get this material back, so that [it is] not coming without the rest of the information which belongs to [it]. Very often a museum has information about a mask or even has not done proper research about the information regarding the mask. So the museum [has an] obligation to produce this information, to do their own research, at their own cost, [and] to give it back with the object.[78] (Guy Buchholtzer)

Since 1993, U'mista has been developing its capacity as an information and resource centre on Kwakwa̲ka̲'wakw culture. Although a significant amount of research has been conducted by academics and others on Kwakwa̲ka̲'wakw communities, until recently original research data and outcomes were rarely shared with the community. Given the importance of this information to rebuilding Kwakwa̲ka̲'wakw knowledge and cultural life, U'mista has expanded its repatriation efforts to include information concerning the Kwakwa̲ka̲'wakw culture wherever it is situated. As discussed earlier in this chapter, the 'Na̲mgis Nation and U'mista have also responded to this problem by establishing research protocols that must be followed by people conducting research on the 'Na̲mgis Reserve.

Reflecting on his research and involvement with the Kwakwa̲ka̲'wakw Centre for Language and Culture in Community, Guy Buchholtzer explains:

> [M]any scholars, many people who write about the community, many people who go there, they often forget about the community as soon as they've done their publications, as soon as they've done their research ... I felt that it was very important that the community regain control over all the information concerning itself, whatever the information is. The community [needs] to look at this information, to judge it, to discuss it, and to supplement it, to evaluate it ... [T]he project consists of first identifying the sources then retrieving those sources, retrieving some material, looking at some material, indexing all this material. And I have a fair knowledge,

> because I have worked for more than a quarter of a century on this issue, where it can be. It's all over the world. I made a feasibility study for the U'mista, and that feasibility study indicated that 70 percent of everything is outside the community. More than 50 percent, perhaps 60 percent is outside of Canada, so that repatriation concerns Canada as well, and I hope that we have the support of Canada [in] repatriating this material to Canada ... Secondly, what is important too is that we are not creating a dead archive or a dead library. What we want to do, and that is in agreement with the elders in the community, is to have a centre where ... those things are going to be discussed, criticized in positive or negative – whatever it deserves. [A]nd to have it integrated again within the community, and the community becomes again – and stays as – the producer of its own culture. Outcomers [people from outside the community] can be invited under, under agreements with the community to look at those materials, to discuss them to do research, but with the agreement of the community and in very clear legal terms. (Guy Buchholtzer)

Although participants acknowledge the importance of having access to material written about them in order to learn more about their language and culture, William Wasden Jr. cautions that such material must be approached with caution:

> You know when Europeans write about us, they've already got an opinion on us because their culture is almost [the] reverse of ours. So there's always going to be some sort of flavour to the way they are going to speak about us and stuff. And, you know, a lot of times they might not understand what these, what these spiritualities and what these pieces and these cultural properties do for us, you know. (William Wasden Jr., part 2)

Some participants express frustration over the removal of data from the community but, at the same time, are grateful that recordings had been made as these have been pivotal in relearning songs, ceremonies, and language. Copies are sufficient, in most cases, to serve the objectives of cultural education and retention and the revival of cultural information and the Kwak'wala language. Those who speak to this issue did not indicate a need for the return of original tapes, archival material, or other records. Sometimes, when budgets allow, the costs are born by the institution receiving the request.

U'mista is engaged in a number of initiatives, other than repatriation, to increase its effectiveness as an information and resource centre, including recording and digitizing oral history in a number of areas. For example, in 1991, U'mista undertook a project to record traditional songs. These have been entered into an audio collection database, and a catalogue record, "which lists whom the song belonged to and the village it came from," has been completed.[79] Family members can request copies of songs "as well as the legends and histories."[80] Such recordings have played a vital role both in learning about and reviving Kwakwa̲ka̲'wakw ceremonies and Kwak'wala itself.

Authenticity and Appropriation of Art: An Artist's Perspective

William Wasden Jr. spoke at length about the challenges faced by Kwakwa̲ka̲'wakw artists.[81] It is now common for Kwakwa̲ka̲'wakw artists to borrow designs and images, such as ancestral crests, from outside of their families or from another tribe. Outside interest in this art and lack of knowledge on the part of some artists has resulted in the commercial sale of images that, in his opinion, should not be shared outside the community without the consent of the appropriate family. He views the use of images, such as emblems and other family images, without proper permission as a form of wrongful appropriation that threatens the cultural integrity of the image. Basil Ambers shares similar concerns about people who are carving totem pole crests and mystic figures, "some Indian and some not." He wonders if the community is "afraid of looking" at this "properly" as it has failed, to date, to take steps to prevent it.

Understanding the need for other artists to support themselves, William Wasden Jr. suggests that families should be responsible for speaking out if they are concerned about the use of a particular image, given the extent to which borrowing has become commonplace among the Kwakwa̲ka̲'wakw. He does not see the sale of images without prior permission as improper and speculates that "[m]aybe the Creator gave us our culture, our wonderful carving style, 'cause he knew how tough the times were going to be." However, the following comments raise difficult questions about what amounts to wrongful appropriation within the community, which images are appropriate for commercial sale, and whose permission is required:

> [I]f people are carving other people's cultural property and the owners don't say nothing about it, then it's kind of like, it's kinda like when somebody, somebody tells a lie and you don't correct them or you don't stand up for the truth and you become a part of it. If that becomes the accepted truth, and you were a part of the lie because you didn't speak up for it ... And, you know, I think people would respect it and respect the, the leaders of those families if they were to say, "You know, I would appreciate it," or whatever, "if you carve my ancestor that you come and talk to me about it first." You know, there would become a more common respect for people and each other over that because it's one thing to be behind the scenes nattering and going on about something, but if it bothers you that much, then go and talk about it.

In his opinion, there is also a difference between ceremonial pieces and pieces intentionally produced for the art market. The "carvers of old" did not sell sacred masks or "major pieces" in the commercial market. Carving at a time when traditions were strong, people could live off the land, and before the anti-potlatch laws and international demand for West Coast aboriginal art exponentially increased its value, they were not faced with the same issues as are contemporary artists who are trying to determine what is and what is not appropriate for sale to outsiders. Wasden Jr. also suggests that new guidelines must be established that include not selling items considered sacred by a particular family or those prepared for ceremonial purposes outside the family. However, in some circumstances, sale of replicas may be acceptable.

Wasden Jr. also considers the use of Kwakwa̱ka̱'wakw images for commercial gain by non-indigenous artists, other than those formally adopted and considered part of the community, to be a form of cultural appropriation. Kwakwa̱ka̱'wakw should not have to "compete with white carvers" who are using their images. He is also concerned about issues of authenticity, accreditation, and cultural integrity. In his interview, he suggests a few strategies for preventing non-Kwakwa̱ka̱'wakw artists from passing off their work as Kwakwa̱ka̱'wakw and for enabling buyers to authenticate items of interest to them. One strategy he proposes is to develop a website that gives information on Kwakwa̱ka̱'wakw artists. He sees U'mista as having a role in developing this resource because the staff have the knowledge and expertise. He also sees it as a way for artists who wish to be on the list to learn more about their own family history and culture and to reduce the need to borrow from others. Some artists have discussed "a stamp or something like that." Although not opposed to it, Wasden Jr. sees this as just "buying into the white man's ways."

Role of Canadian Law and Government

Participants in this study think that cultural heritage must be protected on many levels. The starting point is considered to be with the Kwakwa̱ka̱'wakw themselves because failure to protect their own culture will have deleterious consequences. Reflecting on the meaning of "cultural property," Vera Newman emphasizes the importance of the community's doing its own research while the "old people" are still alive rather than relying on outside experts. For her and others, protection means learning the traditions and living according to the values, beliefs, and principles that the elders teach. It also means being teachers. It means recording and documenting the knowledge of the elders. According to Basil Ambers, these efforts must be accompanied by a respect for Kwakwa̱ka̱'wakw laws: "If we don't look at our laws and don't put teeth to it, then its never going to right itself." Putting forward a canoe gathering called Łaxwe'gila, or "gathering strength," as an example of a recent event that embraced members of the community from "all walks of life," Andrea Cranmer is optimistic the community will come together and emphasize the importance of healing so that "people can get their voice back and be empowered" to develop strategies and to discuss rights that many do not know they have:

> I believe that if we continue to heal as a people, we can continue to make the proper decisions that need to be made for cultural property and all the things that encompass cultural property. And we need to come clean. We need to get our minds clean, our souls clean – all those aspects, we need to come clean with it. And I believe that we can do it, our people can do what needs to [be] done around here. (Andrea Cranmer)

Participants also recognize a strong role for Canadian law and governments in protecting Kwakwa̱ka̱'wakw cultural heritage. All participants called for the Canadian government to acknowledge that the banning of the potlatch was a wrong committed against the Kwakwa̱ka̱'wakw people. Several suggested compensation must be made to the people who had their regalia confiscated, to those who were charged, and to those who were imprisoned for participating in potlatches. One participant draws a parallel between the compensation granted by the Canadian government to Japanese Canadians who had their property wrongfully confiscated during the Second World War. She wonders why the Kwakwa̱ka̱'wakw have not been compensated in the same manner:

> About rightful ownership to the property of all types, cultural, intellectual, anything that belongs to a First Nation, especially ours, they – the government – has to accept responsibility for that ... For instance, the Japanese Internment, where they have extended apologies to those people, extended financial compensation to those people, which is fine. It was wrong that was done against those people, but we are the First Nations of Canada, and here we are still, all these years, a century later, arguing about this. Where is the sense in that? (Andrea Sanborn)

One way to compensate communities harmed by anti-potlatch laws is to fund repatriation initiatives, programs, and First Nations cultural centres. The chronic underfunding of the U'mista Cultural Centre and the Kwakiutl Museum with regard to these and other cultural protection initiatives is a major impetus behind the specific claim discussed below.

U'mista employees and board members commented on the need for existing laws to be strengthened and enforced so as to recognize the importance of material culture. Governments need to work with First Nations communities towards this end. Of particular concern are the limited protections offered by Canada's export control laws and copyright law. These laws are viewed as facilitating, rather than preventing, wrongful appropriation and loss of cultural items and information. Other participants speak in more general terms about the need for laws to protect different aspects of Kwakwa̱ka̱'wakw cultural heritage, including the Kwak'wala language. A common sentiment expressed by those addressing these issues is that outside laws must respect and protect Kwakwa̱ka̱'wakw concepts of belonging and way of life. In the words of Ethel Alfred, "[W]e want laws in place by the government so that people will not disturb our things that are sacred to our people." According to Andrea Sanborn, this means working with Kwakwa̱ka̱'wakw to enact laws that "protect our cultural identity, our cultural objects, our cultural ways" and that make "all the institutions, the dealers, the collectors ... accountable, first to their conscience and, secondly, to the laws."

Participant comments on Canada's export laws are informed by the difficulties U'mista encountered in trying to purchase and prevent the export of the Nowell bead and button blanket. Of particular concern to U'mista is the ability of dealers and collectors to manipulate the permit system to inflate sale prices for items that First Nations may be seeking to have returned. The "Nowell blanket is significant for its artistic merit, but more importantly, because of its exceptional history, craftsmanship, and what it represents to the descendants of Charles Nowell."[82] U'mista tried to purchase this blanket and prevent its export. Exports of cultural items outside of Canada are controlled by the *Cultural Property Export and Import Act*.[83] The Act is designed to discourage the export of cultural objects and to keep objects of national importance within Canada. It does this through export controls that delay permanent export permits and through the provision of repatriation grants, loans, and tax incentives. U'mista received notice of the decision to delay the export of the blanket from the Canadian Cultural Property Export Review Board (CCPERB) because the U'mista Cultural Centre is one of the few First Nations institutions that meets the requirements necessary to receive notice.[84] U'mista applied for a grant under the *Cultural Property Export and Import Act* (*CPEI*), informed the Board of its intent to purchase, and advised Sotheby's (Toronto) of this. At this stage, U'mista understood it would need about Cdn$11,800 to purchase the blanket. Although the *Act* itself places no conditions on grants or loans, the policy at the time was to require organizations applying for funding to contribute towards the purchase price, although in some cases this could be waived. Upon securing a private donor to contribute towards the purchase of the Nowell blanket, U'mista alleges that it was advised that a recommendation for the grant would be made to the minister responsible for administering the *CPEI* and assumed the CCPERB would deny an export permit pending this decision. However, the four-month delay imposed by the CCPERB expired and an export permit was granted to export the blanket to Sotheby's

(New York). One of the reasons cited was that an offer to purchase had not been made to Sotheby's within the delay period, a step U'mista was unable to take before funding was confirmed. Although the estimated value of the blanket was between US$6,000 and US$9,000, U'mista requested a grant for $US18,300 to enable it to bid competitively. Although U'mista eventually received the grant, the maximum amount it was able to bid for the blanket at the auction was US$21,500. At auction the blanket was purchased by a gallery in Ontario for US$24,500, which subsequently agreed to sell it to U'mista for US$30,000. U'mista requested an increase in its grant and received US$27,300. The balance was paid for by private donation.

Problems with the Nowell blanket repatriation and the experiences of another West Coast First Nation resulted in U'mista joining with other partners to research reforms to Canada's export laws:

> Well, one of the problems with the Export Review Board is, of course, the prohibitive costs of ... stopping the export. We'd have to come up with some monies to pay for the pieces, so that was one problem. And the other problem, of course, is a, is – what seems to happen when a piece is to be exported is the price skyrockets. An example is the piece from Bella Coola, where I think a collector bought it for a few thousand dollars and it cost the Bella Coola people I think pretty near a quarter million dollars to get it back.[85] So that was a, that was a real tragedy there, but they did manage to get it back. But, for the most part, lately we've been getting some very good cooperation from the museums in repatriation not only of actual physical property but also for the written materials and the recorded materials. (Bill Cranmer, part 1)

Copyright laws concerning ownership of recorded songs are inconsistent with Kwakwa̲ka̲'wakw understandings of belonging as relayed by the participants in this study. Concern is also expressed about the inability of federal law to protect artists from having their unique style appropriated through unauthorized copies and derivative works. To the extent that these protections exist in Canadian and international law, they are not known or fully understood. As Basil Ambers notes, "a lot of people don't know what our rights are":

> And also, I think there's issues around copyright which need to be resolved because Canadian copyright laws [don't] really take into consideration First Nations customs and what they consider ownership of songs ... [T]here's the material we recorded from Mackenzie in '91. As it stands now, we would retain copyright because it was our equipment. We hired the people. We paid for the information to be collected. But we don't consider ourselves as owners of the material, more [as] caretakers. (Juanita Pasco)

Giving the *Heritage Conservation Act*[86] as an example, Stan Ashcroft and John Pritchard also comment on the inadequacy of existing laws and speak to the importance of educating people about their legal obligations so that they know when they are in breach of them. However, even if people are aware of the limited protections this legislation offers, that is not enough. It is not enough because the scope of property protected by the *Act* is too narrow and because the minister can permit developers to destroy and alter heritage sites that the legislation is intended to protect. According to Stan Ashcroft, what is needed is "a much broader understanding of what constitutes, or at least from the government's side, what constitutes cultural objects for aboriginal people and what should be protected and laws that will provide severe penalties for them being disturbed or taken."

The 1998 claim that U'mista and the Nuyumbalees Cultural Society submitted to the Specific Claims Branch of the Department of Indian and Northern Affairs was made on behalf of fifteen First Nations that, formerly, were part of the Kwakiutl Agency. The specific claim asks the question: "[D]id the passage of the prohibition and its enforcement constitute a breach of the lawful obligation owed by the federal government to the Native peoples of Canada, and in particular, with reference to the facts in the claim, to the Bands of the Kwakwa̲ka̲'wakw filing this Specific Claim[?]"[87] Broadly put, the specific claim alleges breaches of fiduciary duty in three areas: the passage by Parliament of the original prohibition in the *Indian Act* and its subsequent amendments; the role and actions of Deputy Superintendent General of Indian Affairs Duncan Campbell Scott in securing the original prohibition amendment and his actions in enforcing the prohibition against the Kwakwa̲ka̲'wakw; and the role and actions of Indian Agent Halliday in securing the original prohibition, acting as both Indian agent and judge in the trials following the Village Island potlatch, in demanding the forfeiture of regalia and his acquisition of same, and for failing to prevent Sergeant Angerman's improper acquisition of potlatch items. The claim also alleges negligence, breach of the *Indian Act* (statutory duty), and breach of an agreement between Scott and the Kwakiutl Agency Canada to investigate prohibition of the potlatch.

The specific claim was filed because "U'mista wants Canada to accept that what they did was wrong [and to] cover the costs of continuing repatriation of the Potlatch Collection, costs for caring for the Collection, and resources to assist U'mista in language preservation."[88] The only remedy under the specific claims process is monetary compensation. Compensation is being sought for the "harm done to the community or communities by the taking away of the potlatch" and for "articles seized that were never paid for and in particular ... the coppers."[89] Harm includes not only loss of "regalia and the material itself" but also loss of language and the shattering of the social and economic system of the Kwakwa̲ka̲'wakw.[90] Specific examples of breach of fiduciary and statutory obligation by federal agents include the activities outlined in our discussion of the banning of the potlatch. Alleged breaches include Parliament's enacting the anti-potlatch laws based on false information, Canada's enabling Halliday to "convict those very persons who as Indian agent he was supposed to protect," and Halliday and Angerman's creating a scheme to "force people to surrender potlatch regalia and artifacts."[91]

The specific claim was rejected in December 1999. It has since been resubmitted, in February 2005, to the Specific Claims/Claims of a Third Kind Branch, which is where it currently sits. One of the primary reasons that the specific claim was rejected in 1999 was because "the broader category of breach of fiduciary duty *per se*" does not fall within the categories of claims identified in the policy as an area that the federal government is prepared to negotiate.[92] Further, only bands recognized under the *Indian Act* have the status to bring a claim. Therefore, in April 2002, the 'Na̱mgis Nation, on behalf of U'mista and the fifteen tribes, requested an inquiry by the Indian Claims Commission (ICC). The ICC is an independent advisory body that holds public inquiries into specific claims rejected by Canada. It also provides mediation services to help facilitate the process of negotiation. The claim before the ICC is ongoing. If the federal government does not accept the report of the ICC and agree to negotiate the claim, or if a First Nation is unsuccessful at the ICC, the only remaining recourse is to litigate the issue before the courts. At the time of writing, the ICC had not yet completed its investigation of U'mista's claim.

One of the inherent problems with the specific claims negotiation process is that the federal government is not only the defendant in these claims but also the institution that determines the validity of the claims submitted. This has been a concern to First Nations since its inception; it is the reason the ICC was formed; and it is the main rationale behind proposals for the new *Specific Claims Resolution Act*.[93] As John Pritchard explains:

> This is going before the Claims Commission right now, this claim, because it was rejected by Specific Claims West and it was done, we believe it was done on a narrow technical defence. They are claiming that, irrespective of the rights and wrongs here, the injured parties or individuals are not bands as such. So they are taking refuge in that narrow reading of the law. They are saying, in effect, that such things as language, economics, social systems, and so on were not band property as such. If the way that claims tend to work is that expropriation took place through a right of way through a reserve, and that right of way was supposed to be sixty-six feet and took sixty-seven feet, you've got a specific claim here and because it's band property. If you destroy an economic system, a social system, or wreck a language and traumatize people for generations, that's too bad because that's not band property.

Since this interview, the proposed *Specific Claims Resolution Act* has gone through several changes, including expanding the category of eligible claims to include breaches of fiduciary obligation other than those related to funding and delivery of public programs. Given the scope of potential fiduciary obligation claims, it is difficult to determine how this provision will be interpreted. Under the *Act*, if the minister decides not to negotiate a claim it is referred to the ICC. Matters of validity that cannot be resolved through the ICC dispute resolution process and issues of compensation may be referred to an independent tribunal that can make an award binding on the federal government. Although First Nations may make representations concerning appointments to the tribunal, appointments are made by the federal government. Another problem is that the maximum award that can be granted by the tribunal is $10 million.[94]

Conclusion

The not so distant history of the Kwakwa̲ka̲'wakw people was influenced by European settlement, Christian proselytizing, residential schools, legislated discrimination, and forced assimilation. Anti-potlatch laws, as well as other government-sanctioned discriminatory laws and policies, resulted in the significant disruption of Kwakwa̲ka̲'wakw social, economic, political, spiritual, and cultural structures. Not only was material culture illegally confiscated, but the transfer and retention of cultural knowledge, protocols, history, laws, and other information through the potlatch ceremony was severely inhibited. Most participants in this study see the revival of the potlatch ceremony as imperative to successfully strengthening and recovering traditions, values, teachings, beliefs, and the Kwak'wala language. It is central to the continuity of cultural identity and what it is to be Kwakwa̲ka̲'wakw. Factors influencing the urgency and complexity of this process include gaps in cultural knowledge created by the potlatch ban, the passing of knowledgeable elders, decreases in the number of people who can speak Kwak'wala, and the difficulty of maintaining oral traditions and transmission processes if the language is lost.[95]

An important step in addressing the injustices suffered by Kwakwa̲ka̲'wakw, healing from the wounds of acculturation, and strengthening Kwakwa̲ka̲'wakw cultural pride and identity is the repatriation of material culture and information and the creation of cultural centres in the community to house this material and work with the community on language and culture initiatives. Numerous initiatives on the part of U'mista, the 'Na̲mgis, and other Kwakwa̲ka̲'wakw communities have fostered pride, encouragement, hope, and interest in the Kwakwa̲ka̲'wakw culture at home and abroad. Fundamental in the repatriation initiative is an understanding that the value of potlatch regalia lies in the cultural knowledge these items represent, easy access to them so that one may learn from them, public acknowledgment of illegal interference with Kwakwa̱ka̱'wakw property and cultural practices, and the promotion of family and community healing. Unlike some other repatriations, with potlatch repatriations the rationale for return is not based on the need to actually use these items in religious or ceremonial activity. Nevertheless, these items play a fundamental role in rebuilding cultural practices and values. Just as important as the repatriation of potlatch items is the revival and protection of the Kwak'wala language. A variety of strategies have been implemented to deal with this, including the repatriation of oral and written material. A significant barrier to these and other efforts is a lack of human and financial resources.

Participants in this study feel that their cultural heritage must be protected on a number of levels. At the community level, prominent themes are the need to generate Kwakwa̱ka̱'wakw research by Kwakwa̱ka̱'wakw researchers, self-empowerment, recording and documenting the elders' teachings, and community collaboration and discussions. Participants also want the Canadian government to acknowledge the unjust banning of the potlatch and the harm it caused. Some want the government to provide appropriate compensation, perhaps through funding of current and future repatriation efforts, programs, and operations. Others also speak to the importance of collaborating with the government to strengthen and enforce ineffective laws and to take into consideration Kwakwa̱ka̱'wakw concepts of property. Currently, export control and copyright laws indirectly facilitate the loss of cultural objects and information. The second phase of this research program considers these issues of law reform in greater detail.[96]

Notes

1 Interview of Emma Tamilin by Barb Cranmer (9 January 2003), Alert Bay, British Columbia. Transcripts of all interviews are located at the U'mista Cultural Centre in Alert Bay.

2 Miriam Clavir, *Preserving What Is Valued: Museums, Conservation, and First Nations* (Vancouver: UBC Press, 2002) at 119. As several of the individuals interviewed in Clavir's book are Kwakwa̱ka̱'wakw and two of those individuals (Juanita Pasco and Peggy Svanvik) are also participants in this study, it is not surprising that some of the themes that emerge in this research confirm Clavir's prior observations. These include the importance of knowledge and practices associated with cultural objects, such as songs and dances; the role objects have in the restoration, performance, and preservation of ceremonies and the cultural identity of the community; the fact that both families and communities of origin have legitimate interests in the return and preservation of cultural items; and, with regard to the rebuilding of traditional processes, the importance of access to recordings, archival material, and other written documents associated with objects.

3 More extensive quotations from participants can be found online at Project for the Protection and Repatriation of First Nation Cultural Heritage in Canada <http: www.law.ualberta.ca/research/aboriginalculturalheritage>.

4 The Kwakwa̱ka̱'wakw, online: U'mista Cultural Society <http://www.umista.org/kwawa/kwawa.asp>. See also "The Kwakwa̱ka̱'wakw (The Kwak'wala Speaking Tribes)" *U'mista News* (Summer 2002) at 5, which also contains a map of Kwakwa̱ka̱'wakw territories. Issues of *U'mista News* are available from the U'mista Cultural Centre, Alert Bay, BC.

5 Creation stories for most of these communities can be found on the U'mista website, <http://www.umista.org>, and in post-2000 editions of *U'mista News*.

6 U'mista Cultural Society, "Source of Creation Story," *U'mista News* (Fall 2001) at 8.
7 For general information about the U'mista Cultural Society and the potlatch collection history, see online: U'mista Cultural Society <http://www.umista.org>. It is registered under the *Society Act*, R.S.B.C. 1996, c. 433 and is a registered Canadian charity.
8 U'mista Cultural Society, *Annual Report* (31 March 2003) at 1.
9 *Ibid.*
10 *Ibid* at 3. The return of the Potlatch Collection from the National Museum of Man (now known as the Canadian Museum of Civilization) and the Royal Ontario Museum resulted in the creation of two museums. The U'mista Cultural Centre was opened in Alert Bay in 1980, and the Kwakiutl Museum in Cape Mudge was opened in 1979. However, the Kwa-kiutl Museum is no longer in operation, and some of the artifacts from that collection are now held by U'mista. See Maurie Mauzé, "Exhibiting One's Culture: Two Case Studies – The Kwagiulth Museum and the U'mista Cultural Centre" (1992) 6:1 Native American Studies 27.
11 Mauzé, "Exhibiting One's Culture," 27.
12 *Supra* note 7.
13 *Ibid.*
14 *Supra* note 8. For further U'mista initiatives for artists, see Margaret Neufeld, *An Exploration of First Nations Artists in Alert Bay, BC: Connecting to the Art Market from Home* (MA Thesis, UBC Department of Anthropology, 2005) [unpublished].
15 The Kwakiutl Museum is currently closed because of lack of funding. However, the Nuyumbalees Society continues to be a partner in the specific claim. If the claim is successful, funds will be used for the Kwakiutl Museum and the U'mista Cultural Centre.
16 'Namgis First Nation, *Guidelines for Visiting Researchers/Access to Information*, available through the Band Council Office and online: <http://www.law.ualberta.ca/research/aboriginalculturalheritage>.
17 *Ibid.* at 1.
18 *Ibid.* See also *Tri-Council Policy Statement: Ethical Conduct for Research Involving Humans*, online: Government of Canada <http://www.pre.ethics.gc.ca/english/policystatement/policystatement.cfm>.
19 *Supra* note 16 at 3.
20 Interview of William Wasden Jr. was in two parts, both of which were conducted by Barb Cranmer, Alert Bay, British Columbia. Part 1 was conducted on 14 January 2003, while part 2 was conducted on 16 January 2003.
21 Interview of Andrea Cranmer by Barb Cranmer (9 January 2003), Alert Bay, British Columbia.
22 Interview of Andrea Sanborn by Barb Cranmer (9 December 2002), Alert Bay, British Columbia.
23 Interview of Peggy Svanvik (U'mista board member) by Barb Cranmer (15 December 2002), Alert Bay, British Columbia.
24 Interview of Vera Newman by Barb Cranmer (14 November 2002), Alert Bay, British Columbia.
25 Interview of Ethel Alfred by Barb Cranmer (12 January 2003), Alert Bay, British Columbia [translated by Vera Newman]. Ethel Alfred's interview transcript also contains details on how traditional Indian weddings and ceremonies marking the transition of girls into womanhood were carried out in the community before the banning of the potlatch.
26 Interview of Juanita Pasco by Barb Cranmer (5 December 2002), Alert Bay, British Columbia. She is referring here to the export control system under the *Cultural Property Export and Import Act*, R.S.C. 1985, c. 51, discussed in section entitled "Role of Canadian Law and Government" (below).
27 Interview of Bill Cranmer by Barb Cranmer (15 December 2002), Alert Bay, British Columbia. The interview of Bill Cranmer was in two parts. Part 1 was conducted on 10 December 2002, and part 2, with the board focus group, was conducted on 15 December 2002. Both interviews were conducted by Barb Cranmer in Alert Bay, British Columbia.
28 Interview of Spruce Wamiss (U'mista board member) by Barb Cranmer (15 December 2002), Alert Bay, British Columbia.
29 Interview of Christine Joseph (U'mista board member) by Barb Cranmer (15 December 2002), Alert Bay, British Columbia.

30 Interview of Basil Ambers (U'mista board member) by Barb Cranmer (15 December 2002), Alert Bay, British Columbia.
31 The report was drafted by Dr. Jay Powell, professor of anthropology at the University of British Columbia; Dr. Robert Anthony, professor of education at the University of Victoria; and Dr. Henry Davis, professor of linguistics at the University of British Columbia. Doctors Powell, Anthony, and Davis have extensive experience in the areas of First Nations language programs, First Nations education programs, and First Nations languages.
32 Jay V. Powell, Robert Anthony, and Henry Davis, "Review of *Kwak'wala* Language Retention and Renewal Programs 2001 – Draft" *U'mista News* (Spring 2001) at 15. The draft report is reproduced at 15-22 of this issue.
33 *Supra* note 8 at 5 [italics removed]. See also U'mista Cultural Society, *U'mista News* (Spring 2004) at 8.
34 U'mista Cultural Society, *Annual Report* (31 March 1999), Appendix F at 53.
35 *Ibid.* at 11. For discussion of the range of language initiatives in place at the time of writing see *supra* note 8 at 4-6, *ibid.* at 10-16, and Appendix F at 48-54.
36 *Supra* note 34 at 13.
37 *Ibid.* at 49.
38 "The Potlatch Collection History," online: U'mista Cultural Society <http://www.umista.org/potlatch/potlatch.asp>. See also Gloria Cranmer Webster, "U'mista Cultural Centre" (November/December 1965) *Canadian Collector* 64.
39 *Supra* note 28.
40 *An Act to amend and consolidate the laws respecting Indians*, S.C. 1880, c. 28.
41 *An Act further to amend The Indian Act, 1880*, S.C. 1884, c. 27, s. 3. Section 3 reads: "Every Indian or other person who engages in or assists in celebrating the Indian festival known as the 'Potlatch' or in the Indian dance known as the 'Tamanawas' is guilty of a misdemeanor, and shall be liable to imprisonment for a term of not more than six nor less than two months in any gaol or other place of confinement; any Indian or other person who encourages, either directly or indirectly, an Indian or Indians to get up such a festival or dance, or to celebrate the same, or who shall assist in the celebration of the same is guilty of a like offence, and shall be liable to the same punishment."
42 *An Act further to amend the Indian Act*, S.C. 1895, c. 35, s. 6.
43 Gloria Cranmer Webster, "The Potlatch Collection Repatriation" (1995) Special Issue U.B.C. L. Rev. 137 at 138.
44 *An Act to Amend the Indian Act*, S.C. 1918, c. 26.
45 Interview of John Pritchard by Barb Cranmer (21 November 2002), West Vancouver, British Columbia.
46 *An Act Respecting Indians*, S.C. 1951, c. 29, s. 123(2).
47 Interview of Stan Ashcroft by Barb Cranmer (21 November 2002), West Vancouver, British Columbia.
48 *Supra* note 43.
49 *Ibid.*
50 *Ibid.* The official title of the museum is the National Museum of the American Indian. It was created from the G. Heye collections.
51 *Ibid.*
52 See *e.g.* testimony of Arthur Dick, Transcript of Proceedings U'mista (Prohibition of the Potlatch Community Session), Indian Claims Commission (26 February 2003) at 124. The proceedings include detailed accounts of the impact of the potlatch ban by elders Vera Newman, Arthur Dick, Peggy Svanik, Emma Tamlin, Bill Cranmer (26 February 2003); and Harold Mountain and Ethel Alfred (25 February 2003).
53 Christopher Bracken, *The Potlatch Paper: A Colonial Case History* (Chicago: University of Chicago Press, 1997) at 228-29.
54 Electronic correspondence from Andrea Sanborn (7 August 2004).
55 Emma Tamilin also tells of how her grandmother would "run into the bedroom" and "hide under the bed just about" whenever white people came to the door. *Supra* note 1.
56 *Supra* note 28.
57 *Supra* note 43 at 141.

58 *Supra* note 1.
59 *Supra* 43 at 140.
60 Gloria Cranmer Webster, "The 'R' Word" (October 1988) 6:3 *Muse* 43. She is quoting here from notes taken at meetings or from phone calls with ROM representatives.
61 *Ibid.* at 43-44. In the latter article Gloria Cranmer Webster explains that U'mista had in its possession a letter from Duncan Campbell Scott, Superintendent General of Indian Affairs, to Edward Sapir of the Victoria Memorial Museum stating that the potlatch items were to remain the property of the Department of Indian Affairs. This letter was brought to the minister's attention when intervention on behalf of U'mista was sought.
62 *Supra* note 43 at 140. *Financial Administration Act*, O.C. 1987-1701 (14 August) (*Transfer of the Potlatch Collection of Artifacts to the U'mista Cultural Centre at Alert Bay and the Kwakiutl Museum in Cape Mudge*).
63 *Native American Graves Protection and Repatriation Act* 25 U.S.C.A. ss. 3001-3013 (West Supp. 2000). Cultural items are defined in s. 3001(3) A-D of the *Act* and include human remains, associated funerary objects, unassociated funerary objects, sacred objects, and cultural patrimony.
64 *NMAI Repatriation Policy Statement*, reproduced in Barbara Meister, ed., *Mending the Circle: A Native American Repatriation Guide* (New York: American Indian Ritual Object Repatriation Foundation, 1997) 129-33.
65 *Ibid.* at 131.
66 *Supra* note 38.
67 *Supra* note 43 at 140-41.
68 *Supra* note 2 at 140.
69 *Ibid.*
70 *Ibid.* at 140 and 146.
71 In Alberta, the provincial government felt it necessary to enact legislation for the permanent return of such material in order to relieve it of liability. See *First Nations Sacred Ceremonial Objects Repatriation Act*, R.S.A. 2000, c. F-14.
72 *Supra* note 43 at 140.
73 *Ibid.*
74 "The Potlatch Collection History," *supra* note 38. See also *supra* note 43 at 140.
75 *British Museum Act 1963* (U.K.), 1963, c. 24, as am. by *Museums and Galleries Act 1992*, c. 44, s. 11(2), Sch. 8, Pt. I, para. 5(a) [*BMA*]. Under this *Act*, trustees have limited powers regarding the lending or disposal of objects. Only objects that are deemed "unfit to be retained in the collections of the Museum and can be disposed of without detriment to the interests of students" can be taken out of the collection. *British Museum Act 1963* (U.K.), 1963, c. 24, as am. by *Museums and Galleries Act 1992* (U.K.), 1992, s. 5. For further details, see Catherine Bell and Robert K. Paterson, "International Movement of First Nations' Cultural Heritage in Canadian Law," in Catherine Bell and Robert K. Paterson, eds., *Protection of First Nations Cultural Heritage: Laws, Policy, and Reform* (Vancouver: UBC Press, 2008).
76 Jack Knox, "Exposed By a Mask," *Edmonton Journal* (11 August 2002), D8. While the *BMA* restricts disposal of objects, s. 5 lists some exceptions. In particular, see s. 5(c) *ibid.*
77 Personal communication with Andrea Sanborn, Director of U'mista Cultural Centre (17 January 2006). See also Jack Knox, "British Museum Returns Mask to B.C. Band: Potlatch Ceremonial Regalia Taken in 1921 took 30 Years to Recover," *Edmonton Journal* (5 November 2005), A7; and Jack Knox, "The Mask That Has Finally Come Home," *National Post* (6 November 2005), A8. The details of this repatriation are discussed in Bell and Paterson, *supra* note 75.
78 Interview of Guy Buchholtzer by Barb Cranmer (20 January 2002), Simon Fraser University Library, Vancouver, British Columbia.
79 *Supra* note 34 at 20.
80 *Ibid.*
81 Note that all quotes in this section are from William Wasden Jr., part 2, unless otherwise indicated.
82 *Supra* note 34 at 7.
83 R.S.C. 1985, c. 51. For a more detailed discussion of this legislation, see Bell and Paterson, *supra* note 75.

84 This account is taken from "Chronology of Bead and Button Blanket Purchase," appended as C-1 to the 1999 U'mista Annual Report, *supra* note 34. Under current federal policy, only category "A" designated organizations are notified about export applications. Category "A" designation is granted for an indefinite period of time to institutions and public authorities that fall within the legal definitions under the *Act;* receive repeat gifts of cultural objects; are established primarily for exhibiting, collecting, and preserving cultural material; and meet certain legal, curatorial, and environmental standards. See Moveable Cultural Property Division, *Cultural Property Export and Import Act: Designation of Institutions and Public Authorities Information and Procedures,* rev. ed. (Ottawa: Canadian Heritage, 2000) at 6-12.

85 Cranmer is referring to the Nuxalk Echo Mask discussed in Bell and Paterson, "International Movement" *supra* note 75. See also Janet Kramer, *Switchbacks: Art, Ownership, and Nuxalk National Identity* (Vancouver: UBC Press, 2006) at ix-xiii, 87-96.

86 R.S.B.C. 1996, c. 187.

87 John Pritchard, "Making Things Right: The Prohibition of the Potlatch 1884-1951 – A Specific Claim," submission to British Columbia, Specific Claims Branch, Indian and Northern Affairs Canada (January 1998) at 2.

88 *Supra* note 27 (part 2).

89 *Supra* note 47.

90 *Supra* note 45.

91 *Supra* note 47.

92 *Supra* note 45. Under the specific claims policy in effect when this claim was filed, claims could only be brought for non-fulfillment of obligations arising under treaty and other agreements, breach of the *Indian Act* or other federal statutes, breach of obligations arising out of administration of funds, and other First Nations assets and illegal sales or other dispositions of First Nations land. For discussion of the Indian Claims Commission and its role, see <http://www.indianclaims.ca>.

93 [not in force as of 10 January 2006] 2003, c. 23.

94 Mary C. Hurley, "Bill C-6: The Specific Claims Resolution Act," online: Parliament of Canada <http://www.parl.gc.ca/common/bills_ls.asp?Parl=37 and Ses=2 and ls=c6>.

95 See *e.g.* Anne Marie Goodfellow, *Talking in Context: Language and Identity in Kwakwa̱ka̱'wakw Society* (Montreal/Kingston: McGill Queen's University Press, 2005 [McGill-Queen's Native and Northern Series]).

96 See Bell and Paterson, eds., *supra* note 75.

2

The Law Is Opened: The Constitutional Role of Tangible and Intangible Property in Gitanyow

Richard Overstall, in consultation with Val Napoleon and Katie Ludwig

This chapter summarizes and analyzes six of seven interviews conducted by Katie Ludwig between 24 July and 19 November 2002 with knowledgeable persons who are either members of the Gitxsan House of Luuxhon, members of closely related Houses, or have knowledge of the House's interaction in the wider Gitxsan society. Katie is herself a member of the House of Luuxhon. A further interview was conducted with Guy Morgan, who held the chief name Luuxhon at the time. Unfortunately, Mr. Morgan's voice was too soft to be picked up by the interviewer's tape recorder, and he died before the interview could be rescheduled. Luuxhon is a Frog Clan House based in Gitanyow (sometimes called Kitwancool), its ancestral village. The Gitxsan people, including the Gitanyow, have territories and villages in the Upper Skeena and Upper Nass watersheds of the Northwest Coast region of North America.

The interviews and this report are part of a wider study aimed at disseminating information about, among other things, indigenous laws concerning ownership, protection, and control of indigenous "cultural heritage," including "cultural objects," "sacred sites," and "intellectual property." One of the objectives of the study is to examine indigenous concepts of "cultural property." The Pacific Northwest of British Columbia has not been immune to the increased demand by indigenous peoples worldwide for protection of, and the repatriation of, their "cultural heritage." In Canada to date, "cultural heritage" ownership has been regulated in the nation-state system by the common law of property and by heritage conservation legislation. While aboriginal groups have been required to adjust their claims to meet these cultural property laws, the state has yet to adjust its claims to reflect aboriginal peoples' laws.

As the Luuxhon interviews show, the concept of "cultural property" is doubly obscuring. First, it is a term applied by one legal culture (that of the Canadian state) to another legal culture (that of the indigenous peoples of the Northwest Coast) but that the nation-state culture rarely applies to itself. For example, Canadian lawyers talk about ownership of land and tangible objects; about copyright of books, songs, and plays; and about intellectual property rights to inventions and discoveries. But to none of these areas of law do the lawyers usually apply the term "cultural property."[1] The term is applied more consistently to a wide range of aboriginal property, the implication being that aboriginal peoples have a decorative, even a vaguely spiritual, role in Canadian life but that this role does not and should not impinge on the legal, political, and commercial business of the country. This asymmetry of legal classification may reflect a persistent vestige of the colonial mind. This is not to say that Canadian legal categories should be applied to indigenous law; rather, it is to say that indigenous legal terms used in the context of the relevant indigenous legal order should be recognized as being just as valid as the categories of the state legal order.

This brings up the second way in which the concept of "cultural property" obscures Gitxsan law; that is, through its implicit assumption that a part of an indigenous legal culture can be carved out and separate from the rest of that culture. While this may be a valid approach to Canadian legal analysis – for example, looking at the obligations of museums to return certain artifacts or remains – it obscures the significance of objects, images, words, and inventions under indigenous law. Besides being possessions in their own right, many of the objects, and particularly the images, words, and music they contain, have a critical constitutional role in indigenous law. Perhaps this would be less of a concern if there was a general familiarity with the indigenous legal system being considered, but this level of understanding has yet to be achieved.

To date, the law has focused (1) on the obligations of certain institutions – museums and archives – to return or repatriate certain classes of objects and (2) on the conditions the institutions can require indigenous recipients to meet. These conditions mirror the concerns of the institution from which the objects were held and, as such, are narrowly fixed on the physical preservation of the material objects. There has been little discussion of the application of indigenous law to these transactions, and a number of questions remained to be answered:

1 Besides the physical object, reproduction, et cetera, what is the legal nature of what is being returned?
2 To which indigenous persons or institutions should objects properly be returned or loaned?
3 What is the legal nature of those persons' or institutions' possession?
4 Given the inherent power inequalities, what is the obligation of the returning institution to inquire as to the appropriate receiving institution

and the conditions under indigenous law that should properly be attached to the receipt?

5 If objects cannot be returned for some valid reason, what is the legal nature of the holding institution's continuing possession and what is its obligation to allow use or reproduction of objects, images, music, or words by the rightful indigenous holders and by others?

The interviews reported here attempt to begin the process of answering some of the above questions. As such, they look more at the indigenous law that applies to the use and receipt of artifacts and the images on them than at the nation-state law that applies to their repatriation.

The choice to elicit information primarily from one Gitxsan House was made in order to focus each interviewee's attention on his or her role as a participant in the Gitxsan legal order. That legal order is not, of course, exclusively Gitxsan. It is able to interact with its neighbours towards the Coast, including the Nisga'a and Tsimshian, and towards the Interior, including the Tahltan, Wet'suwet'en, and other Athabaskan peoples. Anthropologists call this the Northwest Coast Culture area. The constitutional core of this legal order is made up of a number of family lineages. Each lineage can trace its origin through the mother's line to a founding event that established the group's legal relationship with a specific territory. Over time, these lineages have formed into House groups, each of which is identified as belonging to one of four clans: Frog, Eagle, Wolf, or Fireweed. In practice, through strategic intermarriage, the lineages have woven themselves into a complex cloth that is the society today. Clan identity has an important role in marriage law in that a person cannot marry within his or her own clan. This serves to maintain bilateral relations in the society, which are essential in the governance of small interrelated and intermarried communities. Clan membership also serves as an initial identifier when a House group wants to renew relationships with more distant lineages among other peoples – say, a Gitxsan House wanting to interact with a group on the Coast that shares an ancient history and thus is related.

All these interwoven relationships have evolved without any single overarching authority or institution; for example, there are no clan chiefs and certainly no high chief of the Gitanyow or the Gitxsan. Similarly, there is no governing council or representative assembly. The highest legal and political unit is the House group. The House holds its territory and intangible possessions through its chief. The House authority is subject to witnessing at the feast or potlatch, but while the witnessing chiefs of other Houses can withdraw support of a certain House initiative, they cannot overrule it. For these reasons, it makes sense to investigate indigenous laws about possessions in the context of a specific House – in this case, the House of Luuxhon in Gitanyow.

The interviews were conducted with the cooperation of the Gitanyow Hereditary Chiefs' office. Project leader Catherine Bell, accompanied by Heather Raven, visited the Chiefs Office in Gitanyow in June 2001 to provide information on the research protocols and the role of the community, including the approval of appropriate authorities and the processes for vetting potentially confidential information.[2] On 17 July 2002, further meetings were held between Katie Ludwig, Richard Overstall, and Hereditary Chiefs negotiator Glen Williams and his staff to explain the purpose of the project and the work plan for the interviews that Katie would conduct. Glen offered the support of the Office of the Gitanyow Hereditary Chiefs with regard to administration and said that the work would help Gitanyow in its treaty negotiations, in particular, by demonstrating the relationship of the crests portrayed on poles and blankets with the House territories.

In the Luuxhon case study, the interviews were organized around a set of questions designed to avoid the imposition of Western state constructs of property and ownership. The initial questions were structured around two main themes: (1) how Gitxsan people relate to the world and things in the world and (2) what occurs for the teller and the listener in the telling of the oral history (*adaawk*). In five of the six interviews, these questions were followed by those from the standard set developed for the main project.[3] These initial questions were:

Relations with Intangible Possessions

1. How do Luuxhon members know that songs, crests, and poles "belong" to the Luuxhon or to a particular member of Luuxhon?
2. What does "belonging" mean?
3. How is the relationship of belonging enforced?
4. What are the responsibilities associated with belonging?

Laws about Oral History

5. Who tells and who listens to *adaawk*?
6. How is the *adaawk* told? Why is it told this way?
7. What are the responsibilities associated with telling and listening?
8. What are the changes that are occurring for the Luuxhon members regarding their *adaawk*?

In the interviews, these questions and those from the standard set did not so much elicit direct answers as prompt narratives from which information could be gleaned. This type of response emphasizes the implicit nature of the Gitxsan legal order: it is beneath the surface, felt as much as known, and uncomfortable with abstract questions. The interviews have been reviewed here using precedential analysis, which determines what people have consistently done in the past when faced with these or analogous issues. This is contrasted with normative analysis, which asks about the legal principles or rules involved. Katie Ludwig transcribed all interviews and translated those conducted in the Gitxsan language.

Always Visible: Crests and Names as Intangible Property

Godfrey Good is Gwinu,[4] the chief of a House group closely related to the House of Luuxhon. Both Houses are of the Ganeda, or Frog, Clan. At the time of his interview in July 2002, Godfrey was eighty-six years old. His account of the relationship he and his contemporaries have with so-called cultural property reflects his understanding of the laws that have applied to him and the other chiefs throughout his life.

Godfrey sees that law as emerging in two ways. On the one hand, he describes it as "automatic":

> When a chief dies, this is when the law is opened. It is automatic. No one can break the law when a chief dies. The chiefs will gather, have a feast, and decide what to do. The law is the same today ...
>
> When a chief dies, the law happens automatically. It is in the feast hall that the business is taken care of. If the law is not followed properly, the chiefs will ask why and state that it is not right. The law of our people is very good.[5]

This describes a legal order that applies to the chiefs today as it has in all the past of which Godfrey is aware. The feast is shown to be an occasion that focuses upon legal matters: the communal and implicit nature of the legal order is emphasized; the chiefs gather and decide; no one can break the law. If the law is not followed, the chiefs assume that this is the result of a mistake; therefore, they ask why this mistake was made and say what should be done to correct it.

The automatic nature of the law, operating as it does below the threshold of explicit understanding, also explains Godfrey's difficulty in dealing with the direct questions selected for the interview. For example, when he is asked how the chiefs protect their songs to ensure that no one else uses them, he replies, "I don't know what they do." But he then goes on to tell a story about singing and relates how, at the end of each song, the singer would always acknowledge its owner:

> You know our uncle Albert Douse, when we are out hunting, after we cook and eat, we sit around and start to sing. He sang the song that belonged to a man from Gitanmaax. He would tell who the song belongs to. He knew many songs; he would then say who this song belongs to.

The question is thus answered by the above vignette: songs are protected by the singer's always acknowledging the owner. When the interviewer repeats the direct question after the vignette, Godfrey again says, "I don't know how they used the law."

Yet, in addition to accepting the automatic nature of Gitanyow law, Godfrey appears to appreciate the recognition that laws receive when they are written about and thus made explicit. He asks the interviewer if she has a copy of "the book of the laws of Gitanyow." He is referring to the 1959 British Columbia Provincial Museum (now Royal British Columbia Museum) publication, *Histories, Territories and Laws of the Kitwancool*.[6] He couples his question with the statement, "the law of our people is very good," implying that the communally negotiated museum publication functions as the wider society's acknowledgment of the value of the Gitanyow legal order. The political nature of the book is emphasized by the fact that the monograph is not a codification of Gitanyow law but, rather, a record of certain statements the chiefs at that time thought needed to be made.

There is a second aspect of Godfrey's spontaneous endorsement of the museum monograph. The publication was part of an agreement between the Gitanyow Hereditary Chiefs and the museum. The museum wanted to preserve certain poles that were standing at Gitanyow and move them to Victoria. The chiefs agreed to the poles' removal on two conditions: first, that replicas of the poles be made and raised in Gitanyow at the museum's expense; second, that the museum publish an account of Gitanyow's legal order, with the chiefs having control over its substantive content. This bargain introduces two of the main themes of this analysis of the Luuxhon interviews. The first is that possession of the physical artifact (in this case, poles with representations of House crests on them[7]) appears less important to people than does the right to display those crests in an appropriate legal and social context (in this case, a pole-raising feast). The second theme is that the chiefs associate the physical object not only with the images it holds but also with the legal and political significance of those images (in this case, the link between the crests on the poles and the people's constitutional history and territories).

In Godfrey's view, the law defines the Gitanyow people. "If this law dies out, our people are not good for anything," he says. This statement is made in response to a specific question about a male chief's children's preventing the succession of his name, crests, and authority through a female line. But the answer seems to go beyond that particular point of law. Godfrey recognizes that the law is more than a dispute resolution device: it is also constitutional. The Gitanyow thus centrally define themselves as a people who follow these laws. When they stop following them, Godfrey says, they will cease to be Gitanyow people and will be something else. The constitutional role of the continued stating and following of the people's laws and histories has to be at the forefront of the story that Godfrey relates regarding his efforts to get the crests of his House properly portrayed on his chief's regalia and displayed at feasts and other public occasions.

In Godfrey's story, the things he holds, his "property," are his chief name, Gwinu; a set of *ayuks*, or crest images; and a set of songs – all of which are the unique responsibility of the House of Gwinu. He recalls how he got his chief name when he was about thirty or thirty-five years old:

> Louisa took this name and gave it to me. I didn't care about what they were doing. I didn't know at the time that this was a chief name of high status. Louisa told me to look after this name and honour it: "It is a very important name, make sure that you are always visible. The House of Gwinu is very strong; don't disgrace the name" ...
>
> I thought at the time it was just a name. They kept telling me to take care of this name, uphold its status. I did what I was able to do.

Louisa's instructions to the young and uncaring Godfrey reveal a critical aspect of holding a name: its value is not static but, rather, must be continually enhanced by making the name visible through participation at feasts and by not disgracing it through negligent or selfish behaviour. Participation requires being able to properly host feasts, which, in turn, requires that the House be managed so that it can produce the needed food and goods. Given Gwinu's status in the community today, Godfrey's abilities appear to have been up to the task.

Godfrey gave the account of his receipt of the name in response to a question about the loss of two button blankets with crest images belonging to Gwinu. In his mind, then, the crests and the name are intimately linked. Further, he said that there is a song and a *xwts'an*, or crest pole, that also go with the blankets. The exclusivity of the crests to each House is made clear:

> No one should be able to take this crest that belongs to another chief and wear it. It is not done. That is the Gitxsan law. You are not allowed to wear another's crest. This is our sacred property. These are very important property; our great-grandfathers treasured these.
>
> There is one thing that the chiefs did: no one is allowed to use the crest that belongs to someone else. These crests are on the blankets, headdresses, and rattles. Just the family that owns the crests is allowed to use them.

But note that Godfrey's emphasis is on the wearing and use of the crest by another rather than on the possession of the physical object that carries the crest image. This distinction is maintained in his account of how he and other House members attempted to have duplicate blankets made.

Godfrey names two crests belonging to Gwinu – *Getdimgamaaks* and *Tax bela dim gaak*. Two blankets containing each of these crests came into the possession of K'san,[8] the museum and carving school complex in Gitanmaax, Hazelton, British Columbia, that sells tours and artwork to tourists at a replica nineteenth-century Gitxsan village. Godfrey does not know how the museum obtained the Gwinu blankets, although in another part of the interview he suggests that they may have been sold by Johnson Williams, a previous holder of the name Gwinu. Along with the blankets, other regalia[9] used by the chief in his *naxnox*, or spirit dances, were also sold.

In his interview, Godfrey relates the law on the transfer of feast objects and indicates that it was not followed. "We don't sell these things," Godfrey said simply. Asked if Johnson Williams had said why he did not comply, Godfrey said he had not, but he did offer an explanation: "[T]his is what happened. The members of Gwinu were dwindling. There were very few people in Gwinu's House. I am guessing this is why he did it."

This explanation requires a bit of unpacking. It starts with Godfrey's account of how various objects, including a Raven rattle (*Hax seegam gaak'*), a Raven transformation mask (*Gaagem get*), and other regalia (*gwis haalayt*) were taken by white people from a shed in an abandoned village close to present-day Gitanyow. The time of this incident is not clear from the interview, but it may have been early in the twentieth century. Godfrey says the people of that village had been "cleaned out" by the Ts'ats'awit – an Athabascan people with territories in the Stikine watershed on the northern border of the Gitanyow territories and with whom, in the nineteenth century, the Gitanyow had a number of wars. "Ts'ats'awit" may also be spelled "Tsetsaut." As there is no record of the entire population of Gitanyow being killed at this time, it is more likely that the people temporarily left their village to hide from possible attack.

As well as being abandoned because of war, villages were also depopulated due to introduced epidemic diseases. This depopulation had two effects on the removal of artifacts. As Godfrey relates, the first was that there were simply too few people around to defend their regalia against thieves. The second effect was more subtle. With few members in a House, the chief could not gather sufficient resources to support his or her feast obligations. The time of the greatest decline in numbers was therefore also the time when the people's spirits were at their nadir. It likely seemed to many that the predictions of the missionaries and government officials regarding their complete demise as a people were actually coming true. In such anomic conditions, it is not surprising that some chiefs may have thought they were seeing this demise and that, therefore, their regalia no longer had any useful function. This may be what Godfrey was trying to explain when he said that Johnson Williams sold the blankets because Gwinu's House had so few members.

Godfrey relates how Johnson Williams attempted to get a copy of one blanket made at the K'san museum. When the blanket was completed, however, the museum wanted $7,000 for it, which Johnson could not afford. The museum therefore kept the copy and, as far as Godfrey knows, has it to this day.

At one point, Godfrey asked the K'san museum if he could borrow the duplicate blanket for a pole raising, an important feast occasion for a chief. But someone at the museum told him that he could only have it if he paid the $7,000 that was owed and that he could not borrow it. Godfrey promised to return the blanket but the museum would not relent. Again, it was the ability to wear the blanket – to be "always visible" – that was important to Godfrey, not so much who owned the physical object. There are two things to note about the museum's role: first, that the production of Northwest Coast imagery for the art object market has inflated the price of regalia to the extent that they are often beyond the financial reach of those authorized under their own laws to display them; second, that the museum's narrow vision of its role as preserver of artifacts actually stymies the exercise of the culture it is ostensibly meant to foster.

Godfrey persisted in his attempts to get a blanket he could wear at a feast. He took a picture of the museum blanket and paid an artist $2,000 to make him a replica. The artist made the blanket and then left it at a Prince Rupert shop for some finishing. Unfortunately, the artist owed the shopkeepers money, and, as security for the debt, they seized the blanket and other regalia Godfrey was having made. Eventually, the artist bought new materials and remade them, so Godfrey at last got his blanket and regalia.

In his interview, Godfrey reflects on the lost blankets and his efforts to have them returned: "There is one that the people of Prince Rupert took and the other is at K'san – the old one. It took me a long time to try to get it back, but I couldn't get it back." He was puzzled as to what the people holding them would do with them:

> I don't know if this white person that took these things is aware of the laws of our people – how important these are to us. Our law does not allow other people to wear what belongs to another. The law is still the same today; it is none of their business ...
>
> I just told them that other people cannot wear this blanket and its crest; it does not belong to anyone else. They should know the laws of our people. They have many of our things there.

In Godfrey's mind, there can be no reason to hold crest-bearing regalia if the holder does not have the right to wear and display the crests. Without the right to use the crest, why would anyone want to keep the objects, except out of sheer ignorance?

Godfrey has a solution to the conflict between the need for museums to show objects to the public and the need for the chiefs to be able to exclusively display them in specific legal contexts. He suggests that they be placed in a museum in Gitanyow. Clearly, Godfrey sees a distinction between the museum at K'san, which is outwardly under Gitxsan control, and the museum in Gitanyow. Perhaps he sees the Gitanyow museum as being under the control of the hereditary chiefs so that particular items could be loaned to those who, under Gitanyow law, hold the crests and other images portrayed on them. In this way, if the objects were robust enough, they would be available for people to copy or to use.

In summary, Godfrey tells that each House holds its unique set of crest images on blankets, rattles, poles, and other regalia and that it also holds chief names, songs, and other intangible possessions. In a less fundamental way, the House also holds the actual objects themselves. As Godfrey's account of his succession to the name Gwinu shows, a chief's holding of these House possessions is not a personal property right; rather, the intangible images, music, and words, as well as their tangible depictions on regalia and poles, are held in trust by the chief and the House members for future generations. The trust property is more than a right to display certain images and to perform certain songs and dramas: it is intimately linked with the people's histories, which constitutionally define each group and its relations with other groups, and it connects each group with its territories. It seems that at those times in history when it may have seemed to some chiefs that their trusteeship was ended – that there would be no future generations for whom the trust property would need to be held – was when the objects were let go and outside collectors, such as museums, were able to acquire them.

Button Blankets and Government Grants

In his interview, Godfrey Good set out the law that a House group and its chief hold in trust certain images – *ayuks*, or crests – that are publicly displayed, often on the button blankets worn at certain legal and governmental events. In another interview, a Fireweed Clan chief, Niis Noolh (Ray Jones), from the Gitxsan village of Gitsegyukla, tells how this law was applied in the recent context of a band council project funded by a government grant.[10] Ray's interview offers a case history of how a people's laws can be applied with integrity in the context of displaying images to a non-Gitxsan public outside of the feast system.

Ray relates that, in the late 1970s, he was the band administrator for Gitsegyukla and was always looking for grants to alleviate the chronic unemployment in the village. At that time, there was a Gitxsan dance and singing group that included Gitsegyukla people, some of whom thought that the village should have its own group. As part of the effort to create such a group, Ray obtained a government grant to have blankets made that could be worn by the dancers and singers at their performances. Materials were ordered and a Gitxsan artist was commissioned to draw up the designs.

In Ray's view, the blankets and the designs on them were communally owned by the village. He explained that the money for the blankets was obtained through three government programs and that the funding agencies imposed no constraints in the grant contracts with regard to ownership of the designs. As Ray says, "intellectual property" was not a term that was used at the time. The intellectual property issue was therefore solely in the hands of the hereditary chiefs of the village. These chiefs gave permission for the blanket makers to use generalized images representing the three main clans in Gitsegyukla: Wolf, Frog, and Fireweed.

As a specific example of how the designs were chosen, Ray talks about three different designs for a Grouse blanket ("Grouse" being an alternative name for the Fireweed Clan). But, he emphasizes, there was no specific image that belonged to a House group because that would have been the House's property. The blankets were communal property that represented the clan crests but not the individual *ayuks* of each House. Such generalized images on blankets would have had no role in the feast system and, as such, had no aboriginal law governing them. As much as some chiefs may have wanted the project to supply them with blankets to use in the feast, Ray was clear that, under Gitxsan law, they had to get their own blankets made. Ray also considered the rights of the artist who made the designs: "[B]ecause she produced them ... these are her own creativeness ... and probably that's her own property in one sense. But they were generalized images."

The project group produced about a dozen blankets. Although not mentioned in this interview, one of the blanket makers was Mary Russell (Guxgalga'alsxw), now deceased; however, at that time, she was the matriarch of the House of Luuxhon. Interestingly, Ray is not sure where the blankets are now and thinks that they may have been lost or taken as souvenirs. In any event, there is certainly not the same concern over their fate as there would have been had they been displaying House crests.

Ray's interview indicates that not all images used by Gitxsan and other First Nations peoples are held exclusively by a lineage or a House. Even familiar motifs, such as those commonly associated with the principal clans, can be used in a more communal way. It was important, however, that even though generalized images were used, the hereditary chiefs of the village were extensively consulted on the choice of images and project participants were aware of the law involved. It is not clear whether the same licence would be extended to a non-Gitxsan or a non-aboriginal project. Nevertheless, this account demonstrates another way in which Northwest Coast design can be used publicly without offending the prerogatives of the hereditary chiefs and House groups.

Regalia

In his interview, Robert Good (Sindihl) reviews a number of photographs he took in the summer of 2002 on visits to the Museum of Civilization in Ottawa, the Royal British Columbia Museum in Victoria, and at a chief's funeral in Gitanyow.[11] The museum pictures are mainly of masks and props used in *naxnox*, or spirit dance, performances. Others are of House crests on blankets and, in one case, on a pole. As such, all the images and forms portrayed are held by the head chiefs of specific House groups. Robert identifies each object and, in some cases, says which chief owns the image used. The photographs and the discussion of each picture are recorded in the interview transcript. This account draws out a few themes that run through Robert's review.

The first picture is of a *naxnox* mask that is identified as *Simgyak'.*[12] It is a bird head (perhaps a flicker) with a large beak, the upper mandible of which is split vertically and hinged so that it flies apart to allow a small human figure to spring upright. The strings that manipulate the beak and figure can be seen in the picture. Robert explains that the mask was owned by Luuxhon but that, for a performance, the chief may select a skilled actor who knows how to act out the *naxnox*. During a performance the wearer would sing a song and be accompanied by four small people. Robert also identified an *adaawk*, or formal oral history, that is also associated with the mask. In the *adaawk*, the human figure is shown to be a higher power that has descended from the heavens and that speaks through the bird's mouth. The human figure is identified as a transformation figure that records a time when beings transformed themselves back and forth from spirits to animals to humans more readily than they do now. In this case, the *adaawk* was about a fishing site that was held by Luuxhon. Robert's summary shows the interconnections among a mask, a song, a performance, an oral history, and the ownership and use of a resource territory (in this case, a fishing site). Although Robert gives a very short summary of the *adaawk*, he emphasizes that the transformation figure tells Luuxhon to fish at a certain site. In effect, the spirit of the place (*spanaxnox*) gives the House chief permission to use the site. This permission granting on the part of spirit powers is the underlying legal authority for the right of any House to hold fishing sites and land territories.

Another set of photographs taken by Robert shows the June 2002 funeral of Gordon Johnson, who had held the chief name 'Mali. This occasion would have occurred in one of a series of feasts to transfer the name 'Mali to Gordon Johnson's successor. The succession of the name and the head chieftainship is shown by passing on the 'Mali blanket to the new holder, Glen Williams. Glen is also shown wearing 'Mali's *am haalayt*, the headdress that Godfrey Good said was an important part of a chief's full regalia.

Together, Robert's pictures and his account of them demonstrate the intimate connections between objects that are now in distant museums and the community's ongoing jurisdiction over its people and territories, which is displayed through the actions of the chiefs in the feast hall. In particular, Robert makes explicit the relationship between an image on an artifact that belongs to specific group or lineage, the group's constitutional history, and its territories. As Donald Russell and Victoria Russell emphasize in their interviews (discussed below), it is important for the Gitanyow to have access to items in museums so that they can fulfill their obligations to pass on knowledge, to recreate their identity, and to maintain their legal relationships.

Today's Leaders

As part of the survey of the House of Luuxhon's relationship with the images, words, and territories that belong to it, three younger House members were interviewed. These were all persons who, in addition to their responsibilities as House members, have been involved in the litigation and negotiation of aboriginal rights and title either for the Gitxsan or the Gitanyow.

Herb Russell is Ts'iiwa', a wing-chief name in Luuxhon.[13] In response to questions about how House members know that certain things belong to the House, Herb lists oral histories, feast names, territories, songs, laments, crests, and poles as among the House's possessions.[14] In his mind, the key links are between oral history and territory. When asked about the enforcement of these relationships, he said that the laws dictate behaviour, but he did not elaborate on the processes by which this happens. He did say, however, that a person's main responsibility is to participate in the feast, which, he says, is the way the people govern themselves. For example,

> [t]he traditional way of showing ownership to the land is to repeat the *adaawk* [and] share it with other chiefs. All present at the feast will hear and be witness. The guest chiefs will respond. They will affirm the *adaawk* or they will state it is not correct.

Herb focuses on the telling of the *adaawk* in the feast as a key responsibility for a chief. By listening at the feast, a person becomes familiar with the geographic place names that provide "your deed to the land." This emphasis on place names and territory may, in part, reflect the attention that Gitanyow leaders and researchers have had to place on land issues in aboriginal rights litigation and treaty negotiations. In particular, the Gitanyow have been in court challenging the Nisga'a Final Agreement on the basis that it gave the Nisga'a central government rights over land that is part of the territory of certain Gitanyow House groups.

Thus, when Herb was asked about cultural property, he started with the land and went on to say that its protection was one of the main struggles of the Gitanyow Houses. He referred to the territory of Luuxhon that is on the border of the land claimed by the Nisga'a. There is a landmark that the Gitanyow say is the boundary marker between the Gitanyow House territories and those of the Nisga'a. According to Herb, the Nisga'a have not realized or respected the significance of this marker. When asked about measures to protect cultural property, Herb again refers to the Gitanyow court challenge of the Nisga'a Final Agreement. He characterizes the challenge as an effort to get the provincial and federal governments to acknowledge that they made a mistake in failing to take into account the land of the Gitanyow Houses under the Gitanyow system. Herb places the legal argument solidly within the peoples' own law: "we have to ask permission before we can go on to others' territory."

What an anthropologist might describe as "culturally appropriate processes for determining rights to cultural property," Herb simply refers to as individuals having property for which they are responsible.[15] For example, each "chief of a *wilp* [House group] is responsible for the rattle, headdress, and blanket." Each chief has the main responsibility, but "sometimes it is done by the whole House." This alludes to the trust and responsibility of the chief and House members mentioned earlier.

Herb speaks about the repatriation of museum artifacts very much from the viewpoint of his work as an administrator in the Gitanyow Hereditary Chiefs' office. Nevertheless, he echoes Godfrey Good's emphasis on maintaining control over the crest images rather than simply obtaining the particular object on which they are displayed. As an example of this, Herb tells of his role in getting a pole belonging to Gwinu replicated and erected in Gitanyow. He describes how some parts of the original were decayed and had to be reconstructed from contemporary photographs.

He then discusses Luuxhon's pole, which is also being carved – whether as a replica or not is unclear. In any event, the carving is incomplete and stalled. According to Herb, funds allocated to the Luuxhon pole were diverted by another Gitanyow chief to pay for the carving of a pole for the House of Guxsen, which is in Gitsegyukla, another Gitxsan village. Herb's complaint underscores the complexity of law and politics in a kinship-based society. Although the House of Guxsen is based in another village and therefore, on the face of it, should not be eligible for grants given to Gitanyow, the allocation of funds may have made sense to the chiefs involved, given the social and political relations between the Houses of the two villages.

The general law is that a person cannot marry someone of his or her own clan and, thus, of his or her own House. This is a constitutional law, and it establishes the bilateral relations necessary in societies comprised of closely related and closely intermarried persons. In practice, Houses find it useful to establish a close relationship with a particular House from another clan through repeated intermarriage among members of the two Houses. In Gitanyow, many Frog Clan Houses have established such a relationship with the Gitsegyukla Fireweed Clan House of Guxsen. As it is Gitxsan practice for a woman to move to her husband's village on marriage, it follows that when Guxsen women marry members of Gitanyow Frog Clan Houses, they move to Gitanyow. At present, nearly a hundred members of Guxsen's House live in Gitanyow village. Conversely, one would expect many Gitanyow Frog Clan members to live in Gitsegyukla. The interviewer for this chapter, Katie Ludwig (and others of her immediate family), is an example of this phenomenon. In time, the presence of Guxsen women and their children (who are also Guxsen House members) in Gitanyow will mean that a significant part of the Gitanyow population will be made up of Guxsen House members. From this perspective, it could make political and legal sense for the village chiefs to acknowledge that presence by putting some funds towards the Guxsen pole. This makes legal sense because, under Gitxsan law, what is known as the "father's House" has the responsibility to oversee the carving of the pole of the "mother's House." In this case, the Gitanyow Frog Houses were the fathers' Houses to Guxsen. It is important to note that, although funded by money from Gitanyow Frog Houses, the pole was raised in Gitsegyukla, as it should have been under the people's law.

Issues such as the allocation of funds to carve the Guxsen pole are difficult ones for administrators like Herb. Is his loyalty to his village community, often represented by a band council (which governments use as the conduit for cultural funds), or is it to the more complex intercommunity responsibilities of the Houses and clans under their own laws? Answers to these questions would require careful consideration of the people's own laws and their application to the available evidence.[16]

This reciprocity of responsibilities under the people's own law arises again when Herb gives some context to Robert Good's visit to the Museum of Civilization in Ottawa. Herb explains that, in order for an artifact to be returned, the museum requires that it be identified "through oral history." This raises the difficult question of how a museum might independently verify that the oral history it is being given is, in fact, the full and appropriate one. Herb goes on to give an example of images not being used by the appropriate authority. According to him, the copper shield image used as an emblem by the Nisga'a Lisims Government under the Nisga'a Final Agreement properly belongs to Gitanyow. In fact, Robert Good's photograph collection shows two button blankets stored in the museum in Victoria that depict the copper shield crest. In his interview, Robert identifies the crest as belonging to 'Wii taxhayetxw, a Gitanyow Frog Clan chief. A visual comparison of the crest design shown on a blanket with the Nisga'a Lisims Government emblem on its website shows them to be very similar. The legal issue is that the Nisga'a government does not have the right to use the 'Wii taxhayetxw crest.

Herb goes on to give another example of the illegal use of a crest image. A pole, called 'Wii Sk'imsim, that belongs to the Gitanyow Wolf Clan House of Gwaashlaa'm, has recently been raised in the Nisga'a village of Canyon City. Although there may be members of Gwaashlaa'm's House living in

Canyon City, the rule followed in the case of Guxsen was not followed here. The pole was not raised in Gwaashlaa'm's home village of Gitanyow. Oral history may have been given in an attempt to authenticate the Nisga'a use of the crests on the shield and pole, but it appears that any authenticating was not done according to aboriginal law. That would have required the relevant Nisga'a Houses to have hosted a feast to which the Gitanyow chiefs, along with others with an interest in the crests being displayed, would have been invited as witnesses. Herb characterizes this apparent disregard of the law by saying that the Nisga'a "are not living culturally now." If the issue was the return of certain museum artifacts, how would the museum decide which oral history was correct – the Nisga'a or the Gitanyow? Further, what would the result be if a proper reading of the oral histories showed that House groups in both communities had rights to use certain crest images?

Although Herb is concerned about the unlawful reproduction and use of Luuxhon images, he also discusses the challenges of obtaining access to, and the return of, Luuxhon objects in the custody of museums around the world. Acknowledging that Luuxhon objects have come into the possession of museums through a variety of means, including loans and sales, he indicates that one of the challenges in establishing connections and "getting property back" is a lack of written documentation.[17] Further "many artifacts are quite old and quite brittle." Rather than risk damage by moving them, he suggests that an appropriate response may be for museums or governments to pay for the cost of a replica for the community. Other challenges include museums prohibiting access to certain storage areas, not allowing inspection of all items on lists provided to the Luuxhon, and the high human and financial costs associated with identifying items located in museums around the world. Despite these challenges, the creation of a "federal heritage park" in Gitanyow is the subject of treaty negotiation, as is the repatriation of certain artifacts from the Canadian Museum of Civilization and the Royal British Columbia Museum. Herb anticipates that part of the process will include cooperative management agreements with the two museums, the creation of a facility for the protection and display of items returned, the training of Gitanyow curators, and other forms of capacity building within the community aimed at operating a museum. Herb's skill as a negotiator will be tested as he tries to ensure that the cooperative management agreements secure the return of items to the Gitanyow institutions that own them.

Amsisa'ytxw (Victoria Russell) makes the critical connection between "owning" and "belonging."[18] Clearly, Victoria views "ownership" as a collective responsibility and not as an individual one – "belonging means owning something." Later, she says, "We actually have a place in this world; it makes a difference for me as a Luuxhon House member emotionally because it makes me feel proud to know I own land." Without the land, the songs, the crests, the history, she says, "I would be nothing." As a Luuxhon House member, she "counts for something." This echoes Godfrey Good's statement that if the law dies out, the people are not good for anything. Victoria thus articulates two fundamental points of Gitxsan law: first, a person's rights and responsibilities arise only out of his or her membership in a lineage that operates as a House group in the context of complex reciprocal responsibilities with other Houses; second, the House must hold territories, crests, histories, and songs in order to be recognized, to exist, in fact, as a legal entity within the Gitxsan and wider society.

The interrelatedness of Gitxsan concepts of property and their centrality to Gitxsan identity is demonstrated in Victoria Russell's response to the question, "What does the term 'cultural property' mean to you and how would you define it?"

> For me, cultural property means owning anything that is wood, metal, water. Anything that you can touch. Anything that you can hear or sing that is pertaining to the history of the Luuxhon is owned by us ... as in the Luuxhon House members. It's being passed down to us. Things are passed down so we can survive. Land ownership is for a reason ... Owning what's real, like the land, songs, the crests. Without those material things, the songs, the history I would be nothing. That's why I have those things. It signifies my identity, who I am. That's why I own it. I would have nothing. I would be nothing ...[I]t covers all aspects of our being right from the spiritual stuff to the materialistic stuff. (Victoria Russell)

She elaborates upon this later in her interview:

> I am connected to the land, to my land, to my territory, our territory. The properties that we have, such as the totem poles, the crests, the blankets, the rattles, the aprons – everything is connected to me and that's how I relate myself to the land. That is what you have to keep in mind, is that everything about property relates me back to the land. That's why it's really important that we maintain such properties or obtain our property, such as rings around your neck, because it signifies everything about us, right down to social order, spirituality, the emotional aspect and the physical.

Later in her interview, Victoria distinguishes between the individual possession of an article and the collective possession of the image or representation on it. She uses the example of a chief's blanket. She says that, when an individual "gets the big name," the blanket is passed on to him or her to wear. She characterizes this type of possession as an individual right. But, she says, the House as a whole owns the crest image, which any House member can use on his or her vest or blanket. She characterizes this type of ownership as collective House ownership. Victoria goes on to discuss other examples of these types of ownership with regard to the crests on rattles and the dramatic performances attached to certain feast names in the House. While the name is held by an individual for a while, it is eventually passed on, but the actual activity that goes with it, the *naxnox* performance, is collectively owned. She also explains that the chief is best understood as "the caretaker" of many items, such as headdresses and blankets, "that get passed down." From this account, it appears that some of a House's possessions may pass through the hands of certain individuals whom the House has collectively selected to hold them. But regardless of whether the item is a blanket or a name, eventually the House passes it on to someone else. In this sense, the individual holder could be said to be a trustee rather than an owner.

The telling of the *adaawk* is primarily the responsibility of hereditary chiefs, and it is the responsibility of others to listen and to witness. Witnesses may be called upon to act as mediators if "issues or some misunderstanding" arises within a House. "Telling the truth" is the responsibility of the chief, and "the responsibility of the listener is to make sure they understand what [they] are hearing." The *adaawk* is never told in "one sitting"; rather, it is a "life-long learning session." In her House, Victoria also sees a special role for women with regard to teaching younger members "who we are and where we came from." In a more formal sense, this is the role of House chiefs, both men and women, although they are also mentors. Victoria uses the Gitxsan term *yoohlimx* for this role, meaning "passed on to the next generation." However, she finds that the lack of Gitxsan speakers among the young people is making this transmission more difficult.

Language usage is only one of a number of ways in which the House of Luuxhon is facing changes in how it exercises its relationship to its tangible and intangible possessions. Consider, for example, Victoria's response to a question regarding the importance of protecting historical and ceremonial sites. Like most Gitxsan people, she resists the implication in the question that certain sites on a territory can be carved out for special consideration. Although she is not familiar with all of the Luuxhon territory, she says that it is important to make sure the rivers and creeks "are kept on maps because ... our totem poles tell a story and refer to the sites, which is proof we own the land." Here, as in Herb Russell's discussion of Canadian law, we see the influence of the House's involvement in aboriginal rights and title litigation. The arena of its activities has expanded. Territories are defended not only on the ground but also on maps; the accounting occurs not only in the feast but also in Canadian courts. So, in the broad meaning of the term, language is always changing.

Donald Russell recently assumed the name Luuxhon. He agrees with Victoria that the feast system and telling of *adaawk* is fundamental to the

Gitxsan legal system and to the transmission of knowledge about the Luuxhon. However, like Godfrey Good, he acknowledges the utility of written accounts – such as Michael Bright's book on fishing sites, places, and names – in establishing rights that are recognized outside the Gitxsan legal and social order.[19] Belonging to the House of Luuxhon begins with "transferring names," and the responsibilities associated with belonging include "being informed about traditional values." However, he notes that technology and other outside forces have had a negative impact on the retention of traditional values and learning processes. The inability of youth to understand their responsibilities as witnesses in the feast hall also causes him concern. And the advent of technology has generated differing views on its appropriate use. For example, some individuals have allowed their telling of the *adaawk* to be recorded and some hosts have allowed video cameras and recorders in the feast hall. Others have banned the use of this technology as "part of their cultural protection."

Donald identifies another challenge facing the House of Luuxhon: the inadvertent discovery and destruction of archaeological heritage through resource exploration and development. Research identifying territorial boundaries and the location of resources within those territories is an important step towards the prevention of this type of loss. Of particular concern to him is the protection of burial sites, which need to be marked and preserved.

Conclusion

The dominant theme from the Luuxhon interviews is that possession and the use of the images on certain artifacts is of greater legal significance to House members and their advisors in Gitanyow than is possession of the original objects themselves. Thus, Godfrey Good was less concerned that the museum at K'san held the blanket depicting his House's crests than he was that the officials there would not lend it to him to display at a feast. Similarly, both Godfrey and Herb Russell describe how, at different times, Gitanyow chiefs have allowed the Royal British Columbia Museum to remove old crest poles if the museum paid to have new ones carved and raised.

Robert Good gives a concise account of the legal significance attached to crest images when he summarizes the *Simgyak' adaawk*, or formal oral history. He links the image on a mask to a song, a drama, and the *adaawk*, all of which recreate, through display and performance, the House of Luuxhon's possession of a particular fishing site and of its territories as a whole. Victoria Russell makes the same connection, more abstractly, when she says that, without her House's land, crests, songs, and *adaawk*, she "would be nothing." She says that, as a House member, she "counts for something." Godfrey Good makes the same point even more concisely by saying that the law defines the Gitanyow as a people.

There is an allegorical contrast here: The museums treasure the old, decayed, but original objects; the Gitanyow Houses treasure the ability to recreate relationships with their land and each other through the repeated display of the crest images on new objects. Does this reflect each society's view of aboriginal laws and institutions? The one view being of a decaying culture whose material remnants need preserving; the other view being of an evolving society whose law requires its constitutional elements to be consistently and constantly reaffirmed?

The second theme arising out of this case study involves the importance Gitanyow people attach to the misuse of crests on the part of those not authorized by law to employ them. Godfrey's puzzlement as to why K'san would refuse to allow him to use his House's crest blanket is an example of this. After all, Godfrey muses, the museum cannot use the blanket. Similarly, Herb Russell explains why the Office of the Gitanyow Hereditary Chiefs has an ongoing dispute with the Nisga'a Treaty regarding the aboriginal law governing territory and crests displayed on poles and letterheads. Given the central constitutional role of the protection and display of *adaawk*, crests, and songs, their misappropriation by others is clearly of primary political concern to the House and to the Gitanyow generally.

Gitanyow has dealt with the issue of museum artifacts in two ways: first, by allowing certain objects to be removed from the village if the museum pays for the making and the legally appropriate inauguration of new objects; second, by initiating the building of its own museum, which would be under the control of the hereditary chiefs and which could store old objects in an appropriate physical environment while allowing them to be loaned to their rightful holders for feasts and other occasions.

Many of those interviewed identified the principal things that play a constitutional role for each Gitanyow House group. These are each House's crests, feast names, *adaawk*, songs, *naxnox* dances, and, of primary concern in treaty talks and title litigation, its territories. The Ray Jones interview shows that not all images are House possessions. Those that are not can be more generally used, although the collective permission of the House chiefs in the village is still required. No House possession is personally owned, even by the House chief. Both Godfrey and Herb describe the chief's role as being more that of a trustee than that of an owner. Victoria Russell distinguishes between the House's possession of the crest and a chief's possession, during his or her lifetime, of the physical object – say, a blanket – on which the crest is displayed. Nevertheless, she identifies the House as being the collective owner of the crest, which suggests, in Western legal jargon, that if the chief is a trustee, then the beneficiaries are the House members – past, present, and future. So, if the law defines the Gitanyow as a people, the House is defined by the proper display and performance of its intangible possessions and its protection and use of its territories and fishing sites.

Finally, the interviews suggest that direct questions may not always elicit the answer anticipated, even if the person being interviewed has relevant information and is willing to give it. A more narrative-like interview style is recommended. This may cause difficulties where the interview project is heavily governed by institutional ethics committees as the interview discourse cannot be known and vetted ahead of time. Again, the difficulty may lie with one culture imposing not only its questioning style but also its ethical norms on another. In this case, the use of an interviewer selected not only for her language and social knowledge but also for her legal position in the House may be an example of how cross-cultural ethical issues can be approached in a constructive way.

Notes

1 Heritage conservation legislation and the *Cultural Property Export and Import Act,* R.S.C. 1985, c. C-51 requires that, for the purpose of invoking protections under the legislation, property be classified as property of heritage or cultural value. However, outside these contexts property is "property" and carries with it a system of rights enforceable by the state. Further, within these contexts the law assumes the legitimacy of a market in cultural items and protection of heritage resources has to be balanced against the benefits of economic development.

2 In Gitxsan law, as the study involves members of the Luuxhon House, the appropriate person to speak to the House's approval of it is Luuxhon. He is required to consult with others in the House, as well as with chiefs of closely related Houses, before giving that approval. Consequently, a copy of this report was sent to Luuxhon (Don Russell) to review before its release to the public. It was also sent to all participants, Darlene Russell and Glen Williams (representatives from the Office of the Gitanyow Hereditary Chiefs), and members of the Luuxhon case study research team for comment.

3 A standard set of potential research questions was developed after meeting with prospective First Nations research partners in the summer of 2001 for the purpose of obtaining research ethics approval and funding (see appendix on page 491 of this volume). These processes require the identification of the nature of questions that will be used when conducting research with human participants. Research partners were subsequently encouraged to revise the question set to reflect priorities in their communities and to create their own questions concerning property protection issues and relations. Regardless of the question set used, it was understood that the questions were to be reformulated as necessary to help participants understand them and that questions were to operate as a general guide for a dialogue that might result in a more narrative-like response, depending on the participant interviewed. It was also understood that, to a certain extent, interviews would be guided by cultural interpretations of the questions asked, local protocol, and topics that interviewees felt were most relevant to the issues being raised.

4 According to Robert Good, the name "Gwinu" means "to ask for something." Gwinu will act out this meaning at a *naxnox,* or spirit dance, performance (see Robert Good interview, infra note 11).

5 Interview of Sim'oogit Gwinu (Godfrey Good) by Katie Ludwig (24 July 2002), Gitwangak, British Columbia. Transcripts of interviews with participants who agreed to have their interviews made available to the public have been provided to the Office of the Gitanyow Hereditary Chiefs.

6 Wilson Duff, ed., *Histories, Territories and Laws of the Kitwancool,* Anthropology in British Columbia, Memoir No. 4 (Victoria: BC Provincial Museum, 1959).

7 Crests, or *ayuks,* are images that represent those important events in a House group's history that give the group its identity. The events are more fully recorded in the House's oral history, or *adaawk.*

8 K'san is a registered society with both Gitxsan and non-Gitxsan directors. The society, however, does not acknowledge any formal control of its activities by the Gitxsan Hereditary Chiefs or by Gitxsan laws and institutions.

9 In the course of his interview, Godfrey identifies the main items of a Gitanyow chief's regalia: the blanket (*gwis haalayt*), the headdress (*am haalayt*), and the rattle (*hax seeks*). As noted by the interviewer, the term "*gwis haalayt*" is also, confusingly, used for the regalia as a whole and as a seemingly alternative term for the headdress. "*Haalayt*" refers to the dance (literally, "twirling") that manifests a particular spirit, or *naxnox*, that sometimes uses transformation masks, such as the Raven mask (*Gaagem get*) mentioned by Godfrey. *Haalayt* dances usually precede a feast.

10 Interview of Ray Jones (Niis Noolh) by Katie Ludwig (10 October 2002), Old Hazelton, British Columbia.

11 Interview of Robert Good (Sindihl) by Katie Ludwig (19 August 2002), Gitanyow, British Columbia.

12 This is another transformation mask used at haalayt performances. See note 9.

13 Wing-chiefs are the heads of the constituent families or lineages within a House group and are advisors to the House Chief.

14 Interview of Herb Russell (Ts'iiwa') by Katie Ludwig (15 August 2002), South Hazelton, British Columbia.

15 One of the questions in the standard question set discussed in *supra* note 3 was aimed at determining how property rights and responsibilities were determined within the community. The question is: "What are the culturally appropriate processes for determining rights to cultural property within your community?"

16 For one approach to consideration of applicable law and evidence in the case of ownership of land territories, see N.J. Sterritt *et al.*, *Tribal Boundaries in the Nass Watershed* (Vancouver: UBC Press, 1998).

17 While unsure of how cultural items came into the possession of museums, Don Russell agrees that it is important to have access to cultural items in the possession of museums and that one of the challenges is lack of "historical background" on what is there. Victoria Russell also addresses the importance of access to items, as this would enable a Gitanyow person to fulfill his or her obligations to pass on knowledge and to recreate her/his identity and maintain her/his legal relationships. Interview of Luuxhon (Don Russell) by Katie Ludwig (19 November 2002), South Hazelton, British Columbia; interview of Amsisa'ytxw (Victoria Russell) by Katie Ludwig (15 August 2002), Gitanyow, British Columbia.

18 Victoria Russell, *ibid.*

19 Don is referring to a notebook and map produced by Michael Bright (Ts'tmgwanks) of Gitanyow. See *supra* note 16 at 64-76.

3
Northwest Coast *Adawx* Study

Susan Marsden

This study was initiated as part of the Protection and Repatriation of First Nations Cultural Heritage project discussed in the introduction to this volume. The project was designed to gain insight into issues concerning First Nations intellectual property and heritage resources with a view to discovering or devising legal means to address these issues. There is, however, an inherent contradiction in the design of this project, namely that the issues were predefined in a non-aboriginal context.[1] The concepts of intellectual property and heritage resources arise out of a way of viewing the world that either excludes or is antithetical to that of many First Nations and therefore precludes a real understanding of aboriginal culture and society.

The term "intellect," for example, is defined as "the faculty of reasoning and understanding objectively, one's mental powers"[2] and assumes its opposite, "emotion." The Gitksan word for "to think" is *"ha'niigoot"* and the Tsimshian, *"ha'ligoot"* (literally "used-for-on-heart"). The root word *"goot"* (heart), is a component in the numerous words that convey feelings. For the Gitksan and Tsimshian then, thought arises from the heart – not the heart as the seat of emotions but as the seat of both feeling and thinking.

The term "property" implies separation: this thing that I own is outside of me, is controlled by me, and can be taken from me. There is no equivalent concept in Gitksan and Tsimshian thought. As we will see, for these societies, in cases of what might be considered "intellectual property," it is not so much "I own this" as "I *am* this" and "this *is* me," or perhaps more accurately, "we *are* this" and "this *is* us." Like property, heritage is not something outside of us that has come down from the past, "it is us"; moreover, not only is the identity of our ancestors also our identity, but as their reincarnation, "we *are* our ancestors."

"Resources," like property, is also a concept that flows from the objectification of the world, the transformation of a living, vital, spirit-filled world into a collection of things that exist as potential to be owned, sold, or stolen. For the Gitksan and Tsimshian, there is no separation between people and the cultural "things" collectively called heritage, nor is there a separation between people and the world they inhabit. In fact, central to Gitksan and Tsimshian thought is the principle of respect and an understanding that dividing the world into subject and object – forgetting that animals are our brothers, for example – leads to disrespect and ultimately to catastrophic events.

While it is not within the scope of this study to discuss this way of seeing within a broader philosophical context, it should be noted that when these Gitksan and Tsimshian concepts are considered, they seem to describe not so much another cultural reality as a deeper reality shared by all peoples. While these concepts may be absent from Western secular thought, they are akin to the understandings of some European existential philosophers and to such oriental philosophies as Buddhism.

Concerning this project, however, is it possible to remain faithful to its spirit but to frame the issues it seeks to address in a more indigenous context? How can we avoid the pitfall of acknowledging aboriginal thought only inasmuch as it is comprehensible or compatible with that of non-aboriginal society?

Like the project as a whole, this particular case study of Tsimshian and Gitksan *adawx* was conceived from a perspective outside these cultures and was initially defined as a review of recorded *adawx,* with the purpose of discovering information on the nature of "intellectual property" within these societies. While this initial intent was based on a misunderstanding of the nature of *adawx,* it *is* the *adawx,* within the constellation of cultural institutions of which they are a part, which can help us to develop new and more appropriate perspectives on the issues we are attempting to address.[3]

The Gitksan and Tsimshian, Northwest Coast Nations

The *adawx* and the associated concepts of identity and history are central to Gitksan and Tsimshian society. As John Brown, Kwiiyeehl of the Gisgahaast (Fireweed) clan of the Kispiox tribe of the Gitksan, explained:

> It was customary to transmit the *adawx* so that they may be preserved. A group that could not tell their *adawx* would be ridiculed with the remark, "What is your *adawx*?" And if you could not give it you were laughed at. "What is your grandmother's name? And where is your crest? How do you know of your past, where have you lived? You have no grandfather. You cannot speak to me because I have one. You have no ancestral home. You are like a wild animal, you have no abode." *Niiye'e* and *adawx*, grandfather and history are practically the same thing.[4]

Art Mathews, T'enimgyet of the Laxgibuu (Wolf) clan of the Gitwingax tribe of the Gitksan, also expressed this idea: "Even children had to get names to get into the feast house ... so they don't get embarrassed standing outside the feast hall and somebody walking up to them 'What's your name, where are you from, where is your linkage?'"[5]

As John Brown and Art Mathews describe, identity is defined by lineage and history, and without identity a person is not part of society. Each lineage maintains its history and identity through a sophisticated interweaving of verbal record, song, and image. The verbal record, termed *adawx*, includes ancient songs, or *limx'oy*, and is perpetuated by the memory training of heirs to chiefly positions. The *adawx* tell the history of the origins, migrations, and territories that shaped the unique identity of the lineage. It tells of natural disasters, wars in defence of territory and other extraordinary, often epic, events and is related over many hours at important feasts, or *yukw*. Images, called crests or *ayuuk,* that commemorate the historical events are recorded on totem poles, or *xwtsaan*, housefronts, chiefly regalia, and many of the chief's feasting items. The power of a lineage arising from its history and its place in the world is called *daxgyet* and is a central concept in Gitksan and Tsimshian society. *Daxgyet* means "the strength of a people" and connotes those that are "firmly placed" or rooted.

The *adawx, limx'oy,* and *ayuuks*, their representations on *xwtsaan* and their validation in the *yukw* are not only the manifestation of identity or power, of *daxgyet*, but also the deeds to territories. This relationship between *adawx, limx'oy, ayuuks, yukw,* and title is fundamental to the Gitksan system of land ownership. The *adawx* record the ownership rights, the *ayuuks* are a material expression of *daxgyet,* and the *xwtsaan*, on which the *ayuuks* are carved, is planted in the ground, rooting the lineage and their *daxgyet* in their village and throughout their territory.[6]

The lineage and its territory are woven together by history. Their relationship is an alliance in the deepest sense; in ancient times, when an ancestor first acquired the territory, a cane was sometimes touched to the land to signify the power of the lineage merging with that of the land. The *adawx* of Xamlaxyeltxw of the Ganeda (Frog/Raven) clan of the Gitanyaw (Kitwancool) tribe of the Gitksan, described how this chief and his people first came to own their lands on the Nass River:

> They reached another river which they named Xsigigyeenit, meaning "river above." It was a good salmon fishing river in a good country; they built a permanent village here and put their mark on the river, thus claiming ownership of it ... Once more they moved, leaving their power and mark which made this country theirs. Still travelling they arrived here at Gitanyaw ... by following what is now the Cranberry River (Xsiyagasgiit – "river that descends gradually") ...
>
> The chiefs established themselves at Gitanyaw and raised their poles. The poles gave them their power or coat of arms and gave them the right of

> ownership of all the lands, mountains, lakes and streams they had passed through or over and camped or built villages in. The power of these poles goes unto the lands they had discovered and taken as their own. The power from the house of this chief and his council goes as far as Gitxsits'uuts'xwt, the place of the seagull hunter [Singewin], and includes Xsigigyeenit, the "upper fishing station." The power of the pole still goes on and belongs to Sindihl.[7]

Like the cane, the pole links the lineage to its territory, and through the feast, especially the pole-raising feast, or *baxmaga*, the society as a whole acknowledges this relationship. The term "*baxmaga*" means to "erect upwards." In the *baxmaga*, after the pole is raised, the chief names the mountains, lakes, and rivers of his lineage's territories, thereby recreating and validating the original act of naming that first established the chief's and the lineage's ownership. He recreates the time when his ancestor walked the land and put his power, the power of the pole, or cane, into the land. The names that were created out of the lineage's experience of its land embody the bond between the lineage and the land.[8] Stanley Williams, Gwisgyen, of the Gisgahaast clan of the Gitksigyukla tribe of the Gitksan tells how the boundaries of the lineage's territory are acknowledged in the feast:

> In the chief's houses we have our laws, our laws concerning the boundaries. Each chief knows his own boundaries and this is held in their house. They know where their boundaries are and they know that no one could trespass on a different boundary. They mention their boundaries in the feast hall, and they have chiefs and other Gitksan people listening to him and they are witnessing this while he describes his – the boundary of his territory.[9]

The boundaries are described in the feast by naming the places or natural features at the outer reaches of the territory. Like Stanley Williams, James Morrison, Txawok, of the Laxgibuu clan of the Gitanyaw tribe of the Git-ksan, referred to the naming of boundaries and further explained the Git-ksan concept of boundaries:

> People sitting in the feast hall hear what you saying that identified boundary, and they know where the boundary is. You name the place where the post is, like *an'liidiks*, and they know where the boundary is. It's in the feast, and anyone that is sitting in the feast listen to you, what you said in the feast, *an'liidiks*.
>
> ["*An'liidiks*"] means that landmark where the post on the corner of the boundary, also known as a creek or a mountain, that's never moved, or the creek that they use that's not dry, it always runs, a creek all the time. So that's the reason why they use this boundary, they call *an'liidiks*, it does

> not move. They don't use anything that move. It's still the same today. They never changes. No one can change that.[10]

"An'liidiks" means "place on-firmly placed" and shares the root word *"dax"* with the term *"daxgyet."* As Solomon Marsden, Xamlaxyeltxw, explained, the strength, or *daxgyet,* of the chief is rooted in his land:

> I could talk about my own territory [in the feast] and when I mention my territory, this is where the basis, the foundation of my strength [*dax̀gyet*] with the other Gitksan people, with the territories, I have to describe my land, my territory where my power and my authority is.[11]

James Morrison also alluded to the nature of the relationship between the lineage and the land when he described how the ancestors tell the shared history of the lineage and its territory through the natural forces in the land:

> You have to go out there [to the territory], and sometimes when you feel like to, you have to be out there to be out at the rivers or lakes, wherever you going to sit yourself and feel you can hear the creeks and the rivers to remind you what happened in the past. That's one of those things that people – to go out there and sit in some of those areas and listen to the creeks, what these people in the past used to speak about these territories. That's one reason why they went out there, to listen to this. And you can feel the presence of the creators when you have that – the reflection of this of your territory and yourself.[12]

Stanley Williams explained the relationship between the lineage's history, crest pole, power, and territory:

> We have a totem pole there that contains the history of our territory and the history of our people. The totem pole holds the power wherever the totem pole is, is where your territory is, the power of your territory is there.[13]

Solomon Marsden also referred to this relationship:

> When a chief is planning to raise the pole, it is very important because he thinks back on his territory where he would put all – on this pole he would put all the power and authority that he has and he will put all the crests in his *adawx* on this pole ... and even around this area we see totem poles and it's – the Indians know how important it is to our people, because it shows where our power and authority and jurisdiction is. This is what these poles show where it lies. And this pole is called *xwts'aan* ...

> The pole represents ... the power and ownership of the territory. The ... totem poles that you see standing have these – and they're not just standing there for nothing.[14]

Fred Johnson, Lelt, of the Ganhada clan in the Gitwingax tribe of the Gitksan, described how the crest pole links the lineage with the spiritual world:

> There was a Simooget [Chief] in the sky, Simooget, that gives certain powers with the totem pole and with our *ayuks* and he gives it to us and it is just like cement to us. We see it, just like cement, it is ours.[15]

In his reference to cement, Fred Johnson evokes again the important idea put forth by the other chiefs – that identity and power transcend the material world, yet are firmly rooted and immovable.

The distribution of gifts at the feast honours the relationships of the lineage with others in its society and acknowledges their role in validating its *daxgyet*. As well, by hosting the feast and distributing wealth the chief shows that he has properly overseen the relationship between the lineage and its land and that, as a result, the lineage has prospered. Through the giving out of their wealth, the people of the lineage show that they have fulfilled the law, and this is acknowledged by the guests when they accept their hosts' food and goods.

In one of the few written descriptions of a specific feast, William Beynon described how the Tsimshian – in this case the house of Nisyaganaat of the Raven clan of the Gitsiis tribe – named the territories where each of the foods being distributed had been harvested:

> Then the guests started to eat. As soon as they started eating, one of the leading Gitsiis headmen stood up and said, "Take your time eating, Chiefs, take your time eating, for this is what your grandfathers did. And the meat you are eating is mountain goat taken from the valley of Kiyaks."
>
> Then another stood up and said, "Take your time eating, Chiefs, some of this meat is the seal meat the chief himself caught in his seal traps at the headwaters of Kts'm'at'iin, his own territory."
>
> Then another stood up and said, "Take your time eating, Chiefs, these are the high bush cranberries and crabapples which you will eat gathered by the chief, my master at his own berry grounds at Kts'mkwtuun."
>
> Then they finished naming all the rivers owned by the Gitsiis so as to make them known to the tribes of the Tsimshian, that is why they spoke this way.[16]

Art Mathews referred to this practice in the feast:

> [The territorial names] were announced in various ways. They announced as an *adawx* and they were announced when you bring your soup ... whatever, they announced and said this so and so, this meat comes from, and they specify each mountain or its territory where it comes from. Each creek is mentioned. So in our rule and laws we say that if you eat and digest the words, it's within your very soul. That's why they do these things. [The chiefs from Gitwingax and from all the other villages were present.][17]
>
> All what you take off your territory, then these feasts would be put up, and each – if it was meat or wherever you got the meat – would announce where it came from. It's a show of wealth you would say, and you would mention each name of your territories where it came from ... that's why they do while you are eating this, you digest it, it's within you. It's a spiritual belief that you mention this, that part of the territory where it came from.[18]

This ceremonial distribution of food demonstrates the successful relationship between the chief and his territory, his ability to feed the people, and thus the power of the chief and his lineage. In consuming these foods as the territories are named, the guests acknowledge the *daxgyet* of the host lineage and the ownership of their territories.

As Stanley Williams explained, it is the law that each generation raise a crest pole and host a *baxmaga:*

> This is when the food is given out and the materials are given out. After the guests have eaten and the ... chiefs have been paid for all the help they have given, all the expenses are paid when the totem pole was erected, this totem pole would have all their crests. The reason why this pole is erected because it holds the – power of the – and it holds the power and the law of our people and this is the reason why it's been erected.
>
> If the *'niidil* and Gitwingax, Kitwancool, Kispiox and Gitanmaax chiefs agree with what is going on and what has been said in the feast house by the new chief, then it gives more strength to the new chief that everything is right ... this is the law ... that all the Gitksan people use.[19]

A successful pole-raising feast is evidence that the chief has respected the land, the members of his lineage, and the other lineages in his society and has thereby fulfilled the law.

The role of the chiefs in leading the people and ensuring the peace and prosperity that leads to a successful feast is demonstrated by the *naxnox* rituals that always precede the pole-raising feast. These rituals dramatize *naxnox* names, names representing negative human qualities that flow from a lack of respect for the authority, rights, and territory of others and that threaten the social order. In the *naxnox* performance these qualities are dramatized as a destructive force that threatens everyone but that is tamed by the chief. When these performances are complete, the chief scatters eagle down on his guests to ensure the peace and harmony necessary for the ensuing feast.

Naxnox performances in their totality might be considered an enactment of the process of civilization. The *naxnox* names that are acted out (*e.g.*, stingy, beggar, proud, crazy, restless, hoarder) represent negative human qualities. They are the mirror image of Gitksan and Tsimshian law and its fundamental principle of respect. These human qualities that work against the fulfillment of the law are seen as spirit forces that must be taken on and controlled in the person of the chief. He and the other chiefs in his house are the only ones who have the spiritual strength to mitigate their destructive effect on society. The chief, in controlling one of these forces, takes on its name as one of his own. If the person taking a *naxnox* name is not sufficiently strong, the spirit force in the name controls him and he himself becomes restless, thoughtless, or stupid. Each chief holding a *naxnox* name personally tames that anti-social force for the people as a whole. The full range of such undesirable human qualities is represented in the totality of the *naxnox* names of all the lineages. Through the taming of these aspects of human nature, the foundation of culture is created and the social order maintained.[20]

William Beynon, who devoted his life to recording the history of the Tsimshian and Gitksan, witnessed a number of these *naxnox* performances in Gitksigyukla in 1945. The following is his description of the *bignhaw,* or liar, *naxnox* of the chief T'ewelasxw of the Eagle clan at Gitwingax:

> Then another man came and sat in the middle of the gathering and was apparently indifferent to all the people. The attendants came to him and spoke saying, "All of your guests are here now why don't you dance for them?" He looked about and then calmly stated, "I'm the only chief on the Skeena, I control the water and land and all these totem poles are mine and I am many thousands years of age." This he kept on repeating for a length of time, until the attendants took him and forcibly threw him out of the hall, saying to him, "You liar," using the Tsimshian phrase bignhaw, liar' a naxnox privilege ... of this house.
>
> Immediately after being ejected, the attendants and songsters were in an argument as to whether they had done right in putting out the man. While they were still arguing a large stone was thrown against the building and many men came in terrified and with exclamations, "Why did you put out that *halayt* person, now something terrible has come. We do not know what it is, some very strange being, it is no doubt something come to harm us and destroy us all. Be on your guard." Then another came in with even more terrifying news that this monster or being was destroying everything

in its way. He admonishes the guests and chiefs to be careful lest harm should befall them. Then he turned to the *halayt* attendants and said, "You have invoked the destroying powers of some fearful being. See it come in."

With that there entered a being dressed as a warrior with a bearskin armour, a huge mask about two feet high and the same across and having a barbed lance and quiver of arrows and a bow, and hung from his belt was a *hagaloo'* (war club). The attendants ran around the being in an endeavour to overcome it and it went around as if to grab several of the attendants who fled in terror and the being came to where the guests were sitting and then attempted to try and wreak harm on the guests. The attendants finally overcame it and it fell as if in a stupor and then the singers at the rear of the house [sang] and after, this being began to revive and show signs of life and was able to go to the rear of the house into an enclosure.

After this, the chief T'ewelasxw came forward ... attired in a Chilkat blanket with leggings and an apron adorned with puffin bills. On his head was an eagle headdress, *amhalayt*, which was filled with swans down, *mixk̲'aax*, and the singers singing the *halayt* songs and the chief ... dancing with the rattle, and as he came upon where the visiting chiefs sat, he, nodding his head, scattered the swans down upon the guests.[21]

Naxnox is translated as "supernatural force" or "spiritual power." The power in the *naxnox* name is that of the chief who tames these anti-social forces. Taming is not the same as elimination, however; *naxnox* performances acknowledge the ever-present reality of anti-social forces and the need for the spiritual power of the chiefs to control them on behalf of their people.

Art Mathews described how *naxn̄ox* power overcomes fear and how this strength is part of one's spiritual relationship to territory:

[The *naxnox* is performed at the feast and demonstrates] the spiritual relation you have with your territory ... you relate yourself spiritually to the territories you own in various *naxnox*.

The actual name of showing your *naxnox* is in our language, *luuhetxw halayt* ... which means you're going to show your power which I described as *daxgyet,* is going to be transferred to another person to exact its rightful line of that name. [It] is enacted a day before the *yukw* ... The actual name power is *naxnox* ... it says fearless ... we look anybody in the eye and we don't get scared of them. [The performance] is unforgettable. You could feel the spirit actually coming in you and ... you relate *naxnox* your land to your territory, to the whole house, spirit is given there through *naxnox*. It was a very lengthy – if I went through all the *naxnoxs* that had to be performed, I think they started around one o'clock in the afternoon and they'd end at about four o'clock in the morning.[22]

After the *naxnox* performances, the chief dances the welcome dance in which he scatters eagle down from his *amhalayt* (headdress, literally "good for spiritual power") on his guests. In so doing he moves the feast out of everyday life into a context in which the spiritual aspects of life and the laws of respect, harmony, and balance prevail. Every action is formalized according to the law. Even a higher language is spoken in which words of respect and affection create a mood in which human differences fall away and people focus on the spiritual reality that joins them all. Here events are witnessed in their essence in the light of the law, as part of the flow of spirit through time:

> But when I [Stanley Williams] enter the feast house, I will leave this all behind because this is where our law is. The chief is not supposed to be looking around and talking in the feast house because our ancestors really take the feast house very seriously and our laws seriously. This is why we take everything in that is said in the feast house. We listen closely and we pay attention closely. We learn what is going on in the feast house.[23]

In the feast, the chief, like the crest pole, manifests the spiritual centre of the lineage; in a sense, the pole and the chief are one. The power that flows through the pole also flows through the spinal column of the chief and not only links the lineage to its territory and the animals and plants that feed them but also spreads throughout the society, strengthening the network of human relations forged by this and other feasts.

At the finale of the feast, the chief displays his *hayetsxw*, or copper, and, in so doing, displays both his spiritual centre, in yet another form, and also the wealth of all the feasts held by this lineage over the centuries. The ridge that runs vertically up the lower half of the copper represents the spine of the chief; the crests on the upper half, the power of the chief and his lineage. When the copper is broken and distributed it reinforces, along with the food and goods distributed, the interconnection of all the lineages in the society. At the same time it represents the giving out of many centuries of wealth and the confidence of the lineage that they will continue to live and flourish and create and give away new wealth in the future.

The pole-raising feast also completes the burial of the previous chief and other leading chiefs of the lineage and marks the moment when the current leader is fully acknowledged as a chief. At the same time, the feast establishes the status and worth of the present chiefs and thereby upholds these chiefly names for another generation. These names, like the pole and the copper, represent the cumulative power of the chiefs and their lineage and must be validated and renewed in each generation.[24]

In this way, the history and identity of the lineage and its power and authority are kept alive through each generation. As Solomon Marsden explained, it is one of the chief's main responsibilities to ensure that the knowledge that underlies the *daxgyet* of the lineage is kept alive in his generation and passed on to the next:

> In the beginning when there were Gitksan people here they used to live in big houses, which is known as long houses. There is no rooms in a long house, it's just one big room. The Chief would sleep in the back centre of the house and then they would have their – his brothers and nephews on the sides. Early before morning the Chief would rise and he would tell his brother and nephews and the house members of the *adawx*. He would go over the *adawx* and then he would go over his plans of what they're going to do, if they're going to have a feast, planning a feast. When the – when the older Chief passes on, the new Chief comes on and he does the same thing, and this keeps going on and on and they keep changing Chiefs and they still do the same thing, telling of the *adawx* and what has happened during the lifetime. And this is the reason why today we know the *adawx*, it's been passed on, because this is what they did from the beginning of time.[25]
>
> In the beginning of time when a man becomes a Chief what the law he has to follow is that he sleeps the back centre of the long house and what he does is he takes a name and he's responsible for the house members and we don't write anything down. We don't write – there was no writing down in those days. So what happens as soon as the chief wakes up in the morning, he gets up and he starts telling the *adawx*, what *adawx* they had in that house and then he tell his other house members what to do and how they should do it. And this was the law of the Gitksan people. It gets passed on from generation to generation. And the hard work of the chiefs in the ancient times was to pass the *adawx* and the history from generation to generation and their hard work reached us. This is why we know our adawx and history because this is what the chief did back then passing from generation to generation ... the long houses are really called *Wiluuski yuuhlxamtxw*, which mean where the – where the history of people are.[26]

As Fred Johnson, Lelt, expressed it:

> Showing the other high chiefs that I am a *Simooget* and they would acknowledge whatever I say. And the law will never be lost. And that our nephews will learn that they will follow our traditions, take over our names. The law still exists today, still good today.[27]
>
> Ayuks is power of our forefathers and grandfathers that listened. Beautiful living ... it is something you don't play around with ... it's something that is treasured.[28]

Martha Brown, Xhliyamlaxha, of the Laxgibuu clan of the Kispiox tribe of the Gitksan, referred to this also. "It's a true history. Whatever happens to, to the old Indian people it's old and passed on what today is called generation from generation."[29]

The Gitksan and Tsimshian: Encounters with Foreign Nations

Periods of significant change in the life of a lineage are historical in nature; they add to the identity of the lineage and are recorded in *adawx*. Since, within Northwest Coast societies, people and institutions are intricately interconnected over space and time, the introduction of new and foreign elements provokes changes that move through the network of complex relationships. Encounters with foreign peoples take place at the borders of the nation and are recorded in the *adawx* of the lineages that first experience them. While such encounters were unusual in the thousands of years of Northwest Coast history, the *adawx* that grew out of them record the same ceremonial response as encounters with known groups, the same display of identity in response to the questions documented by John Brown: "What is your grandmother's name? And where is your crest? How do you know of your past, where have you lived?"[30] The following *adawx* relates the first meeting in ancient times of Xamlaxyeltxw and Luuxhon, chiefs of the Raven clan of the Gitanyaw, with the ancestors of the Nisg̱a'a.

> *Xamlaxyeltxw and Luuxhon travelled south along the Nass River looking for a new and unoccupied area that would sustain them. Over many generations, they established new villages at Anxts'imilixnaagets and at Aksnagyalga and laid claim to the surrounding lands. Finally, they settled, after a number of generations, at Winsgahlgu'l and Gitxsits'uuts'xwt. From there they established formal ties with the people of Gitwillaxgyap, an ancient village near what was later Gitlaxdamks, on the Nass River. The people there were a different people and spoke another language.*
>
> *Both Xamlaxyeltxw and Luuxhon gave major feasts at which they identified themselves to these people and at which ties of friendship were formalized. The* adawx *of Xamlaxyeltxw and Luuxhon details these events.*[31]

After living here [at Aksnagyalga] for sometime, they left and came close to a Nisg̱a'a village, at a place named Winsg̱ahlgu'l Ts'ilaasxw (Place of Narrow Canyon). They built their houses at a spot named Sgathlao (in Tsimsyan). This is the name of the house type. It became the crest of the house, a special type with posts leaning inward and supporting big beams. Here they settled. They erected four houses, those of 1. Xamlaxyeltxw, 2. Singewin, 3. Ts'iigwa, and 4. Luuxhon.

Luuxhon did not want to stay there. He preferred to roam about. So he went across the river to the opposite shore and down the river. He travelled until he came to a pretty big river down the Nass and he went up its course until he stopped at a large waterfall. There were plenty of beaver here, in the spring of the year. He was very impressed with the river, as the game abounded.

While he was preparing bear meat and the meat of the beaver he had killed someone appeared in front of him. He called this place Winluundeldehl'aks, Where Meets Water (Where Two Rivers Meet). Those he suddenly met there were his own ... [clan] brothers ... They wept and one of them told them, "You will now become my real brothers. I have taken this river to be mine alone, while my brother Xamlaxyeltxw has already erected a village farther up the river at Winsgahlgu'l" ... At a distance on this river towards the mouth, Luuxhon erected a house at a place called Gitxsits'uuts'xw, People Water Birds or Place of Many Birds.

This encounter is recorded in Xamlaxyeltxw's adawx *as it represents an historic event in the lives of this people, their first meeting with a foreign group since their departure from their homeland. The practice of feasting to establish formal relations was clearly well-developed by this time and the establishment of peaceful relations was accompanied by a full display of* naxnox, *or spirit powers, and* ayuuks.[32]

When he began this house, one of his brothers came to him and said, "We have discovered a village down below us on the main river (the Nass) and the people that live there are fighters and warriors." The Gitksan Luuxhon was now speaking Tsetsaut. He and the rest of the Ganeda at that time were speaking the Tsetsaut tongue. This man said, "These people at the village do not speak the same language as ourselves, but theirs is a foreign tongue."

The younger man and his party prepared themselves to go down to this new village, Xamlaxyeltxw, Hlewa'nst and Tsigwe ... Xamlaxyeltxw was going to this new village to invite them to his *yukw* and announce the establishment of his new village of Winsgahlgu'l. They went to the people who afterwards were known at Gitlaxdamks, the Gitwillaxgyap. It was those people whom Xamlaxyeltxw invited, and they went to his *yukw* at Winsgahlgu'l. In front of those that had come up from this Nass village they placed gifts of bear skins ...

Before the guests had arrived they had painted the front of the houses with a design known as Kawax or Kawangaak, Raven-House-front Painting. It was a single raven and two smaller ravens under each wing. This he exhibited to his guests and he dramatized his name of Xamlaxyeltxw, meaning a person backwards to and backwards, representing his journeys from one place to another.

Luuxhon at that time was working on his own house at Gitxsits'uuts'xw. The rest of the *Ganedas* at Winsgahlgu'l went down to assist him. Luuxhon made a crest that he exhibited, known as *Lademxsimgyet*, Ladder of People, a ladder like an entrance through a being: two huge frogs which were surrounded by many human-like beings. Then he made a huge wooden frog, inlaid with abalone pearl and placed it on the rear platform of the house. Around the edge of this frog were caribou hoofs. He called this *Ganaaw'm La<u>x</u>ptaw'*, Frog On Partition. After that he carved a being wearing a *lanemgayt* (like that on the pole at the present Gitwinhlgu'l) with four layers.

He was now determined to give a *yukw,* inviting the people of 'Wiilaxgyap (Gitlaxdamks), to exhibit his own exclusive crests. He took his guests to his village, but for two days he asked them to fast, as he was also to exhibit a *naxnox* called *Tigyet*. As his guests arrived before the *yukw* proper, he had a *halayt* at which he distributed raw foods, and meats. When his own *yukw* was finished, and he had distributed garments of goats and other animals, his guests departed for their own village.

Xamlaxyeltxw and his people had discovered new territories and a new people at their borders. Their relationship with the Gitwillaxgyap, a previously unknown people, was formalized at their *yukw*, in which the elaborate crests of the lineage, its histories and *naxnox,* established the power of the lineage and its right to the ownership of its territories. The presence of the Gitwillaxgyap at these feasts represented their acknowledgment of Xamlaxyeltxw and his peoples' ownership of their lands and their peaceful relationship with them.[33]

Although these peoples were foreign to each other and spoke different languages, they were both peoples of the Raven clan and, as such, relatives who shared a common ancient ancestry. Where foreign peoples met and could not draw on any shared identity, the establishment of peaceful coexistence took place through marriage. A marriage alliance, as with all new relationships, developed over time and was established through a series of feasts and the distribution of considerable wealth. It followed a period during which each people came to know the other and found mutual benefit in an alliance or a period of warfare or other hostilities such as raiding.[34]

These events recorded in Xamlaxyeltxw's *adawx* took place in ancient times when new territories could still be claimed, probably several thousand years ago. In more recent times, around fifteen hundred years ago, long after the territories of the Tsimshian and Gitksan were well established, large numbers of northern peoples migrated south causing a period of significant political and social disruption for these two nations. The oral histories concerning this period offer a glimpse of the range of responses available to these nations when faced with foreign peoples at their borders. Those foreign groups that had ancestral ties to lineages within these nations were absorbed into existing tribes and formed new house groups among them, while others that had simply invaded Tsimshian territory, settling in remote inlets, were attacked and driven off. The foreign peoples were accepted only after they had demonstrated the power and status they would bring to the tribe by hosting a feast. Here they told their *adawx,* displayed their crests, songs, and *naxnox,* and distributed considerable wealth to show their ability to sustain themselves without relying on the resources of others. In cases where they could not, or where there were insufficient resources for the newcomers, they were expelled and forced to move on to new regions.

During this period, very large numbers of people were assimilated into Tsimshian, Gitksan, and Nisga'a society. The many *adawx* that describe the warfare and political and social upheaval of this period also offer insight into the process by which these challenges were overcome. They relate how these nations retained their institutions and laws in the face of massive immigration and invasion. Their societies adapted to change by becoming more integrated and developing a more complex economy without changing their institutions and their laws.

In the centuries following the re-establishment of stable societies on the northern Northwest Coast, the economy of these societies evolved, resulting in new relationships with the foreigners at their borders. For complex reasons – some arising from this period of change, others from the evolution of transportation technology – trade became a more central aspect of the Tsimshian and Gitksan economies. Exclusive clan and marriage alliances between lineages within and beyond national boundaries created a trade network over the entire northern Northwest Coast region. As well, lineages controlled travel through their territories, and those positioned along important trade routes gained considerable power and economic benefit.

The establishment of alliances and exclusive trade rights had to be formalized through ceremony. The formation of a new alliance with a previously unknown or foreign nation was a historic event and became part of the *adawx* record. Harriet Hudson of the Kitselas tribe of the Tsimshian told the *adawx* of the formation of one such alliance, between the Eagle clan lineage of Gitxhon of Kitselas and the Raven clan group of Hlengwax of Gitlusek, then the first tribe on the Gitksan side of their border with the Tsimshian.

> Ages ago the Kitselas tribe was the uppermost on the Skeena River. Its home village was situated at the canyon. These people of the Tsimshian did not know of any other people above them on the river, and although their hunters went a considerable distance upstream, they never found any other folk living there. There were a great many Kitselas, who made two villages, one on each side of the canyon. One of these was under Gitxhon. His village was on the high part of the canyon and was known as Gitxseex.
>
> One day, a group of young women from the Eagle went out to pick berries. Among these was a niece of the chief Gitxhon. She had gone somewhat farther than the rest and strayed away from them. When it was about dusk, she met some young men who took her and lead her to their camp, which they

reached by night. Next morning, very early, they set off travelling very swiftly, the young woman could hardly understand them, but soon they came to where their canoes were hidden. Then they travelled up the river. For many days they went on, and finally came to a very large village of many people. The young men took the woman to the house of their chief Hlengwax who at once took her for his wife ...

After many years, Gitxhon's niece returned with her children to her uncle's village.

Gitxhon called together all the Kitselas, and presented his nephews and his nieces to his people saying, "These were the ones whom we thought were dead, but are alive. Now I am about to return my niece together with her children to her husband, who is a great chief, and I want you to come with me." Gitxhon then gathered all the coast foods he had, such as dried herring eggs, seaweed, dried halibut, and clams, and all kinds of sea foods. With his folk he set out. When they arrived at Gitwingax, they were greeted by these people and a great *halayt* was at once given by Hlengwax in honour of Gitxhon. After these exchanges, Gitxhon spoke, "My niece has told me how well you have looked after her. She wanted to return after having shown her children to her own people. So, although you have much food, she has brought sea coast treats and this she now places before you. When we return she will remain behind with you." Hlengwax, the Gitwingax chief, replied, "So, what you say is right. I am very happy you are here with us. And I want to proclaim this, that only you shall have the privilege to trade with us, in this way. You may come often to see us. And this will give you also the right to trade with all the other villages above and there are many others [upriver]."

Gitxhon had now come upon a very valuable trading privilege. It was well protected, as his own village was situated in the canyon through which any canoe going up would have to pass. To protect further this watch, he made rope of cedar bark which canoes passing would contact and this would shake an alarm of puffin beaks and deer hoofs. So that anyone trying to go through the canyon at night would shake the cedar rope, thus giving the alarm. Then those in the Gitxhon village would be able to capture the canoe. It was almost impossible to pass through without the knowledge of the Kitselas people.[35]

Sometimes, in more recent times, alliances were created in situations in which no lineage or marriage ties existed by a process the Gitksan called *ne'amex*, making oneself kin. This process also involved feasting and could be formalized by an exchange of chiefly names. Thereafter, during the lifetimes of the individuals involved, they were considered kin. After their death the relationship had to be renewed in some way, or it ceased to exist and the names were returned.[36]

When Europeans first started arriving on the northern Northwest Coast, they were received as were any foreigners. Both peoples sought trade in one form or another and both sought access that excluded others. However, most of the Europeans stayed on or near their ships and failed to understand or ignored the invitations they received to visit various Tsimshian villages. The first encounter between the Tsimshian and the Europeans took place when James Colnett landed in the territory of the Kitkatla tribe in 1787. The first people from Kitkatla to encounter members of the crew were members of the Ganhada (Raven) clan lineage of Saaban at their halibut grounds off Pitt Island. This historical event is recorded in their *adawx*.[37] It was Seeks, however, a chief of the leading lineage of Kitkatla (of the Gispwudwada – Killerwhale – clan), whom Colnett entertained on the ship.

It wasn't until 1792 that a European attended a Tsimshian feast. In that year, Jacinto Caamano's vessel, anchored near the south end of Pitt Island, was approached by Homts'iit, a Raven clan chief of the Kitkatla tribe who danced the peace dance for him. He and his people were invited on board. Homts'iit gave Caamano the gift of an otter skin and Caamano served refreshments, after which Homts'iit exchanged names with Caamano, making them allies. Three weeks later Caamano attended a feast at Tuwartz Inlet. Caamano described a series of feasting events in considerable detail, the first of which took place on 28 August, when Homts'iit visited the ship to invite Caamano to a feast. Since the main elements in these ceremonial invitations are a peace dance and a *naxnox* demonstration, the feathers to which Caamano refers were probably eagle down, the symbol of peace, and his various masks probably represented his various *naxnox* powers:[38]

> Homts'iit came to visit me in the afternoon, accompanied by upwards of forty of his relatives, all singing and bringing feathers. He, together with his nearest relations, arrived in one of two canoes lashed alongside each other. Homts'iit's head appeared from behind a screen formed of brilliantly white deerskin; on it, accordingly as the action demanded or his own particular fancy dictated, he would place various masks or heads of different animals that he proposed to imitate; the deerskin serving as a curtain by which he was entirely hidden when he wished, unseen to put on or change one of these masks or faces. They remained alongside thus for some time, singing and continuing their antics, until Homts'iit with great eagerness explained that he was come to conduct me to his village. Curiosity to see it, as well as the fete for which such extensive preparations were being made, induced me to comply with his entreaties.[39]

Caamano and his men travelled to the village by cutter and were welcomed on the shore by six men with a "very clean deerskin." Clearly, in what follows, Caamano is treated with the highest respect:

> [They] at once dashed into the water up to the waist alongside our boat, making signs for me to sit on the skin to be carried ashore on their shoulders. The moment that I place myself on the deerskin these six fellows hoisted my 150 lb. carcass on their shoulders and carried me at a run across the shingle and up the pretty steep slope leading from it to the village, whither they brought me at a surprising speed. To pass through the narrow doorway of the chief's house, over which was painted a huge mask, it was necessary to make a litter or hammock of the deerskin ... Once inside I tried to get on my feet, but this they would not allow before bringing me to the place for my seat, which was to the right of the entrance. The seat was formed of a case or chest, raised higher than those of the others, fitted for only one person, and covered with a new mat; while a similar one was spread before it. The seats for my officers, ranged on either side of mine, were made in similar manner; those for my men, were formed of mats spread out on the floor. By this time the whole native company, amounting to about eighty people of both sexes, was arranged on the floor.[40]

Caamano described a series of performances, probably *naxnox* displays, by Homts'iit:

> Homts'iit began to emit piercing howls in a pitiful key; after which, throwing back his head as if about to faint, he sat down, clutching at the collar of his cloak, as if wishing to throw it off. Several of his family nearby, who were watching to give him any help that might be necessary, when they noticed this, gathered around him forming a screen so that he might not be seen as changing his garments in which some of the others were assisting him. So soon as he had put on the ones in which he was to show himself, they would break up and sit down out of his way, leaving only a couple of his nearest relations standing by ready to help him as he might require. When he was ready, these also left him, and the actor arose.[41]

The first performances were interrupted briefly when "two tubs or small troughs were brought in, filled with freshly boiled fish for our refreshment."[42] Later Homts'iit presented Caamano:

> with a nutria skin and returned to his place, when all the rest of the Indians rose up from theirs. I thereupon did the same, which being seen by my native escort, they at once got ready my coach (the large deer skin as a litter), put me into it, and quickly carried me down to my boat.[43]

Caamano's departure may have been premature as his boat:

> had hardly cleared the beach before the Indians leaped into their canoes and were making for the ship, which they reached simultaneously with us. Here, started again to sing with even greater vigour than before. I gave them to eat and drink and towards nightfall they returned ashore with expressions of gratitude and pleasure.[44]

Such invitations to attend feasts and to form trade alliances continued along the Tsimshian coast, but there is no record of any other captains accepting them. In 1793, George Vancouver explored the mouth of the Nass River with three vessels. Archibald Menzies, a member of the expedition, recorded descriptions of the invitations by groups in the area to visit their villages:

> Jul 31 We stopped for the purpose of dining [near Hidden Inlet] and were visited by a canoe, in which there were three persons; they approached us with little hesitation, and seemed well pleased on receiving a few trivial presents. They earnestly solicited our return to the head of this little arm, where, it appeared, their chief resided, and who had abundance of furs to barter for our commodities; but as it was out of our way, we declined their proposal; at which they seemed hurt and disappointed, but retired in perfect good humour.
>
> [Returning to Pearse Canal, the boats landed for the night.] Soon after we perceived that we were followed by one of the canoes that visited us at dinner time with [the chief of their party and] a chorus of women singing as they approached our encampment. All the women had their lower lip pierced and stretched round oval pieces of wood ... they staid in a cove close by us all night and were very clamorous and noisy, being joined by another canoe in the night time.[45]

In 1795, the *Ruby*, a British ship out of the United Kingdom, anchored at Wales Passage near the mouth of Portland Canal. The captain, Charles Bishop, described in the ship's log the invitations they received:

> July 16 [About to leave], when a canoe came up the Sound and shortly afterwards another made its appearance. They came alongside with a great deal of confidence and the chief presented me with a curious carved wooden mask. The mask he presented is adorned with teeth. These people appeared to have seldom seen a ship by their curiosity and surprise.[46]

As in previous times, when foreigners invaded their territory, the Tsimshian greeted the crews of the first ships with hostility when they landed on shore – to cut wood, draw water, and explore. From Colnett on, there are descriptions of Tsimshian attacks when the foreigners were perceived to be invading or taking, without permission, what was not theirs.

The intervention of a chief who had an alliance with the captain usually led to a peace ceremony and the end of hostilities.

In all these encounters, the Tsimshian sought to communicate their identity, including their territorial ownership, and to have it acknowledged and respected. Whatever the ships' captains and officers understood of their interaction with the chiefs and others with whom they traded, they knew they would not acquire the trade they desired without following sufficient protocol to satisfy the people. They may not have known that they were acknowledging the legitimate rights of traders and their territory, but they did understand that it was very much to their benefit to have an alliance with the prominent chiefs.

The Gitksan and Tsimshian and European Colonialism

The nature of the forces inherent in this foreign culture were fully revealed to the Tsimshian only over several decades: the symbiotic forces of capitalism and Christianity and their offspring, colonialism, whose roots were to be found in a worldview fundamentally opposed to that of the Tsimshian and other nations of the Northwest Coast. Founded in a European rationalist tradition, it was a worldview based on the separation of intellect and emotion, mind and spirit, to the extent that religion – or rather human understanding of the spiritual aspects of life – became rigorously rational and secular. The emotional and spiritual aspects of human nature were left to find expression in religious fervour, and dogmatism. These foreigners not only believed, like many others, that their way of seeing the world was divinely inspired, but, unlike many others, they also held the unshakable conviction that their way of seeing had to be adopted by all humankind. The leaders of these foreigners for the most part believed that they as individuals had a key role to play in this "enlightenment" of others.

Particularly unfortunate for the Tsimshian was the economic philosophy of the time, a product of the new Protestant religion, which, while defining work as the only way to a righteous life and salvation, at the same time decried the leisure and enjoyment that could come from it. This worldly asceticism resulted in the accumulation of capital and the consequent need to re-invest it in future work. At the same time, salvation became very much an individual enterprise, with each person rationally planning his or her life in accordance with acceptable standards of conduct, thus laying the foundation for colonialism and bureaucracies that spread around the globe. Finally, the philosophy that separated individuals from all that was then deemed to represent the wild, uncivilized aspect of their human nature also separated them from the wildness outside of them, untamed nature, and all peoples who were, according to their philosophy, less evolved in their inevitable progress towards civilization.[47]

The Hudson's Bay Company (HBC), beginning with its first establishment on Tsimshian lands, was part of what Cole Harris described as this "discourse of capitalism [that] turned around management, order and property. As much as possible, it avoided irregularity and uncertainty, and encouraged system. It tended to regulate time, and to commodify nature and work. It valued hard work, thrift, and steady reliability," those qualities internalized through Protestantism.[48] The Company's employees sought to "create familiar, safe spaces for themselves ... [and] to Europeanize and defend patches of land" in the form of forts.[49] The "gentlemen" who ran the forts were men selected for their "system and regularity" to be efficient managers of a commercial empire.[50]

The HBC personnel, like the maritime traders before them, were not intentional agents of British state colonialism; rather, they were more concerned with eliminating their rivals from the fur trade and establishing a monopoly to derive more profit from the trade. The Tsimshian, on their side, were motivated by similar goals and used their clan and marital relationships to ensure that furs did not reach the fort without first providing revenue to them as middlemen. As well, marriage relationships were sought on both sides to facilitate the trade. Ligeex, the leading chief of the Tsimshian, not only offered his daughter in marriage to the surgeon, Dr. Kennedy, but also encouraged the HBC to relocate from the mouth of the Nass River to his land at Laxhlgu'alaams, thus ensuring Tsimshian control over access to the fort.[51]

While no journals recorded the extent of the involvement of HBC personnel in the ceremonial events at Laxhlgu'alaams, the daily logs do contain references to individuals among "the men" leaving the fort to help their Tsimshian wives to prepare for feasts and to attend them. As well, the close relationship between Dr. Kennedy and Ligeex makes it hard to imagine that he did not participate with his wife in the ceremonial life of her people. Certainly, there is every indication that the HBC personnel acknowledged, both in their own terms and through indigenous ceremony, the *daxgyet* of their Tsimshian trading partners and relatives.[52]

The virulence of the European worldview for indigenous societies would not be felt until the arrival of its most aggressive and fundamentalist proponents – the missionaries – followed by the military, surveyors, government officials, settlers, Indian agents, and police, who used the pulpit, schools, laws, regulations, and the constant threat of violence or incarceration to attack the philosophy, social and political structure, spiritual knowledge, economic system, and emotional life that made up the tightly woven fabric of Northwest Coast society.

The missionaries, as the forward flank of colonialism and the spokesmen for its philosophy, attacked the transmission of culture by preaching in churches and schools and then using various forms of coercion against the transmission of Tsimshian knowledge in the longhouses, the Wiluuskiyu-uhlxamtxw, "where the history of the people are." They also attacked the authority of the chiefs and other hereditary leaders and their relationships with each other, their land and the spirits that surrounded them. This proselytizing made little headway among the Tsimshian at the fort, the first to be exposed to it, until the smallpox epidemic of 1862, when the Tsimshian were told that the reason they were dying in the hundreds was their failure to give up their identity and adopt Christianity.[53] The following excerpt from the *Arthur Wellington Clah Diaries and Papers* described the reaction of the Tsimshian:

> June 21 1862 Clah
>
> and all the Indians in Tsimshens they will burned, as all lots the things with fire about in half day, and they wants sacrifices to God, and want they will God take away sickness from them, this the way burned, all bad things, and all the chiefs in Tsimshen burn all his music with teine. Called naxnox, and other kinds we call amiilk [masks], burnt them all. Poor all Tsimshian, they afraid to gone to die. They make God angry and in every year they always telling lies, and stealing. Murder killing another. Drunkenness and fighting. And we never do right in God sight. But we often doing wrong. And in our life and after that, and when all the people done burned all things.[54]

The missionaries and visiting officials, motivated by their own way of seeing the world and their fanatical belief in their "divine" mission, attacked the Tsimshian political and economic system at its heart. After years of receiving their complaints, the government banned the feast, primarily for its economic impacts, which stood in opposition to the essence of Protestant/capitalist thought. The emotional intensity of the opposition to the feast by government officials in the 1870s and their concern with property, civilization, and industry is made clear in the following summary by Douglas Cole and Ira Chaikin:

> The baneful aspects of the potlatch had been brought to the attention of the dominion government soon after Ottawa assumed control of Indian affairs in the newly confederated province of British Columbia. In January 1873, only months after his appointment as Indian superintendent in Victoria, Dr. I. W. Powell commented that potlatches, "quite common" on the coast, retarded civilizing influences and encouraged idleness among the less worthy Indians. Wise administration, he trusted, would in time make them obsolete. Other officers made similar statements.
>
> George Blenkinsop, an agent with the Indian Reserve Allotment Commission on a fact-finding tour of Barclay Sound, reported that, until the

local Indians were cured of their propensity for potlatching "there can be little hope of elevating them from their present state of degradation." Feasting and giving away property took up too much time and interfered with other, more industrious pursuits. "These people," he wrote, "are the richest in every respect in British Columbia and were a proper disposal made of the immense gains they could furnish themselves with every comfort they could possibly wish for."

In October 1879 he [Gilbert Sproat one of the members of the Indian reserve commission] addressed a letter to Sir John A. Macdonald expressing doubt as to whether the federal department "fully appreciates the giant evil which in this inveterate and most pernicious custom has to be met and overcome." The potlatch was "the parent of numerous vices which eat out of heart of people." It produced indigence and thriftlessness, forced women into prostitution and "promoted habits inconsistent with all progress." "It is not possible," he wrote, "that the Indian can acquire property, or can become industrious with any good result, while under the influence of this mania." Sproat was shocked that the federal government, after eight years of administering Indian Affairs in the western province, had done virtually nothing to aid missionaries in their fight against such a soul-corroding system. He urged Ottawa to warn, rebuke and, if necessary, "lay an iron hand upon the shoulders of the people" in order to eradicate an evil that sprawled "like a huge incubus upon all philanthropic, administrative or missionary effort for the improvement of the Indians."

In the face of such reports, Ottawa decided to accept Sproat's recommendation. The deputy superintendent general, Lawrence Vankoughnet, issued instructions to Superintendent Powell, James Lenihan, his newly appointed counterpart in New Westminister, and Sproat himself to discountenance "the foolish, wasteful and demoralising custom." One means to the eradication of the potlatch, Powell hoped, would be through the influence of Band Councils, created under the 1881 Indian Improvement Act. He had no doubt that councillors would be chosen from among "the younger and more advanced Indians" who would be willing to exercise "a vigorous civilizing power" by introducing bylaws or regulations against potlatching. Nevertheless, Powell informed his newly appointed Cowichan agent, with or without a council, the Indians could not be permitted to continue the custom. No law, he admitted, prohibited the practice; its cessation rested entirely upon the persuasion of the agent.[55]

On 7 July 1883 the Canadian cabinet was advised by the prime minister, Sir John A. Macdonald, acting in his capacity as superintendent general of Indian Affairs, that measures should be taken to suppress the potlatch. Cabinet accepted his recommendation that, pending the introduction of legislation at the next session of Parliament, the governor general issue a proclamation discountenancing the custom and requesting that Her

Majesty's Indian subjects abandon it. Less than a year later, on 19 April 1884, an amendment to the Indian Act made engaging in the potlatch a misdemeanor. Outlawed at the same time was the *tamananawas* dance. Both ceremonies were to be declared offences effective 1 January 1885.[56]

As the reference to Powell's strategy makes clear, the Dominion used the Band Council system and legislation in its efforts to destroy the indigenous societies it sought to take over. Historian J.R. Miller describes this policy and the legislation associated with it:

> The statutory instruments that the Dominion utilized to impose political control on the Indian peoples were mainly the Indian Act, in its successive amendments, and the Indian Advancement Act of 1884. Both these statutes aimed at replacing aboriginal political and judicial institutions with Euro-Canadian ones. The Indian Act of 1876 incorporated a provision from an earlier statute that specified electoral mechanisms to select leaders and gave the minister power to instruct a band to use elective practices when vacancies occurred; the 1880 amendment of the Act provided explicitly for setting aside life chiefs and replacing them with elected leaders and headmen. The so-called Indian Advancement Act of 1884 dictated a larger role for the Department of Indian Affairs in both the election and operation of Band Councils. As well, it widened the grounds on which even elected leaders could be deposed by Ottawa.
>
> What was going on was a concerted attack on the Aboriginal, autonomous, and self-regulating qualities of Native peoples, particularly in the West and North. Ottawa, said the Department's report in 1897, "kept before it as an ultimate end, their [Native people's] transformation from the status of wards into that of citizens." Unfortunately, "the hereditary system tends to retard the inculcation of that spirit of individuality without which no substantial progress is possible." That was why "Indian Affairs" policy was "gradually to do away with the hereditary and introduce an elective system, so making (as far as circumstances permit) these chiefs and councillors occupy the position in a band which a municipal council does in a white community."[57]

Powell also indicated another aspect of the government's strategy when he referred to the role it hoped "the younger and more advanced Indians" would play in the destruction of their political and social structures.[58] This approach runs through the documents of the time, which reflect the efforts of the federal government to interrupt the transmission of culture, knowledge, and thought – efforts that escalated to include the forced separation of children from their parents, other family members, and their chief through the institution of residential schools. These efforts to drive a wedge between generations and to pit them one against the other began with European-style housing and missionary schools and were not simply misguided attempts to help people but rather explicit policies designed to achieve assimilation and cultural genocide.

While not immediately apparent to the Tsimshian and Gitksan, the foreigners were using the same legislative approach to attack their ownership of their territories. It is not possible here to adequately present the march of government measures and broken promises that resulted, after decades, in the foreigners overlaying the land with a web of ownership claims and pursuing an economy that ravaged the landscape and destroyed its creatures. In many cases, however, laws were on the books for decades before there was any possibility of enforcement – and enforcement, when it was initiated, was inconsistent in its success.

In the face of this ever-expanding intrusion into their territory and their lives, from the very beginning the Tsimshian and Gitksan defended their territory and preserved their identity, their *daxgyet*. They both perpetuated their own institutions and sought to transform those imposed upon them by reshaping them to their purposes. The feast continued behind blackout curtains and in people's houses or, in more remote regions, in the feast hall; chiefly positions and territories continue to be passed from one generation to the next; exchanges of goods continue between families allied by ties of clan and marriage; children are still educated in their identity at home and now at school. Through it all, for a hundred years, the protests, the delegations, the court cases, the negotiations have continued – from the attempt in 1910 to impose reserves, when Xamlaxyeltxw, Maggie Good of Gitanyaw, told the surveyor Alfred Green, "we do not want reserves, we are not so foolish. We know the land belongs to us and we will hold it till we die,"[59] to 2004, when Sats'aan, Herb George of the Gilseyuu clan of the Hagwilget tribe of the Wet'suwet'en, stated:

> If we have 100 percent of the title interest in our land base, why are we going to give up 95 percent of it to have a relationship? It doesn't make any sense. Why do we have to give up anything? We're not asking you to give up anything. We're not asking you to adopt our government structures. We're not asking you to live on reserves. We're not asking you to live on transfer arrangements from us to live. Question yourself about what you ask of us, because the standard that you set is simply too high. It's higher than your own society can bear.[60]

The chiefs continued to act, as Solomon Marsden and Stanley Williams explained above, within their own indigenous contexts and fulfilled the responsibilities passed on to them by their ancestors. A series of totem pole-raising feasts in Gitksigyukla in 1939 indicates the conviction of the chiefs as they overcame both the potlatch law and the outside influences that had entered their societies through their young people. William Beynon described the sequence of events. In 1936, there was enormous flooding along the Skeena River and many totem poles were destroyed. In 1943, when the potlatch ban was still in effect, "a strong feeling sprung up among the Gitksan villages on the Upper Skeena ... to try and save the remains of these poles and, where these had been totally destroyed, to replace them."[61] Several poles were raised in Gitanmaaxs (Hazelton) and then in Gitwangax and Gitanyaw. At each of these villages ceremonies were "patterned after the older procedures":[62]

> This at first started a controversy among the younger thought and the remnants of the older thought. The younger men, feeling that as they were now in modern times and that these totem poles were simply a reminder to the coming generation of what the right and uses of the totem poles were and that aside from being just a memory of the past [they] also showed the art. These wanted to adopt new methods of erection ceremonies, which were to send out to the invited guests written invitations advising the guests to come at a certain date.
>
> The older men felt that they were reviving more than a memory. This did not simply mean the erection of the pole, but also a display of the many *naxnoxs* in the possession of each of the Houses, these to be dramatized and their songs sung by the members of the House and if necessary all of the village would assist in the rendering of these songs. These olden chiefs also claimed that the dirge songs would have to be sung, also narratives explaining what crests were to be shown on these poles and also as they would be in full costumes, the guests also should come as invited in full regalia and thus show an acceptance of the rights of each pole erected in the same manner as they [had] formerly done. At Kitwancool (Gitanyaw) and Gitwingax the older thought very soon overcame the protests of the younger groups, and messengers they sent out went in groups to represent the clans of the people giving feasts. That is, the *Gisgahaast* group of Gitwangax sent their own men, and the *Ganeda* and *Laxskiik* (Eagle clan) and *Laxgibuu* sent their own, inviting the people of Kitwancool. These were dressed according to their rank and standing, each clan chief being accompanied by his own group.
>
> Now this idea was not acceptable to the younger people of Gitksigyukla who wanted that the ceremonies should be all combined and gotten over with in a few days. Most of the younger chiefs were with this plan and wanted to do everything in a modern way: that no messengers be sent out; and further there would be no formal Indian dancing, that all the dancing would be modern; and no word of mouth invitation. The majority of the younger chiefs wanted this. The older thought said nothing, thus signifying their disapproval to this modern suggestion. 'Wiiseeks, one of the Head

chiefs of the tribe even moved away and went to visit among his wife's people, who were the Hagwilgets. Then another leading chief, Haxpegwootxw, also refrained from making any expression of thought. So, unexpected to the younger group, the older thought took matters in their own hands and were making preparations to send their own messengers to invite their own guests and to proceed to carry out their own ceremonies in the regular prescribed manner. This caused considerable feeling among the younger men, who saw that they were going to be made the butt of many references, so they gathered together and then agreed to the matter being conducted on the old plans.[63]

At the same time as people struggled to perpetuate their societies and *daxgyet,* they also actively resisted government attempts to appropriate their land. In fact the political life of the Gitksan and Tsimshian for the last century and a half has been one of resistance. While the foreigners allocated land according to their newly formed political systems, the owners of the land defended it on the ground. The following chronology by Namaste Marsden conveys an impression of the times:

1898 Indian Reserve Commissioner Vowell was told to "keep his hands off their country," and, while, he intended to establish reserves at that time, he left without doing so.
1907 The provincial and Dominion governments begin their dispute over reserve lands.
1909 Samuel Douse and two other men from Gitanyow are convicted for intimidating two prospectors in their territories. They state they were acting on the authority of a decision made by the Gitanyow chiefs to stop any white man who entered the territories with the object of taking their land.
1910 Albert Douse sent a telegram to Prime Minister Laurier stating that their land was being "surveyed for white men."
1910 Ashdown Green arrived in Gitanyow to be told that they did not want reserves. He prepared surveys but they were not allocated.
1913 Ebert Palmer, Arthur Wilson, and Albert Williams of Gitanyow were charged with molesting the BC land surveyor Harold Price, who had attempted to enter their territories, and were given a suspended sentence.
1915 Albert Williams, the speaker for Gitanyow, addressed the McKenna McBride Commission, ignoring its efforts to obtain specific information about lands for reserves and stating: "It is all good land all the way up to the [Kitwancool] lake and also on the west side of the lake." He produced a map of his own, which encompassed Gitanyow territory, and added: "All different families live where these little red spots are, and that is the reason we signed the petition to get this land back for our own people."
1919 The Indian agent's report describes the Gitanyow's ongoing resistance:

"as usual at every season recurring feature again ... namely, the Indians of Kitwancool tried to resist the entrance of white settlers to the valley ... they seemingly possess qualities of a peculiar opposing type that is almost as effective at times as active resistance."

1919 Stakes are again removed in Gitanyow territory.

1920 Chief Inspector Ditchburn of Indian Agencies received a letter from a settler in the region, stating that a man "possessed with ample Capital" was turned away at "Kitwancool Lake Village," and he was informed by Rattenbury Lands Ltd., on application for a piece of hay land in the Gitanyow's territories, that, "owing" to the Indian attitude, they could not come to terms.

1920 Tom Derrick of Gitanyow threatened a prospector's life when he attempted to prospect in Gitanyow territory on the upper Nass. Derrick warned him that their "hands were clean now" but that if they returned to Gitanyow they would kill them.

1923 A timber cruiser was advised not to enter Gitanyow territories as "the Indians living at Kitwancool Lake would not allow timber cruisers to look over land or timber in that locality."

1924 A forestry engineer is apprehended and brought before Gitanyow hereditary chiefs. Xamlaxyeltxw states, "[W]hen we effect a settlement with the government, we will dispose of the said products on a royalty basis, but until that time no white man shall enter there and you are requested to return at once."

1927 Four Gitanyow leaders are jailed for resisting the creation of reserves, the same year as the *Indian Act* was amended to make raising or accepting monies for land claims illegal. Gitanyow village reserve becomes known as the "Oakalla Prison Reserve." Albert Williams wrote to provincial leaders pointing out that they were not engaged in illegal resistance, stating, "[W]e could not see why any litigation should be necessary, we STILL possess the said mother lands, and this is absolutely LOGIC."

1929 Albert Williams wrote to provincial officials stating that the jailing of their leaders was a "very unlawful way to obtain lands from their owner."[64]

Such protests occurred throughout the territories of the Tsimshian and Gitksan and started considerably earlier on the Coast, in the 1880s. Soon after the initial Tsimshian protests, legal efforts to resolve "land claims" began, and they continue to this day. The Gitksan, a century later, began their landmark *Delgamuukw* case, in which, once again, they attempted to convey who they are to the foreigners on their lands. Over a period of three years, in thousands of pages of testimony, they presented their history and identity. While the first judge had a "tin ear"[65] and did not hear, they received some acknowledgment and respect from the Supreme Court of

Canada. The chiefs and matriarchs made it abundantly clear that decades of efforts to destroy their *daxgyet* had failed. As Stanley Williams stated on their behalf:

> In the beginning we have our own laws that was – that was used by our people, the Gitksan people, *aluugigyet*. These laws were used and after the arrival of white people, they forced us to use their laws, they pushed their laws onto us ... The white people have always tried to make us follow their ways, and they don't realize that we have our own laws and our own ways, and now they say this is – this land belongs to the Crown. This is not true, because the Crown never did – never bought this land from us. When the Queen usually comes, she only goes to Edmonton, to Winnipeg, she never comes here and sees the way – takes in the way we are living, our customs, our traditions, she doesn't see these things. And it's not for us to give our land away to her, this is our land, not hers. As long as we live we will always fight for our land, we will always have our land. We have our – the laws of our ancestors and *aluugigyet,* and we've always – and we've always had this law and we are going to put it into action.[66]

The strength and success of this resistance is made powerfully clear in the testimony of Arthur Mathews, who gave evidence of the unbroken transmission to him of his *daxgyet,* in all its manifestations, from the leaders of his lineage. When he gave this testimony in 1988, he was in his forties and part of a large extended family who shared their responsibilities on the land and in the feast. He had recently taken on the leading chiefly name of the lineage. The scope of his contribution to the case was outlined first by Peter Grant, legal counsel for the Gitksan and Wet'suwet'en in *Delgamuukw:*

> Peter Grant: The focus of Mr. Mathews' explanation of his house's authority system will be his two territories and his fishing sites on the lower Skeena River. He will show how the *adawx* of his *wilnaat'aahl* establish and demonstrate his house's long-term ownership of the territories and fishing sites and how certain historical events on the territory came to be recorded by crests and songs. He will describe how the *adawx* teach house members the laws about their relationship to their territory and the animals on it. The application of those laws to present day management of the territories' resources will be described as well as the management changes made by the house during the witness' own lifetime. Art Mathews will relate how actions by the Federal and Provincial defendants have changed the management options available to his house and the actions he and other house members have taken in response to those changes. In other words there will be some detail about the relationship of this witness and his house to his territory.

And all of this witness' evidence will be related to the jurisdiction exercised at the feast and how his network of kinship-based responsibilities are discharged. However, evidence of these broad relationships can only be found by examining detailed relationships between oral history, territory place names and boundaries, resource law and practice and feast procedures. So in some sense, my Lord, this witness' evidence in some ways will be a paradigm of how the Gitksan houses, and in particular the western Gitksan houses relate to their territory and the historical ties to their territory.[67]

Art Mathews told of the role of *adawx* in his life and in his education:

Art Mathews: I was trained from a young age; these *adawxs* being told to me in short form, in medium form ... when you're just a young kid they just give you the general outline of an *adawx*, and as you get older more detailed ... progressed until the full form of the *adawx* is fulfilled and its full length and the *yuuhlxamtxw gan didils*, everything that's in it you have to understand ... *Yuuhlxamtxw* is when they give you advice on when – how to live your life and show respect to people ... *Yuuhlxamtxw* is wisdom, to give me wisdom, the understanding, the various spirituality of our land. *Gan didils* is the way of life, how to react, how not to react. In other words it's a doctrine of one's *adawx*, it's a realism, it's philosophy, and it's epics, both life and death.[68]

As you grow older the *adawx* expands, in more detail, and everything that's gone into it, the spirituality – we call *sesatxw*, purification. It's a purification, the purifying of your very soul, your spirit, not physically, external.

These types of things, they expand and expand, but with the territorial names, the trails, the cabins, the exterior boundaries. It encloses everything after, it just expands, expands. It's similar like going to university where you hear these lectures daily hammered into you.

... [It takes] up to four months [to tell in its greatest detail]. You fill in the details, it's really vast. Like I said this morning, it covers philosophy, it covers epics. It's life, death, survival, covers everything, covers reincarnation, it covers everything that we do day to day. It covers spirituality, why we have *naxnoxs* today, for instance. [When the *adawx* is taught in detail] [t]his is where we get serious. Just the family hears – a *simooget* tells an *adawx* in its – it's like I described, all these material things, and nobody is allowed to hear this, because wisdom leaking out about our *sesatxw*, how we do it and how we recognize things, hunting signs, all other things they say belongs to that house itself. But actually the actual *adawx* itself publicly is told in the feast halls, but not the secret parts of it. That belongs to the house itself.[69]

At this point Art Mathews told the *adawx* of a woman who was taken away to the world of the bears where she married a bear and had two cubs. When she returned to her people, she taught them the laws of respect for bears. One of the laws taught by the *adawx* is that one should never kill a bear in its den. Art Mathews refers to this and then refers to the special way that bears must be treated if they are killed. He then tells of how this training was completed on his territory:

> I was just talking about our – the loss of the bear, that they'll never kill anybody inside the den, or they will have their cubs inside the den ... [After they killed the bear] they put his body on – they prepared these hemlock branches, where his body was going to be laid after they killed him. This is the instructions left by – and they did. And they followed the instructions right to the T like we said when they field dress him, keep his body off the ground, not to get it dirty.[70]
>
> In our laws, ways, traditions, your grand – your uncle is responsible for field training. When I say field training, it involves hunting, survival and the *sesatxw* that I talked about. I remember one time at Xsigwinlikst'aat at Pacific Place on our berry patch called Winluugan, in the Wilson Creek area. We went out early in the morning. He didn't tell me where we're going. He just said "Come." We went, and we went up the trail to this berry patch, and there he knew a bear den; took me there, and this was around early March. You could see it's starting just to melt at the mouth of the cave. He went, sharpened the end of a stick, so long ... [between two and three feet long] ... gave it to me and said, "Get in there and wake the bear up." With great respect and honour for my uncle, I went in. I went half way in and just like anybody else I chickened out and came crawling back out again. Then he told me about the things, Xpiisoon – I was telling you a while ago that this bear instructed that he'll never kill inside the den, so he told me, "Just go in there. It's not going to kill you. Just wake him up," which I did. I felt better when he told me this from our *adawx*, because I had great belief in the *adawx*, spirits, belief. So I went in there and give it a good poke. I could feel it moving around. I then came back out, and the bear was right behind me. When they're in the den, they're blind anyway. When they come out, they don't know. And he killed him, shot him once. And as the bear was still half dead, you might say, it's still going like that, he grabbed me and rubbed my face on its mouth, indicating that we will be fearless and fear nobody; we would have power, same power as this grizzly had. And that's one of the trainings I had. (13 years old).
>
> Even today, when my mother and father are fishing down at this area, Wilson Creek, Xsigwinlikst'aat, through the training of this great grizzly, we – whatever fish that's too badly damaged by seals and whatever, they're

old, some of them catch them that way, we put them on the beach just a little further down above our smokehouse to feed the bears.[71]

Art Mathews then described the territories of his lineage, Xsigwinlikst'aat and Ts'ihlgwellii, and told how his grandfather had taught him "the boundaries ... of our territory that touches off with some of our relatives from the Kitsumkalum area and the relatives from the Nass. They took me up there to show me where our boundaries start ... and the corner posts."[72] In referring to the specific site called Xsigwinlikst'aat, after which the territory is named, he wove its ancient identity into the present:

> [Xsigwinlikst'aat] is a strategic point. Like I said, that they place the sentinel guard, a watchman at the mouth of the river ... and this, the look-out you might say a first line of defence against intruders, warriors from down river. And it's one of our look-outs. If you are going through somebody's territory you have to stop at this particular place we call *anjok*. The people going through our territories have to report at this *anjok* to the chief that they are going to use your territory to go through it for access of their territory maybe or trading or whatever. The rule specifies the law you have to stop and check in like and tell the owners of that territory your intentions. And then in turn they give you a pilot to go through your territory in a friendly manner. If you do not stop at this particular site, or just using our site for an example but all sites are the same, if you don't report into this *anjok*, then they had – they know you had other intentions. You might not attack this village, but they will stop you and ask for your – whatever intentions you have of governing up – further up the river. Even today people that are riding up and down the river stop off and just chat for a minute and take off.[73]

In addition to protests and court challenges, for decades, Tsimshian and Gitksan leaders have made speeches at conferences and meetings, given interviews, lectured at universities, initiated publications, and feasted members of government, all with the intent of communicating their way of seeing the world, their identity. They have always acted on the assumption that once the foreigners in their midst come to know them, they will respect them. They themselves have always acted from a position of respect in their dealings with foreigners. Were this not the case, they would have pursued violence rather than petitions and court challenges.

While there have been victories over the decades – the repeal of oppressive legislation such as the potlatch law, for example – it is difficult to understand why, in so many cases, these efforts to communicate fall on "tin ears," why those who should hear remain locked in the world of their own thinking, unable to see beyond it and therefore unable to respect other worlds. A statement by Delta-South Richmond Conservative MP John Cummins indicates the degree to which some foreigners have failed to understand:

> Contact with Europeans and other societies did improve the life of Indians in BC whether it was iron tools or firearms ... or the benefits of today's ... health care and society safety net. Most importantly, the stability and security guaranteed by imposition of British rule of law added a certainty to life in Native communities that was lacking. The benefits of European contact are rarely discussed and never considered in the calculation of paying redress for past wrongs.[74]

On the other hand, many who are drawn to aspects of First Nations society do not understand their meaning and importance and therefore fail to respect the society itself. This results in situations that lead to commercial exploitation, cultural commodification, and the appropriation of identity and its material elements – issues this project seeks to address.

Northwest Coast societies have survived in spite of efforts by church and state to impose foreign systems on them through laws, policies, and programs, and in spite of the failure of the foreigners among them to respect and acknowledge their societies. Without significant changes to the way institutions understand and interact with First Nations, the Gitksan and Tsimshian will continue to experience the destructive consequences of these attitudes and approaches.

Conclusion

In conclusion, it would seem that for the Tsimshian and Gitksan the greatest issue associated with what the Euro-Canadian world calls "intellectual property" is the lack of acknowledgment and respect for their identity in its fullest and deepest sense. Every issue that arises can only be understood and addressed in this greater context. The Gitksan and Tsimshian have chosen to make themselves known to the foreigners in their midst in every peaceful way possible. In our attempts to gain insight through this project (Protection and Repatriation of First Nations Cultural Heritage), the danger we face is violating that trust, failing yet again to understand, acknowledge, and respect what we have been told for a century and a half and imposing yet again a process based in foreign ideas and structures.

Notes

1 This contradiction reveals the challenge of this project – namely, whether it is possible to respectfully address First Nations issues with Western notions of property and law.

2 Judy Pearsall, ed., *The Concise Oxford Dictionary,* 10th ed. (Oxford: Oxford University Press, 1999) *s.v.* "intellect."

3 While Gitksan and Tsimshian *adawx* are a primary source for this study, other sources have also been used to describe Tsimshian and Gitksan society. Where necessary, lengthy excerpts are included to maintain the integrity of the *adawx*.
4 Account of John Brown, "The Tradition of Kwiyaihl of Kispayaks" (1920) in Marius Barbeau and William Beynon, *Temlarh'am: The Land of Plenty on the North Pacific Coast 1915-1959* (n.d.), account no. 95 [unpublished, archived at Canadian Museum of Civilization Forklore Division].
5 Direct examination of Art Mathews, Chief T'enimgyet (14 March 1988) in *Delgamuukw v. British Columbia*, [1989] 6 W.W.R. 308 (B.C.S.C.), Proceedings at Trial No. 0843, vol. 73 at 4528.
6 Susan Marsden, "An Historical and Cultural Overview of the Gitksan" (1987) [unpublished, archived at the Gitxsan Treaty Office Library]. Also, Neil Sterritt *et al.*, *Tribal Boundaries in the Nass Watershed* (Vancouver: UBC Press, 1998) at 11-14.
7 Wilson Duff, ed., *Histories, Territories, and Laws of the Kitwancool* (Victoria: BC Provincial Museum, 1959) at 23-24.
8 Marsden, *supra* note 6.
9 Direct examination of Stanley Williams, Gwisgyen (20 April 1988) in *Delgamuukw v. British Columbia*, [1989] 6 W.W.R. 308 (B.C.S.C.), Proceedings at Trial No. 0843, Commission Evidence, Exhibit 446C, vol. 3 at 197.
10 Direct examination of James Morrison, Txawok (18 April 1988) in *Delgamuukw v. British Columbia*, [1989] 6 W.W.R. 308 (B.C.S.C.), Proceedings at Trial No. 0843, vol. 82 at 5133.
11 Direct examination of Solomon Marsden, Xamlaxyeltxw (10 May 1988) in *Delgamuukw v. British Columbia*, [1989] 6 W.W.R. 308 (B.C.S.C.), Proceedings at Trial No. 0843, vol. 95 at 5991.
12 *Supra* note 10 at 5135-36.
13 *Supra* note 9 (April 1988) at 183.
14 *Supra* note 11 (9 May 1988) vol. 94 at 5963 and (11 May 1988) vol. 96 at 6066, respectively.
15 Direct examination of Fred Johnson, Lelt (6 March 1988) in *Delgamuukw v. British Columbia*, [1989] 6 W.W.R. 308 (B.C.S.C.), Proceedings at Trial No. 0843, Commission Evidence, Exhibit. 69 A at 34.
16 William Beynon, "The Feast of Nisyaganaat, Chief of the Gitsiis," in William Beynon, *The Beynon Manuscripts* (n.d.) [unpublished, archived at University Microfilms Inc.].
17 *Supra* note 5 (15 March 1988) vol. 74 at 4607.
18 *Ibid.* (16 March 1988) vol. 75 at 4675.
19 *Supra* note 9 (12 April 1988) vol. 1 at 43.
20 Marsden, *supra* note 6 at 148-65.
21 William Beynon's Kitsegukla (Skeena Crossing) Field Notes (1945) [archived at Ottawa, Canadian Centre for Folk Culture Studies, Canadian Museum of Civilization, vol. 1 at 7-9].
22 *Supra* note 5 (15 March 1988) vol. 74 at 4615.
23 *Supra* note 9 (11 April 1988) vol. 1 at 39.
24 Marsden, *supra* note 6.
25 *Supra* note 11 (6 May 1988) vol. 93 at 5896.
26 *Ibid.* (9 May 1988) vol. 96 at 6060-61.
27 Direct examination of Fred Johnson, Lelt (March 1988) in *Delgamuukw v. British Columbia*, [1989] 6 W.W.R. 308 (B.C.S.C.), Proceedings at Trial No. 0843, Commission Evidence, Exhibit. 69 A at 46.
28 *Ibid.* at 38.
29 Direct examination of Martha Brown, Xhliiyemlaxha (March 1988) in *Delgamuukw v. British Columbia*, [1989] 6 W.W.R. 308 (B.C.S.C.), Proceedings at Trial No. 0843, Commission Evidence, Exhibit. 68 B at 15.
30 *Supra* note 4.
31 Sterritt, *supra* note 6. Excerpt from text at 20-21 and then quoting account of George Derrick, "Origins of Lurhawn in the Groundhog County," in Marius Barbeau and William Beynon, *Raven Clan Outlaws of the North Pacific Coast* (1924), account no. 57 [unpublished, archived at Canadian Museum of Civilization Folklore Division].
32 *Ibid.* at 21-22.

33 *Supra* note 6.
34 Susan Marsden, *Defending the Mouth of the Skeena: Perspectives on Tsimshian Tlingit Relations* (Vancouver: Tin Ear Press, 2000); Susan Marsden, "Adawx, Spanaxnox and the Geopolitics of the Tsimshian" (2002) 135 BC Studies 101.
35 Account of Harriet Hudson, "Gitrhawn's Trading Privileges on the Upper Skeena," in Marius Barbeau and William Beynon, *The Gwenhoot of Alaska: In Search of a Bounteous Land* (1949), account no. 33 [unpublished, archived at Canadian Museum of Civilization Folklore Division].
36 *Supra* note 6.
37 Dorothy Brown of the Kitkatla, "Saaban," in Susan Marsden, ed., *Suwilaay'msga Na Ga'niiyatgm, Teachings of Our Grandfathers* (Prince Rupert: School District 52, 1992).
38 Henry Wagner and W.A. Newcombe, eds., "The Journal of Don Jacinto Caamano" (1938) 2:3 British Columbia Historical Quarterly 189-222, cited in Margaret Seguin, *Interpretive Contexts for Traditional Feasts* (Ottawa: National Museum of Man, 1985) at 28-29.
39 *Ibid.* at 29.
40 *Ibid.* at 29-30.
41 *Ibid.* at 30-31.
42 *Ibid.* at 31.
43 *Ibid.* at 32.
44 *Ibid.*
45 George Vancouver, *A Voyage of Discovery of the North Pacific Ocean and Round the World*, ed. by W. Kaye Lamb (London: The Hakluyt Society, 1984) at 996-97.
46 Charles Bishop, "Excerpts from the log of the Ruby" (1795) [unpublished, archived at the Tsimshian Tribal Council].
47 See *e.g.* William Duncan, *Correspondence, Diaries, Notebooks, Entry Books, Mission Records* (1853-1916) [unpublished, archived at Vancouver: Microfilm, University of British Columbia Library]; Church Missionary Society, *North Pacific Mission Correspondence* (1857-1900) [unpublished, archived at Vancouver: Microfilm, University of British Columbia Library]; Governor James Douglas, *Papers Relative to the Affairs of British Columbia* (London: George Edward Eyre and William Spottiswoode Printers, 1859); Jane Usher, *William Duncan of Metlakatla: A Victorian Missionary in British Columbia* (PhD diss., University of British Columbia, 1969) [unpublished]. See also Max Weber, *The Protestant Ethic and the Spirit of Capitalism* (New York: Charles Scribner's Sons, 1958).
48 R. Cole Harris, *The Resettlement of British Columbia: Essays on Colonialism and Geographical Change* (Vancouver: UBC Press, 1997) at 34.
49 *Ibid.*
50 *Ibid.*
51 Susan Marsden and Robert Galois, "The Tsimshian, the Hudson's Bay Company, and the Geopolitics of the Fur Trade, 1787-1840" (1995) 39:2 Canadian Geographer 169 at 183.
52 Hudson's Bay Company Journals, Fort Simpson, Hudson's Bay Company Archives, Winnipeg, B201a 1-9, 1832-66.
53 *Arthur Wellington Clah Diaries and Papers*, WMS/Amer 140, London, Wellcome Institute for the History of Medicine (Microfilm at 21 June 1862).
54 *Ibid.*
55 Douglas Cole and Ira Chaikin, *An Iron Hand Upon the People: The Law against the Potlatch on the Northwest Coast* (Vancouver/Seattle: Douglas and McIntyre/University of Washington Press, 1990) at 14-16.
56 *Ibid.* at 14.
57 Jim R. Miller, "The Historical Context of the Drive for Self-Government" in Richard Gosse, Roger Youngblood, and James Youngblood, eds., *Continuing Poundmaker and Riel's Quest: Presentations Made at a Conference on Aboriginal Peoples and Justice* (Saskatoon: Purich, 1994) at 41.
58 *Supra* note 55 at 16.
59 Sterritt, *supra* note 6 at 61.
60 Satsan (Wet'suwet'en Chief Herb George), "A Conversation after Dinner," in Owen Lippert, ed., *Beyond the Nass Valley: National Implications of the Supreme Court's Delgamuukw Decision* (Vancouver: The Fraser Institute, 2000) at 537.

61 *Supra* note 21.
62 *Ibid.*
63 *Ibid.*
64 Namaste Marsden, *Gitanyow Historical Research Chronology of Gitanyow Resistance to Incursion on Gitanyow Territories 1884–1928* (2003) [unpublished, on file with author] compiled from the following sources: Author unknown, *Kitwancool Research for Submission to Hugh Faulkner, Department of Indian and Northern Affairs Canada* (n.d.) [unpublished, archived at Gitxsan Chief's office] chap. 3; Robert Galois, "Research Report and Notes: The History of the Upper Skeena Region, 1850 to 1927" (1993-94) 9:2 Native Studies Review 113; and Namaste Marsden, *The Myth of Crown Sovereignty in Gitanyow's Territories: Pre-Contact Gitksan History and Law, Encounters in the Colonial Period 1880-1927* (n.d.) [unpublished, on file with author].
65 Judge McEachern, in *Delgamuukw v. British Columbia*, [1989] 6 W.W.R. 308 did not want a Gitksan matriarch, Mary Johnson, to sing her *limx 'oy* in court, saying, "I can't hear your Indian song, Mrs. Johnson. I've got a tin ear." A cartoon in the *Three Rivers Report* (15 July 1987) showed Mary Johnson replying, "That's OK your highness, I've got a can opener." Walt Taylor, the journalist who wrote the accompanying article, said: "Most of us non-Aboriginal Canadians also wear a tin ear. We are not even aware of the significant sounds we cannot hear." This phrase has come to stand for ethnocentric barriers to understanding. In Don Monet and Skanu'u (Ardythe Wilson), *Colonialism on Trial, Indigenous Land Rights and the Gitksan and Wet'suwet'en Sovereignty Case* (Gabriola Island and Philadelphia: New Society Publishers, 1992) at 43.
66 *Supra* note 9 at 204.
67 *Supra* note 5 at 4514-15.
68 *Ibid.* at 4524.
69 *Ibid.* at 4562.
70 *Ibid.* at 4575.
71 *Ibid.* at 4581.
72 *Ibid.* at 4543.
73 *Ibid.* at 4634.
74 Windspeaker, "Throw Him Out," Editorial, *Windspeaker* (January 2004), online: Aboriginal Multi-Media Society <http://www.ammsa.com/windspeaker/editorials/2004/wind-editorial1.html>.

4

'A'lhut tu tet Sul'hweentst [Respecting the Ancestors]: Understanding Hul'qumi'num Heritage Laws and Concerns for the Protection of Archaeological Heritage

Eric McLay, Kelly Bannister, Lea Joe, Brian Thom, and George Nicholas

In this study, we explore Central Coast Salish Hul'qumi'num customary laws[1] and concerns about the protection of their archaeological heritage. The protection of ancient sites, artifacts, and ancient human remains is a key cultural issue for Hul'qumi'num peoples. The urban, privatized nature of their traditional land base on southeastern Vancouver Island, the southern Gulf Islands, and the lower Fraser River imposes increasing challenges upon Hul'qumi'num peoples to maintain their cultural connections to their ancestral lands. Located in a very rich region of archaeological heritage on the Pacific Northwest Coast, the majority of recorded archaeological sites in Hul'qumi'num territory are now on private property. The incremental destruction of this archaeological heritage by modern land development is a chronic problem that is recurrently witnessed by Hul'qumi'num people across the region. In listening to Hul'qumi'num elders, it is common to hear them assert that this loss of, and disrespect shown towards, their archaeological heritage is contrary to many of their cultural teachings, their *snuw'uy'ulh*, including the assertion of their inherent rights to jurisdiction over, and ownership and management of, their archaeological heritage.[2]

Purpose of This Study

In collaboration with the Hul'qumi'num Treaty Group (HTG),[3] this case study aspires to facilitate respect for, and understanding of, Hul'qumi'num concepts of cultural property and heritage laws.[4] Hul'qumi'num elders strongly recommended that defining the customary laws related to the protection of ancient heritage sites should be one of the HTG's research priorities. To begin to address this issue, we designed this case study in order to better communicate Hul'qumi'num customary laws, traditions, and rules regarding sacred and historical sites, artifacts, and ancient human remains to the government and the general public. We also wanted to stress the importance of protecting these heritage places and objects for future generations.

We have three main goals: first, we attempt to understand Hul'qumi'num customary laws about their archaeological heritage; second, we examine the nature of current problems as expressed by Hul'qumi'num elders; and, third, we seek to understand how the legal environment can be transformed.

To date, there has been little written documentation of the things sacred to Hul'qumi'num peoples. Their strong concern for privacy is in keeping with Coast Salish tradition. However, many Hul'qumi'num elders recognize that concerns for privacy can become problematic if the general public assumes that, since customary laws are not contained in a written record, they offer nothing of importance. As Arvid Charlie explained during our focus group session:

> There's nothing really written down about our sacred things, our sacred ways, sacred areas. We've been brought to question that. Well, other people have said, "Well, you guys must have not very many important sites that's why it's not recorded." You know, when we're trying to look at some ... or something about sacred sites. The answer from our home area is: those things that are really sacred, no one is allowed access to. We didn't share it. We don't share it with just anybody. It was good for that day – we kept our heritage, our culture – but today that almost works against us.[5]

Due to the expressed concerns for privacy of information, we have been very careful to take precautions against sharing any information that participants may deem culturally sensitive.[6]

We summarize our results based on the following sources of information: (1) interviews with twenty-two Hul'qumi'num elders and community members regarding their knowledge of, and experience with, ancient sites, artifacts, and human remains; and (2) an elders focus group session that helped to clarify our understandings of Hul'qumi'num teachings and concerns as well as to explore ideas of how to better protect Hul'qumi'num archaeological heritage. Additional information and quotes are drawn from past HTG Elders Advisory Board meetings. The study is intended primarily as a narrative, rather than as an analysis, of those Hul'qumi'num teachings and concerns that the elders and community members shared with us.

Hul'qumi'num People, Lands, and History

In the Strait of Georgia and the river valleys of southern and eastern Vancouver Island and the Lower Mainland, Island Hul'qumi'num people occupy a central position in the Coast Salish World. We use "Island Hul'qumi'num" to refer to all speakers of Halkomelem, the Central Coast Salish language whose range extends from Saanich Inlet to Nanoose Bay on eastern Vancouver Island. These peoples collectively share a common language, culture, and history. The terms "Hul'qumi'num" and "Hul'qumi'num Mustimuhw" (The People) refer explicitly to the six closely related First Nations who comprise the HTG: the Chemainus First Nation, the Cowichan Tribes, the Halalt First Nation, the Lake Cowichan First Nation, the Lyackson First Nation, and the Penelakut Tribe.

From the beginning of time, Hul'qumi'num myth, history, and customary law embedded the ancestral relationships of the Hul'qumi'num within their territory:

> At the start of the world, the First Ancestors dropped from the sky. These First Ancestors were powerful people. They cleared the world of dangerous creatures and settled the original villages throughout Hul'qumi'num territory. These ancestors were imbued with the powers of transformation. Humans could change to animals. Common things had uncommon powers. Then the Creator, Xe'els, arrived. He went through the land making things as they are today. He transformed the First Ancestors [in]to the deer, [in]to the cedar tree, [in]to the rocks which continue to be found in the land today.
>
> He taught the Hul'qumi'num people about the respect and obligations that were required to live in the world. Xe'els transformations live on today in the animals and places in the landscapes, which carry the history of his work in their Hul'qumi'num names. Hul'qumi'num Mustimuhw recognize the special connections we have to our territory and the resources in it, as we are all descended from those same First Ancestors. We are all related to the living things and places that were touched by the transformations of the Creator.
>
> From these *times immemorial*, Hul'qumi'num Mustimuhw have owned our traditional territories. Hul'qumi'num place names blanket the land. Every bay, every peninsula, every rocky island, every bend in the rivers have Hul'qumi'num names which provide the keys to the extensive knowledge needed to harvest and steward the resources of the territory owned by Hul'qumi'num people. From our ancestral villages, Hul'qumi'num people made extensive use of our territories. The oral histories tell about the family-owned hunting territories and fishing grounds. They tell about the camas-root and berry grounds owned by certain families. They tell about the clam beds, hunting grounds, and fish weirs held in common for the community to use. Our Aboriginal title to our territory has never been extinguished. The rights to harvest and be the stewards of these resources come from the obligations created by the Creator and will continue into the future.[7]

The ancient history of Island Hul'qumi'num culture is situated within the archaeological context of the Gulf of Georgia region, a culture area that encompasses the Strait of Georgia, northern Puget Sound, and the lower Fraser River.[8] This archaeological region is contiguous with the extent of ethnographic Central Coast Salish and Northern Coast Salish cultures, and archaeologists have generally held that, for the last ten thousand years, this region has given evidence of continuous indigenous cultural development. Over one thousand archaeological sites have been recorded in Hul'-qumi'num territory – one of the densest concentrations of archaeological sites known on the Northwest Coast. Approximately 90 percent of these recorded archaeological sites are classified as "shell middens." Although commonly perceived as simply "refuse," these archaeological sites are indicative of past First Nations settlement activity. Formed by the accumulation of stratified cultural deposits over thousands of years, shell midden sites represent some of the most complex archaeological sites in the world.

Today, Hul'qumi'num peoples' cultural connections to their ancestral lands, which are situated in a region of British Columbia that is experiencing strong population growth, are increasingly threatened by private land development. For Hul'qumi'num peoples, the protection of archaeological sites located on private property is an ongoing concern. Most of the waterfront real estate in the region are the location of ancient villages, traditional campgrounds, burial sites, and resource-gathering locations. Archaeological artifacts and ancient human remains are often accidentally unearthed during construction projects for residential housing, road construction, and commercial and industrial land developments. Archaeological sites and their materials are subject to natural erosion from waves and storms as well as to being stolen and damaged by artifact collectors. It is estimated that many unrecorded archaeological sites exist on private property and are destroyed by unregulated land development, although this remains unreported. For Hul'qumi'num peoples, the disturbance of these archaeological sites, their artifacts, and their ancient human remains is a recurring source of cultural conflict with mainstream Canadian society.

Case Study Methodology

Methods and Approach

In late 2002, we decided to focus the study on archaeology – specifically, on ancient heritage sites, artifacts, and ancestral remains. This focus reflects both the concerns expressed by Hul'qumi'num elders and the research priorities of the HTG. HTG staff members drafted a list of potential participants for interviews (mainly elders). In total, twenty-two people agreed to be interviewed, both men and women. The participants are registered under the following tribes: Cowichan, Chemainus, Penelakut, Lyackson, and Halalt. Lake Cowichan was not able to be included in this study. Nevertheless, as, throughout the region, all Hul'qumi'num people are strongly interconnected by family ties, band affiliation does not necessarily reflect where one is from or what one knows. The interviews took place between February and June 2003. Interview questions focused on three general aspects of Hul'qumi'num customs, teachings, and laws regarding their archaeological heritage.[9] First, we asked whether there were Hul'qumi'num teachings about the care, use, and protection of ancient heritage sites, artifacts, and human remains; second, we asked whether Hul'qumi'num customary laws were being respected and whether it is possible to identify some of the issues and circumstances that need to change; and, third, we asked how we could better address Hul'qumi'num interests in their heritage sites in Canadian law and how the legal environment might be transformed.

During interviews, participants were asked to share their knowledge about the topic, and interviewers tried not to interrupt (except for clarification; to comment, if appropriate; or to probe further). The interviewers emphasized that only information that could be made public should be shared. Participants shared what they wanted in a form and at a level with which they felt comfortable. Some information is held by individuals or families, and it is considered inappropriate to share it with outsiders. Interviewers respected whatever level of sharing was most comfortable for the participant in question. Participants spoke mainly in English, but many also used Hul'qumi'num words and phrases.

Themes Emerging from Interviews

To introduce Hul'qumi'num teachings, laws, and beliefs concerning their archaeological heritage, we present one Hul'qumi'num elder's narrative of her personal experience with ancient sites and remains. In the following excerpt, Ruby Peters recounts her visit to the archaeological excavations at the Somenos Creek site in October 1994, when a team of university researchers were conducting large-scale excavations in advance of a residential subdivision development. At the time of her visit, archaeologists had uncovered a large burial feature, which contained three individuals, and included an elaborately adorned child burial. Several major themes concerning how Hul'qumi'num elders understand and relate to their archaeological heritage are revealed in Ruby's interview:

> Some people don't take it serious about human bones. But it's serious. It's really serious. I saw one dig over at Somenos Creek, over here in Duncan. And they had open, open graveyards. And they called, called us over there. And I was at the head of the three open graves. And being a *thi'thu'* [medium or clairvoyant], I can hear them [the spirits]. I can hear them, and when I got there, the man was really, really angry because of the disturbance that was going on because they were, they were studying their bones. What was that, two thousand years old? And they had the open grave. And he was

really angry and he was just growling. He was really, really mad. And I, I just, I just spoke to it and try[ed] to calm that man down. And he wouldn't. He was just so angry. I went to the next one and it was the wife and she was crying. She was crying. So I was just talking to, talking to her in my mind, telling her what was going on. And I went to the next one – there was a little, it was a child, and that child was just crying and scared. He kept saying, "I'm scared, I'm scared" in Indian. Yeah. Just think, this was about six years ago. Eight years ago. And I was still talking to them and praying, standing over those three open graves. And for me that was about fifteen feet, twenty feet away from us, and her daughter just went paralyzed. Just then, she went paralyzed. And she came running to me and she says, "Ruby, Ruby, hurry up! Come and help your niece! Come and help your niece!" So I followed her. I was crying ... I just finished wiping my face and [her mother] got there and she called me. I went to her daughter and it was the right side that was going to paralyze. She couldn't move it. Just couldn't move it anymore. And she said, "Aunty, it just started with my wrist, now it's up to my shoulder." And, I mean, [she] just kept saying, "Do something. Do something." I said, "Have you got any *tumulh* [red ochre, a mineral used in Coast Salish rituals to protect the living against the supernatural]?" Nobody had any *tumulh*. Nobody had anything. So I just prayed. Prayed with my, prayed over my hands and started saying what I had to say, the words I always use, and I brushed her off. And [I was] telling them to let, let her go. That she's there, she's just, ah, she – that she was just there helping. Talking to, talking to the spirit in Indian. But her arm, she was able to move it after. She was able to move it after. But it, when that happened to her, it was the angry one that, that wouldn't listen to me. That was the one that did that. And I didn't get through to him that, that they were just there to help and work.[10] (Ruby Peters)

This Hul'qumi'num elder's experience upon visiting the archaeological excavation is the product of a cultural worldview that differs fundamentally from that of mainstream Canada. As described in the above passage, archaeology is perceived less as a valuable scientific pursuit whose purpose is to learn about the past and more as a socially destructive activity that can cause harm for people in the present. Ruby Peters believed that the disturbance of the ancient burial ground at Somenos Creek not only offended and disrupted relations with the deceased but also resulted in physical danger for the living. Only by conversing with the deceased and using her ritual knowledge could she at least partially restore the requisite balance of relations between the world of the living and the world of the spirits. Her story teaches us that Hul'qumi'num people value their archaeological heritage for its social significance. And it instructs us on how important it is for us to respect Hul'qumi'num customary laws, beliefs, and practices.

In the above passage, Ruby Peters introduces four key themes:

1 There is a perception within Hul'qumi'num culture that their archaeological heritage embodies the physical remains and belongings of their ancestors, whose spirits are believed to remain part of this world. This is important because, in many non-Western cultures, there is no separation between the "real" and "supernatural realms" or between past and present.
2 Hul'qumi'num persons are socially obliged to undertake the stewardship of their ancestral family remains so that they may maintain the appropriate reciprocal relations between the living and the spirit world.
3 Hul'qumi'num culture maintains strict customary laws, inherited social roles, behaviours, and ceremonial practices to control supernatural power and to mediate physical contact with the spirit world, which is inherently potent and dangerous to the living.
4 Due to factors both inside and outside the community, Hul'qumi'num elders today perceive problems in upholding the customary laws associated with their heritage.

The remainder of this chapter explores these four themes by analyzing interviews with Hul'qumi'num elders.

Ancient Sites

Before lookng at what teachings Hul'qumi'num elders are willing to share regarding their ancient sites and remains, it is important to consider how the Hul'qumi'num define their archaeological heritage:

> Teachings about ancient sites ... what's an ancient site? An ancient site could be an old village, the *s-hiilthun*, which is your midden. Midden, I guess, is an early way of saying where you put your garbage, your shells. [I]t wasn't garbage like it is today, it was shells and bones over time that accumulates. That's an ancient site. It could be also important areas such as where [The First Ancestors in the creation era] *Stutson* landed or *Siyalutsu* or *Swutun*.[11] (Arvid Charlie)

> I was asking what a "midden" was. He told me that it's when they find clamshells and the bones of the things that they used to eat a long time ago. I said, "That sounds like a grave." They shouldn't call them middens. That's what we call *shmuqwela*. That's the real word for grave. I don't like how they call them middens.[12] (Roy Edwards)

> When their new sites are a few years old they're called heritage. Our sites have been here thousands of years. Their sites, if they're old, may be a hundred

> and fifty years. They say it's old, but to us that was yesterday. Our ancient sites – since time immemorial. They value their places that [are only] a few years old. To us, our old, much older sites are very important to us. Many of these places have our old people buried in them. So it's not only a heritage site, it's a graveyard. So when I say why not – to me that means a lot – if they can have important places that are only [a] few years old, why not? Why can't we say our places are important to us? Because they are our culture, our heritage. It's about our past and it's our future. (Arvid Charlie)

As Hul'qumi'num elders clearly illustrate, their archaeological heritage is of enduring significance to their cultural identity. Their heritage sites are broadly defined: ancient sites are perceived not only as the tangible remains of ancestral village settlements and cemeteries but also as the sites where the mythic First Ancestors fell from the sky. Hul'qumi'num make no distinctions between either archaeological and historical sites or between historical and mythic sites. As Arvid Charlie asserts, these ancestral sites are an important part of Hul'qumi'num cultural identity: "[T]hey are our culture, our heritage. It's about our past and it's our future."

Many Hul'qumi'num people believe that there should be no conceptual difference made between archaeological sites (of any type) and cemeteries – a point that has significant implications and is discussed at length in this chapter. Ancient burial sites, historical graveyards, human remains, and funerary artifacts dominated the narratives of all the Hul'qumi'num elders whom we interviewed. In fact, the subject of burials so dominated the discussions of heritage issues that, if other site types were mentioned during the interviews, it was usually only as an indirect reference to their importance as burial locations.

Hul'qumi'num elders consider the use of archaeological terms that disassociate the human element from these heritage sites to be especially inappropriate. For example, the application of the general term "shell midden" to their ancient villages and cemeteries is regarded as disrespectful, particularly with its connotation of household refuse. As the direct descendants of this archaeological heritage, Hul'qumi'num elders view their archaeological sites as cemeteries and reject the use of abstract, general terms that detract from a genuine appreciation of their human history. They openly commemorate their ancient heritage sites as the monuments of their ancestors.

Hul'qumi'num Teachings about Ancient Sites and Remains

Hul'qumi'num customary laws, as applied to their heritage, are based on two principles: respect and reciprocity. Therefore, before turning to a more general discussion of Hul'qumi'num customary laws and practices, we provide a close examination of these two principles.

Principle of Respect: Places and Belongings of the Ancestors

If there is one central principle that underlies all discussion about archaeological heritage, it is that the ancestors and their ancestral places must be respected:

> Have I received any teachings from my parents or elders? Yes. I've always been told to be, to be careful and be mindful [of] our, of our ancestors. You always pay respect. It's like when you visit, visit a gravesite, you have to carry yourself in a certain way. You always have to have a prayer in your heart and *tsiit sul'hween* [thank the ancestors] I guess. Thank them, and in a very respectful way.[13] (Charles Seymour)

> As for our teachings, I guess the only teachings that I can speak about are [those that involve] learning from experience with attending funerals, caring for the dead. It's out of respect. And that, I guess that's the only teachings that I can reflect [on] that way. Just respect for our relatives who have gone before us and who have made a path for us in our lives.[14] (Richard Thomas)

> There are very many ancient sites that should be treated with respect. And I think that our non-First Nations people should also treat our ancient sites and human remains with the same kind of respect that they would want their ancestors and human remains to be [given].[15] (George Harris)

It is evident that Hul'qumi'num elders primarily value their archaeological heritage sites and artifacts not as objects or "things" of importance in themselves but, rather, because they embody social values that connect "people," particularly themselves and their ancestors. Respect for ones' forebears is deep-rooted in Coast Salish culture. In their broad social networks, which are based on kinship, knowledge of family history and respect for family relations are essential for maintaining status and social influence. Kinship relations are recognized to extend not only across broad geographic regions but also across generations. Hul'qumi'num people today treat their archaeological heritage as a natural extension of their system of kinship and their customary laws regarding inherited property and mortuary practices.

The Hul'qumi'num elders' belief that their ancestors continue to maintain ownership of their cultural property is most clearly expressed in the discussion of artifacts:

> Ancient objects, when we're finding them, in a way, we cherish it. The people cherish it because it belonged to our ancestors, ancient objects. We don't touch it when it's from a graveyard. We don't touch it when it's in the casket or the little homes [above-ground grave houses] that I remember. We

don't touch that. That belongs to them. And we're forbidden to touch it. But when we find – like, lately, the odd time, people find it. And we cherish it as long as it's not in the graveyard.[16] (Florence James)

With regard to teachings or caring for them, all of these belongings, they belong to individuals. And just, you know, like, you know, take yourself, for example. You know, you're wearing a necklace and probably have earrings and stuff like that, you know, that has some of your essence on there you know to be part of you. What we were told is that person still knows it's theirs. Like if a person finds whatever, like I was talking about that carving, you find something and what if that spirit is like, you know, that's mine.[17] (Sylvia Harris)

We were taught not to take anything from a grave. Even now, you don't do that. You respect the deceased because if you take something from there, something bad will happen to you. And bringing something home from, from a dead person, they'll always follow what they own and they'll want it back. And, and that's when you'll get haunted. And you won't have no rest. You'll be bothered all the time until you return that.[18] (Mabel Mitchell)

It's not a treasure. It's people's belongings, belonging to that person ... if they're digging and they, they have to know it's a grave. But they keep on, you know, like they found a treasure and, and that really just scared me, and, you know, [broke] my heart, you know. How, why did they do that? You know, when they start breaking up the area to find more treasures, which is, wasn't a treasure at all. It was, it belonged to that person or people.[19] (Sally Norris)

People often find old stone tools or ancient objects [while they are] walking along the beach or digging in their backyards. Are there teachings about caring for or handling these? Well, again, it's from the ancient times. And do I say it's mine? Some people say I found it. It's mine. And well, like, let's use the name, we'll say it, for example, eh? Some people say my Indian name is mine. It belongs to me. And [in Hul'qumi'num] teaching ... it's the other way. It's I belong to the name. That's not mine alone, my name, is not mine alone, anybody in my family or from that ancestry can take that name. They belong to the name also. So any artifact, I say it belongs to the old, ancient times.[20] (Abner Thorne)

According to Hul'qumi'num elders, artifacts remain the possession of the ancestor who originally made or used it. They make an important distinction between artifacts that are found in burials and artifacts that are found elsewhere. Artifacts found in graves are recognized to have been deliberately placed there for the deceased and it is understood that they are not meant for the living. Artifacts that are not burial-related are cherished, and the ethics regarding possession of these are comparable to the ethics regarding the holding of an ancestral "name." Like a name, an artifact is not something that an individual owns but, rather, something that is owned by the family, extended household, or group and that the holder must honour through good conduct and pass along to the care of her/his descendants.

Principle of Reciprocity: A Continuity of Relations between the Living and the Ancestors

Hul'qumi'num peoples maintain strong customary laws concerning the dead, and these laws profoundly influence their experiences of their archaeological heritage. Traditionally, in Central Coast Salish society, proper respect for and care of the deceased are family obligations. The many social and ceremonial responsibilities associated with a death in the family do not end with the event of burial but, rather, persist through the generations:

> These burial sites were a family responsibility to see that, to protect them, to keep people away from them.[21] (Ross Modeste)

> As it's been told to me, you know, like if you were the family member, it's up to you to take care of your family member. And then that goes back as far as possible. I mean, today we take care of the graves. (Charles Seymour)

> Our people used to look after our own dead, look after our own dead people. Those were things that were handed down from family to family.[22] (August Sylvester)

> We're always taught to be respectful. For remains, there's all of that teaching with regard to the afterlife, the spirits. And that's why it's, that's why we're always taught to be careful and beware. How we take care of our dead, you know, the process we go through with regard to the preparation, the four days, how we put our people to rest and all of that, you know that, that all has a meaning. How we believe in an afterlife and how we take care of our loved ones, even after they're long gone. (Sylvia Harris)

Hul'qumi'num elders teach that there is an underlying principle of reciprocity that guides one's social responsibility for the deceased. It is the responsibility of the family to ensure that their deceased are afforded a proper funeral, that their burial site and physical remains are respected, and that the needs of their spirits are tended to through the appropriate mortuary rituals. The dead are dependent upon living family members to provide them with food, belongings, and respect.[23] Families who neglect their deceased are morally denounced not only by other families but also by the deceased themselves.[24] Improper care of the deceased becomes a community concern. Any offence to the dead, whether committed through neglect or impropriety, is regarded as dangerous not only for the deceased's family members but also for the entire community.

This relationship between the living and the deceased is reciprocal; that is, it is based on a mutually beneficial exchange. This relationship is exemplified in the following passage:

> I was carrying posts, we were fencing a graveyard, an old graveyard that used to have huts. So it was cleared, brushed out, and we were supplying the fence materials. So we were packing it across, right across the graveyard from that top side where the tractor was with all the posts. And I seen what I thought was a bone when I was carrying this post. On the way back up I looked at it and it was a, looked like part of a skull. That was my first experience with something like that. And I told the guys, "I know what it is. It looks like part of a skull." So several trips later, we're carrying the posts back and forth, carrying one at a time, I seen what looked like part of a jaw. So I gently lifted it up and it was a lower jaw. So there was two pieces: part of a skull, part of a jaw. So I just put them together and that night I asked an elder, "What should I do with it? What should we do with it?" He asked me what I had done with it, and I told him it's, it's laying there on the ground. He says, "Well, you found it. You should tend to it right away. First thing in the morning, you be there and you look after it." So the next morning, I took a friend with me and we went and looked at it and buried it. I go visit it once in a while. I was there a week ago just to visit. I don't know who it was. Part of that was, was said to me was, "Don't be afraid of it. You'll look after it. One day it may look after you somehow." But having said that, this other one's also very important, which is almost opposite. If a person is afraid, they shouldn't be there. Meaning for their own safety, they should avoid these kinds of places or situations. And I really, really believe that. (Arvid Charlie)

Arvid Charlie's discovery of the exposed human remains indicated that he was personally responsible for the care of the deceased, even though he "[didn't] know who it was." Although he understood that they may not be related by kinship, the Hul'qumi'num elder reburied the deceased's remains both out of respect and out of the belief that one may benefit by developing personal relationships with the dead:

> [W]hen you're down [by] the river ... you always hear them [spirits] on the canoes, how they used to ... travel[ ]. You could hear them coming, you could see them. A lot of our young fellas have experienced that, if they[ ]

> use the river. It happened since I was a young fella that they're always around. That you're not supposed to be scared or – our people always, our parents used to just tell us not to get, not to be scared. That they're looking after us. And you have to thank them for being there.[25] (Bernard Joe)

As these accounts indicate, the obligation to care for and respect the deceased is not based solely upon fear; rather, it is understood that it is advantageous to foster relations that can potentially result in supernatural protection, knowledge, and advice.[26] Thus, while the dead are understood to possess dangerous non-human powers that may be used against the living, those who earn their confidence may receive their favour and spiritual guidance. This reciprocal relationship between the living and the dead strongly influences Hul'qumi'num customary laws associated with their archaeological heritage.

Ways That People Care for and Protect Ancient Sites

In our investigation of Hul'qumi'num teachings about their heritage, we found three primary customary laws pertaining to (1) an inherited right to care for the dead, (2) non-disturbance, and (3) avoidance.

Law of Inherited Right to Care for the Dead

In Coast Salish culture, there are stringent customary laws concerning the inheritance of family knowledge, rights, and property. In Hul'qumi'num culture the care of the dead is strictly observed and is considered to be an important inherited family right. It is customary that only certain families are responsible for handling the remains of the dead and mediating with the non-human spirit world.

Based on this customary law, the elders provide a select number of people with intensive education and training concerning this inherited ritual knowledge. As Ruby Peters notes of her inherited role as a *thi'thu'*, or person who has the ability to converse with the deceased, the private knowledge needed to undertake her duties is passed on according to strict rules of descent and is never shared with others:

> I'm a *thi'thu'*. I look after the people. I do a lot of spiritual work, and the things that belong to us, my family, it goes only from mother to daughter, or father to the children, and it doesn't go outside. It stays that way. And it's handed down like that and it's never written. I've been asked so many times to have it written. But my answer is: "No. I will not share what belongs to my family, not even for recording, not even for a video." [I will not share this with] the public because that's the way it is with our family. It's never shared. It belongs to the family and it's passed on that way. All the laws that go with it will be given to them; the words, that will be given to them.

> It will not go outside the family, not to the media, not to anyone outside the family. But directly, it's been like that from the beginning of time, from the First. My, the name *Hwuneem* was one of the First Ones that dropped [from the sky] and that's where that came from. And it's going to stay that way. I'm giving it directly to my children. So, it's true. It's not written. It's not shared, but it does exist. The most sacred – the words, the prayers – everything that goes with it is very important ... the prayers that go along with the things that we do is not shared with anyone. (Ruby Peters)

People recognized as possessing these inherited rights and ritual knowledge may be hired by other families to help them perform their obligations towards their deceased family members:

> Before white man law, we took care of our own dead. There, there were specialties. Someone would prepare the body for burial, the same as a mortician, I guess. But we didn't stuff them with any of the things they do today. There was special people, they still have them today, special people that dig the graves. We're no longer allowed to take care of our own dead [due to provincial regulations].[27] (Ray Peter)

> Our people used to look after our own dead, look after our own dead people. Those were things that were handed down from family to family, just like medicine people. You only teach your grandchildren, you don't teach you[r] children. As it gets handed down, it skips one generation at a time. So always teach the, either a girl or a boy, teach[ ] [them] medicines or teach [ ] [them] how to look after dead people. (August Sylvester)

> When we first moved there ... that was nothing but burial sites there. And we'd – when we put the waterline and water in and sewer line and everything they were finding. But we had asked two elders to lead us in the way of protecting it. So they followed the line and they just kind of used, just wrapped them up in blankets and then they brought them up. That's one place I didn't go, where they brought them. But we trusted these two elderly guys, you know.[28] (Irene Harris)

> Certain time my grandfather, my late grandmother, she was hired to take care of the remains. When the person became deceased, she had the job of bathing them and dressing them and having them ready. And my late grandfather, he used to make the caskets. So that had to have a prayer, and he made it out of – all I can remember seeing was little strips of wood. He made it out of cedar. As you know, cedar keeps well. Even if you put it in the ground, it keeps. And so our people, from what I saw as a little child – and he always had the certain bows of a tree and he'd go there and he'd

> bless the casket and line it and then place the, the body in there. And then my grandmother would bathe them, dress them and, and that was her, her job. And she was a very strong-willed person. She knew the tradition really well. So that was her job. That's what I remember. And I was with her since I was nine months old, as a little girl ... So all the teachings, if it was for the sites and remains, that's how it was taught to us. (Florence James)

In Coast Salish mortuary tradition there existed a number of professional ritual specialists who were hired to perform specific ceremonial roles regarding the care of the deceased.[29] At the death of a family member, Hul'qumi'num families would arrange to hire these specialists from outside of their immediate family. They included morticians, who would wash and prepare the corpse; coffin makers, who would construct the cedar box or casket; ceremonial dancers, who would lead the funerary procession with their cleansing rattles and prayers; pall bearers, who would carry the coffin to the burial site; and ceremonial mourners, who would lament the deceased. A public memorial was held several years after a death, at which time specialists who handled the dead were hired to disinter and rewrap the blankets of the deceased before reinterring her/him. For many years after the funeral and memorial ceremonies families hired *thi'thu'* to conduct burning ceremonials to ritually feed the spirits of the dead. These specialists were engaged to ensure that the appropriate ceremonial practices would prepare the deceased for their final place of rest. These persons were trained to ensure that no harm came to the living as a result of any contact with the deceased.

The role of many of these specialists appears to have greatly diminished since contact. With the introduction of Christianity, provincial cemetery legislation, and the funeral home industry, many of these ceremonial roles have been abandoned, outlawed, or transformed. However, new inherited roles have been created. Perhaps the most important of these new roles, at least with regard to archaeological heritage, is the position of grave digger. Since the abandonment of above-ground interment for the Christian practice of below-ground interment, grave diggers have risen to a prominent position in Hul'qumi'num mortuary life. It is likely that this ceremonial role was originally filled by family members who had the inherited right to physically handle deceased remains (*e.g.,* morticians or specialists who traditionally rewrapped the disinterred remains).

Today, Hul'qumi'num elders maintain that it is these ritual specialists who are responsible for the handling of any ancient human remains that are disturbed by natural erosion, land development, or archaeological excavation. The disturbance or removal of any ancient human remains without the appropriate guidance of these ritual specialists is considered to be against Hul'qumi'num customary law, which recognizes Hul'qumi'num peoples' primary authority to care for the dead as an inherited family right.

Law of Non-Disturbance

How do the Hul'qumi'num practise the principles of respect and reciprocity in relation to their archaeological heritage? The foremost customary law is that these ancient sites and remains should not be physically disturbed:

> Are there ways people protect? [T]hey didn't disturb them. They, it was a burial site, like a white man's graveyard. That's the way they look at it, you know. That's, that it wasn't to be bothered. And I guess I went through that in a way. It's disdainful to see that, like that instance of skeletal remains being brought out in the open to people. (Abner Thorne)

> You don't go digging them up, such as developments or things like that, dig them up today. The worst scenario example would be ... where the city of Blaine [Washington] hired a contractor to go in and [dig] a big hole about eighteen feet deep by about a hundred and eighty feet square, approximately. It was all midden. Many, many remains, skeletal remains and artifacts [were] in there. There's one that's ongoing right now and that's at ... South Pender Island. I went there on one of the investigation trips. And we did see some bones. And we were informed that there was a bone or bones sent somewhere and it was identified as human. And we also did see many artifacts there and we were walking around. And that's ongoing right now and negotiations are being done. We have concerns that the haste to look after it [means that] then we have many things overlooked. Another example can be right here at home, at Somenos Creek, where the developer dug up a bunch of, bunch of our ancestors. Those were put back, but now the guy wants to do some more development there. And that, that's ongoing. So for us, *hwuhwilmuhw* [First Nation people] we do our best not to disturb them. When you cause disturbance, you really bring bad things upon yourself or your family. People responsible, things can happen to them or maybe to one of their loved ones. I need to take it one further. Even if you're not part of the people that wrecked the site, knowing about it makes you responsible to do something about it. (Arvid Charlie)

Hul'qumi'num elders "do [their] best not to disturb" their deceased family members. This customary law of non-disturbance may be seen as parallel to the professional archaeological ethics of site conservation. However, the cultural values behind these seemingly complementary ethics fundamentally differ from one another. For archaeologists, these places are valued as non-renewable cultural resources that represent important sources of information about the past. It is understood that once an archaeological site is disturbed, the information one needs in order to learn about the past is irreplaceably destroyed. For this reason, professional ethics dictate that, for the benefit of future generations, archaeologists minimize their destruction of sites. From a Hul'qumi'num perspective, however, these ancient sites are valued as powerful ancestral places that must be protected out of respect for past generations. Such places were considered *xe'xe* – sacred and spiritually potent. The disturbance of these ancestral places is believed to have mortal consequences for the living. Out of respect and fear of reprisal, Hul'qumi'num customary law instructs persons not to disturb their ancient sites.

However, there are traditional Hul'qumi'num mortuary practices that do intentionally disturb, and even remove, remains of the dead; but this is done only under culturally appropriate circumstances. For example, the ceremonial disinterment and redressing of a deceased family member's remains during a memorial is an ancient Coast Salish mortuary practice, and it continued until recent times. Similarly, the Hul'qumi'num currently engage in the ceremonial removal of human remains that are threatened by such disturbances as those caused by natural erosion. If ancient human remains are removed from a burial site, Hul'qumi'num ethics maintain that, if people are to properly tend to their social relations and to enforce customary law, these bones need to be ceremonially reburied in the same location:

> When they are disturbed, you need to *'a'lhut* [respect them]. You need to look after whatever's been dug up and preferably put it back in the same spot or vicinity. Sometimes it gets impossible to put them back, but every effort has to be made to get them back into the same area. (Arvid Charlie)

> Well, I'll begin [with] my experience with the remains. As a young fella, my dad used to dig. And find bones in the ... and as soon as he found that, I used to help him. As soon as we found it, we'd wrap it with [a] blanket and rebury it. Almost at the place not too far from where we find them. And he's always told me if we, when we do that, we have to say a prayer. In our own way, and he always told me maybe some of our people didn't know our prayers. At that time. So we just said what we – a few prayers for them. It was just like, more like *'a'lhut* in a way. That's why we wrapped them in the blankets. Down here by the rivers there's, every winter there's – the river gets big and the bones start to show up again. Always about three or four we'd have to move. We don't have an answer for – some say we should put some piles of rocks or protect it from caving in again. But when we, when we find remains, we usually put them in a, wrap them up, put them in box and then the, we use our traditional ways. Which is the *shulmuhwtsus*, it's a rattle. That's what we always use when we, when we move them. (Bernard Joe)

> If they've been washed into the river or to the beach, you need to *'a'lhut* – look after them somehow. If the bank is eroding further back, then you need to remove what's in the bank and find a safe place to, to rebury them.

> We have at least two places where the river, riverbank is eroding. And the remains [have] been exposed. We've been taking those remains out of the ground, pick up what's exposed, dig back a little ways, take the remains out of the ground and then rebury them ... at a set aside place for doing that. (Arvid Charlie)

> And if any site was seen where maybe bears got at them and ripped them apart, the families knew who the remains were and they'd tell the family and they'd go up there and make repairs. And maybe even move them. And even up to today, in modern times, there have been cases where the certain ones who have this job of burial and removing of remains and praying to them, they would be called upon to dig them up and move them and rebury them. (Ross Modeste)

The Hul'qumi'num term *"'a'lhut"* (to respect/to take care of) expresses the intention behind the Coast Salish practice of caring for human remains. The removal of human remains to a separate location is permitted only under a restricted set of circumstances, such as their protection of burial sites threatened by natural erosion, flooding, or natural occurrence. With the advent of Christianity in the mid- to late nineteenth century, many traditional above-ground burial sites were disused or abandoned and the human remains removed and buried within consecrated ground in village cemeteries. The removal of entire cemeteries to new village locations has been historically documented and has occurred under culturally appropriate circumstances.[30] However, it is important to state that the customs that allow the intentional disturbance of human remains are not intended to be disrespectful to the dead. Nor is it the intention of Hul'qumi'num elders to disturb remains simply because it might be profitable for the living.

Law of Avoidance

As a precaution against the dangers associated with contact with the dead, Hul'qumi'num elders maintain strict laws to prohibit access to ancient burial grounds, human remains, and funerary artifacts. In particular, persons who are considered *xe'xe* (spiritually potent/vulnerable), such as children and pregnant or menstruating women, were specifically instructed to avoid visiting burial places or to come into contact with any human remains:

> What they call sacred sites, ancient sites – well, they call them sacred, where you might find remains. We were just, we were never allowed to go around them, anywhere near any sacred sites, ancient sites. (Ray Peter)

> At one time, when I was a little girl, they bulldozed the road through there 'cause they talked them into making a road. So that's recently, I was probably

> about just going into school age, Grade 1. And they ploughed the road wide there and all the remains came out of the ground. And there was a little white picket fence around it at my time. And we never walked near it or [went] into it at any time. We never did. And that's what they taught us. And a certain time of the day, we had to be in because of it. So like, four or five o'clock is the latest they'd ever allow us to be out because you weren't to be out when the spirits [were] moving about. That's what they called it. That was my mom's grandfather lived at the point. And so anybody that was deceased [was] placed in those little homes made of cedar. And they shut the door and we were forbidden to go there. (Florence James)

> And it was in our culture, held very sacred, and it was taboo to go to these sites without a reason. So children would be told of this, to keep away from them ... And these sites were held very sacred, probably more so than our present cemeteries because today we know where these cemeteries are. We know where our loved ones are buried. (Ross Modeste)

> But in the certain day, they, they wouldn't bring the remains into a house or anywhere. They just had a little building where they kept it. (Irene Harris)

A marked separation is maintained between the space of the living and the space of the dead. The dead and their belongings are not allowed within the houses of the living, and the living are forbidden to trespass upon the resting places of the dead. This separation encompasses the funerary artifacts and belongings of the deceased:

> I don't think our own people kept such things in their house. Because there are teachings that you can't hold on to those in the house because of the children there. [These things are] [j]ust either brought way up in the mountain and hidden there or just put with the deceased. So with these things, there [is] a *snu'uy'ulh* [cultural teaching] [just as there is with regard to] respect for the deceased.[31] (Ron Alphonse)

> [Finding artifacts while you are] walking along the beach may be different than digging [them up] in another place. So also, [with] along the beach I'd add along the river – erosion. You definitely can't leave [them] there or somebody else is going to come up and pick them up. Some of them were lost by the previous owner but some of them were buried along with the owner at the gravesite. So from what I'm told, if it's a known gravesite, you put it back somewhere there where it won't be eroded again. (Arvid Charlie)

> Those things, they should be returned back to the people that [live near] where they were buried or where they were dug up. Our way is to rebury

everything that was picked up there. It's not to keep and show off in a museum. And those people must've wanted it, [that] is why it's buried with them. (August Sylvester)

The spiritual pollution that results from visiting a burial ground or making physical contact with the deceased's remains or belongings is understood to be life-threatening. The power of death is believed to have such potency that even indirect contact with the deceased can be fatal. For this reason, there are many restrictions on behaviour associated with funerals and on persons who work with the dead. Persons who work with the dead have the inherited right to do so and, thus, have the ritual knowledge with which to protect themselves. These people commonly make ceremonial use of the pigment *tumulh* (red ochre) because it is known to guard against supernatural power. However, even with their ritual knowledge, it is understood that these persons may inadvertently spread lingering spiritual contagion to those around them. Thus, in order to spiritually cleanse themselves, all who come in direct contact with the dead are segregated from the living for a period of days:

Our weak people don't go to the graveyard. But also the other way around, if I go ... [*speaking Hul'qumi'num*] [to the] graveyard or the wake, I shouldn't go visit somebody, whether it's a child or an older person for a certain amount of time. I think that needs to be mentioned a lot of times now, because many of our children today, not only children, they come straight from a funeral and they go visit their elder and that elder is not well. (Arvid Charlie)

When you're a digger, you're not allowed to go near your kids. You have to rinse yourself off; you still can't touch your kids. Lots of restrictions on whatever you do. (Bernard Joe)

There was like a warning, like what I was telling you in the first place, that if you have children not to get involved in it, you know, because you are protecting your children. And so many of the people that were working on the pipeline were told if they found any remains that you had to stay away, not to [ġet] near because it's for the protection of your children. And if your wife was pregnant, that was the most important part of it ... So the longest you ever kept remains was four days, and then they were buried. And then after that, the one to do the burial of the remains. I used to wonder why because my grandfather was one of them. He'd be gone for four days. When I did try to ask, he wouldn't answer me. It was quite a while later and then he told me. He says, "When you work with human remains, you have to sacrifice four days and be able to stay away from your family." (Irene Harris)

The Hul'qumi'num customary law regarding respect for the dead affects peoples' daily schedule. Not only are persons limited in their access to burial grounds, but there are also important restrictions regarding the time of the day at which certain activities can be performed:

> My grandfather used to tell us stories about it and you respect [the] remains of your family and other families. Don't walk around there in the, after the mid-afternoon, that's when they asked us not to be inside the cemetery sites, nowadays. (Florence James)

> My grandfather used to tell us, "You don't go walking around at night time. It's no-no time for people to be out in the night time." And he used to say, just people that kill stay[ ] out in the night time, he used to tell us. [*laughs*]. That's when me and my late brother were kids. Yeah, he said when you go out at night time, if you want to be out at night time, you're looking for trouble. You will find trouble if you stay out at night. That's why you have to just stay home where it's safe. Another thing, when the kids are small yet, he says the people that are in spirit [form], they start coming ... [in] the late afternoon. And he used to tell the kids during that time, you bring them in and let them be out of the people's way that are, you know, going by, walking, or ... people that you don't see. But I think that's true because there has been so [much] of this, you know, people getting sick and the doctor can't see what it is. They don't understand, and that's that, you know. So I think it's very true what the old people used to say a long time ago.[32] (Amelia Bob)

> We don't, we don't move our dead, dead people at night. We only move them in the daytime. The reason is they travel from three o'clock until six in the morning. We're not supposed to move our dead people at that time ... until six in the morning. That would be like taking their body away and moving it somewhere. Then they have to come back and then they have to look for the body – where did their body go? Things like that we don't do. You've got to respect our people. That's why they say you make sure you bury your, your dead before twelve o'clock because they're still home. Later and later, you don't know. You might miss, they're already gone and then you bury them and they don't know where they're at. That's why we've got laws for burial and looking after our people. (August Sylvester)

According to Hul'qumi'num customary law, it is dangerous for the living to be outside at night. It is believed that at dusk, with the setting of the sun, the curtain between the spirit world is drawn open and the spirits of the deceased cross over into the world of the living. Out of loneliness for their family, the spirits of the deceased are known to follow persons home at night, where they can cause soul loss, ill health, even death. Pregnant women and children were especially instructed to be inside "after the mid-afternoon." The exact time of the curfew is debated: some elders say the dead rise after 3:00 p.m., others say 5:00 p.m. or 6:00 p.m. With the rising of the sun, however, all agreed that it was safe for the living to venture outdoors as the deceased would have returned to their rest in the spirit world.

Although the customary law of avoidance instructs people to generally avoid burial sites, there are certain times of the year when people may communally visit burial grounds. The most important of these involved family ceremonies for the remembrance of deceased ancestors:

> But in my times, they had a short time when they wanted to visit and clean. A certain time of year in the spring when everything is growing, they'd clean it. The whole family could get together and clean it and then have lunch together in one of the homes, you know. And that was getting-together time. (Florence James)

> So this is what I learned from my ancestors, like my grandmother and my dad, was to go there at least once a year and clear the graveyards out and to burn food. So that was something all our people did. Sometimes, everybody that had loved ones there would go there and clean the graveyard out, all work[ed] together. (Mabel Mitchell)

> The way, the way that things go and the way that – you know, and at certain times of the year, they used to have elders, all the elders used to get together and they would be burning food for the whole village. And at that time, the children were invited to go because they said that's the only time you give the, your deceased people a feast, that they want to see your, your family too. So all the children were there when they had that feast. (Irene Harris)

> To us, our young ones are always important, whether they're alive or whether they're deceased. Maybe one that goes to show it is how we burn food every now and then. Someday, there'd be a – my family doesn't do it every year because our teaching for that is, they're just starting their journey and they're called back again for another feast. They can't, can't get to where they're supposed to be going. (Arvid Charlie)

At least once a year extended families would gather together to weed and clean their burial grounds and share a meal with their deceased family members. On these commemorative occasions, all persons were invited to their family burial ground, including women and children. The family would hire a *thi'thu'* to perform a "burning ceremony," and a feast would be held in honour of the deceased family members, with food being ritually burned so that it would feed the spirits of the dead. On this day, the customary law of avoidance that separates the dead and the living would be suspended. These annual events were valued as social occasions and as opportunities to instruct the young in traditional ways, when all members of a family's extended relations, living and deceased, were reunited in honour of their kin.

Summary of Emergent Themes

In summary, Hul'qumi'num elders apply strict principles and customary laws to the protection of their archaeological heritage. These principles and laws are based on traditional beliefs that deal with kinship, particularly property rights and mortuary practices.

Hul'qumi'num peoples value their archaeological heritage as monuments of their ancestors. They perceive little distinction between their archaeological heritage sites and their historical cemeteries. For Hul'qumi'num elders, their archaeological sites *are* cemeteries. They believe that their archaeological heritage consists of cultural property that is owned by their ancestors. Hul'qumi'num peoples are obligated to care for their ancestors, who are dependent upon the living for their spiritual needs. A family is obliged to have jurisdiction over and to manage the burial site and cultural property of its deceased members. It is especially important that family members care for the human remains of their ancestors. However, Hul'qumi'num customary laws restrict access to cemeteries and ancestral remains. Professional ritual specialists, who come only from certain families, possess the inherited right to care for the dead.

Any physical disturbance to cemeteries and human remains is strictly prohibited. There are regulations to remove and rebury disturbed human remains, but these are applied only within a restricted set of culturally appropriate circumstances and under the ceremonial guidance of ritual specialists. In general, however, it is prohibited to enter cemeteries or to physically contact human remains.

The Hul'qumi'num maintain a marked separation between the space of the living and the space of the dead. Nevertheless, there are ceremonial occasions during which this customary law is suspended. During memorials and burning ceremonies, families reunite to tend to their cemeteries, to feast, and to honour their ancestral dead. The spiritual potency of death is such that any violation of these customary laws regarding ancient sites and remains may be fatal to the living. Any offence to the spirits of the deceased might be punished by illness, paralysis, or death not only for the offender but also for other members in the community.

Emergent Problems with Regard to Respecting Hul'qumi'num Teachings

An important goal of this study of Hul'qumi'num heritage law involves identifying the problems that Hul'qumi'num peoples currently encounter in the observance of their teachings about their heritage. To this end, we asked the question: What do you think are some of the problems that Hul'qumi'num people face in protecting ancient sites, artifacts, and human remains? In the following section, we examine four themes that emerged from participants' responses: (1) public attitudes about First Nations heritage; (2) land politics; (3) provincial heritage legislation and management; and (4) the research, collection, and repatriation of archaeological materials. We examine these themes both outside and inside the Hul'qumi'num community.

Problems Outside the Community

Public Attitudes: Upholding a Principle of Respect

How Hul'qumi'num peoples perceive public attitudes towards the protection of their archaeological heritage is a primary theme in this study. Essentially, the Hul'qumi'num think that their aboriginal heritage is not publicly valued in British Columbia, that it is not respected as a part of Canadian heritage. In the following excerpt, Hul'qumi'num elder August Sylvester describes his experience assisting at an archaeological site that has been disturbed. Here, he relays a sentiment that is commonly expressed by many property developers in British Columbia:

> I went down there and there's a white man building a home and the people are wondering how to do it. That was a proper burial site until the white people started building there ... It must've been a lot of people there. Must've been a big reserve. How the Indians moved away or lost that park, I don't know. But there is homes there and they're building swimming pools and they're finding artifacts and bones. And they waited a long time before they told anyone that there was a lot of artifacts and bones there. And the guy was just mad because they were there. He was mad because his work got stopped. And he wasn't allowed to go on and build his swimming pool or his basement home. He said that he's losing money. That was his exact words: "I'm losing money." I just told them people nobody told him to build it there. Nobody told him to buy there because that's Indian land. (August Sylvester)

There is a general perception among the Hul'qumi'num who participated in the study that the general public lacks cultural sensitivity towards First Nations heritage. This view contrasts with recent public opinion surveys that indicate that, among the general public within British Columbia and across Canada, there is strong support of both heritage conservation and aboriginal involvement in archaeology.[33] In Hul'qumi'num peoples' experience, however, many archaeological sites have been disturbed by unregulated land development. As expressed in the above example, the fact that so many incidents go unreported is believed to arise from a common public attitude; that is, that the protection of aboriginal heritage sites is an unjustified financial burden and/or a constraint upon private property rights. Hul'qumi'num believe that the general public views archaeological heritage primarily in terms of negative economic cost rather than in terms of positive social benefits. These perceived value differences are a source of contention for the Hul'qumi'num, who make a public appeal to non-aboriginal people to respect the graves of their ancestors:

> You know, if we go to the white man's graveyards, they wouldn't like it. And I don't know why they think that our burial sites is nothing to them.[34] (Simon Charlie)

> To us, it's always hard to understand how the non-natives – their graves there, their graveyards are protected, but when it comes to ours, it doesn't seem to mean a thing. They can bulldoze it, cart the remains away. To us, our young ones are always important, whether they're alive or whether they're deceased. (Arvid Charlie)

> I think one of the things that come[s] to mind when you take a look at ancient sites and burial sites is that – how would the ordinary Canadian or British Columbian feel if we went to their cemetery and dug up their ancestors? I think that it's an insult ... for people not to, not to respect our ancient sites and human remains. (George Harris)

> As for the general public not understanding when we talk about our ancestral remains or our sacred sites, I spoke about this on the radio. And I compared it with people going to Ross Bay and digging it up, and how would the public feel about that? And the bottom line is that, even though we're different, different nationalities than the people down in Victoria, they share the same concerns when, you know, people talk about their ancestors who are buried in that cemetery. They are very concerned, and they don't want people going in there and doing damage and desecration. So, it's just that they need to understand that, you know, that's how we are and that's how we've always been. (Ron Alphonse)

> Through the interview, we've been mentioning the importance of burial sites and what not. And for us, it's important for all of those reasons; but another reason[ ] for us now, in this day and age, is for ... history to place the number of years we have been here ... as a First Nation, as a people. I mean, you know, the *hwulunitum* [white people] should respect that. They

> have their little buildings out there ... they have heritage sites and heritage buildings and all of that, and they, they go to great extents to refurbish like, say, heritage building. So why can't the governments do the same for our people? For our heritage sites and our burial grounds and all of that? (Sylvia Harris)

> I think it, first off, is respect of oneself, respect of one's family. And we put the problem on the other foot [for] these non-native people and say to them, [A]lright, would you do that to your grandmother's grave? Would you do that to your mother's grave? And I'm sure we'd get some response. (Ross Modeste)

Because the Hul'qumi'num elders see archaeological sites as cemeteries, they take great offence at the physical disturbance of these sites. It is common for them to express their moral outrage to the outside community by asking: Wouldn't you take offence to the unearthing of your grandparents? They believe that the fact that most British Columbians do not share their cultural and historical connection to this land contributes to the difference between mainstream Canadian and First Nations attitudes regarding the protection of archaeological heritage:

> I see other people that come to this land – I see Scottish people, or German people, or French people, or people from other lands – they come here and they don't have that timeless connection to these lands. If you were to go to their countries you would see or experience their connection to their timeless attachment with their culture, or what have you. But they come here, and their history starts here about two hundred years ago. And so they don't have that long, time-immemorial kind of connection that we have here.[35] (Joey Caro)

Hul'qumi'num people express a strong attachment to their archaeological heritage, seeing it as part of their cultural identity. They see public attitudes towards their archaeological heritage as being similar to public attitudes towards themselves as aboriginal people in Canada. In the narratives of many Hul'qumi'num elders, the lack of respect they perceive for their archaeological heritage is directly linked to colonialism and to public contempt for aboriginal title.

Land Politics: Preserving Ancestral Relations to the Landscape

Hul'qumi'num peoples' perspectives on archaeology are deeply embedded within modern land politics in British Columbia. For the Hul'qumi'num First Nations, aboriginal title has remained an unresolved issue since the establishment of British colonial interests on Vancouver Island.

The issue of private property constitutes a significant challenge for Hul'qumi'num people who are attempting to maintain their cultural relationship with their ancestral lands. As mentioned earlier, 80 percent of the one thousand recorded archaeological sites are located on private fee simple land in Hul'qumi'num traditional territory. Even though, in British Columbia, strong heritage laws protect archaeological sites on private property, Hul'qumi'num have to deal with the fact that these sites are regularly disturbed by land development. Many Hul'qumi'num elders resent how their archaeological heritage is being destroyed by ever-increasing land-use development, which they view as the continuation of a colonialist policy to break their peoples' cultural connection to their traditional lands. This perspective is clearly articulated by Hul'qumi'num elder Roy Edwards:

> Our people have been moved aside. Rich people are coming in and are moving our people to one side. And that shovel full of dirt is too much for the white people. The Indians shouldn't have that, just a little shovel full of dirt. They are taking acres of land belonging to our Indian people. It's getting to our gravesites. They're moving our old people. It's what the rich white people are doing. Our old people have their graves here and there, wherever they lived, and now that's too much for the white man. They got to move that grave, take it out and put it in the museum. That's what they did to us, the example is right there. They moved us away from the land where our old people used to live and put us in a little bit of dirt. And today, when you look around, that's still too much for the white people. Where we live we are pushing each other trying to find a place. We can't even farm like the way our old people used to, we can't even have a garden where we can grow our berries and things like that. We have to go to a food market to buy what we need; we can't go down to the beach and dig clams or go and fish anymore. I think those gravesites should be fixed right where they are as a marker just like Craig Bay, they fenced that historical graveyard, and you can't touch it anymore. We don't have very much land and it's up to you to understand that. *Si'em nu' siye'ye, huy tseep q'a* [thank you, respected ones].[36] (Roy Edwards)

The unresolved nature of First Nations land issues in British Columbia affects archaeological concerns. In the opinion of the above Hul'qumi'num elder, there is a direct link between the unearthed graves of his ancestors and the displaced living conditions of Hul'qumi'num people today. The external pressures upon their traditional lands and resources are so relentless, he states, that it is not only his people's lands and livelihoods that are being devastated but also "our grave sites." Edwards often states, "Burial sites are our fence posts." In the past, he explains, Hul'qumi'num peoples regarded burial sites as respected landmarks that documented their claim to settle land upon which there were no physical borders.

In 1994, during the notorious land-use conflict at Craig Bay, near Parksville, Island Hul'qumi'num customary laws regarding their archaeological heritage came into direct conflict with provincial politics.[37] The archaeological excavation of 147 graves to make way for a condominium development at Craig Bay incited a blockade of the construction project by the elders of the Sna-naw-as First Nation (formerly Nanoose Indian Band) and neighbouring Island Hul'qumi'num-speaking communities. The ensuing Sna-naw-as lawsuit argued that this ancient burial ground should not be considered an "archaeological site" as provincially regulated under the BC *Heritage Conservation Act*;[38] rather, it should be protected as a "cemetery" under the *Cemetery and Funeral Services Act*.[39] The Crown lawyer argued that, if the Nanoose First Nation was successful, this would stop all development in British Columbia.[40] Ultimately, the court decided that the ancient burial site was "too old" to be legally defined as a cemetery. To resolve the political situation, British Columbia purchased the archaeological site as parkland. This land-use conflict is a well-publicized example of the politics of archaeology and private property among Island Hul'qumi'num-speaking people.

Under Hul'qumi'num customary law, land development on the part of private property owners is not recognized as a culturally appropriate circumstance within which to remove and rebury ancient human remains. Hul'qumi'num elder Ruby Peters expresses this interpretation of the law in the following excerpt, wherein she describes her resistance to the recent large-scale destruction of an archaeological site and burial ground by a luxury resort development at Bedwell Harbour, South Pender Island:[41]

> The one on Pender Island. They were asking us what they were going to do. And I said, "You can't move it because that's where our native people were. And you can't move it to anywhere, it has to be reburied close to where, close to the same location." So they were talking about having a reburial close to the same area. But I don't know where they're going to do it. Because if it's moved it's losing our identity; losing our people, our ancestors being there. Because that's the original ground. So I think it's very important not to move it. (Ruby Peters)

The destruction wrought by modern land-use development contravenes customary law regarding the disturbance of archaeological heritage. It is recognized that the clearance of archaeological sites to make way for property development is not conducted in order to help the deceased; on the contrary, it is often conducted either spitefully or apathetically with regard to their presence. There is a great concern among Hul'qumi'num elders that outsiders will either misrepresent their custom of reburying their ancestors and/or take advantage of it for profit:

> We're kind of in a dilemma here. In moving remains ... one [problem] for sure is erosion ... [such as] by the river or sea. Other similar places would be by the river or by the sea. They need to be *'a'lhut* [respected], moved somewhere. We have to be really careful on solid ground. If we start moving them, it won't take long for developers to find out that we're doing that. Then they'll say it, "Well, you guys moved your ancestors [from] our place here, we're going to do the same and also move [y]our ancestors." So it's a real danger in moving ones that aren't in danger of erosion. There may be certain instances where – I don't want to say this – but there may be certain instances where we need them to be moved ... So we have done it in the past. But I fear if we keep doing that, the developers would use that against us.[42] (Arvid Charlie)

Hul'qumi'num elders fear that, in continuing to bend their customary laws to permit the removal and reburial of ancient human remains that are threatened by development projects, they will eventually undermine their own laws against disturbance and, ultimately, leave these sites vulnerable to exploitation by developers. In the past, Coast Salish peoples considered the desecration of human remains to be so vehemently immoral and dangerous that it is likely that the disturbance of burial sites rarely occurred. However, since outsiders do not share their belief system and now control British Columbia, Hul'qumi'num people have no foundation upon which to enforce their customary laws.

Provincial Law and Management: Appropriating Inherited Rights

In the absence of the power to enforce customary law, Hul'qumi'num people largely rely upon existing provincial heritage legislation and heritage management programs to assert their interests over their archaeological heritage. In contradiction to their negative perceptions of public attitudes regarding aboriginal heritage, the Hul'qumi'num recognize that the provincial government has a strong legislative interest in the protection of their archaeological sites. At least in theory, the 1996 BC *Heritage Conservation Act* is one of the strongest heritage laws in North America.[43] Despite this *Act*, Hul'qumi'num peoples are critical of provincial legislation, which, in their experience, does not address many of their interests or take into account their customary laws about heritage:

> We follow what we call our *snu'uy'ulh* – teachings that tells us not to do these things to other people, peoples' human remains, their ancestors that

have gone before us. Their ancestors, the non-First Nations ancestors, they have what they call their *snu'uy'ulh*. It's written in law, Canadian law and British Columbian law. They call it the *Heritage* [*Conservation*] *Act*, for one example. *The Cemeteries Act*, for another example ... tells them that they have rules that they have to follow with regard to those things, and I think that, that our *snu'uy'ulh*, our rules should be respected every bit as much as any other rules that are set by the governments of Canada and BC. (George Harris)

You know, we don't even have a say on any of our rights and burial sites and grounds unless, all of a sudden, it comes to be known through the government. The government declares it sacred. I mean, what do they know about sacred, you know? To them, it's a sacred site only because they can go and study, you know, remains. (Ray Peter)

As highlighted in court cases such as *Nanoose Indian Band v. British Columbia*,[44] different provincial Acts treat aboriginal human remains in different ways. The *Cremation, Internment and Funeral Services* Act regulates the treatment and disposition of modern and historical human remains, while the BC *Heritage Conservation Act* sets out regulations for the study and protection of archaeological (primarily ancient aboriginal) human remains.[45] Historical burial sites defined as "archaeological sites" appear to receive less public respect than do historical burial sites defined as "cemeteries."

Although the *Cemeteries and Funeral Services Act* (1996) does provide provisions for the exhumation of graves, the scientific study of human remains removed from cemeteries to make way for development is a rare occurrence as the public has a high level of respect for these consecrated grounds.[46] The *Cremation, Internment and Funeral Services Act* also sets out regulations for publicly acceptable behaviour at cemeteries, and these parallel Hul'qumi'num principles of respect with regard to their ancient burial sites. For example, under Part 9, s. 47, "A person must not, on land that comprises a cemetery, mausoleum, columbarium or crematorium, (a) play at any game or sport unless authorized by an operator, (b) discharge firearms other than at a military funeral, (c) drive a motorized device of any kind over lawns, gardens or flower beds unless authorized by an operator, or (d) deposit any rubbish or offensive matter or thing." These provisions are not only stated out of respect for the deceased but also out of sympathy for the feelings of living family members. Again, the issue is the perceived lack of public respect for aboriginal values that seems to underlie legislation that sets out different expectations and sets of public behaviour for the treatment of aboriginal remains than it does for the treatment of non-aboriginal human remains. The fact that Hul'qumi'num peoples do not make a cultural distinction between ancient and historical sites may contribute to this perceived discrimination.

Hul'qumi'num peoples have also criticized the BC *Heritage Conservation Act* and its lack of enforcement as it relates to the conservation of their archaeological heritage:

> We need more than the *Heritage* [*Conservation*] *Act* because people have ways around it. I mean, if, how does it go? If you want to work in a known area, you can still get a permit. Even if the site's older than that magic date of eighteen hundred and something. People are still allowed permits [for archaeology] so, so there's a flaw in the *Heritage* [*Conservation*] *Act*. (Charles Seymour)

> There are laws to protect these [sites/artifacts] and yet they're not very – there's hardly any teeth to that law because a lot of these non-native people get away with what they've done. They say, "[O]h well, it's too late" or "[A]fter fifty years it's now become a museum piece." They put a time limit – fifty years – and, and, you know, our time is forever. (Ross Modeste)

> Today the BC law by itself is very weak, meaning nobody's been charged to the fullest extent. Part of that, there's laws that protect non-First Nation cemeteries, but when it comes to today's developers, they don't seem to want to know or understand – can't be bothered with it. (Arvid Charlie)

> You know the concern we have for the need to protect our ancient sites, artifacts, and, especially, human remains. I think that there's laws in place now that are supposed to protect heritage conservation and protect those sites, artifacts, and human remains. And I think that there's no enforcement, no monitoring. That's a big problem, and basically the bottom line is, I don't think the governments really care. They close a blind eye when there's progress in their mind, that's ultimately [what's] important ... the almighty dollar. Got to keep developing the land. So I think that's a big problem. And it kind of goes back to lack of respect for our ancient sites, our human remains and artifacts ... And when I see things that are contrary to, to what, say, the *Heritage* [*Conservation*] *Act* and destruction of our sites, that means they're not following their own *snu'uy'ulh*. (George Harris)

The main purpose of the BC *Heritage Conservation Act* is to protect archaeological sites from the impacts of modern land development. In practice, however, Hul'qumi'num peoples are of the opinion that the intent of the provincial government is to alleviate archaeological constraints on land developers. In particular, they criticize the provincial process that allows land developers to conduct the large-scale removal of archaeological sites from their properties because it is against their customary laws, which require that they not disturb and that, in fact, they avoid these ancient places. Similar to

Hul'qumi'num customary laws, which allow for the disturbance of sites under certain culturally appropriate conditions, the BC *Heritage Conservation Act* allows for the alteration of archaeological sites under a permit system, as regulated by the provincial Archaeology Branch. However, due to its restricted mandate and minimal government funding, the Archaeology Branch's capacity to monitor violations of the *Act* is minimal. In any case, it is known that few violations of the *Act* have ever been successfully prosecuted under British Columbia's heritage laws.

A critical issue raised in this study involves the lack of an effective role for First Nations in the provincial management of their archaeological heritage. Currently, First Nations in British Columbia are delegated only a minor consultation role in the provincial heritage management process. A majority of the case study participants argued that Hul'qumi'num peoples should be recognized as having the moral and legal authority to protect their own archaeological heritage and that this should be an aboriginal right under future self-government:

> I think that First Nations have to be recognized in terms of the province and the federal government [to] have authority and jurisdiction and management over ancient sites so that we can protect them. (George Harris)

> I think the law is there already regarding our burial sites and relics. So I think the Hul'qumi'num people should be recognized by the British and Canadian law as being coexistent with Canada and BC. If they coexist and recognize that, and if they're not going to, Canada and BC don't really follow their law, then at least recognize our Hul'qumi'num people some way as stewards of our burial sites, if they're not going to be real stewards of our burial sites. (Abner Thorne)

Hul'qumi'num peoples perceive that the provincial government has effectively appropriated their inherent rights to manage their aboriginal heritage. Under the current management regime, Hul'qumi'num peoples are allowed only nominal authority over the stewardship of their ancient sites and ancestral remains. The lack of a meaningful decision-making role in this process undermines the ability of the Hul'qumi'num to fulfill their obligation to care for their ancestors.

Research, Collection, and Repatriation of Archaeological Materials

The Hul'qumi'num interviewees made very few references to archaeologists and the study of their archaeological heritage. This despite a long history of archaeological research in the region, including many recent collaborative archaeological research excavations and regional surveys involving several Hul'qumi'num First Nations. Indigenous groups have often criticized archaeologists for appropriating their cultural heritage. The Hul'qumi'num community does not seem to have a problem with the many university researchers who work with the Hul'qumi'num to protect their heritage and who attempt to learn about Hul'qumi'num culture in a respectful manner. However, it directs strong criticism towards those archaeologists who are perceived to be working against Hul'qumi'num interests. Archaeologists who work in the professional consulting industry are often criticized for facilitating the provincial process that permits property owners to build developments on Hul'qumi'num archaeological heritage sites:

> We're concerned about archaeologists operating in our territory, as well as other First Nations territories, archaeologists who are lacking in the kind of ethics we require. We see instances, over and over again, of consultants being employed who are not looking for evidence of First Nations use and occupation but are looking for evidence of a pay cheque. (Joey Caro)

The perception is that, with regard to archaeological consultants, there is a conflict of interest between business and the conservation of First Nations archaeological heritage. Hul'qumi'num believe that the concerns of such people to minimize financial costs to their clientele results in minimal standards of archaeological research and conservation. In fact, some Hul'qumi'num people question whether the nature of the archaeological consulting industry itself is beneficial to First Nations interests with regard to the stewardship of their archaeological heritage in British Columbia.

There are many artifact collectors, looters, and non-professionals who value archaeological materials simply for the personal profit they can bring. While the extent of the antiquities market in this region is believed to be relatively small compared to what it is other areas of North America, many collectors have large private artifact collections that include ancient human remains. The sale of these archaeological artifacts in local antique stores, flea markets, and, most recently, through Internet auction sites is of great concern to Hul'qumi'num peoples.

> There was a store in Ladysmith. They used to have it advertised that, if the natives didn't have money, [they should] bring their artifacts there and we'll give you five dollars, two dollars. That was all ... they'd give them. [T]hen, when they closed that store, they say artifacts was just full of stuff in their basement that they hid it all the way. One lady told me, she says, "[Y]ou know, all those artifacts went to Italy and Germany." They got a lot of money for it. They didn't sell it around here. They sold it somewhere else. It's the very few things that you see in our museums now that are not, not valuable. It should have been given back. (Irene Harris)

> There are huge private collections of [human] remains and artifacts, and they actually don't go that cheap. Because there was a skull that we had to go and get. From Vancouver somewhere. This person had this human skull on their mantle and they had a candle on top of the skull. So he just let the candle melt on top of this. And it was, you know, one of our ancestors [removed from a site in the Gulf Islands], and some non-native at that party said to that other non-native person, "You better seriously think about returning that." You know, that's pretty disrespectful, and they have quite a bit of insight. They offered the advice [that] if you don't have any problems right now, you will have problems in the future if you don't get this taken care of ... So that skull actually was returned. And reinterred. (Charles Seymour)

> Artifacts, that's a big one today. Many of our artifacts are showing up by erosion, whether it's a flat surface erosion, objects coming up. Whether it's beach erosion, river erosion, and it's hard to tell for some of them whether they were just lost or whether they're part of a burial. I know that some say leave them where they are. I do need to say this – really, today, much of that is impossible to leave there. If we don't, we don't look after it, somebody else will go pick it up and we won't know where it's gone – [whether to] somebody's private collection or sold on the market. (Arvid Charlie)

The collection and sale of archaeological materials by private collectors is viewed as a collective loss for Hul'qumi'num culture. The issue of private collections is closely associated with other challenges Hul'qumi'num peoples face regarding the conservation of their archaeological heritage on private property. There are a greater number of artifacts in private collections within Hul'qumi'num traditional territory than there are in museum collections across Canada. The commodification of artifacts (*i.e.,* as objects of private collection and sale) goes against the Hul'qumi'num belief that these objects belong to their ancestors and, thus, remain the cultural property and responsibility of Hul'qumi'num peoples. If these artifacts include funerary items, then their collection would also be against the customary law of avoidance.

The public collection and exhibition of artifacts by museums is a particular source of concern for many of the Hul'qumi'num who participated in this study:

> There may be artifacts in Victoria in the museum which shouldn't be there. They could have come from gravesites too and [been] moved to the museum ... I guess there's this mentality of just [wanting] to showpiece something from the past, and they're curious because they want to look at it. But with

> us, we have more respect for [the] deceased. We don't make a display of what they owned or wore or used, I guess. (Ron Alphonse)

> I think that, you know, mention a little bit about problems facing [us] from the outside world. Teachings and values of different cultures vary greatly, you know; other cultures, unfortunately, they don't pay attention. And especially for the Hul'qumi'num or any *hwulmuhw*, the burial sites, sacred sites, objects, or whatever. You know, it's not sacred to them ... it's only for ... show-and-tell purposes. [L]ike, take their museums. (Ray Peter)

> Some of these were used for hunting, so that was for primarily survival. And protection of oneself from enemies. So these things that they used to, for protecting themselves from the enemies, would, would be held in high regard and placed in an area where [they] would not be lost. And arrowheads – [s]tone hammers and this sort of thing – that [they] could be placed in an area where [they were] not used as a toy for the children but as a memento of our people of the past. Today people sell them to museums or collectors, and god knows what these people do with them. They put them out [on] display, and that is not the feeling of our people – to put our, our sacred history on display. Certain things, fine, but not some of the things that help our survival. (Ross Modeste)

Many elders criticize the public display of Hul'qumi'num artifacts because it contravenes the customary law of avoidance regarding the belongings of their ancestors. However, some elders express interest in the collection and display of artifacts that are not funerary-related. Abner Thorne, for example, encourages the display of non-funerary artifacts for the purposes of public education as he believes that it shows respect for Hul'qumi'num culture: "so it's there for the people to see it." Many participants also mentioned the repatriation of museum artifacts.

Problems within the Hul'qumi'num Community

Although Hul'qumi'num interviewees indicated that the majority of problems were external to the community, two very serious ones were not: (1) youth education and (2) community capacity.

Youth Education

Many of the Hul'qumi'num elders lamented that the youth in their community do not show any respect for their culture. While recognizing that the values of this new generation are rapidly changing, the elders expressed deep disappointment that young people are not more knowledgeable, or at least involved in learning, about their own culture:

> I think it's today that we have so many young people that really don't know anything about, you know, our values. Our, our way of living, like when we were older. There's not a lot of respect anymore from the young people. (Florence James)

> They don't understand and that's that, you know. So I think it's very true what the old people used to say a long time ago. But when you talk to the young people and try to tell them, they laugh at you. (Amelia Bob)

These concerns about the education of Hul'qumi'num youth extend across the range of their culture, most notably in the practices of the winter spirit dance ceremonials. Hul'qumi'num elders are concerned about educating their youth to respect customary laws about their heritage:

> That's what I say of some people of our younger generations – do that, become pot hunters. So this is the teachings or the respect of people. Some people say they are bothered by things, and maybe because of some of the things they do they get bothered by this. But that's, that's the relics and artifacts that [are] ... useful for teaching our people, and if you know ... [if they find] the extraordinary relics then yes ... [they should] be studied. Yes, okay for our younger people to know what it's all about. (Abner Thorne)

> There are pot hunters, pot hunters [artifact collectors] within our community and the non-native community who dig through these sites and look for artifacts and even remains to sell. That is the only threat, because how do you, how do you make your own people aware? I'm leaning into the language again but with, with lack of language, there's no real, real teachings passed down effectively enough. People aren't aware of the consequences of their actions. So that's why that pot hunter threat exists. There's [a] lack of teachings and awareness. (Charles Seymour)

> And our people, they can't, can't do stuff like that – go in a graveyard and grab something and take it away. That's asking for trouble. We shouldn't have people going around looking for artifacts where they know there is a burial site. Those are hard things to teach our own people 'cause these are our own people that go along the beach picking up the old beads, trade beads. They have a hard time with them. I don't say anything because they're smart children. They went through school already and you can't tell them old things like this. It's too, they've got parents that should tell them, educate them on the Indian ways. We can't, I don't – well, the old teaching is, you don't teach somebody else's children your way. (August Sylvester)

Although the scale and frequency of artifact collecting among Hul'qumi'num youth is unknown, elders from several different communities expressed their concern about it. The Hul'qumi'num community must address the issue of how to educate its youth about their culture and heritage for reasons that go beyond upholding customary laws for the protection of their archaeological heritage. However, it is hoped that educational programs about archaeology may inspire youth to develop an interest in and a respect for their culture.

Presently, there are few educational opportunities for Hul'qumi'num youth to learn about their culture, history, and archaeology. It may be that artifact collecting among youth is a well-meaning, albeit misguided, attempt to discover and learn about their culture and heritage.

Community Capacity

Hul'qumi'num participants identify a second important heritage issue: the current inability of communities to protect their archaeological heritage. Their concerns involve the need for greater community cooperation and the need for more Hul'qumi'num community facilities and institutions:

> For everybody, not just, you know, not just for me, me, me. And that goes for everything, you know. Like not just, not just the burial sites or whatever but everything that we do [is] a community effort. And I think that Hul'qumi'num people, again, I think that we should have a central location to deal with protecting and controlling sites and artifacts in our area. I think that that should be a shared area. (Florence James)

> I think our Hul'qumi'num people should be more involved. A lot of people complain and they know what's going on but they never get involved. They're afraid of being involved in protecting our sites and protecting our lands and our artifacts. And it makes it difficult, you know, just for a, a small group to go when there are so many of us here that should be all working together. And, but when you get, try and organize something like that, only a few people show up. Not everybody wants to be involved, and yet it's usually the ones that complain the most at home that are the ones that don't want to be involved. And, uh, like even our graveyard over here, just [up] the other road, that's really overgrown. A lot of people don't even know that there's a graveyard there. Nobody's ever gone to see it. And it's, it's a shame that, we have such, you know, a large amount of modern tools now, and yet our graveyards are being really neglected. (Mabel Mitchell)

> I think some of the problems faced outside or within our communities in protecting sites, artifacts, and human remains is that, you know, with, with artifacts, the way we are situated now, we don't have a place to bring, we

> don't have our own museum, I guess, to ... or not a museum but a place to hold artifacts and remains until they are dealt with. (Richard Thomas)

> With respect to the artifacts, we've reburied artifacts. And I sometimes think that maybe we should have our – like, different nations have their own museums. I sometimes think that with respect to that that we should do that. That way it's like a learning process for not only our students and our younger people but for the non-First Nations also. (Sylvia Harris)

> I think that out of respect for our ancestors ... that [artifacts] shouldn't leave our territory. They should remain in our territory. That's where I think we need to make a museum so that people can, can observe and look at them so that they can be used for learning purposes for ... all of us – not just young people but for all of us. (George Harris)

Participants said that the current lack of community cultural organizations and institutions for Hul'qumi'num people made it difficult for them to take a greater role in the protection and management of their archaeological heritage. They wanted greater community organization so that Hul'qumi'num people could effectively establish their interests over their cultural heritage. In particular, they believed that the development of a museum would assist in the repatriation of museum artifacts as well as functioning as a central storage facility so that Hul'qumi'num archaeological materials could remain within their territory.

Resolving Disagreements between Different Communities

A complex political issue for the HTG involves its shared territory with other First Nations groups. The HTG's *Statement of Intent: Aboriginal Title Core Territory*, for example, is shared with at least fifteen different First Nations from three major language groups. Although there are many social and economic ties between these First Nations communities, there are few official government agreements or community protocols with which to negotiate the various issues that arise. We asked Hul'qumi'num participants the following question: "If people in different First Nation[s] communities disagree about who should care for these burial sites and human remains and how it should be done, are there ways ... to resolve [these] disagreement[s]?"

Responses indicated that all Hul'qumi'num participants agreed that the principle of respect for their common ancestors takes precedence over any modern political concerns:

> As for the different communities disagreeing about whose burial sites are whose, I know that I've heard from our elders – that we shouldn't be concerned

about whose, whose ancestral remains they are but we have to show the respect that our ancestors deserve. And I guess by just having discussions and agreeing that, you know, there's work that needs to be done and [getting] the work done and then probably by the time the work is done ... any disagreements would be hashed out by then and ceremonies would just strengthen the communities. (Richard Thomas)

I think that there are certain areas where there will be disagreements about burial sites and human remains. And I really feel that ... [the] willingness to resolve the issue has to come from the leadership and the families, community members. They have to make a commitment to resolve the issue, and the best way for that to happen is to rely on our teachings, the teachings coming from our ancestors about how we care for each other ... And ... how we have a common concern to care for all our ancestors and our burial sites, human remains. And ... I believe that if there's an impasse that at least we can maybe agree on someone who could handle it for both parties, handle the human remains or agree on a plan to deal with burial sites. (George Harris)

Hul'qumi'num express the idea that communities should put away their own interests regarding taking care of disturbed ancient human remains in order to "show the respect that the ancestors deserve."[47] Hul'qumi'num customary policy is to recognize their neighbours' legitimate interests in respecting their common ancestors. Shared interests in the management of archaeological issues is to be negotiated and resolved through the mutual recognition of family relations and social ties between communities.

I know we run into problems today about not recognizing each other and having used certain territories or areas. Part of that probably could be addressed by knowing our ancestry lines. Some of us have far-reaching roots. So we all traced our kinship, our genealogy, all of us. I believe there to be less, less of that, I don't know what you call it – animosity or not getting along. (Arvid Charlie)

Yes, usually in the past, people knew who resided in that area and that could be people from various villages. In the past, there was no *Indian Act;* there was no reserve, as we see it today. So people in community A and community B knew who these people were, and they would come together and discuss it and maybe a sacred ritual [would be] put on. Then they decided who would look after it. [This was] usually done through a sacred ritual. (Ross Modeste)

For the other remains that you find in different places, I would say, you know, to mark it and leave it there. And we, we know all our families travelled

> together and went from island to island for their foods. We were all Cowichan peoples at one time; we didn't have differences in community. Everybody loved and cared for one another. And that's a teaching. We don't make each other different 'cause our bloodline – and [our] families are made up of all different famil[ies]. You know, make up the tree and every branch comes, doesn't come from one place. So the people always knew each other and knew their family tree in the oral history. And they'll tell each other, "I'm related to you by your mother or your aunt or your mom's sister." And they know that. It's not written down. And so it's in the memory of the people. (Florence James)

Hul'qumi'num elders offer several examples of neighbouring First Nations communities working together to resolve their interests in their archaeological heritage. These examples include the Nanoose First Nation's 1995 reburial of ancient human remains from the Craig Bay archaeological site and the 2002 museum repatriation of human remains for the Snuneymuxw First Nation:

> I know when the Nanoose had theirs and then they hired everybody. They hired all the diggers, right from Saanich, Esquimalt, Mill Bay, Cowichan, Kuper, Westholme, Shell Beach, and Chemainus Bay. We're all involved in that. They had two diggers for each community. I think that was nice that, having it that way. (Bernard Joe)

> What they did was [in Nanaimo] was they didn't know where these people were from or who they were – if they were Hul'qumi'num people or what. So they had, because of the three nations on our island, they went and they got the sacred ones from Nuu-chah-nulth and Kwakwaka'wakw, and they went down there and each of them did prayers in their own language 'cause they didn't know who our dead was. And when they did that, they had a food burning, offerings of food and that's what they did. They had the three nations of our island, our island only, do it in their own languages. 'Cause they didn't know where the bones [were from], you know. And that was to respect other nations. (Ray Peter)

The above two accounts are examples of First Nations communities recognizing the shared family relations that connect them to their archaeological heritage. They show that, for the Hul'qumi'num, the significance of archaeological heritage is based on its ability to re-establish social relationships between people, both past and present. As demonstrated in the recent incident on South Pender Island, however, disagreements between neighbouring communities regarding the protection of their archaeological heritage do occur, and mutual respect for each other's interests is not always shown.

Summary of Emergent Problems

Hul'qumi'num peoples express deep concerns over their inability to maintain their customary laws with regard to the protection of their archaeological heritage. Modern land politics represents a significant challenge for Hul'qumi'num peoples, and it threatens their ability to maintain their historical connections to their lands and, most notably, their ability to protect archaeological sites located on private property. Hul'qumi'num argue that the provincial government and the heritage resource management industry are undermining their customary laws, which are what enable them to rightfully and appropriately manage their aboriginal heritage. Although issues external to the community are the primary focus of concern, issues within the community also need to be addressed. In summary, Hul'qumi'num peoples require assistance to develop a strategic plan through which to assert their aboriginal right to jurisdiction over, and ownership and management of, the archaeological heritage located in their traditional lands.

Strategic Legal Directions for Respecting Hul'qumi'num Heritage Laws

Guided by the principles and teachings of Hul'qumi'num elders concerning their archaeological heritage, we next examine potential legal directions for Hul'qumi'num peoples to protect their aboriginal heritage in British Columbia and Canada. Discussions with Hul'qumi'num elders clearly identify three main concerns regarding the protection of their heritage: ownership, jurisdiction, and management. We now look at how Hul'qumi'num interests and provincial/federal interests might be worked out through (1) treaty negotiations and (2) amendments to current legislation.

Treaty Negotiations

In British Columbia, treaty negotiations likely hold the greatest potential for achieving a just and equitable reconciliation between First Nations heritage laws and the interests of the Canadian state. With the signing of the Nisga'a Final Agreement in 1998, British Columbia and Canada officially recognized that the Nisga'a Nation has control over its archaeological heritage sites and materials located on Nisga'a lands,[48] and the Nisga'a initiated a process to begin repatriating Nisga'a artifacts from Canadian museums. The Nisga'a Final Agreement has become a template for many other First Nations under the concurrent BCTC process.

Due to the urban, privatized nature of Hul'qumi'num traditional territory in British Columbia, however, the Nisga'a Final Agreement may not be an effective model upon which to base attempts to protect Hul'qumi'num cultural interests in their traditional lands. For this reason, defining a regional role for Hul'qumi'num peoples with regard to jurisdiction over, and ownership and management of, their archaeological heritage located outside future treaty settlement land may be a key negotiation issue for the HTG in the BCTC process.

Ownership of Archaeological Sites as Treaty Settlement Land

Securing ownership of land by treaty may be the most direct legal method of protecting Hul'qumi'num archaeological heritage sites. As is stated in the United Nations Educational, Scientific and Cultural Organization (UNESCO) report on the *Principles and Guidelines for the Protection of the Heritage of Indigenous Peoples:*

> The discovery, use and teaching of indigenous peoples' knowledge, arts and cultures is inextricably connected with the traditional lands and territories of each people. Control over traditional territories and resources is essential to the continued transmission of indigenous peoples' heritage to future generations, and its full protection.[49]

As explained previously, the scale of privatization within Hul'qumi'num traditional territory creates significant challenges to regaining ownership of traditional lands. Over one thousand pre-contact archaeological sites have been recorded in Hul'qumi'num traditional territory. It is estimated that there are one to two thousand archaeological sites in the region that are not yet recorded. On private fee simple land in the region, there are approximately 650 district lots (not including subdivision lots) that are known to contain archaeological sites. The majority of these district lots are waterfront real estate held by residential homeowners. Private land is currently outside the provincial treaty negotiation mandate; however, even if sites were available as willing seller lands to purchase for treaty settlement, it would be a prohibitively expensive and highly unrealistic expectation for treaty settlement.

If land purchase is an option, the HTG will need to make strategic decisions concerning its priorities regarding treaty land selection.[50] Due to high real estate values on southeastern Vancouver Island and the southern Gulf Islands, treaty land selection decisions will need to balance economic, social, and cultural needs for the benefit of future generations. Criteria may have to be developed to prioritize heritage sites of cultural significance to Hul'qumi'num people for treaty land selection purposes. This decision-making process may involve expensive, time-consuming survey projects to ascertain the location, condition, and property status of heritage sites. In summary, treaty land selection is an expensive and impractical strategy for protecting archaeological sites. A longer-term commitment to purchase heritage sites on willing-seller land in the post-treaty era may be a more realistic strategy for regaining ownership of Hul'qumi'num heritage sites.

Additionally, treaty options other than ownership of land may offer more effective methods to resolve Hul'qumi'num interests regarding the protection of their archaeological heritage.

Ownership of Artifacts and Ancient Human Remains as Cultural Property
If Hul'qumi'num peoples cannot own all the lands that contain their archaeological sites, perhaps then can own all archaeological artifacts and ancient human remains located in their traditional territory. According to Hul'qumi'num customary laws, archaeological materials belong to the ancestors. It can be argued on customary, legal, and moral grounds that, as cultural property that was made and used by their ancestors, archaeological artifacts are a form of inheritance – a patrimony – and that this belongs to modern aboriginal peoples. Similarly, Hul'qumi'num customary laws declare that Hul'qumi'num families – not private property owners – have an obligation to make decisions concerning the remains of their deceased ancestors. Therefore, in treaty negotiations, Hul'qumi'num ownership over archaeological artifacts and ancient human remains may provide a powerful tool to protect their interests in their archaeological heritage throughout their territory.

Devolution of Provincial Jurisdiction in Hul'qumi'num Traditional Territory
Following the Nisga'a Final Agreement and recent draft Agreements-in-Principle in the BCTC process, the proposed scope of First Nations governance provides many jurisdictional rights over treaty settlement land, including heritage conservation.[51] Outside of treaty settlement land, however, the Nisga'a Final Agreement clearly recognizes the province's authority to maintain provincial heritage legislation and to manage First Nations archaeological sites.[52] In the post-treaty era, Hul'qumi'num people will likely have the paramount right to develop their own laws and to protect their archaeological sites and materials located on Hul'qumi'num lands. This jurisdictional right may provide the ideal method for ensuring future respect for traditional Hul'qumi'num heritage laws. Significantly, Hul'qumi'num jurisdiction would fill the current gap in the protection of archaeological sites on reserve lands – a gap whose existence is due to the absence of federal heritage legislation.

Although this agreement may be an effective resolution for the Nisga'a Nation, its application to Hul'qumi'num traditional territory would permanently maintain the *status quo*, thus ensuring that Hul'qumi'num peoples would continue to possess limited decision-making authority to protect their archaeological heritage sites outside their reserve or treaty settlement lands. If their treaty settlement land base is limited to Crown land and selected purchased lands, the HTG may have an interest in negotiating more meaningful regional jurisdictional authority over the protection of Hul'qumi'num archaeological sites off treaty settlement land.

While, for reasons of public accountability, British Columbia must retain its authority to maintain provincial legislation on provincial lands, government jurisdiction may involve devolving authority to the HTG within Hul'qumi'num traditional territory. This authority to regulate archaeological heritage may be developed directly in treaty language or through the negotiation of co-management side agreements prior to treaty settlement.

Such delegation of authority to First Nations is envisioned in s. 4 of the BC *Heritage Conservation Act:*

> The Province may enter into a formal agreement with a First Nation with respect of the conservation and protection of heritage sites and heritage objects that represent the cultural heritage of the Aboriginal people that are represented by that First Nation.

The HTG's negotiation of a Section 4-like agreement as an interim measure in the BCTC process would address Hul'qumi'num interests in its archaeological heritage outside of treaty settlement land. However, a Section 4 agreement has never been implemented with any First Nation group in British Columbia. It is suggested that the legal wording of s. 4 may need revision to clarify government intent concerning delegated authority, and that the political process to receive cabinet approval for any Section 4 agreement may be too cumbersome. Unofficially, it is also suggested that most First Nations organizations do not yet have either the current capacity to undertake these provincial responsibilities or the economic basis to finance any heritage resource management programs. Canada, British Columbia, and the HTG may encourage the development of such infrastructure through treaty-related measures to realize these heritage management goals prior to treaty settlement.

Stewardship and Management

Increasing Hul'qumi'num jurisdiction over archaeological heritage through the treaty process could provide a more effective heritage resource management regime in the region. The proposed delegation of provincial authority to Hul'qumi'num government would not necessarily involve restructuring the provincial system; rather, it could involve a decentralized co-management arrangement specific to Hul'qumi'num traditional territory. Delegated authority would be largely restricted to issues pertaining to the co-management of a provincial permit system, with guidelines and protocols for any proposed archaeological research and resource management concerning Hul'qumi'num heritage sites. Promoting the HTG's involvement in the local administration of regional heritage resources would create a strong political will to deliver sustainable management services and to increase the capacity of the province to fulfill its conservation mandate.

To provide local stewardship, the HTG would have to build cooperative alliances with other local organizations, including other First Nations, local government, universities, and the general public. A broadened mandate would fulfill the need for increased heritage management on a local, practical scale, including the monitoring and enforcement of heritage legislation, heritage site management planning and conservation, and public education. The Hul'qumi'num construction of museum facilities would provide local institutions in which to house cultural artifacts.

The establishment of regional archaeological inventory programs led by First Nations organizations could address critical gaps in heritage site inventory information while, at the same time, developing the mutual capacity to more efficiently negotiate heritage issues at the treaty table. The long-term benefit of these inventory programs would be to develop a more comprehensive, accurate provincial database at no cost to private property owners. The achievement of meaningful Hul'qumi'num involvement in heritage resource management would not only resolve Hul'qumi'num interests in their archaeological heritage but would also reduce land-use conflicts, reinforce the historical connections between Hul'qumi'num peoples across their traditional territory, and realize the long-term conservation of heritage sites.

There are many reasons to ensure that Hul'qumi'num interests in their archaeological heritage are included in a treaty, the most important of which is that these treaty rights will provide legal protection under Canada's *Constitution Act, 1982*.[53] The permanence of this constitutional protection contrasts with any protection afforded by federal and provincial government legislation, which cannot be binding on any succeeding government.

While Hul'qumi'num elders are hesitant to identify the location of sacred heritage sites, they realize that the public recognition and provincial registration of archaeological and historical sites is a practical necessity if they are to receive legislative protection that will ensure the preservation of these tangible, culturally significant places on private lands. Intangible places of spiritual significance, such as bathing pools, have no current legislative protection and must be addressed through procedures such as that involved in the identification of cultural landscapes and integrated land-use planning under the *HTG Interim Strategic Land Plan* (2005). The provincial Archaeology Branch restricts access to archaeological site location information, as provided under s. 3 of the *Heritage Conservation Act,* in support of First Nations cultural sensitivities and public conservation concerns around vandalism and illicit artifact collecting.

Amending Existing Legislation

The two main provincial heritage legislations that may be amended to address Hul'qumi'num interests in their archaeological heritage are the *Heritage Conservation Act* and the *Cemeteries and Funerals Act.*

Amending the BC Heritage Conservation Act, 1996

In 2002, the Government of British Columbia announced in cabinet that amendments to the *Heritage Conservation Act* were pending. These proposed amendments were intended to alleviate "archaeological pressures" on private property owners. A discussion paper was circulated among archaeologists, historians, museum researchers, First Nations, and others who comprise the heritage community in British Columbia. It outlined some of the general interests in proposing these amendments. Few of the proposed amendments offer to address any First Nations interests in and/or concerns about their archaeological heritage. Significantly, it was proposed that the provisions (s. 4) that allowed delegation and local management agreements with First Nations be removed. The HTG lobbied for the inclusion of other amendments, such as those dealing with the ownership of archaeological materials and ancient human remains, as well as the revision of a co-management clause. The province's political priorities lie elsewhere, however, and these legislative changes have been put on hold indefinitely. However, legislative change remains a powerful tool for meeting First Nations concerns about protecting their archaeological heritage.

Ownership of Archaeological Artifacts and Ancient Human Remains

The BC *Heritage Conservation Act* is silent on the issue of ownership of archaeological materials. Under s. 13, however, it is a violation under the *Act* to collect archaeological materials from an archaeological site without a permit. By permit, according to provincial policy, any collected archaeological materials must be placed in a designated repository. The *Act* creates a subtle way of controlling the collection of archaeological materials, without making any statements concerning legal ownership. This silence around ownership is reportedly due to the expressed concerns of First Nations in the development of the *Act* in the early 1990s. First Nations regarded such materials as their own cultural property, and they protested the inclusion of language that indicated Crown ownership over their archaeological heritage. However, the silence of the *Act* has created a legal void with regard to the ownership of archaeological artifacts in British Columbia.

The silence surrounding the ownership of ancient human remains is more purposeful than it is over other materials. Under common law, in principle, the human body is considered *res nullius* – the "property of no one." Although the ownership of human bones may not be part of British common law, it may be argued that, under customary law, Hul'qumi'num obligations to next of kin grant them property rights with regard to the possession of ancient human remains for purposes of reburial. Similarly, legislation in the United States, such as the *Native American Graves and Repatriation Act* (*NAGPRA*)[54] and *Charrier v. Bell*,[55] clearly state that Native Americans have legal property rights over their ancestral human remains.

In proposed amendments to the BC *Heritage Conservation Act*, provisions setting out First Nations ownership of archaeological materials and ancestral human remains are important measures for reconciling Hul'qumi'num interests with British Columbia's heritage legislation outside of treaty.

Cemeteries Act

According to Hul'qumi'num principles, archaeological sites are considered the "cemeteries" of their ancestors. Several Hul'qumi'num elders have stated that Hul'qumi'num archaeological sites should be afforded the same consideration as, under provincial law, modern and historical cemeteries. In the Province of Ontario, for example, First Nations concerns over their archaeological burial sites have led to the amendment of the provincial *Cemeteries Act*,[56] which now defines "unapproved Aboriginal peoples burial locations" as "land set aside with the apparent intention of interring therein, in accordance with cultural affinities, human remains and containing remains identified as those of persons who were one of the Aboriginal peoples of Canada."[57] In Ontario, the discovery of ancient human remains and grave goods at archaeological sites is administered under the *Cemeteries Act* rather than under the *Heritage Act*,[58] which regulates provincial archaeological matters. The inclusion of archaeological burial sites under the Ontario *Cemeteries Act* provides some measure of official support for First Nations, without the interference of archaeologists, to respectfully recover ancestral human remains and grave goods that have been disturbed by property development projects.

Developing New Canadian Legislation

The Royal Commission on Aboriginal Peoples in Canada recommended that the federal, provincial, and territorial governments officially recognize aboriginal peoples' rights with regard to heritage conservation.[59] The commission's recommendations included enacting legislation that would recognize aboriginal peoples' ownership of, and some level of jurisdiction over, cultural sites, archaeological resources, burial sites, and spiritual and sacred sites. The HTG hope that the commission's recommendations will serve both to inspire and to guide the development of legislation that explicitly recognizes aboriginal peoples' legal authority with regard to the protection of archaeological heritage in Canada.

Defining Aboriginal Rights in Court

In the last decade, several First Nations have unsuccessfully challenged provincial authority over the jurisdiction and management of archaeological sites in British Columbia. For example, in *Nanoose Indian Band v. British Columbia*,[60] the Nanoose First Nation sought a judicial review of a development permit under the *Heritage Conservation Act* and argued that the ancient site was a cemetery under the former *Cemeteries and Funeral Services Act*. Both these arguments failed. In a more recent case, *Kitkatla v. British Columbia*,[61] the Kitkatla Band argued that the protection of its archaeological sites goes to the "core of Indianness" and should, therefore, fall within federal rather than provincial jurisdiction. Again, the band was unsuccessful in making its claim.

In the future, it may be more constructive for First Nations to argue that their archaeological heritage should be protected as an aboriginal right. According to Hul'qumi'num customary law, Hul'qumi'num peoples have an aboriginal right to jurisdiction over, and ownership and management of, their archaeological sites, artifacts, and ancient human remains, all of which are viewed as their cultural property. Furthermore, Hul'qumi'num peoples have an aboriginal right to protect their dead against physical disturbances. Perhaps establishing archaeological heritage as a judicially recognized aboriginal right would be one way of forcing BC treaty negotiations to take cultural heritage more seriously and, thus, facilitate the drafting of cultural heritage protection with regard to aboriginal archaeological sites and property.

Conclusion

Cultural conflict between the protection of archaeological heritage sites and the pressures of modern land development is a chronic issue for Hul'qumi'num peoples in southwestern British Columbia. Over the last 150 years, Hul'qumi'num peoples have been afforded little political voice in the face of the colonization and alienation of their ancestral lands and resources. In the last decade, the emergent capacity of Hul'qumi'num peoples to assert their aboriginal rights and cultural interests in their land has brought greater public attention to their interest in archaeology. Through the BCTC process, Hul'qumi'num peoples have declared their interest in the constitutional recognition of their aboriginal rights to jurisdiction over, and ownership and management of, their archaeological heritage. Many critics in British Columbia, however, cynically dismiss First Nations interest in archaeology as just another "political tool" to halt land development and to bring greater amounts of land and resources to the negotiating table.

In this case study, we listened to Hul'qumi'num elders and community members talk about their cultural perceptions, customary laws, and concerns about the protection of their archaeological heritage. While underlying and unresolved issues of aboriginal title heighten cultural conflicts, it is clear that Hul'qumi'num peoples' deep-rooted cultural interests in the protection of their archaeological heritage are integral to their distinctive cultural identity.

Hul'qumi'num peoples value their archaeological heritage as part of their relationship to "people" and as something that creates and reinforces social relationships rather than as "objects" of material value. Hul'qumi'num see archaeological sites not as abstract scientific resources but, rather, as the "cemeteries" of their ancestors, their *Sul'hween*. From a Hul'qumi'num perspective, the living have inherent social obligations to care for the remains of their deceased ancestors, who are fundamental figures within extended families. The disturbance of ancient human remains and their belongings disrupt the continuity of relations between the living and the ancestors, whose remains and belongings are considered *xe'xe* (sacred, spiritually-potent) and which possess non-human powers that are dangerous to the living. For this reason, Hul'qumi'num culture has strict customary laws pertaining to the treatment of deceased ancestors and their belongings.

In this study, we found that the Hul'qumi'num have three primary customary laws regarding the protection of their archaeological heritage:

1 Only persons with the appropriate inherited right and ritual knowledge may care for the remains of the deceased ancestors and their belongings.
2 No one may physically disturb any land containing ancient human remains and their belongings.
3 Persons must avoid physical contact with the spirits of the deceased, their skeletal remains, their belongings, and their burial grounds.

These customary laws are based upon principles of respect and reciprocity between the living and the dead. To contravene these customary laws and to upset the balance between the world of the living and the world of the dead is to invite dire consequences for the living, whether in the form of bad luck, illness, paralysis, or death.

Today, the Hul'qumi'num have many concerns regarding the protection of their archaeological heritage, including increasing land development, lack of enforcement of provincial laws, lack of a meaningful role for First Nations governments in provincial heritage management, and the growth of the antiquities market. They are also concerned about educating their youth and increasing community capacity with regard to maintaining their archaeological heritage. Most notably, however, Hul'qumi'num peoples believe that the general public in British Columbia does not value their archaeological heritage as an important part of Canadian heritage.

In this case study, we hope that, by defining Hul'qumi'num customary laws associated with their archaeological heritage and by identifying preliminary legal options for addressing their interests, we can provide some direction to government decision makers, lawyers, academic researchers, and other First Nations who are trying to improve Canadian heritage laws. Further, we hope that, in presenting the words, perceptions, and beliefs of

Hul'qumi'num elders and community members regarding their archaeological heritage, we can begin to improve the relationship between Hul'qumi'num peoples and non-aboriginal British Columbians by providing greater public awareness of the need to recognize that Hul'qumi'num culture and history is an important part of our national heritage.

Appendix: Glossary of Hul'qumi'num Words

'a'lhut	to respect, to care for, to look after
snuw'uy'ulh	teachings, private advice; *sniw'* (abbrev.)
hwulmuhw	aboriginal person
sul'hween/sul'hweentst	ancestor/our ancestors
hwunitum/hwulunitum	white person/white people
thi'thu'	spiritual medium; clairvoyant
mustimuhw	people
tumulh	red ochre
shmukw'elu	graveyard
Xe'els	the Transformer/Creator
shulmuhwtsus	ceremonial cleansing rattle
xe'xe	sacred, spiritually potent
s-hiithun	refuse; midden

Notes

1 In this chapter, we use the term "customary law" to refer to legal practices embedded in the social and cultural milieu of kin-centred indigenous societies such as the Island Hul'qumi'num people. These legal practices are systems of widely recognized and acted upon protocols, rules, and social orders that are held, at times heterogeneously, by members of these communities. We do not intend the use of this term to imply that these legal rules and practices have been codified by colonial governments (as the term is frequently used in the African legal context). "Indigenous law," "Hul'qumi'num law," or "traditional law" could serve as appropriate alternate descriptive terms; however, we do not want to imply a pan-indigenousness with regard to the particular laws we describe, nor do we want to confuse the term "customary law" with "Hul'qumi'num law," which is the term being used for the negotiated law making in treaty negotiations. By using the term "customary law" we wish to emphasize that these traditions, far from being long-past historical beliefs and practices, are contemporaneousness with the ongoing legal orders of the state.

2 A glossary of Hul'qumi'num words used in this report is included in an appendix at the end of this chapter.

3 Established in 1993, the Hul'qumi'num Treaty Group represents six Central Coast Salish Hul'qumi'num-speaking First Nations on southeastern Vancouver Island and the southern Gulf Islands who are jointly negotiating a comprehensive treaty settlement with Canada and British Columbia in the British Columbia Treaty Commission (BCTC) process. The Hul'qumi'num Treaty Group membership, including the Chemainus First Nation, Cowichan Tribes, Halalt First Nation, Lake Cowichan First Nation, Lyackson First Nation, and Penelakut Tribe, together represent a combined membership of over 6,200 First Nations persons in British Columbia. Like most BC First Nations, the Hul'qumi'num Treaty Group membership has never signed any treaty with the Crown. The Hul'qumi'num Treaty Group is currently at Stage 4 of the six-stage BCTC process involving the negotiation of a comprehensive Agreement-in-Principle. The Hul'qumi'num Treaty Group's claim, which is presented in its *Statement of Intent: Aboriginal Title Core Territory*, encompasses a total of 334,000 hectares and includes much of mid-southeast Vancouver Island, the southern Gulf

Islands, and the south arm of the lower Fraser River in southwestern British Columbia. Today, only 1 percent of their traditional territory is set aside as federal Indian reserve land.

4 For more information on this project, and a more detailed version of this study, see online: Faculty of Law, University of Alberta <http://www.law.ualberta.ca/research/aboriginal culturalheritage/>.

5 Hul'qumi'num Heritage Law Focus Group. Facilitated by Eric McLay (7 July 2003) Ladysmith, British Columbia. Participants included elders Arvid Charlie, Irene Harris, Bernard Joe, and Ruby Peters, and researchers Kelly Bannister, Lea Joe, Eric McLay, and Brian Thom.

6 See section below entitled "Case Study Methodology."

7 See online: Hul'qumi'num Treaty Group <http://www.hulquminum.bc.ca/main_inside.html>.

8 See Kenneth Ames and Herbert Maschner, *Peoples of the Northwest Coast: Their Archaeology and Prehistory* (London: Thames, 2000); R.G. Matson and Gary Coupland, *Prehistory of the Northwest Coast* (New York: Academic Press, 1995); Donald Mitchell, *Archaeology of the Gulf of Georgia Area: A Natural Region and Its Subtypes* (Victoria: Queen's Printer, 1971); and Donald Mitchell, "Prehistory of the Coasts of Southern British Columbia and Northern Washington" in Wayne Suttles, ed., *Handbook of the North American Indians*, vol. 7: *Northwest Coast* (Washington: Smithsonian Institution, 1990) at 340-58.

9 Topics included teachings about, experiences with, and protection of Hul'qumi'num cultural heritage, as follows:

1. What has been your experience with ancient sites and remains?
2. Have you received any teachings from your parents or elders about ancient sites, artifacts, or human remains?
3. Are there ways that people care for and protect ancient sites? Can you give us an example?
4. While walking along the beach or digging in their backyards, people often find old stone tools or ancient objects. Are there teachings about caring for and handling these ancient objects?
5. There are many old unmarked burial grounds in the territory. Are there teachings about caring for the dead?
6. If people in different communities disagree about who should care for these burial sites and human remains and how this should be done, are there ways that people agree to resolve their disagreement?
7. Have you, or members of your community, ever been involved in protecting an ancient site or burial ground from threat? Can you tell us about your experiences?
8. What do you think are some of the problems you face from either outside or within the community in protecting ancient sites, artifacts, and human remains?
9. What role do you think that the Hul'qumi'num people should have in owning, protecting, and controlling ancient sites, artifacts, and human remains in their traditional territory?
10. What rights of the Hul'qumi'num people concerning ancient sites and remains do you think need to be recognized by British Columbian or Canadian law?
11. Many people in BC do not share the idea that it is important to protect ancient heritage sites and remains. Many sites have been destroyed because people are either unaware or do not value this heritage. If you had a chance to respond to such opinions, how would you explain why these places are so important? Why do we need to respect them?

10 Interview of Ruby Peters by Lea Joe (30 April 2003), Duncan, British Columbia. Transcripts of all interviews are located at the HTG Treaty Office in Ladysmith, British Columbia. At the time of writing, placement in a public archive had not yet been determined.

11 Interview of Arvid Charlie by Kelly Bannister and Lea Joe (28 April 2003), Duncan, British Columbia.

12 Interview of Roy Edwards by Lea Joe (13 May 2003), Ladysmith, British Columbia.

13 Interview of Charles Seymour by Lea Joe (4 May 2003).
14 Interview of Richard Thomas by Lea Joe (30 May 2003), Ladysmith, British Columbia.
15 Interview of George Harris by Lea Joe (3 July 2003), Ladysmith, British Columbia.
16 Interview of Florence James by Kelly Bannister and Lea Joe (28 April 2003), Kuper Island, British Columbia.
17 Interview of Sylvia Harris by Lea Joe (3 July 2003), Ladysmith, British Columbia.
18 Interview of Mabel Mitchell by Lea Joe (13 May 2003), Ladysmith, British Columbia.
19 Interview of Sally Norris by Kelly Bannister and Lea Joe (24 April 2003), Nanaimo, British Columbia.
20 Interview of Abner Thorne by Lea Joe (26 May 2003), Ladysmith, British Columbia.
21 Interview of Ross Modeste by Lea Joe (7 May 2003), Duncan, British Columbia.
22 Interview of August Sylvester by Kelly Bannister and Lea Joe (30 June 2003), Kuper Island, British Columbia.
23 Pamela Amoss, *Coast Salish Spirit Dancing: The Survival of an Ancestral Religion* (Seattle: University of Washington Press, 1978) at 75.
24 Homer G. Barnett, *The Coast Salish of British Columbia* (Eugene: University of Oregon Press, 1955) at 221.
25 Interview of Bernard Joe by Lea Joe (30 April 2003), Duncan, British Columbia.
26 *Supra* note 24 at 73.
27 Interview of Ray Peter by Lea Joe (1 May 2003), Duncan, British Columbia.
28 Interview of Irene Harris by Kelly Bannister and Lea Joe (14 April 2003), Ladysmith, British Columbia.
29 For a general discussion of Coast Salish Hul'qumi'num mortuary traditions, see Homer G. Barnett, "Culture Element Distributions: IX – Gulf of Georgia Salish" (1939) 1:5 University of California Publications: Anthropological Records 221; Edward S. Curtis, *The North American Indian: Being a Series of Volumes Picturing and Describing the Indians of the United States, the Dominion of Canada and Alaska*, vol. 7, ed. Frederick Hodge (Norwood, MA: Plimpton Press, 1911-14); Charles Hill-Tout, "Report on the Ethnology of the South-Eastern Tribes of Vancouver Island, British Columbia" (1907) 37 Journal of the Royal Anthropological Institute of Great Britain and Ireland 306; Diamond Jenness, *The Saanich Indians of Vancouver Island* (1934-35) [unpublished, archived at Provincial Archives of British Columbia, Victoria, BC]. See also Barbara Lane, *A Comparative and Analytic Study of Some Aspects of Northwest Coast Religion* (PhD diss., Department of Anthropology, University of Washington, 1953) [unpublished].
30 Dorothy Kennedy, *Threads to the Past: The Construction of Kinship and Transformation of Kinship in the Coast Salish Social Network* (PhD diss., Oxford University, 2000) [unpublished].
31 Interview of Ron Alphonse by Lea Joe (15 May 2003), Ladysmith, British Columbia.
32 Interview of Amelia Bob by Lea Joe (4 June 2003), Duncan, British Columbia.
33 David Pokotylo, "Public Opinion and Canadian Archaeological Heritage: A National Perspective" (2000) 26:2 Canadian Journal of Archaeology 88; David Pokotylo and Neil Guppy, "Public Opinion and Archaeological Heritage: Views from Outside the Profession" (1999) 64 *American Antiquity* 400.
34 Interview of Simon Charlie by Lea Joe (14 May 2003), Duncan, British Columbia.
35 Interview of Joey Caro by Lea Joe and Eric McLay (28 October 2003), Ladysmith, British Columbia.
36 Transcript from Hul'qumi'num Treaty Group Elders Advisory Board Meeting (24 July 2003), Ladysmith, British Columbia, with guest, Justine Batten, Director, Archaeology and Registries Branch, Ministry of Sustainable Resource Management.
37 *Nanoose Indian Band v. British Columbia,* [1995] 57 B.C.A.C. 117 (B.C.C.A.) aff'g (1994) [1995] B.C.W.L.D. 084 (B.C.S.C.). For a summary, see Tanja Hoffman, *Out of Time: First Nations, Archaeology, and the Excavation of Human Remains at Qil-Xe'mat (Craig Bay)* (MA thesis, University of Northern British Columbia, 1999) [unpublished].
38 R.S.B.C. 1979, c. 165.
39 *Cemetery and Funeral Services Act*, S.B.C. 1989, c. 21 (repealed 2004) (as replaced by *Cremation, Internment and Funeral Services Act*, R.S.B.C. 2004, c. 35).
40 Richard Watts, "Native Burial Site is Not a Cemetery, Lawyer Tells Court" *Victoria Times Colonist* (2 November 1994) 1.

41 The official geographical place-name for the DeRt-004 site is Egeria Bay, South Pender Island. Poet's Cove at Bedwell Harbour Ltd. is the corporate name of the luxury resort development. Since the site's destruction, people have been referring to the location as "Poet's Cove."

42 Arvid Charlie also noted that his statement can be applied to land developers both on reserve and on private property in Hul'qumi'num territory (personal communication with Eric McLay, December 2003).

43 *Heritage Conservation Act*, R.S.B.C. 1996, c. 187.

44 *Supra* note 37.

45 *Supra* note 39.

46 This *Act* has been changed to the *Cremation, Internment and Funeral Services Act*. The same content in the original quotes from the *Cemeteries Act* Part 3: s. 113 is now in *Cremation, Internment and Funeral Services Act* c. 35, Part 9, s. 47. See online: <http://www.qp.gov.bc.ca/statreg/stat/C/04035_01.htm#part9>.

47 *Supra* note 15.

48 *Nisga'a Final Agreement Act,* S.C. 2000, c. 7. For further discussion of strategies for reform and changes to heritage conservation law, see Bruce Ziff and Melodie Hope, "Unsitely: The Eclectic Regimes that Protect Aboriginal Cultural Places in Canada" in Catherine Bell and Robert K. Paterson, eds., *Protection and Repatriation of First Nations Cultural Heritage: Laws, Policy, and Reform* (Vancouver: UBC Press, 2008).

49 Commission on Human Rights, Sub-Commission on Prevention of Discrimination and Protection of Minorities, *Final Report of the Special Rapporteur: Protection of the Heritage of Indigenous Peoples*, UNESCOOR, 47th Sess., UN Doc. E/CN.4/Sub.2/1995/26 (1995).

50 The results of the 2002 BC Referendum have been used to support the provincial mandate that private land should not be expropriated for treaty settlement purposes. Prior to 2002, Canada and British Columbia had purchased or exchanged willing-seller private lands for treaty settlement purchases (*e.g.* the Snuneymuxw First Nation Agreement in Principle). However, today, such willing-seller private land deals appear to be special circumstances under the BC Treaty Process.

51 Nisga'a Final Agreement (27 April 1999), c. 17:36.

52 *Ibid.* at c. 17:37.

53 The *Constitution Act, 1982,* being Schedule B to the *Canada Act, 1982* (U.K.), 1982, c. 11.

54 *Native American Graves Protection and Repatriation Act,* Pub. L. No. 101-601, 104 Stat. 3048 (1990) (25 U.S.C., [ss. 3001-3013 West Supp. 1991]).

55 *Charrier v. Bell,* [1982] 547 F. Supp. 580. (N.D. LA 1982).

56 *Cemeteries Act,* R.S.O. 1990, c. C.4. "Burial locations" are now called "cemeteries."

57 *Ibid.*, s. 71(4).

58 Ontario *Heritage Act,* R.S.O. 1990, c. 0.18.

59 Canada, *Report of the Royal Commission on Aboriginal Peoples,* vol. 2 (Ottawa: Supply and Services Canada, 1996) at 648-49.

60 *Nanoose Indian Band v. British Columbia,* [1995] B.C.J. 606 (B.C.C.A.) aff. [1994] B.C.J. 2680 (B.C.S.C.). Also see *Nanoose Indian Band v. British Columbia,* [1995] B.C.J. No. 3059 (B.C.S.C.).

61 *Kitkatla v. British Columbia,* [2002] 2 S.C.R. 146.

5

Repatriation and Heritage Protection: Reflections on the Kainai Experience

Catherine Bell, Graham Statt, and the Mookakin Cultural Society

The degree of cultural and societal change arising from government policies of social assimilation, legal prohibition of indigenous religious practices and ceremonies, Christian proselytizing, federal Indian legislation, and other external pressures varies significantly among First Nations within Canada. Although the tensions created by some of these influences continue to be felt, religious ceremonies and social structures associated with those ceremonies have survived and continue to be a vital part of contemporary Kainai (Blood Tribe) life. An example is the annual Sundance, which draws the tribe's religious societies together to perform sacred ceremonies, initiate new members, and transfer knowledge and responsibilities among society members.

Integral to the spiritual life of the Kainai are the medicine bundles held by individuals and societies for a specified purpose and intended to be transferred to other members of the tribe. These bundles consist of numerous items and associated songs, dances, and information used in the performance of spiritual ceremonies and necessary for the transmission of specialized knowledge, healing powers, rights, and responsibilities to individuals within a religious society. Imbued with their own spirit, they require spiritual maintenance and ensure the health, harmony, and well-being of individual bundle holders as well as the broader Blackfoot Confederacy. Consequently, for many years, members of Blackfoot religious societies have sought the return of medicine bundles that were alienated contrary to Blackfoot protocol and have been discovered in the possession of museums and other institutions. The bundles discussed in this report are those that are intended to be transferred to new members of various societies and that are held for the benefit of the tribe.

Pat Weasel Head (Mookakin), Adam Delaney, and other spiritual leaders of the Blood Tribe assisted and advised the Kainai in the repatriation of several medicine bundles in the early 1970s. Since that time, the Kainai have been actively engaged in domestic and international repatriation negotiations.

Activity increased in the 1990s, when the United States enacted legislation requiring federally funded institutions to repatriate to federally recognized Indian tribes sacred and communal property used in religious ceremonies.[1] Although this legislation does not apply to Canadian First Nations, the Kainai sent delegations to various museums in the United States to locate medicine bundles and other important ceremonial items. They hoped the new legislation signalled a general shift in museum policy concerning the repatriation of First Nations sacred and ceremonial objects and that they could work together with the Blackfoot of Montana to bring medicine bundles back home. During this time, they also sent delegations to museums in Canada to discuss repatriation. In 1992, the Task Force on Museums and First Peoples released its report, and it recommended that Canadian museums return to the originating community not only objects that were acquired illegally but also sacred and ceremonial objects and other objects "of an ongoing historical, traditional, or cultural importance to an Aboriginal community."[2] As a result of these developments and the importance of ceremonial items to the religious practices and spiritual well-being of the Blood Tribe, significant Kainai resources have been devoted to the repatriation of sacred and ceremonial items. However, participants in this study emphasize that the protection of Blackfoot language, land, ceremonial sites, and intangible cultural heritage is also vital to the continuity of Blackfoot cultural practices and identity.

In 1998, the Mookakin Cultural and Heritage Foundation (Mookakin Foundation) was established to promote and preserve the spiritual doctrines and observations of the Blood Tribe. The Mookakin Foundation received permission from the Weasel Head family of the Blood Tribe to use the name "Mookakin." Mookakin (Pat Weasel Head), who died on 4 March 1983, was a traditional healer, a prominent elder of the Blood Tribe, and a long-time member of the Sacred Horn Society, to which he became grandfather and adviser.

The Mookakin Foundation's mandate includes the promotion and preservation of the Blackfoot language; the encouragement of the general public's appreciation of Blackfoot culture; the active repatriation of objects that facilitate spiritual doctrines and observances; and the preservation of data and material and cultural objects originating from the Blood community. Pursuant to this mandate, the Mookakin Foundation entered a memorandum of understanding with the Glenbow Museum in Calgary regarding access to sacred materials and archival resources, management of collections, support for training programs, and repatriation of ceremonial items. The foundation has also succeeded in securing the return or long-term loan of numerous medicine bundles and other sacred items from museums in Canada, Scotland, and the United States.[3] Along with the Glenbow and other Blackfoot nations in Alberta, the foundation also played an instrumental role in persuading the Government of Alberta to enact provincial repatriation legislation that enables the transfer of title to sacred ceremonial objects that are in the possession of Alberta's two public museums, and that are claimed by the Alberta Crown, to Alberta First Nations.[4] An equally important goal for the Mookakin Foundation is to facilitate a broader understanding of and respect for Blackfoot laws concerning their cultural heritage.

Methodology

The case study methodology is informed by the broad principles and procedures discussed in the introduction to this volume. The Mookakin Foundation chose to place particular emphasis on the repatriation of objects of spiritual and ceremonial significance. Thus, in-depth interviews were conducted in Blackfoot with six elders and spiritual leaders who are actively involved in the repatriation of medicine bundles.[5] All participants are or were members of the Horn Society, which is recognized among the Blood for its spiritual leadership of the Sundance. Dorothy First Rider of the Blood Tribe, who supervised the research and who has experience in repatriation negotiations, submitted a written report.

According to Blackfoot protocol, it is improper to interrupt elders or to direct conversation one way while they are pursuing another. Consequently, although all interviews addressed the broad set of questions developed for the study, some interviews are more structured than others.[6] Further, because of the subject matter being discussed, the comfort of the participants with the Blackfoot language, and the Mookakin Foundation's mandate to promote and to preserve the Blackfoot language, all interviews were conducted in Blackfoot. Given the difficulty of translating certain Blackfoot concepts and grammar into English, the research team edited the transcripts, where necessary, in order to clarify meaning. Parentheses are used to indicate translator's notes, and square brackets are used to indicate editor's clarifications. However, every effort was made to retain the actual words and the natural flow of thoughts. Participants were asked to review quotes from their interviews to ensure that the original meanings had been maintained. We used computer coded transcripts and individual transcripts that had been marked thematically, along with Mookakin archival material and academic writings, to develop a draft report. This was circulated among participants, reduced in length, and approved by the Mookakin Foundation, as designate of the Blood Tribe chief and council, for publication.

Repatriation

Ceremonial Objects

Ceremonial objects continue to be used by the Blood Tribe to facilitate the transfer of cultural and spiritual information from old to young. Medicine bundles are considered to be living beings in need of spiritual maintenance.

The fact that they have been in the museum for a lengthy period of time and have not been used in ceremonies for many years does not change their animate nature or the responsibility of religious societies and members to attend to their spiritual needs:

> The way you treat those sacred items is the same way you would treat your children. So you have to, you have to ensure that you respect and treat them right, in the same way that you would treat your own children within this house. In the same way that we treat our children with kindness, that is the same way we treat these sacred items. Also, that is my own thoughts on the issue of treating these items with great respect. They will, in turn, treat us in the same fashion. Again, if we care for children, we should treat our sacred items in that respect. Also, including our grandchildren, they will, when we grow old, they will in turn provide us with the same kindness. If we leave our children, then they would also treat us when we get old in the same way. So that goes for the same in respect to our sacred bundles. If we treat them good, then they would in turn treat us good.[7] (Francis First Charger)

> An individual is given this gift. He would be the only one who could use it. He would be responsible to keep it sacred. And these songs with it are also sacred songs and they would also be kept sacred (treated with respect). They are also a part of our culture and they must also be kept sacred. They are also given to us for us to use.[8] (Mary Louise Oka)

> The most important thing is smudging and that these items, as to where they are, need to be smudged in the places that they might be held. The white people that are there in charge, it is one thing that is important, that these white people who are in charge are not able to deal with the spiritual aspect of the item, such as the proper smudging of the items. The sacred items that we use for spiritual activities, which are numerous, that is the way that these things are to be handled and treated. (Francis First Charger)

Bundles held in museums are viewed as orphaned children who have been abducted, contrary to protocols concerning ownership and transfer:

> In our way, the old people would say they have become orphans. And those bundles in museums are all orphans waiting for somebody to adopt them and bring them back and get painted for them so they can be put back into use.[9] (Frank Weasel Head, part 1)

> This is the birthplace of these bundles. Oki, from myself, I was one [of] those that was in charge of one of them to help in raising my, one of my older

> sister's children. The child that I raised is not my own child. It was my nephew, Niskun. Let's say that we have ownership of that child. In my case, I have ownership of this nephew. In the event that there [were] no relatives around and that that child did not have any immediate family, there will always be someone from here, Kainaiwa, that will say, "Here is a child of our people." Even if a child has been put in a home far from here, that person would make an effort to secure that child in his or her care. In the same way, that [is] what is happening in respect to some of these sacred items that have found their way off in different places in the country. Someone at home always will continue to try and pursue the return of that item. Once we have that awareness [of] the whereabouts, they are – we have the exact same feeling about getting back our children. I cannot make reference to those that were given, were sold to the white people. (Francis First Charger)

Once these items are discovered, it is the duty of the Kainai to repatriate them – to bring them home. Often, individual objects reside in the care of religious societies that retain the knowledge, history, and power associated with them on behalf of the larger community. Thus, when the objects under the custodial care of these societies are removed for a period of time, these societies, which are charged with keeping the knowledge and history of the objects as well as with performing the songs, dances, and stories associated with them, are themselves jeopardized. The services formerly offered by the society are not available to the larger community. Also, the society cannot train new members, thus ensuring the survival of the society for the next generation:

> Dennis First Rider: You had previously mentioned the Pigeon Society. They don't exist anymore today? I believe there is only one man alive who is [a] member. [Y]et we still own them [bundles in museums], that sort of thing. If we were to regain these things we lost, how would it be?
>
> Mary Louise Oka: It would be good to regain them so that we could restart them. If there were anyone who is alive today, it would be him who teaches others, if we were to regain those items that they use, those items they use in their ceremonics.

Despite efforts by members of the Horn Society to retrieve their ceremonial items, not all of the bundles integral to their ceremonies have been returned. Even active societies feel the void of missing ceremonial objects, as a complete ceremony cannot be held until all the associated objects are returned:

> But this last Sundance, I spoke to the people ... So, I told them at that time,

> "Today, I will take this opportunity to make reference to our religion." The fact [that] we're [here] and are able to continue to have our camp, those headdresses, those sacred staffs, I was the one that managed to bring them back to our people. Some of them were sold, including some of the Sacred Woman Society headdresses, including Okannii Sun Lodge ... I did sacrifice a lot of personal things in retrieving them, two of the sacred pipes, one of them being Long Time Medicine Pipe and the other one, which I can't remember the name. I brought them back. This helped us to continue our sacred ways ... I tried very hard to try and get everything back together to have a complete Sundance. We're not quite complete yet but we're almost there. There's only one [bundle] out there. If we can get that, then we'll be complete. That's the Horn Society Staff.[10] (Adam Delaney)

Sacred items are also considered to have a role in healing the scars left by colonial oppression, residential schools, and the economic and social hardship imposed in the reserve era. Because these sacred items are viewed as family members whose presence is required for the protection and provision of the community as a whole, receiving items on loan is analogous to having those members come for a visit rather than return home to take their place:

> [A]ya, we were sad, the whole of Kainai was sad when he said that they [bundles] would only be loaned to us. They were given to us. The Creator gave them to us. That is why they [elders] say that they are ours. We only have to take them back. They only have to give them back, so that we can continue to use them ... They are ours. To have them loaned is not to my liking, to have them hold onto them, to have them to remain in the museum. Here, we use them. Every day we pray with the bundles and they protect us. If one was finding difficulties, he would smudge and [use] the bundle so that things would go better and also to help the people here. When the Horns gather, they pray for everyone. [These prayers], they help everyone. (Mary Louise Oka)

Developing New Relationships

Although views concerning the purpose and role of museums vary, a common sentiment among participants is that museums should respect Blood religious traditions and return sacred items. Some participants also express gratitude for the role museums have played in preserving spiritual items that came into their custody and preventing them from being destroyed. In this way, museums are viewed as facilitating the repatriation process. However, as discussed in greater detail later in this study, all participants emphasize that successful repatriations do not occur without proper respect being given to Blood elders and spiritual leaders and without efforts by the

Blood to educate museum personnel, the general public, and government officials about Blackfoot culture. The willingness of museums to receive and act on this information has varied, resulting in both confrontational relationships and successful partnerships. For example, the partnership between the Mookakin Foundation and the Glenbow has enabled the long-term loan of numerous sacred ceremonial items and the enactment of legislation to ensure their eventual permanent return.

Despite these positive developments, participants suggest that, given assertions of power and the wrongs committed by government, museums, and researchers in the past, sharing information with researchers, museum partnerships, and participating in external law reform must be approached cautiously. Underlying this caution are concerns about the assimilative effects of white culture and the improper use and exploitation of cultural information. As Francis First Charger warns, "We are beginning to move to the direction of the white man's way, or we are leaning too much in that direction. Once we start doing that, then we are undermining our own ways":

> All different people, all over the world, were given their own sacred way by our Creator ... We all secure the sweetgrass and those other items we require for the makeup of our sacred bundles, such as the deer, or the buffalo, could be the eagle, and all the four-legged friends that are running around in this place, and the most sacred roots. We do not need to say that we have to travel three thousand miles to get something to complete our sacred bundles ... because they are all around in this area that the Creator gave us. The pipestone that we need, we secure that around the Lethbridge area. Everything that we need is around the Rockies. I can now make reference to those people to the east of us. Their ways are different from us. What they need is what they secure in that area ... They were given those things and that is what makes us distinct from each other in our ways of life. All of these things, the white man disturbed. Still today, they are going abroad and they continue to get involved in matters that they have no reasons to be involved in. They are the ones, the white[s] are the ones that created all of this disturbance. As we are now sitting here, if you were a different Indian person ... I could and I would tell you that you may become part of us, join our way of life, even though you are not part of Kainaiwa or Siksikasitapii, the Blackfoot-speaking people. You perhaps are a Cree person. If I had not sufficient knowledge of our way of life, then I might tell you to join us, my son, because your ways are not the right ways. That is what the white people did to us in this part of the country. (Adam Delaney)

> Yes, laws, we have to be very careful when laws are passed. Especially to us, where it is going to affect us directly, we have to be careful. You just can't

> say this is the way. We have to think carefully ... We have to think [to] include our culture. It should not distort our culture. (Frank Weasel Head, part 2)

> The white man's way of doing ... things and their reasoning ... I try not to get involved in too much. If we start to apply that to our way of life, then we will no longer be stable in our own ways. Today, if there was to be anybody that is going to create instability in our own laws, we would normally say, "Let me get a lawyer and let's let the white man make that decision for us." And this is the way that is going to disrupt our way of life, if we let the white people make those decisions for us. In this way we will have no confidence in our ways. (Francis First Charger)

> Like I was saying, it is the white people that, anything that they do, they have to make money with ... It's bad enough that they took away most our way of life ... Don't matter what company, if they want to come and want to know something, first I will have to assess them before I start revealing information. I will not just start providing them with information. Today, this is where I stand. (Adam Delaney)

> He wrote a book. He kind of done the book right. Once he used my name. I never gave him permission to use my name. He had never asked me ... Our ancestors, [they did] not understand [when] they [had] given an interview. They figured that interview was only for that one person and for his own knowledge. [A] lot of them did not understand or give him permission ... [to] use, write, or make money off of it. (Frank Weasel Head, part 1)

A tension running throughout the interviews involves the desire to protect the Blood Tribe from exploitation and the assimilative effects of external legal, social, and political influences, on the one hand, and the recognition of the need to take advantage of external knowledge, skills, and opportunities to educate the white man and to negotiate effectively, on the other. However, the extent to which white ways can be adopted to help facilitate this process is a matter of disagreement, with some participants emphasizing the need for those educated in both worlds to be leaders in the process and all emphasizing their responsibility as elders and spiritual leaders to selectively share cultural information. Referring to the interviews conducted for this study, Frank Weasel Head says he participated so that others "will respect our rights." However, he shares Adam Delaney's sentiment that community members who "know the white man's way very well" and are "sincere" about Blackfoot ways are the best people to write about Blackfoot culture. Common sentiments are captured in the following quotes:

> That is going to help them understand us better by sharing some of our philosophies. Let's [say] for example, if we were to visit another country, we simply don't take our ways to a foreign country. We need to follow their ways of that, of those people in that country. That is the way I think (or my way of thinking) about these things, especially in the way that we carry out our way of life. We have to bring that awareness to others if we are to expect some understanding from them. And these are the things that are necessary, that we take to those people that we want to retrieve our sacred items from, that we bring that understanding to them so we can have good results in retrieving our sacred items. (Francis First Charger)

> When I talk about participation, I don't only talk of political leaders. I talk of you [Dorothy First Rider] that are directly involved. And there is enough of you well-educated to [be] able to do that. Some of you are better educated than me in both ways 'cause you have the two and you can bind the two together. You are in better shape than I am. Why can't you take the good of our culture and the good of the white man's way and blend the two together? You'll be twice the person I am. So that is what I'm saying. A lot of you go to university. You have degrees, diplomas, whatever you call them. You have those letters behind your name and you also have letters behind your name because you have been involved in our ways and you can blend the two together. (Frank Weasel Head, part 2)

> I've said this about our young people who are getting educated: "I'm hanging on to your coattails to meet us through these problem[s], to get us through, to say, well, okay, 'cause you know white man's [way] and you also know this way. Okay, here is what we can do. Here is how we can protect it." So I'm sort of reversing the role [of elders and younger people] and we have to do that now. (Frank Weasel Head, part 1)

> [T]he reason why you are doing this interview is for in the future, for anyone [of the Blood Tribe] who wants to know about our way of life. This will not be in existence in the future. So that those wishing to learn about this, it will be there for them to look at and hear about them, so that they will be taught about them things, so that those who wish to learn more about this can learn about Indian way[s] of life, so that they may learn by looking at these. (Mary Louise Oka)

Diversity of opinion regarding the extent to which the Blood should engage in "white man's ways" and the pragmatic considerations that must be taken into account if one is to build effective relationships also sometimes result in disagreement regarding the selection of specific repatriation procedures and participants. In addition to spiritual leadership and cultural knowledge about the ceremonial item being sought, factors such as past disagreements between individual community members and museum personnel, limited financial resources and costs associated with travel, and the ability to communicate effectively between cultures may affect the composition of the negotiation team and the selection of elders to guide the process. However, diversity of opinion should not be confused with the overreaching goal of, and support for, the repatriation of sacred ceremonial items. Regardless of differences of opinion, two common sentiments among all participants are (1) the need to respect and not to interfere with the decisions of those elders and spiritual advisors who are asked to participate in a particular repatriation process and (2) the responsibility of all elders and spiritual leaders to assist when asked.

Building Relationships in Alberta

The Lubicon Lake First Nation's boycott of "The Spirit Sings" exhibit at the Glenbow Museum in Calgary was the impetus behind the establishment of a national task force on museums and First Nations. A combined effort of the Canadian Museums Association and the Assembly of First Nations, the task force was mandated to develop "an ethical framework and strategies by which Aboriginal peoples and cultural institutions can work together to represent Aboriginal history and culture."[11] The task force identified three main issues for research and consultation: increased aboriginal involvement in the interpretation of their culture, improved aboriginal access to museum collections, and the repatriation of cultural objects and human remains. But before the task force report was released in 1992, the Glenbow had already taken steps to begin to accommodate First Nations interests in the museum's management and planning.

In 1990, a First Nations advisory council was created to work with the Glenbow in fulfilling the goals outlined in its *First Nations Policy*.[12] A Glenbow First Nations Treaty Seven liaison position was also created and filled. The advisory council meets quarterly and is composed of seven Glenbow staff members, the senior ethnologist (acting as secretary), the liaison officer (acting as chair), one representative from each of the Treaty 7 First Nations (five), and one representative from the Glenbow's Board of Governors.[13] The advisory council's mission is to provide advice on the care and handling of the First Nations cultural material in the collection as well as on the determination of which items and images are appropriate to market through the Glenbow, to assist in the development of First Nations exhibits or programs at the Glenbow, to act as a resource for those who are researching First Nations culture at the Glenbow, and to serve as a liaison between the Glenbow and their communities.[14]

Amidst these comprehensive reforms, Dan Weasel Moccasin approached

Hugh Dempsey (associate director of the Glenbow at the time) and asked for his help in retrieving a Thunder Medicine Pipe Bundle from the Provincial Museum of Alberta (PMA) – now the Royal Alberta Museum.[15] Dan Weasel Moccasin, a traditional ceremonial leader, was in his seventies, and he wanted to pass on his knowledge to his son. However, this required regular access to, and use of, a sacred bundle. Previous attempts to repatriate sacred material from the PMA were not successful. It was hoped that Dempsey's involvement would at least help expedite a loan. Although the PMA agreed that the bundle could be returned for the duration of a ceremony, custody remained with the museum. This was not an acceptable alternative for Weasel Moccasin because the bundle would need to remain in his home if any teaching was to take place.

Dempsey then offered to loan Weasel Moccasin a bundle from the Glenbow collection.[16] The bundle had lain unused and unopened in a Glenbow storage area since its acquisition in the 1960s.[17] A loan agreement was drafted, which stipulated that the bundle would enter the Blood community for three months, then be returned to the museum for three months, with this process continuing indefinitely.[18] The Weasel Moccasins honoured the agreement and began inviting Gerry Conaty (the new senior curator of ethnology) to all events related to the bundle. The stipulation for the return of the bundle was abandoned before the first anniversary of the loan, and a positive relationship between museum staff and the Blood continued. Although museum staff members considered the possibility of unconditional surrender of title to ceremonial items held in the collections, senior government bureaucrats advised them that they could not do this. Consequently, the Glenbow temporarily abandoned plans for full repatriation and, instead, used long-term loan agreements to govern items returned to the Blackfoot community. Following the enactment of repatriation legislation in the United States, in the late 1990s the Glenbow hosted a national workshop for Canadian museums, inviting experts and First Nations to discuss the issue of repatriation and the enactment of repatriation legislation.[19]

In 1998, the Glenbow and the Blood decided to formalize their relationship with the signing of a memorandum of understanding (MOU).[20] Soon after, the Blood accepted an invitation to designate several members to a Blackfoot consultation team that would work with the museum on the development of a new type of museum exhibit.[21] The resulting exhibit, *Niitsitapiisini: Our Way of Life*, marked an important development in the museum's approach in that it included First Nations as full partners in the creation of an exhibit.[22] In response to proposed policy changes to allow access to cultural and ceremonial objects held in the PMA, the Blood also agreed to designate a member to the PMA's Blackfoot Confederacy Advisory Committee on Museum Relations. The committee, composed of members of the Kainai, Piikani, and Siksika, worked on the design and implementation of policy changes and the development of terms of reference.[23] As a consensus-based body of nominated Blackfoot ceremonialists, sanctioned by band council resolutions, it also serves an advisory role to the government with regard to the evaluation of requests for the return of ceremonial objects and/or the use of ceremonial information. Further, by assisting in the development of specific arrangements for each return, it ensures that traditional protocol is adhered to and that government concerns are addressed. Finally, the committee works with the museum to arrange access to ceremonial objects that have been given on loan and to allow museum staff to view them at appropriate times and places. The formation of the committee facilitated long-term loans, while the museum simultaneously maintained the control and preservation of its collections.

Involvement with the museums allowed the Blood to build relationships with museum personnel and to educate them about traditional Blood protocol. For example, Glenbow staff members were able to improve their understanding of Blackfoot culture through discussions and participation in ceremonies, which, in turn, contributed to the staff members' understanding of how sacred objects in the museum should be cared for – beyond usual museum conservation standards.[24] Sacred objects were moved to a secure storage room away from the general collections and were no longer exhibited. Access was restricted to individuals with the appropriate cultural and spiritual qualifications to handle the objects. The museum also accommodated First Nations requests to smudge in the storage area, where sacred items were kept. When the museum began a noisy upgrade to the ventilation systems, the storage area was moved to reduce noise levels around sacred material. Blackfoot consultants were brought in to advise on the movement of the materials and to perform appropriate ceremonies, which included prayers, smudging, and painting staff members involved in the move.

Educating museum staff is essential for developing successful partnerships, increasing awareness about Blackfoot cultural practices, and developing repatriation policies. However, this can be challenging, given the personal nature of the educational process and changeover in museum staff. When communication is abandoned or avoided, relations suffer. As Dorothy First Rider explains:

> Educating and orientating key museum staff members, who are stakeholders in a repatriation project, is an important element to repatriation, but a time[-]consuming process. The drawback to this is that individuals who are educated and orientated eventually take what they have learned, and what they have been sensitized to, with them upon their departure from their current positions. Because this kind of education is not concrete, it cannot be physically left behind for someone else to learn from. New staff members means an educational and orientation process all over again. Personal

> time and commitment from museum staff members have resulted in gaining an understanding and appreciation of the culture, the traditions and values of the community and the society members. These individuals have become a valuable resource to the institution that they are employed with. Unfortunately, once they take on new postings elsewhere, they also take their knowledge with them.[25]

In many repatriations, parties are meeting to discuss cultural issues for the first time. Cultural education occurs through numerous protracted negotiations and is dependent on the patience of Blackfoot elders and spiritual advisors. As the provincial and federal Crowns assert title to many First Nations objects held in public museums in Canada, educational efforts extend beyond museum personnel to government leaders and employees. Although one participant suggested that negotiations should be conducted directly with the federal government based on the treaty relationship, political pragmatism, awareness of provincial assertions of jurisdiction, and specific factual circumstances (such as the refusal to return items on loan) have resulted in the Blood negotiating directly with museums and provincial government officials. Blood band council members and Mookakin Foundation staff members may be present to assist with the negotiations, but their role is more one of political support and facilitation. The important educational role of spiritual leaders and the problem of having foreign policies imposed on First Nations are demonstrated in the following passage from the interview with Adam Delaney:

> It was after Lester had fully explained to her (or them) about our purpose and about our protocol, it was then, it was at that time, the Napiyakii (white woman minister) spoke. She spoke for quite a while, and those that were there with her were more or less assistants to her. We assume that all of them made up a board. It may be that the lady minister was not able to make a decision by herself, either to provide us with our request or refuse our request. I just sat there and listened to her. Upon her finishing her statements, I addressed her to listen to me. I told her that I'm not addressing those others in her party. It is her that I will direct my statements to. "In the way that I understand life, [it] is that you are the leader of this place. That is why you have a title. Now, I am going to make reference to myself. The fact [that] I am a spiritual leader in my community and my people is the reason why I'm here (or that is why they requested that I be present here). I am the holder of the Horn Society Leadership Staff. Today, I'm going to use ... utilize the thing [for what] I was requested to be here for." I then proceeded to provide background information about our way of life and how things are run, also making reference to my previous efforts in retrieving our other sacred bundles. "One thing that the white people make a

> mistake on is after taking all those things that we had as part of our way of life, we may sometimes have to live with it, but one thing you've made a mistake by [is] trying to take our sacred way of life from us. You tend to highlight the fact that you have purchased a pipe from one of us, but those things that you have taken from us, from before, were not sold. It was at those times when our people did not read or write. We believed in other ways, and one of those is our treaty-making process. Perhaps we were not able to secure some of the things that were supposed to be ours. But today, I am going to tell you, on the other hand, I am glad you are here to allow me to tell you those things that you needed to hear ... Now, let me refer to this. Do not put us into one group. We are the Blood Indians, Kainaiwa, part of the Blackfoot Tribe. All of those tribes to the west, to the north, to the south, to the east and further on, in the long distance, those tribes, I cannot speak for them. I cannot speak for them, or request for them, because I believe that each one of us was given our own way of life and that is the way the Creator meant us to be. They all have their own ways, their sacred ways, so I cannot speak for them. Today, as you realize that our sacred bundles are not identical to those of other tribes, it was meant to be that way. They were given their own and we were given our own ... Now, I am going to tell you, [in] those books that you use for reference, you must have some in the library, some here and some at your house, there are many things you have written about us. You have made money on those things you wrote about. The white people make money ... [Y]ou write about us, and you make money with that every day and every month. Our societies come together for many years, and today, I have not acquired full knowledge of our ways. There are many things that are not true about the way you people write about us. Now, the last thing I am going to tell you, one of the things that you used is the boarding school and that is the way of life for us. For these things, I am here speaking on behalf of my people. This is the time we both need our leadership role" ... She then turned to her staff and the people she worked with and stated to them, "I cannot argue with this person. This is the very first time I've heard somebody speak to me in that way. It is true what Adam has told us today, the stories that are in the books that we have are not very accurate. They are far from being accurate." She then stated that the pipe and the medicine pipe were ours [and] just to go ahead and take it home. (Adam Delaney)

Failure (actual or perceived) to listen and offer proper respect to spiritual advisors and elders who have been asked to take on the role of educators and negotiators has sometimes resulted in breakdown of negotiations and the need to draw on the assistance of influential friends from outside the Blood Tribe:

> The Denver Arts Museum repatriation process was a painstaking one that

> resulted in unnecessary hardship [and] emotional turmoil for our society members and leaders and elders. And it could have been a positive experience if key museum personnel were aware, and acknowledged the community ownership concept, along with the protocol in dealing with First Nation people. The repatriation process was eventually successful due, in part, to the political lobbying with members of their board and with the subtle assistance from influential contacts of the Tribe, who interceded on the Tribe's behalf.[26]

Working through Challenges: Difficult Repatriations

Generally, participants in this study relayed positive experiences with repatriation efforts on a national and international level.[27] Positive experiences were associated with good communication, relationship building, mutual understanding, and compromise. However, there were also examples of unpleasant experiences. In Canada, one example is that of the return of the Long Time Medicine Bundle:

> They saw it in a dream, him ... and his wife. The old man and his wife started on the trip (to Edmonton). They had asked for permission to go outside with the pipe, to go around the building (similar to going around the camp). The museum gave them permission, at the [Provincial Museum of Alberta]. They took the bundle outside and when they returned inside, and as she was going to place the bundle back, the old lady told her husband, "I cannot release the bundle. I am trying to untie it but I can't put it down." It was then [he] told his wife, "It wishes to stay with you. It wishes to go home. It is lonesome. Just go back outside with it." The old lady then just started to go outside with her shawl and the way they use them when they handle these holy things. Their faces were painted. As they were going out, they tried to hold on to them, these security guards, but they could not touch them. As they were going to get into the vehicle, another guard attempted to hold them back, but he could not touch them. That is how powerful our Indian way of life is; the bundle is very strong, very holy. They proceeded on home but the museum had phoned ahead to the police to stop them. They even gave them the licence plate number ... The police were unable to stop them and they reached home with it. (Mary Louise Oka)

In this case, several band members who were not involved in the removal of the bundle were threatened with arrest. Frustrations experienced in attempts to explain their innocence to provincial and federal government officials, to locate someone in the federal government to assist them, and to make them understand the importance of not arresting anyone and keeping the bundle in the community resulted in anger and threats to contact the media. Several participants spoke about the ensuing meeting with federal government officials and shared some of the obstacles that they faced:

> I was, we were threatened, to be sent to jail: myself, my wife, Pete and his wife. That was when [the] chief gave me the phone number and I phoned down to Ottawa. I spoke directly to ___ before he went down to Ottawa, that was the time he worked for us here. He knew that at the time, I started pursuing the retrieval of these sacred items ... He was the one that I talked to and that's what I told him: "I'm getting tired of the provincial government and you, the federal government." He did not by name speak about anybody there that deals with these kinds of items, sacred items that belong to the Indians today. He never informed (or gave) me the name of the person that was responsible to deal with these items, never even today. But anyways ... that's what I told him, what this thing was all about. I informed him that I was now tired of the federal government and to serve notice to the federal government that we made treaty with them, and not the province. And I'm getting tired of [their] action, especially now that [they] are taking our sacred ways from us. [I said to him,] "You have managed to take all of those other things away from us, you white people. It's in the area of our religion that you have made a mistake, and now, because you have failed to assist me (or us), it is me that is going to pay. But you remember that you never paid, even though you are saying that you paid for some of the stuff ... out of your pocket. Remember that this money is the taxpayers across Canada. That is what you used to purchase some of them. Now you might say that I never informed you. I'm informing you today what I'm proposing to do. It is me that is tired of that. You have not provided me with assistance. I'm informing you today that I will pay for the radio, the media, [and] newspaper. Maybe the taxpayers of Canada might assist me." "Just wait, Adam. Just wait, Adam. Just hold on. Just hold on," he told me. He then told me, "You are a good friend of mine (or he reminded me)," and I told him, "Yeah." He told me to hang [up] and not speak to those others. I was going to speak to the media. [I] said, "Yes, I will give you two hours." (Adam Delaney)

The next day, federal government officials paid a visit to the reserve:

> The Chief of Culture, a white man, flew in and landed at the administration office. He said that he would meet with the Horn Society. When we were told, we all gathered there at the administration building and met with him. Adam Delaney and Pete Standing Alone were our spokespeople. The man then told us that this time the items are loaned to you. They are not given back to you. You will need to bring them back when you are finished with them. That was when they began to argue with him and told him otherwise. He (Jim) started a smudge but the white man refused the smudge. But they told him that in order for him [the elder who removed the bundle] to talk, that smudging was necessary before he could start talking. (Mary Louise Oka)

It was next to the fire hall, in that area, that is where the helicopter landed. When they came off the helicopter, there were four of them, all carrying a briefcase ... I went downstairs to greet them. I brought them up to chief and council's chambers. The one that was the important person, their leader, was the one that sat on the chief's chair, and I sat there and there were other ones, and on that side, there was a white guy and the rest of my colleagues sat around and [so did] our elders. He then opened his briefcase and took out some documents that he laid on the table. Just when he had got done laying them on the table ... [after some discussion] I then remind[ed] him that it has been three years that we have been talking and every time I meet with you and every time you're leaving the meeting, you keep reminding me that you have to see the board, that you are not the only one that is involved. And I told him, "I guess you're not the leader" (or the boss) and apparently (as I had previously informed my colleagues not to interfere or interrupt in the discussions), I told Mr. ___ that, "You're way down. You're not the boss. But for myself, I'm the boss. Whatever I say is going to be, and these people here, you will not hear them interrupt or say anything. I'm not going to make reference to them." That's when I told him just to leave. (Adam Delaney)

They wanted me to give them back. I said, "No way." Some elders said we're the keeper. There is nothing we can do. They wanted us to bring them back but we just kept them ... it depends on you whites to satisfy white man's law. They wanted a bill of sale for one penny that we brought it back ... The head chief, this is where the respect comes in, turns it over to Adam 'cause he was the leader of the Horn Society. That is not our way and [he] didn't sign it. So [from] that time on, the provincial museum would not deal with the Blood Tribe. They said we stole those bundles ... sometimes we gotta bend our ways a little too. So they wouldn't deal with us. There was no way. Other people had gone up, and they just said, "No way, we won't deal with you" ... But when the new guy came in, he changed and said that is a lie. That is no way to be, so that is when he stated that [he would] permit long-term [loans] but we have to sign for it every year. (Frank Weasel Head, part 1)

But he [white man] had told him why he had taken it. It was then that he finally said, "Go ahead and use it. But in the future, if you begin to sell them again, we will take them back from you. But in the meantime, go ahead and use them as you wish." That is how he finally released it. (Mary Louise Oka)

The return of the Long Time Medicine Bundle is an exceptional situation. It underscores the challenge of reconciling competing concepts of ownership and the distance that had to be overcome to eventually reach an agreement with the province to change laws limiting the ability of museums to repatriate sacred ceremonial items in their possession. The Blood began the process by adhering to their spiritual responsibilities to the bundle and the community, and this resulted in a breach of museum protocol and Canadian law when they removed the bundle from museum control without permission. Government officials then breached Blood protocol when they landed a team of bureaucrats and lawyers by helicopter, demanded a bill of sale for property the Blood considered to be theirs, and refused the smudge. Once the parties communicated and the Blood explained their actions and the centrality of the bundle to their spiritual ceremonies, progress was made and the bundle was allowed to stay.

A similar breakdown in negotiation and communication was experienced with the Denver Arts Museum (DAM). The relationship between the Blood and DAM began in 1997, when tribal members, who were in Denver on other business, discovered that DAM had a substantial collection of Blood sacred objects in its possession.[28] In the winter of 1997-98, the Blood began to negotiate the return of the several Motoki headdresses that were to be used in the summer Sundance. They were able to obtain a loan of the headdresses by having the Glenbow develop a loan agreement that "reflected the physical situation of the loan," obtain all the necessary permits, act as courier for the objects, and co-sign the loan.[29] When the bundles were returned in 1998, the Blood began to intensively negotiate their full repatriation. However, the representative from DAM assigned to work with the Blood was perceived by members of the Blood negotiating team as viewing "his role as a protector ... and the collection as the museum's proprietary right."[30] Further, although not bound by the *Native American Graves Protection and Repatriation Act* (*NAGPRA*), the museum decided to use *NAGPRA* to guide it in its negotiations with the Blood and "to establish a process that would be used as a template for all future repatriation requests by other Tribes."[31] The result, from the perspective of the Blood negotiators, was a "painstaking experience that took four years to conclude."[32]

The *Act* establishes guidelines and standards for the repatriation of human remains, funerary objects, sacred objects, and objects of cultural patrimony to be returned from federally funded institutions to federally recognized tribes in the United States. Sacred items are defined as "specific ceremonial objects which are needed by traditional Native American religious leaders for the practice of traditional Native American religions by their present day adherents."[33] Cultural patrimony is an object of historical, traditional, or cultural importance central to the culture that cannot be "alienated, appropriated or conveyed by any individual" and that is considered inalienable at the time it is separated from the originating community.[34] Further, if a purchase was made in accordance with tribal law, then the museum is not bound to return the objects. The questions in the DAM negotiations, therefore, became: What objects can be alienated, what constitutes a valid alienation, and what defines ownership?[35] The onus was on the Blood Tribe to prove cultural affiliation and to establish that the museum did not have a right of possession.

As bundles are held by a variety of people within a religious society for a variety of reasons, and not necessarily only by those who have a leadership role in a religious society, they do not fit easily within *NAGPRA*'s definition of sacred items. Because they have both individual and communal attributes, they do not fit easily within the definition of cultural patrimony. However, the tribe's position was that bundles are communal religious artifacts that, therefore, cannot be sold by individuals. Individuals within a religious society may obtain possession through proper ceremonial transfer, but "[w]hen transfers take place within any of the societies to new members, the new members are caregivers to the bundles."[36] The bundles belong to the tribe as a whole. Although this was understood by other museums in the United States with which the Blood had positive dealings, DAM's position was that items in its collection were personal property purchased from individuals who had the right to sell them at a time when notions of communal ownership and protocols for ceremonial transfer were in abeyance. The museum conducted an extensive review of archival materials, including correspondence surrounding purchase, and noted the widespread sale of ritual objects on the part of heirs of bundle keepers and the absence of protest and attempts to punish transgressors to back up these claims.[37]

The Blood relied primarily on oral testimony of respected elders and ceremonialists to validate their assertions. As Conaty explains in his paper "Two Approaches to the Repatriation of Blackfoot Sacred Material,"

> [t]he Kainai offered several arguments in rebuttal. First, these bundles were only opened once each year. The alienation may not be discovered for many months, by which time any action may have been futile. Second, the people acting as agents for Walters [an American dealer who initially purchased the bundles] were high ranking Kainai politicians, appointed by Canadian government officials. To whom could the Kainai send their protests? The government overtly and covertly discouraged traditional practices. Who would act on behalf of the Kainai? Third, people are reluctant to condemn another's actions concerning holy objects. It is still a strongly held belief that if one acts improperly they and their family will be punished by the Creator. It is not the place of human beings to act on behalf of the Creator.[38]

The ensuing exchange of information resulted in an evidentiary stalemate, with the Blood feeling that archival documentation was being given priority over the oral testimony of respected members of the community. The Blood Tribe and the Glenbow spent considerable time and money on the process in support of the Blood claim. However, discussions continued, and eventually an agreement was reached detailing the protocols and process by which further negotiations would proceed. The protocol agreement provided a common set of agreed principles from which both parties were to work in further repatriation negotiations. These include:

- that oral history shall be given equal weight to written documents;
- that Elders, members of the sacred societies, and Blood representatives shall be treated with the utmost respect, in keeping with Blood Tribe protocol;
- that outside parties may be consulted to provide information, research, assistance, advice, and recommendations;
- that either party may bring observers and persons with expertise in appropriate topic areas as required; and
- that if discussions break down on any issue, the parties may mutually agree to refer the matter to mediation by an agreed-upon mediator.[39]

The DAM negotiations were further complicated by laws prohibiting the transport of eagle feathers outside the United States and the need to involve the Canadian embassy in the permit process.[40] However, the main impediment appeared to be DAM's conclusion that the bundles in its possession were private property capable of being sold. It was only after the intervention of experts and advocates on behalf of the Blood Tribe, and the visit to the reserve by a member of DAM's Board of Governors, that an agreement was finally reached to repatriate.[41] On 4 April 2000, DAM, the Blood, and the Montana Blackfeet entered into an agreement governing the full repatriation of twenty-three bundles to the Blood Tribe. It was necessary for the Montana Blackfeet to be involved as *NAGPRA*'s creators had not envisioned the return of cultural items to Indian tribes outside the United States. The arrangement was for the bundles to be returned to the Montana Blackfeet, who then returned them to the Blood. On 8 September 2000, with great emotion, the Blood celebrated the return of the bundles to their community.

These two examples give insight into some of the difficulties the Blood faced in attempting to repatriate sacred materials on both sides of the border. In addition to the usual challenges of repatriation, such as cost, distance, personal conflicts, language issues, political pressures, legislative and/or policy requirements, and communication breakdown, the Blood encountered serious confusion and disagreement regarding Blood concepts of property, ownership, transfer, and the validity and enforcement of traditional law.

Concepts of Ownership and Property

Much misunderstanding and conflict surrounding Blood repatriation attempts may be traced to a fundamental divergence between Blood and Western conceptual frameworks pertaining to property. Because the ideology of each is born in a distinct socio-political and economic context, the cultural matrices responsible for defining and delineating the parameters of property as well as the systems of law charged with its regulation and enforcement are, in some ways, incompatible. Property "rights" in land – a defining pillar of English common law – are unknown in traditional Blackfoot culture.[42] This broad conceptual polarity is magnified with respect to cultural heritage and truly represents what Narcisse Blood aptly terms "worlds colliding."[43]

Participants defined cultural property very broadly as their "way of life"[44] and "those things that are given to [them] for [their] existence."[45] It includes "anything within the boundaries of the Blackfoot Confederacy," including "intellectual property" such as "language and ceremonies."[46] However, as Narcisse Blood explains with regard to the danger of defining cultural property, the definitions offered might not be interpreted with sufficient flexibility to include everything that makes the Blood people who they are:

> It sounds complete enough, but, you know, if we take it from our perspective, the issue will always be, "Is that sufficient?" Because we are looking at it in a Western paradigm, [a] Western legal context, because in there, you can twist words. You can do all sorts of things that we don't do in our culture. Yeah, so it sounds good as a start. But then again, how do we do that? That is going to be the big trick. (Narcisse Blood)

When asked about the importance of this cultural property to the emotional, cultural, and spiritual well-being of the community, Narcisse Blood also explains that it is like "the relationship of Rome to the Catholic Church." He asks, rhetorically: "What if we went over there and destroyed Rome, the Sistine Chapel? What would the effects be on Roman Catholics in general?" Although ceremonial objects are very important to contemporary religious practices, the focus and priority given to their repatriation is also a product of the academic classification found in museum policies and repatriation legislation, with the Blood currently repatriating under those categories because of limited resources.

Two areas of tension and confusion with regard to understandings of cultural property in some repatriation negotiations are (1) private versus communal "ownership" and (2) custodial versus personal/proprietary rights. In the case of medicine bundles, the ability of individuals and families to hold communal property for specified uses and benefits has caused confusion about the nature of bundle caretakers. From a Blood perspective, "ownership" is not a term that can be properly applied to the rights and responsibilities of individual bundle holders; rather, bundle holders are caretakers whose responsibility is to use the bundles as intended by the Creator for the benefit of the community and to transfer them to others within the community. This can run contrary to museum policy, which may trace entitlement through direct descendants:

> The Blood understood that museums view their collections as their personal possessions because the museums paid for the articles in their collections and that some articles have been donated from private collectors. Museums will not question the origin of their purchase, nor do they question the donation, especially in relation to religious artifacts and personal articles ... Repatriation [would] be easier if there was an understanding and sensitivity to tribal practices and ... a good understanding of the notion of communal property, especially in relation to sacred artifacts. (Dorothy First Rider)

> For myself, those items that were properly transferred to me, I cannot honestly make a statement that I owned these things outright. They are meant to be transferred on to the next. For the ones that were sold to the white communities, institutions, or individuals, the white people, to them, ownership is another thing. They don't necessarily use First Nation peoples' knowledge and understanding of how these come into the possession of individuals. It is my opinion that these items were born from our own way of life, our own territory. That is my understanding of the origin and their purpose. As I had stated before, these things within the boundaries of our people are the property of the people. Those things that are within this, our territories, these things that are within, they belong to us. We cannot state that these belong to an individual or a family. We have joint ownership of these items. They belong to everybody in our tribe. They were meant to be transferred from one to another and a process has to go on sometimes within a family to another family. Part of the reason why they are transferred to certain people is because these certain people will make specific vows to acquire the rights of that bundle to be transferred to them. Sometimes these reasons relate to illness and other misfortunes. These sacred items were given to us for these purposes. (Francis First Charger)

> To me, that one [*NAGPRA*] kind of threatens our way. It has [been] interpreted [that] ... our bundles became ... owned by individual families or persons of First Nations, instead of our case [where] these belong to the whole community. So when [we] tried to repatriate those bundles, we had a heck of a time proving who owns them. Ownership in our community, in our way, is different from a white man's ownership and view. We believe that

> we don't own thing[s], that they belong to the Creator and [that] bundles [are] given to our people for specific purposes. (Frank Weasel Head, part 2)

> [T]hese things [are] sacred. One is not the owner of them. They are transferred to them. When one has them transferred to them, for four years he will keep it. Then others will have them transferred to them. The Horns is what I had joined, and they are the ones that I know about. When we joined them, we were unable to transfer them for seventeen years, and we kept them for that long. We did not own them. Those that relied on the Horns – like, for a person to be sick or if one was experiencing extreme bad luck, he would rely on the Horns for help. These are the people who are the next in line to be Horn Society members. The same thing for the Motokiks and the Pipe Holders. So no one can say that they belong to them. Those items that are sold, the sacred items, when we get them back, no one can say, "This is mine. I [am] going to take it back." It would remain the same. (Mary Louise Oka)

Further, the concept of communal property and the responsibilities that arise from individual relationships with spiritual objects extend to many forms of spiritual inheritance, whether involving land, objects, or intangible information, and this makes it difficult to use the term "ownership" in any context relating to cultural heritage. Rather, individuals acquire rights and responsibilities of use through clearly defined transfer processes (discussed in further detail in the next section):

> And those songs, those bundles, belong to the Blackfoot Nation. The way my elders (or grandparents), as I call them, Scraping White and all those people, the way they explain them to me, the Creator gave to us, the Blackfoot people. And those are the protocols of our way of life. So when the Creator gave it to them, it was meant to be passed down not only to one family but also to all Blackfoot people. So they have an order they live by. And those orders are a chain of orders and how you live. And that, you might say, [is] a copyright, like in a white man's way, the Creator gave that copyright to the whole Blackfoot Nation. That is how I look at it. All those given to us, they were not going to be owned by one individual. The real ownership of that copyright belongs to the Creator. He is the one that passed it on for us to use. So that is how, for me, how I look at cultural property, intellectual property right[s]. Every member of the Blackfoot Nation owns them and has a right to them. But they have to do certain things to be able to use them. (Frank Weasel Head, part 1)

> There are other items that we use as part of dancing. Those are not necessarily sacred items, but they are subject to a natural (or traditional) transfer

> process. These are, [for] example, (some are referred to as) belts, whips, and other items that are part of dancing gear. These items also are transferred, but the owner has to give testimony as to the origin of these items. Going back to our teepee designs, a lot of these designs are passed down in our families from one generation to the next. (Francis First Charger)

> These things given to us. These things we heal ourselves with, these plants. An individual is given this gift. He would be the only one who could use it. He would be responsible to keep it sacred. And these songs with it are also sacred songs and they would also be kept sacred (clean). They are also a part of our culture and they must also be kept sacred. They are also given to us for us to use. (Mary Louise Oka)

> I can't talk about the Crazy Dogs Society 'cause those rights have never been given to me. Although I can honestly say as a [member of the] Blood Nation I'm part of it, I own part of it 'cause it was handed down to our people. But I have to make that effort to obtain [the] right to use that. So, it's hard to explain that what cultural property, intellectual property ... that is what it means. (Frank Weasel Head, part 1)

Dorothy First Rider suggests that, aside from a general misunderstanding that may be rooted in different concepts of ownership, further confusion may stem from the presentation of offerings regarding certain rights, privileges, and possession of ritual objects. Indeed, the translation of "payment" is actually a mistranslation of a term that, traditionally, meant "tokens of personal offerings." In a Western frame of thought, "payment" is often the only condition for transferring ownership rights, but in Blackfoot culture "[t]he monetary and material goods offered to care for the bundles are not payments, but merely tokens of sacrifice to care for the bundles for a period of time."[47] An example of this process is outlined in the Blood repatriation submission to the Denver Arts Museum:

> The recipient of a bundle will provide material goods to the previous keeper as a show of the sincerity of his/her desire to take on the care of a particular bundle. One is expected to give whatever one is capable of giving. This practice is referred to as "siikapistaan" an ancient term for which there is no English translation. It clearly does not mean purchase or sale. [Blackfoot people] understand this exchange as a show of respect for the power of the bundle and for the status of the owner as someone who has made great personal sacrifices on behalf of all the people. To the Blackfoot, one is not purchasing the ownership of a physical object so much as assuming the role of contributing to the balance of the relational network amongst all of Creation.[48]

The process of *Siikapistaan* is more properly described as a form of reciprocity than as payment in the Western property law sense. The new keeper retains the communally owned object as a private custodian, caring for it on behalf of all members of the present community and for future generations. In some cases, the transfers can be traced back many generations and through many different hands, all of which form part of the oral history of a particular society:

> I am making reference to Pat Weasel Head Senior. I'm still following the belief that we do not have to write or document our way of life. It was in my house, the house that I have given to my son, it was at that place that we held meetings a little while ago. At that time, he seemed to want to provide us with a lot of the [names of] previous holders of the main Staff of the Horn Society. He went on and on, some he knew by name and [there were] others. He could not recall the name[s]. He stated to me that this is the amount that he can recall, and it was twenty-nine [names]. The person that transferred the bundle to me was Fred Weasel Fat. [He] was the twenty-ninth person. Myself, I was the thirtieth holder. Then he would give me these names that he had of the holders of the leadership staff, but [he said], "You will not be included on the list. When you've transferred your bundle, then you will be on the list. Then those ones that I have named before you will be on the list. Then, when you transfer, then you will be on the list. This is as far as I can recall, and those people that will [be] transferred to in the future, their names will then be added to the list [in] this manner. You then will get a chance to know of those ones that held that leadership bundle in the past." (Adam Delaney)

However, as is the case with cultural protocol and societal norms in any other group, this general framework for transfer is subject to certain anomalies, and these can be further sources of confusion and misunderstanding in repatriation negotiations. For example, generally, when another member of the tribe who has made a vow to assume guardianship of a bundle requests a transfer from a bundle keeper, the bundle keeper is under an obligation to transfer.[49] This protocol reinforces the communal nature of ritual objects in Blood society. But, on occasion, a custodial holder may not grant the request of the prospective transferee and may refuse to transfer the item. To an outsider this may seem to reinforce community acknowledgment of individual and proprietary rights to sacred items and may even be used as an example of a present-day abandonment of traditional protocol. However, such a conclusion would be premature, as refusal may be within the duty of the custodian to protect the bundle and to act in the best interests of the bundle.[50] Even so, a situation may arise in which some holders of bundles may claim individual rights or may refuse to transfer:

> [N]owadays, with these bundles that are in museums, family members are saying, "Oh, they belong to my family," "they belong to my father." No. That it's theirs, that it's theirs. It's not theirs. Their father is the one that got painted for them and got transferred. They don't have, they didn't obtain the right to have them. (Frank Weasel Head, part 2)

Disposition of Ritual Objects Outside the Community

Another potential source of tension in repatriation negotiations involves different understandings of what is required for the valid transfer of legal title. From a Western perspective, an individual can acquire legal title by gift or purchase from another person who has valid legal title. Museums will provide written records signed by individuals who donated or sold items to them, evidence of a familial connection to an object, and legislation as sources of their title. However, the Blood have completely different criteria for governing what constitutes a valid transfer not only of medicine bundles but also of the traditional knowledge associated with them:

> [W]e have people like in museums, or the outside people, talking about our ways. They talk about our ceremonies. They keep songs. They do all these things, but they never obtain the right through the proper transfer. It's got to be done through a ceremony. You [have] got to be painted. You give things. Sure they paid for them. They would probably give money, but they never got painted for them through the ceremonies, and that is the important part. Like, if my boy was going to be a medicine pipe or a medicine bundle holder and I never was, even if he didn't pay a dime [and] I put up all the goods for him and in the ceremony he got painted – I don't, those rights don't belong to me. They belong to him 'cause he is the one that got painted for them. He is the one that obtain[ed] the rights for them. All I did [is] paid and supported him. (Frank Weasel Head, part 1)

> For me, I often think and I follow the instructions of my teachers, my grandfathers. It was me that perhaps spent most of the amount for the Sacred Staff that I acquired ... I had to show sincerity in my wish to be part of the Horn Society. Therefore, I [gave] twenty-eight head of horses for my staff, the leadership staff. Also, there were two saddles included. Also, a bridle, the headdress, and a rifle [were] also included. Of course, there were blankets and money. We don't count the money, just the horses. We count twenty-eight heads. On the other hand, the person that was going to transfer to me did not set a price. He never mentioned that this is the amount or this is what you need to give me ... It was Mookakin, Pat Weasel Head, that was telling the people that I was very generous with my offer. It was after that, many years after that, it was ... after I had the leadership staff,

> that was the time he spoke to me. He told me that I will be, "Transferring my sacred staff to somebody, and don't you think of it, my son, that in the future [when] you transfer your bundle to someone, that you are not to expect to get back what you offered as payment for the staff. It was your own doing and generosity. And on the other hand, I'm going to tell you, my children (and he pointed to my colleagues), it's the same for all of you. For what I have told Adam, my children, if you believe in prayer, you don't set the price on your transfer to the next person, to the next group, that are going to run and take care of our sacred ways. Whatever you get at that time, you give thanks for that." (Adam Delaney)

> I do not sing at all. I do not have the voice, but to my knowledge those sacred songs that are part of [the] transfer process within our people, those originated from our own Blackfoot-speaking people. They are required to be part of the actual process of the transfer. Take, for instance, the pipes and the different societies and the Horn Society[ ]. Those songs are specific to them, and those songs are part of the transferring of the rights of the sacred bundles. (Francis First Charger)

> But to me, copyright is when we transfer through a ceremony, like [the] medicine pipe bundle. I have had three of them. When it was transferred to me, I now have a certain right as a medicine pipe holder. Those rights were transferred, and the songs were transferred to me. The rituals were transferred to me. Now I have a piece of that copyright. To me, that is what copyright is. The traditional way is when things are transferred. Now you have a right to use them. And those songs, those bundles, belong to the Blackfoot Nation. (Frank Weasel Head, part 1)

Teepee designs are also governed by strict transfer protocol, with transfer of designs considered to be invalid when conveyed outside these parameters. As with medicine bundles, the origins and purpose of teepee designs are spiritual. They are ceremonially transferred from one tribal member to another. Because of the nature of teepees, they can be easily appropriated by copying their designs or borrowing liberally from them:

> [L]et's say it might be that, for example, that I simply put any kind of design on my teepee, or maybe somebody will do that on their teepee. But in my understanding, like for myself, I would have to make some reference to a previous owner of this design, like Somatopiiapiksi. I would set out to try and secure information on what teepee design he had from other elders that may have knowledge of that design. Of course, that would then be transferred to you along with the special, using special paints to use the full rights

> to the design. Then anybody who sees the teepee will come to [the] conclusion that ... Francis has taken the teepee design of his grandfather. And also acknowledging that you have the full rights, through [the] transfer process, to the teepee and the design and the concept, whatever goes with the teepee, and that is the way of our people. Our elders teach us that ... there might be an individual that, in their dream, the vision would come to them of a teepee design. And that is accepted as a gift from the spiritual side, and that person may put that design on his teepee, going of course through the proper ceremony that provides him with full rights. I happen[ed] to come across this place where a white man had set up some teepees to whatever his liking, in terms of the designs [that] he had on those teepees. I guess this is where we come to again, to the concern that some of our people have fallen into the trap of the white people that exploit our ways and have assisted in going off our path rather than thinking that they – one of our people – that they need to continue to follow our ways. But because of the power of money, they are lured into these kinds of situations. These designs on our teepees, and in the way we get to secure or acquire designs, we need to continue to follow our tradition in that all designs need to go through a proper transfer of the right of those designs. There are a lot of designs that we've lost that were not transferred. (Francis First Charger)

For the Blood, "payment" and title documents may be irrelevant considerations in the final analysis of the validity of transfer. What is important is who specifically underwent the formal ceremonial transfer processes, whether traditional protocol was adhered to during the process, and whether that party met any relevant qualifications of membership during that process. When these key features are not adhered to as required, the transfer is considered invalid and illegal under traditional Blackfoot protocols.

Associated songs, dances, and stories are also transferred along with certain objects. They are considered essential components of a unified whole, symbiotic and indivisible.[51] Conaty and Janes describe the inseparability of songs and bundles this way:

> We have separated the theological principles and tried to explain how the physical objects (bundles) function within that framework. In reality (or, rather our understanding of reality), there is a much more holistic relationship: one cannot isolate songs from ceremonies from bundles; one cannot think of the relational network without including bundles, other beings, ceremonies, etc. To speak of any one part in isolation is to risk making the whole incomprehensible. To remove any part, such as the holy objects, is to risk making the entire worldview dysfunctional and to risk unbalancing the relational network.[52]

If the associated additional essential elements are not passed with a sacred object there is no way for the new holder to properly transfer the object to a future holder. This also voids the transfer under traditional law.

From the perspective of the Blood, many dispositions of sacred ceremonial items outside the community have occurred in breach of traditional law.[53] Participants emphasize that the disposition of these items outside the community can only be understood if one looks at the history of oppression of Blackfoot culture and the poverty of the Blood people at the time such dispositions occurred. Because Blood culture is now in a state of rejuvenation and renewal, and socio-political and legal structures have been restored to full functionality, systems are in place to govern the transference of sacred items, thereby protecting those items from being alienated:

> In Canada, Canadian Federal policies and legislation, such as the *Indian Act*,[54] prohibited the practise of potlatches and the Sundance until the last major amendment to the *Indian Act* in 1953. During the early 1900s, the Blood Tribe was experiencing economic hardships. It was during this time that tribal society members were not transferring any of the tribe's bundles to new "caretakers." This policy, along with economic factors such as the drought of the 1930s, had a major role in feeding the black market that was already flourishing by the late 1930s to the early [19]50s. Employment was even more difficult to attain, rations were hard to come by, the pass system was in place, and it was during this era that a few tribal members capitalized on the black market that was readily available, to buy religious artifacts that were in their possession for a meagre amount. (Dorothy First Rider)

> [W]hat I'm saying is that the laws are already there. Those items should never have been sold. But you have to appreciate the circumstances in and around the sale of those; some of them were taken, some were exploited, our people were starving around that [time], some of them converted to Christianity, and it wasn't the owners, it was their children, their grandchildren, that took those out ... It was not to go hawk to get a bottle of wine. Each story is different on how they left, even some very sad ones. (Narcisse Blood)

> In the past, when the people did not practise our Indian ways too much, it was when they started selling these items (their holy bundles). They sold them to white people, and there are many of them in the United States, some are in Calgary and others in other areas. There they were all kept locked up, and we were unable [to] use them. There were so few left here, but they remained to be the ones that we had for Sundances. I do know, when we joined the Horn Society around the [19]70s, we, the Horns, had [to] fight for those holy bundles, so that we could get them back. (Mary Louise Oka)

Proof of cultural connection, transfer protocols, centrality of bundles to contemporary spiritual practices, and other issues dominant in repatriation negotiations are primarily based on oral testimony shared by spiritual leaders and elders from the community. This is considered by the Blood to be more reliable than "information contained in the literature provided by informants with questionable motive and collectors and ethnographers who are hampered by problems of translation and cultural biases."[55] Knowledge of spiritual practices and transfer protocols is not antiquated or lost because it is "common knowledge," with transfer protocols being witnessed every year as part of the Sundance ceremony.[56] However, sometimes academic writing, written documentation, and outside experts are used to corroborate aspects of a claim. As Adam Delaney explained earlier, because it is made from items located in a particular region, the bundle itself also speaks to its territorial origin. Given this perspective, the Blood challenge the validity of the title to the objects held by museums and collectors, regardless of the nature and extent of the written documentation surrounding an acquisition or whether it is "judged by current legal standards to have been acquired illegally."[57] However, in the minds of some museums and collectors, the documentation of the acquisition and the possession of the objects are sufficient proof of their title absent independent acceptable evidence of theft by a community member or proof that money or goods were not received under the purchase agreement. Even if a museum is required to consider tribal laws in assessing the validity of title (such as under *NAGPRA*), or a museum feels ethically bound to do so (the position taken by some museums in Canada), proof may continue to be an issue if oral histories are scrutinized under Western legal evidentiary standards of trustworthiness and reliability. Concerns about the accuracy of human memory, historical suppression of indigenous culture, contradictions between the oral record and archival material or academic opinion, and the direct interest of those providing information on the return of the items requested can result in hesitation by museums, governments, and other institutions absent independent evidence supporting the claim. As is demonstrated by past repatriation experiences, the resulting situation may involve personal insult, emotional turmoil, dysfunctional negotiations, and a general breakdown in communication.

There are clear lines of authority within Blackfoot religious societies. Elders and spiritual leaders are able to identify the source of their knowledge and right to speak to particular spiritual matters, and those providing evidence in repatriation negotiations are acutely aware of the importance of their decisions to share spiritual information with the broader community and future generations. Those who have the knowledge and spiritual authority to speak to, or handle, specific ceremonial items are commonly known and respected by members of the broader Blood community. If there is more than one person involved, respect for the decisions of those first consulted is required regardless of disagreement. This is because those giving advice are trusted to do things in the best way they understand and to seek advice when they are not sure. These and the ethic of truthfulness inherent in spiritual leadership are all measures of reliability within the tradition of the Blood Tribe. Part of the challenge for non-indigenous institutions is to step outside their own cultural context and to enter that of another culture in order to understand measures of reliability. However, even when museum personnel or government officials are able to do this, or for ethical reasons are prepared to return items purported to be of ongoing cultural importance to an indigenous community regardless of the legitimacy of acquisition, other fears or legal obstacles may prevent them from responding to repatriation requests in any way other than through long-term loans. In Canada, major museums seek to address some of these concerns through repatriation policies and procedures, and, in some instances, provincial laws have been amended to facilitate the repatriation process. The Blood also have their own set of fears concerning repatriation and the legal processes designed to facilitate it.

The Fear Factor

Coupled with the confusion and disagreement surrounding ownership and transfer, there may exist several innate, underlying sources of fear that may determine the tone of negotiations, direct the actions of the parties involved, or alter the spirit of communication surrounding repatriation discussions. Institutions charged with the safekeeping and maintenance of archaeological or ethnographic materials often view their relationship with the larger society as fiduciary in nature. In addition to legal reprisal, museums that infringe the boundaries of their mandate in the deaccessioning of museum materials may face political or social reprisal. Members of the public who may have considered donating personal collections to the museum may withhold those collections due to concern that it may be forced to repatriate some or all of these items. Popular media may seize the opportunity to exacerbate the circumstances. Funders may need to be consulted before a loan or repatriation may occur, and funding sources could be jeopardized.[58] But, aside from consequential damages, museums may fear damage to items that are loaned or repatriated.[59] Items may need to be reburied under traditional law, or access may be restricted to other First Nations.[60] Further scientific documentation, comparative analysis, or future partnerships to display the items in a public venue may be refused.[61] Academic freedom may be limited.[62] Finally, museums may fear that there is deficient capacity at the community level to enforce traditional law and to prevent the subsequent resale of repatriated materials or that loaned materials will not be returned per the terms of loan agreements.[63]

Museums may also fear that the successful, well-publicized repatriation of ethnographic or archaeological materials may result in other bands suddenly evincing a frenzy of interest in museum collections. This concern, coupled with the educational and public mandate of museums, results in some repatriation policies being narrower in scope than others as well as a reluctance to move beyond long-term loans. However, if one studies the successful partnerships that have been established with museums willing to repatriate to First Nations, museums and other public institutions should realize that this fear is unfounded even when tribes seek the return of a broad range of cultural items:

> I think Canadian museums should really look to the example that has been set ... by "[n]obody loses, everybody wins." [T]heir expertise is based on those collections, so the fearful reaction is [that] they're going to clean us out. You know, that is not what we're saying. But look at [the] Glenbow Museum. They're a lot stronger ... I think they can say we have a relationship with the Blood Tribe ... Relationships, in our ways, are very important. The point being that we can cooperate and have lasting friendships as opposed to somebody just reacting to the unknown. Well, we know now. Look at what [the] Glenbow has been able to do. (Narcisse Blood)

Museums also have concerns about legal liability should they return an item to the wrong community as well as with regard to items that are not clearly within the scope of the law or policy governing their repatriation and deaccessioning process. While some fear that First Nations might take advantage of the priority placed on sacred objects by manipulating the cultural and religious parameters,[64] and while others are concerned about honest mistakes or misunderstandings, the fear of being sued can also fuel reluctance to repatriate in cases where oral and written evidence is contradictory or where oral evidence cannot be independently verified. However, participants in the Blood study did not express concern over cultural items being returned to the wrong community. From their perspective, ethical principles and an understanding of Blackfoot protocols make this impossible. Elders can identify the origin of bundles through the physical characteristics of an item as well as through other means. Ethical principles revealed in the interviews include respect for the spiritual practices of different peoples, truthfulness, acknowledging the limits of one's knowledge and authority, taking care of the spiritual needs of bundles, and not speaking on behalf of people other than the Blood. These principles are demonstrated in interview passages given throughout this case study as well as in those reproduced below:

> We always rely on our elders once we have the information as to where one of our sacred items might be. Of course, they always are prepared and ready to go wherever they might be. And that is the advice that they always, and the role they always, provide for us. Also, some of the items that were, or happened to be, in the possession of the white people, we always seek the direction and the proper protocol and process that needs to take place with or on the advice of our elders. When we meet with the white people, we always allow the elders to make statements in respect to a process that reflects our protocol, and we of course always agree to follow their directions. The fact that all of the sacred items differ from each other, it [is] important that whoever you ask ... help from, the advice [that] the elder has, or ... the one with perhaps the knowledge and the right to deal with those items, [that] those directions need to be followed. For myself, those times that I have been asked to provide assistance on ... if I have doubts of certain things, then, as an elder, [I] will seek advice from another knowledgable person. But in the event that I have complete knowledge ... I will simply proceed ... [I]n some cases one would seek an elder's help, but there are times that that person will dispute the advice of that elder. Sometimes, some have come to me to share, or to ask me, [to] make an opinion on the advice of another elder ... and those times that people come to me, where they have already gone to another elder, I simply tell them that I will not be able to help them because they have already sought the help of another elder. And they should follow what he has already instructed or advised him to do. It is only the right thing to do, and, in the first instance, why would you want to go to that elder and then you decide to go to another elder? You should follow what that first one has advised you to follow. It is, in a way, being disrespectful. Also, you do not seek advice of another elder to help you present your arguments against the advice of another elder. That is not the way of our people. Our way is that we try our best as elders in the way that we were made to understand. That is the way we follow in providing advice to others. (Francis First Charger)

> Us, the elders, I will say, the elders used to own these bundles. They know who owns them. They know who those owners were. They are Kainai's holy bundles. They recognized them. That is why they claimed them ... that (person) owns that ... they recognized who the owner was. There [were] also some that belonged to the South Peigan, that also had been written (on cards). But they (elders) did not attend to those, only those that belonged to Kainai. (Mary Louise Oka)

Speaking to the issue of repatriating human remains, Frank Weasel Head explains how difficult it is to reconcile traditional protocol with modern circumstances and the fears he has about facing new challenges:

> Our protocol is, I keep ... the real protocol of our ancestors. I'm not even allowed to view a dead body. The Blood Tribe has never given permission for human remains to be [exhumed by] archaeologists. There [is] a museum in Chicago has twenty-two or twenty-seven freights of it, [of] Blood Tribe human remains. But those were stole[n] from the Blood Tribe burial site. Because of our protocol, how do I deal with that? I can't, I didn't even view them. They wanted me to but I didn't view them. They want to return them, but who can handle them? Really, no Blood Tribe member. And my suggestion to them was, "You wanna return them so much, phone chief and council, and you guys pay [a] funeral home to come and pick them up in Chicago. You pay the expenses now that you don't have any more use for them. You guys bought them, stole them, and the Blood Tribe will provide maybe a mass grave over at the graveyards and bury them." But I can't handle them. So I really don't know, you know, because now, for us, sometimes we say our elders in the past really had it tough. Even previous elders like my dad and Scraping White. I feel we have it tougher now, dealing with these sorts of things, because they never had to deal with this. So a lot of the things for me, I would say sometimes I get stuck 'cause I don't know how to explain certain things 'cause it is hard. I have to almost balance – say what do I know about past ... and almost form a new thing, a new way. So [I am] trying to bring this in the modern way and the old way and try and put them together. And sometimes I get pretty scared, and am I doing right? Am I doing wrong? What would my ancestors say to me? What would people say to me? So, I have to be very careful. (Frank Weasel Head, part 1)

In another interview, Frank Weasel Head speaks to the issue of enacting laws to assist the Blood, the difficulty of communicating across cultures in different languages, the dangers of putting ideas into written form, the dangers of not participating in the process of making laws when initiatives are undertaken by the white man, and his responsibility to future generations:

> Yes, laws, we have to be very careful when laws are passed. Especially to us, where it is going to affect us directly, we have to be careful. You just can't say this is the way. We have to think carefully ... We have to think [to] include our culture. It should not distort our culture. The white man['s] way of thought is very tricky. That is [why] I say it again: we need you. There are some white words – even though they may be small, too – white man can change the meaning to them. Same thing with us. When someone is talking to you, you have to listen really close to what they are saying. Same thing with our language. When someone talks, he will talk of one thing [and] we could translate in three different ways. What you understand may be totally different to what he is saying. It may be far different to what

> we understand. We can understand one another when we are sitting like this. The way we are sitting, what we are talking about, I might use the same words but differently. That is what we need to think about very closely, so we don't interfere with the meaning of what I'm trying to explain to you. Right now, you have seen and read what the museum has written about the objects they have in there. The white men merely ask the person about the object, and the white man merely writes what he hears. He does not know what the meaning is. There are a lot of written mistakes. It is also hard, it still is with our people that wish to partake in our culture. They would simply talk on and on. With me, I am afraid of that. I try very hard to say the truth in what I say ... How are we going to write these laws to protect these? It is dangerous. No, I will say I find it difficult 'cause I'm afraid. I will not say it is difficult. I will say I'm afraid of it. The white man, if you do not have your say, if you do not sit with these white people, for you do not tell the white man what to write, and if the white man merely writes on his own, it will have a different meaning. The next generation will look at it, and he is going to say it is a bad ruling. Right now there are a lot of young people whom I have heard. These young men have written that Red Crow was crazy making Treaty 7. They say if I was there at the time, I would have gone to war. Look[ing] at this is why I find it difficult, because we cannot only think of ourselves. We need to include the far future generation. (Frank Weasel Head, part 2)

As evidenced in passages quoted earlier in this chapter, those who seek the assistance of elders and spiritual leaders in repatriation negotiations fear that elders may have to be patient in the face of the "ignorance" of the white man[65] or that they may be exposed to "unnecessary hardship" and "emotional turmoil."[66] Elders may fear that they will not be respected and that information shared could be misused, misquoted, or decontextualized in a way that does not fairly and accurately represent Blood culture. These and the other fears outlined above contribute to the atmosphere surrounding some repatriation negotiations. They underlie what is said and give context to actions that otherwise may seem confusing. They fuel emotion and they direct communication. But they also reflect a hidden source of common ground: each side values the material at issue, respects the necessity of proper transfer, and fears the consequences of breach of process and protocol within their respective systems. In this sense, even in the most difficult and cumbersome negotiations, one may find common ground and a seed from which to grow a partnership based on mutual respect and understanding. The vast ideological differences pertaining to property ownership and transfer, and the many fears that may inundate repatriation efforts, serve as a backdrop for the specific repatriation efforts of the Blood. Together, they contextualize words and actions, explain attitudes and source emotions.

Legislative Intervention

Even when positive relationships are created and fears associated with negotiating repatriations are overcome, legal barriers can prevent the return of cultural items to First Nations. For example, although the Glenbow worked with the Blood to allow loans of ceremonial items, provincial legislation prevented them from deaccessioning items in their collection for the purpose of repatriation. The *Glenbow-Alberta Institute Act* specifies that objects in the museum's collection are held for the benefit of the people of Alberta.[67] Ministerial approval is required to deaccession items, but prior to the enactment of the *Repatriation Act*, such approval was hard to obtain.[68] Further, as both the Glenbow and the provincial museum were making increasingly extensive loans, the government felt that a consistent and transparent process was required to guide such decisions.[69] Although initially reluctant to support legislation because of negative experiences with the constraints of definitional frameworks in *NAGPRA* and a fear of ruining positive relations developed with museums, some of the participants in the study worked with the Glenbow and the Province of Alberta to craft legislation that would accommodate the permanent return of medicine bundles to the Blackfoot.

The *Repatriation Act* was designed to "harmonize the role museums play in the preservation of human heritage with the aspirations of First Nations to support traditional values in strong, confident First Nations communities."[70] The *Act* provides a process for the Glenbow and the Royal Alberta Museum to return to First Nations in Alberta sacred ceremonial objects, the title to which is vested in the Crown under Canadian law, "used in the practice of sacred ceremonial traditions," and that continue to be "vital for the practice of those traditions."[71] First Nations may initiate a repatriation process by applying to the minister of community development in accordance with the regulations. The minister approves the proposed repatriation, unless in her/his opinion the repatriation would be inappropriate.[72] Upon the successful repatriation of a sacred ceremonial object, the First Nation gains title to the object and holds it on behalf of all the people of that First Nation.[73] The 251 objects previously listed under the Blackfoot agreement were incorporated into the legislation as objects whose title would be transferred upon passage of the legislation.[74] Sacred objects whose title is vested in the Crown but that are not included in the Blackfoot agreement, such as those that exist in the provincial museum of Alberta, can be applied for in accordance with the regulations.

The *Repatriation Act* may be a major stepping stone to the full repatriation of First Nations ceremonial objects in Alberta. However, it began as a result of a partnership that was built on trust and understanding, not legal rights and obligations. Further, it took four years from its enactment to reach agreement on the regulation necessary to transfer title.[75] At the time of his interview for this study, the Blackfoot regulation was not yet in place, leaving Frank Weasel Head wondering whether the legislation would ultimately accomplish what it was intended to and operate to the benefit to the Blood Tribe:

> Now the one in Alberta, we haven't even come to the final stages. We [are] still on how to implement ... the rules and regulations. On that law, we have been helping them. We [are] still having difficulty. So I guess I have [to] wait until I actually see the rules and regulations in place so I can fully comment on it ... I'm not a politician or a lawyer, to really think of white man's laws and how they affect us ... in our ways, but people just didn't understand. [At] contact, we have our own law, our own systems in place. We had all those things in place but they did not understand them. (Frank Weasel Head, part 2)

Despite progress made in Alberta, opinions vary on the desirability of legislative intervention. All participants emphasized the need for education, cooperation, and understanding. Those who spoke to the issue of law reform emphasized the importance of involving both the elders and the younger generation educated in the white man's ways. Some also spoke to the importance of learning from the lessons of *NAGPRA*. One participant specifically identified a need for federal repatriation law. However, all participants are concerned that relying too much on white man's ways can, if the Blood are not careful, undermine internal processes and that, despite their unique cultures, all First Nations might be treated the same. As indicated earlier, whether in the context of defining material culture covered by proposed legislation or finding the right words to incorporate Blood understandings of any agreement reached, participants are also concerned about the "trickiness" of the English language. All participants emphasized the existence of internal laws and processes and the need for these to be respected in any protection and repatriation strategy adopted. Many involved in the repatriation process also understand the legal and political barriers to the process and the rationale for legislated guidelines in Alberta. For these reasons, it is important that the Blood be active participants in any legislative reform:

> *Dennis First Rider*: Do you think it is necessary for the white authority to write regulations, such as these holy items or those things in the museum, in order to protect them?
>
> *Mary Louise Oka*: Yes, they should ... so that they could protect them. So

> that they would not be abused and that the white man would not use them. It was given to us, for us to use them, and they would be kept well.

> Canada needs to seriously examine the need for federal repatriation laws. The law would definitely require First Nation input, and Canada would have to learn from the experiences, both positive and negative, of *NAGPRA*, and entertain a law that would be fair to the museums and to First Nations people. A federal law would have to be pursued immediately, because resource people, mainly elders, from First Nation communities are declining. (Dorothy First Rider)

> It is now you people [Dorothy First Rider and other Kainai members] are those that we now have to rely on to properly arrange these things and say that these are the things that our grandparents – our older brothers, our fathers, our mothers, our older sisters – this is what they had told us. That is how I understand it, and that is the way we could write these properly. *Don't let them write them, my daughter. You write them if there is a need for new rules*. (Frank Weasel Head, part 2, emphasis added)

> *Frank Weasel Head:* The language is different and cultural. Even within our reserve, we have four different dialects. We say we are a Blackfoot Confederacy. The four reserves are different so that the people have to be careful and have to respect that. Also, that is the other thing, sometimes you have groups, AFN [Assembly of First Nations] as you say, a spokesperson [for] all First Nations. But to me, that also worries me because they're way down there. What do they know of our ways?

> *Dorothy First Rider* (interviewer): So, I guess what we have to say is that we have to be careful when we say First Nations participation. It cannot be misconstrued to mean, for example, [by] the political representative that may be AFN. It would be people directly involved in repatriation in our language and religion.

> *Frank Weasel Head:* When I talk about participation, I don't only talk of political leaders. I talk of you that are directly involved. And there is enough of you well educated to [be] able to do that. (Frank Weasel Head, part 2)

One participant touched on another serious challenge – private collection repatriation. However, most did not address the issue of private repatriations. At this point, the Blood strategy in this difficult area seems to be to hope that major museum reforms brought about by legal and ethical challenges will, in turn, lead to a moral reconsideration on the part of private collectors.

Human Remains

Participants relayed very strong views about the removal of human remains from Kainai territory and the storage of human remains in facilities away from those lands. Even the discussion of human remains is taboo, with the disturbance or removal of those materials precipitating an emotional response in those who shared their opinions. Human remains are to be left undisturbed, and the community is to respect the area where the remains are located:

> Now the human remains issues, the way that I was taught by my grandfathers, my spiritual grandfathers, there is something that should be preventable and people have to respect a person that has gone. His remains have to be left there. We always know the gravesite and we always will respect that. (Francis First Charger)

Given traditional methods for treating remains, the Blood do not have ancient burial grounds. Further, under traditional protocol, viewing human remains is strictly forbidden under traditional protocol:

> [W]e don't deal with human remains as you see it now. I'm not even allowed to view a dead body. We would put them up in scaffolds and there they were left alone. 'Cause they have gone back to the Creator and they are to be left alone. 'Cause he has taken them, a person back. Now that person's spirit ... belongs to him. (Frank Weasel Head, part 1)

Despite these historical practices, human remains associated with the Blood Tribe have found their way into the storage rooms of museums and government institutions, many of which in Canada have adopted repatriation, and many museums have, in recent times, adopted liberal policies with clear criteria to expedite the return of those remains. However, as Frank Weasel Head explained earlier, because of the protocol preventing members of the Blood from handling or viewing remains, transporting remains, or executing many other logistical requirements regarding the identification of culturally affiliated remains, there may be a reluctance to retrieve these materials.[76] From his perspective, once human remains are disinterred, the onus should be on those in possession of the materials to return them. This includes providing experts to identify the remains, paying for shipment, and providing personnel to handle them and to reinter them. This duty is necessary in order to bring questionable past behaviour into line with present ethical and moral standards. The Blood role in the process is merely to provide a place for reburial and to advise museum personnel on the necessary protocol that should be adhered to during each stage of the operation.

Protection

Protection and conservation are intertwined with the Blackfoot worldview, with the Blackfoot considering themselves to be stewards of the gifts of language, lands, resources, plants, and animals that surround them. Participants identified language and sacred sites as key areas in need of protection. Although language was not explicitly raised in the interview questions, this focus may have come about because both of these areas are very susceptible to influences operating both inside and outside the Blood community and, given the interjurisdictional nature of these areas, require the establishment of partnerships in any initiative directed at protection.

Land

The Blood celebrate their important relationship with the land, viewing themselves as caretakers of all that is around them. The Royal Commission on Aboriginal Peoples summarized this relationship as follows:

> The land was considered a mother, a giver of life, and the provider of all things necessary to sustain life. A deep reverence and respect for Mother Earth infused and permeated Indian spirituality, as reflected in the Blackfoot practice of referring to the land, water, plants, animals and their fellow human beings as "all my relations." Relations meant that all things given life by the Creator ... the Creator had given them their own territory and entrusted them with the responsibility of caring for the land and all their relations ... Sacred sites were located in mountains and hills. Along with rocks, rivers and lakes these sites were designated for various purposes – vision quests, burial sites, recreational or medicinal uses, Sundances and meeting (council) places within the Blackfoot territorial domain. Each site was named for its unique quality and special rôle in the rituals of the nation and became part of the living landscape to be visited and revisited each year. Gifts were left to pay tribute to the spirits that lived there. Since the spirit (soul) would return automatically to its maker, the people of the plains did not worry about death or the hereafter but concerned themselves with the care of the living things around them.[77]

All participants agreed that more needed to be done to protect sacred sites and the importance of the Sundance grounds to Blood spiritual and social life. However, when prompted about which sites are sacred and should be the focus of protection initiatives, participants were reluctant to prioritize and categorize sites in this way:

> Everything is sacred. Whole Mother Earth is sacred. So those other sites, Writing-on-Stone, where we have our Sundance, Buffalo Jump, those are

> sacred sites. But they also have a bigger significance. That is where part of our existence start[s]. Like the Women's Buffalo Jump, that's where the marriages took place ... When you walk through the whole reserve, it is sacred. Why do we hold it in great significance when we [go by] a teepee ring? Because it is [a] sacred thing. Let's say my house was demolished and we found traces of it. Would we consider it significant or a sacred site? No, because I'm saying, like I said before ... Just because it is a white man's style of a house, we won't consider it sacred. But a teepee we consider sacred. So how can I say which site [is] to be protected? Should I say our Sundance site should be protected or preserved 'cause that is where we gather? And another one that should be preserved is Mookakin Foundation. Another one is Writing-on-Stone. We are making [it] into a national and historical site. We are working with Parks Canada. Hopefully by September, this should be protected. I don't know. So those sites should be protected. Those sites, a lot of the sites are preserved where our beginnings were, from Waterton Lakes to Writing-on-Stone. They all have a connection, but they are all part of our reserve. Those sites need to be respected. (Frank Weasel Head, part 1)

In the Blood worldview, all of Mother Earth is considered sacred. Participants were reluctant to categorize sites into those that need protection and those that don't because all traditional territories are considered to have a relevant place with regard to defining who the Blood are and where they came from. Although the Blood have also realized and acted upon the need to work in partnership with others to protect certain sites, all Blood Tribe land is considered to be connected with the past and to be essential to educating new generations about themselves: who they are, where they came from, and where they are going.

Certain sites are used by elders to supplement and facilitate oral history and traditional knowledge and the passage of that knowledge to the next generation. As physical manifestations of the past, they are interactive tools used in the instruction of others:

> He (Pat) immediately started to tell us stories. He took us over to a campsite teepee ring. He went directly to the actual site ... From what I can gather from Pat, it was in those times that our men went on raids. He stated that this person was ranked high in this activity. He also did manage to take a lot from the enemy on these raids. So, upon his moving off his camp, he left his trademark on the site that he had camped on with rocks by making marks with rocks on the four sides – north, east, south, and west. It was after that that I've heard others make reference to the fireplace on that east end of the ring as the fireplace and the other one on the west as being a

> place for smudging. He (Pat) told us to pay attention to the size of the camp. It was large for those times. It has been there for quite a while. There are two fireplaces referred to as "two stoves." It was because of the size of the teepee that it needed to have two fireplaces to keep it warm. He then, Pat, directed our attention to the location of this camp teepee ring. He was right, that from here, you are able to see quite a ways out there for enemies. It was such that you can detect anybody (or the enemy), even if that person was crawling on the ground. This was the kind of history Pat shared with us that day. It was then my friend Peter asked Pat, "What about at night? How would anybody detect the enemy out there?" Pat replied ... "It was the job for our dogs to alarm us." (Adam Delaney)

Given this important role, it is clear that these sites contribute to the cultural knowledge and sustainability of the Blood people. Each time a site is destroyed or altered, or access to it is impeded, the Blood lose a piece of their culture. Some owners of lands surrounding the Blood Reserve have realized this and have granted the Blood unlimited access to those sites and have purposefully avoided them in their development of those lands:

> [S]omething happened when we were ... making a submission against the Pine Coulee plight. Some of those ranchers came by to us and said: "We support you. On my ranch (or on my property), I have not touched that site. Visit them anytime you want." We have those as well as others that have destroyed those, uh, sites. The person was able to surmise that these must be important ... important enough that he won't put them underground. (Narcisse Blood)

Unfortunately, partnerships of this sort are not universal, and many important sites continue to be threatened by expansive developments around the Blood Reserve. For this reason, the Blood have been active in the protection and documentation of these sites and have sought out new partnerships that would provide better protection and access. They have also initiated internal strategies, including a band council resolution concerning research in relation to archaeological sites and other cultural properties. The protocol is, in part, a response to concern about the way in which outsiders are misrepresenting the sites.[78] However its primary function is to protect Blood cultural heritage, ensure the cultural integrity of information published, and provide the Blood with access to the products of research. It requires the authorization of the chief and council for research to be conducted on the reserve as well as their approval of research outcomes prior to publication, with the Blood Tribe retaining full access to that information.[79] In the resolution, cultural properties are defined as:

> comprised of but not limited to the customs, religion; religious practices, religious artifacts, traditions, language, ancient burial sites; both on and off the reserve, funerary objects, arts and crafts; dating from pre-contact, sacred objects, tools, ornaments, oral history; elders testimonies, and archaeological sites and finds.[80]

The Blood Tribe Research Department also began a Cultural Geography Project that documented the known locations of buffalo kill sites, buffalo jump sites, teepee rings, medicine wheels, and cairns as well as some of the distinctive features of these sites, their cultural significance, and the archaeological materials often found in association with them.[81] Progress has also been made in the protection of Writing-on-Stone. First created as a provincial park by the Province of Alberta in 1957, an archaeological preserve was created within the park in 1977 to protect that area that held the greatest concentration of rock art.[82] In 1981, a portion of the park was designated as a provincial historical resource,[83] and, recently, it was designated a national historic site. Writing-on-Stone has the greatest concentration of Plains people rock art, with over fifty individual rock art sites containing thousands of rock art figures, and it continues to be one of the largest areas of protected natural prairie in the Alberta Provincial Park system.[84] The Blood worked with Parks Canada to have the park recognized as a national historic site. This partnership, and others like it, was encouraged by the report of the Panel on the Ecological Integrity of Canada's National Parks, released in March 2000.[85]

Recommendation 7-4 of the report focuses on cultural sites, sacred areas, and artifacts. What is foremost is ensuring the protection of such historical resources under the auspices of Parks Canada. The return to First Nations of all sacred artifacts and human remains currently in Parks Canada's possession, using proper ceremonies and rites, is advocated, as is negotiating with aboriginal peoples to create a secure and private inventory of sacred areas so that they can be better protected. Facilitating the execution of ceremonies and rites that aboriginal peoples believe necessary for their culture is noted here. The panel also proposes empowering and enabling First Nations peoples to tell their own stories in the parks, including direct participation in interpretive program planning and delivery.

For the Blood, the positive results of these initiatives have been better protection of, and access to, these sites. Also, because the interpretation of the site has been developed in conjunction with the Blood, park facilities are a resource that will, in turn, contribute to the cultural education of the next generation:

> [L]ike Writing-on-Stone. We didn't have hardly any access to it, but now we realize the importance of better access ... [W]e said if we're going to

> participate, access [is] for our young people. Our young people can go there and say this [is] what took place from our ancestors. These are how the writings are here. (Frank Weasel Head, part 1)

Hence, progress is being made in the protection of off-reserve sites of cultural importance. Partnerships are being made; relationships with neighbours, institutions, and governments are being enhanced; and the cultural heritage of the Blood is being documented with new accuracy – a legacy for Blood youth. However, the efforts to protect off-reserve sacred sites is not the only battle in the war raging to preserve the cultural heritage of the Blood people. Throughout the interviews, participants repeatedly mentioned that more needs to be done and more resources are required to preserve and to protect sacred sites on reserve as well as off reserve.

Language and Intangible Cultural Heritage

Those interviewed identified language as the aspect of Blood culture most in need of protection. The language of the Blood is Kainai, a dialect of Blackfoot unique to the Blood, and it is considered the foundation upon which all other advances in education, cultural protection, and revitalization will be built. It also continues to be the medium by which cultural knowledge is transferred between generations of Blood people and is used to sensitize outsiders through communication and sharing of information. But the meaning portrayed in words in Blackfoot is easily lost when these words are decontexualized and alienated from the socio-cultural matrix in which they were born. Complicating matters is the linguistic diversity that is present between First Nations across Canada and among the Blackfoot themselves. Even a direct translation can result in an inaccurate or incomplete meaning when words are stripped from their cultural context. This was one of the major obstacles identified by elders at the time of treaty, and it continues to be a problem today:

> The most important item, and I will tell it to you again, is our language ... and when you translate our language, be careful. Don't translate word for word; interpret what the individual is saying, what that individual means. Don't – word for word doesn't make sense. [You've] got to interpret what the individual is saying 'cause right now, some translators, they translate word for word, and it is a different meaning. (Frank Weasel Head, part 2)

In 1994, the Blood Tribe band council resolved to create a mechanism composed of elders, ceremonial leaders, professional, and members of the Blood Tribe at large to develop and implement a plan that would "ensure that Blackfoot is recognized, used and promoted in every aspect of community life including governmental; administrative including all tribal programs and services; educational; social and recreational."[86] One initiative coming out of this policy development has been the introduction of Kainai into the Alberta-directed curriculum operating on the Blood Reserve. As illustrated in the comments of one participant, though this approach has its challenges, it can be viewed as an opportunity to take the best of both worlds, reconciling the ways of Blood and non-Blood:

> We have to work with Alberta curriculum and say, "[H]ey, language to us is very important." They have to change their ways of testing our children in those tests. And I don't believe in tests [of] children, but they have got to change their ways. Maybe doing some of those tests with our own people, in our language, to enforce that our language stays in place. We can never lose our language. If we lose our language, there is no use talking about this. There is no use. So the process has to take it where government takes action and recognizes the importance of First Nation language. And how [do] they do it? I don't know. This [is] where, I again turn back to the educators. You have to do this. You have to fight for us, for the old people, the young people, for the children, for yourselves. This is what you need. I think if you instill those things into the children ... our leaders ... our educators ... our administrators – our own knowledge – then they would gather the two knowledges and put the two knowledges together, to know how to put that in. (Frank Weasel Head, part 2)

Traditionally, knowledge was passed entirely through verbal instruction and demonstrative action during the recitation of songs and stories and the performance of activities such as hunting, fishing, processing and preparing food, and the performance of ceremonies and dances. As explained earlier in the discussion of concepts of ownership, certain knowledge is also associated with the transfer of bundles. Language was the medium that facilitated the transfer of information in all of these things, and, therefore, recording or writing down such information, even for the purposes of instruction, is inconsistent with traditional processes:

> [I]n the past, there at our Sundance grounds, that is where our people gathered. When we gathered there they would dance, others would play hand games, others would pray there. The songs sung there were all holy songs and there were no recordings. There were no tapes used. (Mary Louise Oka)

> [T]here are many things that those of the Horn Society are told not to speak about. You will, however, see them as they dance out. They will not have their pictures taken. And their songs are a part of the Sundance. And one cannot take them (tape), these things that take songs and what is

> said. It is them (Horns) that can sing them, to use in their ceremonies. Oki. Those that sit inside (the lodge), one is told of what he has done once we all congregate inside (the lodge) of the Horn Society. It is those things that I cannot talk about, what goes on ... inside. It is depending on how one receives the bundle he received, [that is what] would dictate one's behaviour on the inside. He would not be allowed to add, delete, or adjust any portion other than the way he received it. We cannot tell what goes on ... inside. It is holy. They are very sacred. (Mary Louise Oka)

A paradox arises whereby, if the community does not undertake to document its ways, others involved in the documentation may supply inaccurate information that could later be used to document Blood culture and language. However, documentation runs the risk of decontextualizing information and opening a door to cultural appropriation:

> There are those who are against writing or documenting our way of life. Then there are those that it didn't matter to them if we write or did not write it, our way of life. It was after that that I kept thinking about it. That it was true, if we do not write it, or document some of these things, our legends, our way of life [misunderstanding occurs]. I [will] give you an example. A white man, he makes a mistake. The white man believes that, he assumes that all of us Nitsiitapii, the Indian people, we all know all about our way of life. No, just like the way we are sitting here today. If you knew, as an interviewer, then you would not have to come here today. Yeah, and that is the way that some of the white people take us. They assume that everybody knows (or all of us know) about our way of life, especially our sacred ways. (Adam Delaney)

Kainai is viewed as belonging to the Blood community, but it is also the legacy of previous generations and an inheritance to those not yet born. In this sense, the language itself is considered to be communally owned by all who are or will be Blood people. However, there are restrictions to this general rule, such as those governing the transference of names and songs. Names are transferred ceremonially from individual to individual. Once a name is given, it should not be transferred to another without the permission of the owner of the name.

As discussed earlier, some songs belong to the Blood community as a whole. Ceremonial songs are held under the auspices of separate Blood societies, on behalf of the larger Blood community. However, many songs are ceremonial and require the person performing them to be a qualified member of a Blood society and to undergo the proper transfer ceremony to receive the right to perform the song(s). Traditional law still strictly governs the transfer process and the context of its recitation. On occasion, this safety net has failed to prevent the exploitation of songs. At the same time, some see copyright as a possible mechanism for theft rather than as a tool to reduce these dangers:

> *Frank Weasel Head:* Heard one story down in the States that, at a ceremony, this one guy videotaped it and sent it off and copyright[ed] it. The next year, when they were going to do the ceremony, he got the law and said that's mine and was charging them $2,500 to do the ceremony. That is why it is important to protect them. But how do we protect them in the white man's law? Maybe one of these year[s], maybe one of [our] own people [is] going to take [a] video of the Medicine Pipe Dance and he's going to send it off, get a copyright, and he's going to charge the real people that have a right to do it, and he's going to charge them a bunch of money to do it. But how do we protect them?
> *Dennis First Rider:* There was this one person in a situation similar to what you are saying. Do you remember Gladstone and that song he made? Tell us what you think.
> *Frank Weasel Head:* Well, that is a social dance, and this is what I mean about transfers. Go back to the beginning when I talked about transfers. That guy made a song about it, but this guy didn't ask his permission to use the song or he didn't tell him he can use the song. He just went ahead and he used the song without that transfer or without that permission. So yeah, in a way, he owned the right to that song and somebody used it without that transfer or without that agreement (or that permission). So it is almost similar to white man's law. (Frank Weasel Head, part 1)

Although copyright law may be misunderstood, the perception is that Western law is allowed to trump traditional law whenever the two are in conflict. According to this participant, there is already a mechanism in place to transfer such property – a mechanism analogous to "copyright" in a Western paradigm – and it has operated with sufficient potency to prevent exploitation. However, because Western law does not recognize this authority, the traditional mechanism governing transfer is irrelevant to anyone who chooses to act against cultural protocol.

Conclusion

Blood culture has survived and thrived despite the imposition of a foreign legal system. Unbridled policies of settlement, economic development, assimilation and colonization, and the deleterious effects wrought by them – such as disease, famine, poverty, fierce competition for resources, and the virtual extinction of the buffalo in southern Alberta – did not break the ancient chain of transfer of cultural and spiritual knowledge through ceremony, sacred objects and places, tradition, language, dance, and song. However, the cumulative effects of these events have taken their toll on the sustainability of Blood culture, especially when considered alongside the subsequent imposition of the reserve system and residential schools, Christian proselytizing, and the criminalization of indigenous religious practices and ceremonies through the legal prohibition of cultural and spiritual practices.

Academic consideration of the concept of cultural sustainability has largely been explored in terms of how economic or sustenance activities on the land – such as hunting, fishing, trapping (and preserving access to sufficient lands in which to perform these activities) – are integral to the maintenance of culture and how resource planning and management processes can accommodate these uses of the land. More recently, academic notions of cultural sustainability have grown to acknowledge the importance of the social and spiritual values that are intrinsically linked to and perpetuated by those activities.[87] What has become clear in the course of this chapter is that, although the cultural and spiritual values of the Blood are interconnected with economic and subsistence activities, the cultural and spiritual well-being of the Blood transcends those activities and embodies the continued interaction with, maintenance of, and access to cultural heritage. Therefore, the protection and repatriation of cultural heritage (whether in the form of teepee designs, sacred bundles, other sacred or ceremonial objects, or non-ceremonial objects pertaining to cultural patrimony, songs and dances, language, sites, cultural knowledge, design, and intellectual property) and the processes governing the valid transfer, use, and care of that property are essential to the sustainability of Kainai culture and the health of the Kainai community as a whole.

Alienation, destruction, and loss of cultural heritage strikes at the very heart of the Blood's ability to adapt to or resist change. The annual Sundance draws together the tribe's religious societies to perform sacred ceremonies, dances, and songs, and it continues to be a major venue for those societies to initiate new members and to transfer knowledge and responsibilities among existing members. Medicine bundles and the numerous items, songs, dances, and information associated with them are integral to the spiritual life of the Blood and continue to be used in the performance of spiritual ceremonies necessary for the transmission of specialized knowledge, healing powers, rights, and responsibilities to individuals within a religious society. Sites of sacred or historical significance reaffirm the long and intimate relationship of the Blood to the land and continue to be used by elders to supplement and facilitate oral history and traditional knowledge and the passage of that knowledge to the next generation. These things have permeated the very institutions, structures, and activities governing the larger Blood society. Therefore, the loss or destruction of the cultural heritage of the Blood people directly affects the sustainability of Blood culture generally, community health specifically, and the ability of future generations to adapt to or resist the pressures of a changing environment.

This chapter details the various initiatives that the Blood have undertaken to both protect and to repatriate their cultural heritage. Following through with these initiatives has often involved large expenditures of both time and money and has, in many cases, required invasive external audits of Kainai ideology, belief systems, and concepts of property and transfer as well as sacred religious rites and practices. Despite these challenges, the Kainai have remained unshaken in their resolve. Yet not all experiences have been negative, and something can be learned from common traits of positive and negative experiences. Positive experiences were associated with non-adversarial relationships built on mutual trust, respect, and the understanding of cultural differences. Time and resources were set aside to build confidence and understanding, to share concerns and to communicate. Cultural sensitivity training on both sides involved discussions of protocol and obligations and requirements under both Western and traditional Blood law. Negative experiences occurred when parties lost respect for one another or when no opportunity presented itself for relationship building to occur. Problems included failure to adequately assess questions such as the communal nature of property and the legality of its alienation within the cultural context and worldview of the Kainai and without proper regard for the oral testimonies of respected elders and ceremonialists. Communication in these situations was either non-existent, inadequate, or had deteriorated to the point of being regimental and meaningless. An over-zealous adherence to legal definitions, standards of proof, guidelines, policy, and procedure, or an inability or unwillingness to compromise, also typified these situations.

The protection and repatriation of cultural property is a complex, difficult, and politically sensitive issue. But even though the subject matter is complex and the benefits may appear distant, social and legal research needs to press on in this area. The next volume of this research program considers legal and non-legal responses to repatriation and protection issues. This includes consideration of the utility of repatriation legislation and whether indigenous concepts of ownership and transfer can be recognized, accommodated, and empowered in Canadian law. The Kainai study offers many important lessons in this regard, including the following conclusions, which were reviewed and affirmed by participants and the board of the Mookakin Cultural Society:

1 Although this study is cast in the language of property, at the core of the matter is respect for cultural identity and human rights. The Kainai seek respect for their culture and to preserve the integrity and survival of their laws, customs, and practices concerning responsibilities and

transfer of ceremonial and other cultural items. This requires Kainai control over their own forms of cultural transmission, education of outsiders about Kainai culture, and protection and preservation of their cultural heritage, including lands and language.

2 Laws are expressed in different ways among different cultures. The laws of the Kainai concerning proper transfer are rooted in spirituality, oral traditions, and ceremonial protocols that have been adhered to continuously by the Blackfoot people. Violations of these laws can only be properly understood with reference to specific historical, political, and economic circumstances that undermined, but failed to prevent, the continuity of Kainai culture.

3 Legislation can operate to help shift attitudes, overcome legal barriers to return, facilitate respect for First Nations laws and customs, support the continuity of ceremonial traditions and religious practices, and provide opportunity for increased dialogue. For example, like *NAGPRA*, it can require that indigenous laws determine the legal rights of an individual to alienate communal cultural patrimony. However, in an attempt to achieve certainty of title and to apply uniform standards and procedures, legislation can also operate to undermine and to threaten the diversity and survival of indigenous laws and cultures. Strict adherence to definitions, different cultural understandings of words, reliance on written documentation, imposition of culturally biased evidentiary standards, and other problems associated with legal frameworks can generate a lack of flexibility that is detrimental to building positive relationships and achieving repatriation goals. For these reasons, it is important that First Nations play an active role in law reform, that they move beyond consultation and actually participate in drafting, interpretation, and implementation.

4 Those with knowledge and authority to speak to laws concerning cultural heritage are well known within the Kainai community. They are guided by ethics and protocols that ensure that cultural items will be returned to the rightful custodians. Their authority exists independent of the band council. Further, those with authority in one community cannot speak to the laws of another community. Any attempt at law reform must resist placing authority in non-indigenous institutions and respect indigenous decision-making structures.

5 The Kainai appreciate the role museums have played in preserving ceremonial items in their custody and the support of certain museums in the repatriation process. Successful partnerships with institutions such as the Glenbow Museum of Alberta have been instrumental in achieving repatriation goals. The Task Force on Museums and First Peoples has also resulted in increased dialogue, cooperation, and the loan and return of cultural material. However, the existing legal environment

concerning ownership and museum liability may create barriers to return. Legislation may assist to overcome some of these barriers, as was the case in Alberta.

6 There are significant social and economic costs associated with the repatriation process. Financial support for both museums and First Nations engaged in repatriation and protection negotiations would substantially aid in furthering repatriation efforts.

The culture of the Blood Tribe is alive and well. An archaeological excavation did not take place in order to gather data for this research. Living members of the Blood Tribe, participants in this study, have emphasized the importance of repatriating sacred and ceremonial items and have clearly stated that the protection of Blackfoot language, land, ceremonial sites, and intangible cultural heritage from loss, destruction, and appropriation is vital for the continuity of Blood Tribe cultural practices and identity. Although the roles of government and museums are changing, archaic concepts of assimilation and colonization have not been entirely abandoned. Perhaps the dawn of the new millennium is heralding an era of true consultation, negotiation, equal partnership, and meaningful communication between First Nations, governments, and museums; and maybe such discussion will, in turn, spawn a greater understanding of the continuing importance of cultural heritage to the cultural sustainability of the Blood Tribe.

Notes

1 The legislation referred to here is the *Native American Graves Protection and Repatriation Act*, 25 U.S.C.A. ss. 3001-3013 (West Supp. 1991) [*NAGPRA*].

2 Assembly of First Nations and the Canadian Museums Association, *Turning the Page: Forging New Partnerships between Museums and First Peoples* (Ottawa: Canadian Museums Association, 1992) at 9.

3 The Blood have negotiated the return of medicine bundles and ceremonial items from the Provincial Museum of Alberta (now the Royal Alberta Museum), the Glenbow-Alberta Institute, the Canadian Museum of Civilization, the National Museum of the American Indian, the Denver Arts Museum, the Boston Peabody Museum, the Field Museum of Chicago, and, most recently, the Marischal Museum in Scotland.

4 The legislation referred to here and discussed further below is the *First Nations Sacred Ceremonial Objects Repatriation Act*, R.S.A. 2000, c. F-14 [*Repatriation Act*].

5 Although the word "object" is inadequate to describe the multiple dimensions of ceremonial material, the Mookakin Foundation chose to use this term for lack of a better English equivalent. The bundles with which this study is concerned are those that are transferred to authorized members of societies or that are held for the benefit of the community. Six interviews were conducted. Unfortunately, the recording of Marten Heavy Head was inaudible, and the researchers were unable to arrange for a second interview prior to the completion of the case study phase of the project. However, he did participate in the research project symposium in June 2005 and in the review of this study.

6 See appendix on page 491 of this volume. In addition to the standard question set, Blackfoot elders were asked whether they were involved in the process leading up to Alberta's repatriation legislation and, if so, whether legislation was necessary.

7 Interview of Francis First Charger by Dorothy First Rider (31 January 2003), Blood Reserve, Alberta [translated by Dorothy First Rider]. Transcripts for all interviews are held by the Mookakin Society in Standoff, Alberta. At the time of writing, placement in a public archive had not yet been determined.

8 Interview of Mary Louise Oka by Dennis First Rider (17 April 2003), Blood Reserve, Alberta [translated by Dennis First Rider].

9 The interview of Frank Weasel Head was in two parts. First interview of Frank Weasel Head by Dennis First Rider (25 February 2003), Standoff, Alberta (Frank Weasel Head, part 1) [translated by Dennis First Rider]; second interview with Frank Weasel Head by Dorothy First Rider (7 April 2003), Calgary, Alberta (Frank Weasel Head, part 2) [translated by Dorothy First Rider].

10 Interview of Adam Delaney by Dennis First Rider (17 December 2002), Blood Reserve, Alberta [translated by Andy Blackwater and Dennis First Rider].

11 *Supra* note 2 at 1. For further discussion of the litigation that ensued and the task force report, see Catherine Bell *et al.*, "First Nation Cultural Heritage: A Selected Survey of Issues and Initiatives," this volume at 369 and 372-74, respectively.

12 *Glenbow Museum First Nations Policy* (1988, Revised 1995) [on file with the Mookakin Foundation, Standoff, Alberta].

13 *First Nations Advisory Council Terms of Reference* (1996) [on file with the Mookakin Foundation, Standoff, Alberta]. See also *infra* note 21 at 230-31.

14 *Ibid.*

15 The information in this paragraph is taken from Gerald T. Conaty, "Le repatriement du matériel sacré des Pieds-Noirs: Deux approaches" (2004) 28:2 Anthropologie et Sociétés 63 at 66 [translated by author]. Unpublished English version available from Conaty.

16 *Ibid.*

17 *Ibid.*

18 The information in this paragraph is found in *ibid.* at 10.

19 *Glenbow Workshop on Repatriation* (Calgary, 12-14 November 1988).

20 *Memorandum of Understanding between the Mookakin Cultural and Heritage Society and the Glenbow-Alberta Institute* (1998) [on file with the Mookakin Foundation, Standoff, Alberta].

21 Gerald T. Conaty, "Glenbow's Blackfoot Gallery: Working Toward Coexistence" in Laura Peers and Alison Brown, eds., *Museums and Source Communities: A Routledge Reader* (London: Routledge, 2003) 227 at 231.

22 Gerald Conaty and Beth Carter, "'Our Story in Our Words': Diversity and Equality in the Glenbow Museum" in Robert R. Janes and Gerald T. Conaty, eds., *Looking Reality in the Eye: Museums and Their Social Responsibility* (Calgary: University of Calgary Press, 2005) 43.

23 Information about the committee is taken from *Blackfoot Confederacy Advisory Committee on Museum Relations, Draft Terms of Reference* (no date) Standoff, Alberta [on file with the Mookakin Foundation, Standoff, Alberta].

24 Information about the Glenbow's policy for treatment of sacred material is taken from Gerald Conaty and Heather Dumka, "Care of First Nations Sacred Material" (1996) 13 Ethnographic Conservation Newsletter 4.

25 Dorothy First Rider, "Repatriation of Artifacts: Denver Arts Museum Experience" (no date) [unpublished] at 3 [on file with Catherine Bell, University of Alberta].

26 *Ibid.* at 3. For DAM's perspective, see note 28 below.

27 *Supra* note 3.

28 *Supra* note 15 at 69. For DAM's perspective on repatriation, see Roger Echo-Hawk, *Keepers of the Culture: Repatriating Cultural Items Under the Native American Graves Protection and Repatriation Act* (Denver: Denver Arts Museum, 2002). See in particular 171-76. However, it is important to note that officials of the Blood Tribe read this manuscript and concluded that "references to Blood culture, religion and history are generally incorrect" and asked that the discussion of *NAGPRA* as it relates to them be deleted. However, the author retained the references, relying on "first hand experience ... Denver Arts Museum records and other sources." See acknowledgments at vii.

29 *Supra* note 15 at 69.

30 *Supra* note 25 at 2.

31 *Ibid.*
32 *Ibid.*
33 *Supra* note 1, s. 3001 (3)(C).
34 *Ibid.* s. 3001 (3)(D).
35 *Supra* note 15 at 69-70.
36 *Supra* note 25 at 1. The discussion of the position of the parties is taken from documents exchanged between the parties [on file with the Mookakin Foundation, Standoff, Alberta]; the First Rider report, *supra* note 25; and Conaty, *supra* note 15 at 69-70.
37 *Supra* note 15 at 70.
38 *Ibid.* at 71.
39 This agreement, drafted by the Mookakin Foundation, is summarized in Conaty, *supra* note 15 at 71-72.
40 *Supra* note 15 at 69, 72.
41 *Ibid.* at 72.
42 As the *Report of the Royal Commission on Aboriginal Peoples: Looking Forward, Looking Back*, vol. 1 (Ottawa: Supply and Services Canada, 1996) at 63 points out, "[i]n Blackfoot, the word for earth is *ksa'a'hko*, which means 'touching the earth with the feet.' It meant that the land was an original grant from the Creator, and it was a grant to a specific people – not a grant in terms of individual ownership, but a grant in accordance with their world view and philosophy, for 'all my relations.' These relations among all living things were essential in maintaining the continuity of creation, for if the relational network were interfered with, imbalances would occur and the process of creation could come to a halt."
43 Interview of Narcisse Blood by Dennis First Rider (16 December 2002), Blood Reserve, Alberta [translated by Dennis First Rider and Louise Oka Smith].
44 Frank Weasel Head part 1, *supra* note 9.
45 *Supra* note 8.
46 *Supra* note 7.
47 *Supra* note 25.
48 Blood Tribe, *Submission to the Denver Arts Museum for the Repatriation of Blood Tribe Holy Bundles* (1999) [on file with the Mookakin Foundation, Standoff, Alberta].
49 Clark Wissler, "Ceremonial Bundles of the Blackfoot Indians" (1912) 7:2 Anthropological Papers of the American Museum of Natural History 65 at 155. In the words of respected elder Emil Wings, "Holy bundles cannot be withheld. It is not right. They cannot hoard them for themselves. If you follow the Indian way – it can't be refused." Interview with Emil Wings (1996) on file with Kainai Tribal Government, cited in *ibid.* at 12.
50 An example might be a man's requesting a bundle from a women's society. Another example might involve a member who does not practise the traditional ways and who is also known to have substance abuse or debt problems. That member might be tempted to sell a bundle if given guardianship of it.
51 See *e.g.* Brian Noble [In dialogue with Reg Crowshoe, Thunder Medicine Pipe Keeper, Sundance Ceremonialist, and Director, Oldman River Cultural Centre] "*Niitooii*: 'The Same that Is Real' – Parallel Practice, Museums, and the Repatriation of Piikani Customary Authority" (2002) 44 Anthropologica 113 at 123: "Native conceptions of relation to bundles and songs are akin to Aboriginal conceptions of the relation to land: they are understood as being inalienable from the relational network. In contrast, the separating of songs from bundles, societies from ceremonies, exchange relations from the camp arrangement, rights from all of this, derives largely from the modernist practices of anthropology and museology and museum management."
52 Gerald T. Conaty and Robert R. Janes, "Issues of Repatriation: A Canadian View" (1997) 11 European Review of Native American Studies 31 at 34.
53 *Supra* note 48 at 20.
54 R.S.C. 1985, c. I-5.
55 Blood Tribe, *Blood Tribe/Kainaiwa Repatriation Claim for Motoki Bundles, All Brave Dog Society Bundles and Children's Medicine Pipe Bundle* (1998) at 2-3 [on file with the Mookakin Foundation, Standoff, Alberta].
56 *Supra* note 43.

57 *Supra* note 2 at 9.
58 *Supra* note 15 at 66-67.
59 *Ibid.*
60 Kate Morris, "Strategies and Procedures for the Repatriation of Materials from the Private Sector" in Barbara Meister, ed. *Mending the Circle: A Native American Guide to Repatriation* (New York: American Indian Ritual Object Repatriation Foundation, 1996) 73 at 76. And see online: American Indian Object Repatriation Foundation <http://www.repatriationfoundation.org/airorf.html> at 67 reports that "private sector collectors interviewed by the Repatriation Foundation reported that their principle concern is for the physical care of repatriated objects. In some cases, Native Nations may wish to repatriate items with the intent to re-bury, dismantle, or allow them to decompose naturally ... [private collectors] may be unwilling to return objects that they know will be destroyed. Also of concern to private collectors is the possibility that a repatriated object will be re-sold, or that a single individual or Nation might restrict access of other Native Peoples to the material."
61 *Supra* note 52 at 33.
62 *Ibid.*
63 *Supra* note 60.
64 Christian F. Feest, "'Repatriation': A European View on the Question of Restitution of Native American Artifacts" (1995) 9 Eur. Rev. Nat. Amer. Stud. 33 at 37. For a rebuttal to Feest's argument, see Conaty *supra* note 52.
65 *Supra* note 43.
66 *Supra* note 25.
67 R.S.A. 2000, c. G-6, s. 20(2).
68 *Ibid.* s. 20(3). Personal communication with Gerald Conaty, Senior Curator of Ethnology, Glenbow Museum (30 April 2003).
69 Personal communication with Jack Ives, Manager, Archaeology and History (Provincial Archaeologist), Heritage Resources Management (25 June 2004).
70 *Supra* note 4, Preamble.
71 *Ibid.* at s. 1(e).
72 *Ibid.* at s. 2(1) and (2).
73 *Ibid.* at s. 3.
74 *Ibid.* at s. 6.
75 *Blackfoot First Nations Sacred Ceremonial Objects Repatriation Regulation*, Alta. Reg. 96/2004.
76 See quote by Frank Weasel Head at 236, where he elaborates on these points.
77 *Supra* note 42 at 62-63.
78 For example, in his interview, Adam Delaney tells of a barber in Fort McLeod who has a display that he calls a medicine wheel but that, in fact, is a teepee ring, which existed long before the coming of the wheel. See *supra* note 10.
79 Blood Tribe, Band Council Resolution 93-94-7204 A (7 February 1994) [on file with the Mookakin Foundation, Standoff, Alberta].
80 *Ibid.*
81 Blood Tribe Research Department, *Cultural Geography Project* (n.d.) [unpublished, on file with the Mookakin Foundation, Standoff, Alberta].
82 Alberta Environmental Protection, "Writing on Stone Provincial Park Fact Sheet," see online: University of Lethbridge <http://www.uleth.ca/vft/milkriver/wospp.html>.
83 *Ibid.*
84 *Ibid.*
85 Parks Canada Agency, *"Unimpaired for Future Generations"? Protecting Ecological Integrity with Canada's National Parks*, vol. 2: *Setting a New Direction for Canada's National Parks*. Report of the Panel on the Ecological Integrity of Canada's National Parks (Ottawa: Minister of Public Works and Government Services Canada, 2000).
86 Blood Tribe, Band Council Resolution FY-93094-7203 A (2 February 1994) [on file with the Mookakin Foundation, Standoff, Alberta].
87 See generally: Thomas M. Beckley, "The Nestedness of Forest Dependence: A Conceptual Framework and Empirical Exploration" (1998) 11:2 Society and Natural Resources 101;

Adrian Tanner, *Bringing Home Animals: Religious Ideology and Mode of Production of the Mistassini Cree Hunters* (New York: St. Martin's Press, 1979); Richard K. Nelson, *Make Prayers to the Raven: A Koyukon View of the Northern Forest* (Chicago: University of Chicago Press, 1983); Fikret Berkes, *Sacred Ecology: Traditional Ecological Knowledge and Resource Management* (Philadelphia: Taylor and Francis, 1999).

6

Poomaksin: Skinnipiikani-Nitsiitapii Law, Transfers, and Making Relatives

Practices and Principles for Cultural Protection, Repatriation, Redress, and Heritage Law Making with Canada

Brian Noble, in consultation with Reg Crowshoe and in discussion with the Knut-sum-atak Society

> When they took our bundles without paying *Siikapistaan* then they broke the whole system. Now, it's easier for them not to make relatives with us but just to give us back our material objects. But it costs money to make relatives.
>
> – Reg Crowshoe[1]

Preamble: Understanding this Study as Parallel Practice

In this study we focus on the process and practice of the Skinnipiikani (Piikani) people of southern Alberta (and, arguably, the Blackfeet of northern Montana).[2] The Skinnipiikani are one of the First Nations in the Blackfoot Confederacy, which includes the Kainai (Blood), Siksika (Blackfoot) of Alberta, and the Blackfeet of Montana.[3] In particular, we address cultural property and heritage protection within cultural transmission via protocol-driven transfer practices. Protection of cultural knowledge and materials is the central issue and ultimately offers a platform for a more far-reaching discussion of the integrated nature of Nitsiitapii (Blackfoot) law, exchange, and ceremonial practices. While the terms "ownership" and "property" are used, it must be understood that these terms are the only non-Nitsiitapii English-language terms that approximate the outcomes of circle discussions; however, they do not adequately convey the complexity of stewardship rights and responsibilities realized through an integral regulatory practice involving venue, action, language, and song as elaborated in this report.

According to discussion participants, proper redress of heritage-related matters will only be achieved through the full recognition and activation of Nitsiitapii process and practices. At present, Canadian institutions, museums, legal bodies, and agencies of the state continue to ignore or sidestep

Skinnipiikani processes and practices of *Siikapistaan* and *Poomaksin* (payment and transfer) as well as the more general protocols animated by means of venue, action, language, and song. It is the totality of practices and exchanges and the disrupted flow of resources and economics that makes the challenge of cultural, societal, economic, and legal redress so much more difficult for the Skinnipiikani in their relations with non-Piikani institutions.

In attempting to take a practical step in the right direction, this chapter has been designed to respond to and to relay the enactment of authorized collective discussions and decision making. The headings and subheadings are all drawn directly from the discussions themselves. We make a sincere attempt to indicate and reflect the spirit and the full dimensions of these discussions.

Whose Laws? Skinnipiikani, Nitsiitapii, and *Nitooii*

Ultimately, this chapter makes a strong and clear proposal. Protection of Skinnipiikani cultural and heritage property rights in Canada requires the recognition, protection, and activation of Nitsiitapii authority for Skinnipiikani practices. In the dialogue between the Skinnipiikani and Canada, these practices must govern the redress and return of property and future protection measures.

To facilitate this dialogue, we propose a general method of paralleling, which might apply to other First Nations as well. For instance, it was suggested that working with recognized "elders" from each First Nation would allow players to work out parallel terminologies for parallel practices. Here we define several key terms in order to assist in the reading of this chapter and to support the paralleling approach:

1 *Skinnipiikani*: literally "bad hide tanners of the foothills," refers to the Peigan people of southwestern Alberta and northwestern Montana. The participants in this consultation process were exclusively from the Piikani Nation Reserve in Brocket, Alberta, though elder ceremonialists from the Blackfeet (South Peigan) Reservation in Montana were also apprised of this process.
2 *Nitsiitapii:* "real people" is a term designating how Blackfoot recognize themselves, through their socio-cultural practices, laws, and relationships with the Creator, as distinct from other people who do not share those practices. Many Native American societies have an equivalent term, also glossed as "real people." But to be Nitsiitapii is specifically to practise and live by the laws and transfer relations that are discussed here.
3 *Nitooii:* "the same that is real" is a practised way of dual understanding relating to:
   (a) the linked relation between the world of physical things or beings and the shadows that endow them (*i.e.,* that make them real, giving them force and power);[4] and

(b) the paralleling of Nitsiitapii and non-native practices, including practices of law as a means of understanding and recognizing the comparative force and power of these respective practices.

4 *Poomaksin:* the complex of rights and transfer practices of the *Nitsiitapii*. One obtains rights and practices by means of culturally recognized ceremonies involving people, objects, venues, actions, song, and language. *Poomaksin* can govern rights to names, material culture, chiefly headdresses, teepee designs, songs, hunting and gathering of resources, ceremonial bundles, specific ceremonial practices, membership in age-grade societies, territorial boundaries, access to territory, extended kin networks, and much more.

5 *Siikapistaan:* goes hand in hand with *Poomaksin*. It is the act of making a reciprocating "payment" for the rights or privileges obtained. *Poomaksin* cannot be achieved without *Siikapistaan*.

Transfer confers on someone the right to begin and to continue learning about a particular transferred right or practice. Therefore, a transfer ceremony is an induction that occurs only after the rightful elders agree that the particular individual possesses the qualities necessary to carry on protecting the integrity and continuity of the practice. *Poomaksin* is associated with the beginning and ending of a process (*i.e.*, one transfers into a right and, later, transfers it away). It is expected that all transferred participants (*i.e.*, those who have had transferred rights) remember the "mandate" of transferred practice or right and the purpose of their obligations to the mandate. It is also expected that they act in a manner that is true to, and in the best interest of, the survival and integrity of the mandate.[5]

Bundles are of three principal sorts: those that circulate in age-grade societies associated with the Sundance (*e.g.*, Chickadees, Bumblebees, Big Dew Claw, Brave Dogs, Red Coats, Kit Fox) and are transferred to authorized members in the respective societies; those that are communal and held responsibly for the benefit of the entire community (*e.g.*, Thunder Medicine Pipe, Beaver, Sundance Headdress Bundles); and personal medicine bags or those associated with individually kept and used items or, for instance, certain specialized healing practices.[6]

Another important concept is *ahmitoosiman*. This refers specifically to Nitsiitapii "smudge" practices, which revolve around the solemn burning of sweetgrass or sweet pine (or other appropriate herbals) at the outset and conclusion of all ceremonies and formal decision-making meetings. In the most general sense, it refers to everything that takes place between the first and final smudge. As the smoke rises from the burning embers, *ahmitoosiman* visibly links the earth to the sky. *Ahmitoosiman* is also accompanied by and supportive of prayers, and it is meant both to purify the venue, the materials, actions, songs, and participants and to ensure that the ceremony is conducted truthfully, humbly, and with proper "fear" of the powers that give it force (ultimately, the Creator). It often accompanies offerings to share in the smoking of personal pipes in transfer interactions, and it may be used to initiate regular meetings of people whether as family groups or for administrative activity (including band council meetings). Many people smudge morning and night to ensure that their daily lives and their sleep and dreams go well, and smudge is also commonly used in healing practices. *Ahmitoosiman*, while probably the most ubiquitous and familiar of ceremonial practices, is but one common element of the very complex and diverse ceremonial practices that underwrite Skinnipiikani-Nitsiitapii legal and ceremonial practices.

Oral Law, Written Law, and Practice

With regard to their laws, the Skinnipiikani have a performative, orally based practice that is grounded in understandings of the power and authority of the Creator. Nitsiitapii do not codify their laws in written texts. Legal understanding is stabilized, authorized, and derives its force through orally based practice and performance within the context of the proper enactment of ceremonial protocols. In reading what follows, one should understand that these accounts indicate only some of the parameters of practice. They are written descriptions of how the law is expressed in and through key practices and protocols. The full expression of law is that which is enacted, that which is practised. In this way, Nitsiitapii law parallels the common law or judge-made law. Rather than "judges," transferred elders are, quite literally, the arbiters of legal interpretation and transformation.

Features of the Report

The text below is drawn from two circle discussions held at the Oldman River Cultural Centre (OMRCC) in Brocket, Alberta. These were hosted by the Knut-sum-atak, or Brave Dog Society, the ceremonial society with authority for organizing community-wide gatherings of the Sundance and for policing societal relations. A total of twenty-two elders, spiritual leaders, and other members of the Piikani Nation, most of whom hold, or previously held, transferred rights, participated in the discussions.[7] Each discussion is presented as a single section. Working principles derived from the discussions are presented throughout in italicized text and are introduced with the word "principle." They are also listed in the appendix at the end of this chapter.

In order to present parallel ways of identifying the key issues, the text moves back and forth between the voices of the Skinnipiikani participants and that of the non-native writer. For Skinnipiikani, no single author or written text can provide the final word on these or other practices as this is immanent in practice itself; rather, the validation of these texts is supported by the methods used to obtain them – that is, through a process of discussion based on the very principles presented herein.

In the first discussion, "Society Protocols, Traditional Order, Collective Trust: Venue, Action, Language, and Song," the key is understanding venue, action, language, and song as the fundamental elements in Skinnipiikani decision making and legal protocols that govern rights to "cultural property" and Skinnipiikani heritage. While many participants contributed to the discussion, Geoff Crow Eagle Sr. provided the main presentation as he was the one who conducted the major research on the following four elements of practice: (1) ceremonially specific Blackfoot words, manners of speech, and recitations (language); (2) certain prescribed and orderly sets of physical motions (action); (3) the positioning of participants in a circle arrangement according to a formal practice-based set of roles and responsibilities (venue); and (4) drumming-accompanied songs that affirm the participant's rights to that part of the ceremony (song). In combination, these elements bring Nitsiitapii together, while simultaneously invoking and joining all of the physical, embodied, and spiritual dimensions of life.

In the second discussion, "Nitsiitapii Property and Law in Parallel with Canadian Law," we look at the implementation and description of Nitsiitapii law in the context of venue, action, language, and song. The key is understanding the force of Piikani law and the centrality of transfer practices supported by the Skinnipiikani exchange, transfer, and ownership principles achieved through special, relative-making payments known as *Siikapistaan*. Again, many individuals contributed to this discussion, which pivoted around the comments of one respected old lady regarding transfer rights and the respect one has to have for oral laws, including whether one can speak about a given topic. A central commentator in the second discussion is Reg Crowshoe. His comments are often deferred to in accordance with protocol, practice, and recognition of the extent of his transferred rights in many ceremonies; his status as elder in several societies; and his responsibility as keeper, with his wife Rose Crowshoe, of the very powerful, highly respected and feared Small Thunder Medicine Pipe Bundle. The recognition of Reg Crowshoe as the elder who ensures the integrity of the information discussed is an example of the role elders play in transferring rights.

Knut-sum-atak Circle Discussion 1, "Society Protocols, Traditional Order, Collective Trust: Venue, Action, Language, and Song"

The first of the two circle discussions articulated the general principles of Skinnipiikani practice related to law, decision making, protocols, and authority.[8] These principles underlie the rights and transfer practices related to Skinnipiikani cultural materials, knowledge, and practices. The discussion centred on cultural practice and transmission that occur through newly developing tradition-sourced education programs, an activity that was being advanced in concert with those in this project. The understanding was that principles for education apply to the issue of heritage protection and repatriation: they are completely dovetailed practices. In fact, Skinnipiikani practices tend not to have tight categorical bounds. The dividing of practices into education versus law versus ceremony versus material culture versus cultural property is a product of non-aboriginal historical intervention.

In reading through this, one might initially think that these discussions diverge from the issues of cultural property, heritage, and repatriation. To the contrary, we stress that these apparent digressions are essential as they lay the crucial groundwork for understanding the second circle discussion of specialized concepts and practices that must be followed in order to generate effective and long-range responses to these issues.

Collectivity, Support, and Trust

Invoking Support: Relations, Animals, and Rightful People

After the opening smudge and prayer the Knut-sum-atak leader and Thunder Medicine Pipe keeper, Pat Provost, offered some introductory words, whereby he invoked the support of all those present, the rightfully transferred bundle keepers both past and present, and the transferred people (*i.e.*, those who have been transferred membership rights) belonging to the ceremonial societies (such as the Brave Dog and Horn societies):

> We're all coming together to support each other, that's what tonight is about. But what I also understand about tonight is to recognize everybody who is involved in *Ah-tsi-moi-skaan* (prayer), to recognize you guys and bring you out because you are important; your bundles are important. All the people who are Ninaamskaks (Thunder Medicine Pipe Bundle owners), Stsikstaakiiks (Beaver Bundle owners), O'kaks (Sundance Headdress Bundle owners), Knut-sum-ataks (Brave Dogs) and the Horn Society members and former Horn Society members. All these people are being recognized here, from what I understand. So we can gather more often for prayers, so people can get along. Because I feel that everybody's doing their own little individual thing. I think back to when my grandfather opened his bundles. I think they were together back then a lot, they prayed together and they supported each other a lot, during ceremonies being held. I've been fortunate to be involved when I was the youngest, most of us that owned these bundles. When we were younger, when Apohk'soyis (Weasel Tail) first started off with Knut-sum-ataks, and he started into Kinotsosis (Pipe Ceremony). What I recognized then was [that] these old people who ran it, they always came with three or four

> other older guys; so these guys can support them. At a Kinotsosis, there were a lot of older people that showed up to help out, because when a person puts up a Kinotsosis they're asking for help. That's why a Kinotsosis is put up. And they invite the guys that hold the bundles because your prayers are strong, you have bundles in your home that you're smudging and those are the ones being brought together to bring your bundle there, and people are asking for help.
>
> Just like Reg and the staff at the cultural centre asked you to come out tonight because you're important, and they're asking for your prayers so we can have a strong circle here. And support, like whenever there's a ceremony going on, that we'll all feel that you're a part of it. That's from what I understand. When they approached me about this meeting I told him it was a good idea and I want to support it, it's something we all should be involved with. The way things are on the reserve right now, we really need your prayers. Your prayers are what are going to help to get people to help out. Not only that, all we got are deals to having education cutbacks. And when you start praying with your bundles, they are there to help the people so their life can be a little better, people can work together more. It's fortunate to be a part of that, when people all work together and support[ ] each other, or anything that's going on. Any kind of ceremonies, they all came together. I remember going out to the Bad Eagles. There used to be a lot of people from Piikani who supported these things. When the old people were all still alive, they came out and prayed for everybody, all the reserves, chief and council, they all participated.

This opening comment of the Brave Dog leader announces the purpose of the gathering. It recognizes the importance of the stewards of various bundles and societies, and it calls everyone to gather for prayers, the objective being to encourage people to get along. It also serves to remind those present of the integrity of these gatherings and to motivate everyone to continue on with these practices.[9] This provides us with the first working principle:

Principle One: Nitsiitapii practice starts by invoking the support of those present, of rightful transferred bundle keepers both past and present, and the transferred people of the age-grade and other societies.

Collectivity, Sharing, and Equality

The recognition of collective action and good is also grounded in principles of equality and sharing. While transferred bundle keepers are among the most respected people in the community, they are expected to be very generous and humble. The burden of these responsibilities held on behalf of all the people is an important source of their respect. George Gallant illustrates how keepership of the major bundles of the Skinnipiikani was collective rather than individual, even though some people were transferred the right to keep and make proper use of the bundles on behalf of the Skinnipiikani-Nitsiitapii. He very clearly shows how the institutions of the non-native world, from governments to museums, continue to control and oppress the Skinnipiikani people, disrupting their collective lives as sharing, kind, respectful people with traditional lands upon which they live and conduct their lives:

> The way I look at things here is we have to work together. We're all the same, I'm not higher than any of you, and you're not higher than me: we're all equal. We're supposed to be humble people; we're supposed to have respect for one another. But we don't have that respect for one another. We have to work as one, each bundle and pipe[ ] in all the Blackfoot society ... If everybody all works together, we'll be strong. Because today this society we're living under, it's an oppressive society; we're stuck on this little reservation, and we're all fighting over a piece of land. That's not the way it's supposed to be; we're supposed to share. I was fortunate to be raised with some old people and they were all kind people. When they prayed, they prayed for kindness, and they'll have lots to eat. You have to be kind to one another. Today they should pray. Under the system we live [in], we're not a [free] people ... we're controlled. This is my belief, we're all one, and we're all the same ... We don't own those bundles; they belong to the Blackfoot people. That's what I told that guy at the museum. [H]e wanted me to sign a [release] paper, but I told him, "No." The Blackfoot people own that bundle. *You cannot sell that kind of stuff. The white people are the ones who are oppressing [us] today; they want us assimilated. This is where it's important, you have to live by it, but we have to work together.* (George Gallant, emphasis added)

Principle Two: Keepership of the major bundles of the Skinnipiikani is collective (on behalf of the people) rather than individual (for one's own purposes).

Trust and Kindness: The Duty of Bundle Keepers and Ceremonial People
In the face of the ongoing history of cultural and political domination and assimilation within Canada, one of the greatest challenges for the Skinnipiikani today (including the active rightful ceremonial people who have explicit moral duties) is maintaining the manner of kindness demanded by living life as Nitsiitapii and as people with ceremonially transferred rights. People recognize the system of bundles and relations as a gift from the Creator. In humbling themselves to the system and making use of it, they are displaying unconditional trust. One does not "build" trust; rather, one acts with trust. As such, proper respect for the power of the Creator and the

bundles is the basis for striving to be kind to everyone, whether when meeting them, in one's thoughts, or in one's prayers:

> Life is different today. I'm a woman, and I gather the women to sweat, to purify themselves. Today we think mostly white, we don't think native anymore. It's very hard; we have to start Indian thinking. The Indian way is kindness; don't make fun of each other. I'm going to tell you a story of how I started my transfer ... I was told how to dress and I took it, people made fun of me. I didn't pay attention, I just kept walking. The holy spirits gave me the road to walk on and I'm still walking on that path. Today, I greet everyone; it doesn't matter if they're mad at me, I'm still happy to see them and I talk to them. This is when you say we are kind to each other. This is how I greet you and I'm happy to see you. Every morning I pray for you. Iyo Pipe Holder, Iyo Bundle Holder, they will understand [that] the native way of life speaks the truth and gentleness. When I walk through this land of ours, some people will be laughing, saying that I act holy. No, I'm not. I was given the right. My husband is the same; we dream. (Elizabeth Gallant)

It is understood that bundle keepers are meant to embody the moral principles of Nitsiitapii and to be exemplars of these principles in their daily lives. In fact, they are meant to enact through their example – and, even more formally, through the hosting and conducting of ceremonies – all of the moral and legal principles by which Nitsiitapii are governed.

Principle Three: As a moral core, those with transferred bundle rights sustain community respect and support by acting with generosity, humility, supportiveness, sharing, kindness, equality, respect for difference, truthful speech, gentleness, and knowledge of transferred rights and practices.

Ceremonial Society Ways and Transfers

Given the presentation of basic moral principles of sharing, kindness, responsibility, respect, and collective support and action, the discussion turned to the specific pragmatics of the traditional age-grade societies and of bundle-supporting actions. The actual procedures through which morals, values, and, ultimately, Nitsiitapii law or jurisprudence should be advanced were outlined. Geoff Crow Eagle Sr., of the Oldman River Cultural Centre, who is both a transferred elder of a number of age-grade societies and a transferred keeper of parts of the Medicine Pipe Bundle ceremonies, proceeded to present the critical pragmatic features of the traditional societies and their conduct. He was authorized to discuss these matters in this context because the Brave Dog Society had sanctioned this discussion circle. Before considering his comments, however, we explain traditional transfer practices relating to knowledge and property.

Transfers, Protocols, and the Society Lodges of the Sundance

One of the paramount practices bearing upon the circulation and distribution of cultural property and knowledge in relation to the age-grade societies and major ceremonials is that of *rightful transfers*. The Skinnipiikani adhere to traditional transfer practices that, according to the people, they have carried out since the time of Creation. Many tangible and intangible things are subject to ceremonial transfer, including:

1. major ceremonial bundles held on behalf of the entire clan or community (*e.g.*, Beaver Bundle, Natooas Sundance Bundle, Thunder Medicine Pipe Bundle);[10]
2. the many specific practice rights within these ceremonies (*e.g.*, tending fire, drumming, leading ceremony, specific dances, etc.);[11]
3. society membership bundles and regalia, including society leadership regalia;
4. painted teepee designs, both from Creation stories and from dreams;[12]
5. ceremonial paints;
6. medicines (*e.g.*, Horse Medicine Bundle, medicine robes, etc.);
7. chiefs' or leaders' headdresses;
8. personal names, from Creation stories, ceremonies, dreams, etc.;[13]
9. songs; and
10. *iniskim* (buffalo stones)

The transfer of these many forms of "property" – a word used provisionally as it only very loosely applies to these culturally salient forms of "keepership" rights and responsibilities – is achieved by means of protocols.

Principle Four [as noted by Heather Crowshoe-Hirsch]: *The use of the term "property" is inadequate as that which is transferred does not, technically speaking, belong to anyone. The possession of these items is "Creator-given" and, as such, cannot be owned or deemed property as such. Rather than "property," perhaps it is better to say that all of these items are "physical representations of these rights."*[14]

Primacy of Traditional Age-Grade Societies

At the Oldman River Cultural Centre, Geoff Crow Eagle, along with others, had been working with historical records, tape recordings, and other research materials to try to build up understanding of four key concepts of practice: venue, action, language, and song. He first stressed the central importance of traditional age-grade societies with regard to instilling values in young children, pointing out how the erosion of the very principles of kindness came with the introduction of English, a language that, in comparison to Blackfoot, has "anger" and "meanness" in it:

> The important thing of the extraction was some of the stories that the old people had talked about; some of these files were dated back to 1926. In our language, it's very important in our traditional ways. We must carry the language. For the old people, there was no meanness in their language. [At] the turn of the century, when the white man came to our territories, they brought English, and in the English language there was anger. Our ancestors were very humble people, and that is our practice. That practice was ... humbleness, kindness, and respect. Through those stories, I hit a lot of the spiritual connection; people talk about vision quests, societies, and Okan.
>
> If I use this one example, there was a guy named Tom Turned Up Nose. [I]t was 1926. Another reference was George First Rider. In this story, the clans would gather once a year; and in those clans there was age-grade societies from Mosquitoes, Flies, Bumblebees, Young Birds, Doves, Brave Dogs, and so on. These were age societies. This man talked about the discipline of children. He did talk about the mom and the dad and the three children, but the mom and the dad are not responsible for the children, it's the grandparents. These children are sent off to different societies and according to their age group.
>
> This man said that if you don't belong to a society, you're a worthless person and you'll never amount to anything. The parents and grandparents, when the kids were small, their first focus was to send the kids to a society. (Geoff Crow Eagle)

Perhaps the most important dimension of living properly as an age-society member involves adhering to the very structured set of oral and performance-based protocols that society conduct embodies. These protocols offer the core structure for conducting and transmitting the practices:

> If we can keep on with the societies, in societies we talk about the protocols of our people and the respect and humbleness, and [how to] be honest with our empowerment [and] to be kind to each other. All the information that we were getting is extracted from this information. (Geoff Crow Eagle)

Venue, Action, Language, and Song: Four Keys to Society and Transfer Practices

Geoff Crow Eagle also presented the basic format and elements of ceremonial and knowledge transfer practice: venue, action, language, and song. These elements of practice structure the conduct of rightfully transferred people, and the society members and the participants in the ceremonies carefully adhere to them in order to undertake further transfers. Each ceremony is conducted in accordance with a special arrangement of these four elements.

Language: Specialized and Technical versus Everyday

Geoff Crow Eagle first pointed out how the language of age-grade societies and ceremonies is embedded in the four elements of the transfer ceremonies. This language is technically specialized and is distinguished from everyday Blackfoot speech:

> The children were in the age-grade societies. He [the old man] did talk about the language, and why it's so important in our culture. In the song, most of us have had transfers; we all know the importance of transferred rights. In those transferred rights, there are four things ... concepts that are there is the language, there's a technical jargon that's there. Like with the Brave Dogs Society, when they group together they have that technical jargon, they'll talk in their own way. Just the same way as doctors and lawyers, they have their own jargon. The Brave Dogs have a special way of talking too. We know that language is very important. (Geoff Crow Eagle)

His comments raise another fundamental principle derived from the discussion circles.

Principle Five: Technically specific language is a dimension of transfer protocol (i.e., Poomaksin).

One of the participants pointed out how challenging it is to develop and sustain the technical language (what she referred to as "Old Blackfoot") of ceremonies, especially given that many people have faced even more basic challenges in learning everyday Blackfoot itself. Clearly, this is one consequence of historical Canadian policies of language assimilation:

> Very seldom I spoke Blackfoot because I seldom met anyone who spoke Blackfoot. I spoke half and half. One time I went down to Siksika, and I was just speaking English and my late brother-in-law, Raymond Water Chief, told me I should speak Blackfoot because I wasn't a white woman. It's not often that I meet someone who spoke Blackfoot, so I was sort of losing my language. So when I came back here, I tried, I really tried hard. A lot of times I really came out with not very good language. Margaret heard me when I was making mistakes, and she tried to prevent me from speaking Blackfoot. She told me I spoke very broken Blackfoot. A lot of times there [were] very embarrassing situations that happened, especially

> when I was talking to an elder, someone would hear me talking and after would tell me it wasn't the right thing to say. Anyway, I learned; I think today I can speak good Blackfoot. I've learned from Reg and Geoff some of the words that are old Blackfoot that I haven't even heard before. My mother used to speak some old Blackfoot words. She used to tell me to listen and pass it on to my children; I didn't have time to listen to her, I had to run out and play. So I think ... parents, the ones that speak Blackfoot, could help teach their children and start speaking Blackfoot to their children. (Kathleen Grant)

The importance of language lies in recognizing, first, that specific terms and linguistic forms carry specific ranges of meanings that are very different from those embodied in their nearest English language translations, and, second, that ceremonial language has a specificity and power of its own, which is associated with the powers of the ceremony being considered.

Principle Six: Language restoration is crucial to advancing cultural transmission and transfer practices.

Venue: Gathering Place and Sitting Order

Each ceremony is conducted within a teepee circle arrangement, as Geoff Crow Eagle discusses below:

> The second thing we found out was the venue: just like we're sitting here, it's a gathering place. The venue part, it's just like in the Napi legends, [in] those stories there [were] venues. There were technical languages in each part. So that language was very important, and the venue was very important. (Geoff Crow Eagle)

The diagram below shows one such seating arrangement. Each of the positions is to be occupied by someone who has properly acquired the rights and responsibilities of that role.

This diagram suggests the generalized roles associated with each of the seating positions within the teepee circle. The specific arrangement of venue varies in relation to the age-grade society, the ceremonial, or the kind of transfer right issue being addressed. The seating arrangement can be recreated in a meeting room (or a home, for that matter) just as it is laid out within the teepee circle. A repertoire of technical language is associated with each position and role within the circle. It is important to recognize that the bundle, or the bundle issue being addressed, has a position in the venue as well.

Principle Seven: Venue specificity and arrangement is the second dimension of transfer protocol.

Action: Physical Movements
In addition to language and venue, the third element of practice, action, is also important. As Geoff Crow Eagle explains, "the third one was ... action: we have to make motion when you get a transferred right, so we know that these three are very important." Each ceremony adheres to specific protocols. The action element prescribes specific sorts of "ritualized" movements associated with the venue-specific, position-specific roles of the participants. Such actions can include rising to speak, repositioning oneself, a particular dance, or even hand motions.

***Poomaksin* traditional circle**

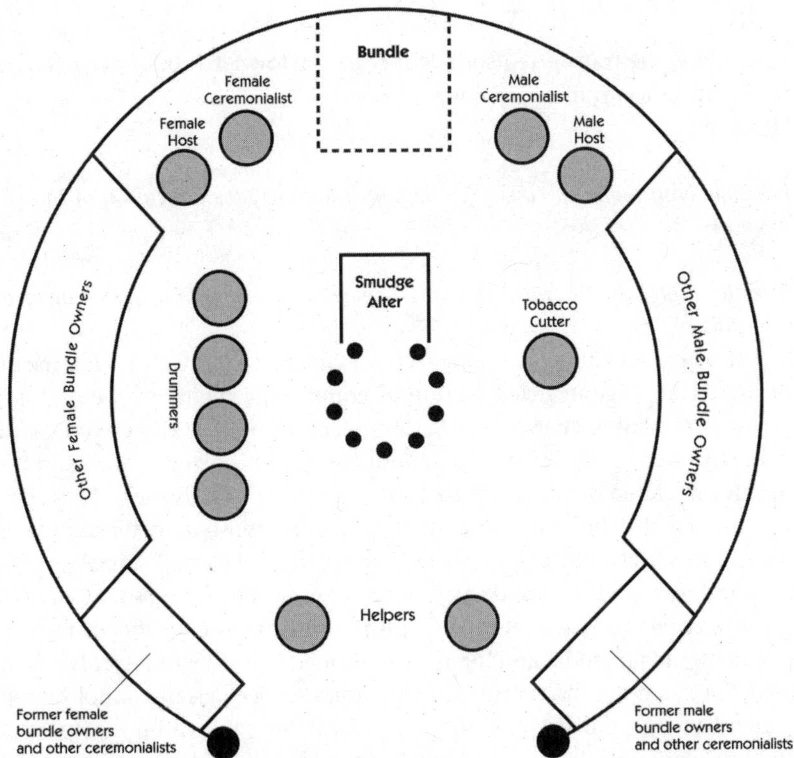

Source: Reg Crowshoe and Sybille Manneschmidt, *Akak'stiman: A Blackfoot Framework for Decision-Making and Mediation Processes*, 2d ed. (Calgary: University of Calgary Press, 2002), 38.

Principle Eight: Action specificity is a third dimension of transfer protocol.

Song: Seal of "Ownership," Credential, or Right

Perhaps the most important element of practice is song. To demonstrate one's transferred right, one has to have the transferred song that goes with that right and the confidence to sing it before witnesses in a ceremonial setting:

> And the fourth thing that is very important is the ownership, when that song is transferred to you then you get that ownership, then your transferred right is complete. If those three are there and one is not there, there's a question. A Siksikakwaan talked about when he gets a transferred right, that song, he must know that song. That's why when I was inducted into the Horn Society I tried so hard to know the songs. Those, we can say, are my degrees. It's so important to know those songs. Myself, my research [was] the songs. I went and did my research and found out the songs are very important. (Geoff Crow Eagle)

Ultimately, the transferred song is the seal of "ownership." Alternately, as in this instance, transferred songs are also described as a "credential" or a "licence."

Principle Nine: Song specificity is the fourth and decisive dimension of transfer protocol.

Integrity (Totality of Venue, Action, Language, and Song) Is a Requirement of Protocol

Separating these elements – song, action, language, and venue – is a means of presenting a generalized picture of common elements of the oral and performance-based character of Skinnipiikani transfer practices and protocols. However, these elements are conducted in an integrated way, and it is in this integrated performance that they gain their effectiveness. These protocols mediate the transmission of what, in non-native terms, would include material culture property (*e.g.*, transferred objects, personal objects, etc.) and intangible or intellectual property (*e.g.*, transferred songs, dances, actions, names, designs, etc.). As with the integrated elements of transfer practices, such material and intangible "property" is integrated and inalienable. For example, the transferred song for a teepee design cannot be separated from the transferred bundle for that design; nor can it be separated from the design itself. If one element is omitted or altered, then the integrity of the entire oral practice is undermined.

Among these four elements, language and song are seen to be the most difficult to recover in communities that have suffered substantial, but not irreparable, cultural loss. Some suggested that the loss of language and song poses the greatest threat to the Skinnipiikani with regard to their ability to sustain their overall practices. That said, the potential for recovery is at hand:

> And all the information is there; some of the people who told these stories have gone on and some are still living. The main thing that we talk about is song and language. Those two are way on top; language is very important. We have to instill that language into our children. How can we do it? How can we [instill] that into our children? Can we build more societies and new songs based on ideas? (Geoff Crow Eagle)

Once more, the transferred songs remain the ultimate element with which to prove one's rights, and it is the element that completes the practices. Geoff Crow Eagle also explains: "If we lose the songs the induction won't be true. If we lose the songs, the transfer wouldn't be true; the three would still be there. They have to be all together." In the following statements, Elizabeth Gallant reiterates the centrality of language and song, and Geoff Crow Eagle expands on this:

> The things that are being taught are very important, legends are very important; they will understand through legends. Legends are very important if they could understand language. Songs: that's what the children should understand. And that's what's so important, when they can understand the language and sing the songs. The spirits that come to us do not understand English, they don't sing in English; but they do understand Blackfoot language and songs, and that's why it's so important that Blackfoot be learned. That's when we can go back to our way of life and our religion. And this is how they [children] will learn as they grow, and will know our way of life. (Elizabeth Gallant)

> When the old people sing, all their songs mean something. The language was the most important thing. You go on the Blood Reserve; you'll see some little kids speaking Blackfoot. But on this reserve, there are hardly any kids who know the Blackfoot language. The way I look at it, we're moving more towards the white ways, rather than going back to our old ways, because we're controlled by the white man. They're the ones supplying our schools, all their ways – where's our ways? Like, what you were saying, teaching the Blackfoot language, songs, and our ways. Our parents, they were self-supporting. The boarding schools took away our self-respect and our respect for other people. (Geoff Crow Eagle)

In the final analysis, it is the restoration of the integrated practices of venue, action, language, and song – as elements of the transfer practices of the Skinnipiikani – that will be the baseline not only for cultural transmission but also for the related matters of cultural material and knowledge protection as well as repatriation. All of these have to be seen as an integrated, total arrangement, and they have to be supported in concert. In fact, it is the disruption of this integrity through the culturally devastating historic policies of the Canadian state, including residential school and other assimilationist policies, that this principle of integration is meant to counteract.

Principle Ten: For the Skinnipiikani, restoring integrated practices of transfer is the means of restoring language, song, and cultural transmission between generations. As they are interdependent parts of the practice, it is crucial that they be restored together and in total, that they not be separated from one another.

Creation Stories at the Heart of Skinnipiikani Social and Moral Order

The depth of Skinnipiikani oral tradition is recognized in the persistence of cycles of stories originating in Skinnipiikani Creation time. In addition to demonstrating the origins, histories, and continuities of certain practices, these stories are the most relied upon source of rules and meanings for the Skinnipiikani social, natural, and moral order. Thus, another matter Geoff Crow Eagle considered in his research "was the Creation: in the past, how did we get that Okan (Sundance) back into our Blackfoot territory?"

Napi and Order

Napi is a mischievous figure who came into the world and who has parallels with the Creation "Trickster" characters of other indigenous peoples.[15] There are hundreds of stories about Napi. Geoff Crow Eagle explains how Napi's exploits made the social and natural order of life understandable. In this instance, he shows how Napi's craziness gets him into trouble when he exceeds a very common stricture of protocol – the four-times repetition of actions:

> The next thing was order – [w]hen Napi came into our world, how Napi made that order. An example: Napi was instructed by the Chickadees and the Chickadees' eyeballs flew away. Napi wanted to know what they were doing, so he told them, "My little Brothers, I would like to do what you are doing." The Chickadees told him not to do it more than four times. That was an order he got into our human race – not to overdo things, or it will backfire. Another story, the coyotes jumping on ice. Napi told the coyotes he wanted to jump on the ice too; the coyotes showed him how to jump on the ice so he can get food. They told him not to overdo it, but he did, and that was another way he brought order to us. Those are our Blackfoot legends.

Principle Eleven: Many key principles underlying the social-natural order are embedded in the Napi (Trickster) stories.

Kutoyiis and Morals and Values

Just as Napi teaches order by his crazy disobedience, which is recounted in so many stories, so the figure Kutoyiis, "Blood Clot," teaches morals and values by taking direct action against those who act immorally:

> Morals and Values: the Legends of Kutoyiis, I'll talk about the Bear Family. [T]he son-in-law was very cruel to his in-laws. The chief and his family took all the food from the camp and hoarded it, so when Kutoyiis came into the camp he told the chief that all his food was in his teepee, and he told him to send his wives one by one. [W]hen each wife [came] into his teepee, Kutoyiis told each one as they came in to lick the fat that was hanging down from the teepee. When they did, he struck them on the throat and killed them; and he did the same thing with the chief, and so the morals and values of this [are that] we should be kind to each other. What we have, we share. Those were the values of Kutoyiis. (Geoff Crow Eagle)

These stories of Napi and Kutoyiis are commonly referred to in an everyday manner, whether by parents, teachers, elders, or among friends. But they are also referred to when people are seeking guidance with regard to proper conduct. Basically, in combination with the fourfold practices of venue, action, language, and song, they help to form the moral basis of decision making and adjudication. Such stories are called upon to help judge the proper behaviour of those making claims to keepership and seeking the transfer of Skinnipiikani knowledge and materials. They demonstrate two key principles arising from our discussions:

Principle Twelve: Many key moral principles and values of the Skinnipiikani are embedded in the Kutoyiis, Blood Clot stories.

Principle Thirteen: Napi and Kutoyiis stories are key sources of principles informing the legal order of the Skinnipiikani.

Elders, Younger Generations, and Transferred Right

Younger Generations and Children in Societies

In the context of education, Reg Crowshoe summed up the set of relations and actions presented by Geoff Crow Eagle. He also discussed the transmission of Skinnipiikani culture between generations:

> The three concepts we're looking at [in] the research ... right now the kids

> are learning the language in school, they're learning their prayer, and they're learning words. When they go home, they don't speak the language. I think when you go to school, they need a physical place to learn; for example, a school, a lesson plan to teach the kids, a teacher, and you need language and symbols (ABCs). Those four will allow you to teach your kids. What are our practices? What are [our] four basic practices; and I think that's what Geoff talked about ... Venue was a place where they gathered, Napi wanted to dance with the mice, the mice gathered in the Elk's skull ... when the gophers were cooking each other. They got together by a fire; it was a place where they got together. If a child can understand that a school is just as important in their culture this way, and the other one you said was language, that's the target there. The other two [were] action and song; when they look at action, it's also the same as teaching someone. So it would be like a lesson plan. When you look at a child to go from Grade 4 to 5, he can't sit in Grade 5 class unless he has a report card. (Reg Crowshoe)

The place of children in ceremonies and practices is something that struck a strong chord among circle discussants. In fact, the issue of intergenerational relations remains one of the greatest driving concerns for the Skinnipiikani, as it does for most First Peoples in Canada, and it was a point that the elders raised time and again. Like other dimensions of practices that have been disrupted by Canada's colonialist and assimilationist projects, the "right" approach to practice in relation to children and young people is continually discussed and reconsidered. This is a fundamental issue for cultural restoration and the attempt to reinforce traditional practices. After reviewing early drafts of this report, Heather Crowshoe-Hirsch remarked:

> Entrusting the continuity of oral cultural practices to children is particularly important to the survival of the traditional practices ... it is part of their identity. In addition, having the ability to function holistically throughout life is important, perhaps the key to survival of the aboriginal way of life and its ability to foster resilience within aboriginal people for further generations to come. (Heather Crowshoe-Hirsch)

In what follows, Pat Provost discusses the importance of immersing young people in the ceremonies, transfers, and material and cultural practices of the age-grade societies:

> Just one quick comment I would like to make, as mentioned earlier about our children and how they don't recognize their culture. Some of the parents hold ceremonies and they take their children, that's something you don't see very often; the parents coming to a ceremony with their children

> and having them sit there and observe everything that's going on. Right now those bundles are coming back and they're travelling, they're going to different people on the reserve; once they start travelling like that to each family, then they get a chance to own a bundle and they start going out and bringing their children out, and [they] teach them. We're blaming them as parents. When the Sundance first started, there was a lot of families that used to camp – they camped with their kids, they brought their kids out. A lot of them joined the Brave Dogs, and when they joined they didn't just own the rattle the parents brought them out, and they were responsible for teaching their kids the role of the Brave Dogs. Right now, with the Brave Dogs, there's a lot of rattles out there and only a handful of people. Another thing is, when there is a Bundle Opening on the reserve, people should come out. Usually it's the same people that come out. Whenever there's a new person that shows up, everyone's glad to see them because they showed up; interest is starting to build up. As bundle holders, we have to start inviting people to come; and sometimes they feel like they don't have the right to go, or they don't know how to go there. (Pat Provost)

The question of how to participate in oral cultural practice is an issue at present because, as Elizabeth Gallant suggested, people are only slowly coming back to these practices:

> The way I understood, I was very young when my grandfather used to open his bundles. All I could get from society was from all day [witnessing what went on]. They'd sing for a Brave Dog. He'll get up and dance; and Chickadees, they get up to dance. There was never any children, [t]he way I understand my grandparents. My grandparents, if they were away, we did the disciplining. Our responsibility was disciplining and respect. When they're of age, they have transfers of whatever they're getting, and that's when they start coming. When [their] turn is, that's when they can come, and that's how I understand it. That's how I was raised, from the old man Crow Flag. But I don't know, things have changed. The way our lives are, we have to know our real life, we challenge it. And another thing is, we have got to be truthful.[16]

Such questioning regarding how to practice among potential participants sometimes inhibits community members from participating. This being the case, it is the responsibility of bundle holders, in their role as stewards, to ensure the members of the community that they are welcome.

Principle Fourteen: The means of resolving confusion and differences of opinion about practices caused by colonialism is to subject the questions to the practices that are activated by rightfully transferred bundle holders and former rights holders. Lifelong engagement with the practices on the part of transferred rights holders is considered crucial.

Addressing Change: Society "Grandparents" as Advisors and Adjudicators
The comments of Pat Provost and Elizabeth Gallant underscore the commitment to working together to talk through uncertainties resulting from the historical disruption of cultural practices that occurred due to their relations with the Canadian state. That said, in Skinnipiikani ways, there is a specific protocol-based recourse to which one may turn on such occasions of uncertainty. In his closing comment in this first circle discussion, Thunder Medicine Pipe Bundle keeper Allan Pard emphasized the importance of recognizing the advisory and adjudicating role of "grandparents" with regard to the age-grade societies. These are people who were once regular transferred members of the societies but who have since transferred their membership, thereby becoming "elders," or "grandparents," to their former age-grade society:

> This meeting, if we're going to use our way of life, you should get grandparents, and the grandparents that you do get will use prayer. It's going to strongly change these meetings. A common way in our Indian practice [is] that we always have to get an elder.[17] If someone still has bundles, that person cannot advise because it's really hard on that person. Furthermore, because he still has the transferred rights along with the bundle ... that's the very reason why that person cannot advise. That's the reason why it's hard for that person, because he has to be holy. It's good, you have to start somewhere to understanding our way. There's a certain protocol to conduct these kinds of meetings; if you're going to use our protocol to learn you have to get a grandfather. In these kinds of meetings we're going to learn the traditional way to conduct traditional meetings. (Allan Pard)

In this Brave Dog circle discussion, Reg Crowshoe was a former transferred Knut-sum-atak member and leader; in other words, he was a grandparent, or elder, to the society. Ultimately, the way to advance and restore traditional practices – whether practices of cultural property redress and transfer, of traditional education in new contexts, or of adjudicating rights – is by following the standards of practice itself, while constantly discussing and adjusting to these orally understood protocols. As an example of this, in the past there have been occasions when transferred Medicine Pipe Bundle holders were simultaneously former holders (*i.e.*, elders or grandparents) to other Medicine Pipe Bundles and who danced with both the pipes. In other words, they exercised both their stewardship and elder, or advisory, responsibilities simultaneously.

Principle Fifteen: Those past rightfully transferred bundle keepers or past rights holders of the age-grade societies are usually recognized as "elders," or "grandparents," to those transferred rights and practices. They may be called upon as advisors and adjudicators on questions of law and protocol associated with materials or practices that correspond to the transferred right being considered.

Knut-sum-atak Circle Discussion 2: "Nitsiitapii Property and Law in Parallel with Canadian Law"

Having discussed the general framework of cultural practices and principles in the first circle discussion, in the second circle discussion we look at how the Skinnipiikani would approach a Nitsiitapii law-driven project for the protection of culture and heritage.[18] After smudging and an opening prayer, the keeper of the Brave Dog Rider Bundle, Herman Many Guns, introduced the general topic for discussion. After this, Reg Crowshoe described for everyone the specific aim of the research project and the discussion:

> Tonight we wanted to talk about cultural protection: how do we protect our culture, how do we protect our smudge? How do we protect that from a white man, who never had any transferred rights [but] takes a smudge, and makes a rattle, and who's dancing around like a Brave Dog, and having ceremonies already without us knowing about it? Somebody takes a picture of the Brave Dogs and puts it on the Internet and sells that picture. [W]ell, whoever buys it can say, "[T]his is my picture, I'm going to dress like this picture." How do we protect it? I think those are some of the things that new technology are bringing. [H]ow do we protect [against] that?
>
> The other thing we talked about was, if we look at the Canadian law, courts, police – and we took out all the authorities – but they don't do that in Canada. I think in Canada we're still scared of the law because it's still strong. In our bundles and our culture, I think if we protect our ways we can start making them strong again. We can use them for things that we need. Because if we don't start protecting that, the old-timers that passed on are going to leave with it, then offshore ethnic people coming in will steal it. [S]o I think those are some of the things that we want to talk about tonight. What do you think about cultural protection? Last time we talked a lot about protocol. But this time we want to talk about cultural protection and we're working with the University of [Alberta][19] and Dalhousie University in Nova Scotia to look at how we look at the concept of protecting our culture. So tonight Brian Noble is here, Brian is no stranger to Piikani; he's been around, and he spent a lot of time with the old man. Right now he lives in Halifax, Nova Scotia. I'll let him talk about the project, how we want to protect our culture.

In his introduction, Reg Crowshoe focused the participants' attention on the issue of appropriation and claims to ownership of Skinnipiikani practices, noting both the tangible and intangible elements of those practices. He indicated that, from the Skinnipiikani standpoint, culture includes all such things in their integrated totality. He also emphasized that the laws governing cultural and intellectual property and that garner the most respect, or "fear," are Canadian laws. In keeping with all the principles mentioned in the first circle discussion, he stressed the importance of redirecting that fear and respect to the sources of Skinnipiikani law by strengthening the bundles as the authority of Nitsiitapii law. Brian Noble offered further context:

> A lot of this has come about because of the worldwide interest in the rights of indigenous people, and a lot of it has to do with these questions of cultural property; nowadays museums are giving a lot back that they weren't prepared to give back in the past. That's because native people have been pressing for this and bringing their messages home to their people. So the issue that comes to the fore along the way when you start looking at this is [that] when things like bundles start coming back into communities, when sacred masks and poles are being brought back into communities on the Coast, the people are bringing back the objects which they have used to express their laws, and even in the way that they come back there's a legal action that takes place, and a lot of people are interested in understanding what those laws are and how to make [them] work better for aboriginal communities. So the basic issue that I wanted to bring today with this research project ... is the issue of how to bestow ... the laws for protecting and preserving *Siikapistaan*. Reg and I have been talking about it. Specifically through protecting and preserving *Siikapistaan*; those means of building relations through payments; *Siikapistaan* and Piikani cultural property and knowledge. (Brian Noble)

Trust, History, Research, and Power

Countering the Cultural "Big Pot": Canada's Universal Indian Approach and the History of Cross-Cultural Misinterpretation

> Political recognition is a prerequisite for advancing this work in any meaningful way. We're struggling not only for independence but recognition. (Reg Crowshoe)

By "recognition" Reg is referring especially to the recognition of the existing culturally based political and legal authority of the Skinnipiikani as a distinct people. Directly related to this is what Herman Many Guns pointed to as the common error that non-native people make when they represent

First Nations peoples as having one common culture: "Canada always kind of throws us all into one big pot, one big culture and ... like we have the same kind of problems. We [live] differently. We [relate to each other] differently. Our language is different; our customs are different."

The melting pot tendency underwrites so many injustices that face indigenous people, and it must be avoided if this project is to be trusted. Universalizing aboriginal peoples across Canada contributes to cultural confusion and undermines any recognition of the differences between aboriginal groups. The following statement clearly shows Skinnipiikani skepticism towards, and suspicion of, non-native initiatives:

> It's like today; we have a hard enough struggle to identify ourselves as Skinnipiikani. And in the way we do things as Skinnipiikani, they have a hard enough struggle. [S]o joining this research, are we just giving more ammunition to the white people to put us into a "melting pot" that we're fighting [to escape] from? (unidentified speaker)

Principle Sixteen: Recognize the great diversity of distinct cultures and practices pertaining to cultural research and ownership; avoid universalizing approaches to aboriginal peoples.

"This Means We Take Control": Research by Others, to Do Our Research and to Do Our Action

To be credible and effective, this research project must have the full trust of the Skinnipiikani community, and this can only be gained by properly recognizing the people, their laws, and their distinctive culture. One male old-timer offered his view on giving control back to the people – control that Canada's previous policies took from them: "Those are some of the beginnings – respect. Some of us went to the residential schools. Protecting our culture takes research. It's there. This is not new to me; you presented this in a different form. When this came, this means we take control."

This same old-timer explained that the Skinnipiikani-Nitsiitapii had as much to offer with regard to knowledge and forms of research as did those who had gained a university education:

> My daughter is going to university. She's into native studies ... but we've got [our own] information which would drown her. Today [we need] someone to begin to understand and respect us, [where we Nitsiitapii] come from. In reality, I know where I've come from. And for another year ... but I'm not too sure this is the course for it – a paper's a paper but to us it's ... this is our life.
>
> So it all starts falling back on [the younger generation] and academia. And

> I've seen it when I was young, and I didn't really [know what would happen]. And [that old man] gave me, oh, I don't know who gave me the name – but the name of [Blackfoot name] I was the one that ... I was the last one that thought I was going to survive. Skinny, always sick, and, my goodness, I was the only survivor today [from my family]. Now I've passed [that name] on.

The power in the old-timer's statement lies both in how it illustrates a native way of thinking and speaking and in how it demonstrates a total respect for the authority and efficacy of Skinnipiikani knowledge and practices.

Principle Seventeen: Ensure that control over research, culture, and heritage lies with the people to whom it belongs and is in accord with cultural practices.

Fear, Danger, and the Force of Ownership Laws: Creator and Canada

Fear, Creator, and the Force of Law: "I'm Stingy of [My Culture and Sacred Way of Life] ... Because I'm Afraid ..."

In the following statement, a female elder explains how dangerous it is to speak of or trade in anything when one does not have the ceremonially transferred rights to it (in fact, the underlying force of Nitsiitapii law is that spiritual sanction will fall upon those who break it):

> This research that you're doing, a lot of people have been asking me different things. I've been brought up the Indian way of life, culture and sacred way of life, by my grandparents. I'm very stingy of it, and I don't like to come right out and talk to somebody about it, especially a complete stranger ... because I'm afraid ...
>
> There are a lot of things in our culture, especially in the sacred way; bundles and all that I was taught to respect ... and there are certain things I hear of but have no rights to come right out and give [them] to somebody, [to] a complete stranger ... Because in the long run, with the Creator, I might hurt myself because some of that [about which] people ask, I'm not entitled to them, to come right out and say things about them. The bundles have histories, especially his bundle [Reg's Small Thunder Medicine Pipe Bundle] ... my grandparents told me stories of how strong that little pipe was, very interesting stories. And out of hearing that I have a lot of respect for it, but I don't have rights to talk about it. I have no rights, I might hurt myself. This is the fear that I carry, and some others too, just like my grandmother has the Sundance Bonnet. I don't have the authority to come out and talk about it, I don't like to come out and say

> it. That's why I'm very stingy, I fear for my culture, to expose it in the outside, because I never know what these people will translate it to different ideas. And where that blame will turn around and come back to me, not only me but also the Creator. Because I have a strong belief in the Creator, this is the way I feel about that. (old lady)

This statement raises many key issues, not the least of which is that the hesitation regarding imparting knowledge to others – something that might be interpreted as an expression of mistrust – is actually a fear of potential reprisal. Also implicit in her comments is the fact that transferred rights include both material things, such as ceremonial bundles, and the stories about the powerful ways in which those bundles work. In other words, knowledge and the tangible things with which they are associated are inseparable from one another, as is the "ownership" of, or right to, these material things.

Principle Eighteen: It must be recognized that rights to material culture, the knowledge of their uses, and the powers that animate them are inseparable from one another.

Sacred Places, Paints, and the Effects of Non-Rightful Disturbance

This same respected old lady discussed the holy ceremonial paint found in sacred locations and how the disturbance of such sites by non-rightful people can corrupt the powers of those sites. These earth-pigment paints are used for the ceremonial painting of both people and sacred objects. Here, she demonstrates how fear of and belief in the Creator is the basis of Nitsiitapii law. She also unambiguously recommends that traditionally rightful aboriginal people, as stewards of the earth and the Creator, should have control over such sacred sites:

> Just like down in Winnipeg, some years back, we went to a Sacred Land Conference. They talked about these different reserves where they have a sacred site and how they lost out on it because the outside world got involved with them too much. Some of them, like up North, they had sacred rocks, where they go and pray and make their offerings, got them turned into a museum, and the outside disturbance ... [now] that thing doesn't do anything anymore because it used to do some kind of miracles and things like that. The main topic was this mountain where we get the Indian paint, the Crow Eagle Reserve, I said, "I used to be brought up there when I was a little girl, with my brother, we used to move up there with my grandparents." I know the ceremonies and what goes on, but I never actually went to the site because I wasn't allowed up there. My grandmother and I would sit back, because we weren't supposed to talk,

> or else they would get nothing. The people that used to go right to the mountain used to come back and give us some paint, some of them would paint their faces; this is what I know of that place, and I know of the ceremonies that used to go on the night before. I'm just trying to explain, and at the end I told them, "What the government should do nowadays, all sacred lands they should turn them back to the rightful owners, us native people, because we know how to go about them." Them, they don't know nothing. And they try to do something, imitate us, and they're not sincere about it, because there's something in you that you really have to open up for the Creator and yourself, not everybody else, to really understand something about these sacred sites and our culture. (old lady)

In this statement, the elder stresses that it is a combination of sincerity and transferred rights in accordance with Nitsiitapii protocols that gives a person the authority to understand and control sacred sites as well as the materials and knowledges derived from them. These materials and knowledges are always integrally connected to the site, even after they are removed from it. Indeed, it is this connection that gives the materials, site, and knowledge their powers. By extension, her statement also suggests that the actions of non-Nitsiitapii jurisdictions to manage, control, and pass laws over such lands is the source of spiritual corruption. Canadian laws are insensitive to Nitsiitapii laws and have no fear of the Creator, who has endowed these sites with their power.

Iniskim *and Paint: The Continuous Nature of Transferred Rights, Ceremonial Rights, and Ownership Rights to Lands and Resources*

The perspective in some Canadian policy and legal and popular thought is that aboriginal peoples had no concept of land rights: they simply roamed the lands taking what they needed for physical survival and, at best, had only a universal collective right to the land rather than personally assigned rights. Reg Crowshoe pointed out the error in this misperception. He also demonstrated how the specialized protocols of venue, action, language, and song mediate and authorize such rights:

> I think it's important what [the old lady] talks about, for example, I've always heard this – I'll call it a myth – that Indians don't own land. White people always say, "Well, Indians don't own land, they moved all over with the buffalo and they can't sell land because they all own it," and it's this romantic, mystifying view of Indians, and how they're connected to nature, they don't own land. But just what [the old lady] talked about, the paint, that paint is transferred; it comes with action, venue, language, and song. You have to go through those four to get it, those are the laws. But white people don't recognize those four. When you have those four

> and you have the right to that paint, then you own part of where you get that paint, then that's property of yours, you can mine it; that's your permission to scrape it off the ledges so that you can use it. Otherwise, if you don't have those four, you can't touch it. Nobody else can touch it, but you have to get those four. So that's a clear indication of laws that say, "If I get to mine that ore, that sacred ore, then I have to get their permission of ownership to do it." So how can white people say that we don't own land? (Reg Crowshoe)

However, to date, Canadian property rights discourse and practices have not adhered to Nitsiitapii protocols, nor have they been modified to accommodate them in parallel or even subordinate ways. Two principles emerge from his statement.

Principle Nineteen: Skinnipiikani-Nitsiitapii practice can assign personalized rights to the use or "exploitation" of lands and resources.

Principle Twenty: Where belief in and fear of the Creator is the force behind Nitsiitapii law, proper adherence to the protocols of venue, action, language, and song through the performance of ceremonies appropriate to the matter under consideration must be the basis of legal conduct.

While the right to sacred paints and their associated sites can be transferred, the finding of *iniskim* (buffalo stones), which are spiritually powerful stones in the shape of bison, confers on the person discovering them a right to the location in which they were discovered, so long as ceremonial protocol is followed to affirm that right. Reg Crowshoe suggested that this is akin to a mineral rights claim in Western legal practice:

> Buffalo stones is another resource. Those buffalo stones are probably taken from the ground again. That's natural resources, that's ownership; if you go through those four, then you own that rock. Just like white people. [T]hey found gold over there, well, they're going to go stake a claim and ownership on that, and then, through the government, they'll get a piece of paper to own that gold. With us it's *iniskim*; we have a process to stake a claim on *iniskim* and paint. Well, how can other people say that we don't have land? We do have land and we have ownership of land. (Reg Crowshoe, emphasis added)

It is fear of the Creator as the source of law that gives force to these rights, and this is what sanctions who is rightfully allowed to speak of them. Likewise, it is important to stress the continuity of rights between such moveable material as *iniskim* and paint, intangibles like songs and stories, and the physical sites in which they originated:

> These are the things [the old lady] is saying, "I don't want those infringed, because we still believe in them." She still feels stingy, [saying], "Yes, we have laws that allows us to own, but I don't want to share them with somebody I don't know because whatever they use, however they use the information, might come back on me, and I would be in trouble, especially if I don't have the right to talk about it." If you have a claim and you found gold on your claim, I wouldn't feel right to talk about your claim and the gold that you're carrying because I don't have the ownership, you have. (Reg Crowshoe)

An important point made above is that both Canadian law and Nitsiitapii law are governed by specific protocols and procedures, and both mediate and validate the assignment of rights of access, use, trade, and confidentiality.

Ultimately, the discussion emphasized that Nitsiitapii law of the Skinnipiikani is the best means of protecting such resources since, among other reasons, its practice is based in and backed up by the fear and force of the Creator who makes things sacred and powerful in the first place. This is as opposed to the fear and force of alien laws, such as those of Canada, which operate according to very different principles. In either form of law, fear is based in some sanction that enables its enforcement. Recognition of the sanctity of things is crucial for Nitsiitapii, as it is for modern Western democratic states and free market economies:

> So, what's my punishment for photocopying a dollar bill and displaying it? (Reg Crowshoe)
>
> Forgery? (old lady)
>
> Forgery ... say, twenty years in jail? (Brian Noble)
>
> But you see, there's Canadian law ... to protect the sacredness of that dollar. But what do we have to protect? We do have our laws. That's why we refuse to talk about them. (Reg Crowshoe)
>
> And because the protocols are there that say, "No you don't" ... unless you have the right. (Brian Noble)
>
> Exactly. (Reg Crowshoe)

Principle Twenty-One: The refusal to speak about something about which one has no rights is legal sanction in action as it is based on a comprehensive "fear" and respect for the source of laws, that source being the Creator.

Principle Twenty-Two: It is vital to determine whether places, objects, substances, stories, and songs are sacred (i.e., *subject to* Poomaksin) *and to ensure that they are not disturbed, removed, or alienated from the community in a manner inconsistent with Nitsiitapii protocol or, specifically, from the people who have rights to them.*

Nitsiitapii Property, *Siikapistaan,* and Exchange: Parallel to but Different from Cultural and Intellectual Property

A fundamental question was eventually taken up in the second circle discussion: What does the term "cultural property," or "cultural resource," mean to Piikani people? In the most general sense, the answer was: anything that people keep in their possession or to which they have rights – including lands, resources, objects, and intangible entities – *and* that is subject to exchange or transfer through Nitsiitapii-Skinnipiikani practice and protocol. A locally relevant set of oral understandings of "cultural property" needs to be articulated and adhered to if the socio-legal integrity of Nitsiitapii protections is to be attained. It was suggested that the appropriate way to achieve this is to get recognized elders from each worldview to work out parallel terminologies for parallel practices.

Tools of Cultural Transmission, What Is Transferred, and What Is Owned

The discussion first turned to ideas paralleling the basic building blocks of language – the alphabet, ABCs. In response to a question from one of the participants, Brian Noble suggested that, in Western law, the alphabet was accessible to all and was not subject to intellectual property rights. However, the assembling of letters into words, and then, for example, into a poem, allows one to use the tools of language to create something that one is able to protect through intellectual property rights. Reg Crowshoe responded:

> So ... whatever I develop with ABCs is my property? So if I made a poem, then it's copyrighted to me because I use the tools of ABC. You can't call ABCs cultural property, but what you made with the ABCs is cultural property ...
>
> So in our culture, we would say cultural property is what the old-timer [anonymous speaker 1] said. When the old man took him to a ceremony to heal him from getting sick ... that healing was his property. I can't re-enact it. But the tools the old man use[d] to heal him are cultural tools ...
>
> [T]he symbols and stuff that he uses to help heal, that's cultural tools, but the cultural property for him to say, "[O]kay, you take this pill and call me back in the morning." That's cultural property, but the tools he used, like the telephone, to say I'm sick, is not cultural property. The knowledge in our culture, the knowledge you get, is when you learn how to use those symbols to read the world ...
>
> So what I'm saying, in the old days, a child is a child; but when you teach that child those cultural symbols like the smudge, the pipe, and the paint, he knows that those are tools that he can use to become a doctor, a lawyer, or Indian chief in the future. That's the cultural knowledge that he owns to get to that, but the tools he uses are the symbols. It's like me, if I want to teach my grandson to be a doctor in the future, then I teach

> him ABCs, and the letters that he puts together with the ABCs and the knowledge that he puts together with that, is what he owns. (Reg Crowshoe)

What Reg Crowshoe is pointing out is that the basic tools of cultural transmission – smudging, protocols, the pipes, and paints, all of which facilitate transfer and transmission – are not the personal instruments of any one person but, rather, are universally available to Nitsiitapii for the purposes of exchange and transmission.[20] They form the communal property of Nitsiitapii, though they may also be transferable tools, as in the case of healing practices, community bundle practices, and so on. What becomes owned by a person individually is that which is specifically transferred to that person by means of these tools and practices, through protocols of venue, action, language, and song, as conducted by a ceremonialist with proper witnesses and participants.

A crucial point, and one that would galvanize much of the concluding discussion for this circle, arose in our discussions of Nitsiitapii property. It is the specific exchange practice that affirms the act of rightful transfer; that being the practice of "payment" – *Sikapistaaway* (the practice of giving *Siikapistaan*) – made by the old-timer:

> That medicine man owns that knowledge, but ... that little bit he used on [the old-timer] ... [The old-timer gives] is *Sikapistaaway,* so he owns it. You know? (Reg Crowshoe)
>
> He owns that part and then he would have a right to talk about that part? (Brian Noble)
>
> If he wants to ... because protocols will tell him that. (Reg Crowshoe)

According to Skinnipiikani laws, you can only talk about what you pay for according to proper protocols. If people speak about it without such payment, they are breaking the laws.[21] It was pointed out that there is a tendency among Euro-Canadian thinkers to see ownership as the central issue, whereas, for Nitsiitapii thinkers, the issues are centred on the obligation to do the right thing and to adhere to the rules of practice. This means that instrumental action associated with venue, action, language, and song is pivotal in any and all determinations of attachment and right (versus ownership).[22] The translational parallels between stewardship and ownership are drawn, but ownership is not the only issue for Nitsiitapii thinkers; rather, what is important is that one possess all the desired qualities of a leader, combined with proper training.

Principle Twenty-Three: All rights of relationship to cultural material, both tangible and intangible – and not solely the right to speak about them – are understood in the context of transfer (i.e., Poomaksin) *and the related system of obligations.*

Redressing the Breakdown of Nitsiitapii Transfer and Exchange Practices

One participant captured the double sense of cultural loss and reconstitution by describing how the disruption to Nitsiitapii principles and practices continued to put Nitsiitapii practices at risk and to raise spiritual dangers for people. She referred to her experience as a Natooas Bundle keeper who has fulfilled what is probably the most exacting and holy vow in Skinnipiikani ceremonies: hosting a Sundance and suffering on behalf of the entire community as a holy Sundance woman. In particular, she underscored how having an oral claim to rights is insufficient *without* the lifelong exposure to rightful practices, the transferred rights themselves, and the direct personal experience of ceremonial practices:

> I think with myself, just starting and learning what I need to know where I'm at right now and what I've gone through that summer, I know that if I do something wrong and I've been taught how to do it and I don't follow those, then I know something is going to happen to me and my family. But somebody that saw or witnessed and went through this, but didn't go through certain sections to get those things to use in the right way, doesn't know the consequence; so for those people who already have transferred rights, they know, "I'm going to talk about this, I can't talk about that, or I'm not going to follow through with this because I don't have that right." (Anita Crowshoe)

> But the ones who were not brought to that attention ... see somebody who was hurt or ... somebody dancing with that pipe or going through an All Night Smoke because somebody else are scared ... [those ones] do not know that. Those are the ones that I get scared of because those are the ones that are causing harm to the ones who are trying to practice the way that we're taught or the ones that say they're from a community but weren't raised in the community and come back and say, "[W]ell, my grandfather was this person, who was a very strong person traditionally, we went through the rites and all that." But because they're related to that person, it's automatically [given respect to] individual because they come from that family to know that they have that. But for that person to say, "[W]ell, I wasn't raised with them, I don't have those transferred rights," and [to] stand up and tell you that, those are the ones that scare me. (Anita Crowshoe)

> I was raised with Joe Crowshoe Sr.; I lived with him and I learned all of these things, now I'm practising the way he taught me. But the thing about it, it's upon me, and I know something is going to happen to me if I do that, but somebody who doesn't know and wasn't raised with it, those are the ones that people will then think, "[W]ell, he says this and

> he says that, he [is] taken for his word value." Because oral is still held [to be] strong by our people. (Anita Crowshoe)

This discussion about having rights to speak of practices and practising rights to lay claims is central to the question of cultural and heritage protection. The unauthorized taking, use, borrowing, modifying, or reproducing of Skinnipiikani transferable songs, materials, and practices are not simply acts of cultural appropriation; rather, they are a full-blown infringement (and corruption) of Nitsiitapii law and practice. The effect of such infringements is the undermining of the intergenerational coherence of Piikani social relations and practices, of being Nitsiitapii. As Anita Crowshoe notes: "People that don't have that right are already doing things, and what's happening is these young ones are seeing this. So their value of who they are, 'Nitsiitapii,' is getting lost; and we, as parents, how do we give that back to our kids? [H]ow do we save them?"

Principle Twenty-Four: Oral claims have to be backed up by transferred right and strong practice experience.

Nitsiitapii Property as the Outcome of Nitsiitapii Transfer Practice

When the question of specific forms of cultural property was raised, it was emphasized that the practices needed protection and that, from there, all such specific forms of ownable or transferable things could be addressed:

> Well, I think we [have to] protect the practices. Because the practice will protect the sites. [*Others express agreement.*] But the other thing is ... do we think the white man's law to protect the sacred sites is more important than the Indian's law, the practice to protect that site? [White man's law] would say, "Okay, I don't want you coming on my land. I'm going to use [white man's law] to protect it."
>
> What about us when we practise *Poomaksin* [transfers]? You know ... if we practise *Poomaksin* then we protect it. And whether it's right or wrong ... *Poomaksin* said there's a right and wrong, but there's a style of how you do.
>
> You know, when I paint your face, I could paint your face this way ... that's right. But, if some ... if the guy next to me paints his face with his middle finger up like this and he paints your face that way, although he's wrong 'cause his middle finger is up ... it's supposed to be down. So now you're fighting about techniques, not the paint that you wore, you know. All of a sudden we're fighting over styles ...
>
> What about painting face, which is important in the first place? And that's what I'm saying. We want to protect the laws ... we have to enforce our laws, our power through our practices and respect them ... those practices. Not style, you know? (Reg Crowshoe)

This centring on practices as the exercise of Nitsiitapii law may provide an answer to the question of new forms and kinds of "property" emerging in Western law.

Principle Twenty-Five: Nitsiitapii stress the overriding authority of practice over specific categories of property or styles of practice.

The Case of Bodily Matter and the Idea of "Nitsiitapii Property"

The question was posed: "What if you're dealing with something like genetic material – blood, tissue samples, something that came from somebody's body from your community, and somebody was misusing it. What kind of law would you appeal to, who would you go [to to] ask, "What should be done about this?" Reg Crowshoe responded: "[The] Creator would ultimately punish them. But if it's anything physical, then it's going to be the societies who are going to be charged with that right to enforce that law, they would."

This prompted the question of the possible distinction between collective property (as in the case of age-grade societies or community bundles) versus personal property (as one might think blood or tissue would represent). Reg Crowshoe explained: "[I]f you were gifted by the spirits with knowledge, or you went out on your own quest to come back with knowledge, it's your personal property. But anything that was transferred to you, then that's community property." He also suggested that the notion of "property" is far more appropriate than is that of "cultural property" or even "culture": "I would say there is our Nitsiitapii properties, whether it's cultural property or not, the word 'culture' is a white man's problem, not ours."

Principle Twenty-Six: Nitsiitapii property is that which is the subject of Nitsiitapii transfer and exchange practices.

Recognizing Siikapistaan: *A Working Principle for Compensation, Redress, and Enforcement*

> The other thing too is risking their lives, they compensated all those soldiers that went to fight in World War Two for Canada; when they came back they compensated them. Who's compensating the ceremonialists that risked their lives against the Indian agent to save our intellectual property? (Reg Crowshoe)

The long history of non-recognition of Nitsiitapii practices prompted questions regarding what has been lost to the Skinnipiikani as a consequence and how to redress these losses in a socially, politically, and economically meaningful way. In fact, as a result of historical colonial relations within

Canada, the Piikani, like many First Nations, are working from a position of profound economic and social disadvantage. The cost of resources necessary to redress this is, at present, incalculable.[23]

> White man asks us if we have resources to protect and put our culture back. The white people took away our cultural materials and told us not to practise. Now, after so many years, white people said, "[H]ere's your smudge stick, here's your smudge box, here's your bundles, here's repatriation, go ahead and practise."
>
> But it's big money to train a person to become a bundle owner, and when they stopped us from paying our tuitions to learn those, our system fell apart and we became poor people. And now you give us a bundle but with no resources to pay for those *Siikapistaan* for us to become teachers again.
>
> [It's as if], as Indians we took Canada and we took all the universities and we put them in the museum and we told the university professors, "[I]f you teach, you're going to jail or you're going to get hung." After eighty years, when all the old professors died off and then we say sorry, "[H]ere's your university, put it back," who's going to teach anybody ABCs to learn how to use that university?
>
> I'm saying the cheapest thing for me to do is give you back your universities, but you teach yourselves how to use ABCs. And the opportunists are just rubbing their hands, one guy knows the three of them, one guy know A, B, and C, but he doesn't know the rest so he's telling the government, "[G]ive the school to me and I'll teach everybody." [A]nother guy can sing, he knows the song, so he says, "[N]o, give it to me, he only knows three letters." So the opportunists start fighting, but the true people, the professors, the few of them that left that know what to do with the ABCs, are not getting the schools. I don't know if that answers your question. (Reg Crowshoe)

What is lacking in the existing repatriation efforts of museums, government agencies, and legislators is recognition of the practices and resources necessary to validate the return of cultural material, lack of support for inclusive, broad-based community participation and development. Without that recognition, combined with the direct application of the protocols of venue, action, language, and song, there is no culturally appropriate power-redressing mechanism for arbitrating return and compensation. As such, those with oral claims, but perhaps not with Nitsiitapii lawful right, may come forward to take advantage of the resources being allocated and the materials being returned.[24]

One proposition involved compensation for loss of elders and teachers – a direct consequence of Canada's past residential school policies and its prohibitions on ceremonies. The idea of compensation is directly related to principles of *Siikapistaan* because the banning of ceremonies and loss of cultural materials disrupted the ceremonial payment arrangements of that institution:

> This money that they're giving to the Healing Foundation, back to the communities, back to the people who have gone to boarding schools, how come they didn't set one up for the ones who practised the ceremonial stuff – even against the laws. They should be compensated ... I'm not saying give it to them. Compensation should have been set there for those people because there are many people in our community that did go through and protect and save the bundles. They risk their way of life just so they can carry on the practice so we have it here. (Anita Crowshoe)

Principle Twenty-Seven: Use principles of Siikapistaan *to provide compensation resources to facilitate reparations for the 100-plus-year loss of elders, teachers, and practices under the colonial policies and practices of the state and its extensions.*

A more nuanced discussion of *Siikapistaan* and its relation to transfers of things and rights followed. In essence, the discussion investigated whether *Siikapistaan* had an effect with regard to making lawful exchanges or arrangements, and, indeed, it appeared that it did:

> In the old days, when a person gets transferred, that's when we, as supporters, we used to give hides as payment. And today, if we look into the past, how much is the cost of one buffalo hide? It's over $1,000. And that's a lot of money in the old days; but when they made payments, [they used] all kinds of hides. Those are what we used for payment. If we count the worth of his payment in the old days and compare it to today, it's worth a lot. (old lady)

Siikapistaan is slightly similar to "consideration" in a contract: in giving something of value, the exchange relationship between the transferor and the transferee is underwritten. Reg Crowshoe explained this in terms of gaining transferred knowledge of practices from a rightful keeper of such knowledges:

> I'll try and say it in English ... now if I had the knowledge to teach the ABCs to Herman, he will come and pay me a *Siikapistaan* to teach him the ABCs. [A]nd once he can see and use the ABCs to expand ... his worldview and say, "[T]his is why I'm going to be a lawyer in the future, using these ABCs," then he'll pay me a tuition or a fee. If he's going to use his knowledge of those ABCs to expand his education, then he's paid me

> *Siikapistaan*. There's a fee for my expertise to teach him. And in certain cases it's a franchise, where every time he's done something a portion of what he's done is paid back to me all the time. (Reg Crowshoe)

The parallels with tuition fees and with franchises are useful but should not be taken as precisely mirrored counterparts to Western contracts or licensing law; rather, *Siikapistaan* signals additional orders of importance – legally, economically, and relationally – for Nitsiitapii as it also produces an ongoing, even perpetual, reciprocal obligation between those involved in the transfer. One of these obligations is to take care of your "teacher," or "trainer," to ensure that others continue to benefit in the same manner as have you. This was built into the system of practices and, historically, provided feedback to the entire social community. Following through on one's obligations, by bringing food or sponsoring a ceremony or circle discussion, ultimately supports the survival of the "institution" that taught the learner, who has gone on to be successful and confident.

Witnessing

The practised legal sanctioning of *Siikapistaan* and transferred rights is achieved through public witnessing, as noted in the following exchange.

> So would the payment of *Siikapistaan*, or lack thereof, have an effect on Nitsiitapii law? (Brian Noble)
>
> *Siikapistaan* is supposed to be done in public. [I]f you don't publicly make a payment, nobody's going to recognize your credentials to come and get help from me, so how are you going to make a living or become a leader? (Reg Crowshoe)
>
> So eventually you run into troubles from the community; sometimes I see some people bring a stick or a horse, but they don't bring the horse necessarily, it just means that they'll bring it later. (Brian Noble)
>
> You ask a person to do something for you, and you ask him how much he will charge, it's up to you. (old-timer)
>
> Is that the basis of all Piikani [legal] relationships? (Brian Noble)
>
> Siikapistaan has to happen ... I would say, yes, that's what holds our laws up. If we don't use *Siikapistaan*, then we don't respect them. (Reg Crowshoe)

One way to think of *Siikapistaan* is as the "glue of transfer rights": without it, the transfer won't "stick" and won't be socially recognized. More important, claiming a transfer right without proper adherence to *Siikapistaan* would be dangerous, and it puts one's social, political, and economic credibility at risk. *Siikapistaan* secures both the transfers themselves and the relationships between those directly involved in the transaction as well as all those with related transfer rights.

Issues of distribution of wealth and resources might appear to produce hierarchical social divisions and inequities. However, in principle at least, *Siikapistaan* is also relative to what the person can afford. Therefore, a rich person and a poor person are effectively equal when they give everything they own, say for a bundle transfer. This is an important point of distinction in contrast to non-native systems, which more often operate according to absolute measures of "worth." Here, one is measured by the relative quality and quantity of one's commitment – a sign of how humble one is prepared to be in taking on the responsibility for the bundle or other transferred right. Humility and commitment are highly valued features in assessing the worth of one's *Siikapistaan*. Even relatively poor people who were especially humble could become highly respected bundle keepers because they could be entrusted with the associated responsibilities of care.

Exchange, Survival, and Making Relatives

Borrowing from key anthropological understandings of reciprocity versus commodity relationships, Brian Noble summed up the generalized contrast between Euro-Canadian and Skinnipiikani transaction and ownership.

> What the [old-timer] is saying made me think of something ... I mentioned before. The non-native [Western European-Canadian] idea of property is based around the idea that something can be exchanged for something else. When two people come together, if I wanted to sell a tape to somebody, that person is going to give me five dollars for the tape. And I give him the tape, and he gives me the five dollars ... he can go his way and I'll go my way, and we never have to talk to each other ever again. And that's the idea of private property, is that all we have to do is exchange the object and we can walk away and never talk to each other again.
>
> But it seems to me when you talk about *Siikapistaan*, when you make that payment to someone and that person gives you something back, then in fact what you have done is, you continued a relationship and made that relationship stronger. [Y]ou can't just walk away after that. Is that part of the idea? Is that the distinction between the [non-native] notion and [the] Nitsiitapii notion of property? (Brian Noble)

The response to this was affirmative, suggesting that a perpetual obligation is created by the exchange:

> I think that part of the notion would say that, in the old days, if I was out

> here in this cold weather we're having today – the elements are going to kill me, but we need a group of us together to survive. So the concept of making relatives, *Siikapistaan* is part of that, [of] making relatives because it's a start of something for us to survive. If you give me something and I paid for it, I'm still obligated to help the community; but it's still understood that the song and the transfer wasn't given to you, you don't talk about it. So that relative building is so important. (Reg Crowshoe)

Relative making is the means to secure a self-regulating social system.[25] Skinnipiikani-Nitsiitapii transfer practice is underwritten by publicly witnessed *Siikapistaan* payments. As such, the practice is socio-culturally, politically, economically, and, therefore, legally far-reaching as it is the means by which communal relationships are forged, altered, strengthened, and judged.

Principle Twenty-Eight: Siikapistaan *is an inalienable and reciprocal counterpoint to* Poomaksin, *which – taken together with language, action, venue, and song – is necessary to affirm rights of keepership, stewardship, relation, and transfer.*

Negotiability, Deferral, and Intercultural Dimensions of Siikapistaan

Certain other nuances were noted in this discussion. One is that *Siikapistaan* can take the form of services in addition to cash or material goods. For example, drumming for ceremonial songs is governed by a whole constellation of transferred rights; some drummers received the rights and then made effective *Siikapistaan* by consistently making themselves available for ceremonies. Payment in-kind, or material payment, then, could be deferred or replaced in some manner, though it would clearly be understood as essential to fully effecting the transfer.

Similar transfer practices among the Pueblo and Sioux were mentioned. Indeed, where the Skinnipiikani may have lost certain cultural-ceremonial practices, there have been transfers with the Sioux, where *Siikapistaan* was paid, as is noted in the following exchange:

> When the Sioux headdress, the Sioux songs and dance were brought up and given to us, we paid *Siikapistaan* on them. We used them. (Reg Crowshoe)
>
> Did they [the Sioux] give up all of their rights or did they give you the rights to use them? (Brian Noble)
>
> Just the right to use them, not all the rights. (Reg Crowshoe)
>
> So they're special rights, and *Siikapistaan* can pay for part of the right. (Brian Noble)
>
> Very specific rights, it's not just a general [right], it's specific. (Reg Crowshoe)

Such rights are specific and apply to everything from chiefs' headdresses to holy ceremonials. An example of the latter is the Sundance, at which there are literally hundreds of transferable ceremonial components for every dimension of the many-day ceremony, and where there are cases in which Skinnipiikani have aquired certain of these rights – such as piercing rights – from other First Nations in order to rightfully exercise the full range of ceremonial components.[26] Of course, this has to be effectively regulated by the elder who transfers or sanctions the partial right and who, through this reciprocal association, becomes a relative to the transferee. This act of relation formation generates its own social sanctions and compels the transferee to learn the practices from the elder.

Principle Twenty-Nine: The ongoing reciprocal dynamic of Poomaksin *and* Siikapistaan *creates relations – or relatives – among people, cultural material, knowledges, places, and so on.*

Decolonizing the Relationship of Canadian Law and Nitsiitapii Law

The overall direction of the second circle led to a sense of:

1 how Canadian (and British and American) colonial non-recognition of Nitsiitapii principles and practices of law, right, ownership, and exchange – all of which are signalled by the idea of "cultural property" and "heritage" as well as "title" in land – have undermined the social, political, material, and moral order of Skinnipiikani society; and
2 how the path to the restoration of Skinnipiikani collective well-being can only be addressed through full and proper support, redress, and recognition of those practices that were ignored and/or undermined by colonialism.

But Canadian law has not simply ignored Skinnipiikani-Nitsiitapii law: it has superseded and elided it. The denial and trumping of Nitsiitapii law is most pronounced in the disruption of the socio-economic order embodied by *Siikapistaan* and transfer practices. Repatriation efforts by museums, while laudatory, demonstrate this very well:

> Would you say that in repatriation, that when the objects were brought back – what Anita was talking about – ... [that] the governments and so forth ... they didn't pay *Siikapistaan*? Is that why it didn't work, why it was an unequal relationship ... why you don't have the resources now? ... Is it because they broke the relationship of *Siikapistaan*? (Brian Noble)

> I think you hit the nail on the head. When they took our bundles without paying *Siikapistaan,* then they broke the whole system. Now it's easier for them not to make relatives with us but just to give us back our material objects, but it costs money to make relatives. In that sense, it goes on to say that building institutions is probably parallel to building relationships. The university needs to build an institution, with teachers and instructors, for that authority for the school to survive; if you don't build that institution and you give them back that school then it's not going to work because there [were] no resources put into it. (Reg Crowshoe)

Just as museums have failed to correct the *Siikapistaan* violation and imbalance, so they have failed to conduct themselves according to the protocols of venue, action, language, and song discussed in the first circle. It is this totality of practices and exchanges – plus the interruption of resources and economic flow – that has been put out of order, making the challenge of cultural, societal, economic, and legal redress and reconstitution that much more difficult for the Skinnipiikani in their relations with non-Piikani institutions.

Obviously, the church and museums alike have been guided by strong ethnocentric and assimilative goals, and the imposition of their moral orders, protocols, and principles have almost always trumped or displaced Skinnipiikani morals, values, and protocols. This dynamic is also seen in contemporary repatriation efforts:

> [You ask] is there any repatriation that has worked? I can't say that I've known a repatriation that has worked because the repatriation process was totally dictated by white people and white laws. [A]nd when that happens, and that bundle is brought back with strings attached to it by white laws, only the people in our community that have been schooled in white laws will be able to control that bundle; and the traditional people that talk about *Siikapistaan* and relation building are left standing on the side. And it's constantly happening: it's divide and conquer. (Reg Crowshoe)

Principle Thirty: Problems in repatriation efforts to date have been caused by not following Nitsiitapii practices, especially in recognizing the inalienability of Poomaksin *and* Siikapistaan *both historically and in the present.*

Transferred Songs as Intangible Markers of Law and Right

Despite this ongoing imbalance, Skinnipiikani, like many aboriginal peoples, recognize that museums remain one of the more receptive, however limited, non-aboriginal institutions with which to deal. As Reg Crowshoe says:

> [T]he songs are coming back, and this is where the love-hate relationship with museums comes in. You hate them for what they did, but you still love them for taping that stuff and hanging on to it. But the love-hate relationship goes back the other way; museums' collections couldn't have existed without the Indian people because they love them to get that material. But when they come to the door, they always think, "[O]h, here comes the thief coming to steal my stuff again." (Reg Crowshoe)

Repatriation actions have tended to bypass the indigenous protocols that are crucial to determining to whom materials should be returned. This was particularly apparent with regard to one key form of intangible "property" – transferred songs:

> So when we talk about songs, it's like saying, I have a copy of a whole bunch of degrees and certificates in my collection. Now do you want to put back your university and your education institutions, then you'll want an example of a degree – whom do I give it to? And how do I know who to give it to? [But] this is where the museums are coming out and saying, "[W]ell, we have the songs, but we don't know nothing about them." If they took those songs and they used the concept of *Siikapistaan* to take them, then they know very well how to give them back. But in this case they didn't. (Reg Crowshoe)

Museum professionals have historically mischaracterized songs as simply examples of cultural or ceremonial expression. As discussed in the first circle, songs are both transferred "property" and the ultimate indicator of "legal" right and cultural credential. One sings the song in ceremonial venues to demonstrate his or her right of transfer to all those actions, objects, and other things that are associated with, and transferred with, that song. Of all repatriable things, transferred songs are central to legal affirmation and to the establishment of community relationships.

Principle Thirty-One: The transferred songs (a form of "intangible" cultural property) are more than simply components of exchange; they are also essential elements of Nitsiitapii jurisprudence, and so they require special attention in future actions related to repatriation and cultural protection.

Jurisdiction: Positioning and Paralleling Canadian and Nitsiitapii Law

The disruption of the state's colonialist actions and its failure to recognize the legal and governing import of Nitsiitapii property was stated plainly:

> Well, it's like any kind of colonialization in any country, or taking over of any country. The first thing you're going to stop is the practice of government. Whether you know it or not, and you want to conquer that group of people, stop the practice of government. [A]nd that's what happened to us. Whether they understood or not, it was in their interest to stop the Indian people from governing themselves. (Reg Crowshoe)

Principle Thirty-Two: Canada's interruption of Poomaksin *and* Siikapiistaan, *as key elements of Nitsiitapii law and governance, effectively disrupted Nitsiitapii practices of self-government.*

The circle reaffirmed that Skinnipiikani-Nitsiitapii laws exist and that people still strive to live by them, even while outside Canadian institutions more or less ignore them. The discussion explored the positioning of Nitsiitapii law. The model of Canadian military law was presented as operating in a parallel, rather than in a subordinate, fashion to Canadian law.

> [I]n the military, if somebody did something – whether it's theft, assault, or murder – they're going to be tried in military court, not Canadian court. So what does the Canadian government do there? They accept [Canadian law as being] ... parallel [with] military law. The example is out there already ... we're just saying we've got culture that is as strong as the military and just as complex. We want to look at considerations of what was taken from us. (Reg Crowshoe)

Reg Crowshoe further used this parallel between military and Canadian law to discuss how, with regard to repatriation actions, Nitsiitapii property rights might be adjudicated:

> If I took military credentials away from the military, how would I know that I'm giving it to the right person back in the military? It's the same thing with the native community; if you took something and were giving it back, how would you know that you're giving it back to the right person? Well, you would study the military community and would follow that cultural process to understand who's going to get it back, let the military community define who's going to get it back. Our practices and community should say who, what, when, where, and how that bundle's coming back.
>
> [And] ... I can name experiences on all my hands and toes [t]hat ha[ve] happened where things were given back by [museums] not using traditional/Indian definition and law and authority ... where things have been given to individuals that'll say, "I have a bundle, I am the bundle, and I will say who gets that bundle back." I don't think the military community

will ever accept anybody taking that stand to say who's going to get any military material.

The authority of Skinnipiikani law must be recognized with regard to the establishment of proper procedures to determine rights, ownership, or stewardship.

Principle Thirty-Three: Skinnipiikani-Nitsiitapii laws have an internal process of deliberation that, in many ways, are akin to common law in Western legal practice.

Nitsiitapii Authority and Oral Precedents for Adjudication and Conflict Resolution: Who Is an Elder?

Some very important specifics with regard to who has adjudication authority were articulated in the second circle discussion, further defining the critical point made by Bundle Keeper Allan Pard in the first circle discussion. Ownership or transfer rights conflicts – as well as alterations to specific principles of law – are to be adjudicated and addressed by *former* keepers (not current keepers) of the bundles in question:

> There's a means of *Poomaksin*, if we say that we have a practice of action, language, venue, and song that gives you authority, and you've died out with it and that family says, "No, that's my bundle," our practices should be given priority to say who gets that bundle, not the family. If my dad died without transferring me the Short Thunder Medicine Pipe Bundle, and I was never an owner, I would have to leave it to the former bundle owners to decide how they're going to handle it. When they decide, I'm just saying, "Have pity on me and transfer me that bundle." If they don't have pity on me or they don't think that I can handle it, then they're going to transfer it to someone else. (Reg Crowshoe)

> [And] [i]t's the former bundle keepers, not the bundle keepers themselves – they can't be involved in the politics of backstabbing. [T]he old people said if there's any of that going on and you're looking after a bundle, to keep the bundle pure just put your head down and walk away because you're still holding a bundle, let the former bundle keepers handle that tough situation; don't embarrass that bundle owner by trying to ask him to make that decision. Don't say anything; just walk away because you're keeping your bundles pure. (Reg Crowshoe)

The former bundle keepers have a *duty* not to make their decisions on the basis of personal whim or interests but, rather, on the basis of prior protocol and practices – all of which are part of Skinnipiikani-Nitsiitapii oral history.

> The former bundle keepers have to use [the] oral history of what was said consistently by the old-timers to make that decision. They wouldn't make a personal decision. They would have to do their research, and they would have to understand the oral protocol. (Reg Crowshoe)

To be sure, such former bundle keepers are what Skinnipiikani would refer to as the elders to bundles or various ceremonial societies. Such transferable age-grade societies have included not only the Brave Dogs, Chickadees, Red Coats, Bumblebees, and Big Dew Claws but also groupings of elders (former keepers) of the larger collective ceremonials, such as the Thunder Medicine Pipes, the Sundance Headdresses, the Beaver Medicine Bundles, and Horse Medicine Bundles. So, for example, in order to adjudicate a transfer right issue related to some element of the Beaver Medicine Bundle, one would convene a meeting of former Beaver Bundle keepers, not current ones. This diversity of ceremonials allowed for addressing all aspects of collective life (*e.g.,* Brave Dogs had policing and organizational functions, Big Dew Claws had functions related to organizing recreational dances and leisure activities, etc.). Where a functional issue needs to be resolved, the question would be put to the elder group according to the appropriateness of the question to the society.

Principle Thirty-Four: Elders of age-grade societies and of bundles are the only persons who may act as adjudicators and arbiters of Skinnipiikani law and practice associated with those particular rights and attendant practices.

Band Council versus Ceremonial Society Authority

The community of elder authorities is separated from contemporary band administration, which is overseen by the elected band council, a political-administrative body established largely as a consequence of *Indian Act* strictures.[27] To date, the band council has taken limited steps to control Nitsiitapii property, and these efforts have not generally followed the Nitsiitapii protection practices described so far but, rather, *Indian Act* bylaw models. Reg Crowshoe argues that ceremonial society protection would be far more forceful and effective than what is found in the Band Council Resolution:

> I think the BCR [Band Council Resolution] says, "Any object that's of the reserve can't be used off the reserve." Whether they [BCRs] work or not, I can say I haven't found them effective because people are still selling information [and] material objects off the reserve and not giving any credence at all to the BCRs. (Reg Crowshoe)
>
> But what I can tell you that's working [with regard to] protection, is transferring to the Chickadee Society those four practices of transfer. [A]nd

> they're holding that cultural practice and information [in] safekeeping ... on the reserve. (Reg Crowshoe)

The very active societies involved with Nitsiitapii transfer and *Siikapistaan* practice today are the ones referred to: the Chickadees, or Niipoomaakiiks, the hosts of these circle discussions; the Brave Dogs, or Knut-sum-ataks; and the keepers of the major communal bundles:

> I would feel that [the Brave Dogs are protecting these rights] because *Siikapistaan* is still a big part of it. The rattles still go within the process of *Siikapistaan*, and that protection still stays there. The bundle owners, same thing, *Siikapistaan* still happens and the protection is still here. But, as politics goes, there are different styles. (Reg Crowshoe)

While these practices are being carried out by these societies, circle discussion participants argue that full community and wider recognition of the ascribed authority and responsibility of the various societies is still lacking. Such recognition would serve to enhance the protection capabilities of the various societies, an example of which would be the policing function of the Brave Dog Society:

> [I]f we talk about giving power to the Brave Dogs to police, then let's give them that power and respect and let's be scared of them. If we just play Brave Dogs, then we'll never have an effective system to protect us. We're telling white people, "[G]ive us the resources, and give us the parallel recognition of policing Brave Dogs so that we can start putting back our systems that we used to have." That's why we brought the Brave Dogs to open the Police and Fire Games in Calgary. At least it took the step [of] recognizing the Brave Dogs Society as a legitimate [body that could provide] fire and policing protection for the community. But nobody else understood it, they just said, "[O]h, what a nice show." (Reg Crowshoe)

Principle Thirty-Five: A contradiction in the means of recognizing authority over cultural materials has arisen with the increasing empowerment of Indian Act *band council administration over Skinnipiikani life and practices.*

The Call for Communally Based Sanction

This all points to one of the cruxes of non-aboriginal consideration of Skinnipiikani ceremony. This is a tendency to view ceremonial practices as quaint cultural performances rather than as seriously respected and effective community-sanctioning practices. But that recognition is also limited within the community itself, and community support needs to be rebuilt over the long term.

There is a two-way relationship here: adhering to oral-based law supports and advances the communal bonds and social order, while communal bonds and social order ensure that the laws are effective and properly sanction individuals and groups within the community:

> In an oral culture, credibility and support of the community is so very important to stay in line. If you break those laws, then you don't get that protection. You don't get that recognition, and you get slowly moved down the line so you're not really respected in the community. I think that's punishment enough. It doesn't have to be [in line with a] Western perspective of what is punishment: let's take [him] to the jail and spend money on him; [g]et him going again to pay his dues. [I]t's not that. I think you're talking two different paradigms here. And you can't cast Western paradigms over an oral culture. I can say that the community is not going to give respect to that person; that's real punishment in our community. In Western paradigms, they say, "Oh, that's not punishment." You have to put them in jail. (Reg Crowshoe)

The salient point is that the power of any sanction will depend on the extent to which the relevant practice is respected and lived in the community itself.

Parallels: Can Canadian Statutory and Common Law and Practice Further Recognize Nitsiitapii Law and Practice?

The crux of the matter was seen as full state recognition of Skinnipiikani-Nitsiitapii protocol and practice, which are the proper means of governing and adjudicating the return and circulation of Nitsiitapii property. Brian Noble indicated that some discussions about new law reform initiatives could move towards the establishment of statutory laws related to heritage property. Reg Crowshoe replied:

> I think you're talking about the sentence that should be put in ... the heritage statutory law that's going to be developed, and I think one of the crucial things there is going to be, how do you work with two paradigms? One cannot trump the other side. So, in order not to trump the other side, you've gotta be able to work with recognition and awareness of both sides. And this is where Rose's concept of ... paralleling came in: *Nitooii.* (Reg Crowshoe)

Nitsiitapii law must be accorded the same degree of practical authority and autonomy as is Canadian common law. One should be parallel to the other, not subordinate to it. In the end, what is called for is a dialogue between laws. The challenge is whether such a dialogue and parallel recognition can be achieved through heritage law proposals and other law reforms or whether an altogether differently conceived, innovative, and brave political and legal project is required for this vitally important task.

Principle Thirty-Six: The final crux of issues involves full state recognition of Skinnipiikani-Nitsiitapii protocols and practices, which are the proper means of governing and adjudicating the return and circulation of Nitsiitapii property.

Principle Thirty-Seven: Any process of discussion and recognition of law and right has to start from the working principle of a dialogue between autonomous laws – Nitsiitapii law and Canadian law – rather than from the presumption that one of these should subordinate or encompass the other.[28]

Or, as one old-timer said, "A paper's a paper, but to us, this is our life. This means we take control."

Appendix: Skinnipiikani Principles for Cultural Protection, Repatriation, Redress, and Heritage Law Making with Canada

The following gathers together the selected key principles for action that emerged from the two circle discussions. In order to set these principles within a larger framework, we reiterate some key general statements from the introduction. These are indicators of important approaches that the Skinnipiikani would welcome to guide future actions. Given all that has been said about the inalienability of practice, people, knowledge, rights, and so on, extracting principles in this fashion has some inherent risks. Therefore, *readers should avoid using any of them outside the context of this study.*

Extracts from Preamble

In relation to rights for culture, repatriation, and heritage, this chapter addresses the complex of stewardship rights and responsibilities realized through an integral regulatory practice involving venue, action, language, and song. It concludes that the proper redress of heritage-related matters will only be achieved through the full recognition and activation of Nitsiitapii process and practice. An important observation is that Canadian non-native institutions, museums, legal bodies, and arms of the state continue to ignore or sidestep Skinnipiikani processes and practices of *Siikapistaan* and *Poomaksin* (payment and transfer) as well as the more general protocols animated by means of venue, action, language, and song. It is this totality of practices and exchanges that has been put out of order, making the challenge of socio-cultural, economic, and legal redress that much more challenging for the Skinnipiikani. To protect Skinnipiikani cultural and heritage property rights in Canada, one must recognize, protect, and activate the authority of Nitsiitapii practices. These practices, in dialogue with Canadian laws, will then govern matters of redress and return as well as current and future protections.

Principles Drawn from Knut-sum-atak Circle Discussion 1

In the first discussion, "Society Protocols, Traditional Order, Collective Trust: Venue, Action, Language, and Song," the key was to understand venue, action, language, and song as the main elements in Skinnipiikani decision making and protocols governing the right to "cultural property" and Skinnipiikani heritage. The following may be interpreted as aspects of lawfully sanctioned proceedings and definitions from the Skinnipiikani.

Principle One: Nitsiitapii practice starts by invoking the support of those present, of rightful transferred bundle keepers both past and present, and the transferred people of the age-grade and other societies.

Principle Two: Keepership of the major bundles of the Skinnipiikani is collective (on behalf of the people) rather than individual (for one's own purposes).

Principle Three: As a moral core, those with transferred bundle rights sustain community respect and support by acting with generosity, humility, supportiveness, sharing, kindness, equality, respect for difference, truthful speech, gentleness, and knowledge of transferred rights and practices.

Principle Four [as noted by Heather Crowshoe-Hirsch]: *The use of the term "property" is inadequate because that which is transferred does not, technically speaking, belong to anyone. The possession of these items is "Creator-given" and, as such, cannot be owned or deemed property as such. Rather than "property," perhaps it is better to say that all of these items are "physical representations of these rights."*

Principle Five: Technically specific language is a dimension of transfer protocol (i.e., Poomaksin).

Principle Six: Language restoration is crucial to advancing cultural transmission and transfer practices.

Principle Seven: Venue specificity and arrangement is the second dimension of transfer protocol.

Principle Eight: Action specificity is a third dimension of transfer protocol.

Principle Nine: Song specificity is the fourth and decisive dimension of transfer protocol.

Principle Ten: For the Skinnipiikani, restoring integrated practices of transfer is the means of restoring language, song, and cultural transmission between generations. As they are interdependent parts of the practice, it is crucial that they be restored together and in total, that they not be separated from one another.

Principle Eleven: Many key principles underlying the social-natural order are embedded in the Napi (Trickster) stories.

Principle Twelve: Many key moral principles and values of the Skinnipiikani are embedded in the Kutoyiis, Blood Clot stories.

Principle Thirteen: Napi and Kutoyiis stories are key sources of principles informing the legal order of the Skinnipiikani.

Principle Fourteen: The means of resolving confusion and differences of opinion about practices caused by colonialism is to subject the questions to the practices that are activated by rightfully transferred bundle holders and former rights holders. Lifelong engagement with the practices on the part of transferred rights holders is considered crucial.

Principle Fifteen: Those past rightfully transferred bundle keepers or past rights holders of the age-grade societies are usually recognized as "elders," or "grandparents," to those transferred rights and practices. They may be called upon as advisors and adjudicators on questions of law and protocol associated with materials or practices that correspond to the transferred right being considered.

Principles Drawn from Knut-sum-atak Circle Discussion 2

In the second discussion, "Nitsiitapii Property and Law in Parallel with Canadian Law," the implementation and description of Nitsiitapii law in the context of venue, action, language, and song was developed, with the goal being to understand the force of Piikani law and the centrality of transfer practices supported by the Skinnipiikani exchange, transfer, and ownership principles achieved through relative-making payments known as *Siikapistaan*.

Principle Sixteen: Recognize the great diversity of distinct cultures and practices pertaining to cultural research and ownership; avoid universalizing approaches to aboriginal peoples.

Principle Seventeen: Ensure that control over research, culture, and heritage lies with the people to whom it belongs and is in accord with cultural practices.

Principle Eighteen: It must be recognized that rights to material culture, the knowledge of their uses, and the powers that animate them are inseparable from one another.

Principle Nineteen: Skinnipiikani-Nitsiitapii practice can assign personalized rights to the use or "exploitation" of lands and resources.

Principle Twenty: Where belief in and fear of the Creator is the force behind Nitsiitapii law, proper adherence to the protocols of venue, action, language, and song through the performance of ceremonies appropriate to the matter under consideration must be the basis of legal conduct.

Principle Twenty-One: The refusal to speak about something about which one has no rights is legal sanction in action as it is based on a comprehensive "fear" and respect for the source of laws, that source being the Creator.

Principle Twenty-Two: It is vital to determine whether places, objects, substances, stories, and songs are sacred (i.e., *subject to* Poomaksin) *and to ensure that they are not disturbed, removed, or alienated from the community in a manner inconsistent with Nitsiitapii protocol or, specifically, from the people who have rights to them.*

Principle Twenty-Three: All rights of relationship to cultural material, both tangible and intangible – and not solely the right to speak about them – are understood in the context of transfer (i.e., Poomaksin) *and the related system of obligations.*

Principle Twenty-Four: Oral claims have to be backed up by transferred right and strong practice experience.

Principle Twenty-Five: Nitsiitapii stress the overriding authority of practice over specific categories of property or styles of practice.

Principle Twenty-Six: Nitsiitapii property is that which is the subject of Nitsiitapii transfer and exchange practices.

Principle Twenty-Seven: Use principles of Siikapistaan *to provide compensation resources to facilitate reparations for the 100-plus-year loss of elders, teachers, and practices under the colonial policies and practices of the state and its extensions.*

Principle Twenty-Eight: Siikapistaan *is an inalienable and reciprocal counterpoint to* Poomaksin, *which – taken together with language, action, venue, and song – is necessary to affirm rights of keepership, stewardship, relation, and transfer.*

Principle Twenty-Nine: The ongoing reciprocal dynamic of Poomaksin *and* Siikapistaan *creates relations – or relatives – among people, cultural material, knowledges, places, and so on.*

Principle Thirty: Problems in repatriation efforts to date have been caused by not following Nitsiitapii practices, especially in recognizing the inalienability of Poomaksin *and* Siikapistaan *both historically and in the present.*

Principle Thirty-One: The transferred songs (a form of "intangible" cultural property) are more than simply components of exchange; they are also essential elements of Nitsiitapii jurisprudence, and so they require special attention in future actions related to repatriation and cultural protection.

Principle Thirty-Two: Canada's interruption of Poomaksin *and* Siikapiistaan, *as key elements of Nitsiitapii law and governance, effectively disrupted Nitsiitapii practices of self-government.*

Principle Thirty-Three: Skinnipiikani-Nitsiitapii laws have an internal process of deliberation that, in many ways, are akin to common law in Western legal practice.

Principle Thirty-Four: Elders of age-grade societies and of bundles are the only persons who may act as adjudicators and arbiters of Skinnipiikani law and practice associated with those particular rights and attendant practices.

Principle Thirty-Five: A contradiction in the means of recognizing authority over cultural materials has arisen with the increasing empowerment of Indian Act *band council administration over Skinnipiikani life and practices.*

Principle Thirty-Six: The final crux of issues involves full state recognition of Skinnipiikani-Nitsiitapii protocols and practices, which are the proper means of governing and adjudicating the return and circulation of Nitsiitapii property.

Principle Thirty-Seven: Any process of discussion and recognition of law and right has to start from the working principle of a dialogue between autonomous laws – Nitsiitapii law and Canadian law – rather than from the presumption that one of these should subordinate or encompass the other.

Notes

1 Reg Crowshoe, Knut-sum-atak meeting: Circle Discussion No. 2 (3 December 2003), Oldman River Cultural Centre (Gift Shop) in Brocket, Alberta. Transcripts of the discussion circles are located at the Oldman River Cultural Centre and are on file with the author. At the time of writing, placement in a public archive was not yet determined.

2 The Blackfeet of northern Montana and the Piikani of southern Alberta were, in pre-colonial times, the same tribal group, and today they continue to share many relations, histories, ceremonial associations, transferred rights, and other exchange connections.

3 The procedures and practices presented in this chapter are, in many ways, complementary to and consistent with those presented and contextualized in an earlier report from the Piikani addressing health-related decision making: Reg Crowshoe and Sybille Manneschmidt, *Akak'stiman: A Blackfoot Framework for Decision-Making and Mediation Processes,*

2d ed. (Calgary: University of Calgary Press, 2002). That report also contains an extensive bibliography of academic, archival, and non-academic sources that are generally and specifically relevant to this chapter.

4 Sákéj (James Youngblood) Henderson uses the concept of "embodied spirit" to capture this integral, inalienable relationship. Sákéj Henderson, "Law Commission of Canada: Indigenous Legal Traditions Workshop" (Workshop presented to the Dalhousie University, Faculty of Law, 30 March 2004) [unpublished] [archived with the author].

5 H. Patrick Glenn, *Legal Traditions of the World* (New York: Oxford University Press, 2000) c. 3 at note 55.

6 Clark Wissler, "Ceremonial Bundles of the Blackfoot Indians" in *Anthropological Papers of the American Museum of Natural History* 7:2 (New York: American Museum of Natural History, 1912) [Wissler]. See also Crowshoe and Manneschmidt, *supra* note 3.

7 Following is a list of the participants in the circle discussion. Most of these people hold, or previously held, transferred rights: Pat Provost, Doris Many Guns, Bryan Jackson, Allan Pard, Geoff Crow Eagle Sr., Heather Crowshoe-Hirsch, Sheena Jackson, Ricky Prairie Chicken, Sidney Bad Eagle, Naomi Windy Boy, George Gallant, Robert Bad Eagle, Dexter Smith Jr., Elizabeth Gallant, Reg Crowshoe, Kathleen Grant, Herman Many Guns, Rose Crowshoe, Dylan Starlight, Mills Big Bull, Deborah Bad Eagle, Anita Crowshoe, and Gordon Many Guns.

A selection of some of the transferred rights represented by participants (transferred songs go with virtually all of these), as either current or former rights holders, includes Natooas, Sundance Headdress Bundle; Thunder Medicine Pipe Bundles (several different bundles, current and former); Beaver Medicine Bundle; Brave Dog Society Bundles (numerous, current and former); Brave Dog Leader Bundle; Brave Dog Rider Bundle; Bundle Drumming (for several different ceremonies); Horn Society membership; Chickadee Society membership; Painted Teepee designs (numerous); Feather Game; Sundance Weather Dancers; Sundance Piercing; Fire and Smudge tenders; personal medicine bundles and *iniskim* (numerous); and bundle-specific ceremonial rights (numerous).

8 Knut-sum-atak Meeting: Circle Discussion No. 1 (21 November 2002) Oldman River Cultural Centre (Gift Centre) Brocket, Alberta.

9 A close reading reveals how the opening statement is metaphorical. He is practising venue, action, language, and song: "venue" is the Brave Dog Society context of the meeting, within which all the dialogue will follow; "action" is the gathering together for the purpose of the meeting; "language" follows the status and transferred rights of those in attendance; "song" is associated with the sanctioned integrity of the objective and the importance of the elders, past and present, who have gathered to attain this objective.

10 Bundles are among the various physical representations of objects that are given specific and specialized mandates to operate, manage, or function in ways helpful to people.

11 These are essentially services and technical support for the ceremony being performed. Not all elements are required in every ceremony, but the ones that are required are often specifically associated with different major transferred bundles.

12 Teepees operate through transferred rights that align with standards of practice for the individual and that do not require the same degree of guidance from an elder as do the major transferred items.

13 While names are transferred, such transfers operate in ways that are outside the scope of this study.

14 Taken from trascripts for the *Poomaksin* case study, Knut-sum-atak Circle Discussion No. 2 (3 December 2003), Oldman River Cultural Centre, Brocket, Alberta.

15 John Burrows, *Recovering Canada: The Resurgence of Indigenous Law* (Toronto: University of Toronto Press, 2002) at 56.

16 It was pointed out that certain matters need to be considered when reading this passage. First, at the time of residential schools, children were simply not around to participate, and there was a general fear of discipline and reprisals that was probably the result of living under what amounted to federal wardship. This appears to be the time when Crow Flag was practising. Second, the practice is usually dependant on the ceremony in question. And third, the best means of resolving this question would be to approach elders involved in the ceremony in question rather than the current transfer holders (*i.e.*, stewards) and practitioners.

17 It is important to know what particular sort of elder you would have to get. Choosing just any elder would not work and could, in fact, simply further distort the oral practice.
18 This second circle discussion was held at the OMRCC (gift shop) in Brocket, Alberta.
19 Professor Catherine Bell, Faculty of Law, University of Alberta.
20 Certain ceremonial rights, including those of whole healing practices and ceremonial leadership, are held on behalf of the community as opposed to forming a simple "commons."
21 It is important to note the implication for museums and researchers as most researchers and museums workers do not have such transferred rights when dealing with collections. This being the case, they are breaking Nitsiitapii law while simultaneously inviting danger both for themselves and for others associated with the tangible or intangible matter being kept or used.
22 Heather Crowshoe-Hirsch, who has been working on band governance development projects on the basis of Nitsiitapii practice later pointed out that all such practice-engagements are regulated by the elders present. Thus, the outcome is a regulated system of governance that, in this case, can transcend many issues and remain functioning and valid because the rules are closely and pragmatically regulated, well taught, and, therefore, consistent.
23 On the extent of transfers and the enormous economic costs of transfer rights payments, see Lucien M. Hanks Jr. and Jane Richardson Hanks, *Tribe under Trust: A Study of the Blackfoot Reserve of Alberta* (Toronto: University of Toronto Press, 1950) at 9-94.
24 Moreover, on legal interpretations of ownership or right, museums and government agents will instead default to Canadian law, thus doing further violence to Piikani cultural practices and risking further disruption to Skinnipiikani social, political, and economic systems.
25 A suggested example in non-native practices was offered by Heather Crowshoe-Hirsch: "The whiteman-Indian parallel to this is in the example of presenting a professional and united front of companies. A company would never allow any employee to make statements on behalf of the company or change, for example, 'the logo color.' These decisions are made by those who know and are familiar with the mandate of the organization. This is similar to making relatives." Telephone interview of Heather Crowshoe-Hirsch with Brian Noble (21 September 2004).
26 Interview of Reg Crowshoe, Piikani First Nation, by Brian Noble (20 August 1992) Brocket, Alberta.
27 *Indian Act*, R.S.C. 1985, c. I-5.
28 In fact, this stance can be seen as part of the doctrinal principles on which Canadian aboriginal law sensibilities and practices are built.

7
Protection and Repatriation of Ktunaxa/Kinbasket Cultural Resources: Perspectives of Community Members

Catherine Bell and Heather McCuaig, in consultation with the Ktunaxa/Kinbasket Tribal Council and the Ktunaxa/Kinbasket Traditional Elders Working Group

The desire for increased control over First Nations cultural heritage is about much more than access to, and preservation of, the physical integrity of objects and sites of significant historic heritage value. At the heart of the movement is an appreciation that cultural objects and sites are integral to a community's cultural identity and are a means to transmit and retain vital cultural knowledge. It is therefore not surprising that the Ktunaxa/Kinbasket Treaty Council (KKTC) (now called the Ktunaxa Nation Council) has developed a broad definition of "cultural resources" and a wide range of strategies to protect and control these resources – a range that extends beyond conventional classifications of property interests and emphasizes the value and importance of these resources to the Ktunaxa Nation.[1] These strategies have been initiated both inside and outside the British Columbia Treaty Commission (BCTC) process. Essential to their approach is an appreciation that improved communication, increased awareness about Ktunaxa/Kinbasket people, and cooperative arrangements that respect the Ktunaxa Nation's jurisdiction are necessary for the effective and efficient preservation and maintenance of Ktunaxa/Kinbasket culture. Thus, although the Ktunaxa Nation asserts that control over cultural resources is an aspect of its inherent right to self-government and that aboriginal rights and title include the cultural rights of the Ktunaxa/Kinbasket people, the assertion and negotiation of legal rights through the BCTC process is only one of several actions taken (one of which includes participation in this research) to retrieve and protect aspects of Ktunaxa cultural heritage.

The KKTC was established in the 1970s to "promote the political goals and social developmental of the Nation."[2] It represents five Canadian bands living within the traditional territories of the Ktunaxa Nation, whose members originate from the Ktunaxa (Kootenai) culture and include one Shuswap band (Secwepemc), which includes descendants of the Kinbasket family.[3] Traditional territories include lands along the Kootenay River and cross both provincial and national boundaries. Ktunaxa communities are located in Windermere, Creston, Invermere, Cranbrook, and Grasmere in southern British Columbia and in northern Montana and Idaho. Traditional Ktunaxa territory also includes parts of southern Alberta and northern Washington.[4] Although the KKTC represents only Canadian bands, it works in cooperation with the Kootenai Tribe of Idaho and the Confederated Salish and Kootenai Tribes in Montana on issues of repatriation and other matters of mutual interest.

This study was designed in collaboration with the KKTC and was implemented in accordance with the methodology and principles articulated in the introduction to this volume. Data are drawn from the KKTC archives and website and from interviews with community members that were conducted from the summer of 2002 to the fall of 2003. A total of fifteen interviews were conducted in Ktunaxa and English. Of those participants interviewed, four are members of the St. Mary's Indian Band, six of the Columbia Lake Indian Band, two of the Lower Kootenay Indian Band, one of the Tobacco Plains Indian Band, and two of the Shuswap Indian Band. Nine had experience or knowledge of the museum industry, archaeology, or archives; nine were involved in the repatriation of objects or human remains; three were band councillors; and three were fifty-five years old or older and were considered elders in their respective communities. Interviews were conducted based on the standard question set.[5] Questions were distributed to participants in advance of interviews. All participants reviewed quotes that were taken from their interviews and used in the case study. Following this process, drafts and the final version of the case study were submitted to the KKTC and the Ktunaxa/Kinbasket Traditional Elders Working Group for comment and final approval, in accordance with KKTC research protocols.

Definition of Cultural Heritage and Cultural Resources

In 1995, responding to input from indigenous peoples and organizations from around the world, United Nations Special Rapporteur Dr. Erica-Irene Daes proposed a definition of indigenous heritage for the purpose of developing international principles and guidelines for protection. Integral to that definition is recognition of the interrelatedness of cultural knowledge, expressions, material culture, and traditional lands.[6] The definition is not restricted to historical manifestations and reflects the idea that cultural heritage is best understood as that which is integral to the distinct identity of a people.[7] There is considerable consistency between this definition and Ktunaxa concepts of cultural heritage. Definitions offered extend beyond conventional legal understandings of property interests, appreciate the inherent limitations of the word "property," and reflect the dynamic nature of Ktunaxa culture. They include all cultural resources – tangible and intangible, animate or inanimate – that are important to contemporary Ktunaxa society and the continuity of Ktunaxa knowledge, identity, and traditions.

This concept is succinctly defined by Margaret Teneese (member of the Shuswap Indian Band and archivist for the KKTC) as anything "that belongs to certain individuals, groups or communities and allow[s] them to practice as a culture."[8]

The first questions asked in the KKTC interview process were, "What does the term 'cultural property' mean to you?" and "How would you define it?" Although some spoke more of the material world than others, all incorporated intangible heritage and knowledge derived from the material world into their definitions. The phrase "cultural property" was uniformly interpreted within the context of a more holistic concept of cultural heritage and, therefore, also includes keepers of traditional knowledge and the Ktunaxa "way of life." Consequently, the word "property" as it is used in Western legal discourse fails to adequately convey Ktunaxa conceptions of cultural heritage. As Gina Clarricoates and Christopher Horsethief explained:

> Cultural properties ... are visible and invisible to the, to Ktunaxa people. Things like the traditions, the beliefs that we have and items that we have that are important to pass on to the younger generations. Some of the things that I like to, to focus on are prayers which [are] invisible and I try to pass that on to the younger people, like my grandchildren.[9] (Gina Clarricoates)

> Well, I think in a broad sense, it refers to anything that has to do with that way of life or the community. But I think specifically it's any value, any thing, any item, any person, even ideas that have to do with who and what we are, things that maintain that way of life. And so I tend to like to be really specific with it, like regalia or remains or idols or things that are used by the people to continue this way of life – the way of life that is moulded around our language and our understanding of who we are in [the] context [of] the rest of the world, what makes us distinct. And that's, for me, an important point. It has to be something that contributes to that distinct quality of who we are, whether it's us in relation to our ceremonial ways, if you want to call it that; our spirituality, if you want to call it that. But I think just those very practical things that we practise, the way of life that we practise, [there] has to be some connection there.[10] (Christopher Horsethief)

All participants agreed that the original definition of cultural property used by the research team "made sense" in their community. That definition includes property integral to the distinctive cultural identity of a particular aboriginal community.[11] One participant also commented that a weakness in United Stated repatriation law is the exclusion of cultural records.

However, everyone interviewed also emphasized that cultural knowledge derived from the material world is as important as the material world itself. The need to preserve the material world is directly related to its utility in preserving and transmitting knowledge from one generation to the next. Wilfred Jacobs and Allan Hunter added that cultural property is the whole land and what is done on the land.[12] A definition of cultural resources that includes only sacred and historically significant sites is too narrow as all traditional lands and, according to Jacobs, "everything within that boundary," are considered cultural property:

> We come from the land. I've read over the definition of property. I do agree that it incorporates objects and places and human remains and whatnot inside here. But I also see that beyond historically significant "places" and moving away from the site-specific area because I do insist on including *amak,* or the territory of the Kootenay, in the definition because ... we don't know where everything, where every significant thing or place is. As my great grandmother told me, she said every square inch of this territory has footprints on it and, and I include that, the territory as cultural property. (Allan Hunter)

Participant observations are consistent with the approach taken by KKTC in its treaty negotiations. After engaging in community consultations, the KKTC adopted the phrase "cultural resources" in documents prepared for the treaty negotiation process. Cultural resources are defined as a "broad set of items that are important to the unique Ktunaxa lifestyle (who we are and how we live) from the past, present or into the future."[13] The term "property" is avoided as the items listed are not viewed as "commodities" but as "resources because of their value and importance to the Ktunaxa." Culture is defined as "always evolving, because culture is who we are, and how we express who we are, at any point in time."[14] Examples of Ktunaxa cultural resources identified by the KKTC include:

1. the Ktunaxa people, particularly the elders;
2. traditions, ceremonies and practices, some of which are inherent rights;
3. physical items or cultural use areas on the land, some of which include: archaeological sites, traditional use areas and sites, structural features, and cultural landscapes;
4. any cultural materials, information inventories or maps associated with these items on the land;
5. items removed from Ktunaxa lands that the Nation feels should be repatriated; and
6. stories, legends, songs, language and language programming.[15]

Rationale

> The strengthening of our traditional culture will improve the awareness and pride within our people and give us greater affiliation with our cultural roots. It will promote the achievement of increased levels of self-esteem amongst the people of our nation.[16]

This quote, taken from a feasibility study on the establishment of a Ktunaxa Nation language and cultural resource centre, encompasses the three main rationales for protection and repatriation of cultural property articulated by members of the Ktunaxa Nation: loss of traditional cultural knowledge, continuity of cultural practices, and improving cultural identity and self-esteem. Of pressing concern to most participants is loss of traditional cultural knowledge. Traditional cultural knowledge is an amalgam of historical and contemporary influences and is used here to describe values, beliefs, customs, practices, and traditions that form part of the Ktunaxa Nation's identity and are connected to the experiences of their ancestors. Levels of traditional cultural knowledge varied among the participants interviewed. Many expressed concern about lack of awareness and further generational loss. All emphasized the importance of learning and expressed concern about the retention and renewal of cultural knowledge in some form. This concern is echoed in discussions on benefits of repatriation with elders and youth in preparation for treaty negotiations. An overview of an early treaty meeting offers the following summary of their views: "We've lost our culture, we don't know who we are. We're grabbing everyone else's culture. We need to get our items back ... to identify how Ktunaxa lived/survived."[17]

Loss of traditional cultural knowledge is attributed to a number of factors, including the removal of cultural material from communities and retention of these items by museums and other institutions. Some participants mentioned how outlawing spiritual practices and ceremonies such as the Sundance and the potlatch under federal Indian legislation facilitated this process. All participants who spoke to the issue of repatriation emphasized that the importance of material culture lies in its meaning and utility to the community. This sentiment is echoed in the following comments:

> [M]y personal view is that when these, when our cultural items were sold and placed in museums, we lost a lot of our traditional cultural knowledge. I'll give an example of the Lower Kootenay people. When I was in the museum, the American National Museum of the American Indian in New York, we saw ... duck decoys. And they were just in perfect condition. Like whoever made them were really, were experts in making the decoys because these decoys looked exactly like the living bird ... They

> used the feathers, the head, the feet, everything, the whole body they used, like the whole duck, they used. [A]nd how they preserved it, I don't know. But they used to use these decoys when they went duck hunting ... I could be wrong, but I don't know of any people, [if] any of our Ktunaxa people today, [know] how to make a duck decoy. I mean, that's one example. That's ... a complete loss of our traditions. [W]ith our items, like our cultural work, artwork being held in museums, they've taken away the, the knowledge from our communities and, you know, placed them far away, where most of our people will never get to and never see. And our children will never see them. So, they don't have a connection to the culture and that's, that's severed. That line is severed. I'll give myself as an example. When I was a young woman, I was a nurse and ... other nurses and doctors would ask me what kind of baskets the Kootenay people made, and I told them that [we] never made baskets. And one of them asked me, "[W]ell, how did you carry your water?" And I said, "I don't know." You know, and I was in my twenties at that time. So I've just named another item that I had never seen. I didn't know that we used, [that] we even wove baskets ... until I was in my forties, [when] I finally saw a basket, and that was at the museum, the Museum of Civilization in Ottawa.[18] (Violet Birdstone)

> It's, it's hard you know, if something is like a sacred object and it's not here in the community, it's hard for us. Especially if it's been removed from the community for generations and that maybe some of that knowledge around that object has been lost. It's hard to, to bring something back when we don't have the knowledge that goes with it because it was taken out of the community. And so it would be important to, to, to seek the elders and say, "What do we do with this?"[19] (Troy Hunter)

Several participants also spoke to the role of the residential schools in undermining cultural identity and individual belonging. One participant explained how the residential school experience traumatized him, tore apart the Ktunaxa as a people, and resulted in the Ktunaxa having to relearn their culture.[20] Responding to a question about the connection of material culture to the spiritual, emotional, and cultural well-being of the community, Margaret Teneese explained:

> And, given the fact that a lot of these things were taken away from us as a deliberate attempt to get us to lose that identity ... in getting it back, it definitely is going to reinforce who we are. [A] lot of people that have been adopted out who are now coming back ... they are like really, totally lost. [If] they have a lot of these things available here, that would help them feel part of the community. They're looking at pictures, listening to

> like, say, their great-great grandparents; they know they're from here. They know that they belong here and it would help them reconnect ... And also you have to understand ... the uniqueness of, you know, their heritage. The Ktunaxa language is like no other language [in] the whole world ... [T]hese individuals are in that kind of, they come back and they can embrace that. It's something that ... is [also] a negative result of these children being taken away, you know, with residential schools that they're in and that, all of that is taken away – your kinship. So we're in school for such a long period of time that we came out, we didn't know who we were related to. So, it's for us as well. (Margaret Teneese)

The passing of knowledgeable elders is another reason offered to explain loss of cultural information. Elders are also needed to interpret and share the knowledge associated with items removed from the community. Consequently, it is important that items be returned while there are still people in the community who can speak to their origin and use. Loss of knowledge is also associated with loss of land and destruction of archaeological sites. Robert Williams echoed the sentiments of others when he said that protection of these sites is necessary "because they tell the story of our past, of how our ancestors lived."[21]

The theme of cultural loss and renewal is also dominant in the feasibility study mentioned earlier. This study, which included a questionnaire distributed to "a randomly stratified sample of ten percent of each band's population," sought as one of its objectives to determine the importance of creating a resource centre on the St. Mary's Reserve to house repatriated cultural material and to increase awareness of Ktunaxa/Kinbasket language.[22] Thirty-two percent of the sample population stated the they "knew something about the Ktunaxa/Kinbasket culture," and 29 percent indicated that they "always teach the traditions/heritage of the Ktunaxa/Kinbasket people to their own people."[23] Eighty-three percent felt it was "extremely important" to establish the centre; 81 percent felt that it would play "an extremely important role in giving back culture and language to the people"; and 79 percent "strongly agreed" that the centre would "greatly improve awareness about ... language and culture."[24] Ninety percent felt that "full access" to cultural material should be "made available to all Ktunaxa/Kinbasket members," and 52 percent felt no access should be given to non-natives.[25] As some cultural material is "spiritually sensitive," the report indicates that "it is not surprising" that full access to these materials is denied to non-natives.[26]

Integral to the proposal for the resource centre is the belief that people who have "been unable to rely on traditional culture to provide them with direction and support" will benefit from an increase in "pride, self-esteem and self-confidence gained by relearning one's language and culture."[27] The study also offers several explanations for cultural loss, including the "thrust of assimilation by European settlers," disease, loss of traditional lands, racial prejudice, and discrimination.[28] On the question of residential schools, the introduction to the study notes:

> There have been many injustices which have removed the language and culture from the Ktunaxa/Kinbasket peoples. The residential schools dramatically restricted the passage of our language and culture to our children. These schools removed the culture from our youngsters and instilled shame on those of us who did not accept the "white man's ways." We have accepted these hardships and embarked on a path of renewing our culture. Today, with the help of our elders, we are strengthening our language and culture and rooting it in our younger generation.[29]

What emerges from the above discussion is a shared belief in a direct relationship between access to, and control over, tangible and intangible aspects of culture and stronger cultural identity. The emphasis given to the protection of spiritual places, the return of spiritual items, and the inappropriate use of spiritual items, places, and songs further suggests that many participants also see a connection between increased protection, local control, and spiritual well-being. In the words of Gina Clarricoates, material culture, information, and the spiritual "blend together and need to be together to evolve." Joe Pierre agreed that the significance of an object may lie in a person's spiritual or emotional connection to it, but he personally found the question hard to answer as his grandparents impressed upon him that the relationship of an individual to a particular item "was an individual thing" and "you just didn't ... unleash ... that kind of information with anybody." This means that, in "some ways" and "some sense," others will never truly know about this connection.[30]

Another rationale offered for greater protection and local control is the need to prevent cultural appropriation; that is, to prevent what participants perceive to be the unauthorized taking or use of an aspect of Ktunaxa culture. An overriding perception is that cultural appropriation harms cultural integrity, survival, and identity as a people. Many forms of appropriation are identified, including degradation and failure to preserve the integrity of cultural information, wrongful removal or restricted access to material culture and information crucial to the continuity of cultural identity, and failure to follow Ktunaxa laws and protocols concerning use and transfer.

When asked, "[Are there any] particular teachings or information that you think are being improperly used by people who are not members of our community?" almost all participants had specific examples to share. This question, unique to the Ktunaxa case study, was included to determine whether community members share similar concerns about the dissemination of cultural misinformation as do representatives of the KKTC who are working on cultural resource issues. Examples given by participants include the desire of trail-riding companies to use pictograph sites as tourist attractions; groups that are not connected to the Kootenay tribes in the United States or the Ktunaxa Nation in Canada holding cultural camps to teach Kootenay "cultural ways";[31] the unauthorized and improper use of Ktunaxa names and songs; tour guides and interpreters having insufficient knowledge about Ktunaxa culture and land use practices; non-native authors failing to give proper credit to people who provide information and/or misrepresenting the history and experiences of the Ktunaxa peoples; people outside of the community "making themselves famous using information about the Ktunaxa regardless of whether it's the truth or, or not";[32] and the tendency of students, academics, and others to use information without permission. These examples demonstrate a common concern among participants regarding the accurate portrayal of Ktunaxa culture, and they also provide some insight into Ktunaxa perceptions of rights arising from original authorship, creation, and association. The notion that aspects of one's culture can be wrongfully appropriated also assumes the existence of relationships in which one group or person has superior rights of use over another.

A related concern is that "teachings or information from other nations ... passed on to the younger generation" are being "mixed up" and confused with Ktunaxa traditions. Gina Clarricoates gave the example of how women are excluded from activities such as drumming, dancing, and food preparation during "women's time." Similar concerns were expressed by elders who attended the treaty nation meeting on repatriation. They emphasized the importance of understanding the distinctions between Ktunaxa and Secwepemc (Shuswap) members of the KKTC with regard to drumming protocols.[33] However, as Joe Pierre explained, Ktunaxa culture is not limited to historical conceptions of what it means to be Ktunaxa: "Everything changes. What could be part of my tradition isn't the same as what my grandparents' tradition was. I think we take some things from the past and, and we use them as part of our lives today."

Protection and Repatriation Strategies

The KKTC's protection and repatriation initiatives form part of a more holistic concept of cultural conservation that includes an assertion of decision-making powers arising from aboriginal title and the right to self-government. Control over cultural resources, including repatriation of resources of historical and cultural significance, was one of the first topics the KKTC selected for negotiation in the BC treaty process. Interests identified for negotiation include "[p]reserving and maintaining the traditional aspects of Ktunaxa culture, and having continued access to resources necessary to support those aspects"; "[f]ull law making and decision making powers on Cultural Resources"; ensuring that all decisions affecting Ktunaxa cultural resources have the agreement of the Ktunaxa Nation and are administered under a "policy and procedure framework defined by the Ktunaxa Nation"; "creating a skilled Cultural Resource workforce"; and ensuring that the nation has the "necessary capacity to effectively meet its Cultural Resource management responsibilities."[34] However, both inside and outside the treaty process, the Ktunaxa Nation recognizes the need to work cooperatively with government, industry, academics, museums, and other institutions with an interest in Ktunaxa culture in a way that respects the jurisdiction and needs of the Ktunaxa Nation.

In July 2002, British Columbia, Canada, and the KKTC released the Interim Negotiating Framework for Cultural Resources.[35] The purpose of the document is to provide a mechanism to structure and monitor the negotiation process. It is not a final representation of the positions or interests of any of the parties. Seven broad areas were identified for negotiation: (1) identification of cultural areas, (2) ownership of heritage sites, (3) access to heritage sites, (4) access by non-Ktunaxa, (5) participation in planning and management of heritage resources, (6) "transfer of cultural materials" from the Royal British Columbia Museum and the Canadian Museum of Civilization, and (7) negotiation of "bi-lateral custodial agreements" for cultural materials.[36] Although the Ktunaxa wish to discuss all cultural areas, British Columbia's "interim negotiating instructions limit current discussions to Provincial Heritage Sites."[37] Repatriation from the two museums named is within the scope of the treaty process as they are provincial and federal institutions that hold Ktunaxa cultural material.

Several KKTC initiatives are designed to facilitate the treaty negotiation process but are not dependent on the process for measurable benefit to the Ktunaxa. For example, in 1999 the KKTC sent approximately one thousand letters to private and public institutions in Canada, the United States, Britain, Sweden, and other European countries that might have Ktunaxa or Kinbasket ancestral remains, items, or cultural records in their possession. Information about the number of items, who made them, their origin, who collected them, and how they came into possession of the institution was requested. Research was required before sending the letter as museums, universities, libraries, archives, heritage departments, and others needed as much information as possible in order to identify Ktunaxa material. Lists of how Ktunaxa material culture was classified by early anthropologists; names of some of the places within Ktunaxa territory that might be associated with Ktunaxa and Kinbasket items; various names for the Ktunaxa Nation and its members; prominent family names; and names of missionaries, art collectors, community leaders, and others who might be involved in the removal of items or the recording of Ktunaxa culture were also identified.[38]

The approximately four hundred responses received varied in content and usefulness, but overall the letter campaign was viewed as a success. In Canada, some institutions provided information even though they were not formally engaged by the BC treaty negotiation process. Some provided repatriation policies that were informed by the principles set out in the Assembly of First Nations and Canadian Museums Association Task Force Report entitled *Turning the Page: Forging New Partnerships between Museums and First Peoples*.[39] Some did not respond or, apologizing for insufficient staff and resources, requested a fee. Others requested more information or explained how they were working towards making the requested information available. Similarly, some institutions in the United States shared information while, at the same time, emphasized that Canadian First Nations were not within the scope of US legislation designed to facilitate repatriation of cultural objects to federally recognized Indian tribes.[40] However, many did not respond, emphasized they had no obligation to First Nations in Canada, or said that they had insufficient resources to respond. Obtaining helpful responses from European countries was more challenging, given the use of languages other than English and the tendency to group Canadian indigenous material into generic classifications.

In February 2000, the KKTC established the KKTC Repatriation Advisory Committee. "The Traditional Use Working Group, made up of Ktunaxa and Shuswap elders" (the Elders Group) forms part of this committee.[41] The purpose of the committee is to provide advice and guidance for the safe return of Ktunaxa material, to help with the continued preservation of Ktunaxa cultural resources, and to help categorize material culture discovered in the possession of other institutions. The committee is composed of Ktunaxa members who are "knowledgeable in Ktunaxa religious and cultural traditions" and who are able to identify and categorize items as sacred, funerary, or of other cultural significance in accordance with definitions imposed by outside legislation or developed through negotiation.[42] The committee works closely with the Kootenai Tribe of Idaho and the Confederated Salish and Kootenai Tribes to repatriate objects from the United States under US law. It is also responsible for developing policy for the proper care and treatment of returned objects and records, and for actively engaging in repatriation activity both inside and outside the treaty process. There are representatives from each of the bands represented by the KKTC as well as from the US tribes.

Another initiative is the traditional use and ethnobotany studies program. This program studies the Ktunaxa Nation's uses of traditional plants in the context of "resource protection, land management, education, economic development and other uses" consistent with sustaining traditional practices.[43] Projects include the creation of a herbarium used for research, comparative work, education in schools, and gathering knowledge of plants from elders and other specialists; the publication of a book on traditional plant uses; and the opening of an indigenous plant nursery.[44] Copies of the book were provided to all households represented by the KKTC and are also sold outside the community. Projects at the time of writing included examining the sustainability and development of resources such as berries, root medicines, and floral greenery.

The ethnobotany program addresses concerns raised by some participants, including sustainability of plant life, retention and dissemination of traditional plant knowledge within the community, and maintenance of traditional relationships with the land. Margaret Teneese referred to knowledge about the uses of the plants, including one "well known" to help with cancer, as "intellectual property" and expresses concern about the destruction and "exploitation of some of those plants." Robert Williams shared similar concerns about "people who claim to be medicine people who come into the area" learn about plants, destroy sites because they don't know how to pick or care for certain plants, and "sell this information to other people that they are supposedly teaching to be medicine men." Several participants emphasized how logging and commercial development are threatening the continuity of traditional plant use and the health of the Ktunaxa. Recalling how one development project destroyed "all the juniper ... on the west side of Columbia Lake," an elder explained that protecting the "spiritual ways," including sacred sites, medicinal plants, and knowledge, should be a priority for protection initiatives.[45] At the very least, when development occurs "people that are knowledgeable" should be able to "check what's in there and [whether] they can save it" or "do something with it ... so it can be ... preserved." Margaret Teneese added that the nation is constantly engaged "in battles" to protect traditional use sites, that destruction is often not necessary in order to achieve development goals, and that some developers "replant with foreign grasses and shrubs."

Like many First Nations, the KKTC has also conducted a traditional land-use study integrating elements of oral history, archival research, and the archaeological record. The Ktunaxa language is unlike any other and assists in the identification of traditional territory through descriptive place names, which imply location and use. The importance placed on this work by the KKTC is consistent with a theme that runs throughout all the transcript data; namely, the importance of preserving cultural landscapes for the survival of cultural practices and the transmission of cultural knowledge. Individual rights of property owners and economic development are the biggest threats to the achievement of these goals.

The activities undertaken in the ethnobotany and traditional use programs raise the broader question of whether traditional knowledge should be documented to preserve its integrity and to facilitate its transfer. While some participants support documenting knowledge, a tension exists between the benefits of documentation and the fear of making information more accessible and vulnerable to exploitation.

Another important KKTC initiative involves the implementation of a code of ethics for researchers. The code takes principles found in contemporary ethical instruments used by academic and other institutions and incorporates them into Ktunaxa/Kinbasket systems of authority, adding obligations to ensure the accurate and fair representation of their culture. The uniqueness of this initiative lies in its recognition of the rights of both the individual and community representatives to be fully informed of research and to control the dissemination of cultural knowledge. The code must be followed by "all persons conducting research projects ... who wish to consult with members of the Ktunaxa Nation and use their oral history, cultural heritage resources, the Traditional Use Study Library, the Ktunaxa Nation archives or other cultural information."[46] If interviews are conducted, participants must be advised of the right to be anonymous, to request that information be treated as confidential, and to withdraw from the research at any time. They must also be provided with information about "the purpose and nature of the research activities, including the potential impacts and possible risks, prior to seeking their consent."[47]

The request to conduct research is reviewed by the Elders Group, the Ktunaxa Treaty Council, and the KKTC. The latter two bodies provide comments and advice, but authority to approve or deny research lies with the Elders Group. This process is designed to help the researcher identify the appropriate community members or groups from whom to obtain the information being sought and to ensure informed consent. It is also intended to provide an opportunity for the resolution of potential conflicts between the research proposed and community interests before research is commenced, to allow for negotiation of issues such as control over dissemination of information, to monitor the accuracy of information gathered about the Ktunaxa and Kinbasket peoples, and to ensure that proper credit is given to elders or others who provide information. Thus, where appropriate, researchers "must ensure that a representative cross-section of community experiences and perceptions is included in their research," credit must be given in the final report to all participants, and research results must be provided to the Elders Group, the Ktunaxa Treaty Council, and the KKTC so that they may provide comment before a final product is completed.[48]

The KKTC has also developed archives to protect records that have legal, fiscal, administrative, historical, and cultural value. They are used by the KKTC to prepare for treaty negotiation and are accessible to Ktunaxa citizens and non-natives. The archives include photographs, recordings, historical records, archaeological reports, environmental records, and administrative records. Easy access to such material is considered vital not only to prepare for treaty negotiations but also to facilitate revival, preservation, and transmission of cultural knowledge. However, inadequate storage facilities have limited the amount of resource material that can be stored and more detailed or specialized material must be borrowed from other collections. Further, as part of the treaty process, it is necessary to collect "endless volumes of maps, documents, books, and other printed and photographic materials."[49] Given the rationale for repatriating cultural material and the impact of the treaty negotiation process, it is not surprising that the Ktunaxa Nation's repatriation efforts include cultural records and a new facility to house cultural material.

In the early 1990s, the Ktunaxa/Kinbasket Language and Cultural Department conducted the feasibility study discussed above in order to determine the extent of community support for such a facility as well as for an "ecomuseum." The ecomuseum, or living museum, concept is one that recognizes the importance of heritage sites within Ktunaxa territory, acknowledges the tourism potential of some of these sites, and provides employment and training opportunities for Ktunaxa Nation members as heritage resource personnel. Although it includes a more traditional museum facility and archives, the ecomuseum also includes an experiential recreation component intended to provide a more "'hands on' educational experience where patrons would be guided through traditional, or culturally modified areas" such as petroglyph sites, "alpine game-drive sites[,] and prehistoric mines."[50] Eighty-one percent of the participants in the feasibility study felt that the proposed resource centre would have "an extremely important role in giving back culture and language to the people."[51] The five highest ranked uses for the facility were a cultural learning centre, the education of future generations, a language learning centre, a research library/centre, and a centre for housing and displaying of artifacts.[52] Other activities envisioned for the centre were "language lessons, tool making lessons, trapping, hunting and fishing lessons, spiritual teaching, and traditional plant and medicine teaching."[53] Eighty-five percent of the participants were also "very interested in the concept of a major heritage/cultural tourism attraction in the Kootenay areas which would create jobs for the Ktunaxa/Kinbasket peoples."[54]

The activities envisioned for the language and cultural resource centre and ecomuseum are consistent with the rationale for protection and repatriation identified by participants in this case study. Margaret Teneese passionately articulated the issue of access and reflected on the desire of young people to reconnect with the knowledge of their ancestors and to keep traditions alive:

> Some of these things, you know, shouldn't be in museums in the first place. Where they are now in the museum, it's really not that conducive to us learning what we are, in a museum a thousand miles away. And you

> know, we're looking at a population that's impoverished, yet you expect us to go out to Ottawa to go and enjoy these things. (Margaret Teneese)

Another benefit associated with having cultural material housed on Ktunaxa territory is that it would enable non-natives who want to study Ktunaxa/Kinbasket cultural material to acquire greater knowledge and appreciation than they would have done before they were compelled to visit Ktunaxa territory, meet members of the Ktunaxa Nation, and interpret cultural material within its appropriate context. However, participants also indicated that not all material culture returned to the Ktunaxa would end up in a Ktunaxa museum. John Nicholas felt that each band should also have its own display of material culture as physical proof of its occupation and longevity.[55] As discussed below, some cultural material is considered sacred or spiritual and should not be on public display. Other material is considered to belong to descendants of specific individuals and families.

Museums have offered support for a Ktunaxa Nation facility in a variety of forms, from providing professional training in curating, preservation, cataloguing, and museum design to donating display cases.[56] It is anticipated that some cultural material necessary for the resource centre will be repatriated as part of the treaty process. Institutions outside of the process have also expressed some willingness to enter into repatriation discussions. Profits from the development of a golf course and resort complex on Ktunaxa land have enabled the Ktunaxa to take the first step in facilities development by opening an interpretive centre on the St. Mary's Reserve. As it is not known how much material will be returned, it is difficult to determine the size and costs of an appropriate facility. However, the main challenge has been to obtain sufficient funds for construction, operation, and training. Margaret Teneese explained the problem this way:

> We were thinking about establishing museums. We went out there just to let them know that we were interested in repatriating. When we met with them, they told us then that, that they weren't interested in repatriating to us unless we met some of their conditions: ... we were to build a museum up to their standards. And, we looked into different funding to build museums and much of what was out there was, they would only pay a third of what the museum would cost, which was $300,000 and we have to, would [have to] ... raise the rest. And at that time, that was only talking to one museum that had our, our holdings, and that was the conditions they, they put on us. (Margaret Teneese)

The Ktunaxa language is considered to be an integral part of Ktunaxa identity. It is taught in the Ktunaxa Independent School System, promoted through the KKTC language program, identified as a cultural resource in need of protection in treaty negotiations, and utilized in traditional use studies and other KKTC publications. Retention of language is central to all plans for Ktunaxa heritage protection and to all attempts to create and reclaim Ktunaxa cultural records (such as audiotapes and transcriptions of oral literature).

Study participants also emphasized the importance of language to the retention of culture. According to Joe Pierre, "one of the far most important things" that has been done in his community involves the revival of the Ktunaxa language in the school system. Gina Clarricoates agreed but emphasized that Ktunaxa language loses its meaning outside of the context of the actual histories and experiences of the Ktunaxa people. Allan Hunter also emphasized that protecting language and controlling education must be a top priority. He said that the community had a "responsibility to share our language with our children." One way to protect language is to use it. In order to keep the Ktunaxa language alive, it is important to use it to name places as well as in everyday conversation. Nelson Phillip explained that immersion is the best way to learn the language as, when he takes classes, once he leaves them he is immediately "back to English again" because his peers do not speak Ktunaxa. Sharing oral traditions in the Ktunaxa language also helps to protect traditional knowledge and to control its use.

Concepts of Ownership and Belonging

Although there are many similarities between Western and Ktunaxa concepts of ownership, the former cannot adequately describe participants' perceptions of their relationship to material culture, information, and land. However, references to non-consensual appropriation, the employment of words like "ours," rights of alienation, control over use, and the ability to exploit aspects of cultural heritage for economic gain suggest that the relationship of Ktunaxa to material culture, information, and land also has proprietary aspects. For example, Ktunaxa individual and family items may be alienated as one wishes. However, all study participants also felt that descendants and the broader Ktunaxa community should continue to have rights of access, use, and control, regardless of how items came to be removed from the community. Although rights are often expressed in terms of the human right to cultural survival, they are "proprietary" in nature. The community's rights are based in its cultural connection to the object, giving it both superior claim rights to non-Ktunaxa citizens and attendant responsibilities.

Participant transcripts reveal several influences on Ktunaxa concepts of ownership, including concern for the respectful use and representation of Ktunaxa cultural heritage; control over matters considered to be essential to the survival of Ktunaxa cultural identity; and traditional values, beliefs, customs, and practices. Given the social and economic realities of contemporary aboriginal communities, it is not surprising that participants also spoke to the responsible commercialization and exploitation of cultural resources.

Intangible Cultural Heritage

The overriding perception is that intangible heritage forms part of a people's identity and that unauthorized appropriation is disrespectful of Ktunaxa culture and protocols. For example, several participants express concern about the inappropriate use of sacred names and words by non-Ktunaxa citizens and the ability of non-Ktunaxa citizens to acquire exclusive use of names through the operation of intellectual property laws.[57] At the same time, the concept of individual ownership is not easily applied to traditional ways of controlling use, which rely on notions of belonging and respect:

> A good example of that is the use of the word "Nipika." That's our word for, like, [the] Creator. And there's companies that use that word ... a wilderness lodge bed and breakfast ... [T]o me it's no different than if we were to call the casino that we just opened up, say, the "Holy Mary Jesus Christ Casino" or something like that. (Troy Hunter)

> Our names, I think that, in law, I think you can use, have a copyright on it; but that, to me, that contravenes our traditional ways because copyrighting something, like a name, like a sacred name, means that you own it, and in our belief, we cannot own that name, as a nation or as people. So there's a conflict right there between public law and our own traditional beliefs and our own traditional laws. You know, it's, it's something that really has to be debated, and I think that the elders' knowledge in areas like intellectual property is really important because you know they'll help us decide what route to go. (Violet Birdstone)

Fortunately, because the Ktunaxa language is unique and complex, the improper use of names and words is not a frequent occurrence.

Most participants expressed the need for greater control over the use of Ktunaxa songs. Although one participant was concerned about an instance in which some First Nations people inappropriately sang a special Ktunaxa song as a powwow dance song,[58] most expressed concern over inappropriate use by non-natives. These concerns include singing songs without permission, academics recording or reproducing songs without permission, non-Ktunaxa citizens having inappropriate access to sacred songs, and the inappropriate reproduction and copyright of Ktunaxa songs. Discussing the repatriation of recordings, Margaret Teneese said that if museums could "understand that some of these songs are sacred and they're not for public consumption," and if they could "abide by what our wishes are," the nation might not be in such a hurry to get recordings back. She also told the story of a university student who recorded songs for a slide presentation that was subsequently used by someone else without the permission of the individual or the community.

Most participants did not directly address the individual and collective nature of entitlements to use and control songs. However, the use of phrases such as "whose song" and "somebody's song" and discussions about the transfer of songs, permission to use songs, and responsibility to prevent the misuse of songs suggest that songs belong to individuals who create or are given them. Everyone who spoke to the issue of "sacred songs" suggested that the community also has an interest in, and entitlement to, control over proper use. The issue is not communicated as one of respecting rights of exclusive possession or original authorship so much as one of cultural appropriation and lack of respect for Ktunaxa/Kinbasket protocols. The transcript data also reveal an awareness of the difficulty of controlling use of information already in the public domain, errors generated by attempts to document Ktunaxa songs, and concern over the impact of intellectual property law on Ktunaxa rights of use and enjoyment. Although one participant questioned whether copyright law could be used to protect Ktunaxa intellectual property, most did not fully understand copyright law and viewed it as a means to facilitate the appropriation of Ktunaxa intangible heritage by non-natives:

> Some of our sacred songs are already, have already been written. I've seen it in books, written by anthropologists. The anthropologists came around ... and recorded some songs and have actually written them into music. And I don't think that they got permission from the people that time, at that time to do that ... [W]hen they start writing, it's, they have a copyright to whatever they write ... and by rights those songs belong to that anthropologist now because he wrote them. So, I guess if we sing it ... you know, we're contravening their copyright law. (Violet Birdstone)

> [W]e're talking two different, two different cultures here. In the copyright law, that song belonged to that person. In our traditional ways and our Ktunaxa traditional ways, I don't think there's anything in our traditional ways that says that a non-Indian can own a song. I'd be very surprised if there was because those songs belong to us as First Nations people and, as far as I know, it can never belong to a non-Indian. (Violet Birdstone)

Not all songs are considered sacred, but many are intended for specific uses by specific individuals and societies. The keeper of the song is the person who has the right to share it and to determine who is entitled to sing it:

> For instance, it's been the case where I sang with the Chief Cliff Singers for a couple years, and Mikey, the lead singer, composed those songs or other songs were given to him. But even though I sang with them people a lot of the time because I like to record stuff, people would come to me and ask for recordings of them. [T]hat's one of those things where it's up to him. You have to go and ask him. And you couldn't go to the culture committee because all those elders down there would never say you can use his music for this. And you couldn't go to the Tribal Council and ask them. (Christopher Horsethief)

Christopher Horsethief also discussed how songs can be distorted and lose their power and meaning when non-Ktunaxa record and document them:

> So, and that's one of those things that, you know, the Jesuits were really good at writing down everything. Unfortunately, on the one hand, we could get a lot out of maybe looking at that or reading that or seeing what they had to say. But at the same time, it kind of dilutes it, and once it's broken down, it's not that – what's the word I'm looking for? I mean, when I learn it and I sit down with an old lady and she shares a song with me and I learn it and she says this is a song for you. This is for you to use, and there's usually some context, use it here or use it there, use it to remember, or use it – usually it's kind of, you use it for yourself and your family. And if that was ever really written down, that I think would take away from what is unique about it. You know, you can't take the piano role of notes and then match them up, you know, with a genre of music from our community. It just, it doesn't work like that. So that, I think, is really different 'cause it tends to – if someone tries to reinterpret, based on those other notes, it's not, it's not going to work. And I think it could actually be of more harm than good. (Christopher Horsethief)

The KKTC ethnobotany program suggests that certain plant knowledge may be viewed as belonging to the Ktunaxa Nation and that it is sometimes appropriate to share and extract economic benefit from this knowledge. However, few participants directly addressed this issue. One participant emphasized that the community was in a "Catch-22" situation because of non-aboriginal commercialization and exploitation:

> [I]t's kind of like a Catch-22 because the nation knows about these plants that they have used for years, hundreds of years, yet they don't want to tell the non-natives about them. So the non-natives are destroying them through their acts of, daily acts of logging or dams or whatever, and they don't know about the plants 'cause the First Nations won't tell them what it looks like, and you have to tell them about it. But if you do that, they'll

> turn around and exploit it anyways ... Exploit it and commercialize it and make money off it if they can. So what do you do? You could take those plants and mass produce them yourselves and set up like a greenhouse where you have control over it, and if it's getting commercialized so be it. Get in on it, and yet you still have the plant 'cause you're cultivating it yourself. (John Nicholas)

Joe Pierre explained that "only a very limited group of people" have knowledge about the names and uses of plants. There is a need to control access to such information as some people want to keep it to themselves – and "rightfully so." When asked about the improper use of medicinal knowledge, one elder replied: "that is ours and it should stay ... as ours." It should be "handed down, down, down" to children and kept by the Ktunaxa and Kinbasket people.[59] Discussing the transmission of cultural information and the use of the Internet to teach the Ktunaxa language, Gina Clarricoates said that information about medicines should not be included on the KKTC website because "it [would] lose its value." This is because once it is exposed to the public, "it seems that it doesn't have the strength to do what it's supposed to do." The appropriate process is for a knowledgeable elder to identify a successor and to "take that person and say, you are going to be my successor and I will share this with you." However, elder participation in the ethnobotany publications and the discussion of documentation (above) indicates that some knowledge is considered appropriate for dissemination outside the community.

What flows from the discussion of names, songs, and medicinal knowledge is the idea that they do not always fit easily into either category of individual or collective ownership. Further, although there is a general sense that such information can be shared with non-Ktunaxa under appropriate circumstances, participants said that it was important to maintain a continuing supervisory authority in order to control proper use. Although some participants recognized the challenge of controlling information within the public domain, the overriding sentiment was that sharing information should not automatically result in unrestricted public access. One method of upholding these principles and controlling appropriation and disrespect involves developing internal guidelines for information sharing. The code of ethics for researchers attempts to do this and is consistent with the preservation of relationships and responsibilities. It also reflects the individual and community dimensions of cultural information by requiring that both individuals and community representatives be fully informed and that they consent to any research that draws on Ktunaxa knowledge and cultural information. The code also responds to concerns about researchers' misrepresentation, misuse, and copyright of information and enables the enforcement of Ktunaxa protocol through the law of contract.

Tangible Cultural Heritage

Participants commonly understood that historical material culture "belongs" to individuals and to the Ktunaxa people. These layers of interest are derived from individual acts of creation, familial connection, and the cultural value of the item to the community of origin. Although several participants suggest that families of origin have the primary entitlement, there is also uniform acknowledgment that the community has an interest in material culture for its educational value. The few items that have been repatriated to date have been returned as a result of direct negotiation with family members. However, even those involved in private repatriations of family property recognize the importance of community access. Some participants also acknowledge that the community may acquire an interest in objects returned through private repatriations by providing the money necessary to buy an item back.

Participants were asked about culturally appropriate processes for determining rights to cultural property in the community as well as about safeguards to help ensure that property is returned to the correct community. Although some participants appreciated the importance of returning cultural items to the correct community or family, they also pointed to such identifiers as the use of specific family or community designs, marks, styles, and patterns; the existence of museum and archival records and photographs; and the use of the Ktunaxa language in recordings. In their opinion, these identifiers, combined with the assistance of elders, should provide the necessary safeguards.

All participants spoke to the importance of involving knowledgeable elders and community members in resolving ownership and distribution issues. Christopher Horsethief also indicated that caution should be exercised when relying on museum records. He emphasized that, under Ktunaxa protocols, some property is not capable of being transferred outside the community or by individuals. The following passages reflect common sentiments:

> You, you would try to have as many people, I would assume to be involved in an advisory capacity, people that have knowledge in regards to what certain pieces look like. There are things that you can look for if we're talking about a vest, a buckskin vest with beadwork on it. There used to be certain people that had a different thing that they always included in how they did their beadwork, and it was their own personal signature. It's just those kind of things ... You ... can look at old photographs and you can talk to other family members, make comparisons maybe even with pieces that they still sort of have in their possessions. But I think at the end of the day, I think there could probably still be ... a piece of property returned to the wrong person or the wrong community. I think that can happen. (Joe Pierre)

> [I]tems have to go back to the community as a whole, and they'll determine what'll happen with them. The items should never just go back to a family or an individual because there's a lot of danger with that. And if it is something that is supposed to go back to that individual or someone in their family, the elders are going to know. And a lot of times, I think it's still possible to figure out where a particular piece of regalia came from, and those elders can make a decision [about] what should happen from there. And as a community and as a group, we should be a part of that discussion. (Christopher Horsethief)

When asked about laws concerning the proper care, use, and control of material culture, some participants spoke about processes for determining entitlements rather than specific rules outlining entitlements. One participant indicated that property individually owned is governed by personal rules concerning care and use that are passed down to family members. Throughout the transcripts there is also a general sense that some individual items can be donated or sold outside the community but others cannot – for example, medicine bottles. Processes for distributing property upon death and information on how to properly care for certain items have also been interrupted by the fact that non-community members have removed and retained these things:

> In our traditional way, when we, when a person dies, all their property is, their estate is put together, and before anything is done with the estate or the property ... there's certain steps that have to be taken ... then the estate can be distributed. [M]y concern is that when a person – if a person donates or sells or makes an item, an art item, and sells it to the museum, that's fine. That's their choice. [B]ut when a person's property was stolen from them by someone else and then sold to a museum, to a collector, and that item is in the museum, when that person dies, our traditional law has been broken because all their items have not been gathered. Like, all their belongings have not been gathered because our law is that, all the, all the belongings, the whole estate, has to be gathered and put together in one place. (Violet Birdstone)

The above discussion reveals that participants recognize individual, family, and community interests in cultural items derived from acts of creation, familial connection, and the cultural knowledge an item represents. Violation of Ktunaxa laws concerning transfer is not the primary basis raised for asserting rights over material culture in the possession of museums, even though continued retention may interfere with certain protocols. Although some participants distinguished between stolen items and those rightfully transferred and identified limits on the right to alienate ceremonial items, all emphasized the importance of having access to cultural items – regardless of their nature or mode of acquisition – in order to acquire the knowledge that they represent. Participants attributed the loss of cultural items to the actions of individual band members, but they also strongly felt that significant loss could not have occurred independent of Canada's legal and political environment, which intentionally undermined aboriginal cultures.

Those participants who spoke about Ktunaxa laws respecting land did so in terms of entitlements and responsibilities. However, they emphasized that the concept of ownership does not adequately describe their relationship to the land. As one elder explained, "[W]e are stewards[ ] of the land. That's all I can say is, hey, we were put here for that."[60]

Traditional Territory and Cultural Landscapes

Ktunaxa culture is embedded in the relationship between the Ktunaxa and their traditional territory. For this reason, participants identified pictographs, cave paintings, traditional use sites, and ceremonial sites as sites in need of protection. Gravesites were also included, out of respect for ancestors and concern over the respectful treatment of their remains. There is a sense of urgency in the voices that spoke to these issues, and that sense of urgency is linked to concerns that the Ktunaxa are insufficiently protected under Canadian law and that they need stronger internal policies. Some felt that, in order to ensure their preservation and the cultural knowledge and norms associated with them, spiritual sites should always remain within the control of the KKTC.

Several participants discussed the impact of private property and development on archaeological gravesites and emphasized the need for developers to treat human remains with respect. One participant also raised the issue of souvenir hunters digging up archaeological sites and removing artifacts. Although some felt that gravesites should be left undisturbed, given the Ktunaxa custom of burying the dead throughout the territory in unmarked graves and the current political climate (which supports economic development over culture), most recognized the practical difficulties of taking this approach. It is commonly believed that most developers and private owners do not directly notify the nearest band about the discovery of human remains and archaeological sites, thus ensuring that no action can be taken on behalf of the band. Some participants also emphasized the inadequacy of existing laws:

> I think human remains is the most important for us as – not only us, the Ktunaxa people, but as aboriginal people, to protect our gravesites – because historically we're known to have buried persons wherever they died. And so our graves are everywhere. I think that protecting our graves

> is the most important. And I think we have to protect the gravesites whenever they're found. Through some kind of legislation or [on] our own, with our own communities or with our own band councils or tribal councils, I think that we should have some kind of a policy in place, stating that we want these sites protected. (Violet Birdstone)

> Well, it, it's hard to get a grasp on your physical, cultural evidence, like archaeological remains and stuff like that, because so much of it is on private properties and you can't go on that property to retrieve anything. So much of it has been collected by non-native people already ... between the sites and the mountains. They have their own private collections. The [Ktunaxa] nation doesn't have any type of policing agencies to go around and, you know, demand stuff back or even resources to get stuff back from private collectors. And, like I said, private lands is a whole different issue. You can't even get on private lands without the authorization of the landowner. (John Nicholas)

> Why am I not too keen on laws? Because sometimes laws are broken and then [*laughs*] they find ways to go around it. See, if a homeowner, like, says that this is my property. Why should I get in touch with them? ... I got to get in touch with the province, the nation ... all these people. They're going to get upset and break the law and do what they have to and won't say nothing until they're at the end, when all the damage is done to – well, the items. See, when you find it, first finding out, it should be secured and ... somebody [should] look at it right away and then say, "[W]well, thank you for letting us know. We'll do what we can right away, and we won't hold you back in your job or project." (Gina Clarricoates)

Although most participants expressed negative views about developers and private owners, some provided examples of good will and cooperation. However, problems still arise, such as the inability to inter remains without them first being removed by archaeologists and then repatriated to the community. Pat Gravelle gave the example of a private owner who was developing a lakeside campground and discovered the remains of a young girl and her father.[61] The developer notified the appropriate government department, and the operation was shut down until excavation could occur. However, the band had to go "through a big process to get the remains back." An overriding theme throughout the transcript data is that more money is needed to finance costs associated with protection and repatriation efforts. As Robert Williams explained, costs are also associated with reburial, and even when developers are being cooperative, disagreement arises over costs:

> We did find some up in Columbia Lake and I was involved in the first day of – we were getting the excavation part set up and I was there when they pulled the bones up. And the problem with that was [the company] caused the bones to be moved to the side, and what they had said was that they owned from fifty feet from the tracks ... and it was their responsibility ... [to deal with] everything that happened in there. But when it came down to it, they wouldn't pay for the bones to be removed. Even though they were the ones that caused the damage. They said it was the landowner's responsibility to pay for that. 'Cause it was on the landowner's land, even though they owned fifty feet from the tracks.

Those who speak about gravesites speak with equal passion about the threat to spiritual places and harvesting sites arising from commercialization, private ownership, Crown ownership, development, and acts of vandalism. Areas used for hunting, gathering, and fishing; petroglyph sites; cave paintings; hot springs; old Sundance grounds; and old campsites were all mentioned in these discussions. Participants were concerned about destruction, and they also made it clear that they should not be denied access and rights of removal with regard to areas of cultural significance, even if these are located on private lands:

> [W]e have a lot of these big developments that are happening, like ski hills and things like that, golf courses and whatnot, and they have a tendency to, to alter a lot of things because of the nature of it. We're constantly in battles with them. It's really difficult to have our concerns addressed. [I]t seems to me this mindset that we – we have the profit side, and then we have the, we're trying to protect, you know, certain things on one side and ... they won't work together. In fact, they can [work with] one another, and I think that's sort of like where we need to be going with what's happening in, in our traditional territory. A lot of these areas, they don't need to be destroyed. (Margaret Teneese)

> Well, when we talk about berries, our food ... we're already competing with the animals, the wildlife over them, and to have commercial harvesters come in and just sort of clear out an area is disheartening. You know, you have to drive around to lots of places just to find a good patch that hasn't been touched ... [O]ur peoples used to take care of the grounds, the places that they picked the berries. Every year they would return to the same place and they would even use fire to control, you know, overgrowth and stuff, so that it was, it was a managed resource. And, and now it's like it's a free for all. (Troy Hunter)

> Well, definitely there are important sites that should be protected. Like

> places that have pictograph paintings on them or hieroglyphic scratching on rocks. Those are important things ... And even stuff like hot springs. That used to be important to us and now it's all commercialized. We even have to pay to go sit in them – [s]piritual places, places where people went on their vision quests. A lot of them are, well, unknown or on private property, and we can't access them anymore. Just those kinds of things that we know are there, yet we have no access to them. Just because of them being on private property or under provincial or national parks standards – stuff, you know, stuff that we have no control over at this moment in time. (John Nicholas)

Although the value of these places and the resources that they provide to the Ktunaxa cannot be adequately measured in monetary terms, a few participants discussed issues of compensation and economic opportunity. Implicit in these discussions is an understanding that cultural rights have been lost through appropriation, exploitation, and economic forces not easily overcome. For example, Lucille Shovar suggested that, because Ktunaxa are no longer able to control and have free access to hot springs within their traditional territories, they should get a percentage of the revenue. Similarly, John Nicholas suggested that, if commercial plant harvesting cannot be stopped, the Ktunaxa should see some economic benefit.

Almost all participants had some level of familiarity with the *Heritage Conservation Act,* and all expressed concern about its enforcement.[62] Although opinions vary on how to improve the legislation, all who spoke to this issue agreed that the *Act* is ineffective and does not protect traditional use and other heritage sites within Ktunaxa traditional territory. Several spoke to the need for greater Ktunaxa Nation involvement – through notification, enforcement, and cooperative resource management – in the protection of their heritage.[63] Protection is not necessarily inconsistent with economic development; rather, some participants emphasized the need to work together cooperatively to shift development away from important sites, to recover archaeological items, or to take other action deemed necessary by the community:

> We have the *Heritage Act, Conservation Act,* but I don't think it goes far enough, and there's no enforcement of it now, you know. [I]t's written in there, it all sounds good and even, but there's no enforcement. Actually, there's maybe individual cases where, let's say, the CPR would come to us and [say] they found remains and, you know, rather than just not dealing with them at all, they did reach us, the, the band ... But we have the big developments that have no enforcement at all, and they're just going ahead and they don't have anybody that, you know, they feel they, they should go to. So, it's, it's really not consistent. (Margaret Teneese)

You can't just look at it from the revenue side of the ledger, but you've got to look at the other things too. Like, what's bringing people into this area is not just, you know, the tourism. It's what, you know, the value-added, which is, you know, the First Nations history. [A]nd to destroy all that, then you don't have anything. I think that those two could work together and I'm sure, like within our traditional territory, we, we could probably [have] a treaty, to be able to enforce some of these things. (Margaret Teneese)

Yeah, they've got the *Heritage Act* and nobody does anything. To tell you the truth, 'cause even those pictographs are basically kind of vandalized too. You know, they're slowly going away, so who looks after those? Now I guess we'd have to ask the Canadian government or policy makers or whatever and say, you know, you make all the laws you want but those laws you make are still broken.[64] (Lucille Shovar)

I think what we have to do is work with the BC *Heritage Conservation Act* and make it a little stronger and have, have it recognized by the BC government. And raise the fines and make sure they are followed up on. Like, if you're going to fine somebody for destroying something, make sure that the branch follows up on it and just not look the other way anymore. They need to deal with these problems. As a nation, I think we have to get more, more involved in this capacity for consultation and possibly to go up to full management so that we have a say in what's happening to us, us and the objects that are out there and being destroyed. (Robert Williams)

[I]t's mostly for the logging business or, like, gravel pits, and they don't actually protect sites ... if they find a site a ways down that is dug, they work around it. They leave it standing but it isn't protected because, after all, the other trees are gone in that area, the rest just fall over, and the site is exposed. So even though they have those little things, what they call machine-free zones and management zones, what they do is they tear down the trees around the site but it doesn't help. It just becomes a bare area in there after they go in and log it. (Robert Williams)

So I mean, just last year, there was that incident ... where they reported archaeological sites and fenced the area off from partiers that went up there on weekends and tore up the ground and everything like that. They fenced it off. What happened was they went back up there and the fence had been torn down again and the partiers were partying back in the area in the exact same spots that they were before. And the *Heritage Conservation Act* says that someone should get fined for destroying archaeological

> sites, especially if it's a reported one. And there's nothing that's been done about that through the Archaeology Branch. So that's just, that kind of makes me lose my trust in the *Heritage Conservation Act* as far as protecting the archaeological sites goes. It would be nice to see a nation agency that kind of had the same rights to go around and enforce laws like that, just to keep everybody on the up and up you know, not destroying archaeological sites and any other protected sites in the area that are important to the nation. (John Nicholas)

Parts of the Ktunaxa traditional territories are within national parks. Participants expressed concern about restricted access to some areas, lack of public acknowledgment of Ktunaxa connection to the land, and tour guides misrepresenting the history of the land. Troy Hunter gave the following example:

> The paint pots at the Kootenay National Park is a Ktunaxa site. And protecting it is one thing, and protecting it is happening because it's in a national park. But it must also be available to Ktunaxa people for access and use, as with any other sacred and spiritual sites that we have, whether they're in parks or not. (Troy Hunter)

Some participants also address the problem of having to identify sites for protection. Identifying them risks exposing them to exploitation, particularly in an environment where laws concerning their protection are not being enforced and cannot be enforced by the Ktunaxa. Further, the locations of some sites are not intended to be known to the public and, therefore, cannot be identified and protected through conventional legal means:

> Like, there should be a law for protection of sacred sites but I have a problem with that ... because, in our traditional way, sacred sites, the identification of sacred sites is not for public knowledge ... I don't think we could go out and start red flagging these places. You know, as long as our cultural leaders and cultural elders know these sites, I think that should be honoured by provincial law. (Violet Birdstone)

> Well, I think you got to first of all educate the people that are in the area and expose them to whatever it is you're trying to protect and educate them on what it means to you. Show them that it's, you know, spiritual or religious or has some meaning to you so that they respect it that way. It's hard to do that with some things that are valued [by] some people because once you expose them to it, they turn around and try to make that dollar off it. But you'd have to team up with some of the non-natives that live in the area and go over and set some laws down that you both

> agree are fair and go about enforcing them in the right way. You can't have all natives enforcing the rules because the non-natives are going to turn against them because they don't want to be bossed around by a group of natives. And then you have, on the other hand, non-natives enforcing laws on natives. That is wrong. They've got to have something to do with the natives personally. One-sided just doesn't work. They have to get together, sit down, and make some rules and regulations that are fair to everybody, I guess. If it means having to expose ... things that you don't really want to show people, so be it. You have to show them to gain their respect and let them know what it means to you. (John Nicholas)

Despite these concerns, the feasibility study on the language and cultural resource centre discussed earlier demonstrates that the population is not opposed to tourism and making Ktunaxa heritage known and available to the greater public, where such access is appropriate. Indeed, 85 percent of the participants in that study supported the development of "a major heritage/cultural tourism attraction in the Kootenay areas that would create jobs," and 81 percent were "very interested in pursuing experiential recreation as a form of future development in the area of tourism."[65] The latter would involve Ktunaxa and Kinbasket peoples in selecting appropriate sites and as guides and interpreters. This study and the discussions on repatriation that follow also suggest that employment and revenues from tourists is an anticipated ancillary benefit to repatriation. However, it is not emphasized. Further, given the concern over return and care of spiritually sensitive material, full access by the public is not supported by either study.

Repatriation

Material Culture

In repatriation literature and policy it is common to distinguish material considered sacred, spiritual, or ceremonial from other cultural material. Three participants (including two elders) indicated that the repatriation of these items should be a priority. An overriding sentiment is that spiritual items must be handled properly and should be returned along with other cultural material important to the community. Robert Williams suggested that, in some circumstances, improper handling could result in the inability to use items in ceremonies. Although ceremonies can be held without ceremonial items, the return of the latter is still considered vital for community well-being and the continuity of cultural knowledge. Troy Hunter provided the following example:

> The pipe is a sacred object. It's used for ceremony. And I know that there are museums that have pipes from the Ktunaxa. And when I look around

> the community today, I see very few people that hold those pipes. So how it affects the spiritual, emotional, and cultural well-being of the community is that's one less cultural resource that we have because they have been taken away. And that's just one example. There's, there's others. (Troy Hunter)

Certain items, such as bear claws, pipes, and medicine bundles, are clearly identifiable as spiritual or ceremonial in nature. However, the spiritual nature of objects is generally highly personal and difficult to define. For example, in treaty consultations concerning repatriation, elders and youth said any attempts to define what is sacred "should not be too specific" as the "items are personal," and "each person has his own definition."[66] For museums these are "just material things," but for the Ktunaxa the sacred nature of the item is "very deep within the soul."[67] They also emphasized that views of what is sacred vary between the Ktunaxa and the Secwepemc members of the KKTC.

Gina Clarricoates explained that the life force of an item may also compel its return home regardless of its location or how it was acquired. She shared a story about a pipe she discovered in a second-hand store. At first, the shopkeeper wanted to sell it, and then he just returned it "because things were happening in his store." The "pipe was crying to be let out of the case it was in" and wanted to go back home.

A common view among participants is that the cultural value of an item is not just measured by the necessity of its use but by the cultural knowledge it represents. Thus, cultural materials that signify everyday use, like clothing, baskets, utensils, and other similar items, are as important to repatriate as are sacred materials of a spiritual, religious, or ceremonial nature.[68] However, one participant suggested that, given his experience with repatriation legislation in the United States, limiting repatriation claims to "important" items is the most realistic approach:

> I think that everything should be brought back but I also know that that is never going to happen. Things like fish weirs and baskets and arrowheads and pottery chips, I don't really see a use in fighting for those things that we can still make. You know, and I think you kind of have to draw a line and choose wisely. There's some things that are crucially important, like bundles and pipes and things like that. And then there are other things ... So I think it's a good opportunity to maybe, I don't like to say trade or give away, but when it comes to the time ... to plan for, you know, what's going to work best for everyone, getting those important things back and giving on some other things – you know, giving them something to work with, because that was a big discussion in the States. You know, it's not ever going to be the case that we get everything back.

> And museums and universities, the Smithsonian, and groups like that, they want to have something. They're not going to just ever give up. It's the other things that we can't really live without ... [that] should be back in the community. (Christopher Horsethief)

Although some participants were aware of First Nations claims based on violation of customary laws, none of them asserted rights to repatriation on this basis. Issues of lawful ownership were raised, but emphasis was placed on moral obligations arising from the government-sanctioned oppression of Ktunaxa culture and the need for current possessors to understand the importance of returning Ktunaxa material to the survival of Ktunaxa identity. The complexity of the situation is revealed in the following quote:

> I'm not really sure what's right and what's wrong because, like, these things are there. They're not there because we chose them to be, and in some cases where they were stolen, they [were] stolen by somebody ... so that the holders of these probably don't even know where they ended up and the – not all, not all of them ended up in the museum. Some of them ended up in private collections, and that's one of the things that I found out is that a lot of these things didn't go to the museums, even though they're taken by one person. There were collectors back then too ... and there was a time when, in recent history, where people thought they were vanishing and so there was sort of a grab for a lot of these things. But what might've spurred that is, you know, the laws enacted by the *Indian Act,*[69] the potlatch ... And so, whether that institution has that right or individuals have a right to it, with the generations left here now, I think they still have a right to them, and this is the manner that a lot of them were taken because in, in our natural ways, these things would've been just handed down to the people of the next generation. (Margaret Teneese)

Participants appreciated the role museums have played in protecting cultural items, but some also viewed them as temporary custodians of cultural property and thought that they should return requested items when the community was ready for them. Some participants also saw a role for museums in training First Nations in museological practice and developing collaborative exhibits. However, opinions on the role of museums varied. Some are reproduced below.

> On the personal side, speaking as a person that worked in an institution at a provincial museum level, I think it was fortunate that some people had the foresight to go out and recognize certain material cultural things ... I'm sure a lot of children, the younger people in our community, wouldn't

have a clue what these things were. And I'm glad that we did have institutions like this; but at this particular point, I think the [Ktunaxa] nation is ready to be able to portray what our, who we are as a people, and we're going in that direction. (Joe Pierre)

I think they play a huge role because they do have a lot of objects and people as well and resources [for] dealing with a lot of things, maybe in their own culturally specific ways, ... you know, where they put things behind glass for people to "ooh" and "aww" over and [un]wrap ... mummies and stuff like that, just to see what's in them. But I think they can play a bigger role in terms of bridging and assisting in tribal protection and preservation and repatriation and education, interpretation, and in coordinating, you know, things that need to be done, and assisting us in repatriating everything back. I think they can play a role in assisting ... the tribe and the tribe's desires ... rather than going against it. (Allan Hunter)

I don't think they should have any right in controlling them. As for protecting them, they've been protecting them long enough I think. We know just as much as they do about how to protect them these days. (John Nicholas)

They don't have a role. They should not have those objects. They should not have those objects in their custody and they should be returning all of those cultural objects back to the owners, which is, in our case, the Ktunaxa. If they hold any of our Ktunaxa objects in their museum, it's not right and they should be returning those to us.[70] (Diana Cote)

Most participants had positive attitudes towards Canadian museums. Positive experiences are generally associated with open communication, appreciation of Ktunaxa interests in cultural objects, willingness to return, and relationship building. However, participants also identified numerous barriers to repatriation, including the need to be familiar with diverse repatriation policies and procedures, the difficulty and expense of gaining access to information and identifying cultural items located outside the community, conditions imposed by outside institutions, the absence of proper facilities in the community, and the dangers posed by chemicals used to preserve certain cultural items. Any negative experiences with museums are directly related to these challenges. A consistent message is that the Ktunaxa are in the initial phases of inquiring about repatriation and forming internal policy. Participants acknowledged that approaches and priorities may change, depending on the objects at issue and the deaccessioning policies of various institutions:

> And there's also a danger, you know, if you set up a board that says we're going to get elders from five communities and we're going to follow their guidelines to do everything, well there's differences between here and just even the next community up the road on how to deal with things. So, I mean that's not a very positive thing to say about the future of that relationship. But I think it's their [the museum's] responsibility because they have the things and so they should probably facilitate that discussion and be thorough, and I think positive things could come out of it. But it's not going to be just a quick or easy discussion, [it'll be] very resource-intensive. (Christopher Horsethief)

> I don't know of any private collectors that are willing to hand over their items to us without being paid for it. So, we don't have money. And I don't know of any museum that just says, "[W]ell, here," you know. I mean, yes, I was reading about how they repatriate objects in Alberta ... They put them out for a long-term loan and the institution does not expect to get them back. I think that is a mechanism that we could use, but the problem with that is that we would have to negotiate with ... the museum as to what is sacred. And I would argue that practically everything that they have, except for the art for sale, would be considered sacred. (Troy Hunter)

Margaret Teneese suggested that the task force on relationships between Canadian museums and First Peoples has had an impact on improving relations and has increased contact between museums and First Nations. However, participants still expressed concerns about insufficient funding, balance of power in negotiations, and the ability of museums to impose conditions on return. The frustration created by the need for facilities and the imposition of conditions is demonstrated in the following comments from Margaret Teneese and Christopher Horsethief, who have worked with museums in Canada and the United States on repatriation issues:

> You know, a lot of the communities and institutions responded and they gave me lists of what they have in their museums and ... we were pleased with that. And again, we're in the same dilemma of, okay, do we have a place big enough for all of this? And again, it's always getting money. (Margaret Teneese)

> Sometimes I know that it was really, with some of the bigger institutions and especially with different universities, [that] they thought they were going to be in a position to start calling shots with things. If we give you this back, you've got to hold it like so and so. And even with the archaeological

> collection, they had to, the tribes had to build a really big archaeological repository to get anything back. And on the one hand, that was probably good. There are certain conditions you should have in a building to keep things like that in proper condition. But if it's regalia or a bundle or anything like that, institutions have no say. Again, they never understood what it's for. They never will completely understand why it is important. They never saw it as part of a living, breathing thing. So, it's been the case I know where some people were saying, well, we'll give this back, but we want to make sure, you know – like the little asterisk with the rules and conditions. And it's like, well, that's just not the way things are done. And once it comes back into our community, our community brings it back in the way it is appropriate for us. It doesn't matter how it's appropriate for you. You don't know what a fan is used for. You don't know why that basket is important. You'll never understand why a bundle is kept the way that it is. And we do. So it's not ever going to be the case that we're going to have a good working relationship when someone is trying to tell us this is how you're going to have to take care of it, of something. Because they just – they never, they never completely understand it. They never had that appreciation of how it works in the community. And if you don't, then you shouldn't be trying to set rules for things like that. (Christopher Horsethief)

Throughout the discussions on repatriation, a feeling emerged that it was crucial to have cultural items returned while elders are still alive to explain their use and meaning. At the same time, the lack of resources to gather information from institutions and to build proper facilities to store and preserve items was viewed as a major obstacle to their return. The Ktunaxa concept of preservation is concerned not just with maintaining the physical integrity of the object but also with maintaining its meaning and utility to the Ktunaxa Nation. The role that cultural items have in transmitting knowledge is not always possible given that repositories of cultural objects and records are located outside the community and are not easily accessible to Ktunaxa citizens. Such a role will also be undermined if returned items are not properly cared for once back with the Ktunaxa. Consequently, the concept of a museum and conventional conservation practices are not necessarily inconsistent with Ktunaxa goals. However, several participants believed that the Ktunaxa should be the ones to determine which items should be preserved and displayed.

One of the potential challenges that the Ktunaxa face in negotiations with museums and other public institutions is the perception that the knowledge of museum personnel is more accurate or complete than Ktunaxa knowledge. However, participants consistently held that expertise regarding ownership, distribution, proper care, and interpretation of Ktunaxa culture lies with elders and other knowledgeable members of the Ktunaxa Nation. In the following passages, Christopher Horsethief elaborates on elder expertise with regard to the care and interpretation of material culture:

> People have to remember that they got it from a living, breathing people and they didn't ever come and get a collection from us, and we told them, like, this is our basket number 372 and it's used for this. [*Laughs*] ... I mean, you have to learn the whole way. Like those old people will tell you, you can't just write it down. You have to go and do it. So if we were studying place names, they would say, "[W]ell, we're not just going to tell you the name and then you write it down on a map" ... And so anytime you're dealing with people that ... take a lot of pride in those collections, they've spent their whole life determining all these wonderful things about it, but they'll never have the understanding. So that's just the most, I think the biggest stumbling block in a discussion like this. I mean, you got to remember, no matter how well you know it, you don't know it as well as we do 'cause this is where it came from. (Christopher Horsethief)

The challenges to repatriation are intensified in dealings with private collectors. Some collectors concerned about the preservation of items either refuse to return them or impose conditions upon their return, while others will sell items back with no conditions attached. Financial resources to purchase and store items is an issue regardless of whether they are in public or private collections. Some participants also noted that, once items are in the hands of private collectors, the law works in the collectors' favour. Unlike public institutions, private collectors may not appreciate ethical arguments for repatriation.

Several participants emphasized the importance of returning, rather than loaning, cultural items. They explained how a system of loans does not work for skeletal remains or objects of spiritual or ceremonial significance. However, some indicated that loans or replicas might be appropriate in certain circumstances, such as when it is agreed that items are to be preserved but proper facilities are not available, when private collectors refuse to return originals, or when items requested depict Ktunaxa culture but have not been created by Ktunaxa citizens:

> Why is it important to have this property returned rather than loaned for a particular purpose or on a long-term basis? Personally, I'm really quite comfortable either way. As long as we do get some of these pieces returned and, you know, if it's on a long-term basis that's fine. I mean, it could mean that again, if we do get some pieces returned, that it would probably

> [be] housed in a facility and maybe at that particular time it's not conducive to us doing proper care ... I think we have to kind of share our knowledge with people, and if [that] means having to refrain from taking everything back into our possession, fine. (Joe Pierre)

> I guess talking about direct experience about returning property there is, there is one that I could talk about, and that's the BC Archives, [which] has a collection of paintings. The artist that did the paintings is not a native person ... [I]t's very beautiful, very colourful to look at, very well detailed. And it's an important, it's a very important body of work that depicts our ancestors' way of life and it's our culture that is continuing. And in setting up the Interpretive Centre, I first of all purchased the slides from the archives of the objects or the paintings. And then in terms of using those slides to have them enlarged and to have them exhibited on the walls, I wrote and I said, "[C]an you give us free use for permanent exhibition, the use of these photographs, artwork?" And they wrote back and said yes, that they will waive any exhibition fees on that. [A]nd so we have copies of these original paintings that are important and beautiful to look at. It brings up the question though: are replicas, are copies, appropriate? (Troy Hunter)

> There's a lot of things that were taken inappropriately, and so for an institution to say this belongs to us but we will loan it to you and you have to pay to use that, that's probably inappropriate. The other thing is that the connection to the object may be so strong that there would be no way that this is going to go back. Once we have it here, it's like we'll probably have a welcome home ceremony, you know, to say we missed you and we're not going to let you go again. It depends upon which object we're talking about. And then again, how do we use that object if it's used in an exhibit? In an interpretive centre is one thing, but if it's used in a cultural setting for it's original use, well that's, that's entirely different. And I think that there's a spiritual connection, a spiritual bond to items with people, and if you bring these together and the bond becomes one, then it's really difficult to separate that object back without doing something to the spirit. And that's why it's important that once that bond has been re-established or reconnected, that it isn't broken. (Troy Hunter)

Some participants acknowledged that their material culture also had a role in educating non-Ktunaxa citizens about Ktunaxa culture, but most felt that this function is secondary to its cultural meaning for communities of origin. Given this, participants discussed the benefit of partnerships with museums that involve Ktunaxa citizens in the interpretation of objects and collections management. Such partnerships are viewed as beneficial not only to the Ktunaxa but also to the museums because they ensure the proper interpretation of Ktunaxa items. However, at the heart of these discussions is a shared belief that the Ktunaxa should determine what should be returned, that they should be able to use items as deemed necessary, and that spiritual items should not be used by those who do not have the appropriate knowledge of, or connection to, them. These points are eloquently expressed by Margaret Teneese and Christopher Horsethief:

> [I]f they could understand that some of these songs are sacred and they're not for public consumption and [if] they [could], you know, put their mind, change their mind a bit so that they [could] sort of abide by what our wishes are, we probably wouldn't be so in a hurry to get them back. Because as long as they're in there, they can change the rules a bit and not have the public use them as much as they have been. Then we would feel a lot better that they are being protected there and that they're, that they're not being used for things like, that are inappropriate. If they can work closer with us, then we'd establish a relationship with them because I – as much as the museums feel that they are reaching out to First Nations and things like that, I kind of think that they still have their own agenda. (Margaret Teneese)

> [I]f you're going to set up a display and label things on there, you know, that can be a really difficult thing ... Because of the way our language works and the different dialects and different things like that, I think it would be really difficult for an institution to take something out of a book. Maybe what Schaeffer had wrote, let's say he did a big thing on baskets, you know, and called them one thing. But again if, if you don't go into the community where those words still mean something and they're tangible [so] that you can still touch this process of making baskets and what they're used for and how they're made and all of those individual things that go in there – you know, if you don't have that communication with the community and have some kind of a relationship, I mean even in that sense, probably mislabelling things could be a really difficult thing because old people like to see our name on things. And if ... the words are inaccurate, there's been a lot of cases where that's been difficult for people. (Christopher Horsethief)

Allan Hunter acknowledged the complexity of overlapping claims but nevertheless called for Ktunaxa participation in the interpretation of Ktunaxa items and sites to ensure accurate portrayal and respect for Ktunaxa history:

> [O]ne of my experiences once was being asked by somebody from across the mountains to come to Fort Steele with a travelling exhibit from the

> Head-Smashed-In Buffalo Jump. And they wanted to do their interpretive displays there. But upon further investigation, I found that there's no reference to the Ktunaxa using that site at all. The archaeology that's been done on it and everything, that has not really even mentioned Ktunaxa at all. Yet a vast amount of the stone – that's stone tools and chippings – that are there had to be "top of the world" and other Kootenay sources [sites]. And the Kootenay have been here for over ten thousand years. And so I found that even, even at that level the tribal relations, where another tribe, our neighbours, are interpreting stuff, I felt that it should be important that we were all also mentioned and given our, our place in history ... I found out later that it was a lot to do with the political situation of the day. When they established Head-Smashed-In, it had to be something to do with one ownership of the land, and they didn't want treaty issues and all of the other kinds of overlapping issues. (Allan Hunter)

All participants agreed that museums should facilitate the process of returning cultural items and should inform bands about the content of their collections. As discussed earlier, participants also agreed that it is the responsibility of both the requesting First Nation and the museum to ensure that property is returned to the correct community. Also common throughout the interviews is an understanding that it is unethical to claim a right to items that originate in another indigenous community.

Ancestral Remains

Repatriation of ancestral remains is a highly emotional issue. Participants spoke with passion about how storage of remains is a violation of human dignity and demonstrates a complete lack of respect for the Ktunaxa as a people. Several identified ancestral remains as a priority for return. Anger, frustration, shock, and hurt are common emotions expressed by those who speak to this issue:

> You know, the scientists take our ancestors' bones and study them and, you know, in the name of science, and yet it's, on the other hand, it's, it just shows complete disrespect for a human race ... They wouldn't do that to their own grandmother and yet they're taking our grandmothers and grandfathers away and placing them in a scientific lab for students to learn on, you know, to learn from. They have to take a step back in the name of science and take a look at themselves and their own principles and ethics and, you know, what really are they doing and who is it benefitting? (Violet Birdstone)

> I don't care who has them or where they came from. I don't care if they came out of a national park. If they're human remains and you know

> where they came from ... then they have to be returned ... Somebody has got to come forward and say this is a basic human right. You can't go to a graveyard and dig someone up and say we're going to take this. I mean, people would just be in a fury over that. It would be hugely controversial and it would be a violation of, you know, everybody's right to die in peace or however you want to say that. But it's not the case that we're extended that type of respect. Our people are in boxes. They're labelled with numbers. I even saw one of the cases we were looking at where the bones, it was written right on the bones in permanent pen, the lot number, and that, to me, that's just wrong. If you knew that that person came from this area you know ... that's where it belongs; you should be reburied there. And there should be no discussion. It needs to be a right 'cause as soon as you open up the door and put a bunch of asterisks beside it, saying, you know, "as long as these conditions are met," then you might as well be writing more numbers on those bones because if you're dead ... your community is supposed to take care of you a certain way. And that's been violated in a certain manner. You owe it to that person and their family and their community. Their family is still alive. Just because you don't know specifically who they were, you can't just go and take them out and put them in, you know, "Chris' museum of human remains" and label them and box them. So, first and foremost, the remains have to be given back. It has to be recognized as something that is important and as something that bothers us. Just because it's more generations back than we can count on our hands doesn't mean that it doesn't count and that it doesn't matter. If you're talking about law and what the government can do to make things better in this situation, it's getting those people back to where they belong. (Christopher Horsethief)

Referring to problems encountered in the repatriation of ancestral remains in the United States, Christopher Horsethief explained that items buried with an individual must also be returned for reburial:

> They wanted to keep something he was wearing and send the bones back, and every one was just, like, no, you can't. That was, you can't, if it was not separate from that person when that happened. You can't separate it now. And that was big. And there was a case at the last minute where they tried to pull that. They said everything was ready to go and all of the bones are here, and then they asked, "[W]hat about the things that were with them?" And they said, "[N]o, we never had an agreement about that." And what I was told at the time when someone, when there's a burial and there's remains, everything is part of it. You can't separate it out and say, you know, this necklace he was wearing is not part of it. Or this bundle he was with, or if he was travelling and had his implements

> with him, that, that's all part of him ... Whatever was in that burial, you can't separate it out. That's a really dangerous thing to do. (Christopher Horsethief)

Troy Hunter suggested that ensuring that remains are returned to the appropriate community of origin is the joint responsibility of current custodians and the owners of the traditional territory where the remains were found:

> [A] neighbouring tribe has been repatriating human remains and has been burying those remains, and they've been inviting the press to these burials, saying they're reburying their ancestors. Yet, this neighbouring tribe lives within our traditional territory. It's what we call an overlapping area. How do we know for certain that they were not repatriating Ktunaxa human remains? And I don't think that they asked us when they repatriated those objects. I don't think the museum asked us, "Hey, we're repatriating these things to this neighboring tribe. Do you have a concern?" It's like, "[Y]ou bet. It's part of our traditional territory too." Those may be our ancestors, and that is why the communication needs to involve all parties. (Troy Hunter)

Most of the museums and other public institutions in Canada with which the KKTC has dealt appreciate the sensitive nature of this issue, view themselves as custodians of ancestral remains, and have policies in place to facilitate their return. These policies reflect the recommendations of the Canadian Museums Association and First Nations Task Force report, which offers the following guidelines:

1 Remains of individuals whom evidence indicates are remembered by name must be offered for disposition at the request of the families, their descendants or clan, upon notification of the appropriate First Nations, community, tribes, clan or family members.
2 Human remains which evidence indicates may be affiliated with a named First People must be reported to that Nation, community, clan, tribe or family.
3 Upon agreement and in cooperation with the museum, the appropriate First Nations group may work with scientific interests for a mutually agreed upon period, and may have the remains re-interred according to the appropriate traditional or other religious practices of the First Nation or Aboriginal community.
4 The treatment and disposition of remains and associated burial objects that are ancient or that cannot be affiliated with a named First People shall be decided through discussion and negotiation with an advisory

committee of First Peoples. The First People may work with scientific interests for a mutually agreed upon time period and may have the remains re-interred in a manner consistent with local traditional practices.

5 Museums that acquire human remains through any means must involve the appropriate First Nation in the treatment and disposition of the remains.

6 The retention of Aboriginal human remains for prolonged periods against the express wishes of First Peoples is not acceptable.[71]

In the spirit of this report, the Royal British Columbia Museum (RBCM) and some other Canadian institutions have been proactive in identifying remains, notifying First Nations, and inviting them to make repatriation requests. Participants spoke positively about their experiences repatriating remains from the RBCM and commented on the helpfulness of the staff. However, even in the presence of this good will, problems associated with the cost of personally escorting remains home and community readiness have at times resulted in a lengthy and costly process.

An overriding concern is the need to follow proper protocols for collection and reburial. These protocols are known to a limited number of individuals within the community, and these people teach them to others. Given the specialized nature of this knowledge and the limited number of people who carry it, one participant active in the process of reburial supported documenting burial protocols. Although some participants understood the need for forensic study to determine the age of remains and, where relevant, cause of death, some clearly stated their opposition to the scientific study of remains. As discussed earlier, this is a deeply emotional issue and is associated with issues pertaining to respect for human dignity. Some also expressed concern about non-Ktunaxa citizens handling the remains.

International Repatriations

Although the KKTC has just begun a campaign to repatriate from institutions outside Canada, preliminary investigations reveal similar obstacles to those faced inside Canada. Of particular concern is the cost associated with research and the identification of material, access to information (including costs of reproduction), lack of consistency in institutional repatriation policies, lack of proper storage facilities, the need to become familiar with a different set of laws, and varying degrees of cooperation. Varied responses to the mail-out campaign discussed earlier indicate that it is sometimes necessary to conduct site visits in order to identify the location of Ktunaxa property. Such visits are a crucial part of the identification process even when an institution has provided inventories or pictures of Ktunaxa property. This generates additional costs associated with international travel. As the Ktunaxa territory extends over the Canadian and American border, and as cultural items are sold and donated across borders, most international negotiations and visits have been to museums and other institutions in the United States. However, one of the problems is the scope of *NAGPRA*, which only applies to federally recognized Indian tribes. To address this problem, the KKTC works in partnership with Ktunaxa tribes in the United States and with the Kootenai Repatriation Committee. The purpose of this committee is to help museums develop guidelines to identify Kootenai material within the scope of *NAGPRA*, develop a repatriation policy in consultation with knowledgeable people within the community, develop a treatment plan for objects that remain in museums, and assist in developing a process to determine cultural affiliation as required by the *Act:*

> We're dealing now with a different country and the Ksanka people, down in Montana, they're under *NAGPRA* and ... that's what they are governed under right now ... some very specific laws in which museums deal with First Nations down there. We're kind of in a good position because it's mainly up to the museum, in their good, you know, faith, to bring ... these things back. And by talking with other tribes, they've been quite good about getting, giving these things back. The other challenge I, I also see, too – and again, we're dealing with different laws altogether – would be international. Things that may be across, like in Europe, places like that, and again we're dealing with a whole different set of laws that, that we'll find, we'll probably, when the time comes, find out how that's going to work. Right now, there hasn't been a whole lot of effort in really looking for things over there other than writing some letters and that. (Margaret Teneese)

The challenges faced in domestic and international repatriations underscore the need for indigenous peoples to learn from each other's experiences and to share information at both the local and international level. Some participants indicated that they had attended conferences and participated in workshops with this objective in mind.

Concepts of Law and Law Reform

Although participants did not often articulate specific rules, they acknowledged the existence of Ktunaxa law and appreciated that different laws, or "ways," apply, depending on the material or information at issue.[72] All noted the existence of people or processes within the community to help ascertain these values in the event of doubt. It is also apparent that the Ktunaxa community is composed of diverse individuals with varied expertise, just as is any other community and, also like other communities, certain individuals are considered to be "legal" experts. Most participants, when asked about what prevents the community from exercising its laws in relation to cultural property, interpreted this question as: What prevents the community from practising traditional ways? Obstacles identified include institutions placing conditions on repatriation, provincial land and resource policies, failure to resolve treaty issues, and failure of governments to appreciate how the land provides for First Nations.

When asked, "What rights to cultural property do you think need to be recognized in Canadian law," participants offered a variety of responses that reflect their personal repatriation and protection priorities. Thirteen participants noted the need for laws that facilitate repatriation and protection of ancestral remains and spiritual items. Thirteen spoke more generally to the need for the law to recognize Ktunaxa ownership of all cultural items originating from their community. All participants expressed doubt that the enactment of outside laws will be sufficient protection. This doubt arises from a perception that existing property laws facilitate cultural appropriation, concerns over lack of enforcement, problems associated with *NAGPRA*, and failure of outsider laws to promote and support internal laws and processes.

Participants were also asked to discuss laws that threaten Ktunaxa efforts concerning protection and repatriation. Due to varying degrees of knowledge about federal and provincial laws, some had difficulty answering this question. However, most participants talked about how outside law facilitates the appropriation and/or destruction of their cultural heritage. For example, Allan Hunter argued that most laws, like the *Indian Act*, threaten Ktunaxa culture and that, historically, "laws were created to allow people to use the lands and to take ownership and without regard to who was there first and how they were using the land." Diana Cote agreed that it is because of the *Indian Act* that Ktunaxa culture has been lost and community members are unhealthy:

> [T]he Indian Act took our culture away and as a result of that we are in the situation that we're in right now, which is we have unhealthy members in our community. We have lost our culture. We have sad families because it took that ability to be a family away. So it's probably the worst thing that ever happened to the First Nations people in Canada. (Diana Cote)

Others acknowledged this problem but still saw a role for outside law:

> [T]here's various books that you can get that have the language written in it, and I guess if you look at the *Copyright Act* and how long it goes to protect stuff like that or, or who gets to call it ownership because they wrote the book, you know, that – those would be legal mechanisms that can be used to extract from what we already have here ... So, you know,

> we need a, like an international instrument, a legal instrument that can say this language is unique to the Ktunaxa people and [that] all of the words within their language are unique and therefore are protected against use of any kind and that they have full and complete ownership of all of the words in their language. And if somebody wants to use it, to call their business a name, that they have to go, come to us, and request something like that and then that would be good. But that's what's important. There are no ... laws to protect these things. (Troy Hunter)

> I was going to say that a law needs to be passed that all private owners need to give up. I mean, sure, you could maybe compensate them something, but I think the government needs to do that, not the individual or the community or the nation or whatever. It was something taken away from them without their permission. (Lucille Shovar)

A common sentiment throughout the interviews is the desire to protect the cultural integrity of information as well as to have continued access to, and control of, information. Protection must not be limited to specific words or creations, be they of individuals or communities; rather, it must also be extended, in the form of respect, to that which gives these phenomena meaning to Ktunaxa. In an article on intangible aboriginal cultural heritage, Gordon Christie offers an explanation consistent with the understandings reflected in this study:

> Such activities as storytelling, music, dance, dramatic re-enactments and presentations, carvings and paintings, rituals, ceremonies and the content of the stories, songs, dances and ceremonies, touch more directly on more or less transparent expressions of – that which an Aboriginal people would identify as what is valuable or essential to their self-identity. But as such they do not themselves, by themselves, comprise the culture of a people. What may be directly touched on by such activities ... are the values, principles and beliefs that inform the physical manifestations, which give them meaning, truth and validity (if only to the people who live through these meanings). These sources of meaning are what are seen and felt by Aboriginal peoples to be worthy of protection, as the "cultural property" that they wish to have respected appropriately in regard to its preservation, development and transmission.[73]

Those familiar with Canadian laws in the area of land and site protection spoke mostly to the need to reform and enforce existing laws rather than to create new ones. However, Violet Birdstone is of the opinion that specific laws need to be enacted to protect gravesites. She argued that First Nations gravesites should get the same protection as cemeteries and that a separate law that overrides others is necessary to protect graves both on and off reserve.

Few participants spoke specifically to the issue of repatriation legislation. Margaret Teneese and Christopher Horsethief indicated that, if such legislation were to be enacted, we need to learn from the problems associated with *NAGPRA*. It is not outside law *per se* but, rather, the potential for its strict interpretation and lack of flexibility that raises concern. One participant also emphasized that existing laws that support museum ownership are a threat to the protection of Ktunaxa property:[74]

> I found that that all depends who you, who you talk to ... [A] lot of them [American museums] said that they were willing to repatriate and a lot of them also said that we wouldn't have to go through cultural affiliation and all this ... So, that was one of my main concerns, is that we would have to prove that under *NAGPRA* in the States. That's what they have to do. They have to prove that, even though there's a paper trail that says these are Ktunaxa, they still have to get the documentation and things like that. (Margaret Teneese)

> There were people still sending us their accession list years after they were supposed to. They were just dragging their feet and just being pissy about it, for lack of a better term. So having some kind of teeth to that, if you do have remains and you know where they came from, notify the appropriate people and help them set up a way or maybe recognize the existing manner ... for [dealing with] those kind of things. And providing support if they know how to get things back and take care of them, then they should be allowed to do that. I mean, if we know and the community has accepted that there's certain ways that we take care of that, then that should be good enough. (Christopher Horsethief)

Underlying these discussions is a general recognition that repatriation laws will not be effective without the development of strong and respectful relationships between natives and non-natives. Improved communication is seen as essential.

> [T]here was one informal situation where a person had a private collection and they passed away and they gave the collection to Kootenay culture. And it was mostly photographs, and it said as long as you cite us when you use these photos, you can use them. I mean it was good because it was people from Elmo and Dayton and Hot Springs, and they gave it all back and said. "[Y]ou guys deal with it the way you think it is appropriate. My father had a good relationship with your community. He took

> lots of pictures and however you see to work it out." And that was a situation that wasn't a law. (Christopher Horsethief)

> They have to consult with First Nations ... When I say transparency, I mean don't just go to the chief or the council and say "this is it" and then go back and write [that] they consulted with the First Nations and the chief said there's no concerns. That's not involving the community. The chief doesn't know everything or the leader of the community doesn't know everything about each individual community member ... You hold community information meetings, you hand out pieces of paper, brochures; you can do it by email and, to a limited extent, put some information on the websites. But you know, I don't think that the internet is the best way to reach an aboriginal community. The best way to reach an aboriginal community is to come to the community and bring slides, PowerPoint presentations, handouts, and to talk and to make personal connections. Don't just come to the chiefs and councils or to a staff member of an organization and say that we have consulted with you. (Troy Hunter)

Although participants had different opinions regarding priorities and strategies for protection and repatriation, they agreed that more can be done within the community to protect cultural heritage. Some participants emphasized the need to formalize internal laws, policies, and procedures and argued that the role of outside law should be to facilitate these internal processes. Two participants also raised the need for greater communication regarding existing policies and strategies among Ktunaxa members:

> Right off the bat, Ktunaxa law, we need to create our own laws and, and then have them recognized by, by other governments and have them incorporate it into their laws. Something like that. But rather than changing their laws and looking at their laws and how we want their laws to fit us, we need to create our own laws. And that's just, you know, we need a listing of our laws and whatnot [and] that needs to be done, and [we need to] ratify that somehow amongst ourselves and then have that recognized as legitimate law. And with laws there needs to come enforcement. (Allan Hunter)

> I think legislation needs to be enacted that if there's cultural significance in this area, that the aboriginal community that is there or close by needs to do the laws for protecting it. Like the pictographs, it should be Ktunaxa that make laws or policy on how it should be protected or who can use it or who can go near it – those kinds of things. It shouldn't be the parks or whoever say[s] they own it now. (Lucille Shovar)

[W]e need to write down our own laws. We need to practise our own laws. So I don't believe that we need to legislate anything in Canadian laws because we already have our own and they've worked for centuries, beyond centuries. So I don't – I think the only type of laws we need are our own. We just need to incorporate those back into our lives again. (Diana Cote)

Participants also demonstrated appreciation for the complexity of enacting laws in Canada, given overlapping government jurisdictions and the public/private nature of property rights:

But when you do have the old argument about people having ownership [of] things that are out in the public, and especially with things that are happening with the Internet, *et cetera,* people that have done research, it's out in the public domain. And how do you actually ... [protect] those? You know, like especially intellectual property. I always found that to be a tough one, and I don't know how, how a group of people or individuals, when an individual can put protection over that, aside from putting a copyright over it and having, having maybe that kind of protection. But at the end of the day, it's always kind of [a] really fuzzy, grey area for me. I don't really have any firm beliefs on that. (Joe Pierre)

[W]hen you say Canadian law, there's lots of jurisdictions and then there's also land status. Is it public? Is it private? Is it being developed? Is it in an area where the Ktunaxa people and the province have some kind of a way to work things out? Is it somewhere that is in an area that has already been disturbed? Is it going to be disturbed? You know that it's difficult to envision any one law that could cover all of that. (Christopher Horsethief)

I think when we talk about law ... we have traditional laws that, they're not the same as the system according to the courts and stuff like that. And it's hard for us to assert our laws because our jurisdiction sometimes is not recognized. If a long time ago, somebody did something that was wrong, they would be told, you know, either leave forever or ... go and take coup against the enemy. Things like that. [W]ell, it's hard to, to do that because of the neighbouring communities, non-native communities that have their laws in place. (Troy Hunter)

The enactment of *NAGPRA* in the United States acted as a catalyst for many tribes, including the Kootenai Tribe of Idaho and the Confederated Salish and Kootenai Tribes, to develop internal guidelines and processes for ensuring the protection and repatriation of cultural items. Although this was a positive outcome of legislative reform, participants spoke of the need for greater consultation early in the law reform process, including with regard to any initiatives that may arise from this study:

> And of course nobody from the legislation came out and asked us before. It was like everything else: they asked us after. "Here's our law. What do you think?" Well, we looked at [it] and we said, "[W]e kind of think you should have come to us in the beginning [*laughs*]. That way we maybe could've come up with something better." (Christopher Horsethief)

> If this is going to reach a level, if this study is going to reach a level where legislation is going to be put in place for protection of cultural property, real consultation [should] take place with First Nations peoples so that it really does protect us, protect our cultural property. Because often legislation is put in place with good intent, but in the end, it does nothing for the – nothing to, you know, protect the person. Instead, it might inhibit whatever the legislation was put in place for. (Violet Birdstone)

Given the emphasis on control and protection, the data also suggest that any legislative initiatives concerning intangible heritage should facilitate respect for Ktunaxa concepts of ownership and protocols for responsible use.[75] This may mean amending existing federal and provincial laws or creating new ones that facilitate community control over the use of certain images and ideas or creating new laws to facilitate the return of cultural records. Of particular concern is the need for a mechanism to enforce Ktunaxa laws:

> I guess we've created the Ktunaxa research code. I am aware of that. I think, as for having that ... enforced by provincial or federal law is, is another thing that ... needs to be incorporated, I guess, sort of like the treaty. (Allan Hunter)

> There has to be something stronger than the convention on copyright because copyright lasts only fifty years after the death of an author or fifty years from the time that a photograph has been taken. This does not protect our language. Our language is our language, Ktunaxa people. (Troy Hunter)

Conclusion

Participants in this study interpreted cultural property within a holistic concept of cultural resources that includes intangible cultural heritage, keepers of traditional knowledge, and the Ktunaxa "way of life." The Ktunaxa prefer not to use the word "property" because "cultural resources are not commodities" but, rather, important and valuable aspects of their "unique lifestyle."[76] Of pressing concern to participants is the loss of cultural knowledge and determining how to strengthen and renew that knowledge. Loss is attributed to a number of factors, including the removal of cultural items from communities; the destruction of, or inability to gain access to, traditional lands and sites; the outlawing of spiritual practices; and forced assimilation through the residential school system. All participants linked the importance of protection and repatriation initiatives to self-esteem, community well-being, and the retention of cultural memory, practices, and identity.

The Ktunaxa are engaged in a variety of strategies to protect and control their cultural heritage both inside and outside the BC treaty process. Through treaty negotiations, they hope to "retrieve important Cultural Resources that were lost, and to preserve important Cultural Resources that are left."[77] Cultural resources are considered an integral part of aboriginal rights and title, which include not only "use and occupation of the traditional territory" but also "the culture that stems from that use and occupation."[78] Treaty objectives include repatriating items of "historical or cultural significance," access to resources necessary to support "traditional aspects of Ktunaxa culture," jurisdiction and law-making powers over cultural resources, involvement in cultural resource management, control over acquisition and dissemination of cultural information, language programming, and the ability to ensure "that the interpretation of Ktunaxa culture and heritage is accurate and culturally sensitive."[79] The code of ethics for researchers is intended to respond to some of these concerns by placing greater control over research in the Ktunaxa community with the Ktunaxa authorities.

Some participants identified the Ktunaxa language as one of the most important areas of Ktunaxa culture in need of protection. Throughout the report, participants acknowledged the importance of education in the Ktunxa language and the responsibility of community members with regard to language use, revival, and transmission. Because of the importance of language and of learning its correct and original use, the Ktunaxa also seek the repatriation of recordings, writings, and other Ktunaxa oral material.

All participants spoke of how important the repatriation of material culture is to the retention of cultural knowledge and practices, regardless of its mode of acquisition. Although some participants indicated that repatriation and the proper handling of spiritual items should be a priority, it was commonly held that the cultural value of an item is not just measured by use in ceremonial activities but also by the cultural knowledge associated with it. Consequently, the cultural items and records the Ktunaxa want repatriated are not just those of a spiritual, religious, or ceremonial nature. Acknowledging individual, familial, and community interests in cultural items, all participants emphasized the importance of involving knowledgeable elders in ascertaining the appropriate rules for ownership and distribution. Although issues of lawful acquisition were raised, the emphasis was on moral obligations arising from government-sanctioned oppression and the need for current possessors of Ktunaxa material to understand that the return of some items is crucial to the survival of Ktunaxa identity. Some participants acknowledged that cultural items also have a role in educating non-Ktunaxa about Ktunaxa culture, but most felt that this function is secondary to the meaning these items hold for their communities of origin. Given this, some addressed the importance of effective partnerships with museums holding Ktunaxa material. All agreed that it is time for Ktunaxa to take control of the preservation and the use of some Ktunaxa material. However, the financial and human resources associated with acquiring information, locating items, training staff, and building an appropriate facility within the community are a significant barrier to achieving this objective. Throughout the report there emerged a feeling that it is urgent to have significant cultural items returned while elders are still alive and able to explain their use and meaning.

Participants also spoke to the importance of repatriation and the reburial of ancestral remains and items accompanying them. Storage of ancestral remains is a violation of human dignity and demonstrates lack of respect not only for Ktunaxa laws but also for the Ktunaxa as a people. Most museums and public institutions that the Ktunaxa have dealt with appreciate the sensitivity of this issue and have policies in place to facilitate return. Several participants commented on the positive experiences they had working with Canadian museums, such as the RBCM, in bringing their ancestors home.

The effects of the destruction and development of Ktunaxa land are highlighted in participant discussions of heritage burial sites. The inability to rely on existing heritage protection laws leaves them feeling vulnerable to further desecration and exploitation. Through examples such as the *Heritage Conservation Act*, participants spoke directly to the inadequacies of existing legislation and, in particular, to the issue of enforcement. Provincial parks regulations and private property prevent unfettered access to ceremonial places and traditional hunting and gathering places. Whether speaking to the issue of existing heritage conservation legislation or proposed repatriation legislation, participants indicated in various ways that legal solutions are not enough: what is also required is adequate resources to implement and enforce the rules, changes in the attitudes of non-natives, and improved communication. All participants agreed that more could be done within their own communities to protect cultural heritage and that the role of outside law, if any, should be to facilitate internal laws and processes. Participants also demonstrated an appreciation for jurisdictional issues raised by the process of law reform and the need to learn from repatriation experiences under legislation enacted in the United States.

Notes

1 The phrase "cultural resources" is used in all documents prepared for treaty negotiation as they are not viewed as "commodities" but "resources because of their value and importance to the Ktunaxa." *KKTC Cultural Resources Interest Statement* (12 November 1998) [archived at KKTC offices, Cranbrook, British Columbia].

2 "Ktunaxa Nation Council," see online: Ktunaxa Nation <http://www.ktunaxa.org/who/kktc.html>.

3 *Ibid.* For more historical information and Ktunaxa communities, see "Who Are the Ktunaxa?" online: Ktunaxa Nation <http://www.ktunaxa.org/who/index.html>.

4 The five bands living within Ktunaxa traditional territory in Canada are the Columbia Lake Band, the Lower Kootenay Indian Band, the Shuswap Indian Band, the St. Mary's Indian Band, and the Tobacco Plains Indian Band. The Kootenai Tribe of Idaho and the Confederated Salish and Kootenai Tribes are located in the United States.

5 The standard question set is included in the appendix on page 491 of this volume.

6 Commission on Human Rights, Sub-Commission on Prevention of Discrimination and Protection of Minorities, *Final Report of the Special Rapporteur: Protection of the Heritage of Indigenous Peoples,* UNESCOOR, UN Doc. E/CN.4/Sub.2/1995/26 (1995). Dr. Daes defines the heritage of indigenous peoples as follows:

> 11 The heritage of indigenous peoples is comprised of all objects, sites and knowledge the nature or use of which has been transmitted from generation to generation, and which is regarded as pertaining to a particular people or its territory. The heritage of an indigenous people also includes objects, knowledge and literary or artistic works which may be created in the future based upon its heritage.
>
> 12 The heritage of indigenous peoples includes all moveable cultural property as defined by relevant conventions of UNESCO; all kinds of literary and artistic works such as music, dance, song, ceremonies, symbols and designs, narratives and poetry; all kinds of scientific, agricultural, technical and ecological knowledge, including cultigens, medicines and the rational use of flora and fauna; human remains; immoveable cultural property such as sacred sites, sites of historical significance, and burials; and documentation of indigenous peoples' heritage on film, photographs, videotape or audiotape.

7 Marie Battiste and (Sákéj) James Youngblood Henderson, *Protecting Indigenous Knowledge and Heritage: A Global Challenge* (Saskatoon: Purich Publishing, 2000) at 65.

8 Interview of Margaret Teneese by Laura McCoy (26 August 2002), Cranbrook, British Columbia. Transcripts of participants who agreed to have their entire interviews made available are located in Cranbrook at the KKTC Archives. At the time of writing, placement in a public archive had not yet been determined.

9 Interview of Gina Clarricoates by Laura McCoy (8 October 2002), Cranbrook, British Columbia.

10 Interview of Christopher Sanchez (Horsethief) by Laura McCoy (19 February 2003), Cranbrook, British Columbia.

11 *Supra* note 5.

12 Interview of Wilfred Jacobs by Laura McCoy (18 December 2002), Creston, British Columbia; interview of Allan Hunter by Laura McCoy (16 December 2002), Cranbrook, British Columbia.

13 *Supra* note 1 at 1.

14 *Ibid.*

15 *Ibid.*

16 Ktunaxa/Kinbasket Language and Culture Department, *Ktunaxa/Kinbasket Language and Cultural Resource Centre Feasibility Study Report* (n.d. 1992?) at i [archived at KKTC Archives, Cranbrook, British Columbia].

17 *Overview of Treaty Nation Meeting* (6 and 7 November 1998) at 1 [archived at KKTC Archives, Cranbrook, British Columbia].

18 Interview of Violet Birdstone by Laura McCoy (2 October 2002), Cranbrook, British Columbia.

19 Interview of Troy Hunter by Laura McCoy (9 October 2002), Cranbrook, British Columbia.
20 Interview of Nelson Phillip by Laura McCoy (25 November 2002), Windermere, British Columbia.
21 Interview of Robert Williams by Laura McCoy (19 February 2003), Cranbrook, British Columbia.
22 *Supra* note 16 at 2.
23 *Ibid.* at 18 and 19.
24 *Ibid.*
25 *Ibid.* at 19.
26 *Ibid.* at 3.
27 *Ibid.* at 2-3.
28 *Ibid.* at 1.
29 *Ibid.*
30 Interview of Joe Pierre by Laura McCoy (9 December 2002), Cranbrook, British Columbia.
31 *Supra* note 18.
32 Allan Hunter, *supra* note 12.
33 *Supra* note 17.
34 *Supra* note 1 at 2 and 3.
35 *Cultural Resources Sub-Agreement Interim Negotiating Framework Public Information Draft* (10 April 2002) [archived at KKTC Archives, Cranbrook, British Columbia]. At the time of writing, a final agreement on these issues had not been reached and negotiations were proceeding based on the 2002 framework agreement.
36 *Ibid.* at 2. These are consistent with matters of cultural heritage negotiated in the Nisga'a Treaty. See Nisga'a Final Agreement, online: Indian and Northern Affairs Canada <http://www.ainc-inac.gc.ca/pr/agr/nsga/nisdex_e.html>. Enacted by the British Columbia legislature as the *Nisga'a Final Agreement Act*, S.B.C 1999, c. 2 and federally as the *Nisga'a Final Agreement Act*, S.C. 2000, c. 7.
37 *Ibid.*
38 See *e.g.* Letter from Margaret Teneese to Specific Claims West, DIAND (19 July 1999) [archived at KKTC Archives, Cranbrook, British Columbia].
39 Assembly of First Nations and the Canadian Museums Association, *Turning the Page: Forging New Partnerships between Museums and First Peoples*, 3d ed. (Ottawa: Canadian Museums Association, 1994).
40 The legislation referred to is the *Native American Graves Protection and Repatriation Act*, 25 U.S.C.A. ss. 3001-3013 (West Supp. 2000) *[NAGPRA]*. Although First Nations in Canada do not fall under *NAGPRA*, they have successfully partnered with Indian tribes in the Unites States to repatriate under this legislation.
41 Repatriation Advisory Committee Terms of Reference (4 February 2000) [archived at KKTC Archives, Cranbrook, British Columbia].
42 *Ibid.*
43 "Ktunaxa Ethnobotany," online: Royal BC Museum <http://www.livinglamdscapes.bc.ca/cbasin/ktunaxa/introduction.htm>.
44 *Ibid.*
45 Interview of Anonymous by Laura McCoy (9 October 2002), Fairmont, British Columbia.
46 *Code of Ethics for Researchers Conducting Research Concerning the Ktunaxa Nation* (November 1998) available by request from the Ktunaxa Treaty Council. It is reproduced on our project website at <http://www.law.ualberta.ca/research/aboriginalcuturalheritage>. The code is a living document and processes are sometimes adjusted, depending on the nature of the research.
47 *Ibid.*
48 *Ibid.*
49 *Supra* note 16 at 8.
50 *Ibid.* at 4.
51 *Ibid.* at 18.
52 *Ibid.* at 4.
53 *Ibid.*

54 *Ibid.*
55 Interview of John Nicholas by Laura McCoy (17 January 2003), Cranbrook, British Columbia.
56 *Supra* note 16 at 6.
57 Participants demonstrated some knowledge of intellectual property law but often had an incomplete understanding of it and/or confused different areas of law such as patent, copyright, and trademark. However, an overriding perception is that Western intellectual property law facilitated the appropriation of Ktunaxa intangible heritage.
58 *Supra* note 18.
59 *Supra* note 45.
60 *Ibid.*
61 Interview of Pat Gravelle by Laura McCoy (24 April 2003), Grasmere, British Columbia.
62 R.S.B.C. 1996, c. 187.
63 Participants commonly felt that there was a need for the Ktunaxa to become more involved in protecting and maintaining sites. Later in the case study, we included concerns about enforcement of legislation in the discussion of concepts of law and law reform. We raised the issue of cooperative development in earlier discussions about private ownership and commercial development as well as in later discussions about site identification.
64 Interview of Lucille Shovar by Laura McCoy (29 November 2002), Cranbrook, British Columbia.
65 *Supra* note 16 at 20.
66 *Supra* note 17.
67 *Ibid.*
68 See *e.g.* passage from interview with Violet Birdstone, *supra* note 18 at 316-17 of this chapter.
69 R.S.C. 1985, c. I-5.
70 Interview of Diana Cote by Laura McCoy (13 August 2003), Invermere, British Columbia.
71 *Supra* note 39 at 8-9.
72 It is important to note that all cultures do not express their legal principles in the same way and that it is inappropriate to apply the concept of law as clearly articulated rules to First Nations cultures. See *e.g.* Val Napoleon, "Looking beyond the Law: Questions about Indigenous Peoples' Tangible and Intangible Property" in Catherine Bell and Robert K. Paterson, eds., *Protection of First Nations Cultural Heritage: Laws, Policy, and Reform* (Vancouver: UBC Press, 2008).
73 Gordon Christie, "Aboriginal Rights, Aboriginal Culture and Protection" (1998) 36:3 Osgoode Hall L.J. at 450.
74 *Supra* note 18.
75 For further discussion on how legislation can help to facilitate respectful negotiation, see Catherine Bell, "Restructuring the Relationship: Domestic Repatriation and Canadian Law Reform" in Bell and Paterson, eds., *Protection of First Nations Cultural Heritage, supra* note 71.
76 *Supra* note 1 at 1.
77 *Ibid.* at 2.
78 *Ibid.*
79 *Ibid.* at 2 and 3.

Part 2: Experiences across the Nation

For the Anishinabek, law is taught, in part, "through the stories of a character known as Nanabush, the Trickster."[1] Nanabush's behaviours are entirely contradictory because they are at once charming and cunning, honest and deceptive, kind and mean. Nanabush's actions and stories can cause one to think and perhaps also to be uncomfortable. Stay with the discomfort – it is an important place.

Nanabush is draped along the top of the large metal T-shaped sculpture outside the concrete bunker that is the Faculty of Law at the University of Alberta. He is a law professor after all. So, the spring air is delicious, the sun is warm, and the snow is just starting to melt. Nanabush has been spending time at the law school – attending classes and faculty meetings, and hanging around the library. What a jumble of passions, hilarity, mind-numbing boredom, constipated bureaucracy, competition, fast friendships, and exhilarating high energy – downright Trickster-like! Maybe it is not that different from teaching law among the Anishinabek: Nanabush is going to have to think about that one some more.

And right now, Nanabush is amused. He has been eavesdropping on discussions abut cultural heritage and is musing on the cleverness of sleight-of-hand tricks and how fooling the eye can fool the mind. He heard someone saying, "We've lost our culture." And there was something else about the *Indian Act* being the thief. And there is talk about evolving relationships, recovery of cultural items, the role of museums, development, respecting ancestors, joint initiatives, land claims, conservation strategies, rights, ethics, law – and lots of other complicated stuff. Nanabush is wondering what all this means. Has another Trickster been around? Nanabush decides that there is an optical illusion on the loose. True, he concedes, the stuff of culture has changed, but people survived and are rebuilding. So why on earth are they looking for culture outside of themselves? Curious. He must listen more.

Nanabush thinks he hears somebody laughing in the distance. Tarantula? Bobtail? Weget? Clown? Or maybe Wisakedjak?

Val Napoleon

Note

1 John Borrows, *Recovering Canada: The Resurgence of Indigenous Law* (Toronto: University of Toronto Press, 2002) at 56.

8
First Nations Cultural Heritage: A Selected Survey of Issues and Initiatives

Catherine Bell, Graham Statt, Michael Solowan, Allyson Jeffs, and Emily Snyder

Increasingly, issues of ownership, protection, and repatriation of First Nations cultural heritage are gaining attention in Canada. Modern treaties, museum and government policies, band-level initiatives, litigation, and enactment of provincial repatriation legislation in Alberta confirm the importance of these issues. Against this backdrop Canadian museums and federal and provincial governments have demonstrated a willingness to relinquish and share control over many cultural items and heritage sites. However, in addition to stories of success and cooperation, there have been challenges, which, like the case studies in this volume, raise questions about the need for law and policy reform. In this chapter we provide snapshots of some repatriation and protection experiences and initiatives in Canada over the last twenty years. We draw examples from a number of sources, including media reports, legal literature, museum policy, and submissions from First Nations other than our formal research partners. These snapshots are not intended to thoroughly address all sides of a given issue, nor is this chapter intended to be a comprehensive examination of all experiences and initiatives; rather, we have assembled what we believe to be helpful illustrations that will provide the reader with a starting point to explore repatriation and protection experiences beyond those detailed in the case studies in this volume.

Repatriation

Evolving Relationships between Museums and First Nations

Museums in Canada have played, and continue to play, an important role in the protection and repatriation of First Nations material culture. Museums are not only concerned about physical preservation and access to material culture for the purposes of education and research but are also engaged in numerous initiatives that demonstrate their commitment to the living cultures of First Nations and other aboriginal peoples of Canada. For example, the Canadian Museum of Civilization (CMC), provincial museums, and other major museums that hold public and private collections are involved in recording and preserving cultural knowledge through written, visual, and oral records; collaborative research; improving access to collections through visitor programs, travelling exhibits, loans, digitization of collections, and other means; co-management and consultation in proper care, use, and display of First Nations material; museology training programs; and efforts to obtain funding and meet other conditions necessary under federal law and policy to prevent the export of important First Nations cultural material. Developments in technology have also increased access to collections and enabled the creation of data bases in First Nations communities, such as the one created by the Vuntut Gwichin of over eight hundred Gwichin items held worldwide.[1] Some of these initiatives, such as the role of museums in cultural documentation, have been in place for many years. However, the expansion of initiatives in the last fifteen years or so, and fundamental changes in political and professional relationships between Canadian museums and First Nations, have also arisen out of controversy and the recommendations of the Task Force on Museums and First Peoples (the Task Force).[2]

More complex in the process of relationship building is the issue of the repatriation of cultural items. As the case studies in this volume illustrate, prior to the Task Force recommendations, some museums were already responding to requests by First Nations institutions, such as the U'mista Cultural Centre, to repatriate items confiscated under discriminatory laws or illegally acquired under Canadian law. There are also examples of the repatriation of sacred ceremonial material, such as the CMC's 1989 return of the Starlight Bundle to the Tsuu T'ina. In explaining this decision, the CMC "stressed the importance of the bundle to the band in conducting tribal ceremonies, its intended use in educating young Sarcees about their heritage, and the band's assurances that the bundle would be well preserved."[3] However, in the early years repatriation occurred on a more *ad hoc* case-by-case basis, not all requests met with success, and museums did not have specific repatriation policies in place. Increased awareness of, and attention to, the issue of repatriation was brought about by events leading to the Task Force, contemporary land claims, and enactment of repatriation legislation in the United States.[4] Today, several major Canadian museums have specific aboriginal repatriation policies in place and deaccessioning inside and outside of these policies is based on contemporary ethical standards maintained within the museum community.

In this section we offer highlights of evolving relations between museums and First Nations in Canada, including repatriation legislation and examples of contemporary museum policy. More detailed accounts of some of these developments from the perspective of research participants are found in the case studies included in this volume.[5] Rather than repeat what has already been discussed in the case studies and is elaborated in the second volume of our research (such as Alberta's repatriation legislation and the return of potlatch materials), these initiatives are either omitted here or raised only briefly.

Controversy and Change: The Glenbow Experience

In 1988, controversy developed over an exhibit of First Nations items held in connection with the 1988 Winter Olympic Games in Calgary. Although a court application to remove a False Face mask from the exhibit was ultimately unsuccessful, the Task Force on Museums and First Peoples was subsequently created. As part of the Games, the Olympic Arts Festival hosted a special exhibit entitled "The Spirit Sings" at the Glenbow-Alberta Institute. The exhibit, considered the flagship attraction of the arts festival, included in its collection masks lent by other institutions. Controversy erupted over the display of a Mohawk False Face mask originating from the region of southern Quebec and that was on loan from the Royal Ontario Museum (ROM). False Face masks are used in healing ceremonies by Mohawk medicine societies, and some are considered so sacred that it is forbidden for non-natives to view them. The Lubicon Lake First Nation organized a boycott of the exhibit.[6]

Upon learning of the exhibit, the Mohawk Nations of Kahnawake, Akwesasne, and Kanesatake (plaintiffs) filed a statement of claim seeking the return of the mask and other objects in the exhibit as well as an injunction to prevent the display of the mask. They were initially successful. On 15 January 1988, Justice Shannon of the Alberta Court of Queen's Bench granted an interim injunction pulling the False Face Mask from the exhibit.[7] However, a second hearing was held two weeks later to enable cross examination of the plaintiffs on their evidence. At the second hearing, the Court heard from the ROM, which claimed that it had acquired the mask, along with other items, from the Chiefswood Collection, which belonged to Evelyn H.C. Johnson of the Six Nations Band of Indians. Her will bequeathed the mask, among other artifacts, to the ROM. The Mohawk denied that the mask or any part of the collection belonged to Johnson. They argued that she could not have had legal title to the items because, under Mohawk law, False Face masks are not subject to individual ownership; rather, they are the communal property of the Medicine Society of the Mohawk Nation and the Iroquois Confederacy.[8]

The ROM claimed the mask had been displayed publicly on several occasions and was the subject of published photographs, articles, and catalogues. It argued "no claims to ownership or possession of the Mask had been asserted by anyone at any time since the Mask came into the possession of the ROM."[9] The Mohawk denied knowledge of public exhibitions or publications about the artifact.[10] Upon learning that the ROM had possessed the mask for sixty-six years and had displayed it at various institutions without complaint, Justice Shannon denied a further injunction. The Court held that the applicants had failed to show that irreparable harm would result from the continued display of the mask – a prerequisite necessary to obtain prohibitive injunctions in Canadian law. The mask was returned to the ROM after the exhibit concluded.

In the wake of the controversy, the Glenbow Museum in Calgary worked to improve its relationship with First Nations, and in 1990 it established the First Nations Advisory Council (discussed in Chapter 5, this volume). The council's work has increased awareness and understanding of First Nations cultural practices among museum staff. The Glenbow also entered agreements for indefinite long-term loans of sacred and ceremonial objects, such as medicine bundles, for ceremonial use. However, efforts to actually repatriate objects were hampered in part by the *Glenbow-Alberta Institute Act* (*GAIA*), which specified that objects in the museum's collections are held for the benefit of the people of Alberta.[11] These difficulties were ultimately resolved through the enactment, in 2000, of the *First Nations Sacred Ceremonial Objects Repatriation Act* (the *Repatriation Act*)[12] and an amendment to the *GAIA*.[13] The *Repatriation Act* provides a process for the Glenbow and the Provincial Museum of Alberta (now the Royal Alberta Museum [RAM]) to return to First Nations in Alberta sacred ceremonial objects – the title to which, under Canadian law, is vested in the Crown – "used in the practice of sacred ceremonial traditions" and that continue to be "vital" for the practise of those traditions.[14]

Cross-Border Repatriation: The Scriver Blackfoot Collection

Alberta's repatriation legislation was also deployed to facilitate the cross-border repatriation of the Theodore Last Star Medicine Pipe Bundle to the Montana Blackfeet. The bundle was originally acquired by the RAM as part of the Scriver Blackfoot Collection from Montana artist Bob Scriver in October 1989, for US$1.1 million.[15] The Blackfoot of Canada eventually requested repatriation of the bundle under Alberta's repatriation legislation and returned it to the Montana Blackfeet. Although the *Repatriation Act* is limited in application to First Nations in Alberta, Premier Klein supported extending "the spirit of the legislation south of the border."[16]

The collection was started by Thaddeus Emery Scriver, a merchant in Browning, Montana, when he was issued a federal licence in 1907 that allowed him to trade with the Indians.[17] Government assimilation policies, systemic poverty, and the influence of the church provided an atmosphere ripe for collecting as the Blackfoot "went underground" with some ritual practices and no longer engaged in others.[18] Sons Harold and Bob (a renowned artist) continued their father's legacy, and by the time the collection was scheduled for sale it contained over fifteen hundred individual items, including medicine bundles.[19] Some of the bundles were collected from a Canadian who brought them into Montana to be sold. Other ceremonial items were gifted or sold to Bob Scriver as ceremonies had either gone underground or were in abeyance:[20] "Many of the elders feared for the loss and destruction of ceremonial items after they passed away and to ensure their preservation brought them to the Scrivers."[21]

Bob Scriver, who died in 1999, was known among the Blackfeet as Sik-Poke-Sah-Mah-Pee.[22] Born and raised on the reservation, he had many close personal contacts with the Montana Blackfeet. He was given his name in the summer of 1969 when, during a transfer ceremony, he became the recipient of the Little Dog Thunder Medicine Pipe.[23]

Why then was the collection sold to a museum in Alberta? As Scriver aged, the question of what to do with his collection of bronze sculpture, artifacts, and taxidermy became pressing as family members were unable or unwilling to assume responsibility. The building housing the collection was in poor condition and under threat of fire. Scriver tried, without success, to sell it to some museums in the United States. The family may also have feared that returning the collection to the Blackfeet could result in items being sold to private collectors.[24] The director of the RAM was very interested in the collection and persuaded him to sell it. Further, much of the collection is thought to have originated in Canada. Scriver felt a connection to Edmonton as he had once lived there, and he was persuaded by the promise of an area devoted to the collection.[25]

Reg Crowshoe of the Piikani Nation viewed the sale as an "asset to the Blackfoot," but he cautioned that "if it's going to be sitting in the museum all locked up, then it's not going to help anyone."[26] Crowshoe explained that the bundles "are like a spiritual roadmap telling us where we're [Blackfoot] going and how we're going to get there."[27] However, Chief Earl Old Person was surprised by the sale as he thought that these items would one day be returned to the Montana Blackfeet community.[28]

Adding to the complexity of the Scriver acquisition was the prior publication of Scriver's book entitled *The Blackfeet: Artists of the Northern Plains* (1990), which includes colour photographs of medicine bundles and other ceremonial items. Many Blackfoot assert that displaying the contents of a medicine bundle outside of a ceremony is forbidden under Blackfoot law, and some even consider looking at the pictures in Scriver's book sacrilege.[29] Scriver maintained that "all ceremonial bundles and items in this collection have lost their power for some reason or another."[30] According to Blackfeet tradition, he claims, objects given or sold without a ceremonial transfer remain in inactive status as artifacts only. However, the Blackfoot studies in this volume suggest that there are differing views on this issue and that the power of such bundles and the responsibilities to attend to their spiritual needs may remain active.[31]

Getting the collection from Billings, Montana, to Edmonton, Alberta, was a complicated affair because the collection contains several pieces with eagle feathers as well as parts of endangered species. Endangered species laws in the States made it illegal to take eagle feathers and other parts of endangered animals across the border. On the Canadian side, the material did not require an import permit because there was no counterpart to the *Bald Eagle Protection Act*, and all of the material had been collected prior to the *Convention on International Trade in Endangered Species of Wild Fauna and Flora*.[32] After considerable diplomatic effort, the required permits were eventually obtained from the United States.

Soon after the collection arrived at the RAM, Montana Blackfeet activists demanded the return of several sacred items. RAM acquired legal title to the entire collection under Canadian and US law, the Blackfeet argued that, morally, they had a better claim. The history of the collection further complicated matters. It is reported that the collection was the result of dealings with Southern Piikani (Piegan), artifact dealers, and Canadian Blackfoot who came "south to visit, race horses and celebrate."[33] Furthermore, sacred artifacts "circulat[ed] freely throughout the whole of the Blackfoot Confederacy ... [s]teadily moving from family to family, from band to band, traded and re-traded. A single pipe-bundle may have had thirty or more owners."[34]

The matter was not resolved until after the enactment of Alberta's *Repatriation Act*. The Blackfoot in Canada requested that certain items from the Scriver collection be repatriated to them under the *Act* so they could give them to the Montana Blackfeet. On 1 July 2002, Canadian Blackfoot and American Blackfeet gathered on a ranch in Montana to celebrate the return of the Theodore Last Star Thunder Medicine Pipe to the Montana Blackfeet.[35] It was the first ceremonial opening of the bundle since 1942.[36] Similar cooperative arrangements have been used to repatriate objects to First Nations in Canada from the United States under US repatriation legislation.

Canadian Museum Repatriation Policies

Also arising from the "The Spirit Sings" controversy was a conference sponsored by the Assembly of First Nations and the Canadian Museums Association on the relationship between Canadian museums and First Peoples, which ultimately led to the establishment of the Task Force. The Task Force made a series of recommendations for policy reform in a number of areas, including increased involvement of aboriginal people in the interpretation of museum collections, training, support for cultural institutions, improved access to collections, and repatriation. Bell and Paterson summarize key features of the report relating to the repatriation of "sacred" objects and "cultural patrimony" as follows:

> The report distinguishes between objects that are judged to have been (by current legal standards) "acquired illegally" and those "obtained legally." In the former case, the objects should be returned, together with a transfer of title, to the originating cultural group or individuals. In the latter situation of presumed legitimate acquisition, museums are to negotiate, upon request, returns of sacred and ceremonial objects and other objects of special importance with appropriate Aboriginal communities on a case-by-case basis, taking into account moral and ethical concerns as well as legal considerations. The Task Force Report also outlines three alternative strategies, in addition to the physical return of objects accompanied by a transfer or return of legal title. It suggests that museums lend sacred and ceremonial objects for use by Aboriginal communities and that museums allow the replication of materials in their collections. Finally, the report encourages museums to engage in shared management of their collections of Aboriginal material by involving First Nations in such areas as defining access, determining storage conditions, and recognizing the traditional ownership systems of originating cultures.[37]

The Task Force report also addresses the repatriation of human remains and associated burial objects. Disposition recommendations flow from three different categories: remains of persons known by name, remains affiliated with a named First Nation, and remains that cannot be affiliated with a First Nation. In the latter situation, the Task Force recommends that remains and associated objects "be treated and disposed of after consultation between museums and representatives of Aboriginal peoples."[38]

Also in the 1990s, repatriation and heritage protection were being raised as issues in modern land claim and treaty negotiations. These factors and the desire to maintain positive relations with First Nations influenced the development of specific repatriation policies relating to material culture by some of the major museums in Canada. Some museums (*e.g.*, the Manitoba Museum and the Royal Saskatchewan Museum) were in the process of developing or revising policies at the time of writing, and many continue to respond to repatriation requests under general deaccessioning policies.[39] Because there is no national organization monitoring the implementation of the recommendations, details on the extent to which they have been adopted or modified are unavailable. However, the date and content of policies we examined suggest that the Task Force and modern land claim and treaty negotiations have influenced policy development in major Canadian museums.

It is beyond the scope of this review chapter to include all existing and developing policies. Existing repatriation policies vary among institutions but they share in common a willingness to consider the return of items articulated in the Task Force report as well as options that fall short of return. Some also address the nature of proof required and the potential of competing claims within and between communities. Further, policies usually operate in addition to other deaccessioning processes. For example, given a compelling case that does not fit within a specific repatriation policy, museums may also repatriate on a case-by-case basis under general deaccessioning policies. We consider key features of three sample policies and processes here: the Canadian Museum of Civilization, the Royal British Columbia Museum, and the Manitoba Museum. Each of these are incorporated institutions that receive public funds and are repositories for government-owned property and items acquired through purchase and donation.

Canadian Museum of Civilization (CMC) The CMC has been working with aboriginal peoples to resolve repatriation issues for many years. Under the *Museum Act,* the CMC may loan or dispose of items in its collection subject to approval by the Board of Trustees and terms on which an item was acquired or is held.[40] In all decisions to repatriate, the CMC is now guided by its Repatriation Policy and is committed to balancing the interests of First Nations with the corporation's obligation to hold collections in trust for all Canadians."[41]

At the CMC a repatriation request may be made within treaty, self-government, and comprehensive claims processes and on a case-by-case basis by Aboriginal individuals and governments. The Repatriation Policy was "developed in the spirit of the recommendations" of the Task Force and covers "human remains and associated burial objects, archaeological objects and related materials, ethnographic objects, and records associated with these" that are not bound by repatriation provisions under treaties with First Nations.[42] Where a request has been made in writing and "overlapping or competing claims from other groups are resolved," the CMC may repatriate human remains and directly associated burial items "demonstrably linked" to the requesting Aboriginal government or individuals and "objects which have demonstrably originated with the Aboriginal society and were employed by traditional curers and/or definitively related to traditional and ongoing religious practice."[43] Under this policy, objects are repatriated to an aboriginal government, unless "the requestor is an individual or group of individuals with an undisputed historical relationship to the objects and the objects are demonstrated to have been acquired under conditions that were illegal at that time" or "the Aboriginal Government has designated in writing a duly constituted organization, such as a cultural centre, to assume responsibility for the material in question."[44] Requests are reviewed according to four criteria: "the historical relationship" of the requestor to the item claimed, "conditions under which the materials requested were acquired," the potential for competing claims, and whether "the character of the objects" meet the criteria set out in the policy.[45]

Objects remaining with the CMC may also be the subject of custodial agreements with an aboriginal government. All repatriations are approved by the Board of Trustees.

Repatriation achieved through treaty, comprehensive land claim, and self-government negotiations may be broader in scope. In its 2006-7 Corporate Plan, the CMC reported that it was actively engaged in discussions with approximately thirty-four First Nations, most in British Columbia, but some of which were in Labrador, Quebec, Ontario, and the Northwest Territories.[46] Negotiated repatriations are also presented to the Board of Trustees for approval prior to the federal caucus' review of the draft treaty, self-government, or land claim agreement. An example of large-scale repatriations possible under this process is the Nisga'a Treaty, which is discussed later in this chapter.

In addition to these programs, the CMC runs a Sacred Materials program. This program, which has been running since the 1990s, involves the CMC inviting and paying for representatives from two or three First Nations to visit the CMC every year to view items and records in its collection, to make recommendations on care and handling, to provide ceremonial care and, if desired, to discuss repatriation requests.[47] "[E]xperiences and practices in regard to repatriation" are also shared at conferences, "working meetings of curators and directors," and through publications.[48]

Like many other museums, the CMC also has a specific policy for the repatriation of human remains and associated mortuary objects. "In order to safeguard the collections held in trust for the peoples of Canada and to prevent any improprieties regarding remains and objects," repatriation and "rights to remains and objects are determined on a case by case basis and may be demonstrated through ancestral-descendant relationships or valid historical connections between an individual or family group and the remains and (or) objects in question."[49] The CMC reserves the right to conduct a "thorough inventory and scholarly documentation" for the "purposes of scientific inquiry and heritage preservation."[50] Several major repatriations of remains have occurred in accordance with this policy, including repatriations to the Mohawk Nation Council of Chiefs (1998); Six Nations Council (Iroquois) at Ohsucken, Ontario; the Haida Nation (Haida Gwaii/Queen Charlotte Islands); and the Kitigan Zibi Algonquin located near Manawaki, Quebec.[51]

Royal British Columbia Museum (RCBM) The RBCM has an "Aboriginal Material Operating Policy" that acknowledges that "Aboriginal materials ... [are] part of the intellectual and cultural heritage of the respective Aboriginal peoples," responds to "initiatives of the provincial treaty negotiations," and facilitates the "return of human remains, and cultural objects which may have been acquired under circumstances that render the Museum's claim invalid, to originating Aboriginal communities, when it is the wish of those Aboriginal communities."[52] Pursuant to these objectives and enabled by amendments to the *Museum Act*, the RBCM is committed to:

- The return of human remains and associated burial objects, upon the request of an Aboriginal community with a demonstrable claim of historical relationship to those objects in question.
- The return of objects that may have been acquired under circumstances that render the museum's claim invalid, at the request of an Aboriginal community with a demonstrable claim of historical relationship to those objects in question.
- Negotiating with Aboriginal communities on the return of material of spiritual significance or essential to cultural survival, at the request of an aboriginal community, bearing in mind the Provincial interests and in the context of ongoing treaty negotiations.[53]

Sacred and ceremonial items "of religious significance and essential to the continuation of ceremonial and ritual life among Aboriginal people" may be returned and in the case of "ceremonial and religious material, the claimant must demonstrate that the materials are needed by a traditional Aboriginal leader or leaders for traditional Aboriginal practices."[54]

The policy also addresses other RBCM objectives consistent with Task Force recommendations, such as the repatriation of human remains, the increased involvement of aboriginal peoples in the interpretation of their culture and history, and the cooperative management of aboriginal cultural objects. The RBCM is also a partner in the treaty negotiation process and, like the CMC, is, through this process, engaged in the repatriation of items and the development of custodial agreements. These approaches to repatriation are facilitated by ss. 5(7) and 5(2)(b) of the *Museum Act*, which provide that the RBCM must "at the request of government ... transfer all of its interest in possession of an artifact" where conditions in a treaty or other agreements with the government have been met, and that it may dispose of items in its collection "after considering the cultural significance of the objects," the "public interest in retaining the objects," and "in accordance with ethical and other standards" adopted by the RBCM.

Manitoba Museum The Manitoba Museum has been involved in issues pertaining to the repatriation of sacred materials since the mid-1970s. Like other museums, it continues to hold such materials for diverse reasons at the request of individuals and communities and enables spiritual care through a variety of means. In some instances where the community has decided it "is not ready to receive" sacred materials, the museum has acted as a "Keeping Place, or as one elder put it, 'Sanctuary' for objects in 'transition' as they make their way back into the communities."[55] Along with representatives from other institutions that hold prairie material, staff of the museum and representatives from First Nations communities meet to discuss issues of common concern, including but not limited to matters of repatriation. What is apparent from these and other experiences is that repatriation "is a complex issue for communities."[56] For example "there are still outstanding issues in the community regarding customary use, ownership (bloodline or communal), etc., coupled with internal and external politics that must be addressed," including counter-claims by organized groups on behalf of those no longer practising their traditional ceremonies.[57]

At the time of writing, repatriation procedures at the museum were under review. The procedures applicable to aboriginal material have developed in "response to advice and consultation received from various members in the Aboriginal community," "experiences of other heritage institutions," and "in the spirit" of the Task Force.[58] The new draft policy appears broader than other museum policies specific to repatriation. Of particular interest is express consideration of "cultural duress" in assessing claims by individuals or groups to illegally acquired material.[59] The museum may also repatriate "objects which have demonstrably originated with a particular ceremonial aboriginal or non-aboriginal society or organization and were employed by traditional ceremonialists and/or definitively related to traditional or ongoing religious practice."[60] This is different from the 2002 Manitoba policy, which required a demonstration of need "for ongoing practice of traditional religions."[61] However, all Manitoba museum policies and procedures are currently under review, so this could change.

Like other repatriation processes, the Manitoba process needs to take into consideration the mandate of the museum, professional ethics, negotiations between aboriginal peoples and government, and laws relating to cultural objects (such as the inability to deaccession an item subject to restrictions imposed on donation without first having such conditions legally removed). The new procedures also address repatriation in the context of land claims, self-government, and treaty processes. Assuming the categories of existing policy are maintained, the museum will also consider the return of human remains and "directly associated burial objects," ethical conditions that render the museum's claim invalid, and material of "spiritual significance *or* essential to the cultural survival."[62] Repatriation of human remains is directed by provincial legislation and policy. Remains and directly associated burial objects are only repatriated to an aboriginal government or an organization designated in writing for that purpose.[63]

Competing Claims: University of Winnipeg Anthropology Museum

Sympathetic to the interests of First Nations, museum personnel have engaged in repatriations pursuant to formal and informal processes. Despite good intentions, challenges can arise when clear deaccessioning policies are not in place or are not followed. For example, items requested for use in ongoing ceremonial activity may be claimed by individuals, religious societies, families, and communities of origin. In some instances, it may not be clear how an item came to be housed in a collection, and it may not be possible to trace clear affiliation to a particular individual or group. An example of the complexity of repatriation and problems that can arise in the absence of detailed records for deaccessioning is illustrated in media accounts and the Manitoba auditor general's report on repatriations by the University of Winnipeg (U of W) anthropology museum. A forensic audit in 2002 revealed that eighty-nine ethnological items listed in the catalogue could not be located.[64] It is alleged that some ceremonial items repatriated to a First Nation group that did not create them and that the deaccessioning process did not always comply with museum policies and procedures.[65]

The museum began to acquire its collection in the late 1960s and early 1970s, when American patrons of a remote fishing lodge in the Berens River area of northern Manitoba began buying large numbers of artifacts from the local First Nations, particularly, the Pauingassi.[66] Professor Jack Steinbring of the U of W Anthropology Department travelled to the community to collect as many of the artifacts as he could, believing the historical material culture of the groups might soon be completely lost and with the understanding it was going to be protected for the benefit of the community. He eventually acquired 400 items, 240 of which were from Pauingassi.[67] The Pauingassi maintained contact with the university, and on occasion an elder would come to examine Pauingassi artifacts and give talks to university students.[68] As late as 1996, the chiefs and tribal council wrote letters praising the mutually advantageous relationship and supporting the university's continued research, preservation, and stewardship activities.[69]

In September 1999, U of W history professor Dr. Jennifer Brown, who had for many years conducted research with the community of Pauingassi, received a letter from the Anthropology Department stating that some items had been removed from the collection and had "entered back into the traditional spiritual community."[70] The letter identified nine people with whom the repatriation was discussed at length. However, according to Brown, the Pauingassi had no knowledge of the transfer. Of the nine names on the list, eight were not from Pauingassi and the one that purported to be from Pauingassi was unknown to anyone in the community. Several were from the Three Fires Midewiwin Society in Wisconsin, a society consisting of three major tribal groups that practise the Midewiwin way of life,[71] and one was a Manitoba member of the Three Fires Society.[72] Brown's further investigations revealed that more items were missing from the collection than had been originally thought, and some seemed to have been removed without sufficient documentation regarding their disposition.[73]

A representative from the Three Fires Society who received six of the artifacts indicated that he did not believe the Pauingassi's claim to have knowledge.[74] His understanding was that the repatriation occurred with the full knowledge and consent of members of the Pauingassi community and that the controversy was contrived.[75]

This case became increasingly complex as there were conflicting accounts between First Nations and the U of W museum, conflicting claims within First Nation communities and between First Nation groups in Canada and the United States, as well as debate among museums and museum curators in Canada. A member of the Three Fires Society questioned whether the Pauingassi community would even benefit from the return of these items.[76] Eddie Benton Benai, the leader of the Three Fires Society, described the conflict over the repatriation as follows: "It's not a White matter. It's not a Christian matter. It's an Indian; it's a Native issue. That's it."[77] He did not want the items returned to the Pauingassi if they were going to end up back in a museum or in the hands of those other than First Nations.[78]

Due to the complexity of the situation and the numerous conflicting accounts surrounding the repatriation, provincial auditor general Jon Singleton conducted a forensic audit of the museum between November 2001 and February 2002. This audit revealed that eighty-nine artifacts were missing.[79] Fifty-eight of these artifacts were from the Northern Ojibwa collection and thirty-three related specifically to the Pauingassi.[80] The report revealed that deaccessioning occurred over a period of time and culminated with the delivery of two water drums (including one belonging to a Pauingassi medicine man named Fair Wind) and two birch-bark scrolls (from the Jackhead First Nation) to the Three Fires Society in 1998. Apparently, a raven headdress, originally collected from the Little Grand Rapids area, was deaccessioned at the same time as were the drums and scrolls. The headdress, however, was never located.[81]

The auditor general found that the policies and procedures governing museum repatriation and deaccessioning were not always followed and that documentary and inventory records were not always complete. His report concluded that the transfer of the drums and scrolls to the Three Fires Society may have invoked the *Cultural Property Export and Import Act* [*CPEIA*],[82] and he suggested that the university seek legal advice regarding the situation.[83] He also noted that no formal documentation requesting the repatriation of artifacts was available for review; that neither the individuals who assembled the collection nor the communities from which the artifacts were collected were adequately consulted or made aware of the repatriation; and that the museum did not report to or consult with the department chair in relation to the repatriation, as per the museum policy manual.

Although the auditor general's report underscores some of the problems that can arise despite good intentions when repatriation proceeds without adherence to clear procedures, Singleton also indicated that he was "encouraged by the University's response to [the] findings and recommendations, and [was] particularly impressed by the University's determination to be a part of the process of dealing with the future impact of past actions."[84] The university and the anthropology museum were also working closely to improve their policies, particularly concerning repatriation.[85]

On 21 June 2002 (National Aboriginal Day), members of the Three Fires Society met in a private ceremony in Winnipeg with representatives of the Pauingassi community to return the two water drums, a drum rim, a drum plug, and two drum sticks.[86] The remaining items in the collection were never found.

International Repatriation: The Haisla Spirit Pole

The Haisla First Nation of Kitlope in northern British Columbia has been successful in the repatriation of a spirit pole that was taken from their community. The pole had been given to Sweden as a gift and was held at the National Museum of Ethnology in Stockholm. The unusual saga told here is drawn from media reports, the Haisla website, and documentary films. It began in 1862, when smallpox decimated the Haisla. The population of four villages in the Kitlope area plummeted from 3,500 to 57. When the smallpox epidemic raced through Misk'usa, the entrance to the Kitlope wilderness about six hundred kilometres northwest of Vancouver, the great Eagle chief G'psqoalux lost his family and all his clan. In his grief, the chief went into the forest, where he had a spiritual experience that reunited him with the spirits of his lost loved ones. In commemoration, the chief commissioned two carvers to make a mortuary pole that was erected at Misk'usa in 1872.[87]

In the 1920s, Olof Hansson, Swedish consul for British Columbia stationed in Prince Rupert, became very interested in totem poles and wanted to acquire one to give to his country as a gift. In 1927, the Indian agent at Bella Coola wrote to the Department of Indian Affairs in Ottawa requesting that Hansson be permitted to obtain the G'psgolox (also known as the Haisla and Misk'usa) totem pole. He wrote: "[The] reserve is uninhabited and very isolated. The chances are that the pole, if not removed, after some time will fall down and be destroyed."[88] In January 1928, the deputy superintendent general of Indian affairs gave permission to acquire the pole, given that "the Indian reserve was uninhabited and very isolated" and "provided that the Indian owners [were] willing to dispose of it."[89]

Gerald Amos, lead treaty negotiator for the Kitamaat Band, explains that, when Hansson went to get the pole, the village was empty.[90] However, according to Haisla elder Louisa Smith, "[j]ust because that place had nobody there doesn't mean it was abandoned."[91] Further, some accounts of the removal of the pole maintain that, in 1929, upon their return from a fishing trip, the Haisla discovered that the pole was gone.[92] It had been removed and shipped to Sweden, where it was displayed outside for six months before being moved into storage for more than forty years. It was then put on display in 1980, when the museum built a new gallery to house its native collections.[93] Sixty-one years after the pole was taken, a photograph in the anthropology text alerted the community to its location.

In 1991, the Haisla sent a delegation to Sweden to request the pole's return, and in 1994 the Swedish government granted permission to return it.[94] The Museum was concerned about the preservation of this "world treasure."[95] It had cared for the pole for decades and wanted its preservation to continue. At the same time, museum personnel appreciated the complexity of the situation, given the cultural significance of the pole to the Haisla. Totem poles can denote tribal and family identity, tell stories, mark historical events, and commemorate family. When a totem pole falls, it is left to go back to Mother Earth. Among the Haisla there were also dilemmas. The pole had been taken from the Haisla, but its preservation could be seen as a symbol of healing and could be used to educate their people and others about Haisla history. Had the pole remained in the community, it would have deteriorated. Further, the Haisla discussed whether the pole should be housed according to the standards set out by the Museum or whether they should put it back in the ground and let it return to the earth, as is cultural tradition.[96]

The facility that the Museum originally requested was beyond the financial means of the Haisla. The Kitamaat Village Council and elders granted approval to Ecotrust Canada, an organization with a good working relationship with the Haisla Nation, to spearhead a repatriation campaign. A website was launched, and brokering arrangements were made with the David Suzuki Foundation, the Rockefeller Brothers Fund, the Endswell Foundation, and the Museum. Money was and is being raised to build the facility, to provide curatorial training for Haisla staff at the UBC Museum of Anthropology, and to carve two replicas of the pole – one to be raised at the Misk'usa village site and the other to be sent to Sweden as a gift.[97] In August 2000, a ceremony was held to celebrate the raising of the Haisla replica pole at Misk'usa. In September that same year, in order to raise public awareness of the project, Haisla carvers returned to Sweden to finish carving the other pole.

The pole "began its long journey home" on 15 March 2006.[98] When the pole first arrived back in Canada, the UBC Museum of Anthropology temporarily housed it. At the time of writing, the Haisla planned to transfer the pole to a temporary spot in Kitamaat, British Columbia, while awaiting the construction of a community cultural centre.[99] In a Government of British Columbia news release, BC Assembly of First Nations Regional Chief Shawn Atleo was quoted as saying that, with the return of the original pole, "[w]e are building new relationships based on respect and recognition. The return of cultural property is integral to maintaining and passing on our culture, teachings and languages, and to reclaiming our identities."[100]

Dealers and Private Sales

Mount Newton Crossroads Bowl
In the 1890s, the Mount Newton Crossroads Stone Bowl was discovered in a field in Saanich, British Columbia. The field was located off reserve lands but within the traditional territory of the Saanich people.[101] The bowl, believed to be between 1,500 and 2,500 years old, is a thirty-six-centimetre sandstone sculpture of a woman holding a bowl in her lap. The Saanich people named the bowl *Sddlnewhala,* meaning medicine bowl.[102] Medicine men and women used the bowl in female puberty ceremonies. An artifact dealer purchased the bowl in the summer of 1993 from the last surviving member of the family on whose property it had been found. The bowl was purchased after the RBCM refused to buy it, citing its policy at the time of not purchasing artifacts.[103]

An application for an export permit under the federal *Cultural Property Export and Import Act* was filed in April 1993. The dealer intended to sell the bowl to a man in Chicago for $58,500.[104] An expert examiner from the RBCM recommended the export permit be denied, citing the importance of the bowl. A letter was sent to the Canadian Cultural Property Export Review Board to have the application reviewed. The review board imposed a three-month delay period, during which institutions and public authorities within Canada were solicited to make a fair offer to purchase the bowl and keep it in Canada.[105]

Barbara Winter, curator of the Simon Fraser University (SFU) Museum of Archaeology and Ethnology, was notified of the pending export and notified the Saanich Nation.[106] With only two months before the export delay period expired, the Saanich Nation considered four options: purchasing the bowl, working with a federally designated class "A" museum that could buy the bowl, seeking a court injunction, or allowing the bowl to be sold.[107] The first option was particularly problematic as some First Nations find it offensive that they should have to buy back their own sacred objects in order to prevent their export.[108]

The Canadian Cultural Property Export Review Board could not extend the delay period since there was no provision in federal legislation to do so. However, under intense pressure from First Nations, the public, the media, and the museum community, the dealer granted a forty-five-day extension. During this time, the SFU museum, as a class "A" museum under the *CPEIA,* was able to apply for a Movable Cultural Property Grant to purchase the bowl. Buying the bowl was a difficult ethical decision for the museum. Ultimately, it decided to purchase it because it wanted to help the Saanich Nation and did not want to see it exported, as has happened with many other bowls.[109] The Archaeology Branch of the Government of British Columbia contributed 30 percent of the asking price, and the federal government awarded the museum a $40,000 cultural property grant. These large grants allowed the museum to purchase the bowl and the Saanich Nation to stand by its position that it would not buy back its own bowl.[110] The export was prevented and legal proceedings were unnecessary.

In order to avoid offending both Canadian archaeologists (who disagree with the evaluation, trade, and barter for artifacts) and First Nations (who would claim that the object belongs to them), the SFU Museum of Archaeology and Ethnology immediately executed a transfer of title of the bowl to the Saanich Native Heritage Society. A custodial agreement was also signed, under which the museum would care for the object and the society could request the bowl for display purposes or traditional use.[111] Because of the transfer of title, the museum can only make *recommendations* for care and use of the bowl when it is in Saanich possession.[112] Significantly, of the sixty-eight known seated human-figure bowls from British Columbia and Washington State, sixteen are in private collections and the rest are in North American and European museums. This is one of only two bowls currently owned by a First Nation.[113]

Medicine Bundles of the Siksika First Nation

In 1974, two sacred bundles mysteriously disappeared from the Siksika Reserve near Gleichen, Alberta, ninety kilometres east of Calgary. The bundles contained two eagle feather headdresses, named Red Bird and Yellow Bird, respectively, that were used in the mid-summer Sundance ritual on the reserve. The headdresses originate from the Motoki Society, which means Women's Buffalo Society, and date back to the 1800s. The whereabouts of the bundles was discovered three decades later, when a Montana dealer tried to sell them back to the Siksika. It is unknown how the Montana dealer acquired the items. The Siksika refused to buy back what they felt was already theirs and, upon learning the bundles would be sold to a buyer in Japan, contacted the RCMP and Canada Customs. The dealer was later detained at the Coutts, Alberta, border crossing, at which time the bundles were seized and held until an expert could conclusively authenticate them.[114]

In January 2000, the dealer was charged in Montana with selling two other headdresses in the United States.[115] He faced charges in Canada under s. 159 of the *Customs Act*[116] for smuggling goods into Canada and s. 40 of the *CPEIA* for attempting to export from Canada objects included on the Export Control List. He was further charged under ss. 6(2) and 8(c) of the *Wild Animal and Plant Protection and Regulation of International and Interprovincial Trade Act*[117] for attempting to export animal parts without a permit and possession of animal parts for the purpose of distribution.

In November 2001, a special ceremony was held in the Siksika Deerfoot Sportsplex to officially return the medicine bundles. A trunk containing the 150-year-old bundles was accepted by Angeline Leather, spiritual leader of the Women's Buffalo Society, in keeping with Siksika tradition, which holds that only women may handle these bundles.

Modern Treaties and Claims

At the heart of land claims and modern treaty agreements are language, culture, and protecting a way of life. However, Canada's first modern land claim settlements did not include specific references to the repatriation of cultural material or human remains.[118] In 1993, the Yukon Umbrella Final Agreement was signed between the Council for Yukon Indians and the Governments of Canada and Yukon, to provide a framework for negotiating land settlement claims involving Yukon First Nations.[119] Chapter 13 includes a reference to repatriation issues. Section 13.4.3 provides:

> Government, where practicable, shall assist Yukon First Nations to develop programs, staff and facilities to enable the repatriation of Moveable and Documentary Heritage Resources relating to the culture and history of Yukon Indian People which have been removed from the Yukon, or are retained at present in the Yukon, where this is consistent with the maintenance of the integrity of national or territorial collections.

In conjunction with the signing of the Umbrella Final Agreement, final agreements were also signed by the Vuntut Gwitchin First Nation, the First Nation of Na-cho Nyak Dun, the Champagne and Aishihik First Nations, and the Teslin Tlingit Council. None of these agreements, or subsequent Yukon final agreements, speaks to issues of repatriation beyond what is provided for under s. 13.4.3 of the Umbrella Final Agreement.[120]

The limited treatment of repatriation under early land claim agreements, which for a long time were restricted in scope by the federal government and excluded self-government negotiation, can be compared to the more recent Tlicho (Dogrib) Agreement, signed on 25 August 2003.[121] It is the first combined land claim and self-government agreement in the Northwest Territories. The agreement affects 39,000 square kilometres of land between Great Slave Lake and Great Bear Lake. Section 17.3.1 of the agreement provides:

> It is an objective of the Parties that Tlicho heritage resources[[122]] which have been removed from the Northwest Territories be available for the benefit, study and enjoyment of Tlicho Citizens and all other residents of the Northwest Territories. The attainment of this objective may include the return of such resources to the Northwest Territories, on a temporary or continuing basis provided that:
>
> (a) appropriate facilities and expertise exist in the Northwest Territories

which are capable of maintaining such Tlicho heritage resources for future generations; and

(b) such relocation is compatible with the maintenance of the integrity of public archives and national and territorial heritage resource collections.

The agreement stipulates that achieving this objective will involve the cooperative efforts of the governments of Canada, the Northwest Territories, and the Tlicho.[123] While human remains of Tlicho ancestry and associated funerary objects are included in the definition of "heritage resources," these items are not contemplated in the above provisions; rather, the agreement includes a specific clause dealing with such matters. Section 17.3.4 provides:

> At the request of the Tlicho Government, government shall:
>
> (a) deliver any human remains and associated grave goods that were found in Tlicho burial sites in the Northwest Territories and subsequently removed from the Northwest Territories and are still held by government to the Tlicho Government in accordance with applicable legislation and government policies; and
>
> (b) use reasonable efforts to facilitate the Tlicho Government's access to Tlicho artifacts and human remains of Tlicho ancestry that are held in other public and private collections.

The most extensive treatment of repatriation is in the Nisga'a Final Agreement, a treaty and land claim agreement covering an area in the Nass River Valley of northwestern British Columbia, which came into force on 11 May 2000.[124] It includes provisions for the transfer or shared custody of hundreds of Nisga'a artifacts held by the CMC and the RBCM. Chapter 17 of the agreement represents the first time that a treaty with a Canadian First Nation has dealt in detail with the repatriation of cultural material in possession of government institutions.[125]

Appendices L-1 and L-2 list all artifacts in the permanent collection of the CMC, as of the effective date of the agreement, that have been identified as Nisga'a artifacts. Appendix L-1 includes 109 Nisga'a artifacts, primarily sacred and ceremonial items, to be transferred from the CMC to the Nisga'a Nation without condition. This represents approximately 25 percent of the Nisga'a objects held by the museum and includes headdresses, masks, rattles, soul catchers, and charms.[126] Appendix L-2 includes 283 Nisga'a artifacts to be shared by the CMC and the Nisga'a Nation. Custodial agreements relating to these items are to "respect Nisga'a laws and practices relating to Nisga'a artifacts and comply with federal and provincial laws ... and the statutory mandate" of the CMC.[127] Included are items such as spoons, earrings, baskets, arrows, and masks. Any Nisga'a artifacts permanently acquired by the CMC after the effective date are to be added to Appendix L-2, unless the museum and the Nisga'a Nation agree to include them in Appendix L-1.[128] This procedure is also to be followed if it is determined that another artifact in the collection of the museum is a Nisga'a artifact.[129]

Appendix L-3 and Appendix L-4 set out all artifacts in the permanent collection of the RBCM, as of the effective date of the agreement, that have been identified as Nisga'a artifacts. Appendix L-3 lists 180 Nisga'a artifacts to be transferred without condition from the museum to the Nisga'a Nation (more than 40 percent of the museum's Nisga'a collection). Appendix L-4 lists 244 Nisga'a artifacts to be held by the RBCM.[130]

The agreement also speaks to future ownership and acquisitions. For example, "[a]n artifact originally obtained from a Nisga'a person, a Nisga'a community, or a Nisga'a heritage site is presumed, in the absence of proof to the contrary, to be a Nisga'a artifact."[131] Any Nisga'a artifacts discovered within Nisga'a lands, after the effective date, will be considered property of the Nisga'a Nation unless another person establishes ownership of them.[132] Additionally, any Nisga'a artifacts discovered outside of Nisga'a lands that come into the permanent possession or under the control of British Columbia or Canada will be lent and possibly transferred to the Nisga'a Nation.[133] Human remains of individuals of Nisga'a ancestry removed from a heritage site will, subject to federal and provincial laws, be delivered to the Nisga'a Nation. The Nisga'a have not yet repatriated objects or remains as they are still in the process of building a cultural centre to house them.

Protection

Heritage Protection in Treaties and Land Claims

The Nisga'a Final Agreement also contains provisions for the protection of cultural heritage. It acknowledges that Nisga'a citizens have the right to practise the Nisga'a culture and to use the Nisga'a language.[134] Also under the agreement, the Nisga'a Lisims Government is recognized as another level of government, responsible for intergovernmental relations between the Nisga'a Nation and the governments of Canada and British Columbia.[135] Chapter 11 allows the Nisga'a Lisims Government to make laws "to preserve, promote, and develop Nisga'a culture and Nisga'a language, including laws to authorize or accredit the use, reproduction, and representation of Nisga'a cultural symbols and practices, and the teaching of Nisga'a language."[136] However, this right does not include "jurisdiction to make laws in respect of intellectual property, the official languages of Canada or the prohibition of activities outside of Nisga'a Lands."[137]

Transfer of cultural property is also addressed. The Nisga'a Lisims Government may make laws regarding the devolution of the cultural property of a Nisga'a citizen who dies intestate. For the purposes of this section, cultural property includes "ceremonial regalia and similar personal property associated with a Nisga'a Chief or clan."[138] In the event that Nisga'a law, in this respect, should be in conflict with either provincial or federal law, the Nisga'a law will prevail. Heritage sites on Nisga'a lands continue to be managed by British Columbia but only until such time as the Nisga'a Government has developed the necessary processes to manage these historical resources and to preserve them from proposed land and resource activities that may affect the sites.[139]

Similar protection powers associated with self-government are contained in the Tlicho Agreement. The government of the Tlicho First Nation has the power to legislate with regard to Tlicho spiritual and cultural beliefs, language and culture, traditional medicines, and heritage resources.[140] Heritage resources are dealt with in detail under Chapter 17 of the agreement. Under s. 17.2, custodianship of heritage resources on Tlicho lands is vested in the Tlicho government. In the event that Tlicho heritage resources are discovered outside Tlicho lands, but within the Northwest Territories (NWT), the Tlicho government is to be notified. Archaeological permits pertaining to heritage resources on Tlicho lands require the written consent of the Tlicho government. With respect to Tlicho heritage resources elsewhere in the NWT, consultation with the Tlicho government is required prior to issuing a permit. All such archaeological permits require "site protection and restoration [plans], where applicable,"[141] and must detail how "materials extracted" will be handled.[142]

Regardless of whether they address self-government, land claim agreements are concerned with the management, preservation, and promotion of culture and heritage. For example, under the Yukon Umbrella Final Agreement, First Nation ownership extends to heritage resources found within the traditional territory of a First Nation if they are "directly related to the culture and history of Yukon Indian People."[143] The agreement also acknowledges the underdeveloped nature of Yukon First Nations heritage resources relative to non-First Nations heritage resources. It stipulates that Yukon First Nations will be given priority in the allocation of government program resources for Yukon heritage resources development and management. This preferential allocation is to continue "until an equitable distribution of program resources is achieved,"[144] after which Yukon First Nations are to continue to receive an equitable portion of government resources. Furthermore, the government will facilitate the preparation of an inventory of heritage resources relating to Yukon First Nations.

As this is a framework agreement, it allows for specific provisions to be inserted into any subsequent final agreements to be made. For example, s. 13.4.6 allows for provisions in respect to heritage parks and sites, rivers, and routes. The Champagne and Aishihik First Nations Self-Government

Agreement used this section to recognize, in Schedule A, the cultural and heritage significance of heritage routes and to require consideration of their significance and any adverse effects relating to land development.[145] The Vuntut Gwichin Final Agreement also provides for greater control over heritage sites through land management and governance. The Vuntut Gwichin have joint management of two important heritage sites (Rampart House and LaPierre House), have been engaged in heritage documentation projects to assist in the assessment of applications for access to traditional territories, and have jointly developed a management plan with the federal and Yukon governments for a national park within their territory that includes important heritage sites (such as caribou fences).[146] In the Selkirk First Nation Final Agreement specific provisions are included establishing Fort Selkirk as a designated heritage site.[147] Schedule A calls for fee simple title to lands comprising Fort Selkirk to be transferred to the Government of the Yukon Territory and the Selkirk First Nation as tenants in common. Additionally, historic site designation under the *Historic Resources Act* is specified.[148]

First Nation Heritage Conservation Strategies

Kitkatla: Litigation to Protect Culturally Modified Trees

In an action that proceeded to the Supreme Court of Canada, the Kitkatla First Nation of the Kumealon Lake region in British Columbia sought to halt the removal of culturally modified trees (CMTs). International Forest Products Ltd. (Interfor) was issued a forest licence and began logging in the central coast area of British Columbia in 1982. As of 1994, Interfor regularly notified the Kitkatla of its forest development plans, as required by provincial forestry regulations, though the Kumealon area was never specifically mentioned in these reports. The Kitkatla entered treaty negotiations concerning aboriginal rights and title to this area in 1998.

During this time, Interfor applied to the Minister of Small Business, Tourism, and Culture for a site alteration permit under s. 12 of the *Heritage Conservation Act* (*HCA*), authorizing the removal and processing of CMTs found on the cutblocks.[149] The permit was issued on 31 March 1998. The Kitkatla disputed the legality of the permit and commenced legal proceedings. Requests were made for injunctions to stop logging in the Kumealon Lake area until the issues of aboriginal title and rights were resolved. In October 1998, the chambers judge set aside the site alteration permit and directed the minister to reconsider the decision after finding that there had been insufficient notification and consultation with the Kitkatla.[150]

Pursuant to the court order, the minister embarked on the reconsideration process. The Kitkatla petitioned for the denial of the site alteration permit, asserting the existence of aboriginal title and rights. The minister responded that any such determination of aboriginal rights was beyond the scope of the permit-granting procedure. Justice Wilson of the BC Supreme Court agreed.[151] The site alteration permit was reissued, requiring that all fallen CMTs be preserved, together with 76 of the 116 trees still standing in the cutblocks.

On appeal before the British Columbia Court of Appeal,[152] the main issue was whether the province has jurisdiction under s. 92(13) of the *Constitution Act, 1867*[153] to enact legislation protecting heritage property that also allows for the alteration, removal, and destruction of aboriginal heritage objects and sites located off reserve lands. The Kitkatla argued that provisions in the *HCA* relating to aboriginal heritage property are unlawful because such matters are properly within the jurisdiction of the federal government under the federal *Indian Act*.[154] Additionally, the Court was asked to consider whether, even if the impugned *HCA* provisions applied, the minister must consider whether aboriginal rights are affected before issuing a site alteration permit.[155]

The Court of Appeal upheld the decision of the trial court, ruling that the *HCA* was a law of general application and was not aimed at aboriginal peoples or at impairing their status. Further, the Court determined that the impugned provisions did not strike at the core of Indianness.[156] On this point, Justice of Appeal Prowse parted company with the majority, finding that the impugned legislation did affect the core values of Indianness and Indian society and was, therefore, beyond the scope of provincial jurisdiction over property and civil rights.[157] However, the majority rejected the Kitkatla's argument concerning the value of the CMTs. Justice Braidwood referred to them as trees of "ethnic" and "scientific" significance, which are "altered through the removal of bark strips" and are so "common" in the province that literally thousands are reported and registered annually.[158] While not disputing that such modifications are the work of Aboriginal people living in the area, he determined that "it is not possible to tell which Aboriginal group culturally modified the trees."[159] In contrast, the Kitkatla described CMTs as "living museums of Aboriginal culture."[160] Matthew Hill, an elected hereditary chief of the Kitkatla Nation, explained:

> CMTs become even more important as a way to know our ancestors and their way of life. By studying the location and the details of how the forest was used in the past, we can learn about our own culture even when there are no people alive to tell us about those place or those uses. It is like the spirit of our dead ancestors still have a way to speak to us and our children.[161]

The Supreme Court of Canada determined there was insufficient evidence to support the Kitkatla's claim. No jurisdictional issues were engaged because the provincial statute did not affect the core values of Indianness and, therefore, did not invoke the federal power over native affairs. It was the Court's opinion that the permit struck a balance between protecting aboriginal heritage and the exploitation of provincial natural resources. While the Kitkatla's claim ultimately failed, some cause for hope may be found in the judgment, where Mr. Justice LeBel states:

> In some future case, it might very well happen that some component of the cultural heritage of a First Nation would go to the core of its identity in such a way that it would affect the federal power over native affairs and the applicability of provincial legislation.[162]

First Nations Land Management Strategies

As the case studies demonstrate, First Nations communities have been developing internal mechanisms to control the flow of information and to address heritage protection. For example, the Stó:lō Nation of the Fraser Valley in British Columbia has developed a heritage policy manual to protect, preserve, and manage the Stó:lō heritage.[163] The manual is based on guiding principles drawn from a series of interconnected Stó:lō teachings. For example, ownership and caretaking responsibility related to heritage artifacts is based on the teaching that "'artifacts' *belong to those who made them*."[164] As such, determining an artifact's lineage is important. It is Stó:lō policy that ownership of, and jurisdiction over, all Stó:lō heritage sites and objects not directly linked to a family or individual remain with the Stó:lō Nation. Another teaching speaks to conservation issues, which require that one take no more than one needs. It applies to development, planning, and research and particularly to archaeologists whose work causes destruction. This teaching is reflected in the Stó:lō policy that resource and land-use planning should conflict with heritage interests as little as possible. The policy requires mitigation and/or compensation when negative impacts cannot be avoided. The Stó:lō Nation has also established cultural protocols for archaeological work, such as wearing *temelh* (red ochre) as a means to address the impacts to archaeological sites and the disturbance of Stó:lō ancestors.

Included in the policy manual are heritage resource assessment requirements. All potential developments within Stó:lō territory must consider and assess their impact on Stó:lō heritage resources. Heritage resource studies take two forms: overview assessments and heritage resource impact assessments. They are to be conducted by experienced researchers under conditions contained within the Stó:lō Nation Heritage Investigation Permit.[165] An investigation permit is required prior to commencing any archaeological or cultural resource work within the traditional territory of the Stó:lō Nation. Working without a permit or in contravention of the permit issued will result in a notation on the researcher's record and may exclude the researcher "from future permit holding capacity."[166]

The policy manual also addresses the collection of Stó:lō heritage artifacts. It identifies two general categories of collection: "incidental finding and collection" and "investigation project-related collection."[167] Incidental findings are to be left as they were found, unless there is an immediate threat to the preservation of the object, in which case collection is most appropriate. In either case, the Stó:lō Nation archaeologist is to be contacted immediately. Findings related to projects carried out under the auspices of an investigation permit are to be investigated "in-field" (*i.e.*, recorded, described, and analyzed) and left as they were found. Artifact locations are then to be plotted on site maps. Collection is appropriate when significant or rare objects are identified that require further study or when the preservation of the objects is at risk. Collected artifacts are to be housed in appropriate curatorial facilities. If the objects are part of an existing collection (*e.g.*, at the SFU Museum of Archaeology and Ethnology, the UBC Museum of Anthropology, or the RBCM), they will be added to the collection on the basis that the institution "maintain[s] the artifacts on behalf of and in trust for the Stó:lō and other associated First Nations."[168] Otherwise, two options are available. If the First Nations parties involved agree, the artifacts will be curated at the Stó:lō Nation Material Culture Repository.[169] As an alternative, collected artifacts will be curated at one of the above-mentioned institutions, subject to the condition that it be on an "in-trust" basis.

First Nations have also enacted laws creating heritage conservation schemes and permit systems similar to those administered by provincial governments. For example, in 1997 the Kamloops Indian Band enacted a heritage conservation bylaw that applies on reserve lands.[170] The bylaw establishes the Cultural Resources Management Department (CRMD), which is to administer a heritage protection trust fund, to act as an advisor to the band council, and to liaise with governments on heritage management issues. The CRMD also assumes responsibility for heritage protection and for promoting public awareness. Heritage areas and associated artifacts or human remains are protected from excavation, damage, and other forms of desecration through a permit system administered by the band. All material found or excavated is declared to be the property of the band. Failure to comply with bylaws can result in stop-work orders, summary conviction, or fines.

The Skeetchestn Band's Territorial Heritage Conservation Law controls archaeological study and other heritage investigation within the band's territories, on and off reserve, again through a permit system. Although it is not an enforceable bylaw to the extent that it applies off reserve, it has been successfully applied in negotiations over the Pembina Pipeline worksite and a proposed cutblock in the 100 Mile House Forest District.[171]

First Nations employ a wide range of other strategies to protect cultural and heritage sites, such as land-use plans designed to protect sensitive areas and other natural areas considered particularly important in sustaining relationships with the land. While these and other sites are important to First Nations, the land's significance extends beyond archaeological, sensitive, spiritual, and other identified areas in need of protection. Some First Nations have also gained greater control over the management of reserve lands under the federal *First Nations Land Management Act (FNLMA)*. This was enacted in 1999, with the initial support of fourteen First Nations.[172] The *Act* enables First Nations who opt in to manage their lands and resources, enact laws respecting their lands, and create summary conviction offences.[173] Land codes enacted pursuant to this legislation may deal with heritage conservation. For example, the Nipissing First Nation Land Code requires community consultation before enacting any band council laws affecting heritage sites.[174] As of October 2005, thirty-six First Nations opted into the *FNLMA*. Significantly, if a First Nation negotiates a self-government agreement, the *FNLMA* will no longer apply to it.[175]

Joint Initiatives, Designations, and Co-Management Agreements

First Nations have sometimes worked successfully in partnership with government to utilize protection mechanisms that exist in Canadian and international law. An example is the protection of Head-Smashed-In Buffalo Jump. For almost six thousand years, the Plains Indians hunted the buffalo, herding them over Head-Smashed-In Buffalo Jump (located northwest of Fort Macleod in southern Alberta) through V-shaped drive lanes to their death below.[176] In 1979, the Province of Alberta sought to protect this site by making Head-Smashed-In a provincial historical site.[177] In 1981, UNESCO declared it a world heritage site, thus joining it with such similarly designated world attractions as the Egyptian pyramids, Stonehenge, and the Galapagos Islands. A ten-million-dollar interpretive centre, funded by the Alberta government, was officially opened. The interpretation of the centre's themes represents the viewpoint of both aboriginal peoples and European archaeological science. Interpretation at the centre is provided by members of the Piikani Nation.

First Nations have also acquired greater control over heritage management through cooperative management agreements. An example is the Whitefish Lake First Nation (WLFN) cooperative management agreement, which involves a consensus-based, multi-stakeholder decision-making process. It has allowed the WLFN in north central Alberta to influence government land-use planning in its traditional lands. Shortly after signing the agreement, it became apparent that an inventory of known cultural resources in the area was needed. This investigation was conducted in cooperation with Alberta Community Development, Alberta Lands and Forests, and the Canadian Circumpolar Institute.[178]

The cultural inventory has documented known gravesites, sacred sites, historic sites, and archaeological sites within traditional WLFN territory. By the end of 2000, a total of forty individual burial sites had been documented, many of which were previously unmarked or had existed only in the memory of community elders. Alberta Sustainable Resource Development subsequently placed these lands under either consultative notation (CNT) or protective notation (PNT). Consultative notations are used to alert developers and others to the interests of a particular group. Protective notations ("reservations") are placed by public agencies in consultation with the public land manager, show allowable land uses, and may give management guidelines for integrating different uses on the land.[179] Local knowledge of fish and wildlife patterns and habitat, berry locations, mineral licks, and nesting grounds have also been documented and placed under PNTs or CNTs. Documented local knowledge is being entered into a geographic information system (GIS), as are traditional place and feature names, which will allow prospective land developers to digitally overlay their plans in order to determine an acceptable development strategy.[180]

Another interesting initiative is the Sliammon First Nation Crown Lands Referral Tool Box. Following the *Delgamuukw* case, which affirmed constitutional protection of aboriginal title in British Columbia and the duty to consult bands concerning developments affecting their lands,[181] many bands were flooded with land resource referrals but lacked both the capacity and the infrastructure to respond. The manager of the Sliammon Crown Land Referrals and Resources Department was determined to bring people together to discuss this issue and worked with Ecotrust Canada to make this happen. A two-day workshop, which generated a list of action items (including the idea for a toolbox), was held in November 1999. Together, Ecotrust Canada and the Sliammon created the toolbox and launched it as Kla-soms Kwuth Tooqen, which means "Answer with Strength." Accessed through the Aboriginal Mapping Network, the site includes Crown land referral case studies, sample agreements and protocols, a listing of government and First Nations contacts, and an analysis of relevant case law.[182]

First Nations have also entered into successful partnerships with Parks Canada. An example is the agreement with the Haida to co-manage the Gwaii Haanas Park Reserve, also recognized as a world heritage site. Part of the management program includes the Haida Gwaii Watchmen, a group of First Nations volunteers charged to watch over the natural and cultural heritage of several sites on South Morsbey Island. During the summer months, up to five Watchmen live on-site in longhouse-style cabins at each of five designated heritage sites. While their main responsibility is protecting the sites, they also limit access to twelve visitors at one time and provide insights into Haida culture.[183]

Language and Intangible Heritage

Language Protection

As the case studies demonstrate, First Nations are engaged in various language revitalization projects.[184] An example is the Daghida Project, a joint research effort between the community of Cold Lake First Nations and the University of Alberta, which is intent on revitalizing the Dene Suline language and the distinctive dialect spoken at Cold Lake.[185] The project identifies three major components: (1) linguistic research, (2) language retention and education efforts, and (3) cultural preservation and revival. A chief aim of the project is the development of materials for both language learners and linguistic researchers. An elders' advisory group has been established to be the main language resource for the community, to guide the project activities, and to provide advice on issues such as language documentation and cultural renewal efforts. Ongoing and proposed project activities include "an adult Dene language and literacy class, Dene language festivals, cultural and linguistic immersion camps, an immersion day-care or Head Start program, and school age curriculum development as well as teacher education and language education at the post secondary level."[186] Fluent Dene speakers are being asked to share personal narratives, traditional stories, community histories, and songs that will be recorded and archived. These materials could then be used in schools or for broadcast via radio, TV, or the Internet to reach youth and the young-adult community. A bilingual Dene/English dictionary, a university-level Dene language textbook, and a Dene language website are also envisioned. A Dene Suline interpretive centre has also been proposed.[187]

The Musqueam, located in the Greater Vancouver area, have taken a different approach to language revitalization than have many other First Nations communities: they have been working within the parameters of the BC public education system. The incorporation of the Musqueam language into the public school curriculum has contributed to an increase in self-esteem in Musqueam students and has raised the profile of the language as a distinct form of the larger language group, Hul'qumi'num.[188] One aspect of the program involves the teaching of traditional stories in English and Hul'qumi'num, thus allowing aspects of the Musqueam worldview to enter the educational forum. The curriculum requires the active involvement of elders and family members in a variety of ways, including home assignments and homework. The University of British Columbia offers several courses in Hul'qumi'num, and the band hopes to use these courses to train future Musqueam language instructors.

Many other initiatives are under way to protect First Nations languages. Government-supported initiatives at the time of writing include the Aboriginal Languages Initiative, through which Heritage Canada provides funding for language revitalization programs.[189] A task force was also struck in cooperation with the Assembly of First Nations to consult with First Nations and to make recommendations to the minister of heritage regarding language revitalization and protection.[190] The Government of Canada aboriginal place names project has also helped with language preservation by charting aboriginal place names across Canada and changing the official names of some locations back to their aboriginal designations.[191] Some communities have strong teaching programs in place, and some have also been trying immersion programs. An example is the Haida Nation Skidegate Immersion Program, which has been implemented in many community institutions, including daycares, preschools, elementary schools, high schools, youth groups, and seniors lodges.[192] Despite these efforts, First Nations languages continue to be in a state of crisis.

Snuneymuxw First Nation: Petroglyph Protection

To the extent possible, First Nations have also used intellectual property (IP) legislation to protect cultural images and other information from what they perceive to be wrongful appropriation. For example, the Dancing Man and Kingfisher petroglyphs have been reproduced on everything from jewellery and postcards to T-shirts.[193] Acting on the advice of legal counsel and treaty negotiator Murray Browne, the Snuneymuxw decided to use IP law to protect these images. The Snuneymuxw contacted the Registrar of Trademarks to request that public notice be given of the adoption and use of the petroglyph images in question.[194] If recognized as "official marks," the images could be protected under Section 9(1)(n)(iii) of the *Trademarks Act*. The Snuneymuxw Band Council needed to satisfy the Registrar of Trademarks that it met the two-part test applied to evaluate public authority status. The test, adopted by the federal Court of Appeal,[195] requires that (1) a significant degree of control must be exercised by the appropriate government over the activities of the body, and (2) the activities of the body must benefit the public.[196] It was determined that the Snuneymuxw First Nation qualified as a public authority, and ten of its most popular petroglyph images were recognized by the Trademarks Office as official marks subject to Section 9 protection. As such, the Snuneymuxw have the right of exclusive use and reproduction of the images and can apply to the federal Court of Appeal to remedy unauthorized reproductions.

Unlike regular trademarks, which are subject to renewal every fifteen years, official mark protection is indefinite (subject only to withdrawal of the mark by the public authority in question or further to a court decision). Following official mark designation, signs posting the images were covered up, the annual Dancing Man Music Festival kept its name but stopped using the popular figure, the local museum stopped selling certain items, and artists who wished to continue to use the images expressed a willingness to pay royalties. The local museum also applied and received a federal heritage grant to make cement copies of the originals, under the condition that it consulted the Snuneymuxw and received their consent.[197]

Community Research Protocols

In July 1999, the Grand Council of Mi'kmaq appointed a group of Mi'kmaw leaders, elders, educators, and other professionals to study issues of cultural and intellectual protection, with a particular focus on research conducted on the Mi'kmaw people. Research protocols were created, and the Mi'kmaq College Institute at the University College of Cape Breton administers them. At the same time, the Mi'kmaw Ethics Watch was created to review proposals for research conducted among and with the Mi'kmaw. The protocols reflect the underlying principle that "Mi'kmaw knowledge is collectively owned, discovered, used and taught and so also must be collectively guarded by appropriate delegated or appointed collective(s) who will oversee guidelines and process research proposals."[198] The protocols require that participants be recognized and treated as equals and that respect be shown for the language, traditions, and standards of Mi'kmaw communities in which research is conducted. In order to ensure "accuracy and sensitivity of interpretation," researchers are required to solicit Mi'kmaw participation in interpretation and/or review of any conclusions drawn. Similar research protocols have been established by other First Nations, all of which incorporate traditional laws, community systems of authority, and local values.[199]

Ancestral Remains and Burial Grounds

Repatriation of Ancestral Remains

This topic was already addressed briefly under repatriation. Most museums are prepared to return ancestral remains to lineal descendants and descendant First Nations provided sufficient proof of connection, provision for scientific study if required, and absence of competing claims (or some combination thereof).[200] However, First Nations have concerns about how the process should occur, costs of repatriation, and the difficulty of asserting the right to internment based on discovery on traditional lands rather than genetic connection to the community. An example is Kitigan Zibi Anishinabeg First Nation's attempt to repatriate remains removed from Algonquin territory. Responsibility to repatriate the remains was viewed not only as a matter of ancestral responsibility but also as a matter of connection to traditional territory and moral obligation.[201]

In July 2002, the *Ottawa Citizen* revealed that human remains were dug up 160 years ago on land in Gatineau, where the CMC and the Scott paper plant now sit.[202] Many remains have also been removed from surrounding areas since 1883 (*e.g.,* from Aylmer, Morrison, and Allumette Island) and some have found their way into the CMC collection.[203] Articles in the *Ottawa Citizen* prompted the Algonquin Nation, led by the Kitigan Zibi, to call for the return and internment of the remains. The CMC was prepared to repatriate the remains "after [their] archaeologists ... determined, to the best of their abilities, which of the human remains are Algonquin" and on condition that there was "broad consensus" among the Algonquin communities of both Quebec and Ontario.[204] However, the CMC also maintained that some of the remains predated Algonquin settlement. The Kitigan Zibi contacted all other Algonquin nations that may have lived in the areas at issue in order to ensure that they had no objections to their repatriation request. After much discussion, it was decided that a reburial would take place on Kitigan Zibi land. Approximately ninety boxes of remains, including those originally in dispute, were repatriated and reburied in June 2004.

Many Canadian museums have been proactive in contacting First Nations communities to return remains in their collections. For example, the ROM approached the Wikwemikong Heritage Organization in Ontario to repatriate two crania. The only stipulation was that Wikwemikong get local First Nations involved so as to avoid potential disputes regarding origins and return. The process took about four years. This was mainly due to community concerns that it be done properly, and, as a consequence, consultations took place in several communities. In the end, "these remains were transferred directly to a lodge in which ceremonies were conducted for these ancestors until reburial took place."[205]

The amount of effort on the part of communities to negotiate and to prepare for the repatriation of ancestral remains is significant. This is demonstrated in the efforts of the Haida repatriation committees from Massett and Skidegate, respectively. The Haida Nation promotes repatriation based upon mutual respect, cooperation, and trust and does not view repatriation as the substance of treaty negotiation or other external legal mechanisms. The committees have contacted over two hundred museums and, based on responses from those museums, have successfully negotiated the return of several hundred remains from museums across Canada and the United States. Recently, the Field Museum in Chicago returned the remains of 160 Haida ancestors, and the committees continue to seek return from other museums. A letter from the band council and hereditary chiefs, recognizing the committees' authority to negotiate, ensured that museums would deal directly with committee members. Essential to the committees' successful repatriation efforts was the support of community members. Working as one, members of the communities of both Massett and Skidegate developed ceremonies and dedicated "many hours to fundraising, making bentwood burial boxes, button blankets, and arranging the travel logistics and museum negotiations."[206] Through this process, the young people became more engaged in the culture and learned to make their own regalia.

Children made over 100 button blankets in which to wrap the remains, and high school students assisted in decorating the bentwood burial boxes.

Control and Responsibility over Activity on Traditional Lands

In August 1999, a most remarkable find was made in Tatshenshini-Alsek Park, when three hunters came upon preserved remains at the margins of a glacier. Tatshenshini-Alsek Park in northwestern British Columbia is located within the traditional territory of the Champagne and Aishihik First Nations (CAFN) and is administered under a 1996 management agreement between the province and the First Nations. The park, along with protected areas in Yukon and Alaska, "comprise[s] the largest international protected area in the world" and is a designated United Nations World Heritage Site.[207] Along with the body were several artifacts, including a hand tool, a wooden dart, a woven hat, a fur garment, and a small hide pouch. The party did not disturb the remains and promptly notified authorities in Whitehorse, Yukon, who alerted the CAFN.[208]

CAFN representatives visited the site to confirm the find, inviting along Yukon Heritage Branch and BC Parks Branch staff to assist. Once the find was confirmed, the director of the BC Archaeology Branch was notified and a recovery operation was mounted. "Following their initial visit to the body discovery site, CAFN Heritage staff met with Elders and members, who suggested that the discovery be referred to as 'Kwaday Dan Ts'inchi' in Southern Tutchone, meaning 'long ago person found.'"[209] Initially, the remains where recovered and flown to Whitehorse, where they were stabilized and stored at the Yukon Heritage Branch facility. Shortly thereafter, a partnership agreement was negotiated between the CAFN and the province, with the BC Archaeology Branch acting as its representative, and the remains were transferred to the RBCM in Victoria.[210] While some of the artifacts were also transferred, most remained with the Yukon Heritage Branch under a separate management agreement with the CAFN.[211]

The Kwaday Dan Ts'inchi Agreement sets out the terms governing the research and care of the remains and associated artifacts. Central to the agreement is a requirement that the remains "be treated with respect and dignity throughout the scientific examinations."[212] The agreement establishes a management group, consisting of six members, three selected by CAFN and three by the BC Archaeology Branch. The group, which governs by consensus, is charged with determining the terms for scientific study of the remains. Responsibility for final disposition of the remains rests with the CAFN.

Despite initial reservations, the First Nations agreed to DNA testing of the body. In fact, in a unique mix of science and culture, the CAFN provided their own funding to expand the DNA testing to include CAFN members in the hope of discovering a living relative.[213] Cultural sensitivity was, however, an ever-present issue. For example, Beattie *et al.* report that the CAFN members identified the small hide pouch found with the remains as the deceased's personal medicine bag: "Because of its cultural significance and the private nature of such pieces, this item was not opened, nor subject to any form of scientific study, documentation or close scrutiny."[214] It is also assumed that documenting traditional stories from CAFN and neighbouring First Nations elders will aid in understanding the discovery:

> It is important that the find, which is indicated as dating to several hundred years before non-aboriginal contact in this area, is yet recent enough to allow confident interpolations from local oral histories. It will serve as a bridge between the local and regional aboriginal understanding of the area's past, and the archaeological and scientific interpretations of this past.[215]

The remains of Kwaday Dan Ts'inchi and associated artifacts have since been returned to the CAFN. The experience is said to have raised many issues among the CAFN concerning the role of science and community values and beliefs regarding the dead.[216] In the end, Kwaday Dan Ts'inchi was laid to rest. While most of the associated artifacts were retained, the medicine bag was cremated along with the remains.

Municipal Development and the EPCOR Burial Dispute

In September 1999, Edmonton Power (now known as EPCOR) announced plans to expand the Rossdale Generating Plant on the north side of the North Saskatchewan River. In existence since 1891, the plant has grown over the years to cover most of the area originally occupied by Fort Edmonton, its cemetery, and an aboriginal burial ground. News of the planned expansion angered many who had been calling for the plant's closure and for having the site receive a provincial historical designation.

Archaeological finds confirm that the Rossdale Flats area has had a significant aboriginal presence for nearly eight thousand years. The Fort Edmonton cemetery and aboriginal burial grounds date back to the early 1800s, when the North West Company and the Hudson's Bay Company created the cemetery just outside of the fort. Later, the St. Joachim Mission (in the 1840s) and the Protestant cemetery (in the 1870s) became part of the fort cemetery. While the City of Edmonton has plotted the boundaries of the fort cemetery, it is acknowledged that an unknown number of aboriginal people are buried outside of the cemetery's boundaries.

According to the City of Edmonton, "Over time, Aboriginal people were forced from the area and the burial grounds and cemetery were paved over in some areas, and disturbed by ongoing construction of transportation and utilities infrastructure by the City of Edmonton and by Edmonton Power/EPCOR."[217] During the 1960s, workers who were installing a gas line uncovered human remains in the vicinity of the cemetery. However, disturbances to the site occurred prior to that time, and the continual pattern of disturbances has been of particular concern to descendants. Approximately thirty human skeletons have been uncovered in the area over the years.

EPCOR applied to the Alberta Energy and Utility Board (AEUB) for approval for the expansion project, and a hearing was held, which lasted six weeks. In May 2001, the AEUB announced that the EPCOR expansion project was in the public interest, as required by the *Hydro and Electric Energy Act* (absent from the *Act* is a definition of "public interest").[218] It was also determined that the AEUB would defer to Alberta Community Development with regard to assessing heritage resources on the site. Under s. 20 of the *Historical Resources Act*, the minister of community development may place this designation on any historical resource, the preservation of which is deemed to be in the public interest.[219] This protective measure means that no one may disturb the resource in any manner without the express consent of the minister.

In March 2000, members of the Blackfoot Nation's First Thunder Society, the Papaschase First Nation, and Concerned Citizens for Edmonton's River Valley gathered together to honour the dead buried beneath Rossdale Flats near EPCOR's power plant.[220] They hoped that the high-profile meeting would pressure the City of Edmonton to declare the EPCOR grounds a provincial historic site, rally support to exhume and relocate the bodies, or even pressure the provincial government to amend Alberta's *Repatriation Act*. However, EPCOR maintained that the site was not on its land, and the municipal and provincial governments did not immediately act to protect or relocate the burials.

In May 2001, the Papaschase First Nation Society attempted to secure an injunction against EPCOR after workers discovered the bone fragments of an adult, a small infant, and a child while digging the underground component of the plant expansion.[221] The excavation was one hundred metres away from where the external boundaries of the fort cemetery were said to be, and this renewed debate about whether further industrial development should continue in that portion of the river valley. The injunction failed, and work continued on the site. Shortly after excavation resumed, another intact skeleton was discovered inside the EPCOR fence line. All work was stopped, and EPCOR stopped its operation to review the situation. Both the Papaschase First Nation and the Métis Nation of Alberta requested that the project be shut down permanently and that the boundaries of the burial grounds be expanded to protect the area from future disturbances.

In June 2001, the minister of community development issued a notice of intention in relation to designating three buildings on the Rossdale site as provincial historic resources. The Alberta Historical Resources Foundation held a stakeholders hearing into the proposed designation. The foundation's recommendations were then forwarded to the minister, who officially confirmed the designation in October 2001. While the lobbying effort to have the aboriginal burial grounds protected under the *Historical Resources Act* had failed, the provincial designation for the three buildings indirectly served the needs of the First Nations involved. The EPCOR expansion project called for the destruction of two-thirds of the Low Pressure Plant, one of the protected buildings. Given the minister's recent designation of the site, approval for its destruction was very unlikely. In November 2001, EPCOR announced its decision to cancel the project, and shortly thereafter the City of Edmonton began working with the Edmonton Historical Board and over 180 stakeholders to develop a plan.[222]

In August 2005, the remains of eight aboriginals and European-Canadians that had been unearthed between 1967 and 2001 were laid to rest in the burial ground. Construction of a memorial and interpretive centre was scheduled for the spring of 2006.[223] Plans for the memorial are to reflect the perspectives of the cultures of those interred in the cemetery, and any writing on the memorial will include First Nations languages, English, and French.

The dispute highlighted gaps in provincial legislation concerning human remains which were not clearly articulated within the parameters of cemeteries legislation and the *Historical Resources Act*. At the time of writing, the Province of Alberta was conducting consultations concerning this problem.

Litigation and Confrontation

First Nations have turned to the Canadian Courts to protect burial sites.[224] For example, in 1987, Nipigon Power Limited (Nipigon) marked the High Falls location on the Namewaminikan River near Beardmore, Ontario, as a potential site for a hydroelectric project. The lands in question were claimed by the Sand Point and Rocky Bay First Nations as part of their traditional territories; however, neither nation is party to the proceedings discussed below. The applicant, the Poplar Point Ojibway First Nation, was formed in April 1988 and is not recognized by the Government of Canada as a registered Indian band within the meaning of the *Indian Act*. They were not included in the 1850 Robinson Superior Treaty, despite a lineage in the region that can be traced back to at least 1814 in Roman Catholic church records.[225]

Due to their uncertain legal status, the Poplar Point Ojibway First Nation was not consulted when the Ontario Ministry of Natural Resources and Nipigon began planning the hydroelectric project (only officially recognized First Nations were consulted). Upon hearing about the development in the summer of 1991, the Poplar Point Ojibway First Nation initiated legal action to stop the project. According to their elders, the High Falls area was a sacred place and a human burial ground. However, when asked to pin-point precise locations of gravesites, the elders were either unable or unwilling to do so. Some elders explained that, as children, they were told that High Falls was a sacred place where the dead were sometimes buried. They were never given precise details as to where the graves were, and they would never have presumed to ask. Others pointed out that to provide descriptions of the gravesites could compromise the sacred character of the area or even allow sensitive information to fall into the hands of looters.[226]

Following unsuccessful attempts to halt the project, construction continued uninterrupted from September 1991 to September 1992. On 9 September 1992 an employee found a skull and two bones during site excavations, and the Ontario Provincial Police were called to investigate. News of the discovery quickly spread, and the band again intervened to stop construction, imposing what was widely described as a blockade upon the area.

In Ontario, when human remains are discovered, an initial determination is made as to whether a criminal investigation is appropriate. If it does not appear to be a criminal matter, the Cemeteries Branch of the Ontario Ministry of Consumer and Commercial Relations takes over; this is the agency responsible for administering the *Cemeteries Act*.[227] Professor Scott Hamilton of Lakehead University undertook an archaeological investigation, ordered by the Registrar of Cemeteries under s. 70(1) of the *Cemeteries Act*, to determine the origin of the site. Issues addressed in the investigative report included a determination of the cultural origin of the remains, an assessment of the boundaries of the burial site, the style and manner of internment, a description of any artifacts accompanying the remains, and an opinion as to whether or not internment at the site was done "in accordance with cultural affinities."[228] The investigation was carried out under the guidance of elders of the Poplar Point Ojibway First Nation and with the participation of the chief and other Poplar Point members. The need to "protect the sanctity and confidentiality of sacred sites," as well as "respect the value of Poplar Point First Nation's oral history and knowledge" was also recognized.[229]

According to Hamilton's preliminary report of 28 September 1992, the recovered remains were of an adult male Amerindian who had been deliberately buried at the site. While radiocarbon dating would be necessary to determine the actual antiquity and possible cultural affiliation of the burial, he estimated it to be at least two hundred years old and possibly even several thousand years old. However, the Poplar Point Ojibway First Nation was not prepared to permit further scientific analysis of the remains, which was viewed as a further affront to the deceased. On 8 October 1992, court proceedings were launched by counsel for Chief McCrady and the First Nation, seeking an order compelling the Registrar of Cemeteries to declare a large tract of the High Falls watershed an unapproved aboriginal peoples cemetery,[230] as well as an injunction to stop further site construction. The matter was adjourned on terms that required that no flooding of the area occur during the adjournment period.

Hamilton completed his final report on 12 October 1992. Central to his report was an acknowledgement of the spirituality of the High Falls burial site and its contemporary relevance to First Nations cultural practice. According to Ojibway teachings, he writes, "[w]herever the ancestors are buried, their voices are transmitted through the water flowing across the landscape. It is at special places such as High Falls where these voices are transmitted and amplified so that they may be heard by the living descendants. This makes High Falls an important sacred place in traditional Ojibwa cosmology."[231] Using the spiritual criteria of the elders and referencing this to the physical dimensions of the knoll, Hamilton estimated that more than four thousand square metres of area had been "severely damaged or completely destroyed by construction activities."[232]

In order for the Registrar of Cemeteries to make a ruling regarding a burial, specific boundaries for the site must be established.[233] In a letter to the registrar, Hamilton explained his inability to provide such markers:

> [I]t reflects a notion of the bounded "sacred precinct" of a cemetery. This is a Judeo-Christian concept that has little relevance to Native spirituality. The burial(s) is an important secondary element of a much larger sacred system that involves the whole falls area. The current regulatory process is addressing the secondary element, but is ignoring the larger sacred issue.[234]

While only one burial was recovered at High Falls, Hamilton did not rule out the possibility of other burials. Only subsurface archaeological inspection of the falls could conclusively answer that question, and this was not possible in light of the prohibition imposed by the band, along with the time and financial constraints cited by Hamilton.

By definition, under s. 71(4) of the *Cemeteries Act*, an "unapproved Aboriginal peoples cemetery" is one that includes the remains of more than one individual. However, counsel for the Ministry of Natural Resources wrote to the Registrar of Cemeteries and expressed a willingness to deal with the site as an "unapproved Aboriginal peoples cemetery," even though only one set of remains had been found. On 2 November 1992, the Registrar of Cemeteries declared the site to be an "unapproved aboriginal peoples cemetery" within the meaning of s. 71 and directed the parties to enter into a site disposition agreement pursuant to s. 72(2) of the *Cemeteries Act*.

On 17 November 1992, the Poplar Point Ojibway First Nation applied for a judicial review disputing the definition of the site. The applicants submitted that the registrar was biased and/or conveyed a reasonable apprehension of bias; that flooding for the hydro project would have serious negative effects on the freedom of conscience, worship, and religion of the applications; and that the definition of the site infringed their rights under

s. 15 of the *Canadian Charter of Rights and Freedoms* by discriminating against aboriginal people who considered the falls to be part of the High Falls cemetery.[235]

The application was heard before a three-member panel of the Ontario Court of Justice. It was the view of the Court that "the Registrar, in the circumstances of this case, acted fairly to each party."[236] The Court also found that the spatial limit placed upon the definition of "burial site" by the *Cemeteries Act* and regulations "is not based upon religion, religious beliefs nor the contravention of anyone's freedom of religion or conscience. The sole criterion is the site of the human remains."[237] Similarly rejected was the contention of a Section 15 *Charter* (equality rights) violation.

While it was asserted that more burials existed at High Falls, the Court noted the lack of actual knowledge or evidence put forward to support the contention. It was further acknowledged that, while the *Cemeteries Act* gives the registrar the power to order an investigation, it does not mandate an investigation;[238] and even once an investigation is begun, there is nothing in the *Cemeteries Act* that compels the registrar to accept all or part of the investigation report.[239] As such, the Court concluded that the registrar acted appropriately, within the scope of his mandate, in making his determination. The application for judicial review was dismissed.

Under the terms of the site disposition agreement, the "unapproved Aboriginal peoples cemetery" was limited to an area on the south and west side of the knoll; it was ruled that completion and operation of the High Falls dam and reservoir would not materially affect the site.

Conclusion

This chapter and the case studies in this volume underscore the many issues associated with protecting and repatriating First Nations cultural heritage in Canada. While there are many successes, there is also struggle. At the core of the struggle there sometimes lies "[a] ... gulf between Western concepts of private property and the primacy of the relationship between property and identity in Aboriginal societies."[240] Challenges include (1) reconciling the important role of museums with increased First Nations demands for repatriation; (2) combating the lucrative private trade in aboriginal material culture; (3) protecting traditional knowledge from misappropriation in what is arguably a legislative vacuum; and (3) attempting to tackle all of the above on the international stage. Central to all these considerations is the very real need for capacity building and for more resources in order to develop better and more protection initiatives, to challenge laws that are not working, to finance repatriations, to build and maintain cultural heritage facilities, to develop site protection programs, and to support collaborative initiatives, and so on.

Despite the challenges, progress is being made. Many of the stories shared speak to partnerships between museums and First Nations and changes in museum policy. The common theme of the success stories reviewed above is a strong relationship based on equal respect among the parties. When true partnerships are forged between First Nations and, for example, governments or museums, the potential for equitable solutions increases exponentially. The Glenbow/Kainai partnership and cooperation between the BC government and the Champagne and Aishihik First Nations serve as examples. However, as discussed in this and the next volume, the complexity of Canada's existing legislative and policy environment may place limits on the ability to develop truly equal partnerships.

Notes

1 Personal communication from the Vantut Gwichin (2 June 2003).

2 Assembly of First Nations and Canadian Museums Association, *Turning the Page: Forging New Partnerships between Museums and First Peoples,* 3d ed. (Ottawa: Canadian Museums Association, 1994). Although major public institutions have taken steps to implement some of the recommendations, adoption is neither universal nor uniform. To date there has not been a follow-up with museums regarding implementation, but the Canadian Museums Association recently applied for funds for this purpose. For further discussion, see Trudy Nicks, "The Task Force on Museums and First Peoples" (1995) Special Edition U.B.C. L. Rev. 143; and Catherine Bell, "Restructuring the Relationship: Domestic Repatriation and Canadian Law Reform" in Catherine Bell and Robert K. Paterson, eds., *Protection of First Nations Cultural Heritage: Laws, Policy, and Reform* (Vancouver: UBC Press, 2008).

3 Rebecca Clements, "Misconceptions of Culture: Native Peoples and Cultural Property under Canadian Law" (2001) 49 U.T.L. Rev. 1 at 9.

4 The legislation being referred to here is the *Native American Graves Protection and Repatriation Act,* 25 U.S.C.A. ss. 3001-3013 (West Supp. 2000).

5 See in particular Catherine Bell *et al.*, "Recovering from Colonization: Perspectives of Community Members on Protection and Repatriation of Kwakwa̱ka̱'wakw Cultural Heritage," this volume; Catherine Bell, Graham Statt, and the Mookakin Cultural Society, "Repatriation and Heritage Protection: Reflections on the Kainai Experience," this volume; Catherine Bell and Heather McCuaig, "Protection and Repatriation of Ktunaxa/Kinbasket Cultural Resources: Perspectives of Community Members," this volume.

6 Canadian Press, "Sacred Mohawk Mask to be Displayed at Museum, Judge Rules" *Winnipeg Free Press* (29 January 1988) 12. See also *infra* note 7.

7 *Mohawk Bands of Kahnawake, Akwesasne and Kanesatake v. Glenbow-Alberta Institute,* [1988] 3 C.N.L.R. 70 (Alta. Q.B.).

8 *Ibid.* at para. 8.

9 *Ibid.* at para. 8.

10 *Ibid.* at para. 4.

11 R.S.A. 2000, c. G-6, s. 20(2).

12 R.S.A. 2000, c. F-14 [*Repatriation Act*]. For further discussion see Bell, "Repatriation" *supra* note 2 ; and Bell *et al.*, "Repatriation and Heritage Protection" *supra* note 5 at 238-39.

13 *Supra* note 11 at 20(3).

14 *Repatriation Act, supra* note 12, s. 1(e).

15 Larry Johnsrude, "Bundles of Contention" *Edmonton Journal* (18 March 2001) E3.

16 Larry Johnsrude, "Return Blackfoot Artifacts – Klein" *Edmonton Journal* (29 March 2001) A3.

17 Bob Scriver, *The Blackfeet Artists of the Northern Plains* (Kansas City: The Lowell Press, 1990)

at xv. "This was a document that the federal government required from every merchant or trader doing business on the reservation in those days."

18 *Ibid.* and Philip H.R. Stepney, "Bob Scriver: The Man and the Collection" in Philip H.R. Stepney and David J. Goa, eds., *The Scriver Blackfoot Collection: Repatriation of Canada's Heritage* (Edmonton: Provincial Museum of Alberta, 1990) 5 at 11, quoting speech by Robert M. Scriver.

19 Stepney, *ibid.* at 5. "Bonnets, moccasins, leggings, gauntlets, dresses, war shirts, vests, beaded capes, jackets, awl pouches, jewellery, capotes, toys, dolls, dance costumes and accouterments, amulets, drums, scrapers, fleshers, parfleches, carrying pouches, plateau bags, snare and pack saddles, bridles, decorated britching, horse and dog travois, teepees, backrests, trade goods, rifles, bows and arrows, clubs, knives and sheath, rattles, Sun Dance necklaces, medicine pipes, beaver, natoas, horn society and other bundles, and a host of other items are all contained in the collection."

20 Personal communication with Mary Strachan Scriver (14 June 2004). See also Larry Johnsrude, "Historic Art Languishes in Basement" *Edmonton Journal* (27 December 2001) B1 at B2. In a later communication dated 22 June 2004, M. Scriver lists eighteen "small bundles" labelled sacred by the Canadian who sold them and ten "major bundles of established importance." Bundles and other ceremonial items that remain in the museum's possession are discussed in Patricia A. McCormack and Karen L. Robbins, "A Survey of the Scriver Blackfoot Collection" in Stepney and Goa, *supra* note 18, 105 at 129-33.

21 Stepney, *supra* note 18 at 8.

22 The name means "He who likes his back fat burned black." Many Blackfeet names are derived from idiosyncrasies about eating or sleeping or other parts of daily life.

23 *Supra* note 17 at xvi. The ceremony is also discussed in Stepney, *supra* note 18. The Little Dog Thunder Medicine Pipe was not included in the collection sold to the museum and was intended to be "transferred in the proper manner at some future date to someone [deemed] worthy." Robert M. Scriver, quoted in Stepney, *supra* note 18. The location of this bundle is currently unknown. Mary Strachan Scriver, given the name Meek-skim-yahkee and wife of Bob Scriver at the time of the bundle transfer, suggests that, according to Blackfoot law, the bundle belongs to her. She is trying to locate it so it can be properly transferred to a tribal member. Personal correspondence with Mary Strachan Scriver, *supra* note 20 (14 June 2004).

24 Ron Chalmers, "Blackfeet Demand to Test New Legislation on Aboriginal Artifacts: Alberta Paid $1.1 M to Montana Estate for U.S. Collection" *Edmonton Journal* (2 July 2001) B3.

25 Helen Plishke, "Blackfoot Artifacts Make Rich Exhibit" *Edmonton Journal* (23 May 1990) B3.

26 *Supra* note 15.

27 *Ibid.*

28 *Ibid.*

29 *Ibid.*

30 *Supra* note 17 at xvii. See also *supra* note 18.

31 See *e.g.* Bell, Statt, and the Mookakin Cultural Society, "Repatriation and Heritage Protection" *supra* note 5 at 206-8; and William E. Farr, "Troubled Bundles, Troubled Blackfeet" (1993) 43:4 Montana: The Magazine of Western History 2.

32 16 U.S.C. ss. 668-668d (1940) and *Convention on International Trade in Endangered Species of Wild Fauna and Flora* (3 March 1973) reprinted in 12 I.L.M. 1085, online: <http://www.cites.org/eng/disc/text.shtml>. For further discussion, see Philip H.R. Stepney, "Repatriation of the Scriver Blackfoot Collection" in Stepney and Goa, *supra* note 18 at 17; and Catherine Bell and Robert K. Paterson, "International Movement of First Nations Cultural Heritage in Canadian Law" in Bell and Paterson, eds., *supra* note 2.

33 Farr, *supra* note 31 at 6. See also *supra* notes 15 and 16.

34 Clark Wissler, "Ceremonial Bundles of the Blackfoot Indians" (1912) 7 Anthropological Papers of the American Museum of Natural History 273-76, cited in Farr, *ibid.* at 11. See also *supra* notes 15 and 16.

35 Larry Johnsrude, "Natives Celebrate Return of Sacred Bundle" *Edmonton Journal* (7 July 2002) A1.

36 *Ibid.*
37 Catherine Bell and Robert K. Paterson, "Aboriginal Rights to Cultural Property in Canada" (1999) 8:2 Inter. J. Cult. Prop. 167 at 198. The Task Force report provides at page 9, *supra* note 2 that "[e]ven in cases where materials have been obtained legally, museums should consider ... transfer of title of sacred and ceremonial objects and of other objects that have ongoing historical, traditional or cultural importance to an Aboriginal community or culture. This involves case-by-case negotiation with the appropriate communities based on moral and ethical factors above and beyond legal considerations."
38 *Ibid.* For further discussion, see also Robert K. Paterson, "Ancestral Remains Institutional Collections: Proposals for Reform," in Bell and Paterson, *supra* note 2.
39 Information about repatriation policies was obtained online or by request from twelve federal and provincial museums in Canada or museums structured as Crown corporations that receive public funds. We also contacted the Glenbow Museum, Museum of Anthropology (University of British Columbia), and Parks Canada because of their reputations for developing responsive policies in this area. There is no central collection of museum, university, or government agency policies and few public or private museums or government agencies have their policies online. At the time of writing (2006), Parks Canada and six of the museums we contacted had specific aboriginal repatriation policies and guidelines in place or under revision relating to objects in their collections (Canadian Museum of Civilization, Manitoba Museum, Royal Saskatchewan Museum, UBC Museum of Anthropology, Royal British Columbia Museum, Royal Ontario Museum). Provincial guidelines outline procedures for the Glenbow Museum and Royal Alberta Museum under Alberta's repatriation law for sacred ceremonial items. They do not have specific policies for items that fall outside the scope of this legislation. We contacted some universities and governments but did not do a comprehensive review of university and government agency policy nor did we contact private museums. In 2007, Janine Andrews (Executive Director, University of Alberta Museums and Collections Services) and Corinne Marceau conducted a survey of museums, government agencies, and universities concerning repatriation policies that covered funerary objects and ancestral remains as well as other cultural materials. They sent twenty-one surveys and received eight responses. They found that, in addition to the above, some universities (including the University of Alberta) also have aboriginal-specific policies.
40 S.C. 1990, c. 3. Disposition is addressed in ss. 6, 9, 12, and 15.
41 "Summary of Corporate Plan (2003-4 to 2007-8)," see online: <http://www. civilization.ca/societe/corpsm03/corp03e.pdf> at 10. It is also guided by the *Museum Act*, *ibid.*, and the Task Force Recommendations.
42 "Repatriation Policy," online: <http://www.civilization.ca/cmc/repat/repat00e.html> at 1. The original policy came into effect on 1 May 2001, s. 1 "Purpose."
43 *Ibid.*, s. 6.1.
44 *Ibid.*, s. 6.3. Similar limitations may not apply to repatriation through other CMC processes.
45 *Ibid.*, s. 5.3.
46 "Summary of Corporate Plan (2006-7 to 2010-11)" online: <http://www.civilization.ca/societe/corps06/corp06e.pdfat10>.
47 *Ibid.*, and note 42, "Introduction."
48 *Supra* note 46, and note 42, "Introduction."
49 "Canadian Museum of Civilization Policy on Human Remains" (202) at 2 [Human Remains Policy]. The policy has been in effect since 1991 and is available from the CMC.
50 *Ibid.*
51 See press releases issued by the CMC with respect to these repatriations, online: <http://www.civilisations.ca/media/show_pr_e.asp?ID=6407>. See also same URL ID=557 and ID=39. Some of these repatriations are discussed later in this chapter and in Paterson, "Ancestral Remains" *supra* note 38.
52 Royal British Columbia Museum, "2003 Aboriginal Material Operating Policy A.1-1," at 3, online: <http:www.royalbcmuseum.bc.ca>.
53 *Ibid.* at 3; *Museum Act*, R.S.B.C. 1996, c. 326, s. 5.

54 *Ibid.* at 4.
55 Personal communication with Katherine Pettipas, Manitoba Museum, to Kim Cordeiro (5 June 2007).
56 *Ibid.*
57 *Ibid.* And see "The Manitoba Museum Repatriation Procedures" (Under Revision 2002) at 1 [unpublished] available from the Manitoba Museum, Section 4: Competing Claims [*Repatriation Procedures*].
58 *Repatriation Procedures, ibid.*
59 *Draft Repatriation Policy* (March 2005) at 3 [unpublished] available from the Manitoba Museum.
60 *Ibid.*
61 *Repatriation Procedures, supra* note 57 at 5.
62 *Ibid.* at 2-3.
63 *Supra* note 59.
64 Manitoba, Office of the Auditor General, *Investigation of Missing Artifacts at the Anthropology Museum of the University of Winnipeg* (Winnipeg: Office of the Auditor General, 2002) at 3 and 9 (Auditor General: Jon W. Singleton) [Singleton Report].
65 Cheryl Petten, "Missing Artifacts Lead to Auditor General's Scrutiny" *Windspeaker* 20:4 (August 2002) 7. See also *ibid.* at 9-12.
66 Interview with Professor Jack Steinbring by Maureen Matthews (19 April 2002) on *Fair Wind's Drum*, CBC Radio, Toronto, CBC Radio Archives. Also aired (28 April 2002) on *This Morning,* CBC Radio, Toronto, CBC Radio Archives.
67 Quoting Mathews, *ibid.*
68 Len Kruzenga, "Artifacts Spirited into the US by Ojibwe Cultural Society: But University's Transfer of Items to Group Sparks Fierce Controversy" *The First Perspective* 10:9 (September 2001) 2.
69 *Ibid.*
70 Interview of Jennifer Brown by Maureen Matthews (19 April 2002) on *Fair Wind's Drum,* CBC Radio, Toronto, CBC Radio Archives.
71 Midewiwin refers to the "society of the Mide or Shamans, or Grand Medicine Society of the Ojibwas." Singleton Report, *supra* note 64 at Appendix A.
72 *Supra* note 70.
73 Interview of Eddie Benton Benai by Maureen Matthews (19 April 2002) on *Fair Wind's Drum,* CBC Radio, Toronto, CBC Radio Archives.
74 *Ibid.*
75 *Supra* note 66.
76 *Supra* note 68.
77 *Supra* note 73.
78 *Ibid.* See also Nick Martin, "Judge Guides Sacred Native Objects Home: Sinclair says Items Now Held in US Will Likely Be Returned to First Nation" *Winnipeg Free Press* (17 October 2001) at A10.
79 *Supra* note 64.
80 *Ibid.* at 3.
81 *Ibid.*
82 R.S.C. 1985, c. C-51. The report concluded that the deaccessioned objects may be classified as Group II objects as defined by the Canadian Cultural Property Control List, thereby requiring expert assessment to determine whether an export permit was required and, if so, whether it should be issued. For further discussion of the *CPEIA*, see Bell and Paterson, "International Movement," *supra* note 32.
83 *Supra* note 64 at 3-4.
84 *Ibid.*, at 1.
85 *Ibid.*, "Response from the University of Winnipeg," at 20-23.
86 Len Kruzenga, "Extensive Investigation Launched into Museum Practices, Missing Artifacts" *The First Perspective* 11:8 (August 2002) 5.
87 Stephen Hume, "Return of the Spirit Pole" *Vancouver Sun* (2 June 2000) A13.
88 Letter from Iver Fougner to the Secretary, Department of Indian Affairs (16 December

1927), Ottawa, Library and Archives Canada (RG 10, vol. 4087, file 507, 787-2B), cited in "Chronology," online: Haisla Totem Pole Repatriation Project <http://www.haislatotem.org/chronology/chron_main.html>.

89 Letter from the Deputy Superintendent General to Iver Fougner (11 January 1928), Ottawa, Library and Archives Canada (RG 10, vol. 4087, file 507, 787-2B), cited in "Chronology," *ibid.*

90 *Supra* note 87.

91 *Ibid.*

92 Craig Jacobson, "Welcome Home: G'psgolox Pole Returns Home to Kitimaat Village after 80 Years," online: Ecotrust <http://ecotrust.org/nativeprograms/gpsgolox_totem_pole.html>.

93 Jeff Lee, "A Totem Pole Comes Home: A Swedish Museum Is Returning the Artifact to the BC Band That Carved It 134 Years Ago" *Vancouver Sun,* 1 March 2006, online: <http://www.canada.com/vancouversun/voices/story.html?id=3e5069ae-097b-42ef-a1d2-6d8253c5112f and p=2>.

94 "Chronology," *supra* note 88.

95 *Supra* note 87.

96 Gil Cardinal, *Totem: The Return of the G'psgolox Pole* (Ottawa: National Film Board, 2003).

97 *Ibid.*

98 "Haisla Totem Begins Return Trip from Stockholm" *CBC News* (14 March 2006) online: CBC News <http://www.cbc.ca/story/arts/national/2006/03/14/totem-haisla-return.html>.

99 *Supra* note 88.

100 News release, Office of the Premier, Ministry of Aboriginal Relations and Reconciliation, Government of British Columbia (21 June 2006), quoted in "Aboriginal Celebration Marks Historic Repatriation," online: Government of BC <http://www2.news.gov.bc.ca/news_releases_2005-2009.2006OTP08-000836.pdf>. In 2006 the Stone T'xwelátse, an ancestor figure of the Stólō-Ts'elxwéyeqw people, was likewise returned. T'xwelátse was removed from Stó:lō territory and eventually became part of the collection of the Burke Museum in Seattle. In is now residing temporarily at the Museum of Anthropology at the University of British Columbia and was featured in a high school program on repatriation. David Schaepe, senior archaeologist and co-manager of the Stó:lō Research and Resource Management Centre, explains how the Nooksak Tribe used US repatriation law to facilitate the return of T'xwelátse (personal communication with author, 18 January 2008):

> [A]fter 15 years of efforts led by Herb Joe (T'xwelátse) ... Stone T'xwelátse was repatriated from the Burke Museum in Seattle, Washington. Originating among the Stó:lö of British Columbia, an official *NAGPRA* repatriation request was submitted in 2005 by way of T'xwelátse's family members and executive council of the Nooksack Tribe, abutting the international border of northern Washington State. The application presented arguments that Stone T'xwelátse met the legal definition of both an Object of Cultural Patrimony and Native American Human Remains. While the US federal government did not recognize the application of Native American Human Remains to Stone T'xwelátse – a transformed human and ancestor of the Ts'elxwéyeqw Tribe – the family's efforts succeeded under the category of Object of Cultural Patrimony ... After a celebration of their ancestor's return, Nooksack family members handed him over to their Stó:lō relatives north of the border, ending a 114-year absence from the community.

101 Patrick Walker and Clarine Ostrove, "The Aboriginal Right to Cultural Property" (1995) Special Issue U.B.C. L. Rev. 13.

102 Diana Henry, "Back from the Brink: Canada's First Nations' Right to Preserve Canadian Heritage" (1995) Special Issue U.B.C. L. Rev. 5 at 8.

103 *Ibid.* at 9.

104 Ian Dutton, "Saanich Group Fights to Rescue Native Artifact," *Victoria Times-Colonist* (4 September 1993) A5.

105 *Supra* note 102 at 9.
106 Barbara J. Winter, "New Futures for the Past: Cooperation between First Nations and Museums in Canada" (1995) Special Issue U.B.C. L. Rev. 29 at 33. The *Act* requires that certain institutions be notified but not First Nations.
107 *Supra* note 102 at 9-10.
108 *Supra* note 106 at 33.
109 *Ibid.* at 34.
110 *Supra* note 102 at 10.
111 Appendices 1 and 2 (1995) Special Issue U.B.C. L. Rev. 321.
112 *Supra* note 106 at 34-35.
113 *Ibid.* at 32. See also Kathryn Bernick, "The Lillooet Stone Bowl: A Case of Luck" (1986) 18:4 The Midden 2.
114 Larry Johnsrude, "Black Market Grows for Sacred Artifacts: US Man Tried to Sell Headdresses to Alberta Siksika Band" *Edmonton Journal* (12 April 2001) A6.
115 *Ibid.*
116 R.S.C 1985 (2d Supp.), c. 1.
117 S.C. 1992, c. 52.
118 "James Bay and Northern Quebec Agreement and Complementary Agreements," online: Indian and Northern Affairs Canada <http://www.aincinac.gc.ca/pr/agr/que/jbnq_e.html>.
119 "Umbrella Final Agreement between the Government of Canada, the Council for Yukon Indians and the Government of the Yukon," online: Indian and Northern Affairs Canada <http://www.ainc-inac.gc.ca/pr/agr/umb/index_e.html>.
120 Including final agreements signed by the Selkirk First Nation (1997), the Little Salmon/Carmacks First Nation (1997), and the Tr'ondek Hwech'in First Nation (1998).
121 Tlicho Agreement, online: Indian and Northern Affairs Canada <http://www.aincinac.gc.ca/pr/agr/nwts/tliagr2_e.html>. Provisions concerning ownership, protection, and repatriation of archaeological material have also been included in the Labrador Inuit Land Claim and the Tsawwassen, Lheidli T'enneh, Sliammon, and Maa-nulth negotiations.
122 For the purpose of this agreement, "heritage resource" means:

(a) a site with archaeological, historical, or cultural significance that includes a burial site; or
(b) an artifact, object, or record of historical or cultural significance that includes human remains and associated grave goods found in a burial site.

123 *Supra* note 121, s. 17.3.2.
124 Nisga'a Final Agreement, online: Indian and Northern Affairs Canada <http://www.ainc-inac.gc.ca/pr/agr/nsga/nisdex_e.html>. Enacted by the British Columbia legislature as the *Nisga'a Final Agreement Act*, S.B.C. 1999, c. 2; and enacted federally as the *Nisga'a Final Agreement Act*, S.C. 2000, c. 7.
125 Bell and Paterson, *supra* note 37 at 203.
126 *Ibid.*
127 *Supra* note 124, c. 17 at para. 18.
128 *Ibid.*, c. 17 at para. 12.
129 *Ibid.*
130 *Supra* note 124, App. L-4 at 424. No explanation is given for the use of the word "held" in relation to the RBCM as opposed to "shared" in relation to the CMC. Both instances refer to "custodial agreements."
131 *Supra* note 124, c. 17 at para. 6. No time limitation, such as "after the effective date," is specified in this section.
132 *Ibid.*, c. 17 at para. 40.
133 *Ibid.*, c. 17 at paras. 41, 42.
134 *Ibid.*, c. 2 at para. 7.
135 *Ibid.*, c. 11 at paras. 1 and 3, respectively.
136 *Ibid.*, at para. 41.

137 *Ibid.*, at para. 42.
138 *Ibid.*, c. 11 at paras. 115-16.
139 *Ibid.*, c. 17 at paras. 36-39.
140 *Supra* note 121, s. 7.4.4.
141 *Ibid.*, s. 17.2.8(a).
142 *Ibid.*, s. 17.2.8(c).
143 *Supra* note 119 at para. 13.3.2.
144 *Ibid.* at para. 13.4.1.
145 Champagne and Aishihik First Nations Self-Government Agreement, online: Indian and Northern Affairs Canada <http://www.ainc-inac.gc.ca/pr/agr/ykn/casga_e.html>.
146 *Supra* note 1.
147 Selkirk First Nation Final Agreement, online: Indian and Northern Affairs Canada <http://www.ainc-inac.gc.ca/pr/agr/selkirk/sfa_e.html>.
148 S.Y. 1991, c. 8.
149 R.S.B.C. 1996, c. 187.
150 *Kitkatla Band v. British Columbia (Minister of Small Business, Tourism and Culture)*, [1999] 1 C.N.L.R. 72 (B.C.S.C.). For discussion of the use of litigation to protect sacred places, see Michael Lee Ross, *First Nations Sacred Sites in Canada's Courts* (Vancouver: UBC Press, 2005).
151 *Kitkatla Band v. British Columbia (Minister of Small Business, Tourism and Culture)*, [1999] 2 C.N.L.R. 176 (B.C.S.C.).
152 *Kitkatla Band v. British Columbia (Minister of Small Business, Tourism and Culture)*, [2000] 2 C.N.L.R. 36 (B.C.C.A.).
153 [U.K.], 30 & 31 Vict., c. 3 [*Constitution Act, 1867*].
154 R.S.C. 1985, c. I-5.
155 For an in-depth analysis of the B.C.C.A. decision, see Catherine Bell, "Protect ing Indigenous Heritage Resources in Canada: A Comment on *Kitkatla v. British Columbia*" (2001) 10:2 Int'l J. Cult. Prop. 246.
156 This is a term of art used to describe the federal jurisdiction over "Indians" under s. 91(24) of the *Constitution Act, 1867, supra* note 153. "Indianness" encompasses core values of aboriginal societies, status under the federal *Indian Act, supra* note 154 and aboriginal rights.
157 *Supra* note 152.
158 *Ibid.* at paras. 28-30.
159 *Ibid.*
160 *Ibid.* at para. 130.
161 *Ibid.*
162 *Kitkatla Band v. British Columbia (Minister of Small Business, Tourism and Culture)*, [2002] 2 S.C.R. 146 at 181.
163 Stó:lō First Nation, *Stó:lō Heritage Policy Manual* (5 May 2003) [unpublished, available from the Stó:lō First Nation] at 3. Stó:lō heritage is defined as "all aspects of Stó:lō culture and lifeways – both tangible and intangible – of the past, present and future" at 8. Information also provided by personal communication with Dave Schaepe, Senior Archaeologist/Co-Manager, Stó:lō Research and Resource Management Centre (20 December 2007).
164 *Ibid.* at 5 [emphasis in original].
165 *Ibid.*, Appendix 1 at 31. Permit terms and conditions require, for example, that all staff working on the project be familiar with the Stó:lō Nation Heritage Policy; that at least one Sto:lō individual be hired for the project; that the Stó:lō Nation archaeologist be given an opportunity to consider and respond to any proposed recommendations relating to cultural sites identified during the project; and that, in the event that human remains are found during the project, the permit holder will stop work immediately and inform the Stó:lō Nation.
166 *Ibid.* at 23.
167 *Ibid.* at 24.
168 *Ibid.* at 26.
169 Stó:lō Nation, *Stó:lō Material Culture Repository Operating Policy and Procedures Manual* (5 May 2003) [unpublished, available from the Stó:lō Nation]. The repository is administered

by the Stó:lō Research and Management Centre of the Stó:lō Nation/Tribal Council, which has had an archaeological collection since 1985. Its collection consists of donated surface finds within the traditional territory and some archaeological material uncovered by permitted archaeological investigations. To date, there are no repatriated items in the collection.

170 Kamloops Indian Band, *Heritage Conservation By-Law* (1997) [available from the band]. A more recent bylaw was not available at the time of writing.

171 Online: Skeetchestn Indian Band <http:www.skeetchestn.ca/Skeetchestn%20NEWS%20BRIEFS.html>.

172 S.C. 1999, c. 24.

173 *Ibid.*

174 See *e.g.* Nipissing First Nation Land Code, s. 13.1(b), online: Framework Agreement on First Nations Land Management <http://www.fafnlm.com/LAB.NSF/0/d6440826ec-45f4d985256d5d006a4a2f?OpenDocument>.

175 Brian A. Crane *et al.*, *First Nations Governance Law* (Markham: LexisNexis Butterworths, 2006) at 119.

176 Gordon Reid, *Head-Smashed-In Buffalo Jump*, rev. ed. (Calgary: Fifth House, 2002) at 11, 12.

177 *Ibid.* at 24.

178 David C. Natcher, "Institutionalized Adaptation: Aboriginal Involvement in Land and Resource Management" (2000) 20:2 Canadian Journal of Native Studies 263 at 274.

179 See "Reservation/Notation Program," online: Government of Alberta, Sustainable Resource Development <http://www3.gov.ab.ca/srd/land/APL_Reservation_Notation.html>.

180 *Supra* note 178 at 275.

181 [1997] 3 S.C.R. 1010.

182 Online: Aboriginal Mapping Network Crown Land Referrals Toolbox <http://www.nativemaps.org/>.

183 Neil Rayner, "The Haida Gwaii Watchmen Program: Preserving Gwaii Haanas" *Dreamspeaker* (Winter 2001), online: Indian and Northern Affairs <http://www.ainc_inac.gc.ca/nr/nwltr/drm/w2001/index_e.html>.

184 See also Marianne Ignace and Ron Ignace, "Canadian Aboriginal Languages and the Protection of Cultural Heritage," this volume.

185 Heather Blair *et al.*, "Daghida: Cold Lake First Nation Works Towards Dene Language Revitalization" in Barbara Burnaby and Jon Reyhner, eds., *Indigenous Languages across the Community* (Flagstaff: Northern Arizona University, 2000) 89 at 89-98. See online: Indigenous Languages across the Community <http://jan.ucc.nau.edu/~jar/ILAC/>.

186 *Ibid.* at 94.

187 *Ibid.* at 96.

188 Neil Rayner, "Revitalizing Aboriginal Languages: Completing the Circle of Language and Culture" *Dreamspeaker* (Spring 2000) 6 at 7. See online: Indian and Northern Affairs Canada <http://www.ainc-inac.gc.ca.login.ezproxy.library.ualberta.ca/nr/nwltr/drm/s2000/ral_e.html>.

189 "Aboriginal Languages Initiative," online: Canadian Heritage <http://www.canadianheritage.gc.ca/progs/pa-app/progs/ila-ali/index_e.cfm>.

190 Discussed in Ignace and Ignace, *supra* note 184.

191 "Aboriginal Place Names," online: Indian and Northern Affairs Canada <http://www.ainc-inac.gc.ca/pr/info/info106_e.html>.

192 *Supra* note 188 and Ignace and Ignace *supra* note 184.

193 Murray Browne, "Snuneymuxw First Nation: Using the *Trade-Marks Act* to Protect First Nation Petroglyph Images" (Sacred Sites panel discussion at the Protecting Knowledge Conference, Vancouver 2000) [unpublished] [archived with author]. The challenges of using existing IP legislation to address First Nations concerns are explored in chapters by Rosemary Coombe, Mohsen Ahmed, Robert Howell, and Kelly Bannister in Bell and Paterson, *supra* note 2.

194 *The Trademarks Act*, R.S.C. 1985, c. T-13 s. 9(1)n(iii) provides a public authority can give

public notice of its adoption and use as a mark for "wares and services," thereby preventing its adoption by anyone else for business or other purposes.

195 *Ontario Association of Architects v. Association of Architectural Technologists of Ontario*, [2003] 1 F.C. 331.

196 Canadian Intellectual Property Office (CIPO), "Public Authority Status Under Sub-Paragraph 9(1)(n)(iii)" Trade-Marks Journal 49:2501 (2002) 249, online: Industry Canada <http://strategis.ic.gc.ca/sc_mrksv/cipo/tm/tm_journal2002/ 2oct2002.pdf>.

197 Adrienne Tanner, "Image Problem" *Province* (Vancouver) (13 February 2000) A22.

198 Online: Mi'kmaq College Institute, University College of Cape Breton <http://mrc.uccb.ns.ca/mci/default.htm>.

199 See *e.g.* Bell and McCuaig, "Protection and Repatriation," *supra* note 5 at 324-25.

200 For further discussion, see Robert K. Paterson, *supra* note 38.

201 Gilbert Whiteduck, "Address" (delivered at the First Nations International Symposium on Repatriation hosted by the Kitigan Zibi in Maniwaki Quebec) (August 2005) [unpublished]. See also the CMC website at <http://www.civilizations.ca/media/show_pr_e.asp?ID=640> for their account of this story.

202 Randy Boswell, "Upon Human Bones: A Search for Artifacts from an 1843 Archeological Dig Yields a Cache of Stories about the Birth of the Capital, the Progress of a Nation and an Enduring Clash of Cultures" *Ottawa Citizen* (1 July 2002) A1.

203 Randy Boswell, "Museum Returns Ancient Native Bones: But Aboriginal Groups Angry Some Bones Withheld" *Edmonton Journal* (31 December 2002) A12.

204 *Ibid.* citing CMC president Victor Rabinovitch in a letter of reply to the Kitigan Zibi chief Jean-Guy Whiteduck. See also CMC website at <http://www.civilizations.ca/media/show_pr_e.asp?ID=640> for an account of this story.

205 Personal communication from Wikwemikong Heritage Organization, Ontario (2 June 2003).

206 Personal communication with Lucille Bell, Heritage Officer, Haida Repatriation Committee (2 July 2002). Information on this repatriation is also derived from presentations made by members of the Haida Repatriation Committee at the Aboriginal Repatriation Extravaganza (24 May 2004, Masset Haida Gwaii) and First Nations International Symposium on Repatriation (August 2005, Maniwaki, Quebec).

207 Preamble to the Tatshenshini-Alsek Park Management Agreement between the Champagne and Aishihik First Nations and Her Majesty the Queen in Right of the Province of British Columbia [on file with the authors].

208 Owen Beattie *et al.*, "The Kwaday Dan Ts'inchi Discovery from a Glacier in British Columbia" (2000) 24 Canadian Journal of Archaeology 129 at 132, 136-37.

209 *Ibid.* at 135.

210 Kwaday Dan Sinchi Agreement, 31 August 1999 [available from Champagne and Aishihik First Nations and on file with the authors]. Preferred spelling "Kwaday Dan Ts'inchi."

211 *Supra* note 208 at 132-33.

212 *Supra* note 210.

213 Arctic Athabaskan Council, "Examples and Effects of the Utilization of Traditional Knowledge in the Yukon" (14 March 2003) [unpublished, prepared for the Canadian Biodiversity Office, Environment Canada] at 24.

214 *Supra* note 208 at 137.

215 *Ibid.* at 144.

216 Personal communication with Sheila C. Greer, consulting anthropologist working with the Champagne and Aishihik First Nations (4 November 2003).

217 "Traditional Burial Ground and Fort Edmonton Cemetery Program Statement" at 1, online: The City of Edmonton <http://www.edmonton.ca/CityGov/CommServices/TraditionalBurialGroundsProgramStatement.pdf>. For a general discussion of events and legal proceedings leading to provincial designation see Lynn Parish, "Power to the People" (April/May 2002) 26:5 Law Now 32. For more detailed discussion, see Pamela Cunningham, *infra* note 223.

218 R.S.A. 2000, c. H-16, ss. 2(a)-(b), 9.

219 R.S.A. 2000, c. H-9.

220 Charles Mandel, "Rossdale Burials Honoured" *Edmonton Journal* (22 March 2000) B5.
221 Elinor Jackson, "Skeleton Discovered at Edmonton EPCOR Plant" *First Nations Free Press* 8:11 (November 2001) 10.
222 *Supra* note 217.
223 Pamela M. Cunningham, *The Meeting Place at the Bend in the River: An Examination of the Fort Edmonton Cemetery/Aboriginal Burial Ground* (MA Thesis, University of Alberta, 2006) [unpublished].
224 Another example is *Touchwood File Hills Qu'Apelle District Chiefs Council Inc. v. Davis, Lindsey and Sinclair et al.*, [1987] 1 C.N.L.R. 180 at 181, where an injunction was granted under the *Heritage Property Act*, S.S. 1979-80, c. H-2.2 and *Kitkatla*, *supra* notes 150, 151, and 152.
225 Scott Hamilton *et al.*, "New Solitudes: Conflicting World Views in the Context of Contemporary Northern Resource Development" (1995) 19 Canadian Journal of Archaeology 3 at 4.
226 *Ibid.* at 6.
227 R.S.O. 1990, c. C-4.
228 O. Reg. 133/92, s. 2(2)5.
229 *Poplar Point Ojibway Nation v. Ontario*, [1993] O.J. No. 601 at para. 33.
230 *Supra* note 227, s. 70(4) reads: "An unapproved Aboriginal peoples cemetery is land set aside with the apparent intention of interring therein, in accordance with cultural affinities, human remains and containing remains identified as those of persons who were one of the Aboriginal peoples of Canada"; per s. 71(5): "'[U]napproved' means not approved in accordance with this Act or a predecessor of this Act."
231 *Supra* note 225 at 15.
232 *Ibid.*
233 *Supra* note 228, s. 2(2)2.
234 *Supra* note 229 at para. 51.
235 Part I of the *Constitution Act*, 1982, being Schedule B to the *Canada Act 1982* (U.K.), 1982, c. 11 [*Charter*].
236 *Supra* note 229 at para. 65.
237 *Ibid.*
238 *Supra* note 227, s. 70(1).
239 *Supra* note 229 at para. 65.
240 *Supra* note 155 at 248.

Part 3: Reflections on Selected Themes

The Trickster is known to the Gitksan as Weget (Raven). Weget has many teaching roles, including the development of critical thinking and reasoning skills.[1] Weget looks around and wonders why aboriginal peoples have become so preoccupied with the assertion of the cultural attributes that characterize how "different" their group is from everyone else.

Weget is of the opinion that the basis for establishing respectful relationships between aboriginal peoples and the Canadian state is the recognition that aboriginal peoples are self-defining groups with shared histories. Aboriginal peoples should not have to keep trying to be, or proving that they are, different and culturally distinct. That was just a trick Weget played at the Supreme Court of Canada when it decided *Van der Peet*.[2] People weren't supposed to actually believe it or take it seriously. It was one of Weget's biggest jokes, but nobody got it. Weget also shakes his head sadly at the now too common themes that echo through the aboriginal discourse across Canada, namely (1) a tragic and heroic past, (2) exploitation, and (3) resistance and healing.[3] Weget wonders what will happen when aboriginal groups start to lose aspects of their cultural and political difference.

He begins to groom his most beautiful and, he notes, cosmopolitan feathers. Clearly, he is going to have to dream up another trick. A really good one that will make the people laugh at themselves again. But simpler this time so people will get it, because Weget hates laughing alone. Yes, we all need a really good belly laugh.

Weget stops and listens carefully. Darn! With all these Tricksters around it is hard to relax. Is somebody laughing at him? He is sure he hears a Trickster giggle somewhere.

Val Napoleon

Notes

1 Mary Jane Smith, "Placing Gitxsan Stories in Text: Returning the Feathers – Guuxs Mak'am Mik'Aax" (PhD diss., University of British Columbia, Faculty of Education, 2004) [unpublished].

2 [1996] 2 S.C.R. 507. See John Borrows, *Recovering Canada: The Resurgence of Indigenous Law* (Toronto: University of Toronto, 2002) at 57.

3 Tim Schouls, *Shifting Boundaries* (Vancouver: UBC Press, 2003) at 69.

9
Canadian Aboriginal Languages and the Protection of Cultural Heritage

Marianne Ignace and Ron Ignace

The significance of the indigenous language is addressed in many of the case studies of this volume, and, at least in a symbolic if not in a functional sense, takes a prominent and essential place in the discussion of indigenous cultural heritage and property rights. Indeed, participants perceive language to be "at the core" of shaping First Nations identities, culture, histories, and connection to land. However, within Canada, aboriginal peoples face the reality that the vast majority of the approximately sixty languages of the Inuit, Métis, and First Nations peoples are in a precarious and endangered state. For example, the 2001 Canada Census indicated that only about 20 percent of aboriginal people who reported had an aboriginal mother tongue, a decrease of 3.5 percent since 1996.[1]

Given this depressing and sobering situation, and the emphasis given to language in the case studies, the purpose of this chapter is to (1) discuss the continuing significance of aboriginal languages for the protection of aboriginal cultural heritage and (2) explore ways to address the continuing survival of aboriginal languages not only as symbolic markers of indigenous identity but also as living aspects of aboriginal peoples' identities and cultures. A useful distinction in this respect is that between the symbolic functions and the practical functions of a language.[2] The protection of indigenous cultural heritage invariably involves the protection and revitalization of indigenous languages. This involves the active transmission of cultural knowledge and the active use of language in communities. It is important to distinguish between (1) the *communicative* and the *practical* function of a language as a tool in everyday communication and (2) the symbolic function of one's ancestral language (which is perhaps no longer used and spoken in everyday life) as a marker of identity, cultural distinctness, and wisdom. Language protection and survival, in turn, requires practical and long-term community-driven efforts, including the "banking" of linguistic knowledge through documentation and archiving; the restoration of that knowledge in the adult and caregiver generation; and the intergenerational transmission of language to younger generations. The reflections of case study participants on strategies for language retention are consistent with this position. For languages that have almost ceased to be used in everyday communication, this is a daunting task. Today, community education institutions take on essential functions of language transmission that are often connected to, and at times controlled by, outside agencies. This reality raises further questions. Can languages be protected or even revitalized through legislation? What are the pitfalls in communities' efforts to protect languages? How can communities protect their autonomy over their language and the communicative content and knowledge contained in that language? These issues are connected to appropriation, copyright, cultural autonomy, and intangible intellectual property rights.

The State of Canadian Aboriginal Languages

Surveys by linguists,[3] the Assembly of First Nations (AFN),[4] and particular language communities and regional organizations[5] have shown that the vitality of aboriginal languages in Canada varies by region and across speech communities. Only a few languages, notably dialects of Cree, Ojibway, and Inuktitut, are considered to have significant numbers of speakers of all ages and thriving intergenerational transmission. Some smaller languages, including Mi'kmaq, Tsilhqot'in, Denne Suline or Chipewyan, Carrier, Gitksan, and Mohawk still have speakers in the child-bearing range, although their use in the home, and thus the in-home transmission to young children, has diminished. For most other languages, including most of the thirty or so languages of eight diverse linguistic families represented in British Columbia, the situation is difficult. Some, like Nuxalk, Haida, all Coast Salish languages, and Ktunaxa, have merely a handful of elderly speakers left. Others, like the Interior Salish, Sm'algyax (Coast Tsimshian), and South Wakashan languages (Nuu-chah-nulth and Kwak'wala), and the Dene languages in northern British Columbia, Yukon, and the Northwest Territories, have a small number of elderly speakers left, but intergenerational transmission has virtually ceased. As we have seen in many endangered indigenous language situations, once a language is reduced to a small, shrinking body of elderly speakers with no younger speakers being raised through intergenerational transmission, it can face sudden decline and death, often in the course of a decade or two. This is the situation aboriginal languages in Canada are now facing or nearing.[6]

The current situation of language loss has nothing to do with the intrinsic properties of these languages but, rather, with a fluke of biogeography that took on a momentum of its own during the last century and with political processes of colonization, economic expansion, and globalization.[7] In this chapter, we do not discuss in detail the oppressive policies, practices, and issues that have led to the alarming decline of indigenous languages in Canada, the

United States, and other parts of the world. Here in Canada, the main culprits are the Indian residential school system, which literally beat aboriginal languages out of two or three generations of children; the predominance of English (or French) in the workplace; the subsequent dominance of English since the late 1960s in the public education system; and the contemporary dominance and pervasiveness of English in all walks of life. Fewer and fewer people know or have occasion to use their indigenous language.

The speed at which a language declines once intergenerational transmission is lost is demonstrated in the example of the Secwepemctsin (Shuswap) language. Secwepemctsin is one of the three northern Interior Salish languages spoken in the interior of British Columbia. In surveys conducted during the late 1980s and early 1990s by the AFN, Secwepemctsin, as spoken in several communities in the Secwepemc/Shuswap Nation, was rated as an "enduring" language.[8] While the number of fluent speakers (as reported by younger, non-fluent adults) was likely inflated in these surveys, figures and data compiled since that time give us an idea of how fast the linguistic knowledge and ability of a nation of speakers can decline once mother tongue transmission stops. A 1995 survey reported that only 3.5 percent of Secwepemc people, or slightly over three hundred people, peer-evaluated one another as speakers of Secwepemctsin. Most of these were in their sixties or older.[9] Since then, many elders have died, so this number has shrunk to about 250. As the numbers decline, so does the detailed knowledge of the language and the ability of the few remaining speakers to communicate in it due to the geographic distance of reserve communities, dialect divisions, and lack of opportunity to socialize and use the language.

Although intergenerational transmission has stopped in most homes, and school programs have had limited success, there are glimmers of hope. For example, an immersion program for the Adams Lake First Nation is producing young children with good proficiency in the language, and home language efforts are also achieving some success. Through courses delivered as part of a First Nations/university partnership program, including "master-apprentice" training with fluent speakers/elders, some adults have gained proficiency in the language and are now teaching it.[10] However, as the case studies in this volume show, aboriginal groups have, with limited successes, also engaged in other efforts to revive indigenous languages (*e.g.*, reintroducing them through ceremonies, through recording traditional songs on CDs, and through using other modern media that appeal to children).[11] The studies support the findings of the 2005 foundational report of the Task Force on Aboriginal Languages and Cultures (TFALC), which indicate that there is an urgent need for Canada to recognize its linguistic heritage and to enable the protection and revitalization of aboriginal languages. The report calls for national intervention and enduring support for indigenous language initiatives. As part of its guiding principles, the report states:

> We believe that Canada must truly make itself whole by recognizing and acknowledging our First Nation, Inuit and Métis languages as the original languages of Canada. This recognition must be through legislation and must also provide for enduring institutional supports for First Languages in the same way it has done for the French and English languages.[12]

What Is at Stake? Implications of Language Loss

> If you don't breathe, there is no air.
> If you don't walk, there is no earth.
> If you don't speak, there is no world.
>
> — a Navajo elder's words[13]

Indigenous groups and individuals worldwide have professed a deep and far-reaching connection to their collective and individual identities, which are rooted in their indigenous languages. Fishman notes that if you take language away from cultures, "you take away its greetings, its curses, its praises, its laws, its literature, its songs, its riddles, its proverbs, its cures, its wisdom, its prayers."[14] Similar sentiments are echoed in the case studies. In the words of Vera Newman, "if we don't have our language, we don't have a culture."[15] The point is also eloquently made by Elizabeth Gallant:

> The things that are being taught are very important, legends are very important; they will understand through legends. Legends are very important if they could understand language. Songs: that's what the children should understand. And that's what's so important, when they can understand the language and sing the songs. The spirits that come to us do not understand English, they don't sing in English; but they do understand Blackfoot language and songs, and that's why it's so important that Blackfoot be learned. That's when we can go back to our way of life and our religion. And this is how they [children] will learn as they grow, and will know our way of life.[16]

The AFN has expressed similar views about the importance of preserving aboriginal languages:

> The Aboriginal Languages were given by the Creator as an integral part of life. Embodied in Aboriginal languages is our unique relationship to the Creator, our attitudes, beliefs, values, and the fundamental notion of what is truth. Aboriginal language is an asset to one's own education, formal and informal. Aboriginal language contributes to greater pride in the history and culture of the community, greater involvement and interest of

> parents in the education of their children, and greater respect for elders. Language is the principal means by which culture is accumulated, shared and transmitted from generation to generation. The key to identity and retention of culture is one's ancestral language.[17]

Not surprisingly, the report of the Royal Commission on Aboriginal Peoples (RCAP) also emphasizes the vital function of language in the transmission of culture and the importance of funding language initiatives. Language is recognized as "the principal instrument by which culture is transmitted from one generation to another, by which members of a culture communicate meaning and make sense of their shared experience. Because language defines the world and experience in cultural terms, it literally shapes our way of perceiving – our world view."[18]

The above quotes underscore the view shared by many indigenous communities that indigenous languages are the spiritual, cultural, and social essence that defines them. Each language contains collective cultural, spiritual, ecological, and intellectual knowledge and wisdom and carries it through many, many generations of speakers. The far-reaching connection between language, cultural identity, spirituality, and well-being is also expressed in the titles of reports whose purpose is to alert us to the danger that aboriginal languages may well become extinct. For example, a recent report by the Aboriginal Language Services, Government of Yukon, is entitled *We Are Our Language*.[19]

Like indigenous speakers, linguists also appreciate and celebrate the complex storehouses of knowledge contained in languages. The famous linguist Edward Sapir, who began by studying Germanic and Hebrew scholarship and then devoted much of his career to studying North American indigenous languages, noted that "[l]anguage is the most massive and inclusive art we know, a mountainous and anonymous work of unconscious generations."[20] Noting that the vast intellectual reservoirs of indigenous languages were "intellectual archives," linguist Michael Krauss suggested that "[e]very time we lose a language, it's like dropping a bomb on the Louvre."[21] Another linguist, Marianne Mithun, who collaborated extensively with Mohawk people and with Californian aboriginal peoples while recording and reviving their languages, concluded:

> Language represents the most creative, pervasive aspect of culture, the most intimate side of the mind. The loss of language diversity will mean that we will never even have the opportunity to appreciate the full creative capacities of the human mind ... There is not a language in North America that fails to offer breathtakingly beautiful intricacy. For descendants of speakers to discover this beauty can profoundly enrich their lives, much like the discovery of music, literature, or art, if not more.[22]

Through its grammatical structure, each language also includes fascinating and different ways of categorizing experience.[23] Examples from the Secwepemc language (Secwepemctsin), Haida, and Heiltsuk show how different languages express different ways of conceptualizing the world.

Secwepemctsin, the Secwepemc language, distinguishes between three kinds of evidentials. These are grammatical elements attached to verbs that express the nature of evidence, or the source of information for a given statement. When a Secwepemctsin speaker talks about something that has happened, he/she always indicates whether the issue that is reported is known to the speaker because (1) he/she had first-hand experience of what happened, (2) he/she knows that something happened from hearsay (someone having reported it to him/her), or (3) physical evidence shows that something has happened.

Consider the following examples. If someone says, "tscentés re Fred re tsitcws," this means "Fred fixed up his house." When the verb *"tscentés"* has no suffix, this means that the person who uttered the sentence personally experienced the action or, in other words, was there when Fred fixed up his house. If someone says, "tscentés-ekwe re Fred re tsitcws," this also means "Fred fixed up his house"; however, the use of the suffix *"-ekwe"* indicates that the speaker knows this from hearsay, from someone who was there or who knew Fred fixed up his house. Thus, *"-ekwe"* (pronounced "uka") is an evidential suffix. If someone says, "Tscentés-enke re Fred re tsitcws," this means that Fred fixed up his house and that the speaker knows this from physical evidence. When he/she saw the house, it was freshly painted and had new windows, a new roof, and perhaps other new parts as well. Thus, *"-enke"* is also an evidential suffix. Unlike the suffix *"-ekwe,"* which involves hearsay, *"-enke"* involves the perception of physical evidence.

By using such evidential suffixes consistently in everyday speech or in storytelling, Secwepemctsin speakers constantly remind one another of the status of knowledge or evidence of various pieces of information. In English, we can include such information by adding additional sentences. We can say, "Someone told me he fixed his house," or, "I noticed that he fixed up his house." However, these involve elaborations and choices of speech (which can also be omitted). In Secwepemctsin, the categories of grammar themselves encode this information and are an intrinsic part of the utterances made by speakers of the language. Many other aboriginal languages have evidential particles, although each language has unique ways of expressing the status of evidence of an utterance. Two more examples follow.

It has often been said that, in aboriginal languages, relations and concepts are not so much expressed by talking about "things" as by the actions and movements of the concepts upon one another. In other words, aboriginal languages perceive the world through verbs that express being and dynamic relations among entities in flux rather than through static things and their qualities. For example, in Haida, when you want to say that something "is blue," you express it as a verb. Consider the following examples:

1 In the sentence "Ajii miidiigee.uu guhlalgang," or "This blouse is blue," the concept "to be blue," derived from the root "*guhlahl,*" is expressed by adding a verb suffix to the word "blue."
2 "Ayaad.uu yaanangaagang" means "Today, it's foggy" (Today+emphasis+foggy+verb+present). The concept "to be foggy" is an action rather than a quality of a noun (*i.e.,* the weather), as it is in English.

By adding further prefixes and suffixes that express the shape and dynamic location of verbs, the Haida language is enormously creative with regard to evoking complex images through verbs. For example, the sentence "kun aduu tldaaltl'xas"[24] means "A canoe full of men [is] coming around the point [towards the speaker]," without mentioning the canoe as a thing; however, it builds the shape of a canoe, expressed through the prefix "*tl-*," into an action involving a number of things coming towards the speaker. As linguist Jeff Leer has noted, "one of the first things the student of Haida has to learn is to orient himself to a new system of ordering words within a sentence, and a system of building words with ordered parts which is more detailed and productive than anything we are accustomed to in English."[25] The speaker of Haida can thus refer to, or allude to, the shape and consistency, motion or direction, and action of something on something else without even mentioning it as a "thing."

Yet another example of the connection between linguistic categories and the cognitive ordering of the world involves the deictic words and particle words in Salish and Wakashan. Deictics are "pointing words." In English, we are used to having pointing words refer to something that is either "here" or "there," or involving the two dimensions "this" or "that." English-language pointing words are thus organized in a simple binary fashion; in Salish languages, pointing words are much more complex. First of all, they involve three dimensions: whether something is close to the speaker (this here by me, or here by me); close to the addressee (that thing near you, or there by you); or away from both speaker and addressee (that thing way over there). Additional dimensions concern whether the object or person referred to is visible (present), invisible (absent), or real or hypothetical, and, when objects or people are in motion, whether the motion is towards or away from the person speaking.

In Heiltsuk, a Wakashan language, the here-near-speaker/there-near-addressee/over there distinction is added to the verb in the third person. Every time a person speaks about a thing or person doing something, (*e.g.,* "the dog ran away" or "the boy ate some fish") the speaker indicates, by way of a suffix added to the verb, whether the dog or the boy is close to the speaker, close to the person to whom the sentence is told (the addressee), or away from both speaker and addressee. The speaker also indicates whether the dog is visible or invisible to the speaker.[26]

These examples demonstrate that languages organize experience in unique and different ways and, within them, contain different possibilities of thinking. Loss of indigenous languages is a crisis faced not only by indigenous peoples but also by humankind: if linguistic diversity becomes reduced from thousands of ways of thinking to a few dozen, then we are all reduced.[27] As linguists Ofelia Zepeda and Jane Hill express it:

> Even this vastly reduced reservoir of linguistic diversity [among North American native languages] constitutes one of the great treasures of humanity, an enormous store-house of expressive power and profound understandings of the universe. The loss of the hundreds of languages that have already passed into history is an intellectual catastrophe in every way comparable in magnitude to the ecological catastrophe we face today as the earth's tropical forests are swept by fire. Each language still spoken is fundamental to the personal, social and – a key term in the discourse of indigenous peoples – spiritual identity of its speakers. They know that without these languages they would be less than they are, and they are engaged in the most urgent struggles to protect their linguistic heritage.[28]

Kanien 'keh á :ka (Mohawk) scholar Christopher Jocks adds:

> Another potential that is impaired when language is endangered is the potential of a community to grow, and for its members to find new, creative solutions to the problems they face. Patterns of thinking and perception and prioritization encoded in their original language can easily be lost with that language, making it increasingly difficult to *frame* problems – and to solve them – in any but the dominant culture's terms.[29]

Jocks poignantly examined the real-life impacts of language erosion. Although he hesitates to embrace the view that "without our languages we are no longer Native people,"[30] he fears that

> without our languages it is all too easy for us to become cartoons, caricatures of ourselves. Not only does ceremonial work too easily become rote and formalistic, but when we must depend on English-language contextualization, it becomes easy for us to adopt and incorporate alien images and understandings of ourselves without knowing it.[31]

By examining what is lost in the translation of the Kaianeren 'k ó :wa, or "Great Law" of the Longhouse, from Mohawk to English, he shows not only how nuances and unique essences of knowledge, perceptions, and strategies of negotiating meaning are lost but also how new ones derived from English language and culture replace them, thus distorting, changing, and simplifying indigenous concepts expressed in Mohawk. David Crystal notes, "as each language dies, another precious source of data – for philosophers, scientists, anthropologists, folklorists, historians, psychologists, linguists, and writers – is lost. Diversity ... is a human evolutionary strength, and should be safeguarded as an end in itself."[32]

The Legal Protection of Indigenous Languages

In the post-Second World War era, a number of declarations, covenants, and conventions have dealt with the protection of indigenous cultural property, intangible intellectual property, and heritage and, thus (although not explicitly as such), indigenous language. These include:

1 The *Universal Declaration of Human Rights*, 1948, which lays down the basic principle against discrimination on the grounds of language.[33] Article 2 provides that "[e]veryone is entitled to all rights and freedoms set forth in this Declaration, without distinction of any kind, such as ... language."

2 The 1966 *International Covenant on Civil and Political Rights*, which establishes the rights of cultural expression, states in Article 1(1) that all peoples have the right of self-determination. By virtue of that right, they freely determine their political status and freely pursue their economic, social, and cultural development.[34] Without making particular reference to language rights, it makes reference to cultural expression as a basic human right.

3 The 1992 *Declaration on the Rights of Persons belonging to National or Ethnic, Religious and Linguistic Minorities*, which stipulates in Article 1(1) that signatory states shall develop legislation to protect the "national or ethnic, cultural, religious and *linguistic identity* of minorities within their respective territories," and notes, *inter alia*, in Article 2(1) that "[p]ersons belonging to national or ethnic, religious and linguistic minorities (hereinafter referred to as persons belonging to minorities) have the right to enjoy their own culture, to profess and practise their own religion, and to use their own language, in private and in public, freely and without interference or any form of discrimination."[35]

4 The 1976 *International Covenant on Civil and Political Rights*, which states that "[i]n those states in which ethnic, religious or linguistic minorities exist, persons belonging to such minorities shall not be denied the right, in community with the other members of the group, to enjoy their own culture, to profess and practise their own religion, or to use their own language."[36]

5 Article 28 of the 1989 *International Labour Organization (ILO) Convention 169 concerning Indigenous and Tribal Peoples in Independent Countries,*[37] which requires that "children belonging to the peoples concerned shall, wherever practicable, be taught to read and write in their own indigenous language or in the language most commonly used by the group to which they belong" and that "adequate measures shall be taken to ensure that these peoples have the opportunity to attain fluency in the national language or in one of the official languages of the country." The article provides, at the same time, that "measures shall be taken to preserve and promote the development and practice of the indigenous languages of the peoples concerned."

6 The 1989 *Convention on the Rights of the Child,* which sheds light on another aspect of the language issue in education.[38] It emphasizes the fact that language also has to be considered as an educational value. Article 29 sets up that "States Parties agree that the education of the child shall be directed to ... the development of respect for the child's ... cultural identity, language and values." A 2004 UNESCO position paper regarding education in a multilingual world reaffirms the value of local mother tongues as the medium of instruction where the shift to English or regional/national lingua franca has become prominent and has led to devaluation of local vernacular languages, especially indigenous languages.[39]

7 Article 14 of the 1994 United Nations *Draft Declaration on the Rights of Indigenous Peoples,* which states: "Indigenous peoples have the right to revitalize, use, develop and transmit to future generations their histories, languages, oral traditions, philosophies, writing systems and literatures, and to designate and retain their own names for communities, places and persons. States shall take effective measures, whenever any right of indigenous peoples may be threatened, to ensure this right is protected."[40]

Translating such documents into tangible rights and measures of protection on the ground is difficult. In fact, the rhetoric of global declarations, often decades in the making, has proven to be discouraging for indigenous people(s) at the local level. For example, the 1989 *Convention on the Rights of the Child* has not led to legislation, or even a moral readiness on the part of political jurisdictions in most parts of North America, to prioritize, let alone implement, education in an endangered aboriginal language. Nor has the mention of language rights in earlier covenants and declarations had any effect on the protection of precarious languages; rather, national and provincial governments have by and large ignored the existence of indigenous languages, tacitly relying on the ability of aboriginal people to use English.

Can Languages Be Saved through Legislation?

> A shrinking language minority cannot be saved by the actions of well-wishers who do not belong to the minority in question. In particular, its shrinking cannot be halted by the action, however benevolent and intelligent, of a modern centralised state. It can be saved only by itself, and then only if its members acquire the will to stop it shrinking, acquire the institutions and financial means to take appropriate measures, and take them.
>
> — Desmond Fennel[41]

Language Legislation and Legal Strategies

For some time, numerous nation-states in the developed and developing world have created legislation to protect indigenous or endangered minority languages contained within their boundaries. In most cases, language policies have done little to enhance the vitality of indigenous languages or to increase the number of speakers. Suzanne Romaine has noted that the ineffectiveness of indigenous or minority language legislation is often attributable to the "weak linkages" between grand declarations about language rights and language protection in legislation, on the one hand, and tangible policy instruments that enable the maintenance of languages in practice, on the other.[42] At a minimum, effective language legislation must be accompanied by an enduring political and financial commitment to support language education programs, institutions, and local community initiatives. Two examples of indigenous language legislation and its pitfalls demonstrate this point:

1 Despite the fact that Gaelic has been recognized as an official language since the establishment of the Republic of Ireland in 1919, Gaelic has almost given way to English because efforts to protect it by making it a second language that is compulsory in schools neglected to nourish the mother tongue transmission of Gaelic in the home and community.

2 The *Native American Languages Act of 1992 (NALA)* states that the United States will take action to ensure the survival of Native American languages, including preserving, protecting, and promoting the rights and freedom of Native Americans to use, practise, and develop their languages.[43] However the *Act* does not provide for financial resources or enforcement mechanisms, and a recent Senate bill to adjust this situation died on the floor in 2005. *NALA* thus is viewed as having done "too little, too late" for the *de facto* revitalization of the large number of critically endangered aboriginal languages in the States.[44]

Indigenous languages with a wide base of speakers have sometimes received other forms of legal recognition that have similar pitfalls and problems. For example:

3 Article 48 of the 1993 Peruvian Constitution makes Spanish the official language of Peru, although it also designates Quechua and Aimara and other indigenous languages as official languages in "zones" where they are predominantly spoken. However, as Serafin M. Coronel-Molina has pointed out, this official language status has not been accompanied by large-scale efforts to revalorize it after centuries of colonizers' efforts to devalue the language, and bilingual education for Quechua-speaking children remains available to only a small percentage of indigenous students.[45]

4 Of the thirty-one Mayan languages, twenty-one are spoken in Guatemala. Guatemala's 1985 Constitution recognizes Mayan languages as part of the cultural patrimony of the nation and mandates bilingual education in Indian areas of the country. In 1991, the Guatemalan government established and began to fund the Academy of Mayan Languages, which marked a significant milestone for Mayan control of their own languages.

5 The *1992 European Charter for Regional or Minority Languages* was created to provide a legal instrument to protect the numerous indigenous and non-indigenous minority languages of the European Union. It has had positive impacts on attitudes towards regional and indigenous languages in Europe and has provided a measure of funding for language protection initiatives. However, because it is European nation-states that ratify the *Charter,* it is up to the state governments to recognize whether a particular language exists within its boundaries.[46]

6 The creation of the State of Israel in 1948 enabled, within it, the restoration of Hebrew as a spoken language. Hebrew is sanctioned and enforced through policies that make it the language of Parliament, education, and other official walks of life. Hebrew is often cited as one language that has been successfully revived. It is noteworthy that the revitalization of Hebrew was enabled by the creation of a nation-state that could authoritatively create specific policies and resource institutions to bring the language back.

Of special note among indigenous language measures is the status of the Maori language (Te Reo Maori) within the State of New Zealand (Aotearea Maori). Unlike the diversity of aboriginal peoples and languages in Canada or the United States, the Maori comprise a single indigenous people within the State of New Zealand. Although represented by a single language and a single culture, the Maori nonetheless have a number of dialects and consist of local traditional groups, crosscut by regional and geographic differences. The Treaty of Waitangi, signed and delivered by the British colonial government and the chiefs of the Maori in 1840, significantly, and in contrast to Canadian First Nations treaties, has a written bilingual version.[47] Since the 1980s the Waitangi Tribunal has interpreted concerns raised by Maori according to the spirit and intent of the Waitangi Treaty. The tribunal has accepted the Maori people's continuing ability to protect their language and culture as an issue of redress. This has led to the establishment of Maori as the "other" (next to English) official language of New Zealand. This outcome was also heavily influenced by a grassroots-driven revitalization movement of Te Reo Maori, with "language nest" preschools, schools, and adult immersion programming.

In Canada since the 1980s, the federal, provincial, and territorial governments have taken various legal measures to address minority languages (*i.e.,* French outside of Quebec) and heritage languages as well as aboriginal languages. An example is the Canadian *Official Languages Act,* which recognizes French and English as the "official languages" of Canada and was amended in 1988 to incorporate s. 23 of the *Charter of Rights and Freedoms,* which guarantees minority language educational rights to French-speaking communities outside Quebec and, to a lesser extent, to English-speaking minorities in Quebec.[48] Despite this, the 1991 Canada census returns show that the use of the French language among French minorities outside of Quebec, Ontario, and New Brunswick, which have high concentrations of speakers, has been steadily declining.

The Northwest Territories *Official Languages Act* guarantees the equality of French and English, along with the five First Nations languages and Inuktitut/Inuinnaqtun, in the Territories.[49] However, according to observers, it has not halted the decline of aboriginal languages in the NWT to date. As Freda Ahenakew, Brenda Gardipy, and Barbara Lafond found, "While the Act has had many positive effects in the NWT, it has not, on its own, been able to reverse the language shift."[50] As numerous observers have stated, the *Act* focused far more on the translation of government documents and access to services in the official languages than it did on home and community-driven efforts to maintain intergenerational mother tongue transmission. Although addressed through policy rather than legislation, the Yukon Territory provides aboriginal language services similar to those provided in the NWT. However, a recent study revealed that Yukon languages have continued to decline, and it appears that these services have had almost no effect on the maintenance and revival of aboriginal languages at the grassroots level.[51]

Arguably, indigenous languages also receive some protection in the Canadian *Constitution Act, 1982*. Section 35(1) states that "[t]he existing Aboriginal and treaty rights of Aboriginal peoples of Canada are hereby recognized and affirmed."[52] While the interpretation of this section is still debated by the Canadian public and politicians, on the one hand, and aboriginal peoples, on the other, the Supreme Court of Canada, in *R. v. Sparrow*, has held that "a generous, liberal interpretation of the words in the constitutional provision is demanded."[53] Aboriginal peoples have maintained that aboriginal rights include the right to learn, use, and have services provided in one's aboriginal language. Adopting legal discourse, it is integral to their distinctive cultural identities. Based on several Supreme Court of Canada decisions, First Nations have also argued that the federal Crown, represented by the minister of Indian affairs, has a fiduciary obligation to protect the rights and interests of First Nations peoples, including their languages. However, there is no Canadian case law directly on point.

Section 15(1) of the *Canadian Charter of Rights and Freedoms* guarantees that "[e]very individual is equal before and under the law and has the right to the equal protection and equal benefit of the law without discrimination and, in particular, without discrimination based on race, national or ethnic origin, color, religion, sex, age or mental or physical disability."[54] While language rights for languages other than French and English are considered to be included, there is no specific mention of them. However, s. 27 of the *Charter* states that it "shall be interpreted in a manner consistent with the preservation and enhancement of the multicultural heritage of Canadians." Aboriginal peoples have argued that equality means protection and access to services in their own languages that is equal to that given in English and French languages.

Since the mid-1970s, language has also received attention in special agreements between the Crown and First Nations. The James Bay Cree and Inuit, through the James Bay and Northern Quebec Agreements, hold special language education rights that are implemented by locally controlled school boards.[55] The James Bay Inuit immediately implemented exclusive Inuktitut instruction at the primary school level. The James Bay Cree, after initial failed attempts to improve literacy rates and education through English instruction, implemented Cree as the primary language of instruction for elementary grades and, to a certain extent, at the secondary level. It appears that, for the James Bay Cree and Innu, autonomy in education has enabled them to maintain their language among the younger generation, with the help of K-12 schooling. Outside of schooling, the Cree language continues to be spoken in the home and community.[56]

In Quebec, aboriginal languages are exempt from the implementation of Bill 101, the French Language Charter, which severely restricts education and services in languages other than French. Before this exemption, aboriginal peoples in Quebec, such as the Kahnawake Mohawk, had already begun to revive their language in opposition to having the French language imposed on them through legislation. In effect, Bill 101 was a catalyst for the establishment of Mohawk immersion programs and other community efforts to revive and preserve the Mohawk language.[57] In addition, as recent demographic and statistic data from the 1996 and 2001 Canada Census suggest, the Cree languages of Quebec (Attikamekw, Montagnais-Naskapi), along with Inuktitut, appear to be in an impressive state when compared to the state of similar languages outside Quebec.[58]

In at least a small effort to fund aboriginal language programs in British Columbia, in 1990 the Province of British Columbia passed the *First Peoples' Heritage, Language and Culture Act*[59] "based on the principle that Native People themselves should take the leadership role in preserving their culture and languages but that other sectors of society have responsibility to share in the costs of a cultural initiative that will benefit all British Columbians."[60] However, as of early 2006, the BC government has not provided secure funding for the foundation it created to implement the *Act*.

Despite these initiatives, the reality in Canada is that, in 2006, French and English were federally recognized as the "founding languages" of Canada, with the sixty or so languages that pre-existed the political creation of a country by speakers of English and French having no place in the past or present of this nation. The Task Force on Aboriginal Languages and Culture has questioned this status quo and has strongly recommended the creation of legislation that (1) recognizes aboriginal languages as the original languages of Canada and (2) is accompanied by a commitment to provide more resources to aboriginal language revitalization and preservation within communities. As TFALC notes, the legal recognition of French and English as "founding languages" and as national languages – to the detriment of aboriginal languages – has translated into enormous disparities in the provision of resources.[61] For example, the 2005 proposal of $5 million a year and the commitment of $160 million over ten years for First Nations, Inuit, and Métis languages is only a very small fraction of the funding provided to promote the French and English languages. French language funding over five years from eight different government departments totals $751.3 million. In Nunavut, French speakers receive $3,902 per capita in funding for language services and programs, whereas Inuit receive $44 per capita for similar programs and services.

Following legislation and policy proposed earlier by the AFN and the Confederation of First Nations Cultural Centres, TFALC proposed

> [t]hat Canada enacts legislation that recognizes, protects and promotes First Nation, Inuit and Métis languages as the First Languages of Canada. This legislation, to be developed in partnership with First Nation, Inuit and Métis peoples, must recognize the constitutional status of our languages; affirm their place as one of the foundations of First Nation, Inuit and Métis nationhood, provide financial resources for their preservation, re-vitalization, promotion and protection; and establish the position of First Nations, Inuit and Métis Language Commissioner.[62]

However, as previously argued, legislation can at best be an enabling factor that will provide the necessary prestige, recognition, and financial resources for the on-the-ground initiatives, language preservation, and revitalization programs requisite for *de facto* language renewal.

Some Pitfalls in Language Restoration

Having pointed to the importance and necessity of promoting and legalizing the role of indigenous languages within the policies and fabric of a nation-state, it is important to remind ourselves of some of the pitfalls of relying on government policy and legislation. In our introduction, we mentioned the difference between the symbolic and practical functions of languages. Attitudes towards a language operate at a different level than does actual use of a language, and a positive attitude about one's mother tongue or ancestral language alone does not translate into speaking the language in everyday life.[63] Successful language legislation for critically endangered languages must not only concern itself with planning to improve attitudes towards language but also with acquisition planning in order to create practical ways and incentives to restore use of language in everyday communication as well as in culturally and ceremonially important functions.

A second issue identified by language speakers/elders and language planners is the fact that producing second-language speakers of an indigenous language will not necessarily preserve it. The fate of Irish/Gaelic during the twentieth century, after it received legal recognition in the Republic of Ireland, is a case in point. While the Irish government focused its efforts on promoting Gaelic as a second language to be learned by Irish children in schools, it neglected to protect Gaelic in the Gaeltacht – areas in Western Ireland where Gaelic was still used and spoken, but where transmission was declining because of the increasing domination of English.

Language planners have repeatedly argued that the key to restoring a language is to restore its intergenerational mother tongue transmission.[64] For critically endangered languages that have no able speakers in the parent generation, the recreation of intergenerational mother tongue transmission is a difficult task. As initiatives in certain parts of the world have shown, early childhood to adult immersion projects can produce important milestones in revitalizing the language.[65] However, we will need to find out from future generations of second-language learners whether languages that are aggressively revitalized through long-term immersion will also be revitalized as home languages by graduates who become parents. Only time, or perhaps initiatives enabled by policy and driven by communities that encourage such home efforts, will tell.

One might argue that "banking," or archiving, indigenous language knowledge will suffice to keep that knowledge intact and make it available to future generations. However, as elders in the case studies and other speakers often note, archiving a language, as opposed to keeping it alive among present and future generations, does not amount to breathing new and ongoing life into it. The archived written or audio/video-recorded speech of the last speakers of a language is but a pale impression of what a living language represents. Leanne Hinton has observed that a language "preserved" and stored only in archives rather than in the minds and words of speakers is like "pickled" produce as opposed to tasty and fragrant fresh produce.[66]

Protection of Linguistic Knowledge

In light of the objectives of the research program of which this volume forms a part, we also must ask: How can aboriginal groups protect the knowledge expressed in their language? This question leads to issues of copyright over linguistic materials in printed form and multimedia form, and to issues involving the intellectual property right over knowledge as produced through research.[67] Of particular interest to aboriginal groups are the products of academic and applied linguistic research, including orthographies of the language. In other words, who controls the alphabet? Who owns the fonts? Who controls access to language information?

Numerous language communities, sometimes anecdotally and sometimes with detailed documentation, have complained about the "linguistic theft" of elements of language knowledge from their elders. This is when outsider researchers copyright the products of language knowledge, be it in dictionaries compiled from the words and knowledge of speakers of the language or from stories recorded from the last speakers and storytellers. Whether such violations of copyright (*i.e.*, the right to copy these products) are real or imputed, they must be understood as part of the wider issue of outsiders' appropriation and use of indigenous groups' linguistic and cultural knowledge. These violations must be understood in light of the imbalance of power and resources that aboriginal groups face *vis-à-vis* the exploitation of their tangible and intangible cultural heritage by members of the dominant society. The fact remains, as demonstrated by case studies in this volume, that on the ground level an aboriginal language group usually has few resources, let alone legal protection, to deal with such issues.[68]

From the point of view of the *de facto* protection of languages, there is another issue. Nora Marks Dauenhauer and Richard Dauenhauer discuss copyright and intellectual property rights among southeastern Alaskan aboriginal languages whose speech communities have strong traditions of tangible and intangible property and who express group *rights* to property. Sharing is important for language preservation: "Ownership is only half the traditional equation; the other half is stewardship and transmission to the next generation and to the grandchildren ... We appreciate the fear of desecration, but we believe that the risks of sharing information are less dangerous at the present time than the risk that it may otherwise be lost forever."[69]

While issues of "linguistic theft" have vexed the consciousness of aboriginal groups, especially given the little recourse that is available, it has had another significant impact. In many instances, elderly speakers of critically endangered languages, along with some younger people, have become increasingly reluctant to share knowledge, even within their own speech communities. The notion is that, if linguistic and cultural knowledge is kept private, it cannot be appropriated by outsiders. However, such measures often prevent individuals who want to learn their language from having access to linguistic knowledge (stories, songs, written materials, and curricula). Examples of this are, within some communities, the existence of organizations that have exclusive ownership of all publications in the language and the existence of one group that has exclusive ownership of the computerized fonts through which learners and speakers can write the language. In other cases, there has been unease among speech communities and their members, or dialects, regarding who controls the authority over the language in its printed or performed form.[70]

How might the intellectual property rights of a speech community be made compatible with the production of language materials from within, or by, a large organization? An example is FirstVoices, a project launched by the First Nations Language, Culture and Heritage Council of British Columbia. The project's objective is to assist First Nations groups to archive their languages and to make linguistic knowledge available to members of their speech communities (or, with discretion, to outsiders) through the Internet. In designing its Web-based multimedia dictionaries for aboriginal languages, FirstVoices implemented community contracts that gave First Nations communities the opportunity to designate a First Nations organization, as represented by a password holder, as the steward of the language. It has also, through the use of passwords, provided the possibility for communities to choose either to limit uploaded materials to exclusive use by members of the speech community or to make them accessible to wider audiences. Currently, FirstVoices is working with some thirty language groups in British Columbia and Yukon, less than half of whom have sanctioned public access to their language.[71]

The Intellectual Appropriation of Language: Teaching Methods and Curricula

We wish to raise a final point that is often overlooked by those interested in intellectual property rights issues as they affect languages. Nonetheless, it is an issue of significant concern to the knowledge, wisdom, and cultural expression contained in languages. If, as we show below, indigenous languages are subjected to various pressures involving a "colonization of consciousness," the very integrity of the worldview contained in the languages is at stake.[72] Appropriate curricula must be created to avoid this consequence.

In the 1970s, when aboriginal languages were first taught in schools in Canada (and in the United States and other countries dominated by Western/European pedagogies), the content was heavily influenced by the curriculum used for teaching primary grades in English/French and other Western European languages. In other words, aboriginal language teachers were coached to teach abstract numbers (which, in the North American/European curriculum teach essential intellectual skills such as sequencing), colours (which teach discrimination and comparison), and noun objects (like animals, which teach visual discrimination and comparison). In aboriginal languages, which often have multiple number systems that count objects according to their shape or animate nature, and in which abstract colour terms are rarely used without reference to things, Indo-European noun-verb distinctions often do not apply. Such categories, to the dismay of elders/speakers, distorted aboriginal languages and were taught with a great deal of unease. However, with time, this approach to language became internalized as cultural knowledge, even though twenty or thirty years earlier, the first generation of fluent-speaker language teachers struggled to find the requisite number and range of abstract colour terms in their languages and/or had to remind one another to count in abstract numbers. Essential linguistic skills in particular aboriginal languages, like using intricate systems of lexical classifiers or suffixes to indicate the kind, shape, or class of objects or actions, have rarely entered the curriculum. Thus, the intellectual wealth of aboriginal languages, demonstrated in this volume, rarely becomes the focus of aboriginal language curriculum in second-language instruction. A language's unique ways of organizing experience through complex grammatical structures like deixis, evidentials, verbal affixation, and lexical categories often disappears into the themes and content translated from the categories used by the dominant language. Some thirty years after this curricular appropriation, many aboriginal language teachers (who often function in a context in which they are symbolically and materially dominated by a "public" education system run by "trained" teachers and administrators) still struggle to be true to their languages as they devise curricula.

Likewise, teaching methodologies borrowed from teaching English as a Second Language (ESL) often force categories of Western/European thinking on aboriginal languages. Thus, language teachers often find themselves borrowing modules and templates derived from ESL, which then have to be "fit" into the categories of thinking, grammar, and lexicon of their own languages. Teaching methodology often relies on English templates that are often suggested through professional development. An example is total physical response (TPR) teaching, a methodology that was once enthusiastically embraced by indigenous language teachers but that has significant cultural and linguistic shortcomings when applied to specific aboriginal languages. TPR relies on the teaching of commands, which are then carried out as actions by the learners in order for learners to internalize what is said.[73] While "user friendly" and non-stressful, the protocols of interaction among aboriginal language speakers (and learners), which in at least some cultural contexts focus on personal autonomy and non-interference, do not always lend themselves to imperatives. Moreover, linguistic forms taught through TPR commands have a certain purpose in ESL as the English imperative also represents most verb forms. Many aboriginal languages, however, have far more complex ways of expressing action through verbs, which include marking singular and plural action in the verb root itself, transivity and ergativity, the nature of evidence and control over the action on the part of the actor, and so on. In other words, the structural complexities of an aboriginal language are rarely represented in TPR instruction modules and require tremendous adaptation. If simply transferred into the aboriginal language, they result in distortion.

Finally, the imposition of English (or French) language knowledge onto aboriginal language does not rest here. An additional way in which indigenous language, knowledge, and wisdom is compromised involves the increasing tendency by First Nations organizations to translate the agreements they enter into with provincial or federal bodies into an aboriginal language. Portions of contractual agreements, treaties, and resource-sharing and resource stewardship agreements are translated into the aboriginal language once they have been conceptualized and developed in English by aboriginal and non-aboriginal policy advisors and bureaucrats. Here, again, we are alerted to the symbolic function of language. This translation is merely an after-thought to the intents and purposes of the English language text and serves to legitimize the existence of the aboriginal group rather than its knowledge and ways of thinking and being. As Frank Weasel Head and many other aboriginal language speakers and elders have suggested, such documents should be developed first and foremost by paying attention to the protocols and the ways of thinking, speaking, and existing that are expressed in aboriginal language traditions.[74] However, this rarely happens on the ground, especially when only a handful of elders know and speak the language and, in any case, are usually absent from the tables where political decisions are made or policy documents drafted.

In the end, we see aboriginal language revitalization efforts handicapped, ironically, by the "colonization of consciousness" that derives from well-intentioned efforts in which the dominant society imposes its categories of meaning and practices of speech on the way aboriginal languages are taught. Repossessing autonomy over our languages means we must become conscious of these pitfalls. It also means that breathing new life into aboriginal languages can only be achieved by putting our languages to work as living artifacts in our own communities without uncritically surrendering to external methodologies and ways of teaching them. We are hopeful that future legislation, as recommended by the recent Task Force on Aboriginal Languages and Cultures, will do its part to enable and support this difficult task. The work is up to us.

Acknowledgments

The authors gratefully acknowledge the research assistance of Michael Sinclair. We would also like to thank and acknowledge the many elders and aboriginal language teachers in First Nations communities who have shared their knowledge with us.

Notes

1 See Statistics Canada, *2001 Census: Analysis Series, Aboriginal Peoples of Canada – A Demographic Profile* (Ottawa: Minister of Industry, 2003) at 9, online: <http://www.12.statcan.ca/english/census01/products/analytic/companion/abor/pdf/96F0030XIE2001007.pdf>; Statistics Canada, "Aboriginal Peoples Survey 2001 Initial Findings: Well-being of the Non-Reserve Aboriginal Population" (Ottawa: Minister of Industry, 2003) at 29, online: <http://www.statcan.ca/cgi-bin/sownpub/freepub.cgi?subject=3867#3867>.

2 Lynn Drapeau, "Perspectives on Aboriginal Language Conservation and Revitalization in Canada," CD-ROM: *For Seven Generations: An Information Legacy of the Royal Commission on Aboriginal Peoples* (Ottawa: Libraxus, 1997). As Drapeau points out, while the practical function of a language as a tool of communication may be severely eroded, its symbolic function of expressing group identity and cultural connection may well continue on. Drapeau alerts us to the fact that, while the use of a language may be severely eroded, the members of the speech community may well continue to view their language as important. In short, attitudes about a language often operate at a different level than does the actual use of the language. See also Marianne Ignace and Ron Ignace, "The Old Wolf in Sheep's Clothing? Canadian Aboriginal Peoples and Multiculturalism" in Dieter Haselbach, ed., *Multiculturalism in a World of Leaking Boundaries* (Munster: Lit Verlag, 1998) 57; and Nora M. Dauenhauer and Richard Dauenhauer, "Technical, Emotional, and Ideological Issues in Reversing Language Shift: Examples from Southeast Alaska" in Lenore A. Grenoble and Lindsay J. Whaley, eds., *Endangered Languages* (Cambridge: Cambridge University Press, 1998) 57.

3 See Dale M. Kinkade, "The Decline of Modern Languages" in Robert H. Robins and Eugenius M. Uhlenbeck, eds., *Endangered Languages* (Oxford: Berg Publishers, 2001) 157; Eung-do Cook, "Amerindian Languages of Canada" in William O'Grady and Michael Dobrovolsky, eds., *Contemporary Linguistic Analysis: An Introduction* (Toronto: Copp Clark Pitman, 1987) 259; Michael Foster, "Canada's Indigenous Languages: Past and Present" (1982) 7 Language and Society 3.

4 See the following pamphlets produced by the AFN: Mark Fettes, *A Guide to Language Strategies for First Nations Communities* (Ottawa: AFN Language and Literacy Secretariat, December 1992); *Towards Rebirth of First Nations Languages* (Ottawa: AFN and Literacy Secretariat, 1992); and Ruth Norton *et al., A Time to Listen and the Time to Act: National First Nations Language Strategy* (Ottawa: AFN, 2000).

5 See Federation of Saskatchewan Indian Nations (FSIN), *Aboriginal Language Survey* (Saskatoon: FSIN, 1998) [unpublished]; Assembly of Manitoba Chiefs Committee on Education, *The Manitoba First Nations Languages Survey: A Report* (Winnipeg: Manitoba First Nations Education Resource Centre, 1999); Dixon Taylor, *British Columbia First Nations Language Survey* (Victoria: First Peoples' Culture, Heritage and Language Foundation, 2003); Northwest Territories Ministry of Education, Culture and Employment, *Revitalizing, Enhancing and Promoting Aboriginal Languages Draft Report* (2000) [unpublished] [Northwest Territories Draft Report]; and Government of Yukon, *We Are Our Language: Sharing the Gift of Language – Profile of Yukon First Nation Languages* (Whitehorse: Aboriginal Language Services, 2004).

6 Mary Jane Norris has carried out several excellent analyses of the current state of Canadian aboriginal languages using macro-data from the Canadian census and post-censal survey data.They show the powers, and some limitations, of statistical data analysis for throwing light on the state of languages. Interestingly, they point to the strength of indigenous languages in Quebec as opposed to much of the rest of the country, an important issue in light of language legislation and policy. See Mary J. Norris and Lorna Jantzen, "Aboriginal Languages in Canada's Urban Areas: Characteristics, Considerations and Implications" in David Newhouse and Evelyn Peters, eds., *Not Strangers in These Parts: Urban Aboriginal Peoples* (Ottawa: Policy Research Initiative, 2003); Mary J. Norris, "Canada's Aboriginal Languages" (Winter 1998) Canadian Social Trends 8; Mary J. Norris, *The Diversity of Aboriginal Languages in Canada: Patterns and Trends* (Ottawa: Department of Canadian Heritage Aboriginal Affairs Branch, 2004), online <http://www.pch.gc.ca/pc-ch/pubs/diversity2003/Norris_e.cfm>; Mary J. Norris, "From Generation to Generation: Survival and Maintenance of Canada's Aboriginal Languages within Families, Communities and Cities" in Joe Blythe and McKenna Brown, eds., *Maintaining the Links: Language, Identity and the Land – Proceedings of the Seventh Conference of the Foundation for Endangered Languages,* 11-24 September 2003, Broome, Western Australia. See online: <http://www.ogmios.org>.

7 Daniel Nettle and Suzanne Romaine, *Vanishing Voices: The Extinction of the World's Languages* (Oxford: Oxford University Press, 1999); see also Marianne Ignace, *Backgrounder Document for Taskforce on Aboriginal Languages and Cultures* (2005) [unpublished, prepared for the Government of Canada, Department of Canadian Heritage].

8 See AFN, *Towards Linguistic Justice for First Nations* (Ottawa: AFN Language and Literacy Secretariat, 1990); and AFN "Rebirth," *supra* note 4.

9 Marianne Ignace, *Language Curriculum Framework Assessment* (report prepared for Secwepemc Cultural Education Society and School District no. 24, Kamloops, British Columbia, September 1995) [unpublished]. See also Nathan Matthew, *Secwepemc Language Nest Immersion Project* (report prepared for the Secwepemc Cultural Education Society, Kamloops, British Columbia, May 1999) [unpublished].

10 For a discussion of this and other examples, see Marianne Ignace and Ron Ignace, "*Secwepemc* Language Acquisition in the Home: Sharing the Experience" (Paper presented to Stabilizing Indigenous Languages Symposium, Victoria, British Columbia, June 2005) [unpublished]; Sandra I. Lai and Marianne Ignace, "A Preliminary Analysis of *Sepwepemc* Language Acquisition by a Young Child" in *Proceedings of the 33rd International Conference on Salish and Neighbouring Languages* (Seattle: University of Washington Press, August 2000).

11 See *e.g.* Brian Noble, in consultation with Reg Crowshoe and in discussion with the Knut-sum-atak Society, "*Poomaksin*: Skinnipiikani-Nitsiitapii Law, Transfers, and Making Relatives: Practices and Principles for Cultural Protection, Repatriation, Redress, and Heritage Law Making with Canada, this volume at 268-69; Catherine Bell *et al.* in consultation with Andrea Sanborn, the U'mista Cultural Society, and the 'Namgis Nation, "Recovering from Colonization: Perspectives of Community Members on Protection and Repatriation of Kwakwaka'wakw Cultural Heritage," this volume at 45-46; and Catherine Bell *et al.*, "Repatriation and Heritage Protection: Reflections on the Kainai Experience," this volume at 247.

12 Task Force on Aboriginal Languages and Cultures (TFALC), *Towards a New Beginning: A Foundational Report for a Strategy to Revitalize First Nation, Inuit and Metis Languages and Cultures* (Report to the Minister of Canadian Heritage, 2005) at 3 (Chair: Ron Ignace) [unpublished]. While Ron Ignace was the chair of the task force, the opinions reflected in this chapter are those of the authors and not the TFALC. The limits of legislated solutions are discussed later in this chapter. For a critical assessment of the limited impact of legislation on endangered languages, see Suzanne Romaine, "The Impact of Language Policy on Endangered Languages" (2002) 4:2 International Journal on Multicultural Societies (UNESCO) 197.

13 Paraphrased by Akira Yamamoto from a Navajo elder's words, PBS-TV Millennium Series, *Tribal Wisdom and the Modern World*, hosted by David Maybury-Lewis, aired on 24 May 1992, in UNESCO *infra* note 39.

14 Joshua Fishman, "What Do You Lose When You Lose Your Language?" in Gina Cantoni,

ed., *Stabilizing Indigenous Languages* (Flagstaff, AZ: Northern Arizona University, 1996) 80 at 81.

15 Bell *et al.*, "Recovering from Colonization," *supra* note 11 at 43.

16 Noble, *"Poomaksin," supra* note 11 at 273.

17 AFN, *Rebirth, supra* note 4 at 14.

18 Canada, *Report of the Royal Commission on Aboriginal Peoples: Gathering Strength, (RCAP)*, vol. 3 (Ottawa: Supply and Services Canada, 1996) at 602.

19 Government of Yukon, supra note 5.

20 Edward Sapir, *Language: An Introduction to the Study of Speech* (New York: Harcourt, Brace and World, 1921) at 220.

21 Cited in Mark Abley, *Spoken Here: Travels among Threatened Languages* (Toronto: Random House of Canada, 2003) at 126.

22 Marianne Mithun, "The Significance of Diversity in Language Endangerment and Preservation" in Lenore A. Grenoble and Lindsay J. Whaley, eds., *Endangered Languages* (Cambridge: Cambridge University Press, 1998) at 189.

23 While speakers of indigenous languages have consistently pointed out the connection between linguistic expression and culture, the "Sapir-Whorf hypothesis," which addresses the interconnection of thought, language, and reality, has alternately intrigued some linguists and been shrugged off as empirically unverifiable by others. Recently, however, it received renewed attention. See John J. Gumperz and Stephen C. Levinson, eds., *Rethinking Linguistic Relativity* (Cambridge: Cambridge University Press, 1996).

24 From John Swanton, "The Haida Indian Language" in Franz Boas, ed., *Handbook of North American Indian Languages* (Washington, DC: Bureau of American Ethnology, 1911) 233.

25 Jeff Leer, "Introduction" in Erman Lawrence, *Haida Dictionary* (Fairbanks: The Alaska Native Language Centre, University of Alaska, 1977) at 58. For a recent comprehensive, but technical, linguistic work on the Haida language, see John Enrico, *Haida Syntax* (Omaha: University of Nebraska Press, 2004).

26 Of course, aboriginal languages also organize experience differently from Indo-European languages in terms of the lexical categories, or words, they employ. For examples, see Leanne Hinton, *Flutes of Fire: Essays on Californian Indian Languages* (Berkeley: Heydey Books, 1994); and Nettle and Romaine, *supra* note 7 at 72-77.

27 On language diversity and the intellectual capacity of humankind, see *e.g.* Ken Hale *et al.* "Endangered Languages" (1992) 68 Language 1; Ken Hale, "On Endangered Languages and the Importance of Linguistic Diversity" in Grenoble and Whaley, *supra* note 2 at 32; and David Crystal, *Language Death* (Cambridge: Cambridge University Press, 2000) at 32-67. For detailed discussions about the connection between biodiversity of species and the intellectual "biodiversity" of languages, see Luisa Maffi, ed., *On Biocultural Diversity: Linking Language, Knowledge and the Environment* (Washington: Smithsonian Institution Press, 1999).

28 Ofelia Zepeda and Jane H. Hill, "The Condition of Native American Languages in the United States" in Robert H. Robins and Eugenius M. Uhlenbeck, eds., *Endangered Languages* (Oxford: Berg, 1991) 135 at 135.

29 Christopher Jocks, "Living Words and Cartoon Translations: Longhouse 'Texts' and the Limitations of English" in Grenoble and Whaley, *supra* note 2, at 217, 232-33 [emphasis added].

30 *Ibid.* at 35.

31 *Ibid.* at 36.

32 Crystal, *supra* note 27 at 53.

33 *Universal Declaration of Human Rights*, GA Res. 217(III), UN GAOR, 3d Sess., Supp. No. 13, UN Doc. A/810 (1948) 71.

34 *International Covenant on Civil and Political Rights,* 19 December 1966, 999 U.N.T.S. 171, arts. 9-14, Can. T.S. 1976 No. 47, 6 I.L.M. 368 (entered into force 23 March 1976, accession by Canada 19 May 1976).

35 *Declaration on the Rights of Persons Belonging to National or Ethnic, Religious and Linguistic Minorities*, GA Res. 47/135, UN GAOR, 47th Sess., Supp. No. 49, UN Doc. A/47/49 (1993) [emphasis added].

36 *International Covenant on Civil and Political Rights*, *supra* note 34, art. 27.

37 *Convention (No. 169) concerning Indigenous and Tribal Peoples in Independent Countries*, 27 June 1989, 72 I.L.O. Official Bull. 59, 28 I.L.M. 1382.
38 *Convention on the Rights of the Child*, 20 November 1989, Can. T.S. 1992 No. 3, 1577 U.N.T.S. 3.
39 UNESCO, "Education in a Multilingual World," online: <http://unesdoc.unesco.org/education>.
40 *Draft Declaration on the Rights of Indigenous Peoples*, 28 October 1994, 34 I.L.M. 541. This language is now included in the recently adopted Article 13 of the *United Nations Declaration on the Rights of Indigenous Peoples,* GA Res. 295, UNGAOR, 61st Sess., UN Doc. A/RES/61/295 (2007). Article 13 adds, "states shall take effective measures to ensure this right is protected and also to ensure indigenous peoples can understand and be understood in political, legal, and administrative proceedings, where necessary through the provision of interpretation or by other appropriate means."
41 Desmond Fennel, "Can a Shrinking Language Minority Be Saved? Lessons from the Irish Experience" in Einer Haugen, J. Derrick McLure, and Derick Thomson, eds., *Minority Languages Today: A Selection from the Papers Read at the First International Conference on Minority Languages Held at Glasgow University from 8 to 13 September 1980* (Edinburgh: Edinburgh University Press, 1981) 32 at 39.
42 Romaine, *supra* note 12 at 203.
43 *Native American Languages Act*, Pub. L. No. 101-477, s. 102, 104 Stat. 1153 at 1167 (1990).
44 Romaine, *supra* note 12 at 210.
45 See Serafin M. Coronel-Molina, "Functional Domains of the Quechua Language in Peru: Issues of Status Planning" International Journal of Bilingual Education and Bilingualism (1999) 2:3 at 166-80; see also Nancy Hornberger, *Bilingual Education and Language Maintenance: A Southern Peruvian Quechua Case* (Providence: Dordecht-Holland, 1988). Article 48 of the Peruvian Constitution states, "son idiomas oficiales el castellano, y en las zonas donde predominen, tambien lo son el quechua, el aimara y las dem s lenguas aboriginas, segun la ley" (the official languages [of Peru] are Spanish, and in the areas where they dominate, also Quechua, Aymara and the other aboriginal languages, according to the law). Article 3 of the Constitution prohibits discrimination on the basis of language, among other things. The Constitution of the Republic of Peru is available online: <http://pdba.georgetown.edu/Constitutions/Peru/per93.html>.
46 See Romaine, *supra* note 12 at 203-4 for a discussion of this problematic aspect of the *European Charter for Regional or Minority Languages*. By definition, languages included in the charter are those with a European cultural tradition, which have a territorial base and which can be distinguished as separate languages. Excluded are recent immigrant languages from outside.
47 Reprinted as Schedule 1 of the *Treaty of Waitangi Act 1975* (N.Z.), 1975/114, 33 RS 907.
48 *Official Languages Act*, R.S.C. 1985, (4th Supp.), c. 31.
49 *Official Languages Act*, R.S.N.W.T. 1988, c. O-1.
50 Freda Ahenakew, Brenda Gardipy, and Barbara Lafond, eds., *Voices of the First Nations* (Toronto: McGraw-Hill Ryerson, 1995); see also Northwest Territories, Draft Report, *supra* note 5.
51 *Supra* note 5.
52 *Constitution Act, 1982,* being Schedule B to the *Canada Act 1982* (U.K.), 1982, c. 11.
53 *R. v. Sparrow*, [1990] 1 S.C.R. 1075, 70 D.L.R. (4th) 385.
54 *Canadian Charter of Rights and Freedoms*, Part I of the *Constitution Act, 1982*, being Schedule B to the *Canada Act 1982* (U.K.), 1982, c. 11.
55 James Bay and Northern Quebec Agreement, ss. 16, 17 in the *James Bay and Northern Quebec Native Claims Settlement Act 1976-77*, c. 32; Northeastern Quebec Agreement, s. 11 in *An Act approving the Northeastern Québec Agreement,* R.S.Q., c. C-67.1.
56 See Barbara Burnaby, *et al.*, "Native Language for Every Subject: The Cree Language of Instruction Project" in Jon Reyhner, Gina Cantoni, and Robert N. St. Clair *et al.*, eds., *Revitalizing Indigenous Languages* (Flagstaff: Northern Arizona University, 1999).
57 See Michael Hoover, "The Revival of the Mohawk Language in Kahnawake" (1992) 21:2 Canadian Journal of Native Studies 269.
58 Statistics Canada, *supra* note 1; for further discussion, see Norris, *Diversity, supra* note 6;

and Ignace, *supra* note 7.

59 *First Peoples' Heritage, Language and Culture Act*, R.S.B.C. 1996, c. 147.

60 British Columbia, Legislative Assembly, *Official Report of Debates (Hansard)*, (30 May 1990) at 9928 (Hon. Weisgerber), online: <http://www.leg.bc.ca/hansard/34th4th/34p._04s_900530p.htm#09947>.

61 Task Force, *supra* note 12 at 86.

62 *Ibid.* at 79.

63 See *e.g.* Ignace and Ignace, *supra* note 2; and Drapeau, *supra* note 2.

64 See *e.g.* Joshua A. Fishman, "Bilingualism with and without Diglossia: Diglossia with and without Bilingualism" (1967) 46:2 Journal of Social Issues 28; Joshua A. Fishman, *Reversing Language Shift: Theoretical and Empirical Foundations of Assistance to Threatened Languages* (Clevedon, UK: Multilingual Matters, 1991); Joshua A. Fishman, "What Do You Lose When You Lose Your Language?" in Reyner *et al.*, *supra* note 56. Leanne Hinton and Ken Hale, eds., *The Green Book of Language Revitalization in Practice* (San Diego: Academic Press, 2001); and Crystal, *supra* note 27.

65 The examples most often cited in the literature on language revitalization are the Maori language immersion schools, including Te Kahanga Reo (language nests), followed by school immersion programs (Kura Kaupapa). See *e.g.* Jeanette King, "Te Kohanga Reo: Maori Language Revitalisation" in Leanne Hinton and Ken Hale, eds., *ibid.* at 119-28; Augie Fleras, "Redefining the Politics over Aboriginal Language Renewal: Maori Language Preschools as Agents of Social Change" (1987) Canadian Journal of Native Studies 1; Augie Fleras, "Te Kohanga Reo: A Maori Renewal Program in New Zealand" (1989) 16:2 Canadian Journal of Native Education 78. And for more cautious assessments, see Richard A. Benton, *The Maori Language: Dying or Reviving? A Working Paper Prepared for the East-West Center Alumni-in-Residence Working Papers Series* (Honolulu: East West Centre Association, 1991).

66 Hinton and Hale, *supra* note 64 at 12.

67 Intellectual property law questions are explored in further detail in the second volume of this research. See Catherine Bell and Robert K. Paterson, eds., *Protection of First Nations Cultural Heritage: Laws, Policy, and Reform* (Vancouver: UBC Press, 2008).

68 See *e.g.* concerns relayed by participants in community case studies in this volume in Catherine Bell *et al.*, "Recovering from Colonization," *supra* note 11; Catherine Bell *et al.*, "Protection and Repatriation of Ktunaxa/Kinbasket Cultural Resources: Perspectives of Community Members" at 328-32.

69 Dauenhauer and Dauenhauer, *supra* note 2 at 91-92.

70 In British Columbia, some of these issues were brought to the forefront by a BC College of Teachers bylaw – created in the early 1990s with the input of First Nations advisors – to implement a teaching certificate for First Nations language and culture teachers that would be issued by a "First Nations Language Authority," which, in turn, would sanction an applicant as a "proficient speaker" of the language. Aboriginal groups themselves, sometimes according to linguistic divisions or dialect divisions, needed to constitute themselves as First Nations Language Authorities, with each setting their own standards for "proficiency."

71 Personal communication with Peter Brand, FirstVoices Coordinator, First Peoples' Cultural Foundation, Victoria (June 2005). For the FirstVoices website, see online: <http://www.firstvoices.ca>.

72 This term is borrowed from John and Jean Comaroff, "The Colonization of Consciousness" in Michael Lambek, ed., *A Reader in Anthropology of Religion* (Malden, MA: Blackwell Publishers, 2002), which gives examples of changes in the mode of thinking, lexicon, and functions of the Tswana language in Southern Africa upon the arrival of missionaries and other colonial agents.

73 See James Asher, "The Total Physical Response Approach to Second Language Learning" (1969) 53 Modern Language Journal 3; Stephen D. Krashen, *Second Language Acquisition and Second Language Learning* (Oxford: Pergamon, 1981).

74 Bell *et al.*, "Repatriation and Heritage Protection," *supra* note 11 at 233-34.

10

Canada's Policy of Cultural Colonization: Indian Residential Schools and the *Indian Act*

Dale Cunningham, Allyson Jeffs, and Michael Solowan

Although at the time of its implementation many officials considered Canada's Indian policy to be inevitable and even benevolent, it is no secret what the Government of Canada originally intended for the first inhabitants of this country. In 1895, a solution to the "Indian problem" was presented to the Canadian Parliament:

> If it were possible to gather in all the Indian children and retain them for a certain period, there would be produced a generation of English speaking Indians accustomed to the ways of civilized life, which might then be the dominant body among themselves, capable of holding its own with its white neighbors; and thus would be brought about rapidly decreasing expenditure until the same should forever cease, and the Indian problem would be solved.[1]

One hundred years later, on behalf of the Government of Canada, federal cabinet ministers Jane Stewart and Ralph Goodale apologized to aboriginal peoples:

> Sadly, our history with respect to the treatment of Aboriginal people is not something in which we can take pride. Attitudes of racial and cultural superiority led to a suppression of Aboriginal culture and values. As a country, we are burdened by past actions that resulted in weakening the identity of Aboriginal peoples, suppressing their languages and cultures, and outlawing spiritual practices. We must recognize the impact of these actions on the once self-sustaining nations that were disaggregated, disrupted, limited or even destroyed by the dispossession of traditional territory, by the relocation of Aboriginal people, and by some provisions of the *Indian Act*. We must acknowledge that the result of these actions was the erosion of the political, economic and social systems of Aboriginal people and nations ...

> One aspect of our relationship with Aboriginal people over this period that requires particular attention is the Residential School System. This system separated many children from their families and communities and prevented them from speaking their own languages and from learning about their heritage and cultures.[2]

These excerpts serve as bookends for a period of Canadian history during which the federal government sustained an assault on the integrity of First Nations culture.

Our intention in this chapter is to address how the erosion of First Nations culture was fuelled by official government policy and how the establishment of a residential school system was key to this. Although implicit in any discussion of continuity and revival of First Nations culture, the corrosive effect of the residential schools and other assimilationist policies on First Nations cultural knowledge is explicitly raised in many of the case studies in this volume. For many participants it was important that we provide greater detail on federal law and policy, elaborate upon the relationship between assimilationist policy and cultural loss, and comment on strategies that may address the harm done. To this end, we consider (1) the historical origins of the Indian residential school system (IRS), (2) the IRS and *Indian Act* cultural prohibitions, (3) the impact of the IRS and the *Indian Act* on First Nations language and culture, and (4) legal and other options for redress for harm done to First Nations language and culture. We conclude by looking at some theoretical concerns.

Historical Origins of the IRS System

From Church to Government Control

The seeds of the Canadian IRS system were first sown in the seventeenth century by Roman Catholic missionaries and later by other Christian denominations as they sought to evangelize and Christianize aboriginal peoples.[3] The first boarding schools were established in what is now central Canada. However, by the early nineteenth century, missions and boarding schools were established on the western Prairies, beginning in 1820 with Anglican minister John West's foray to the Red River.[4] With the signing of the seven numbered treaties in the 1870s, Canada was expected to fulfill obligations to educate aboriginal peoples.[5] The missionaries had been involved in the negotiations, and government promises "gave the churches a lever" to push for money that might assist or expand religious-based instruction.[6] In anticipation of increased settlement by Europeans, Canada and the churches were prepared to collaborate in the education and, it was anticipated, the eventual assimilation of aboriginal people.[7]

When the residential school system was at its peak, there were eighty institutions operating across the country: forty-four Roman Catholic, twenty-one Church of England (Anglican), thirteen United Church, and two Presbyterian.[8] Throughout much of their long history, statutory authority for the residential schools tended to be broad, permissive, and reactive.[9] This was especially true during the early years when the system was expanding. Consistent with this trend are early indications that the government was attempting to delegate responsibility for day-to-day operations to the churches.

The growth and development of the federal Indian bureaucracy closely parallels the expansion of the IRS system. The Imperial Indian Department, established in 1755, was a "branch of the military," and its goals were directed towards establishing and maintaining "the commercial and military alliances with tribal nations upon which the welfare of British North America depended."[10] However through the mid-nineteenth century and into the post-Confederation era, officials adopted a more paternalistic stance. The prevailing view came to be that Indians would need government assistance "through education and every other means" to prepare them "for a higher civilization."[11] These values were eventually crystallized in the *Indian Act* of 1876, which established the first modern version of the Department of Indian Affairs (DIA).[12] The cabinet minister heading it was referred to as the superintendent general of Indian affairs. However, in practice, this official also controlled a more "politically significant" portfolio, leaving the day-to-day running of the department in the hands of the senior bureaucrat, the deputy superintendent general.[13]

During its formative years, the DIA developed an inward-looking orientation. Because the people it was responsible for were not enfranchised and their well-being did not generate widespread interest among the non-aboriginal public, senior officials in the department did not think that they needed to develop external allies.[14] This state of affairs also allowed the DIA to pursue policies that, with rare exceptions, were unlikely to be scrutinized and that had no mechanisms by which they would be rendered accountable to the aboriginal people whom they were intended to benefit.[15]

Evolution of State "Indian Policy": The "Civilization" of Aboriginal People

In British North America of the 1600s and 1700s, British imperial Indian policy focused on maintaining military alliances and trade relations with aboriginal peoples, which, in practice, meant "seeking aid or neutrality from Aboriginals in war, and their friendship in peace."[16] Nonetheless, the British Crown's colonialist intentions found their way into legislation as early as 1670, when the British Parliament conferred responsibility for aboriginal relations upon the colonial governors: "As you are to consider how the Indians and slaves may be best instructed and invited to the Christian religion, it being both for the honour of the Crown and of the Protestant religion itself, that all persons within any of our territories, though never so remote, should be taught the knowledge of God and be made acquainted with the mysteries of salvation."[17] While Confederation and the passage of the first *Indian Act* was still over two hundred years away, the state's policy of civilization through religious conversion was firmly established.

The 1800s saw a steady influx of settlers encroach on aboriginal territories. The stabilization of the military situation in North America led to the declining importance of aboriginal peoples as allies in war, and they came to be viewed "less as warriors or potential warriors and increasingly as a barrier to progress, or even as a nuisance."[18] In practice, this meant that the Crown no longer dealt with aboriginal peoples as though they were distinctive peoples or sovereign nations, as was the case in earlier efforts to protect Indian lands.[19] By 1830, the nature of relations between aboriginal peoples and the evolving Canadian state had fundamentally changed, and, when the "Indian" department was transferred from military to civilian control, it became clear that the mission was now to "civilize" aboriginal people. As F.G. Stanley explains:

> It was the civil authorities who talked about helping the Indian to adjust to the changing world in which he was living, of educating Indian children, of saving the native peoples from ethnic extinction by helping them survive in what was becoming a white man's world. In brief, their motivation was honest and well-intentioned; their means, cultural assimilation.
>
> Social Darwinists argued, therefore, that the Indians must be helped to adjust themselves to their inevitable fate; they would have to adapt themselves to the white man's economy by learning to live and think like white men. The school teacher, the missionary, the farm instructor would make the Indians of Canada into dark-skinned white men.[20]

What followed were a series of legislative measures whose explicit aim was the creation of these "dark-skinned white men."

Instruments of "Civilization": Indian Residential Schools and the *Indian Act*

Pre-1867

The 1844 Bagot Commission of Inquiry report provided the impetus for developing social engineering policies intended for the "benefit of the Indians."[21] The commission considered evidence given by missionaries, Indian agents, and superintendents – people associated with aboriginal people. However, aboriginal people were never consulted, a state of affairs that continued until the 1845-47 meetings of the Joint Committee of the Senate and House of Commons. In testimony before the Bagot Commission,

Assistant Superintendent J.W. Keating described what would come to define Indian policy in Canada:

> Most men are also closely attached to habits and institutions of their forefathers, and have a natural and almost praiseworthy aversion to change them, and these medicine men are the real barrier to improvement. Educating the children, and placing them among already settled and civilized Indians, who pay regular attention to farming, would be the readiest mode of bringing the heathens to the right way.[22]

A number of policy principles are discernable: (1) the subversion of the authority of elders and medicine men; (2) the accomplishment of (1) through education, whose purpose is to replace traditional values with European values; (3) the use of farming to establish a pattern of settled life; and (4) the "civilization" of the "heathens" through Christian conversion. While missionaries in Canada had long used education as a tool of assimilation, in 1846, with the establishment of residential industrial schools, the government took a direct role.[23] On-reserve day schools, though a treaty promise, found little favour with government officials and missionaries because of the clash of values between what was taught in the classroom and what was taught in the home.[24] Day schools were phased out as residential schools grew in number, and it was at residential schools, which were often located at great distances from reserves, that those charged with the education of aboriginal children pursued their civilizing mission – far from potential interference by traditional languages, customs, and spirituality.

In keeping with the government's goals of protection, civilization, and assimilation, legislation was passed in 1850 to protect Indian lands and to place control over Indians living on those lands with the government.[25] Government officials believed that such protection was necessary only for a limited time as it would be rendered redundant once wholesale assimilation occurred.[26] *An Act for the Better Protection of the Lands and Property of Indians in Lower Canada* vested all Indian land and property in a commissioner of Indian lands.[27] It also offered the first definition of an Indian – someone of Indian blood reputed to belong to a particular tribe – and included the spouses, children, and adopted children of such individuals. The following year the *Act* was amended to exclude non-Indian males married to Indian women. The Upper Canada legislation, *An Act for the protection of Indians in Upper Canada from imposition, and the property occupied or enjoyed by them from trespass and injury*, required the Crown's consent for any conveyance of Indian lands.[28] Tax and debt repayment exemptions for Indians were also included in the statute.

In addition to the *Acts* referred to above, the 1857 *Act for the Gradual Civilization of the Indian Tribes in the Canadas* made clear the government's intention to eradicate aboriginal culture and to assimilate aboriginal peoples into mainstream Anglo-European Canadian society.[29] One means of accomplishing this was the IRS system; another was the prohibition of ceremonies such as the potlatch of the West Coast peoples and the Sundance of the Plains Cree. The legislative impetus behind both was expressed through the *Indian Act*.

Post-1867

Residential Schools and the Indian Act

In 1867, under s. 91(24) of the *Constitution Act*, the federal Parliament was responsible for "Indians and Lands reserved for Indians."[30] Therefore control of Indian education fell to the federal government, even though education was generally a matter for provincial legislatures.[31] The first post-1867 reference to Indian education was contained in s. 11 of *An Act providing for the organization of the Department of the Secretary of State of Canada, and for the management of Indian and Ordinance Lands*.[32] This 1868 precursor to the *Indian Act*[33] stipulated that:

> The Governor in Council *may*, subject to the provisions of this Act, direct how and in what manner, and by whom the moneys arising from sales of Indian Lands, and from the property held or to be held in trust for the Indians ... shall be invested from time to time, and how the payments or assistance to which the Indians may be entitled shall be made or given, and may provide for the general management of such lands, moneys and property, and direct what percentage or proportion thereof shall be set apart from time to time, to cover the cost of and attendant upon such management under the provisions of this Act, and for the construction or repair of roads passing through such lands, and *by way of contribution to schools frequented by such Indians*.[34]

The permissive language in this statute was to become typical of future provisions concerning the IRS system.[35] The government repeatedly used the term "may" when authorizing cabinet to make regulations related to schools and the students attending them. Further, it appears that relatively few regulations were in fact enacted.[36]

However, the 1868 provision was sufficient to ground authority for the "manner and extent" of school funding in the government.[37] It also made clear that money for Indian schools would be generated from sales of lands and other assets that the government held in trust for Canada's aboriginal peoples, in effect ensuring that aboriginal peoples would pay for the very system established to eradicate their culture.[38]

In 1879, Nicholas Flood Davin was sent to the United States to investigate the industrial boarding schools that were a cornerstone of the "aggressive civilization" policy pursued by the US government.[39] His *Report on Industrial Schools for Indians and Half-Breeds* extolled the success of the American model, which relied upon the virtues of toil, Christian faith, and prosperity.[40] Davin recommended the Canadian government enact a version of the policy, contracting with various churches that were already running missionary schools and, thereby, harnessing their "religious zeal and heroic self-sacrifice."[41] Incorporating religion into education was important because any attempt to civilize the Indian population would "take away their simple Indian mythology" and supply them with "a better" spiritual view.[42] According to Davin, "The Indian is a man with a tradition of his own which make [sic] civilization a puzzle of despair."[43]

Children could be agents of change for their race, provided they were "kept constantly within the circle of civilized conditions."[44] In addition to Christian religion and English, they were to learn skills that would help them succeed as farmers. Boys were to be taught cattle rearing and agriculture, while girls were to be taught sewing, bread making, and other skills appropriate for a "farmer's wife."[45] Stock and supplies would be provided to the schools, which were encouraged to become self-supporting. Costs were viewed as relatively modest: $125 per year for each pupil in schools where attendance was thirty or fewer.[46] This could be reduced to $100 at larger schools and maybe "even less when the school is of considerable size."[47]

The government acted on Davin's report, establishing schools to operate on a half-day system, with one half of the day being spent on traditional curriculum and the other half being devoted to practical pursuits. The department's attempt to transform aboriginal children into model Anglo-European Canadian citizens is evident in annual reports that refer to the need to rescue the Indian child "from the uncivilized state in which he has been brought up" by bringing him under influences that would "effect a change in his views and habits of life."[48]

Churches running the schools would attend to the children's moral development, which meant replacing "pagan superstition" with the "virtues of our civilization."[49] Both the DIA and the churches identified the elimination of aboriginal languages as a central tenet of the civilization process. The DIA proclaimed that Indian people would remain "permanently disabled" unless the English language was adopted because "so long as he keeps his native tongue, so long will he remain a community apart."[50] Department officials made it clear that the "use of English in preference to the Indian dialect must be insisted upon."[51]

Criticisms of the program focused upon costs, which were viewed as extravagant. Regulations were passed in 1892 to establish per capita grants as a method of instituting "economic management."[52] The regulations "distinguished between the government and management" by church authorities.[53]

Maintenance, salaries, and expenses were to be funded from the per capita grant, and management was to "conform to Indian Affairs' rules and maintain a certain standard of instruction and dietary and domestic comfort."[54] DIA officials were to inspect the schools and report on the facilities.

There were already eleven industrial schools (housing more than one thousand students) and twenty-two boarding schools (housing about five hundred students) under government authority when the first direct statutory reference to residential schools was incorporated into the 1894 *Indian Act*.[55] The boarding schools tended to be modest in size, generally housing between ten and fifty students, while the industrial schools were much larger and were intended to offer a higher level of training (although over the years the actual differences tended to blur).[56] Sections 137 and 138 provided power to establish industrial and boarding schools, enforce compulsory attendance by threat of fine or imprisonment of parents, and to fund the schools.[57]

The coercive nature of the compulsory attendance provisions did not provoke much concern during parliamentary debates. When questioned briefly about them, Superintendent General of Indian Affairs T. Mayne Daly defended the measures, saying: "[Indian] parents have interfered and taken boys away just when they were beginning to learn a trade."[58] His department's budget for the schools received far more attention. Daly sought to reassure the House that the money was a good investment: "The children come with nothing on them but a blanket and are clothed, fed and educated and treated as parents would treat their children."[59] In his 1894 annual report, Deputy Superintendent General Hayter Reed dismissed the heavy-handed provisions, arguing that compulsory school attendance was "reasonable" given that Indians "who are to an extent a privileged class" were able to take advantage of education services funded by the state.[60]

Cultural Prohibition and the Indian Act: *Potlatch and Sundance Ceremonies*

At the same time that residential schools were being used to assimilate Indian children, family members who remained at home were prohibited from engaging in certain ceremonies integral to their cultural, political, and spiritual life. An example is the banning of the potlatch and Sundance ceremonies. While a full examination of the historico-cultural complexity of these ceremonies in the context of increasing interaction between aboriginal and European cultures is not intended here, there can be little doubt that the potlatch and Sundance ceremonies played a central role in the cohesion and reproduction of the aboriginal cultures of which they were a part. In their study of the Southern Kwakiutl potlatch, Philip Drucker and Robert F. Heizer described the potlatch as "an institution of maximum importance" for the Southern Kwakiutl.[61] Katherine Pettipas, in her examination of government repression of indigenous religious ceremonies on the Prairies, describes the importance of the Sun, or Thirst, Dance with regard to social, political, educational, and spiritual functions.[62]

Missionaries and Indian agents lobbied Ottawa to impose legislation banning potlatch ceremonies because they perceived them to be obstacles to "progress" towards assimilation to European ways. In 1883, the issue of a legislative ban on the potlatch was before the House of Commons, and it was decided that a royal proclamation "discountenancing the custom and requesting in her Majesty's name that Her Indian subjects abandon the same" would be sufficient to eradicate "the heathenish and worse than useless custom" of the potlatch.[63] Not long afterwards, in April of 1884, Bill 87 resulted in an amendment to the *Indian Act* that made participation in the potlatch a misdemeanor punishable by imprisonment.[64]

Legislation opposing the Thirst Dance, or Sundance, did not appear until 1895. Objections to this cultural practice were similar to those to the potlatch. Missionaries and government officials shared the view that the celebration of these ceremonies was anathema to their shared goal of civilizing (*i.e.,* assimilating) the "Indian." The Sundance both negated the missionaries' work on the children in residential school classrooms and kept aboriginal adults from maximizing the potential of their government-mandated homesteads under the tutelage of the farm instructors.[65] The 1895 amendment to the *Indian Act* was intended to put a stop to the Sundance. In 1914, 1918, and 1932-33 subsequent amendments strengthened the prohibition of this cultural practice.[66]

Assessing the impact on aboriginal people of the prohibition of the potlatch and Sundance is a complex task because these prohibitions were only one part of a broad colonial policy of assimilation. The legislative prohibition of cultural practices occurred in concert with the work of missionaries in the government-mandated IRS system, and all of this occurred in the context of the increasing encroachment of large numbers of settlers and their European socio-economic system. However, it is clear that the West Coast potlatch and the Prairie Sundance were integral to the social, political, religious, and economic systems of their respective aboriginal peoples. As Maggie Hodgson writes: "Taking away these and other ceremonies meant taking away the ideas, values and principles basic to community mental health. With the ceremonies went security, ideology, rituals, belongings, beliefs, access to resources, time together, healing and justice."[67] Not surprisingly, during this time many items of spiritual and other significance were also separated from the community, some ending up in museum and other collections. There is also a recognizable link between the loss of aboriginal cultures brought about by colonial policies of assimilation, of which residential schools and the legislative prohibition of cultural practices were central features, and contemporary aboriginal social issues. Several of the case studies in this book attest to this. Other serious consequences also ensued. Put bluntly, "to hear that there is more poverty, more death, and more violence in the native community than in any other community in Canada has such a familiar ring that our eyes glaze over and our ears wait impatiently for what comes next."[68]

Impact of Indian Residential Schools and *Indian Act* Prohibitions on Language and Culture

Instruments of Education: "Learning by the Lash"

By the latter part of the nineteenth century, Canada had developed a policy of assimilation, which entailed a three-part policy for the education of aboriginal children: (1) separation (which entailed the removal of children from family and community); (2) socialization (which entailed a precise pedagogy for resocializing children); and (3) assimilation (which entailed a scheme for integrating graduates into the non-aboriginal world).[69] Replacing aboriginal languages with English was key to this cultural assault. Children were beaten for speaking their language. In order to "kill the Indian in the child" and cut the artery of culture that ran between generations and connected child to parents and community, the operators of residential schools were required to physically punish children for speaking their languages.[70]

The strict and rigid regimens of residential schools relied on discipline and punishment to enforce compliance. Corporal punishment became the general form of discipline in the operation of residential schools. These schools became cultures of punishment and then cultures of abuse:

> Isolated in distant establishments, divorced from opportunities for social intercourse, and placed in closed communities of co-workers with the potential for strained interpersonal relations heightened by inadequate privacy, the staff not only taught but supervised the children's work, play and personal care. Their hours were long, the remuneration below that of other educational institutions, and the working conditions irksome. Thus the struggle against children and their culture was conducted in an atmosphere of considerable stress, fatigue and anxiety that may well have dulled the staff's sensitivity to children's hunger, their ill-kempt look or ill-health and often, perhaps inevitably, pushed the application of discipline over the line into abuse and transformed what was to be a circle of care into a violent embrace. Although there were caring and conscientious staff, not every principal, teacher or employee was of the desired moral character; outside the gaze of public scrutiny, isolated from both aboriginal and non-Aboriginal communities, schools were opportunistic sites of abuse.[71]

Experts have confirmed the connections that aboriginal people have drawn between the IRS system and the resulting dysfunction in their communities.

For example, N.R. Ing, L. Bull, and others have detailed the social pathologies produced in individuals by their experience with the IRS system:

> The survivors of the Indian Residential school system have, in many cases, continued to have their lives shaped by the experiences in these schools. Persons who attend these schools continue to struggle with their identity after years of being taught to hate themselves and their culture. The residential school led to a disruption in the transference of parenting skills from one generation to the next. Without these skills, many survivors had difficulty in raising their own children. In residential schools, they learned that adults often exert power and control through abuse. The lessons learned in childhood are often repeated in adulthood with the result that many survivors of the residential school system often inflict abuse on their own children. These children in turn use the same tools on their own children.[72]

Adding these individual "social pathologies" to the broader cultural impacts on First Nations people brought about by the residential school system raises the question: What options are available to redress the cultural damage done?

Centrality of Language to Aboriginal Culture

At the conclusion of the First Nations Cultural Heritage Symposium,[73] which was attended by members of those communities featured in the case studies in this volume, several common themes and fundamental principles were identified as being central to the preservation and protection of aboriginal cultural heritages. Among these, language was identified as essential and as being at the core of aboriginal culture. The following statements, which were accepted by the participants, confirm this tenet:

> Language is key in shaping First Nations identities, culture, history and connection to the land. Without language one's history is lost. Without language, verbal record identification of traditional territories and ownership rights is jeopardized.
>
> Cultural transmission of traditional knowledge, rights and entitlements is connected with one's ability to understand and speak the language.
>
> Language revitalization is a prerequisite for all other aspects of cultural continuity and restoration. Challenges confronted in language revitalization include passing of knowledgeable elders, lack of support both within and outside communities, and lack of funding for language training.[74]

The importance of language as a primary foundation of First Nations culture and the damage caused by residential schools is emphasized again and again in the case studies in this volume. As well, by drawing on the interviews and narratives that make up these case studies, we find powerful illustrations of the centrality of language in the words of the participants, some of whom are residential school survivors. By way of example, we draw on the *Poomaksin* and Kainai studies (Chapter 6 and Chapter 5, respectively).

Poomaksin *Case Study*

The centrality of language to Skinnipiikani culture is expressed in the oral and performance-based practice of their laws. Laws are not codified in written form: "Legal understanding is stabilized, authorized, and derives its force through orally based practice and performance within the context of the proper enactment of ceremonial protocols."[75] The *Poomaksin* study is devoted to an examination and understanding of "venue, action, language, and song as the fundamental elements in Skinnipiikani decision making and legal protocols that govern rights to 'cultural property' and Skinnipiikani heritage."[76] While recognizing that the four elements – language, action, venue, and song – are an integrated totality, language and song are the most important because of the potential difficulty of their recovery in communities that have suffered substantial cultural loss.[77]

> When the old people sing, all their songs mean something. The language was the most important thing. You go on the Blood Reserve; you'll see some little kids speaking Blackfoot. But on this reserve, there are hardly any kids who know the Blackfoot language. The way I look at it, we're moving more towards the white ways, rather than going back to our old ways, because we're controlled by the white man. They're the ones supplying our schools, all their ways – where's our ways? Like, what you were saying, teaching the Blackfoot language, songs, and our ways. Our parents, they were self-supporting. *The boarding schools took away our self-respect and our respect for other people.*[78]

The author of the study, Brian Noble, concludes his discussion of the key elements of language, act, venue, and song in relation to cultural transmission with the following statement:

> In the final analysis, it is the restoration of the integrated practices of venue, action, language, and song – as elements of the transfer practices of the Skinnipiikani – that will be the baseline not only for cultural transmission but also for the related matters of cultural material and knowledge protection as well as repatriation. All of these have to be seen as an integrated, total arrangement, and they have to be supported in concert. *In fact, it is the disruption of this integrity through the culturally devastating historic policies of the Canadian state, including residential school and other*

> *assimilationist policies, that this principle of integration is meant to counteract.*[79]

Kainai Case Study

The authors of the Kainai study point out that their interviewees identified language as the aspect of Blood culture that was most in need of protection. Further, they emphasize that the Kainai dialect of Blackfoot, which is unique to the Blood, is considered to be the foundation upon which future progress in education, cultural protection, and revitalization will be built.[80] Participants stressed that their language continues to be the medium through which cultural knowledge is transferred from one generation of Blood to the next.[81] Participants identified the need to integrate the Kainai language into the existing provincial curriculum:

> We have to work with Alberta curriculum and say, "[H]ey, language to us is very important." They have to change their ways of testing our children in those tests. And I don't believe in tests [of] children, but they have got to change their ways. Maybe doing some of those tests with our own people, in our language, to enforce that our language stays in place. We can never lose our language. If we lose our language, there is no use talking about this. There is no use. So the process has to take it where government takes action and recognizes the importance of First Nation language. And how [do] they do it? I don't know. This [is] where, I again turn back to the educators. You have to do this. You have to fight for us, for the old people, the young people, for the children, for yourselves. This is what you need. I think if you instill those things into the children ... our leaders ... our educators ... our administrators – our own knowledge – then they would gather the two knowledges and put the two knowledges together, to know how to put that in.[82]

Spoken, as opposed to written, language was the medium through which the transfer of cultural information and knowledge was traditionally accomplished. Such knowledge was passed entirely by means of "verbal instruction and demonstrative action during the recitation of songs and stories and the performance of activities such as hunting, fishing, processing and preparing food, and the performance of ceremonies and dances."[83] There was no recording of such information, even for the purpose of instruction, as this would be contrary to traditional processes.[84]

> [I]n the past, there at our Sundance grounds, that is where our people gathered. When we gathered there they would dance, others would play hand games, others would pray there. The songs sung there were all holy songs and there were no recordings. There were no tapes used.[85]

Study participants also expressed concern that the documentation and recording of tradition could result in misinformation, decontextualization, and cultural appropriation:

> There are those who are against writing or documenting our way of life. Then there are those that it didn't matter to them if we write or did not write it, our way of life. It was after that that I kept thinking about it. That it was true, if we do not write it, or document some of these things, our legends, our way of life [misunderstanding occurs]. I [will] give you an example. A white man, he makes a mistake. The white man believes that, he assumes that all of us Nitsiitapii, the Indian people, we all know all about our way of life. No, just like the way we are sitting here today. If you knew, as an interviewer, then you would not have to come here today. Yeah, and that is the way that some of the white people take us. They assume that everybody knows (or all of us know) about our way of life, especially our sacred ways.[86]

Among the Kainai study's summary comments is one that concludes that Blood culture has survived and even thrived despite policies of settlement, economic development, assimilation, and colonization.[87] However, it is also acknowledged that the sustainability of Blood culture has been negatively affected by the "imposition of the reserve system and residential schools, Christian proselytizing, and the criminalization of indigenous religious practices and ceremonies through the legal prohibition of cultural and spiritual practices."[88]

Although they expressed this in particular and different ways, case study participants identified language as fundamental to the preservation, protection, and revitalization of cultural heritage. Also, each case study identified residential schools as part of a larger process of assimilation that First Nations people endured at the hands of the Canadian state and from which they still, individually and collectively, bear "cultural scars" in the form of loss of language and cultural heritage. Similarly, in previous sections, links have been drawn between the provisions of the *Indian Act* designed to prohibit cultural practices such as the potlatch and the Sundance and the impact on aboriginal cultures. Quotations selected above, and others from the *Poomaksin* case study, offer poignant illustrations of the nature of this impact.

Legal and Other Options for Redress for Harm to Language and Culture

Legal Options

The harm suffered by survivors of residential schools and other discriminatory laws and policies is now the subject of legal redress and, in some communities, influences strategies for cultural revival and renewal. The limited ability of the law to respond adequately to cultural loss claims underscores the importance of also seeking redress outside the legal framework. Ken Cooper-Stephenson examines the utility of tort law (*e.g.*, assault, negligence, and infliction of suffering) as a legal means of redress for the state wrongs committed against aboriginal children within the IRS system.[89] As Cooper-Stephenson observes, the application of conventional tort law to those aspects of residential school abuse cases dealing with claims of individual victims against individual perpetrators and/or claims against government and institutional defendants (churches) is relatively unproblematic, apart from the usual problems pertaining to evidentiary issues, liability, damages, limitations, and the like.[90] Where problems arise is in the application of conventional tort law to the broader claims for cultural damage (and the associated damages that flow from it), which go beyond the individual to the community and cultural level:

> The residential school experiment led to many Aboriginals suffering hardship and abuse, including sexual abuse. Many Canadian Aboriginals continue to endure the effects of the removal of children from families to be institutionalized in residential schools. Loss of culture, family, connection and trust, to name but a few losses, coupled with memories of physical and sexual abuse has resulted in many [aboriginal people] being unable to properly function as parents and members of communities. Often this has been played out through substance abuse, contact with the criminal justice system, poor health and early death.[91]

As alluded to above, claims for physical and sexual abuse fall squarely within the existing tort doctrines of battery and assault, and, while a less well-recognized doctrine, the emotional and mental damages flowing from such assaults fit within the ambit of the tort of indirect infliction of physical and mental suffering.[92] Combining these torts with the concept of vicarious liability moves residential school claims beyond the liability of individual perpetrators and opens the door to the institutional liability of the government (who provided funding) and the churches (whose personnel were involved in the operation of the schools). The foundation of vicarious liability is not based on the direct fault of the employer institution (government and/or church) but, rather, on the "perceived distributive fairness of making the employer internalize the cost of the general activity involved."[93] The tort doctrines of assault and battery and infliction of physical and mental suffering do little, however, to advance claims for cultural damages.

The doctrine of negligence can also move liability beyond individual perpetrators of physical and sexual abuse to those who knew or ought to have known such abuse was occurring, or might occur, and did nothing to prevent it. The duty of care in negligence renders individuals and institutional entities liable for acts or omissions that might foreseeably cause harm to others, where a sufficiently direct and proximate connection can be established between the victim and the negligent person or institution.[94] In the residential school context, liability for negligence may adhere to the employers and supervisors of abusers for failing to stop the abusive conduct. And while there are questions of how far back the duty of care may go and how far forward it may apply to the successors of those who were abused, it may be that an action by second-generation plaintiffs for lives affected by the dysfunctionality of their abused parents could find purchase in the doctrine of negligence.[95]

Still among the conventional tort-like doctrines, the action for breach of fiduciary duty may provide a means for finding government and institutional liability in the context of residential school claims. While the traditional focus of fiduciary duty is breach of trust, with the associated emphasis on disloyalty and putting one's own or others' interests ahead of the beneficiary's interest, if this "private" fiduciary duty owed to particular individuals (*e.g.*, by parent to child) is coupled with the "public" fiduciary duty that the Crown owes to aboriginal people, it may assist in a claim for breach of fiduciary duty in the context of residential school litigation.[96]

The courts have established that the Crown owes a fiduciary duty to aboriginal peoples and that this duty is equitable and enforceable.[97] Such a duty cannot be delegated and requires that the Crown deal in the best interests of aboriginal peoples. This might lead one to think that this *sui generis* form of fiduciary duty, combined with the fact that the government, in pursuing its residential school policy, was dealing with vulnerable children, would make this an obvious form of redress. However, as Vella and Grace point out, breach of fiduciary duty has proved to be a disappointing avenue of redress.[98]

In *Wewaykum*, the Supreme Court of Canada held that an attempt to find a "plenary Crown liability" in the fiduciary relationship with aboriginal peoples "overshoots the mark";[99] rather, fiduciary obligations arise in relation to specific aboriginal interests. The Court made it clear that fiduciary protection is most likely to be successful with respect to land, although it did not categorically rule out finding that duty in other contexts.

In residential school cases, the courts have frequently found that a fiduciary relationship was owed to aboriginal students, but they have been "exceedingly reluctant" to find a breach.[100] However, in 2003 the Supreme Court of Canada may have opened the door slightly on this issue in *K.L.B. v. British Columbia*.[101] The case involved the abuse of children at the hands of foster parents. The Court held that the public fiduciary duty law was similar to "the fiduciary obligations of the Crown toward Aboriginal peoples, which have been held to include a requirement of using due diligence in advancing particular interests of Aboriginal peoples."[102] Although the Court did not find a breach of fiduciary duty in this case, it held that such a breach could be found where a government interest was placed ahead of the interests of the children or where acts were committed that "harmed the children in a way that amounted to betrayal of trust or disloyalty."[103]

In its management of the residential school system, the government consistently behaved in just such a manner by placing budgetary concerns over the well-being of children, by failing to fulfill promises to educate them in a manner that would enable them to participate in society, and by consistently turning a blind eye to the substandard level of their education and the brutality of their treatment. With respect to the substandard education provided at residential schools, there is the possibility that references in certain treaties to some measure of Crown responsibility for teachers and education might permit the possibility of a claim for treaty breach.

While, as mentioned above, traditional tort doctrine has a role to play in certain aspects of residential school claims, it must also be recognized that tort law, at least in its conventional form, is limited in its application to the historically, culturally, and factually complex legacy of IRS abuse. Canadian tort law has a narrow, individualist focus, which, at best, provides only a limited and indirect way of addressing the deeper issue of reparations for what we have broadly described as cultural damages. It must also be recognized that the application of law and the process of litigation can be time-consuming, expensive, and psychologically damaging to claimants.

Cooper-Stephenson suggests that the tort doctrine might be expanded to encompass reparation for wrongs such as cultural harm by extending the reach of traditional damage assessment to include losses experienced by the claimant's social group and even by as-yet-to-be-conceived children; by expanding the interests protected by tort law to recognize cultural harm as actionable by, for example, building upon the protections for "dignity" (as already recognized in defamation) and for protection from intentional infliction of emotional harm (again, as already recognized); by defining causality to recognize the social pathologies produced by the residential school system; and by incorporating into tort law the norms of international law so that collective harm to sectors of the community is sufficient to ground a damages award against the state.[104]

More complex are general claims for cultural loss arising from *Indian Act* prohibitions. While not dealt with here, claims such as the specific claim discussed in the U'mista case study are unique and illustrative.

Non-Legal Avenues for Redress of Harms Caused by IRS and Legislative Prohibition of Cultural Practice

While avenues of legal redress are, if successful, largely confined to individual financial compensation for damages proven, there are many who view individual compensation as only part of the answer. We conclude by briefly examining examples from two different categories of initiatives that try to deal with the continuing impact of the IRS system and the assimilative effects of *Indian Act* cultural prohibitions.

On 23 November 2005, an agreement in principle outlining a comprehensive settlement package was reached between all parties involved in the long-standing IRS litigation, and on 8 May 2006, a final version of this agreement was signed by all parties.[105] At the time of writing, this agreement in principle was not yet certified by the courts, but it is very likely that the proposed comprehensive settlement package will be implemented. Articles 7 and 8 of the agreement are of particular interest here. Article 7 deals with truth and reconciliation and commemoration, while Article 8 is concerned with healing. These sections represent initiatives that are separate from the individual compensation that is also included in the agreement in principle. The programs anticipated include (1) individual and community healing initiatives to be conducted through the Aboriginal Healing Foundation (to be funded by Canada in the amount of $125,000,000);[106] (2) commemoration initiatives, events, and projects concerning the history and impact of residential schools on aboriginal peoples at both national and community levels (to be funded by Canada in the amount of $20,000,000);[107] and (3) a truth and reconciliation process to report to the public regarding what happened in residential schools (to be funded by Canada in the amount of $60,000,000).[108]

It is unfortunate that several years of litigation were required before a settlement agreement in principle was reached. While recognizing that the agreement in principle must still be successfully implemented, it is nevertheless breathtaking in its expansiveness and willingness to contemplate avenues of redress far beyond the conventional boundaries of compensation typically considered in the settlement of litigation. Canada commits, in the conventional manner of settling tort actions, not only to providing substantial individual compensation for damages suffered from abuses in residential schools but also to providing substantial funding for the programs and initiatives identified above. This seems a genuine attempt to acknowledge and to begin to ameliorate the cultural devastation visited upon generations of aboriginal people by the IRS system and to begin to build a positive relationship between aboriginal and non-aboriginal Canadians. Should implementation of the settlement contemplated by the agreement in principle be fully realized, Chief Phil Fontaine's contention that it is "historic" and "the largest and most comprehensive settlement package in Canadian history" will not be an overstatement.

Language loss is a substantial part of the cultural harm caused by the IRS. Thus, in order to adequately address the full extent of this harm, it is crucial to address language. The case studies mentioned throughout this chapter reveal that, with regard to non-legal avenues for redress, language and repatriation are key. As an alternative to payments, repatriation is a viable means to address cultural harm because it supports the continuity and revival of cultural practices. Positive repatriation experiences are based on trusting relationships such as that between the Blood and the Glenbow Museum. Negative repatriation experiences with museums and other institutions were the result of their failure to consider the individual and communal nature of bundles, the legality of alienation within the context of the Blood culture and worldview, and the oral testimonies of respected elders and ceremonial practitioners.[109] Communication in these situations was absent or inadequate, or, even worse, was regimented and meaningless, as evinced by a blinkered adherence to legal definitions, standards of proof, guidelines, policy and procedure, and an inability or unwillingness to compromise. In their closing commentary, Bell *et al.* conclude that, despite the complexity, difficulty, and political sensitivity of the subject matter of repatriation, legislation in which indigenous concepts of belonging and transfer are recognized, accommodated, and given power are necessary if aboriginal and non-aboriginal peoples are to move forward in an equal partnership.

Some Concluding Theoretical Concerns

A certain unease necessarily accompanies an attempt to comment critically on the Canadian state's colonization of aboriginal peoples. Unease stems from the fact that these endeavours apply the language and assumptions of the colonizers to analyze the situation of the colonized. This is precisely the case here, where the terms, concepts, and assumptions of the Canadian legal culture are utilized to speak about avenues of redress available to aboriginal peoples for cultural harms caused by the operation of residential schools and the legislated prohibition of cultural practices. As is suggested by Richard Overstall[110] and Susan Marsden,[111] we must be aware of how our use of Anglo-Canadian analytical concepts and assumptions obscures an understanding of First Nations concepts and First Nations assumptions about the matters in question, be they cultural harm, cultural property, property rights, intangible versus tangible property, or whatever. We must be aware that Anglo-Canadian legal and property concepts arise out of a worldview that is often antithetical to that of First Nations and, thus, may preclude an adequate understanding of aboriginal cultures.

While our efforts in this research project may represent the beginning of a journey by scholars and legal practitioners down the road to a greater understanding of aboriginal legal systems and culture, it is just that – a beginning. As scholars, legal practitioners, law makers, and non-aboriginal members of Canadian society generally, we all have a long way to travel before the destination of understanding is anywhere in sight.

Notes

1 Government of Canada, *Annual Report of the Department of Indian Affairs* (Ottawa: Queen's Printer, 1895) at xxvii.
2 Excerpts from Jane Stewart P.C., M.P., and Ralph Goodale P.C., M.P., *Statement of Reconciliation: Learning from the Past*, addressed to aboriginal peoples on 7 January 1998.
3 Jim R. Miller, "Troubled Legacy: A History of Native Residential Schools" (2003) 66 Sask. L. Rev. 357 at 358.
4 *Ibid.* at 359.
5 *Ibid.* at 361. Miller noted that most of the treaties specified or implied that the schools would be located on reserves.
6 John S. Milloy, *A National Crime: The Canadian Government and the Residential School System 1879 to 1986* (Winnipeg: University of Manitoba Press, 1999) at 54.
7 See also Harold Cardinal, *The Unjust Society: The Tragedy of Canada's Indians* (Edmonton: M.G. Hurtig Ltd., 1969) at 53.
8 Canada, *Report of the Royal Commission on Aboriginal Peoples: Looking Forward, Looking Back*, vol. 1 (Ottawa: Supply and Services Canada, 1996) at 265.
9 Susan M. Vella and Elizabeth K.P. Grace, "Pathways to Justice for Residential School Claimants: Is the Civil Justice System Working?" in Joseph Eliot Magnet and Dwight A. Dorey, eds., *Aboriginal Rights Litigation* (Markham: LexisNexis Canada, 2003) at 202.
10 *Supra* note 8.
11 *Ibid.* at 277.
12 *Indian Act*, S.C. 1876, c. 18 (39 Vict.) s. 2.
13 *Supra* note 8 at 278.
14 Harry B. Hawthorn, ed., *The Politics of Indian Affairs* (Ottawa, Indian Affairs Branch: The Queen's Printer, 1966). Reprinted in Ian A.L. Getty and Antoine S. Lussier eds., *As Long as the Sun Shines and Water Flows: A Reader in Canadian Native Studies* (Vancouver: UBC Press, 1983) at 173.
15 *Ibid.*
16 John Leslie and Ron Maguire, eds., *The Historical Development of the Indian Act* (Ottawa: Treaties and Historical Research Centre, Indian and Northern Affairs Canada, 1978) at 2.
17 *Ibid.* at 3.
18 Robert J. Surtees, *Canadian Indian Policy: A Critical Bibliography* (Bloomington: Indiana University Press, 1982) at 31-32.
19 E. Brian Titley, *A Narrow Vision: Duncan Campbell Scott and the Administration of Indian Affairs in Canada* (Vancouver: UBC Press, 1986) at 2.
20 George F.G. Stanley, "As Long as the Sun Shines and Water Flows: An Historical Comment" in Getty and Lussier, *supra* note 14 at 13-14.
21 Province of Canada, *Journals of the Legislative Assembly of Canada, 1844-1845*, Appendix EEE, "Report on the Affairs of the Indians in Canada," 20 March 1845, cited in John Leslie, *Commissions of Inquiry into Indian Affairs in the Canadas, 1828-1858: Evolving a Corporate Memory for the Indian Department* (Ottawa: Indian Affairs and Northern Development, 1985) at 81-96.
22 Canada, Parliament, *Journals of the Legislative Assembly of Canada*, App. T (II Vict., 24 June 1847), Minutes of Evidence, App. 2: Supplementary Report to the questions proposed by the Commission on Indian Affairs.
23 Suzanne Fournier and Ernie Crey, *Stolen from Our Embrace: The Abduction of First Nations Children and the Restoration of Aboriginal Communities* (Vancouver: Douglas and McIntyre, 1997) at 53-54.
24 *Ibid.* at 55.
25 "The early history of tripartite relations between Indian nations and the Crown in British North America during the stage of displacement can be described in terms of three phases in which first protection, then civilization, and finally assimilation were the transcendent policy goals." *Supra* note 8 at 263.
26 *Supra* note 19 at 4.
27 S.C. 1850, c. 42.
28 S.C. 1850, c. 74.

29 S.C. 1857, c. 26.
30 *Constitution Act, 1867* (U.K.), 30 & 31 Vict., c. 3, s. 91(24).
31 *Ibid.*, s. 93.
32 *An Act providing for the organization of the Department of the Secretary of State of Canada, and for the management of Indian and Ordinance Lands*, S.C. 1868 (31 Vict.), c. 42.
33 *Supra* note 12.
34 *Supra* note 32 at s. 11 [emphasis added].
35 *Supra* note 9 at 202.
36 Despite an exhaustive search, no *Indian Act* regulations related to the residential schools sections of the various acts could be located. The following sources were searched: Gail Hinge, *Indian Acts and Amendments, 1868-1950* (Ottawa: Minister of Indian Affairs and Northern Development, 1983); Minister of Indian Affairs and Northern Development, *Contemporary Indian Legislation, 1951-1978* (Ottawa: Minister of Indian Affairs and Northern Development, 1981); Canada Privy Council, *The Consolidated Orders in Council of Canada: Under the Authority and Direction of His Excellency the Governor General in Council* (Ottawa: Queen's Printer, 1889); Canada Privy Council Statutory Orders and Regulations Division, *Statutory Orders and Regulations Consolidation 1949* (Ottawa: King's Printer, 1950); Canada Privy Council Statutory Orders and Regulations Division, *Statutory Orders and Regulations: Consolidation 1955* (Ottawa: Queen's Printer, 1955); Canada Statute Revision Commission, *Consolidated Regulations of Canada, 1978* (Ottawa: Queen's Printer, 1978); Canada, *The Canada Gazette* (Ottawa: Queen's Printer, 1883-1946), vols. 25-26, 35, 38, 39, 40, 42-43, 46-47, 51, 54, 60, 61-83. Where there were gaps in the University of Alberta Law Library collection, searches were made through the index to parliamentary debates as the 1894 version of the *Indian Act* indicated regulations were to be "laid before both Houses of Parliament within the first fifteen days of the session next after the date thereof" (s. 12). No regulations associated with the *Act* were found using this process. A search was made of the *Official Report of the Debates of the House of Commons of the Dominion of Canada*, vols. 37-102, covering the period 1884 to 1910-11, and also of Canada, *The Canada Gazette Part II Statutory Orders and Regulations* (Ottawa: Queen's Printer, 1952-53), vols. 85-86, without success.
37 *Supra* note 9.
38 *Ibid.*
39 Nicholas Flood David, *Report on Industrial Schools for Indians and Half-Breeds* (Ottawa: 1879), online: <http://www.canadiana.org/ECO/mtq?doc=03651> at 1.
40 *Ibid.*
41 *Ibid.* at 12, 13.
42 *Ibid.* at 14.
43 *Ibid.* at 10.
44 *Ibid.* at 12.
45 *Ibid.* at 2.
46 *Ibid.*
47 *Ibid.*
48 Government of Canada, *Annual Report of the Department of Indian Affairs* (Ottawa: Queen's Printer, 1889) at xi, cited in RCAP, *supra* note 8 at 339.
49 *Ibid.*
50 Government of Canada, *Annual Report of the Department of Indian Affairs* (Ottawa: Queen's Printer, 1895) at xxii-xxiii, cited in RCAP, *supra* note 8 at 341.
51 LAC, RG 10, vol. 3674, file 11422-25, MR C10118, to H. Reed from the Deputy Superintendent General, 24 August 1890, cited in RCAP, *supra* note 8 at 341.
52 Order in Council P.C. 2810, cited in Vella and Grace, *supra* note 9 at 203. It does not appear that this regulation was published. The appropriate volumes of *The Canada Gazette* (on microfilm) were searched without success. Canada, *The Canada Gazette* (Ottawa: Queen's Printer, 1892) v. 25-26.
53 Vella and Grace, *ibid.*
54 *Ibid.*
55 *House of Commons Debates*, 37 (22 June 1894) at 4864-69 (Hon. Thomas Mayne Daly).

56 *Ibid.*
57 *An Act further to amend "The Indian Act"* S.C. 1894 (57 & 58 Vict.), c. 32. Note that these changes remained unchanged for the 1906 revision, *Indian Act*, R.S.C. 1906, c. 81, ss. 9-11.
58 *Supra* note 55 at 5552.
59 *Ibid.* at 5553.
60 Government of Canada, *Annual Report of the Department of Indian Affairs* (Ottawa: Queen's Printer, 1894) at xxii.
61 Philip Drucker and Robert F. Hezier, *To Make My Name Good: A Re-Examination of the Southern Kwakiutl Potlatch* (Berkeley: University of California Press, 1967) at 52.
62 Katherine Pettipas, *Severing the Ties That Bind: Government Repression of Indigenous Religious Ceremonies on the Prairies* (Winnipeg: University of Manitoba Press, 1994) at 60. The importance of these ceremonies is also discussed by participants in the case studies. See, in this volume, Catherine Bell *et al.*, in consultation with Andrea Sanborn, the U'mista Cultural Society and the 'Na̲mgis Nation, "Recovering from Colonization: Perspectives of Community Members on Protection and Repatriation of Kwakwa̲ka̲'wakw Cultural Heritage"; Brian Noble, in consultation with Reg Crowshoe, and discussion with the Knut-sum-atak Society, "*Poomaksin:* Skinnipiikani-Nitsiitapii Law, Transfers, and Making Relatives: Practices and Principles for Cultural Protection, Repatriation, Redress, and Heritage Law Making with Canada"; Catherine Bell *et al.*, "Repatriation and Heritage Protection: Reflections on the Kainai Experience."
63 Forrest E. La Violette, *The Struggle for Survival: Indian Cultures and the Protestant Ethic in BC* (Toronto: University of Toronto Press, 1973) at 38.
64 *An Act further to amend the Indian Act, 1880*, S.C. 1884, c. 27, s. 3; *The Indian Act*, R.S.C. 1886, c. 43, s. 114.
65 *Supra* note 19 at 165.
66 S.C. 1914, c. 35, s. 8; S.C. 1918, c. 26, s. 7; S.C. 1932-33, c. 42, s. 10.
67 Maggie Hodgson, "Rebuilding Community after the Residential School Experience" in Diane Engelstad and John Bird, eds., *Nation to Nation: Aboriginal Sovereignty and the Future of Canada* (Concord, ON: Anansi Press, 1992) 101 at 102.
68 Tim Schouls, John Olthuis, and Diane Engelstad, "The Basic Dilemma: Sovereignty of Assimilation," in Engelstad and Bird, *ibid.* at 12-13.
69 *Supra* note 8 at 337.
70 *Ibid.* at 365-66. Accounts are also given by participants of the impact of residential schools. See *e.g.*, Bell *et al.*, in consultation with Sanborn *et al.*, *supra* note 62 at 43-44 and also in this volume Catherine Bell *et al.*, in consultation with the Ktunaka/Kinbasket Tribal Council and the Ktunaka/Kinbasket Traditional Elders Working Group, "Protection and Repatriation of Ktunaka/Kinbasket Cultural Resources: Perspectives of Community Members" at 317-19.
71 *Supra* note 8 at 367.
72 INAC, file E6757-18, vol. 13, Memorandum for the Deputy Minister from J. Cochrane, 6 June 1992, and attachment, "First Nations Health Commission – May 1992 – Proposal, Indian Residential School Study, Draft No. 4," cited in RCAP, *supra* note 8 at 379. For further information see L. Bull, "Indian Residential Schooling: The Native Perspective" and N.R. Ing, "The Effects of Residential Schools on Native Child-Rearing Practices" (1991 supplement) 18 Canadian Journal of Native Education 1.
73 First Nation Cultural Heritage Symposium, 18 and 19 June 2005, Lister Centre, University of Alberta, Edmonton, Alberta.
74 *Ibid.* in *Summary of Common Themes and Fundamental Principles* agreed to and shared among symposium participants, online: <https://www.law.ualberta.ca/research/aboriginal culturalheritage>. Also see Marianne Ignace and Ron Ignace, "Canadian Aboriginal Languages and the Protection of Cultural Heritage" in this volume, for an examination of the centrality of aboriginal language and cultural identity.
75 Noble *supra* note 62 at 261.
76 *Ibid.* at 262.
77 *Ibid.* at 272-73.

78 *Ibid.* at 273 (Geoff Crow Eagle) [emphasis added].
79 *Ibid.* at 273-74 [emphasis added].
80 Bell *et al.*, "Repatriation and Heritage Protection," *supra* note 62 at 246.
81 *Ibid.*
82 *Ibid.* at 247 (Frank Weasel Head, part 2).
83 *Ibid.*
84 *Ibid.*
85 *Ibid.* (Mary Louise Oka).
86 *Ibid.* at 248 (Adam Delaney).
87 *Ibid.* at 249.
88 *Ibid.* at 250.
89 Ken Cooper-Stephenson, "Reparations for State Wrongs: Tort Law's Political and Theoretical Role" (paper presented to the conference entitled Residential Schools Legacy: Is Reconciliation Possible? March 2004) [unpublished].
90 *Ibid.* at 1.
91 Antonio Buti, "Responding to the Legacy of Canadian Residential Schools" (2001) 8:4 Murdoch U, Electronic J. of L. at para. 15, cited in Cooper-Stephenson, *ibid.* at 2.
92 *Supra* note 89 at 4.
93 *Ibid.* at 5.
94 *Ibid.* at 5-6.
95 *Ibid.* at 6.
96 *Ibid.* at 8.
97 *Guerin v. Canada*, [1984] 2 S.C.R. 335.
98 *Supra* note 9 at 232.
99 *Wewaykum Indian Band v. Canada*, [2002] 4 S.C.R. 245 at para. 81.
100 *Supra* note 9 at 232.
101 *K.L.B. v. British Columbia*, [2003] 2 S.C.R. 403.
102 *Ibid.* at para. 40.
103 *Ibid.* at para. 50.
104 *Supra* note 89 at 10-14.
105 Indian Residential Schools Resolution Canada, Final Agreement, 8 May 2006, online: Government of Canada <http://www.irsr-rqpi.gc.ca/english/ news_10_05_06_AIP.html>.
106 *Ibid.* at Article 3.
107 *Ibid.*
108 *Ibid.*
109 Bell *et al.*, "Repatriation and Heritage Protection," *supra* note 62 at 251.
110 Richard Overstall, in consultation with Val Napoleon and Katie Ludwig, "The Law Is Opened: The Constitutional Role of Tangible and Intangible Property in Gitanyow," this volume at 92-95.
111 Susan Marsden, "Northwest Coast *Adawx* Study," this volume at 114-15.

11

Owning as Belonging/Owning as Property: The Crisis of Power and Respect in First Nations Heritage Transactions with Canada

Brian Noble

> [There are] many issues associated with protecting and repatriating First Nations cultural heritage in Canada ... At the core of the struggle there sometimes lies "[a] ... gulf between Western concepts of private property and the primacy of the relationship between property and identity in Aboriginal societies."
>
> – Catherine Bell *et al.*[1]

In this chapter I take up two central points from Bell's decidedly anthropological observation – respect and difference. These points are among those most forcefully transmitted by the First Nations participants in this project. It is upon their statements and positions that this chapter is grounded. I identify respect as a crucial transcultural touchstone for developing practices of political relationship between Canada and First Nations. The "gulf" between concepts of property is demonstrated through the profound disparity between participant and non-aboriginal (especially Euro-Canadian) social and political understandings surrounding practices of ownership and transaction, and the relation of this to problems of identity and autonomy.[2]

My analysis considers First Nations positions on the ownership and protection of cultural heritage primarily within the context of liberal state conditions animated by histories of colonial hierarchy and power. Western law and property practices continue to displace, or "trump," historic and contemporary indigenous law and property practices. For example, some of the case studies demonstrate a stark contrast between practices emphasizing "owning as property" and "owning as belonging" – a contrast that goes to the heart of social and political formation. The phrase "owning as property" describes a system that emphasizes property as a commodity capable of individual ownership and alienation for the purposes of resource use and wealth maximization. In contrast, "owning as belonging" places greater emphasis on transactions that strengthen relationships of respect and responsibility between people and what they regard as "cultural property." It assumes a largely inextricable connection and continuity between people and the material and intangible world. Differing understandings of ownership have long preoccupied anthropologists,[3] but very rarely have anthropological considerations been applied to such a rich array of thematically unified and indigenous-sourced case studies. The promise of these case studies is that they afford an opportunity to see clearly the fuller and deeper contours of the ongoing crisis regarding respect for First Nations practices of owning and transaction of cultural property and heritage. This crisis also raises larger questions regarding power, recognition practices, and how to conceive of the mutual "sovereignties" of First Nations and the Canadian state – yet another interest of contemporary anthropological inquiry.[4]

While cultural property, repatriation, and heritage issues are the focus of the case studies, my focus is an analysis of the economic, political, and cosmological philosophies informing them. I look at how, and in what contexts, ideas of respect, transaction, autonomy, and power collide, and I seek to offer clues regarding how we might imagine new legal and political arrangements. Drawing on the cumulative findings of the studies, I consider a modest proposal advanced by one participant for parallel reciprocal "recognition spaces" as opposed to a singular approach to rights recognition that continues to privilege the Canadian state. The premise is that the parallel model can go much further in redressing fundamental, historical imbalances of power and issues of respect in cultural heritage relations than can the singular model. It does so, in part, by being resolutely serious about the existence of the crisis in power and respect between Canada and First Nations and by allowing for the advancement of First Nations autonomous practices of "owning as belonging" rather than acquiescing to the problematic liberal political trend of translating First Nations practices into various versions of "owning as property."

The first half of the chapter concentrates on examining some of the entangled issues arising in the case studies – issues of respect, difference, power, and owning – as a means of honing and restating some critical questions suggested by the overall project. This is followed by a discussion of possible strategies of recognition that arise from and address crises of respect and power.

Respecting Difference through Ways of Owning

First Nations in Canada continue to experience locally variable conditions of economic disparity, political marginality, and social inequality and, with regard to relations of power, are subordinate to the Canadian state. In this historical and contemporary context, First Nations peoples have long been facing economic practices that are preponderantly based on Western liberal notions of property and autonomy. Indigenous practices of owning and autonomy, and the social and political differences engendered by them, have largely been eclipsed.[5]

The case studies have brought home the importance of respecting difference. For example, in the *Poomaksin* chapter, Herman Many Guns remarks, "Canada always kind of throws us all into one big pot, one big culture and ... like we have the same kind of problems. We [live] differently. We [relate to each other] differently. Our language is different; our customs are different."[6] Similarly, in the *Adawx* case study, Susan Marsden concludes: "for the Tsimshian and Gitksan the greatest issue associated with what the Euro-Canadian world calls 'intellectual property' is the lack of acknowledgment and respect for their identity in its fullest and deepest sense."[7] Narcisse Blood of the Kainai describes this quite plainly and aptly as "worlds colliding."[8] To reiterate, there is a deep and pervading crisis in Canada with regard to respect for difference.

The explicitly collaborative nature of this project has brought us face to face not only with respect for difference in the general sense (as in you are Hul'qumi'num, Kainai, or Haida and I am Anglo-Canadian or Indo-Canadian, etc.) but also in the more specific sense of considering how First Nations societies and the wider plurality that makes up Canadian society *practise respect for difference differently.* This contrast in forms of practice is evident in different practices of ownership: how one owns, how one transacts, how one relates to the matter that is being transacted, and how social (and natural) relations are made, reinforced, weakened, or broken. In every sense then, owning is a relational term. It signals both the *kinds* of attachment between people and things and the *modes* of making and breaking such attachments when people transact culturally important matters.

Listening carefully to the words of those participating in this project, one gradually comes to see that the central distinction between owning as property and owning as belonging is repeatedly asserted as a key to the crisis in matters of cultural heritage. While expressed in different ways, this basic distinction came up over and over again. For example, in her response to the question, "What does cultural property mean to you?" Andrea Sanborn described how totalizing the idea of owning things cultural is to the Kwakwa̲ka̲'wakw: "[C]ultural property, to me, is anything about us, for us, given to us by our Creator and is ... to be used by all of us with respect."[9] This positions Kwakwa̲ka̲'wakw ideas of ownership far from Western notions of transacting alienable "property," which implies the *severability* of things from "us." In addition, she couples this deep sense of attachment to an obligation to respect. Bell *et al.* are explicit about this sense of belonging in Kwakwa̲ka̲'wakw practices:

> The traditional concept of "belonging" associated with masks, dances, stories, and songs does not anticipate wrongful appropriation but, rather, common knowledge and compliance with Kwakwa̲ka̲'wakw protocols on use and responsibility. Relationships of "belonging" were traditionally

> demonstrated through performance and verified through being witnessed by the community. Songs, dances, and masks were an integral part of family identity.[10]

Implicit in the distinction between owning as belonging and owning as property are the problems of (1) who should exercise power over indigenous cultural property and (2) the internal and external means by which this issue might best be resolved. This leads to a consideration of the issue of power imbalances and, in particular, whose practices of owning and transaction are given greater or lesser agency, accorded greater or lesser primacy, and in what circumstances. Exploring concepts of ownership also leads to a consideration of how differences in power among individuals, and between individuals and the state, are affected by owning. Along with political philosophers, anthropologists have recently considered the connection between liberal state power and the apportioning exercise of exclusive property rights.[11] What continues to be lacking is a persuasive analysis of how to bring non-Western practices of owning into a mutually powerful relation with, alongside, or against Western property practices in matters of cultural heritage. Few have considered the complex and pragmatic issues of whether and how Western laws, policies, programs and other initiatives may be effectively advanced by strong forms of mutual respect for *both* distinctive and shared ways of engaging ownership and difference.[12]

Given all this, in a project that also queries the validity and impact of the possible reform of Canadian/First Nations heritage law, one could reformulate its central question as follows: Is there a mutual and deeply respectful way for multiple indigenous laws and practices relating to ownership of things cultural to coexist and co-relate with Canadian laws and practices of heritage ownership? To answer this question it is imperative to discuss the possibility of *mutual respect* across divides of difference and to explore, as Mary Ellen Turpel suggests, how "each culture is capable of sensitivity to the basic conditions of difference."[13] This, too, is an implicit theme echoing throughout the case study reports. Thus, an even more basic question is: How might we move together from cursory to very deep forms of mutual respect for difference? With this in mind, I now consider contrasting and overlapping ideas of respect.

Differentiating Respect: Duty and Awe

Respect can be a complex and slippery concept, especially when considered in a transcultural context. The case studies suggest that First Nations and Euro-Canadian notions of respect are often divergent. In the English lexicon, "to respect" is defined in terms akin to the verbs "to defer," "to heed," or "to pay attention," as is discernible in the *American Heritage Dictionary* entries: "1. To feel or show deferential regard for; esteem. 2. To avoid violation of or interference with: respect the speed limit. 3. To relate or refer to; concern."[14] However, in everyday practice, acts of respect are not simply demonstrative in the manner posed by these definitions. They are also framed in terms of exchange or transaction: one *pays* or *owes* respect and *earns* respect; one *gives* and *receives* respect; one *gains* or *loses* respect. Often respect conjures the creating or sustaining of balance or imbalance, pointing to reciprocal power transactions in the making (or breaking) of relationships.

As an everyday act of discursive power, respect usually requires the voluntary humbling of oneself to another.[15] A related question then becomes, How humble need two parties be to create balance? Further, to really respect people or their society, can you be humble towards them some of the time but not all of the time? How much respect is owed to redress histories of deeply hurtful disrespect? Put in strictly transactional terms, we might ask: How do we calculate depth with regard to respectful relations and debts of respect owed?

It follows that, depending on the measure of obligation and reciprocity applied in the interchange, respect will be strong or weak, deep or superficial. In a more cursory form, respect is offered by momentary acts of deference, such as lowering one's head, speaking reverently, not speaking out of turn. This is what people often do in a courtroom, in ceremonies, or while listening to a teacher or an elder. On their own, these are gestures, rhetorical acts, and expressions – ephemeral exchanges of respect.

In a much stronger and deeper form, such as that most often discussed in the case studies, one pays respect by *recognizing*, humbling oneself, and acting upon the source of power and authority of the other not simply in the moment but also in the perpetual unfolding of relations. In this sense of respect, people act not because they are forced to do so nor because they are fulfilling a moral duty. In this way, notions of respect articulated by participants contrast with the Western individualist philosophy expressed most famously in Kant's ends/means, or dutiful, formula of respect – *achtung*[16] – which demands that one "[a]ct in such a way that you always treat humanity, whether in your own person or in the person of any other, never simply as a means, but always at the same time as an end."[17]

Consider, for example, the multiple layers of respect invoked by Hul'qumi'num speaker Roy Edwards when discussing human remains:

> The old people said, when you see remains, honour it, "'ethu 'i'ch mustimukw" [Take care of each other]. If you take care of them, they'll help you. You help them, they help you later on. They will thank you for the little bit of respect you showed them. Help each other, never argue. If you argue, you never know, it might be your children they will take it out on. Always be careful, help each other. Honour and respect.[18]

There is a contrast between a Kantian dutiful deference to the humanity of persons and a relational and visceral awe and fear for the sources of power giving life and authority to persons – as is frequently noted in the case studies.[19] Unlike Kant's ends/means distinction, in First Nations thinking the concepts of ends and means practically evaporate, collapsing into one another in a relational process. Everything is Creator-given. One is part of creation and is always being cared for by others, so one needs to take care of others. If one cares for others, things will go well for all and there will be no retribution. Whether living or deceased people; tangible or intangible things of the earth, water, and sky; or things "cultural," every animated *thing* and every animated *being* needs to be respected since we are always in a relationship of exchange with all of this, with all of them.

Participant understandings of respect go considerably beyond the ephemeral acts of cursory, deferential expressions of respect. These are profound, highly consequential, and enduring exchanges of respect. In transactional terms, profound respect extends into the past and far into the future of all relationships, and it is produced and maintained through greater degrees of reciprocity. While it may be hard to continue to respect others if they do not respect you, one needs to respect them all the same since we cannot escape the fact that we are mutually entangled. From this perspective, there will be consequences if one does less than this.

As an observer of Canadian-First Nations relations, it is my sense that Canada has mostly extended a cursory form of respect in these relations, usually in consequence of implicit or explicit moral and legal senses of duty. This occurs despite the fact that First Nations peoples attempt to practise and call for stronger forms of mutual, transactional, and relational respect in their relationships with Canada. For example, case law and public pressure have resulted in governments developing more meaningful consultation processes to address the impacts of resource development on First Nations lands rather than developing an enduring deep form of respect for rights, interests, and difference. The consequence is a historic and ongoing imbalance in power surrounding exchanges of respect in First Nations-Canadian state relations. Differing principles and practices of respect also help us to understand the historic incapacity of Canada to generate lasting beneficial relations with its indigenous peoples.

So, where might we look to see how contrasting notions of "respect" intersect in legal relations between Canada and First Nations concerning ownership of cultural property? One telling occurrence appears in Bell *et al.*'s survey of repatriation and heritage law in this volume, where the authors cite the text of the Nisga'a Final Agreement.[20] The Nisga'a Final Agreement incorporates other agreements negotiated with the Royal British Columbia Museum (RBCM) and the Canadian Museum of Civilization (CMC) to return certain Nisga'a items from their collections. While those to be returned by the CMC are mostly of a sacred or ceremonial character, those to be returned by the RBCM are wider in scope. Both museums are to negotiate custodial agreements with respect to Nisga'a items remaining in their collections as well as with respect to those that might be acquired in the future. Paragraph 15 provides that the Nisga'a "share possession" of items remaining in the CMC collection, and Para. 17 specifies that the terms of sharing are to be set out in a custodial agreement that must "respect Nisga'a laws and practices relating to Nisga'a artifacts and comply with federal and provincial laws of general application and the statutory mandate of the Canadian Museum of Civilization."[21]

The vagueness of the phrase "respect Nisga'a laws and practices relating to Nisga'a artifacts" stands in sharp contrast to the legal precision and obligatory nature of the phrase "comply with federal and provincial laws of general application and the statutory mandate of the Canadian Museum of Civilization." Where Nisga'a law is general and unspecified, but something that parties must "respect," the relationship with federal and provincial laws and with the mandate of the CMC are something with which parties must "comply." This could be due to a number of factors, including Nisga'a oral traditions, understandings of respect, the nature of material at issue (included, among other items, are spoons, earrings, baskets, and arrows), the reluctance of the CMC to be obliged to comply with laws not clearly articulated in a manner familiar to it, and the retention of custody by the CMC, which must act within the confines of Canadian law. However, the choice of words still offers insight into power differentials and respect for different legal orders. While Canadian law is held to operate through a very robust and traceable obligation of compliance, First Nations practices are limited to an unspecified notion of "respect" – and this is within the terms of a Western legal instrument that could readily have incorporated some kind of instruction on how one goes about properly respecting Nisga'a law on its own terms.[22]

Through this kind of statement, respect for Nisga'a law is subordinated and displaced by respect for Canadian law. One has to treat difference differently, and this applies to differences in laws as much as it does to differences in social formations and practices. Without more clarity regarding the sort of practices that constitute respect and that must be respected, a non-First Nations reader or government interpreter of this text might conclude that a gesture of deference and reverence would suffice or, at most, that the internal legal machinations of the Nisga'a, once resolved, would ultimately be subject once and for all to the laws of Canada. Although Nisga'a law is paramount in some areas, there are still other important areas (*e.g.*, environmental protection, timber processing, etc.) in which federal or provincial law will prevail should there be a conflict. Even in those instances in which Nisga'a law is formally recognized as paramount, it is no different from the federal or provincial laws when it comes to appeal:

the system under which all parties resolve legal conflicts is represented by the courts of Canada. Nowhere in the Final Agreement is there an explicit or implicit notion that the Nisga'a system could be the decisive venue for resolving such conflicts.

If the case studies in this volume are a useful guide to thinking about practices of other First Nations in Western Canada, and I believe they are, then one might interpret respect for Nisga'a laws as the enduring, profound, relational, and transactional sort of awe discussed so far. It is this strong practice of respect, which should apply not simply in Nisga'a territory but also in Nisga'a's dealings with provincial and federal jurisdictions. This is likely the form of respect the Nisga'a had in mind in agreeing to this wording.

This gets at the next puzzle I wish to address. Specifically, if we are to discuss the possibility of coexistence and respect for difference in practices in which First Nations and mainstream Canadian ideas of heritage or cultural property meet, we need to also ask: Is it necessary, and is it respectful, for any set of laws or practices to be able to trump others?

Trumping Inseparability

Consideration of respect for difference and practices of difference have led us to questions about the legitimization of different practices of law and cultural property. These questions have historical underpinnings. Despite almost twenty-five years of First Nations political and legal engagement in a post-section 35 constitutional environment, the crisis pertaining to respect for indigenous control of indigenous lives persists in Canada, and much of this crisis still crystallizes around questions of respect for "ownership."[23] Heritage and culture are but one element of this larger issue. Comprehensive claims, aboriginal rights and title litigation, and various efforts in law reform have been moving ahead since 1982, all grappling with questions of control, respect, co-management, and partnerships.

Protection, repatriation, and control, what we might call "effective ownership" of cultural heritage, are inseparable from the larger historical crisis of power between Canada and First Nations that s. 35 is intended to address. Heritage and culture are part of a broader struggle that is rooted in European-aboriginal contact, which occurred over two hundred years ago. Whether framed as a crisis of power or as a crisis of respect, the inherent dilemmas concern *who owns* (*i.e.*, controls) and *who has say over ownership* (*i.e.*, arbitrates the practice of owning and transaction) not just things cultural but also lands, resources, sea beds, knowledge, bodily matter, lives, rights, relationships, and more.

It is worthwhile, therefore, to look more carefully at distinctions between First Nations and mainstream Canadian notions of owning. Many of the community participants in this project have stated directly that cultural property is part and parcel of an inalienable, completely interconnected complex. Echoing Andrea Sanborn and other members of her community, Kwakwaka'wakw participant Andrea Cranmer provided details regarding the idea that cultural property consisted, literally, of everything that the Kwakwaka'wakw own:[24]

> Okay, my whole existence as Andrea is cultural property. It's who I am. It's all the traditions of the Kwakwaka'wakw that belong to me and belong to our people. It's the language, the Kwak'wala language and, most importantly, our values we have as a people, *maya'xala*, which means respect or treating someone good or something good. It's protecting all our songs and dances and history. It's protecting our land because all the land base comes out of our creation stories in this area. That's cultural property. So those are the things. It's family passing on family values and the history of each family and all the treasures they own culturally.[25]

This matter of the inseparability of indigenous practices from that upon which they act reminds us yet again of the complex issue of how one owns all of this. It also anticipates the eventual challenge we face in addressing whether and how multiple ways of distinctive owning and transacting can coexist in a respectful and uncompromising way.

Virtually all the case studies discuss problems with the use of the terms "property" and "ownership." The Kwakwaka'wakw tended to speak of owning in terms of belonging, of entitlements and responsibilities that are transferred intergenerationally through complex clan relations. Similarly, the Ktunaxa/Kinbasket report states: "Although there are many similarities between Western and Ktunaxa concepts of ownership, the former cannot adequately describe participants' perceptions of their relationship to material culture, information, and land."[26] Instead, we find statements such as that of one Ktunaxa elder, "[W]e are stewards[ ] of the land. That's all I can say is, hey, we were put here for that."[27] In Gitanyow, owning as belonging also means that which makes a person real, and it entails a complete relation between one's attachment to things cultural and one's attachment to the land. Amsisa'ytxw (Victoria Russell) explains this: "'We actually have a place in this world, it makes a difference for me as a Luuxhon House member emotionally because it makes me feel proud to know I own land.' Without the land, the songs, the crests, the history, she says, 'I would be nothing.'"[28]

In a different vein, Hul'qumi'num speaker Abner Thorne inverts the relation of belonging: "Some people say my Indian name is mine. It belongs to me. And [in Hul'qumi'num] teaching ... it's the other way. It's I belong to the name. That's not mine alone, my name, is not mine alone, anybody in my family or from that ancestry can take that name. They belong to the name also."[29]

In other instances, concepts of transferred rights and responsibility were set directly against ideas of property. One Skinnipiikani speaker, Heather Crowshoe-Hirsch, notes:

> The use of the term "property" is inadequate as that which is transferred does not, technically speaking, belong to anyone. The possession of these items is "Creator-given" and, as such, cannot be owned or deemed property as such. Rather than "property," perhaps it is better to say that all of these items are "physical representations of these rights.[30]

There is a curious parallel between Crowshoe-Hirsch's final statement and the now mainstream legal concept of Western property, which sees it not as a thing but, rather, as a bundle of rights to which certain things are subject. However, in Skinnipiikani terms, the physical object represents the abstract right, whereas in Western thinking the abstract right is an adjunct to, not a representation of, the object of transaction. That said, the two approaches diverge on the distinction of Skinnipiikani "property" as '"Creator-given" and so specifically subject to the highly distinctive practices of *Poomaksin* (reciprocal transfer) and *Siikapistaan* (reciprocal payment).

It is clear that, while there are some consistencies in certain principles underlying concepts and practices of ownership, the case studies demonstrate a remarkable diversity of specific means for differentiating how people own, or form attachments to, cultural property. All of the case studies point to very strong attachments and obligations associated with owning and transacting items of significant cultural value to the community. Among these significant materials are clan and ceremonial items (*e.g.*, clan crests in carved work or shawls, songs that signal rights to territory, and ceremonial bundles for community healing). Just as important, transfer and other forms of exchange of cultural property tend to strengthen, deepen, and extend social and emotional connections among people, their histories, their material productions, their knowledge, their lands, their kin groups, and the Creator, rather than to effect a separation, as would be expected of the predominantly Western understanding of property as commodity.[31]

While participants emphasize the importance of tangible and intangible cultural property to revival and to the continuity of cultural knowledge and identity, to reduce this connection to a simple relation between property and identity is to be too narrow. Modes of exchange, and relationships and obligations created through exchange, are also crucial to social and political formation. In this light, there is an astonishing consistency between the First Nations case studies and the generalized anthropological distinction between commodity exchange and gift exchange systems as articulated by Chris Gregory.

Gregory describes commodity exchange as "an exchange of alienable objects between persons who are in a state of reciprocal independence which establishes a quantitative relationship between the objects exchanged."[32] He contrasts this with gift exchange systems based on "an exchange of inalienable objects between persons who are in a state of reciprocal dependence that establishes a qualitative relationship between the persons involved in the exchange."[33] Notably, commodity-centred practices amplify and sustain an impersonal separation. Parties remain "in a state of reciprocal independence" by being able to *alienate* the objects in the transaction. In gift-centred practices, it is the *inalienability* of the objects being transacted that amplifies the reciprocal social dependence of the parties.

To some extent, Gregory's contrasting systems reduce complex, culturally diverse practices of transaction to a strict categorical opposition – one that we ought not essentialize. However, his representations get at radically different relations of power and respect regarding the way in which people engage each other at the moment of transaction and far into the future once the transaction is completed. Understood in this sense, that which has been (and is still being) trumped in historic and contemporary relations between Canada and First Nations is not only First Nations systems of ownership and transaction but also their central mode of economic, social, and political formation.[34] Relationships and obligations created through transactions of things cultural are central elements of self-definition – the socio-political fabric that First Nations refer to and mobilize in fashioning their self-determination. In practice and effect, by means of privileging liberal property transaction, Canada is trumping and displacing, though as the case studies demonstrate not fully erasing, the crucial inseparability of First Nations people from their land, their societies, their modes of governance, their material heritage, their knowledge, their practices, and much, much more.

Of course, while Gregory's contrasting systems are highly germane to this argument, the complex manner in which a First Nation conducts its social and economic life in relation to cultural property can only be understood in specific historical and contemporary contexts pertaining to particular First Nations/state relations. However, all participants in this research attest to how Western property law and the commodity exchange system are privileged over their own.[35] They contend, as in the Ktunaxa/Kinbasket study, "that significant [cultural] loss could not have occurred independent of Canada's legal and political environment, which intentionally undermined aboriginal cultures."[36]

Given the historical and contemporary legal, social, economic, and political environment, it is little wonder that Canadian laws continue to engender incommensurability between First Nations practices of owning as belonging and predominant Canadian practices of owning as property.[37] It is also not surprising that participants frequently expressed hesitation regarding the effectiveness of Canadian law to address this issue in practical ways.

For example, Ktunaxa speaker Gina Clarricoates remarks, "Why am I not too keen on laws? Because sometimes laws are broken and then [*laughs*] they find ways to go around it."[38] Hul'qumi'num speaker Charles Seymour agrees: "We need more than the *Heritage [Conservation] Act* because people have ways around it ... If you want to work in a known area, you can still get a permit."[39] However, caution is necessary as legislation directly constrains one's practices and rights, including those that would otherwise be protected by customary legal claim.

Intercultural Recognition through Cultural Property?

What I have proposed thus far is that, in the larger Canadian society, the idea of owning is dominated by notions that *privilege property*, whereas in First Nations societies *owning privileges belonging*. However, it should be remembered that members of First Nations and the wider pluralities constituting Canadian society understand both owning as property and owning as belonging.[40] Why? One reason is that we have lived on these lands together for more than two centuries. Another is that we have all experienced the connective social force of inalienable reciprocity (*e.g.*, gift giving with an implicit expectation of return) and the easy disconnective force of alienable trade (*e.g.*, buying consumable goods with money). We are already, and have long been, "intercultural," which Marilyn Strathern describes as "the condition of already inhabiting one another's cultures."[41] In the end, we can talk about these differences because we *all* have a sense of these two subsidiary ways of engaging the world: property and belonging. Essentially, most of us have the basic skills for developing mutual respect for how we differentiate notions of "ownership."

What happens when we bring together the interculturality of owning practices with ideas of cursory or deep forms of respect? What is the best way to secure and extend the strong forms of respect that have for so long eluded Canadian law and politics? How do we get beyond the history of non-recognition when thinking about law reform, policy development, and programming initiatives? Is it possible to produce an outcome that fully recognizes and respects the highly varied social practices of owning as belonging?

In response to these questions I present two propositions: one from Australia and one derived from the Skinnipiikani community study. The first proposition includes the idea of "recognition spaces" – an idea that has emerged in the context of Australian aboriginal land rights discourse.[42] Coined by aboriginal Australian lawyer and land negotiator Noel Pearson, the term was meant to describe the sort of recognition afforded by the 1993 *Native Title Act*, which arose after the famed *Mabo* decision of 1992.[43] Where, in Pearson's words, *Mabo* states that "native title is not a common law title but is instead a title recognized by the common law,"[44] native title has to be sourced outside the common law. Citing Pearson and the workings of the *Native Title Act,* Mantziaris and Martin summarize the notion of recognition space as follows:

> A space within which the Australian legal system gives formal recognition to the relations between indigenous people and their physical environment (e.g., land and waters), which have been defined by the traditional laws and custom of the indigenous group.[45]

This proposition supports the idea that legislation can recognize and respect indigenous peoples as the driving force in defining their own laws and customs regarding what is ownable, how people own, and how they belong or relate to the land.[46]

Anthropologist James Weiner has offered a number of strong arguments regarding how the idea of recognition space hinders a fuller comprehension of intrinsic differences between cultural practices.[47] The central critique is that recognition presumes two things: (1) the ability to communicate indigenous ways in a manner cognizable to the Western legal system and (2) that there is a fixed and recognizable notion of First Nations cultures and laws. This has two implications. First, it subtly fashions First Nations cultural practice into something that is commensurable with and understood by Western law and culture. For example, although a First Nation may consider an item and the songs associated with it as inextricably linked, in order to be recognized in Canadian law, the item and song may have to be treated separately under separate categories of property law. Second, Weiner points out that the bracketing of indigenous law places it in a separate domain from Western law, as though the two sets of laws have nothing to do with one another. This is contrary to the nature of cultural interaction and relational practices such as treaty making, which are at the heart of First Nations principles of respect.

There are other, more ominous, practical effects of adopting a simple recognition space concept. For example, in the instance of the *Native Title Act,* the authority for formally recognizing indigenous law remains squarely in the authorized domain of the Australian legal system. Indeed, Povinelli argues that indigenous law is cunningly made to perform according to the needs of the Australian multicultural state by the very recognition work undertaken by the courts and in the implementation of legislation.[48] Like some Nisga'a laws under the Nisga'a Final Agreement, indigenous law is still subordinated and subjected to the definitions of Western law. Such legal entailment exercises are quite familiar to us in Canada, where decisions such as *R. v. Van der Peet* have specifically framed the terms for what can be understood as aboriginal "custom" deserving of protection as a constitutional right when asserted independently of claims to title. As framed within the aboriginal rights deliberations of Chief Justice Lamer: "the test for identifying the aboriginal rights recognized and affirmed by s. 35(1) must be directed at identifying the crucial elements of those pre-existing distinctive societies."[49] Legitimate rights-bearing customs are recognized through non-indigenous doctrines of contact, continuity, and change.

As legal scholar Robert Cooter explains, "courts do not invent custom, but by articulating it, they shape it decisively."[50] They make the determination of what is customary and "indigenous" and, in so doing, have the power over the sorts of social arrangements that any given custom or customary law can regulate. Of course customary law operates independently of judicial recognition, but in the event of conflict, recognition by external courts determines what laws shall prevail. Judicial recognition is given within a narrow context and only as specific cases arise, without consideration of the broader social, cultural, economic, and historical contexts in which they are embedded. This can put limitations on what may be seen as acceptable customary practice.

As noted in the Ktunaxa report, "Most participants, when asked about what prevents the community from exercising its laws in relation to cultural property, interpreted this question as: What prevents the community from practising traditional ways?"[51] This statement tells us, yet again, that we cannot separate the practice of First Nations law from the totality of social, political, and economic practice. How is it that one aspect of custom – laws in relation to cultural property – can be defined outside of the totality of customary law or outside the context of relations with other First Nations or Western legal systems?

A vital point is that legislation and other legal acts of recognition reflect the views of those who subscribe to the social and political discourse from which the act of recognition emerges and in which it is authorized. Legislation creating recognition spaces remains an extension of the rule of the state. It may well represent an honest and even conditionally respectful attempt to provide an inclusive view of the practices of others. Nonetheless, it is highly questionable whether legislation can escape its own social field of force.[52] We need simply ask the question: If First Nations people want to appeal an application or interpretation of a legislative regulation recognizing their customary practices, where can they turn? The jurisdiction is with Canadian courts. But does the power of recognition always have to be so?

Beyond Trumping: Parallel Recognition Spaces

So, where do we begin to look for stronger ways to accord enduring, motivating, and mutual respect? While the case studies are replete with examples of First Nations practices and understandings being trumped by Canadian law, there are few examples of how to move beyond this situation.

There is mention of treaty negotiation in the general sense, provided such negotiations are underwritten by the activation of First Nations practices of recognition. For example, as then Gitanyow chief Godfrey Good suggested, hunting rights may be recognized through song. Speaking of his uncle, he explains: "He sang the song that belonged to a man from Gitanmaax. He would tell who the song belongs to. He knew many songs; he would then say who this song belongs to."[53] The acknowledgment of hunting territory rights by means of owned and transferable intangibles such as rightful songs could be built into treaty understandings, negotiations, and agreements. For example, evidence of aboriginal title could be advanced through the singing of songs rather than through speaking and written documents. In terms of strong translegal reciprocity, this is the sort of distinctive practice that needs to be *respected* when we speak of comparably distinctive ways of exercising Gitksan law, Stó:lō law, Nisga'a law, Secwepemc law, and so on.

The need for mutual and uncompromising respect is also addressed in the Skinnipiikani community study. As Reg Crowshoe put it:

> [H]ow do you work with two paradigms? One cannot trump the other side. So, in order not to trump the other side, you've gotta be able to work with recognition and awareness of both sides. And this is where [the] concept of ... paralleling came in: *Nitooii*.[54]

Nitooii translates into "the same that is real." In this concept of paralleling, each and every Western legal action, definition, or differentiation is set against the alternative culturally based rights or legal practice of a First Nation in the context of an everyday issue in need of regulation or judgment. The *Poomaksin* report of the Skinnipiikani is a partial demonstration of this practice. Laws concerning verbal interchange on rightful topics are demonstrated in practice, while, at the same time, being spoken about and expanded upon.

The Skinnipiikani community study's process for addressing cultural heritage followed the protocols and practices of the Sundance and Brave Dog Society in order to achieve a strong sense of rightful interaction, positions, and principles. A similar process could apply, for instance, in the case of child custody disputes. Such disputes could be directed simultaneously and in parallel to both provincial court processes and to Skinnipiikani-Nitsiitapii processes. The latter might be associated with major community bundles that have clear protocols regarding venue, actions, language, and songs. Thunder Medicine Pipe Bundles, for example, are transferred to rightful holders from specific clans and, therefore, readily invoke the kin-related connections and commitments of those clans. In such a process, the players, family members, and disputants would engage in a proceeding within, for example, the general context of an All Night Smoke ceremonial hosted and led by transferred bundle keepers. Everyone would sit in the prescribed circle arrangement for witnessing and would observe the ascribed statuses for discussion, protocols for ordering speech, and songs for affirming rightfulness. Both the authority of the bundles and of the non-Piikani laws would be activated, addressed, and paralleled in this arrangement. The generalized functions of ceremonialist, host, drumming support, ceremonial service, and advisory support would be filled, adapted, and directed towards the terms of the legal dispute and the issue it is addressing. Opening with smudging and prayer, the action follows the appropriate protocols but focuses upon pointed discussion and adjudication in an environment of practice-driven customary authority, support, common witnessing, and responsible participation.[55]

Such a process could just as readily be applied to discussions concerning the rightful repatriation of cultural materials, for instance. Indeed, it is the authority and rightfulness of cultural materials that would be used by practitioners to deliberate on such rights being considered in relation to other cultural materials held outside the community. In relation to the broader landscape of First Nations involvements in Canada, this sort of approach would be sourced in the practices of right and law of each First Nation and would operate, therefore, according to the culturally specific rules and principles of respect, autonomy, and authority of the First Nation in question.

The general notion of dual or parallel practice is evident in the comments of other First Nations participants in this volume. For example, John Nicholas of the Ktunaxa/Kinbasket makes reference to balanced, dual practices with regard to the regulation of sacred sites:

> You can't have all natives enforcing the rules because the non-natives are going to turn against them because they don't want to be bossed around by a group of natives. And then you have, on the other hand, non-natives enforcing laws on natives. That is wrong. They've got to have something to do with the natives personally. One-sided just doesn't work. They have to get together ... If it means having to expose ... things that you don't really want to show people, so be it. You have to show them to gain their respect and let them know what it means to you.[56]

To be sure, one has to consider whether a parallel recognition process implies the engagement of two self-determining parties and sovereign nations, even in a provisional sense. That is a much larger conversation than what we can offer here as it necessitates addressing the matter of how to manage disputes and conflicts among parties. That said, the potency of paralleling is in how it accords a mutual respect, thereby offering an unthreatening means of advancing such a conversation. Another question is whether, by way of Western law reform, it is possible to create *parallel recognition spaces* where the First Nations practices formally recognize and respect the authority of Canadian laws and, reciprocally, where Canadian laws formally recognize and respect the authority of the First Nations laws.

The Kainai report demonstrates the potency of mutual, reciprocal recognition in Kainaiwa relations with the Glenbow. As Narcisse Blood remarks:

> [L]ook to the example that has been set ... by [the] "[n]obody loses, everybody wins" [policy] ... look at [the] Glenbow Museum. They're a lot stronger ... I think they can say we have a relationship with the Blood Tribe ... Relationships, in our ways, are very important. The point being that we can cooperate.[57]

Parallel recognition and respect by the Glenbow and Kainai have resulted in repatriation, enactment of repatriation legislation that acknowledges the legitimate moral interests of the Glenbow and Blackfoot tribes in Blackfoot material and that enables transfer of title, and co-management agreements for Kainai material remaining in the Glenbow's possession.

While one might argue that the Kainai-Glenbow relationship may not yet be the full-blown manifestation of the parallel recognition spaces discussed above, by underscoring the principle of the necessary mutuality of respectful interaction, it certainly moves in this direction. The Kainaiwa case study emphasizes how mutual and enduring respect is the crucial touchstone for successful repatriation negotiations and for creating powerful relations:

> Positive experiences were associated with non-adversarial relationships built on mutual trust, respect, and the understanding of cultural differences ... Negative experiences occurred when parties lost respect for one another or when no opportunity presented itself for relationship building to occur.[58]

Similarly, in 2001, Reg Crowshoe of the Skinnipiikani identified a relationship he referred to as "re-repatriation." Re-repatriation involves the ongoing reciprocal trade of cultural matter between public institutions/government museums and First Nations – trade that extends mutual respect for distinct practices in perpetuity.[59] This proposition, perhaps not surprisingly, mirrors historic First Nations understandings of the treaty relationship as opposed to such modern versions as the Nisga'a Final Agreement, which appear to skew to conventional contractual principles of certainty.[60]

Ultimately, then, what Reg Crowshoe points us to is the development of strong parallel and reciprocal recognition spaces rather than state recognition practices, such as the Nisga'a Final Agreement, *NAGPRA* in the United States, or Australia's *Native Title Act*. It returns us to the premise that each society has within it all the capacities and sources of authority to engage universes of natural and social relations. It gets at the idea of two (and more) coexisting worlds of practice, both fully activated, differentiating difference by their respective means, both fully respectful of the interests of the other, reciprocally engaged with each other (or at least moving in that direction). When First Nations and Canadian practices are paralleled, the mutually respectful dialogue we have so far been unable to achieve, or have achieved only very rarely, may emerge.

Conclusion: The Deeper Challenges of Cultural Property

> In the beginning we have our own laws that was – that was used by our people, the Gitksan people, *aluugigyet*. These laws were used and after the arrival of white people, they forced us to use their laws, they pushed their laws onto us ... The white people have always tried to make us follow their ways, and they don't realize that we have our own laws and our own ways, and now they say this is – this land belongs to the Crown. This is not true, because the Crown never did – never bought this land from us ... And it's not for us to give our land away to her [the Queen], this is our land, not hers ... [W]e've always had this law and we are going to put it into action.
>
> – Stanley Williams[61]

When First Nations peoples assert that they *belong* indivisibly to their cultural property, they are stressing the all-encompassing idea of *owning as belonging*, an idea that is fully animated by culturally distinct, practised systems of internal legal sanctions. This idea recapitulates the often-heard statement by First Nations peoples that they also belong indivisibly to the land. In the case studies we repeatedly encounter this very easy move between indigenous attachment to land and indigenous attachment to things cultural. As Stanley Williams notes above, these are implicitly and explicitly connected matters that are enmeshed within and protected by the power of indigenous law.

In addition to asserting the power of Gitksan law, Williams reminds us that the Crown did not make use of its ("her") own inherent system of property transaction to acquire Gitksan territory. Moreover, he suggests that "it's not for us to give our land away to her." How, or indeed why, would a people give away that to which they belong? Given such strong commitments to their inherent inseparability from the land, to suggest they could give the land away is to suggest they could give themselves away. From all that is presented in this volume, it appears that this same premise applies to the relations to certain forms of cultural property, which are also indivisible from the people and the land. It follows that to ignore that is to commit a deeply disrespectful act.

If future discussions of First Nations cultural property move forward by privileging non-First Nations ways and non-First Nations procedures for recognizing ownership, or if the notion of owning as property dominates the notion of owning as belonging, we will have done little to find a fulsome, strong form of respect. If, for example, these issues continue to be resolved solely through legislation and legal decision-making processes external to First Nations communities, at best we will have merely performed dutiful acts of deference, arguably the easier kind of respect. We will have sidestepped what all these case studies call for – a deep, robust, reciprocal, and enduring respect across state-enacted divides. In my view, this is the most fundamental challenge posed by the First Nations contributions to this project and to any future initiatives it might trigger. It is the challenge that Canada must address if it is to avoid perpetuating the existing crisis of power and respect.

Charles Seymour, a Hul'qumi'num elder, reminds us of the gift of respect he has received. His sense of care and honour towards the ancestors could as easily apply to the culturally important tangible and intangible matter described throughout these reports:

> Have I received any teachings from my parents or elders? Yes. I've always been told to be, to be careful and be mindful [of] our, of our ancestors. You always pay respect. It's like when you visit, visit a gravesite, you have to carry yourself in a certain way. You always have to have a prayer in your heart and *tsiit sul'hween* [thank the ancestors] I guess. Thank them, and in a very respectful way.[62]

Gauging from the case studies, such teachings are familiar terrain for First Nations peoples, and they continue to recognize and act upon the challenges they pose. The more difficult challenge lies with Canada and the Canadian polity. The simple question to which we must return, over and over, is: How deeply respectful are we actually prepared to be?

Notes

1 Catherine Bell *et al.*, "First Nations Cultural Heritage: A Selected Survey of Issues and Initiatives," this volume at 404.

2 I use the term "transaction" throughout this chapter in a broad anthropological sense to refer to practices of exchange in all their cultural diversity, in local contexts, and in historical flux. In a general way, transaction can refer to the exchange or transfer of goods, tangible and intangible things, rights, land, knowledge, even people (as in marriage exchange). Following standard dictionary meanings, it can also refer even more broadly to interpersonal or intergroup, even interspecies, exchanges as in "a communicative action or activity involving two parties or things that reciprocally affect or influence each other."

Merriam-Webster Online Edition, *s.v.* "transaction," online: <http://www.m-w.com/dictionary/transaction>. A broad concept like this is useful with regard to addressing views raised by indigenous peoples that they do not simply enter into exchange with people but, indeed, with animals, land, spirits, objects, "cultural property," the Creator, and more. Significantly, I use the term to embrace multiple possibilities of exchange practices, so I am not intending to signal narrow legal notions of transaction from, for instance, sale of goods or contract law; rather, those specific forms are not excluded from this idea and can stand as examples. In relation to this, see my discussion of Strathern's proposition of an "owner," *infra* note 40.

3 *Infra* note 11.

4 Michael Asch, "Self-Determination and Treaty-Making: Consent and the Resolution of Political Relations between First Nations and Canada," online: <http://hobbes.law.uvic.ca/demcon/papers/Asch_Demcon_f2-1.doc> in Mario Blaser *et al.*, eds., *In the Way of Development: Indigenous Peoples, Life Projects and Globalization* (London, New York: Zed Books in Association with International Development Research Centre, Ottawa, 2004); Robert Paine, "Aboriginality, Multiculturalism, and Liberal Rights Philosophy" (199) 64:3 *Ethnos* 325; Noel Dyck, ed., *Indigenous Peoples and the Nation-State: "Fourth World" Politics in Canada, Australia, and Norway* (St. John's: Institute of Social and Economic Research, Memorial University of Newfoundland, 1985); Harry B. Hawthorn, ed., *A Survey of the Contemporary Indians of Canada*, vol. 11 (Ottawa: Queen's Printer, 1967); and see Ronald Niezen, *Defending the Land: Sovereignty and Forest Life in James Bay Cree Society* (Boston: Allyn and Bacon, 1998).

5 Canada, *Report of the Royal Commission on Aboriginal Peoples: Restructuring the Relationship*, vol. 2 (Ottawa: Supply and Services Canada, 1996) in particular, "Part Two: False Assumptions and a Failed Relationship."

6 Brian Noble, in consultation with Reg Crowshoe and in discussion with the Knut-sum-atak Society, "*Poomaksin:* Skinnipiikani-Nitsiitapii Law, Transfers, and Making Relatives: Practices and Principles for Cultural Protection, Repatriation, Redress and Heritage Law Making with Canada," this volume at 281.

7 Susan Marsden, "Northwest Coast *Adawx* Study," this volume at 146.

8 Catherine Bell *et al.*, "Repatriation and Heritage Protection: Reflections on the Kainai Experience," this volume at 223.

9 Catherine Bell *et al.* in consultation with Andrea Sanborn, the U'mista Cultural Society, and the 'Na̲mgis Nation, "Recovering from Colonization: Perspectives of Community Members on Protection and Repatriation of Kwakwa̲ka̲'wakw Cultural Heritage," this volume at 39.

10 *Ibid.* at 64.

11 See, for instance, the following works (and their extensive bibliographies): Katherine Verdery and Caroline Humphrey, eds., *Property in Question: Value Transformation in the Global Economy* (London: Berg, 2004); Christopher M. Hann, ed., *Property Relations: Renewing the Anthropological Tradition* (Cambridge: Cambridge University Press, 1998); Marilyn Strathern, *Property, Substance, Effect: Anthropological Essays on Persons and Things* (London: Athlone Press, 1999).

12 See, for example, Rosemary Coombe *et al.*, "Bearing Cultural Distinction: Informational Capitalism and New Expectations for Intellectual Property" in Willem Grosheide, ed., *Articles in Intellectual Property: Crossing Borders* (Utrecht: Mollengafica/Intersentia, 2006).

13 Mary Ellen Turpel, "Aboriginal Peoples and the Canadian Charter: Interpretative Monopolies, Cultural Differences" (1989-90) 6 Can. Hum. Rts. Y.B. at 14, 45, quoted in Gordon Christie, "Law, Theory and Aboriginal Peoples" (2003) 2 Indigenous L. J. at 113.

14 *American Heritage Dictionary of the English Language*, 4th ed., *s.v.* "respect," online: <http://www.bartleby.com/61/4/R0180400.html>.

15 Though this chapter has a different approach to the question, in enlightenment terms the concept of "respect" has been thoroughly examined by Immanuel Kant. See his propositions on the idea of respect in dutiful – and therefore moral – relations between modern subjects in *Groundwork of the Metaphysic of Morals*, trans. H.J. Paton (New York: Harper and Row, 1964) at 437-38.

16 But contrast Kant's use of the term *achtung* with the connotation of respect in another German vernacular term for respect, *ehrfrucht*, meaning both fear and honor. According to the twentieth-century Roman Catholic theologian and religious popularizer Romano Guardini: "Respect is a strange word, this combination of fear and honor. Fear which honors; honor which is pervaded by fear. What kind of fear could that be? Certainly not the kind of fear that comes upon us in the face of something harmful or that causes pain. That kind of fear causes us to defend ourselves and to seek safety. The fear of which we shall speak does not fight or flee, but it forbids obtrusiveness, keeps one at a distance, does not permit the breath of one's own being to touch the revered object. Perhaps it would be better to speak of this fear as "awe." See online: <http://www.jknirp.com/guarda.htm>. While a theologian himself, as an Enlightenment thinker Kant held God in a separate, transcendent sphere beyond human reason. *Achtung* (literally "attention" or "regard") would have been a far less problematic term on which to base his naturalistic philosophical maxims than would a term like *ehrfrucht*, which contains an awe for otherwoldly powers and their sanctions against improper conduct.

17 *Supra* note 15 at 429. This is Kant's "Formula of the Ends in Itself," which is one of the four elements of his "categorical imperative," described in his *Groundworks of the Metaphysics of Morals*.

18 Eric McLay *et al.*, "*'A'lhut tu tet Sul'hweentst* [Respecting the Ancestors]: Understanding Hul'qumi'num Heritage Laws and Concerns for the Protection of Archaeological Heritage," online: <http://www.ualberta.ca/research/aboriginalculturalheritage/researchpapers.htm> at 57.

19 See Michael Asch, "Some Considerations on Law, Ethics and Repatriation"(Paper presented to Glenbow First Nations Repatriation Workshop, Calgary, Alberta, 12-14 November 1998) [unpublished]; and Michael Asch, "Self-Determination of Indigenous Peoples and the Globalization of Human Rights Discourse: The Canadian Example" (Draft paper presented to CONGLASS III, July 1997, New York University) [unpublished]. See also various papers from the conference entitled Consent as the Foundation for Political Community, University of Victoria, British Columbia, 1-3 October 2004, including <http://www.hobbes.law.uvic.ca/demcon/papers/Jeremy Webber> "Challenges of Consent" [unpublished]; Val Napoleon, "Living Together: Gitksan Legal Reasoning as a Foundation for Consent" [unpublished], available online: <http://www.hobbes.law.uvic.ca/demcon/papers/>; and Asch, *supra* note 4. Also Leroy Little Bear, "Aboriginal Relationships to the Land and Resources" in Jill Oakes *et al.*, eds., *Sacred Lands: Aboriginal World Views, Claims, and Conflicts* (Edmonton: University of Alberta Press, 1998) 15; and Leroy Little Bear, "Aboriginal Rights and the Canadian 'Grundnorm'" in Rick Ponting, ed., *Arduous Journey: Canadian Indians and Decolonization* (Toronto: McClelland and Stewart, 1986) 243.

20 Nisga'a Final Agreement, online: Indian and Northern Affairs Canada <http://www.ainc-inac.gc.ca/pr/agr/nsga/nisdex_e.html>. Enacted by the British Columbia Legislature as the *Nisga'a Final Agreement Act*, S.B.C. 1999, c. 2, and federally as the *Nisga'a Final Agreement Act*, S.C. 2000, c. 7 [Nisga'a Agreement]. Bell *et al., supra* note 1 at 385-87.

21 Nisga'a Agreement, *ibid.*

22 There are no clear statements either about the nature or operationalizing of "Nisga'a laws" in the Nisga'a Final Agreement; however, the subordination and incidentalizing of Nisga'a law in relation to a hierarchy of jurisdiction is laid out in c. 2, para. 53, "General Provisions" of the Nisga'a Final Agreement: "If a Nisga'a law has an incidental impact on a subject matter in respect of which Nisga'a Government does not have jurisdiction to make laws, and there is an inconsistency or conflict between that incidental impact and a federal or provincial law in respect of that subject matter, the federal or provincial law prevails to the extent of the inconsistency or conflict." While one must acknowledge that, in c. 11, Nisga'a Governance, the Nisga'a are assigned authority to make their own laws in such areas as government, citizenship, culture and language, property on Nisga'a lands, marriages, social services, health, child custody, education, and so on, these would be laws developed within the constraints of the Nisga'a Constitution and its attendant practices. Closer critical analysis needs to be paid to the subtle distinction in the Final Agreement between references to "Nisga'a law" and the "Nisga'a Constitution." My preliminary suggestion is that Nisga'a law refers to those customary practices that are more fully activated

by the modes of respect discussed earlier in this chapter, while the Nisga'a Constitution may well establish procedural techniques that are potentially less consistent with those modes of respect. In other words, it appears that the Agreement itself privileges a more non-Nisga'a practice of written law making through its legally fashioned Constitution, which is subtly displacing and subordinating unwritten customary law based in principles of reciprocity, obligation, and enduring respect. Certainly, these issues are complex and deserve a more thorough analysis than I am able to provide in this chapter.

23 *Constitution Act, 1982*, being Schedule B to the *Canada Act, 1982* (U.K.), 1982, c. 11. Section 35 provides that the aboriginal and treaty rights of the aboriginal peoples of Canada are "recognized and affirmed."

24 *Supra* note 9 at 39-40.

25 *Ibid.*

26 Catherine Bell *et al.*, in consultation with the Ktunaxa/Kinbasket Tribal Council and the Ktunaxa/Kinbasket Traditional Elders Working Group, "Protection and Repatriation of Ktunaxa/Kinbasket Cultural Resources: Perspectives of Community Members," this volume at 327.

27 *Ibid.* at 107.

28 Richard Overstall, in consultation with Val Napoleon and Katie Ludwig, "The Law Is Opened: The Constitutional Role of Tangible and Intangible Property in Gitanyow," this volume at 107.

29 *Supra* note 18 at 159.

30 Taken from transcripts for the *Poomaksin* case study, *supra* note 6. Knut-sum-atak Circle Discussion No. 2 (3 December 2003), Oldman River Cultural Centre, Brocket, Alberta.

31 I say "predominantly" given that the very idea of "commodity" is, in itself, an analytical formulation, as Marilyn Strathern reminds us: "Of course many anthropologists have argued that the commodity never was the pure product which its standing as an analytical category made it out to be" at *supra* note 11 at 25.

32 Christopher A. Gregory, *Gifts and Commodities* (London: Academic Press, 1982) at 41-43. For an overview of how complex and convertible reciprocity and commodity processes can be see, see C.A. Gregory, "Exchange and Reciprocity" in Tim Ingold, ed., *Companion Encyclopedia of Anthropology* (London: Routledge, 1994) at 919-39.

33 Gregory, *Gifts and Commodities, supra* note 32 at 41-43.

34 Arguably, all the First Nations in this report have had historical reciprocity relations in their systems of transaction. The most familiar of these practices are expressed in the Northwest Coast potlatch and winter ceremonials, and the Sundance complex of the Blackfoot. Both of these types of ceremonials have made their way into the interior of British Columbia.

35 This has transpired through historic colonial expansion into and encroachment upon all aboriginal territories in Canada and, with that, through the hegemonic assertion of liberal political economic regimes. The political effort to quash First Nations exchange practices has also been effected through the rule of law, through the banning of First Nations ceremonies (such as the potlatch and Sundance), causing significant disruption – though not wholesale loss – of such socio-economic attachments and means of transacting. Dimensions of this history of cultural suppression are discussed throughout the case studies presented in this volume. See also Katherine Pettipas, *Severing the Ties That Bind: Government Repression of Indigenous Religious Ceremonies on the Prairies* (Winnipeg: University of Manitoba Press, 1994).

36 *Supra* note 26 at 334.

37 For a critical discussion of radical incommensurability, see Elizabeth Povinelli, "Radical Worlds: The Anthropology of Incommensurability and Inconceivability" (2001) 30 Annual Review of Anthropology 319.

38 *Supra* note 26 at 335.

39 *Supra* note 18 at 180.

40 In a recent article on innovation and property, British social anthropologist Marilyn Strathern (in conversation with James Leach) offered a working definition of "an owner" as,

quite simply, "somebody with something to transact." Marilyn Strathern, *Commons and Borderlands: Working Paper on Accountability and the Flow of Knowledge* (Oxon: Sean Kingston Publishing, 2004) at viii. Such a definition may be helpful in moving beyond oppositional categories and developing ownership terminology within an intercultural context as it is inclusive of differing concepts and practices of ownership. It allows for transactions of commodities (buying, selling, trading of alienable property), reciprocity transactions, transactions with the land (hunting, gathering, planting), transactions of people (marriage and kin relations), transactions with the Creator and other creative forces, transactions of respect, and so on. Strathern's definition also allows for any combination of such practices.

41 *Ibid* at 1.

42 Community case studies of this very project are such a space. They provide a venue for recognizing the social, land, and transactional relations of different First Nations peoples, where interests in indigenous peoples' tangible and intangible cultural matter intersect with interests of the Canadian state.

43 *Mabo and Others v. Queensland (No 2.)* (1992), 175 C.L.R. 1 (H.C.A.); *Native Title Act* 1993 (Cth); Noel Pearson, "The Concept of Native Title at Common Law" (1997) 5 Australian Humanities Review, online: <http://www.lib.latrobe.edu.au/AHR/archive/Issue-March-1997/pearson.html>.

44 *Ibid.*

45 C. Mantziaris and D. Martin, *Guide to the Design of Native Title Corporations* (Perth, Australia: National Native Title Tribunal, 1999) 1.

46 A recognition space, produced in the context of legislation like Australia's *Native Title Act*, or of the *Native American Graves Protection and Repatriation Act*, Pub. L. No. 101-601, 104 Stat. 3048 (1990) in the United States still narrows its considerations to "law," whether substantive common law or what is termed aboriginal "customary law." As James Weiner points out, see note 47 below, Western law, in itself, is not the total fabric of social practice but, rather, a "codification" of that totality. In contrast, what we hear about First Nations law in the community reports is that it is something that is inherent in the totality of practices. It is, in the words of Marcel Mauss, a set of total prestations.

47 James Weiner, "Eliciting Customary Law" (2006) 7:1 Asia Pacific Journal of Anthropology 15.

48 See Elizabeth Povinelli, *The Cunning of Recognition: Indigenous Alterities and the Making of Australian Multiculturalism* (Durham and Londong: Duke University Press, 2002) at 184-85.

49 *R. v. Van der Peet* [1996] 2 S.C.R. 507 at para. 44.

50 Robert Cooter discussing laws in Papua New Guinea, quoted in James F. Weiner, "The Foi Incorporated Land Group: Law and Custom in Group Definition and Collective Action in Kutubu Oil Project Area, PNG" (2001) State, Society and Governance in Melanesia Project, Working Paper 01/2, online: <http://rspas.anu.edu.au/papers/melanesia/working_papers/workingpaperjamesweiner.pdf>.

51 *Supra* note 26 at 353-54.

52 On "social fields of force," see William Roseberry, "Hegemony and the Language of Contention" in Gilbert M. Joseph and Daniel Nugent, eds., *Everyday Forms of State Formation: Revolution and the Negotiation of Rule in Modern Mexico* (Durham: Duke University Press, 1994) 355.

53 *Supra* note 28 at 96.

54 *Supra* note 6 at 305.

55 While some readers might see this as resembling sentencing circle processes, a crucial difference is that the process suggested here is socio-culturally specific and socio-culturally derived. It activates the lawful authority of transaction and respect implicit in the practices of the respective First Nation, and, although it is not subordinated to the legal determinations of non-native jurisdictions, it certainly promises to provide a means of producing a viable dialogue and collaborative set of outcomes with them.

56 *Supra* note 26 at 340.

57 *Supra* note 8 at 234.

58 *Ibid.* at 251.

59 Brian Noble, "Nitooii – The Same that is 'Real': Parallel Practice, Museums, and the Repatriation of Piikani Customary Authority" (2002) 44 Anthropologica 113.

60 See Asch, *supra* note 4.

61 *Supra* note 7 at 142 (Stanley Williams).

62 *Supra* note 18 at 158 (Charles Seymour).

Concluding Thoughts and Unanswered Questions

Val Napoleon

> Coyote, Coyote, please tell me,
> What is magic?
> Magic is the first taste of ripe strawberries, and
> Magic is a child dancing in a summer's rain ...
>
> Coyote, Coyote, please tell me,
> What is power?
> It is said that power is the ability to start your chainsaw with one pull.
>
> – Peter Blue Cloud/ Aroniawenrate, *The Elderberry Flute Song*[1]

While an appreciation of cultural and geographic specificity remains critical in order to avoid superficial generalizations of First Nations peoples, a reading of this volume should expose some larger patterns and a commonality of issues. The cultural content of the case studies is applicable only to the First Nations partners, but the composite of the studies can be extrapolated to provide larger lessons. Treated in this way, the case studies serve to create a new landscape with serious questions for consideration. Some of these are considered in this volume and others are considered in the second volume. Some remain to be answered.

The case studies create a telling picture of a number of First Nations groups and how they survived. There is a sense of retraction during the worst years of colonization. Perhaps as people lost control over lands and the larger economic, political, and social matters, they began to focus more attention on those things that remained within their control. This defensive turning inward enabled some cultural practices to be maintained (and written about in the case studies), but it is still unclear how these remaining practices, when taken literally and perhaps even out of the frame of a complete indigenous legal order, might be usefully applied to contemporary issues. How can they be applied to the ongoing struggles over lands, resources, and political control that are taking place in the communities, courts, and political and corporate boardrooms?

What becomes apparent, not surprisingly, is that the legal orders and laws of First Nations peoples have been undermined and, for many groups, are now incomplete. This is the lay of the land now made visible, and so this must be the starting place for future discussions about cultural heritage and other governance matters. The goal is not to go back in time. For some, it is to draw on existing and emerging indigenous legal principles to deal with belonging, conflict management, governance, and the current relationship with the Canadian state. What are the intellectual processes within the indigenous legal orders that enable or enabled deliberation, reasoning, and, most important, dissent and consent? In considering the case studies, what are the principles that may be derived from the cultural practices relating to cultural heritage? How might they be reconciled with current decision-making processes regarding cultural heritage and other matters? What can or should be done, if anything, to facilitate recognition, respect, and change through external Canadian legal, ethical, and policy frameworks? These are some of the many challenging questions explored in further detail in the second volume.

What would the Trickster do with these questions? How would the Trickster deal with the contradictions within our work (and all work has its inherent contradictions)? Recall that the role of the Trickster is to enable us to reconcile the past with the present so that we may imagine a future that makes sense, however transitory. The Trickster also uses humour and the bizarre, the profane, and the insane to demonstrate that which is funny, bizarre, profane, and insane but that has become cloaked in a normalcy born of familiarity and habit. Most likely, the Trickster would ask whether we are protecting the remnants of First Nations societies rather than looking at the larger structural issues and problems that First Nation peoples are experiencing. And we have to think about this question. According to the Trickster, sometimes to get rid of a log jam you have to blow it up – at least intellectually. Because of this, sometimes people think the Trickster is mean, but she is not: she just makes us see differently by drolly holding up the lens of the bizarre, the profane, and the insane.

Note

1 Peter Blue Cloud/Aroniawenrate, *The Elderberry Flute Song: Contemporary Coyote Tales* (Buffalo: White Pine Press, 1982) 131, cited in Rupert Ross, *Returning to the Teachings: Exploring Aboriginal Justice* (Toronto: Penguin Books, 1996) at 72. According to Ross, the song shows how the Trickster "loves to poke fun at the conceit that anyone, human *or* superhuman, has anything close to a profound understanding of Creation. In the first verse, Coyote sets you up to expect nothing but cosmic wisdom, and in the second, he crashes you back to earth again." In part, Coyote is a way of acknowledging uncertainty and uncontrollability.

Appendix: Standard Question Set

Interview questions and areas for research were designed in consultation with First Nations partners prior to the submission of applications for funding. Originally, we worked with the concept of cultural property to define the scope of our research. Our definitions and questions were framed within a property law context in response to research needs identified by First Nations partners in the early planning stages and in order to demonstrate the potential legal implications of our research to university and funding bodies. However, as is discussed in "Introduction, Methodology, and Thematic Overview," we struggled with this approach and, as research planning progressed, encouraged First Nations to reframe the questions to be more suitable to community understandings and priorities. As a result, this question set was used, with modification, in the Kainai, KKTC, *Poomaksin*, and U'mista studies. Unique questions were designed for the Luuxhon and Hul'qumi'num studies.

Questions were used as a guide for the interview process and as a starting point for conversations. They were simplified and, in some studies, translated into different languages or cultural understandings. Certain questions may have been omitted or emphasized, depending on the experience of the participant. Participants were also encouraged to elaborate on issues that were of the greatest concern to them. Interviews and group discussions were guided by participant interpretations (and sometimes reformulations) of questions asked, local protocols, and topics they considered important with regard to understanding concerns relating to the protection and repatriation of cultural heritage.

Answers to these questions revealed similar and different concepts of ownership and property. In our analysis, we eventually adopted the descriptor "cultural heritage" rather than "cultural property" as it is more consistent with participants' understandings.

1 What does the term "cultural property" mean to you? How would you define it?
2 In conducting this research, we have defined cultural property as being property integral to the identity of a particular aboriginal community. It includes objects of significant historical, ceremonial, or religious importance; intellectual property (*e.g.*, medicinal knowledge, songs, music, dances); sacred and historically significant places; and human remains and tissues. Does this definition make sense in your community?
3 What types of cultural property are a priority for your community to protect and control? Why?
4 Are there historical and ceremonial sites that are important for the community to protect?
5 What are some of the challenges faced in protecting and controlling the cultural property you have identified?
6 What are your laws or traditions regarding "ownership," care, use, and transfer of this property that you can share with us?
7 Does anything prevent you from being able to practise some or all of these laws or traditions the way you would like to practise them? (Example)
8 What are the culturally appropriate processes for determining rights to cultural property within the community? (How do we know who has rights/responsibilities to this property?)
9 What is the relationship of the property we are discussing to the spiritual, cultural, and emotional well-being of the community?
10 What role do you think Canadian museums should have in protecting and controlling aboriginal cultural objects in their custody?
11 Have you, or members of your community, been involved in getting property returned from a museum, public institution (*e.g.*, university), or private collector in Canada? Can you tell us about your experience?
12 Have you, or members of your community, been involved in getting property returned from a museum or private collector outside of Canada? Can you tell us about your experience.
13 Has the community taken any steps, that you are aware of, to try to protect and control the property we have discussed? (Example)
14 What rights of the ______ people to cultural property do you think need to be recognized and protected by Canadian law?
15 What types of laws do you think are necessary to protect cultural property in your community?
16 Can you think of specific laws that have helped protect, or threatened, ownership or protection of cultural property in or from your community?
17 Is there anything else you would like to say before this interview ends?

Contributors

Kelly Bannister is a research associate with the POLIS Project on Ecological Governance (Faculty of Law and School of Environmental Studies) at the University of Victoria and an adjunct professor in the School of Environmental Studies. Her work on the Project for Protection and Repatriation of First Nations Cultural Heritage was supported by a postdoctoral fellowship from the Social Sciences and Humanities Research Council of Canada. She has a BSc and an MSc in microbiology/biochemistry and a PhD in ethnobotany/medicinal plant chemistry. Her main research interests are in ethics and indigenous intellectual property rights with regard to research involving biodiversity and traditional knowledge.

Catherine Bell is a professor of law at the University of Alberta specializing in aboriginal legal issues, property law, community-based legal research, and dispute resolution. She has published extensively on First Nations and Métis legal issues, including book chapters and articles on repatriation and aboriginal rights to material culture. She is the author of two books on the Métis settlements of Alberta and is co-editor of *Intercultural Dispute Resolution in Aboriginal Contexts* (2004, UBC Press). She has also acted as an advisor to First Nations, Canadian governments, and Métis organizations, including the U'Mista Cultural Society. She is the principle investigator and coordinator of the SSHRC-funded research on protection and repatriation of First Nations cultural heritage, which led to the publication of this volume.

Dale Cunningham has practised law in Edmonton since 1999 and has been with the firm of Field LLP since 2001. He practises general litigation with a primary focus on aboriginal law and is a member of the firm's legal team representing aboriginal clients pursuing claims for abuse suffered while at government-run residential schools. Dale has been a guest speaker on residential school issues at the University of Alberta Faculty of Law and at various conferences and workshops sponsored by aboriginal groups in Alberta and the Northwest Territories.

Prior to practising law, Dale was a sectional lecturer in sociology at Grant MacEwan Community College in Edmonton and has also taught courses at the University of Alberta's Faculty of Business and its Department of Sociology.

Marianne Ignace is the academic coordinator of the Simon Fraser University Aboriginal Program in Kamloops and is associate professor of anthropology and First Nations studies at SFU and an associate faculty member of the SFU Department of Linguistics. Her doctoral dissertation on Haida discourse and kinship, *The Curtain Within*, was published by UBC Press in 1989. Since the mid-1980s, she has carried out research on Secwepemc language and culture, including work with elders from all seventeen communities. During the past fifteen years, she has also worked on aboriginal language teaching and curriculum in the Secwepemc Nation and with Haida, St'át'imc, Nuxalk, Hilzaqvla, and Sm'algyax language teachers and elders. In 1998, she wrote the *Handbook for Aboriginal Language Program Planning in British Columbia*. She is the mother of eight children and, through using Secwepemctsin (Shuswap) in the home with her younger children, has experienced the rewards and challenges of keeping a First Nations language alive.

Ron Ignace is a member of the Secwepemc Nation. He was elected chief of the Skeetchestn Band from 1982 to 2003 and served as chairman of the Shuswap Nation Tribal Council for several years. He was also a founding member and chair of the Assembly of First Nations Chiefs Committee on Aboriginal Languages from 1997 to 2003; a founding member of the Secwepemc Cultural Education Society (SCES) and was its president from 1987 to 2003; and co-chair of the aboriginal university partnership between SCES and Simon Fraser University in Kamloops, British Columbia, where he has taught courses in the Secwepemc language and First Nations studies. He was a member and chair of the First Peoples' Cultural Foundation of British Columbia from 1995 to 1999 and is presently chair of the National Task Force for (Inuit, Métis, and First Nations) Languages and Cultures appointed by the Canadian minister of heritage.

Allyson Jeffs graduated from the University of Alberta Law Faculty in June 2006. She worked as a research assistant for Catherine Bell and Dale Cunningham. Allyson is now a lawyer with the Edmonton law firm of Ackroyd LLP. A former journalist, she has covered political and social justice issues for the *Edmonton Journal* and the *Calgary Herald*.

Lea Joe is a member of the Cowichan Tribes and works as negotiations projects assistant for the Hul'qumi'num Treaty Group. Lea has participated in community-based research projects at the HTG involving land-use planning, traditional land use and occupancy, the identification of culturally significant lands, place names inventory, park co-management, and eligibility and enrollment. Lea's research resulted in HTG publishing *In the Footsteps of Our Ancestors: Interim Strategic Land Plan for the HTG Core Territory*. Lea received a BA in First Nations studies and a certificate in human resource management. She is the proud new mom of Madison Amber, born in 2005.

Susan Marsden is currently the curator of the Museum of Northern British Columbia, in Prince Rupert, BC. After graduating from the University of Toronto with an honours BA in philosophy, and from the Professional Development Program at Simon Fraser University, she moved to Gitanyow, where she married and raised a family. She was adopted into the House of Gwin'uu and participated actively in Gitksan community life. She has worked as a teacher in several Gitksan communities, developed culture and language curriculum for the Gitksan and Tsimshian, coordinated research for the Gitksan Wet'suwet'en Tribal Council in preparation for *Delgamuukw v. A.G.*, and coordinated and conducted research for the Tsimshian Tribal Council. As curator of the Museum of Northern British Columbia, she has overseen the development and design of its new facility and its evolving role as a cross-cultural institution. She is the author of several articles on Northwest Coast oral history and co-author of *Tribal Boundaries in the Nass Watershed.*

Heather McCuaig has a background in sociology and law. She worked as a research assistant to Professor Bell and was called to the Alberta Bar in September 2005. She practices in Lethbridge in the areas of family law, wills and estates, criminal law, and civil litigation. She is active with the Legal Aid Society and sits on the Board of Directors for the Bluefox not-for-profit organization in Lethbridge.

Eric McLay is an archaeologist who specializes in the Coast Salish region of the Northwest Coast. Eric has been working with the Hul'qumi'num Treaty Group since 2001, assisting in treaty negotiations and the development of heritage policy for the protection of culture and heritage. Eric has a strong professional interest in integrating First Nations in heritage site management and helping to reconcile aboriginal interests over ancestral cultural property.

Val Napoleon is from northeastern British Columbia and is of Cree, Saulteaux, and Dunneza heritage. She worked as a community activist and consultant in northwestern BC for over twenty-five years, specializing in health, education, and justice issues. Val received her LL.B. from the University of Victoria in 2001 and was called to the Bar in 2002. She is completing a PhD at the Faculty of Law at the University of Victoria. Val joined the University of Alberta in 2005 to teach in the faculties of law and native studies.

George Nicholas is associate professor of archaeology at Simon Fraser University, Burnaby, British Columbia. He was founding director of Simon Fraser

University's Indigenous Archaeology Program in Kamloops (1991-2005). Since moving to British Columbia in 1990 from the United States (he is an American citizen), he has worked closely with the Secwepemc and other First Nations and, for fifteen years, has directed a community-based, community-supported archaeology program on the Kamloops Indian Reserve. His research focuses on the archaeology and human ecology of wetlands, hunter-gatherers past and present, intellectual property rights and archaeology, indigenous archaeology, and archaeological theory – all areas within which he has published widely. He is a member of the Society for American Archaeology's Committee on Curriculum and currently serves as editor of the *Canadian Journal of Archaeology*.

Brian Noble is assistant professor in Dalhousie's Department of Sociology and Social Anthropology. He has worked with Canadian First Nations for the last two decades, addressing matters ranging from traditional knowledge and intellectual property rights to relations with the Canadian state and international regimes of law. His current anthropological research addresses the socio-political conditions allowing for the rise of indigenous law and the processes animating recognition of indigenous land, resource, and knowledge rights in global arenas. He has worked with Piikani Blackfoot, Shushwap, Kwakwa̱ka̱'wakw, Mi'kmaq, and Cree communities and is now developing projects involving these people as well as indigenous activists in Papua New Guinea and Colombia.

Richard Overstall has a past life as a mining geologist, sawmill worker, farm labourer, and land- and river-use activist. For the past twenty years, he has worked as a lands and resources researcher for aboriginal peoples in northwestern British Columbia, principally the Gitxsan and Wet'suwet'en. For and with them, he has coordinated the non-aboriginal expert evidence for the trial of the *Delgamuukw* aboriginal title case, advised on treaty and consultation negotiations, managed wildlife surveys, produced and researched documentary films, and designed justice and education programs. Richard graduated from the University of Victoria Law School in 2000 and currently practices law in northern British Columbia.

Heather Raven, BA, LL.B. (UBC) is a member of the Brokenhead Ojibway First Nation located in Manitoba. She was called to the British Columbia Bar in 1987 and practised employment law in Vancouver prior to her appointment at the Faculty of Law, University of Victoria, in 1992. She teaches courses in employment law, contracts, secured transactions, legal mooting, and indigenous law. As part of her commitment to public service, she has served on several boards, commissions, and foundations, such as the Law Foundation of British Columbia, the British Columbia Police Commission, and the British Columbia Public Service Appeal Board. She currently serves on the Health and Social Development Advisory Committee of the Vancouver Foundation.

Emily Snyder was the research manager for the Faculty of Law and the Faculty of Native Studies at the University of Alberta until she began doctoral studies in sociology. She received her Bachelor of Arts degree in criminology from Saint Mary's University. Emily then completed a Master of Arts degree in sociology at Carleton University before moving to Alberta.

Michael Solowan received his Bachelor of Arts, with distinction, from Trinity Western University and then spent five years living and working in Sweden. Upon returning to Canada, he obtained a Bachelor of Laws, also with distinction, from the University of Alberta, where he served as research assistant to Professor Catherine Bell. Michael is the City Solicitor for the City of Leduc, Alberta.

Graham Statt is the Executive Director, Resource Consultation and Traditional Use, Alberta International, Intergovernmental and Aboriginal Relations. In this role, he is continuously challenged to work through cross-cultural issues towards solutions that respect the culture, history, and unique place of aboriginal people in Canadian society. Graham acted as a research assistant to Professor Bell and defended his MA (anthropology) at the University of Alberta in Edmonton under her supervision. In his thesis, he considered the viability of using cooperative management agreements with First Nations as a way to satisfy the duty of the Crown to consult and as a mechanism to enhance the cultural sustainability and self-sufficiency of First Nations in Alberta.

Brian Thom is senior negotiation support for the Hul'qumi'num Treaty Group. He has a central role in tripartite negotiations on land, governance, resource management and fiscal relations, and is lead negotiator on park co-management and land-use planning. He has led community-based research on territorial boundaries, traditional land use and occupancy, and community land-use planning. He received his PhD in anthropology from McGill University in 2005 and has written and published articles on local land tenure systems and intangible cultural property, social meanings of oral tradition, the role of culture in relations of power between the state and indigenous peoples, and Coast Salish culture and history.

Other members of the academic team contributing to the second volume of essays are: Michael Asch, Mohsen Al Attar Ahmed, Nicole Aylwin, Rosemary J. Coombe, Melodie Hope, Robert Howell, Darlene Johnson, James Nafziger, Robert K. Paterson, Roch Ripley, Bruce Ziff, and Norman Zlotkin.

First Nation Contributors

Hul'qumi'num Treaty Group

The Hul'qumi'num Treaty Group (HTG) represents the treaty interests of six

Hul'qumi'num-speaking Coast Salish First Nations located on southeast Vancouver Island and the southern Gulf Islands: the Chemainus, Cowichan, Halalt, Lake Cowichan, Lyackson, and Penelakut First Nations. HTG is actively involved in research related to the social, economic, and cultural needs of its member nations, including heritage protection and repatriation issues as they relate to treaty.

Ktunaxa Nation

The Ktunaxa Nation consists of five bands as well as a Kinbasket clan of Shuswap living in the southeastern section of British Columbia. For thousands of years the Ktunaxa existed in the area known as the Kootenay region. Ktunaxa territory is not confined to British Columbia as it includes areas as far south as Missoula (Montana) and Spokane (Washington). The Ktunaxa language is unique: it is not associated with any other language in the known world. Repatriation of human remains and artifacts is part of the ongoing work of the Ktunaxa Nation.

Luuxhon House/Gitanyow

The present villages of the Gitksan are Gitanyow, Gitwangak, Gitsegyukla, Kispiox, Glen Vowell, and Gitanmaax. The fundamental political unit in Gitksan society is the House Group, which is a matrilineal descent group. Each House is part of a larger clan grouping. All Gitanyow Houses can trace their ancestry to early Frog (Ganeda) and Wolf (Lax Gibuu) clan peoples. Their House territories are in the Nass and Skeena watersheds of northern British Columbia.

The partners in this volume are the Luuxhon House of the Frog Clan in conjunction with the Office of the Gitanyow Hereditary Chiefs. The Gitanyow Huwilp Society acts on behalf of Gitanyow Houses in a number of different areas, including treaty negotiations, promoting the involvement of House Groups in conservation management and sustainable development, developing programs and services, and promoting and facilitating Gitanyow culture and laws.

Mookakin Cultural Society

The Mookakin Cultural and Heritage Foundation of the Blood Tribe (Kainai Nation) is named after one of the Blood Tribe's foremost spiritual leaders in order to acknowledge the contribution he made to the preservation of culture and spiritual practices. He was also known as Pat Weasel Head, a Medicine Pipe Bundle keeper, a member of the Horn Society, and later a Grandfather to the Horn Society. He was also a renowned healer and herbalist. His knowledge and advice governed the Blood in the successful repatriation of several medicine bundles in the 1970s. In keeping with its namesake, the Mookakin Foundation was established in 1998 to promote and preserve the spiritual doctrines and observances of the Blood Tribe, to promote and preserve their unique language and history, to encourage an appreciation by the general public of Blackfoot culture, to encourage and actively pursue repatriations of objects and articles that facilitate spiritual doctrines and observances, and to preserve data, material, and cultural objects of the Kainaiwa people.

Oldman River Cultural Centre

Participation in this research was undertaken by the Oldman River Cultural Centre of the Piikani (Peigan) Nation under the leadership of Dr. Reg Crowshoe in partnership with Dr. Brian Noble (sociology and anthropology, Dalhousie). The cultural centre, located on the Peigan Reserve, is mandated to protect and preserve the cultural heritage of the Blackfoot culture and Piikani Nation. The centre has been actively involved in repatriations of cultural and ceremonial objects.

U’Mista Cultural Society

The mandate of the U’mista Cultural Society is to ensure the survival of all aspects of the cultural heritage of the Kwakwa̱ka̱’wakw. To facilitate this mandate, it has a board of directors composed of members of the Kwakwa̱ka̱’wakw First Nations and has established a cultural education centre that permanently houses repatriated potlatch items, conducts cultural-based research, archives cultural data, and promotes cultural activities of significance to the community. Communities serviced by the U’mista Cultural Society include Kwagu’ł (Fort Rupert), Mama̱liliḵa̱la (Village Island), ‘Na̱mgis (Alert Bay), Ławit’sis (Turnour Island), Da̱’naxda’x̱w (New Vancouver), Ma’a̱mtagila (Estekin), Dzawada̱’enu̱xw (Kincome Village), Ḵwikwa̱sutinux (Gilford Island), Gwawa’enux̱w (Hopetown), ‘Nak’waxda’x̱w (Blunden Harbour), Gwa’sa̱la (Smiths Inlet), G̱usgimukw (Quatsino), Tłatła̱siḵwa̱la (Hope Island), Weḵa̱’yi (Cape Mudge), and Wiweḵ’a̱m (Campbell River).

Index

Note: This book features First Nation concepts of cultural heritage that are difficult to capture using conventional indexing techniques and categorizations. However, as this book is also intended for those who may not be familiar with these concepts or cultural differences, we have intentionally adopted search entries and categorizations that we hope will facilitate the location of information by all readers. For example, the practice or performance of a ritual may be a way of expressing law even though it is not specifically identified using the words "law" or "protocol." Although we include an entry for "laws," we also point the reader to its expressions in other forms (*e.g.*, "transfers") and in specific contexts (*e.g.*, "songs and dances") through references to other portions of the index (*e.g.*, "cultural heritage") and text. Tension and the Trickster remain with us to the end.

Aboriginal Languages Initiative, 394-95
Act for the Gradual Civilization of the Indian Tribes in the Canadas (1857), 446-47
adawx (or *adaawk*) (Gitksan and Tsimshian oral histories): accounts of formalization of alliances through ceremonies, 127-30; connections with ceremonies and territorial lands, 103-4, 105-7; defence in *Delgamuukw*, 142-45; encounters with other foreign groups, 127-28; first encounter with ancestors of the Nisga'a, 125-27; in Gitksan (also Gitxsan) law, 95; link with identity and history, 115-17; manifestation of title to territories, 116-17; pole-raising feasts and acknowledgement of territorial rights, 117-23; responsibility of chiefs, 104, 109, 123-24; role in Gitksan legal system, 109-10; on Tsimshian formation of alliance with Gitksan, 128-29
Ahenakew, Freda, 429
Aishihik First Nation. *See* Champagne and Aishihik First Nations
Alberta Energy and Utility Board (AEUB), 400
Alberta Historical Resources Foundation, 400-1
Alfred, Ethel, 40-41, 44, 48, 49, 50, 55, 58, 59-60, 63, 82
Algonquin, 396-97
Alphonse, Ron, 168, 174, 184
Ambers, Basil, 44, 45, 47, 49, 67, 71, 79, 80-81, 83
Amos, Gerald, 380
An Act for the Better Protection of the Lands and Property of Indians in Lower Canada (1850), 446
An Act for the protection of Indians in Upper Canada from imposition, and the property occupied or enjoyed by them from trespass and injury (1850), 446
An Act providing for the organization of the Department of the Secretary of State of Canada and for the management of Indian and Ordinance Lands (1868), 447
ancestral remains: different treatment of aboriginal vs. other remains (legislation), 179, 403; museum policy (*see* museums; *and names of individual museums*); *Native American Graves Protection and Repatriation Act* (*NAGPRA*, US), 195; need for respect, 22-23, 42. *See also* archaeological sites (Hul'qumi'num); burial customs; burial grounds; Kwaday Dan Ts'inchi; laws

(Kainai/Blood); repatriation, ancestral remains; *and individual First Nations, e.g.,* Kainai/Blood, cultural heritage; *and specific legislation, e.g., Cemeteries Act*

Angerman, Sergeant, 53, 54, 56, 84, 85

archaeological sites. *See* archaeological sites (Hul'qumi'num); burial customs; burial grounds; cultural heritage, protection; heritage sites; *and individual First Nations, e.g.,* Ktunaxa/Kinbasket First Nation, cultural heritage

archaeological sites (Hul'qumi'num): ancestors' continuing ownership of burial artifacts, 158-60, 168-69, 192; collection and sale of materials, 181-84; danger to the living from the deceased, 155, 161, 165, 169-71, 172, 198; definition, 156-57; dense concentration now in private hands, 153, 176, 191; exhibition of artifacts in contravention of Hul'qumi'num law of avoidance, 183-84; Hul'qumi'num view of archaeological excavations, 154-56; inability of Hul'qumi'num to protect heritage, 186-87, 190; land-use conflicts with developers, 176-78; law of avoidance (of burial grounds, human remains, funerary artifacts), 167-72, 198; law of inherited right to care for the dead, 162-64, 169, 172, 198; law of non-disturbance of ancient sites and remains, 165-67, 172, 177-78, 198; principle of reciprocity: continuity of relations between the living and the ancestors, 160-62, 198; principle of respect: places and belongings of ancestors, 157-60, 198; protection required, 23, 153, 173-75; red ochre, use of, 155, 169; resolving disagreements among First Nation groups, 187-89; respect and care of deceased as family obligations, 160-62, 172, 192, 198; significance in cultural identity, 156-57; South Pender Island development, 177-78, 189; threat of strong white population growth, 153; treatment of aboriginal vs. other remains, 179; viewed as cemeteries, 157, 172, 177, 196. *See also* burial customs (Hul'qumi'num); Hul'qumi'num Treaty Group (HTG), cultural heritage; laws (Hul'qumi'num)

Arthur Wellington Clah Diaries and Papers, 135

Ashcroft, Stan, 38-39, 53-54, 58, 75, 84

Assembly of First Nations (AFN): activities regarding Kwaday Dan Ts'inchi, 398-99; and Canadian museums (*see* Task Force Report on Museums and First Peoples); on endangered state of aboriginal languages, 418-20; language as essence of culture, 420-21

Atleo, Shawn, 381

Bagot Commission of Inquiry (1844), 445-46

Beattie, Owen, 399

belonging. *See entries beginning with* ownership/belonging concept

Benai, Eddie Benton, 379

Beynon, William, 119, 121-22, 139-40

Birdstone, Violet, 20-21, 317, 328, 329, 333, 335, 339, 349, 355-56, 359

Bishop, Charles, 132

Blackfeet: Artists of the Northern Plains (Scriver), 371

Blackfeet (Montana), 370-72

Blackfoot Confederacy: Advisory Committee on Museum Relations, 213-14; EPCOR dispute over ancestral remains, 400; language, 205, 246-47; Nitsiitapii (Blackfoot) law, 259-61, 301; protocol on speaking with elders, 205; worldview on conservation and protection, 242, 255n42. *See also under* Brave Dog Society; Glenbow Museum; Kainai First Nation (Blood Tribe); Mookakin Foundation; Piikani First Nation; Scriver Blackfoot Collection; Skinnipiikani First Nation, cultural heritage

Blenkinsop, George, 135-36

Blood, Narcisse, 223, 231, 234, 244, 467, 481

Blood Tribe. *See* Kainai First Nation (Blood Tribe)

Blue Cloud, Peter (Aroniawenrate), 489

Bob, Amelia, 170, 185

Brave Dog Society (Knut-sum-atak) (Skinnipiikani): advisory responsibility of "grandparents," 278; authority and approval of use of information, 16, 261, 266; description of, 261, 302; host of Skinnipiikani case-study discussions, 16, 261, 278, 279, 303; intergenerational transfer of knowledge, 276-77; keeper of major bundles, 260, 303; language, technical, 269; opening and participating in circle discussions of transferred people, 263-64, 266, 278, 279, 303; possible policing function, 302-4. *See also* Skinnipiikani First Nation, cultural heritage

Bright, Michael, 110

British Columbia Provincial Museum. *See* Royal British Columbia Museum
British Columbia Treaty Commission (BCTC), 312
British Museum, 76, 90n75
Brown, Jennifer, 378
Brown, John, Kwiiyeehl, 24, 115-16, 125
Brown, Martha, Xhliyamlaxha, 125
Browne, Murray, 395
Buchholtzer, Guy, 36, 38-39, 45-46, 77-78
Buffalo Stones *(iniskim),* 285
Bull, L., 452
burial customs (Hul'qumi'num): ancestors' ownership of burial artifacts, 158-60, 168-69, 192; ancient remains not to be disturbed, 165-67, 172, 177-78, 198; annual family ceremonies to remember ancestors, 171-72; archaeological excavations against customary laws, 154-56; cultural sensitivity lacking in Canadian public, 173-75, 179; danger to the living from the deceased, 155, 161, 165, 169-71, 172, 198; disinterment and redressing of remains, 164, 166-67; exhibition of artifacts in contravention of law of avoidance, 183-84; inherited right to care for the deceased, 162-64, 169, 172, 198; principle of reciprocity between living and ancestors, 160-62, 198; principle of respect due to ancestors, 157-60, 198; professional ritual specialists for care of the deceased, 164, 172; red ochre, use of, 155, 169; removal of remains strictly regulated, 164-65, 166-67, 172, 177-78; separation of living and dead, 167-72. *See also* archaeological sites (Hul'qumi'num); laws (Hul'qumi'num)
burial customs (Kainai/Blood), 236, 241-42
burial grounds: EPCOR dispute in Edmonton, 399-401; Kainai/Blood protocols regarding remains, 236, 241-42; Ktunaxa/Kinbasket, 334-36, 361; Kwakwa̲ka̲'wakw, 42; litigation re Nipigon Power High Falls project, 401-4; Luuxhon, House of, 109, 110; need to respect ancestral remains, 22-24, 42. *See also* ancestral remains; archaeological sites (Hul'qumi'num); *and under individual First Nations and laws, e.g.,* Hul'qumi'num, cultural heritage; laws (Hul'qumi'num)

Caamano, Jacinto, 130-32
Canadian Charter of Rights and Freedoms, 430
Canadian Cultural Property Export Review Board (CCPERB), 82-83, 382
Canadian government: apology to aboriginal peoples, 442-43; assimilationist policies, prohibition of potlatch ceremonies and Sundance, 53, 58, 449-51, 486n35; assimilationist policies' impact on First Nations culture, 86, 136-38, 209-11, 249-50, 269-70, 442-43, 450-55; assimilationist policies prohibiting aboriginal languages, 27, 43-44, 59, 86, 269-70, 319, 418-19, 451-52; assimilationist policy of residential schools, 443-44, 445-49; breach of fiduciary duty claims by First Nations, 37, 84-85, 457-58; Department of Indian Affairs, 444; Imperial Indian Department, 444; Indian policies and actions post-1867, 447-51; Indian policies and laws pre-1867, 445-47; legal options for redress by aboriginal peoples, 456-58; mission to "civilize" aboriginal peoples, 444-45; negotiations with Kainai re cultural heritage, 215-16; "parallel reciprocal recognition spaces," 466, 476-82; "recognition space" for First Nations law and culture, 476-78; role in protecting Kwakwa̲ka̲'wakw heritage, 81; truth and reconciliation process with First Nations, 459. *See also* colonialism, effects of; *Indian Act* (1876); laws (Canadian)
Canadian Heritage, Department of, 2, 394-95
Canadian Museum of Civilization: activities re First Nation collaborations, recording and preserving cultural heritages, 368-69; agreement re Nisga'a artifacts, 385-86, 470-71; negotiations for return of Gitksan artifacts (Gitanyow), 107; negotiations with Kainai First Nation (Blood Tribe), 204, 253n3; negotiations with Ktunaxa/Kinbasket Tribal Council, 321; repatriation policies, 374-75; repatriation within treaty, self-government, or land claims agreements, 374-75; return of confiscated potlatch regalia (Kwakwa̲ka̲'wakw), 55, 69, 73-74; return of Starlight Bundle to Tsuu T'ina, 368; Sacred Materials program, 375. *See also* museums; *and see under* repatriation, *e.g.,* repatriation (Kwakwa̲ka̲'wakw)
Canadian Museums Association. *See* Task Force Report on Museums and First Peoples

Caro, Joey, 175, 182
case studies. *See* research project
Cemeteries Act (ON), 196
Cemetery and Funeral Services Act (BC), 177, 179
Champagne and Aishihik First Nations, 384, 387-88, 398
Charlie, Arvid, Luschiim, viii-ix, 19, 151, 156-57, 161-62, 165-69, 171, 174, 178, 180, 183, 188
Charlie, Simon, 174
Chemainus First Nation, 152, 153
Christie, Gordon, 355
Church of England (Anglican), 444
Clans (Gitksan), 94, 101-2
Clarricoates, Gina, 314, 319, 320, 327, 331, 335, 341
Clavir, Miriam, 72-73
Coast Salish. *See* Hul'qumi'num Treaty Group (HTG); laws (Hul'qumi'num)
Cole, Douglas, 135-36
Colnett, James, 130
colonialism/colonization, effects of, 18, 20. *See also* Canadian government; *Indian Act;* laws (Canadian); residential schools; *and under individual First Nations*
community research protocols (guidelines and ethics), 15-17, 38, 77, 324, 396
Conaty, Gerry, 213, 221-22, 230-31
Confederated Salish and Kootenai Tribes in Montana, 313, 322
Confederation of First Nations Cultural Centres, 431
Constitution Act, 1982, 194, 429-30, 447
Convention on the Rights of the Child (1989), 426
Cooper-Stephenson, Ken, 456, 458
cooperative management agreements, 392-93
Cooter, Robert, 478
Coronel-Molina, Serafin M., 428
Cote, Diana, 18, 343, 354, 358
Cowichan Tribes, 152, 153
Craig Bay land-use conflict, 177
Cranmer, Agnes, 57
Cranmer, Andrea, 7, 26, 39, 40, 43, 44, 47, 51-52, 59, 61-62, 64, 71, 81, 473
Cranmer, Barb, 38
Cranmer, Bill, xi, 42, 43, 44, 74, 83
Cranmer, Dan (Kwakwa̱ka̱'wakw potlatch), 57
Cranmore Ethnographical Museum (England), 76
Cree language, 418, 430-31
Cremation, Internment and Funeral Services Act (BC), 179
crest images and designs (Kwakwa̱ka̱'wakw), 66, 79-80
crests *(ayuks):* exclusive to each House, 98; generalized Clan images vs. individual House *ayuks,* 101-2; illegal use of images, 106-7, 111; as intangible property, 96-101; links with *adaawk,* 104-7; physical possession vs. right to display, 97, 98-101, 110-11; portrayal of historical events, 116
Crow Eagle, Geoff, Sr., 262, 266-75
Crowshoe, Anita, 289-90, 292, 293
Crowshoe, Reg, 7, 262, 275-76, 278, 279-80, 284-85, 287-88, 291, 292, 293-94, 296-304, 371, 479, 481
Crowshoe, Rose, 262
Crowshoe-Hirsch, Heather, 267, 276, 474
Crystal, David, 425
cultural heritage: basic issues, 5; Creator as giver of cultural property, 17, 39, 67, 79, 208-9, 225-26, 267, 467, 470, 474; demand by indigenous peoples for control, 1, 26-27; effects of colonialism (*see* colonialism/colonization, effects of); intangible cultural heritage (*see* cultural heritage, intangible); need to recognize distinctiveness of, 19; protection (*see* cultural heritage, protection); redress (*see* cultural heritage, redress for harm); repatriation (*see* repatriation); UN definition, 313, 362n6. *See also* cultural heritage, intangible; cultural knowledge; *and under individual First Nations and laws, e.g.,* Kainai First Nation (Blood Tribe), cultural heritage; laws (Kainai/Blood)
cultural heritage, intangible: appropriation and misappropriation of, 25-26, 79, 319-20; inseparability of cultural heritage, integrated whole, 6, 65, 93, 207, 230-31, 250, 255n51, 472-76, 482. *See also* community research protocols; cultural heritage, protection; cultural knowledge; elder knowledge; intellectual property; *and specific forms of intangible heritage, e.g., adawx;* crests; languages (aboriginal); *specific forms under individual First Nations, e.g.,* Kainai First Nation (Blood Tribe), cultural heritage, teepee designs; ownership/belonging concept
cultural heritage, protection: ancestral remains, gravesites, and burial grounds, 396-404; archaeological sites (*see*

archaeological sites [Hul'qumi'num]); consultative or protective notations (AB), 393; cooperative management agreements, 392-93; costs, 27, 334-40; First Nation land management strategies, 390-92; importance for revival of cultural knowledge, 1-2, 18-19; Kamloops Band heritage conservation bylaw, 391; legislation and law reform (*see* laws [Canadian], protection of cultural heritage); litigation in Canada (protection and repatriation), 141-45, 369-70, 388-90, 399-404; by museums, 367-68; *Native American Graves Protection and Repatriation Act* (US), 195, 220-21; parks, provincial and national, 107, 245-46, 339, 393; priorities for protection, 23, 40-42; provincial heritage protection legislation (*see also Heritage Conservation Act* [BC]); *Historical Resources Act* (AB); *and under individual First Nations,* cultural heritage), 23-24, 84, 180-81, 290-91, 337-39, 361; Skeetchestn Band Territorial Heritage Conservation Law, 391; Skinnipiikani/Nitsiitapii/*Nitooii* laws, 258-61, 279-80; Stó:lō Nation Heritage Investigation Permit, 390-91; strategies for, 26-27, 386-93, 398-404; traditional knowledge, protection of, 404; traditional use studies, 315, 322-32; treaty and land claims negotiations, 190-94, 312, 320-21, 360, 373, 384-88, 470-72 (*see also individual entries for modern treaties and agreements, e.g.,* Tlicho [Dogrib] Agreement); UNESCO heritage site designation, 349, 392; UNESCO's principles and guidelines, 191. *See also* cultural heritage, intangible; cultural heritage, redress for harm; heritage sites; languages (aboriginal), protection and revitalization; ownership/belonging concepts; *and under individual First Nations, e.g.,* Gitksan First Nation, cultural heritage

cultural heritage, redress for harm: claims of breach of fiduciary duty, 37, 84-85, 457-58; claims of negligence, 456-57; claims of vicarious liability, 456; language loss, 459-60; repatriation, 460; under tort law, 456; tort law, limitations, 458; truth and reconciliation process, 459. *See also* cultural heritage, protection; repatriation; *and under individual First Nations, e.g.,* Gitksan First Nation, cultural heritage

cultural knowledge: "banking" of linguistic knowledge, 417, 432-33; importance of language preservation, 4, 24-25; linking of heritage sites, land, and territory, 23, 104, 243-44; loss in residential schools, 4; loss in residential schools (Ktunaxa/Kinbasket), 316-18, 319, 360; loss in residential schools (Kwakwa̱ka̱'wakw), 4, 43-44, 59, 86; loss of language in residential schools, 43-44, 59, 86, 269-70, 319, 418-19, 451-52; plant and medicinal knowledge (Ktunaxa/Kinbasket), 330-31; repatriation and cultural knowledge/associated information, 19-20, 33-34, 72, 75, 77-79, 105, 205-7, 316-20 (*see also under* repatriation); research on protection of, 2; transfer with medicine bundles (Kainai/Blood), 203, 205, 250. *See also* elder knowledge

cultural property: definition problems, 6-7. *See also* cultural heritage; cultural heritage, intangible; *Cultural Property Export and Import Act;* elder knowledge; *and under individual First Nations, e.g.,* Gitksan First Nation, cultural heritage; ownership/belonging concept (Gitksan)

Cultural Property Export and Import Act, 2, 82-83, 379, 382-83

Cummins, John, 146

Daes, Erica-Irene, 313

Daghida Project (language), 394

Daly, T. Mayne, 449

Dancing Man petroglyph (Snuneymuxw), 395-96

Dauenhauer, Nora Marks, 433

Dauenhauer, Richard, 433

David Suzuki Foundation, 381

Davin, Nicholas Flood, 447-48

Dawson, Amos, 56-57

Declaration on the Rights of Persons Belonging to National or Ethnic, Religious and Linguistic Minorities (1992), 425

Delaney, Adam, 203-4, 208, 210, 215-16, 218-19, 227, 229, 232, 244, 248

Delgamuukw case (Gitksan), 141-45

Dempsey, Hugh, 213

Denver Arts Museum, 216-17, 220-22

Draft Declaration on the Rights of Indigenous Peoples (UN, 1994), 426

Drucker, Philip, 449

Eagle Clan, 94

Ecotrust Canada, 381, 393

Edwards, Roy, 156, 176-77, 469-70

elder knowledge: acquired through research, ix-x; attaining status of learned elder, ix; elders as transmitters of knowledge and history, viii-ix; respect for, viii, 208-9, 216-17. *See also* cultural heritage, intangible; cultural knowledge; *and entries for individual First Nations*

Elderberry Flute Song (Blue Cloud), 489, 490

Endswell Foundation, 381

EPCOR (Edmonton Power) dispute, 399-401

European Charter for Regional or Minority Languages (1992), 428

False Face mask controversy (Mohawk), 369-70. *See also* "Spirit Sings" exhibit

Fennel, Desmond, 427

Field Museum (Chicago), 397

Fireweed (Grouse) Clan, 94, 102

First Charger, Francis, 5, 7, 206-7, 209-11, 224, 226, 230, 235

First Nations Confederacy of Cultural Education Centres: sponsor of current research, 2

First Nations Land Management Act (FNLMA, 1999), 392

First Nations Language, Culture and Heritage Council of British Columbia, 434

First Nations partners. *See* research project

First Nations Sacred Ceremonial Objects Repatriation Act (AB, 2000), 238-41, 370

First Peoples' Cultural Foundation, 2

First Peoples' Heritage, Language and Culture Act (BC, 1990), 431

First Rider, Dorothy, ix-x, 205, 214-15, 224, 226-27, 231

FirstVoices project, 434

Fontaine, Phil, 459

Frog Clan, 94. *See also* Luuxhon, House of

Gallant, Elizabeth, 25, 266, 273, 277, 420

Gallant, George, 264-65

George, Herb, Sats'aan, 138

Gitanyow (also, Gitanyaw) (Gitksan, also Gitxsan), 92, 125-27

Gitanyow Hereditary Chiefs, 94-95

Gitksan (Gitxsan) First Nation: chief's responsibilities, 19-20, 101, 104, 108-9, 117-24; defence of territory and identity against Europeans, 138-41, 145-46; defence of territory in *Delgamuukw* case, 141-45. *See also* Gitksan (Gitxsan) First Nation, cultural heritage; research project

Gitksan (Gitxsan) First Nation, cultural heritage: *adawx* (*adaawk*) and identity/history and territorial rights, 115-17, 125, 142-46; blankets and designs, 101-2; chief's responsibilities, 19-20, 101, 104, 108-9, 117-24; colonialism, impact of, 133-46; concept of cultural property, problem applying, 92-93, 114-15; concept of intellectual property, problem applying, 114-15, 146; constitutional role of cultural objects, 6-7, 93, 97, 111-12; crests *(ayuks)* and portrayal of historical events, 116; formalization of alliances through ceremonies, 127-30; intangible possessions/property, 95, 96-101; language survival, 418; legal matters focus of feasts, 96; manifestation of title to territories, 116-17; *naxnox* ritual, 120-22; ownership/belonging concept, 19-20, 95, 101, 108-9, 111; physical possession of objects vs. right to display, 97, 98-101, 110-11; pole-raising feasts and territorial rights, 117-23; potlatch, 135-38, 449-50; principle of respect, 115; songs *(limx'oy)* and dances, 116, 479; territory ownership and lineage, 115-18, 142-46; totem poles *(xwtsaan),* crest poles, feast poles, 97, 105, 106-7, 116-23; trade a central part of economy, 128; Weget (Raven) the Trickster, 415; Westerners' lack of respect for identity, 146. *See also adawx* (or *adaawk*) (Gitksan and Tsimshian oral histories); crests *(ayuks);* cultural heritage, intangible; House groups; laws (Gitksan); Luuxhon, House of; ownership/belonging concept (Gitksan); repatriation (Gitksan); songs *(limx'oy)* and dances (Gitksan)

Glenbow-Alberta Institute Act (GAIA), 238, 370

Glenbow Museum (Glenbow-Alberta Institute): assistance in repatriating material from Denver Arts Museum, 220, 222; deaccessioning First Nations' objects, 238; False Face mask controversy, 369-70; First Nations Advisory Council, 212, 370; *Glenbow-Alberta Institute Act (GAIA),* 238, 370; partnership with Mookakin Foundation, 21, 204, 209, 252; positive relationship with Kainai/Blood, 212-14, 481; "The Spirit Sings" exhibit, 212, 369, 372. *See also* museums; repatriation (Kainai/Blood)

Good, Godfrey, Gwinu, 96-101, 110, 111, 113n9, 479

Good, Maggie, Xamlaxyeltxw, 138

Good, Robert, Sindihl, 102-4, 110
Goodale, Ralph, 442-43
Gough, Meagan, 9-10
G'psqoalux pole (Haisla Spirit Pole), 380-81
Grace, Elizabeth K.P., 457
Grant, Kathleen, 270
Grant, Peter, 142-43
Gravelle, Pat, 335
gravesites. *See* burial grounds
Gregory, Chris, 474-75
Gwaii Haanas Park Reserve, 393
Gwinu, House of: chief's "property," 97-98, 113n9; chief's responsibilities, 19-20, 101, 104, 108-9; House possessions held in trust by chiefs, 101, 111; legal and political role of cultural objects, 97; nature of law, 96-97; people defined by law, 97; physical possession of objects vs. right to display, 97, 98-101, 110-11

Haida First Nation, 393, 395, 397-98, 423
Haida Gwaii Watchmen, 393
Haisla First Nation, 380-81
Haisla Spirit Pole, 380-81
Halalt First Nation, 152, 153
Halkomelem language (Hul'qumi'num), 151
Halliday, William, 36, 53-55, 84, 85
hamat'sa (in potlatch ceremony), 48, 49
Hamilton, Scott, 402-3
Hansson, Olaf, 380
Harris, Cole, 134
Harris, George, 158, 174, 179, 180-81, 187, 188
Harris, Irene, 163, 168, 169, 171, 182
Harris, Sylvia, 159, 160, 175, 187
Head-Smashed-In Buffalo Jump, 349, 392
Hebrew language, 428
Heiltsuk language, 423-24
Heizer, Robert F., 449
Heritage Conservation Act (BC): amending to protect cultural heritage, 1-2, 195; case regarding jurisdiction over aboriginal heritage property, 388-90; Craig Bay land-use conflict, 177; delegation of authority in s. 4, 193; indigenous laws not taken into account, 178-79; lack of enforcement, 84, 180-81, 337-39, 361; lack of role for First Nations, 181; silent on ownership of ancient human remains, 195-96; treatment of aboriginal vs. non-aboriginal remains, 179
heritage sites: ceremonial, spiritual, sacred, and other heritage lands, sites, places, 23-24 (*see also under individual First Nations, cultural heritage, e.g.,* Kainai First Nation (Blood Tribe), cultural heritage); cultural landscapes, 334-40; First Nations' connection to the land, 23-24. *See also* archaeological sites (Hul'qumi'num); burial grounds; cultural heritage, protection; Luuxhon, House of; *and specific heritage legislation, e.g., Heritage Conservation Act* (BC); laws (Canadian); *laws of specific First Nations, e.g.,* laws (Hul'qumi'num)
Heye, George, 55
Heye Foundation, 55
Hill, Jane, 424
Hill, Matthew, 389
Hinton, Leanne, 433
Historical Resources Act (AB), 400-1
Histories, Territories and Laws of the Kitwancool (British Columbia Provincial Museum), 97
Hodgson, Maggie, 450
Horn Society, 11, 205, 207-8, 247-48
Horsethief, Christopher, 22, 314, 330, 332-33, 342, 344-46, 348, 350-51, 356-57, 358-59
House groups (Gitksan), 94, 101-2
Hudson, Harriet, 128-29
Hudson's Bay Company, 133-34
Hul'qumi'num Treaty Group (HTG): case study, 3, 11, 150-51, 153-54, 200n9, 491-92; First Nations members, 152, 199n3; history and lands, 151-53; land issues in BC unresolved, 175-78; oral histories of territories, 152; themes emerging from interviews, 154-56, 172. *See also* Hul'qumi'num Treaty Group (HTG), cultural heritage; laws (Hul'qumi'num); research project
Hul'qumi'num Treaty Group (HTG), cultural heritage: archaeological heritage significant for identity, 154-56; cultural sensitivity lacking in Canadian public, 173-75, 179; Hul'qumi'num to protect heritage, 186-87, 190; inability of land-use conflicts with developers, 176-78; languages (Halkomelem, Musqueam), 151, 394; oral histories of territories, 152; ownership/belonging concept, 158-60, 191-92, 195-96; protecting cultural heritage by amending existing legislation, 194-96; protecting cultural heritage by defining aboriginal rights in court, 196-97; protecting cultural heritage by developing new Canadian legislation, 196; protecting cultural heritage through treaty negotiations, 190-94; protection problems, 173-87;

repatriation, 182-84; threat of strong white population growth, 153; youth education necessary, 184-86. *See also* archaeological sites (Hul'qumi'num); burial customs (Hul'qumi'num); cultural heritage, intangible; laws (Hul'qumi'num); repatriation (Hul'qumi'num)
Hunter, Allan, 26, 315, 327, 339, 343, 348-49, 357, 359
Hunter, Troy, 25, 317, 328, 337, 341, 347, 351, 355, 357, 358, 359

Indian Act (1876, 1894, plus amendments): authority of band councils vs. that of ceremonial societies, 302-4; banning of potlatches, 53-54, 89n41, 137, 231, 447, 450; banning of Sundance and Thirst Dance, 450; goal of destroying indigenous culture, 18, 53, 58-60, 354, 444, 447-51; oppression according to First Nations, 4-5; paternalistic attitude toward aboriginal peoples, 444; precursor to, 447-48; residential schools and, 447-49; threat to Ktunaxa culture, 354. *See also* Canadian government; laws (Canadian)
Indian Claims Commission (ICC), 85
indigenous knowledge. *See* cultural knowledge
Ing, N.R., 452
intellectual property law (Canadian): copyright, 16-17; copyright on recorded songs, 83; Dancing Man petroglyph (Snuneymuxw) as official marks, 395-96; lack of recognition of First Nations jurisdiction over intellectual property, 8, 25-26; protection for indigenous knowledge, 2; World Intellectual Property Organization (WIPO), 2. *See also* cultural heritage, intangible
International Covenant on Civil and Political Rights (1966, 1976), 425
International Forest Products Ltd. (Interfor), 388-90
International Labour Organization (ILO) Convention 169 concerning Indigenous and Tribal Peoples in Independent Countries (1989), 426
Inuit, James Bay, 430
Inuktitut language, 418, 429-31
Investigation of Missing Artifacts at the Anthropology Museum, University of Winnipeg (Singleton), 379-80

Jackson, Michael, 69
Jacobs, Wilfred, 315
James, Florence, 159, 164, 168, 170, 171, 185, 186, 189
James Bay Cree, 430
James Bay Inuit, 430
Janes, Robert R., 230-31
Jocks, Christopher, 424-25
Joe, Bernard, 166, 169, 189
Johnson, Evelyn H.C., 369
Johnson, Fred, Lelt, 119, 124
Johnson, Gordon, 'Mali, 103
Jones, Ray, Niis Noolh, 101-2
Joseph, Christine, 44, 51, 57, 65

Kainaiwa/Blood language, 246-49. *See also* Blackfoot Confederacy, language
Kainai First Nation (Blood Tribe): on Canadian law reform, 208-12; case study, 11, 205, 251-52, 491-92; ownership/belonging concepts, 19, 220-28; participation in Alberta repatriation legislation, 5, 238-41; on repatriation legislation (*see* repatriation [Kainai/Blood]); research protocols, 26-27, 244. *See also* Glenbow Museum; Kainai First Nation (Blood Tribe), cultural heritage; Mookakin Foundation; research project
Kainai First Nation (Blood Tribe), cultural heritage: authority to speak and ethics involved, 233-34, 252; authorship and copyright issues, 12, 17; band council vs. ceremonial society authority, 15, 204-5; Blackfoot language, 205, 246-47; building relationships with museums, 212-17; burial customs and protocols, 236, 241-42; Cultural Geography Project, 245; cultural sensitivity training for museums, 214-15; definition of cultural property, 244-45; Horn Society, 11, 205, 207-8, 247-48; impact of Canadian "civilizing" actions, 455; impact of external influences, 209-12, 249-51; importance of social and spiritual values, 250-52; inseparability of songs, dances, stories, and medicine bundles, 207, 230-31, 255n51; intangible cultural heritage and language, 246-49; language and its protection, 246-49, 454-55; on law reform and white man's ways, 210-11, 236-42; medicine bundles, 203-7, 216-22, 225-33, 250; names, 250; *Native American Graves Protection and Repatriation Act,* 220-21; on negotiations with Alberta (*see* repatriation [Kainai/Blood]); on negotiations

with Canada re cultural heritage, 215-16; oral histories, 222, 227-28, 232, 243-45, 250; ownership concepts, 19, 220-28; protection vital to First Nation identity, 204, 242-46; reasons for repatriation efforts, 20; relationship with the land, 242-46, 255n42; repatriation from museums, 21; sacred items as means to heal colonialism's scars, 208, 249-51; sacred sites and land, protection, 242-46; songs and their transfer and protection, 229, 230-31, 247-49; stories, 230-31, 243-44, 247-48; Sundance, 11, 203, 205, 250; teepee designs, 229-30; threat by developments around reserves, 244; title, requirements for valid transfer, 205, 228-33; traditional knowledge and documentation, 247-48; transfer protocols, 19, 206, 225-28, 229-33, 248-49, 252; Writing-on-Stone Provincial Park (rock art), 245-46. *See also* cultural heritage, intangible; laws (Kainai/Blood); medicine bundles (Kainai/Blood); ownership/belonging concept (Kainai/Blood); repatriation (Kainai/Blood)

Kamloops Indian Band, 391

Keating, J.W., 446

King, Jonathan, 76

Kingfisher petroglyph (Snuneymuxw), 395-36

Kispiox Tribe (of Gitksan), 24

Kitigan Zibi Anishinabeg First Nation, 396-97

Kitkatla First Nation, 197, 388-90

Kitkatla v. British Columbia, 197, 388-90

Kitwancool village. *See* Gitanyow (Gitksan, also Gitxsan)

K.L.B. v. British Columbia case, 457-58

Knut-sum-atak Society (Skinnipiikani). *See* Brave Dog Society

Kootenai, 312. *See also* Ktunaxa/Kinbasket Tribal Council

Kootenai Tribe of Idaho, 313, 322

Krauss, Michael, 421

K'san museum, 98-100, 111

Ktunaxa/Kinbasket Traditional Elders Working Group, 313, 322, 324

Ktunaxa/Kinbasket Tribal Council (KKTC), 3, 10-11, 312-13, 491-92

Ktunaxa/Kinbasket Tribal Council (KKTC), cultural heritage: archives, 324-25; British Columbia Treaty Commission (BCTC), 312; Canadian laws for protection, 354-59, 361; Canadian undermining of culture, 475; commercialization possible if responsible, 328, 340; concern over cultural appropriation, 319-20, 328-32, 364n57; cultural landscapes and traditional territory, 334-40; cultural resource centre necessary, 318, 325-26; cultural/spiritual sites, 318, 334-37; definition of cultural resources, 312, 314-15, 359-60; development of archives, ecomuseum, cultural resource centre, 324-26; ethnobotany program, 322-23; gravesites, 334-36, 361; *Heritage Act* and lack of enforcement, 337-40, 361; identification of sites for protection, problems with, 339-40; identity of people and, 312, 316, 318-19, 328, 355; intangible cultural heritage, 328-32; Interim Negotiating Framework for Cultural Resources, 321; land-use study, 323-24; language uniqueness and retention, 323, 326-27, 360; loss of traditional cultural knowledge, 316-19, 360; material culture's importance to community, 316-17, 341-42, 345, 347, 360; museum support for Ktunaxa facility, 326; names, 328, 331-32; in national parks, 339; oral histories, 323-24; ownership concept of intangible heritage, 328-32; ownership concept of tangible heritage, 332-34; ownership concept re territories, sites, graves, 334-37, 361; plant and medicinal knowledge, 330-31; rationales for protection and repatriation, 316-20; research protocols and ethics, 15-16, 26, 324, 360; residential schools' impact on identity, 317-18, 319, 360; role in transmitting knowledge, 345; songs and dances, 328-30, 331; stories, 315; strategies to protect, 15-16, 26, 312, 320-26, 360; traditional use studies, 315, 322-32; transfer protocols, 319-20. *See also* cultural heritage, intangible; laws (Ktunaxa/Kinbasket); ownership/belonging concept (Ktunaxa/Kinbasket); repatriation (Ktunaxa/Kinbasket)

Kwaday Dan Ts'inchi, 398-99

Kwakiutl. *See* Kwakwa̱ka̱'wakw

Kwakiutl Museum, 69, 88n10

Kwakwa̱ka̱'wakw: case study, 34, 38-39, 491-92; chief's roles in society, 42, 47; 'Na̱mgis Nation, 3, 35-36, 38-39, 77, 449-50; ownership/belonging concept, 47, 50-51, 60-69, 467-68, 473; people and territory, 34-36. *See also* Kwakwa̱ka̱'wakw, cultural heritage; research project; U'mista Cultural Society

Kwakwaka’wakw, cultural heritage: appropriation of images, 79-80; authenticity and appropriation, artist’s perspective, 79-86; commercial art market, 67-68; crests, 64, 79; cultural property, definitions and protection, 39-42; disruption of culture by European settlement, 55-60, 86; family creation stories, 64-65; language importance and revival, 24, 34, 37, 39-40, 42-46, 59-60, 86; loss in residential schools, 4, 43-44, 59, 86; masks, 20, 39, 40, 60, 64-65, 71, 76; names, 39, 64; ownership/belonging concept, 47, 50-51, 60-69, 73, 467-68, 473; petroglyphs, 42; priorities for protection, 40-42; protection of lands, harvesting areas, heritage sites, 42; revival of, 33-34, 41, 60-62; role of Canadian law and government in protecting, 80-86; stories, 46, 50, 51, 56, 64-65; strategies for protection, 41-42; traditions around “belonging,” 63-65, 467-68, 473; traditions dynamic and changing, 65-69; transfers and transfer ceremonies, 46-47, 50-51, 63, 65, 86. *See also* cultural heritage, intangible; Kwak’wala language; laws (Kwakwaka’wakw); potlatch (Kwakwaka’wakw); repatriation (Kwakwaka’wakw); songs and dances (Kwakwaka’wakw); U’mista Cultural Society

Kwakwaka’wakw Centre for Language and Culture in Community (KCLCC), 36, 45

Kwak’wala language: importance to culture, 24-25, 34, 37, 39-40, 42-43; link with ceremonies, 25, 42-43, 61; retention and revival efforts, 25, 34, 37, 44-46; suppression due to potlatch ban, 59-60; suppression in residential schools, 43-44, 59, 86

Lake Cowichan First Nation, 152

languages (aboriginal): assimilationist policies of government, 27, 43-44, 59, 86, 269-70, 319, 418-19, 451-52; Blackfoot, 205, 246-47; elimination the goal of government, 448; endangered state, 417, 418-20, 438n6; essence of culture and identity, 14, 24-25, 417, 420-25, 452-53; Haida language, 395, 423; Halkomelem language (Hul’qumi’num), 151; Heiltsuk, 423-24; implications of language loss, 420-25; intergenerational transmission crucial for survival, 419; Inuktitut, 418, 429-31; Kainai/Blood, 246-49, 454-55; Ktunaxa/Kinbasket, 323, 326-27, 360; Kwak’wala (Kwakwaka’wakw), 24-25, 34, 36-37, 39-40, 42-46, 59-61, 86; potlatch ban and language suppression, 53, 58-60; practical vs. symbolic functions of language, 417, 437n2; redress for language loss, 459-60; residential schools and language loss, 43-44, 59, 86, 269-70, 319, 418-19, 451-52; Salish, 423; Secwepemctsin (Shuswap), 419, 422; Skinnipiikani, 267-70, 306-7, 453-54; Wakashan, 423. *See also* languages (aboriginal), protection and revitalization; and *under individual First Nations*, cultural heritage

languages (aboriginal), protection and revitalization: Aboriginal Languages Initiative, 394-95; aboriginal place names project of government, 395; Adams Lake First Nation immersion program, 419; “banking” of linguistic knowledge, 417, 432-33; “colonization of consciousness” or intellectual appropriation, 434-35, 436, 460; Cree language in agreements, 418, 430-31; Daghida Project for Dene Suline language, 394; FirstVoices project, 434; funding of language protection programs (BC), 431; Haida Nation Skidegate Immersion Program, 395; intergenerational transmission, 417-18, 432; for Kwakwaka’wakw language (*see also* Kwak’wala language), 34, 36, 37, 42-46; language and information repatriation, 38-39, 45-46, 77-78; legal protections in place, 425-26; legislative and legal strategies for protection, 427-32; “linguistic theft” and intellectual property rights, 433-34; Musqueam efforts, 394; problems in language restoration, 427-28, 432-33; restoration among adults and caregivers, 417; teaching methodologies, 435-36; translation of agreements, 436; vitality of, 418. *See also individual First Nation languages, e.g.,* Kwak’wala language

laws (Canadian): benefits and detriments of cultural heritage laws, 8; claims process and conflict of interest, 85-86; export laws, 2, 81-83, 379, 382-83; failure to address indigenous peoples’ rights, 1; First Nations’ preference for indigenous laws, 5; inadequacy of existing laws, 84; intellectual property (*see* intellectual property law [Canadian]);

ownership (*see* ownership concept [Canadian]); "parallel reciprocal recognition spaces," 466, 478-82; precedence over aboriginal laws, 19, 249, 297-98, 470-72, 475-76, 477, 485n22; "recognition space" for aboriginal law and culture, 476-78. *See also* Canadian government; cultural heritage, protection; intellectual property law (Canadian); respect; *and* cultural heritage *under individual First Nations; and specific laws, e.g., Act for the Gradual Civilization of the Indian Tribes in the Canadas*

laws (Canadian), protection of cultural heritage: Canadian vs. First Nation concept of ownership, 468-72; *Cemeteries Act,* 196; complexity and need for caution in formulating, 236-37, 239-41, 252; in conjunction with Skinnipiikani/Nitsiitapii/*Nitooii* laws, 258-61, 279-80, 304-5; current legislation dated and inadequate, 1-2, 4-5; failure to enforce, 23-24; *Heritage Conservation Act,* 178-81, 193, 195-96, 337-39, 361; land claims issues, 175-78; law reform needed, 353-59; legal action to protect High Falls area, 401-4; legal protection of indigenous languages, 425-32; "parallel reciprocal recognition spaces," 466, 476-82; recognition of indigenous legal terms, 92-93; *Repatriation Act,* 238-39; role of Canadian law and government, 80-86

laws (First Nations): Creator the force behind law, 152, 222, 261, 283-86, 306, 308; culturally bounded, 5-6; First Nations' preference over Canadian law, 5; impact of *Indian Act,* 20; need for recognition of validity, 93; oral nature of, 25; precedence of Canadian laws, 19, 249, 297-98, 470-72, 475-76, 477, 485n22; on proper use of cultural heritage, 25-26; "recognition space" provided by government for aboriginal law and culture, 476-78; respect for (*see also* respect), 18-20; role of potlatch, 50-51, 60. *See also* laws *(individual First Nations); also under individual First Nations,* cultural heritage; ownership/belonging concept; repatriation. *Laws and protocols are discussed under specific entries, such as adawx;* burial customs; crests; names; songs and dances; transfers

laws (Gitksan): about oral histories, 95; complexity in kinship-based society, 105-6; concept of cultural property, 92-93; concept of intellectual property, 114-15; constitutional law, 93-94, 97, 101, 105-6, 111-12; constitutional role of cultural objects, 6-7, 93, 97, 111-12; on display of images, 101-2; individual vs. collective possessions, 19-20, 108-9, 111; legal culture/order, 92-95; legal matters and feasts, 96, 101; on marriage, 105; on names, 96-101; nature of, 96-97; people defined by law, 97; physical possession of objects vs. right to display, 97, 98-101, 110-11; on repatriation/use of cultural objects, 93-94, 106; role of *adaawk* and feasts, 109-10; songs, protection of, 96; on territorial rights and feasts, 117-23; on use of crest images *(ayuks),* 106-7, 111. *See also adawx* (or *adaawk*) (Gitksan and Tsimshian oral histories); Gitksan (Gitxsan) First Nation, cultural heritage; laws (First Nations); Luuxhon, House of; ownership/belonging concept (Gitksan); potlatch (Gitksan)

laws (Hul'qumi'num): based on principle of reciprocity between living and ancestors, 160-62, 198; based on principle of respect due to ancestors, 157-60, 198; definition of "customary law," 199n1; law of avoidance (of burial grounds, human remains, funerary artifacts), 167-72, 198; law of inherited right to care for the dead, 162-64, 169, 172, 198; law of non-disturbance of ancient sites and remains, 165-67, 172, 177-78, 198; protecting cultural heritage by amending existing legislation, 194-96; protecting cultural heritage by defining aboriginal rights in court, 196-97; protecting cultural heritage by developing new Canadian legislation, 196; protecting cultural heritage through treaty negotiations, 190-94; provincial laws undermining customary laws, 178-81, 190; respect and care of deceased as family obligations, 160-62, 172, 192, 198; times of day for living to be outside, 170-71. *See also* archaeological sites (Hul'qumi'num); burial customs (Hul'qumi'num); Hul'qumi'num Treaty Group (HTG), cultural heritage; ownership/belonging (Hul'qumi'num)

laws (Kainai/Blood): Creator the force behind law, 222, 225-26; on names, 248; need for mutual respect in repatriation, 239; need for respect for traditional laws, 239; protocols regarding human remains, 236, 241-42; respect and reconciliation with other external laws, 210-11, 236-41; on songs and their transfer and protection, 248-49; on teepee designs, 229-30; on title, requirements for valid transfer, 228-33; on transfer of medicine bundles, 19, 206, 225-28, 229-31, 248-49, 252. *See also* laws (First Nations); Kainai First Nation (Blood Tribe), cultural heritage; medicine bundles (Kainai/Blood); ownership/belonging concept (Kainai/Blood); repatriation (Kainai/Blood); transfers and transfer ceremonies (Kainai/Blood)

laws (Ktunaxa/Kinbasket): concepts, 353-54, 364n71; on inheritance, 333; need for formalization by Ktunaxa, 357-58, 361; obstacles to practise of, 354; songs, 328-30, 331; on use and transfer, 319-20. *See also* laws (First Nations); Ktunaxa/Kinbasket Tribal Council (KKTC), cultural heritage; ownership/belonging concept (Ktunaxa/Kinbasket)

laws (Kwakwa̱ka̱'wakw): access to resources, 39; inheritance, 63; names, 39, 64; stories, 46, 50, 51, 56, 64-65; territorial rights, 47, 60-61. *See also* Kwakwa̱ka̱'wakw, cultural heritage; ownership/belonging concept (Kwakwa̱ka̱'wakw); potlatch (Kwakwa̱ka̱'wakw); transfers and transfer ceremonies (Kwakwa̱ka̱'wakw)

laws (Luuxhon) on intellectual property, 97, 98, 100-2, 106-7, 110-11

laws (Skinnipiikani-Nitsiitapii): acquiring transferred rights and authority for Skinnipiikani practices, 259-61; advisory and adjudication authority, 278-79, 301-2, 307; band council vs. ceremonial society authority, 15, 302-4, 309; belief in and fear of the Creator force behind law, 283-84, 285-86; Canadian denial of Nitsiitapii law, 297-98; Canadian laws more respected or "feared," 280; Canadian non-payment of *Siikapistaan,* 258, 298-99; creation stories key sources of legal order, 274-75, 307; on display of medicine bundle contents, 371; means of protecting rights and resources, 286; *Nitooii* (dual understandings), 259-60, 479; Nitsiitapii, definition of, 259; oral-based performative practice, 261, 453; oral law, written law, and practice, 261; "parallel recognition spaces," 479-80; positioning and paralleling with regard to Canadian law, 300-1, 304-5, 479-80; requirement to practise and live by the law, 259; songs as indicators of rights, 299-300, 309. *See also* laws (First Nations); Skinnipiikani First Nation, cultural heritage; ownership/belonging concept (Skinnipiikani); Skinnipiikani principles on property and law; respect; transfers (Skinnipiikani)

Leather, Angeline, 383-84

Leer, Jeff, 423

Lenihan, James, 136

Little Dog Thunder Medicine Pipe, 371

Long Time Medicine Bundle repatriation, 217-20

Lubicon Lake First Nation, 212, 369. *See also* "Spirit Sings" exhibit

Ludwig, Katie, 92, 95

Luuxhon, House of: *adawx* on meeting with Nisga'a ancestors, 125-27; case study and interview questions, 11, 95, 491-92; chief's responsibilities, 19-20, 101, 104, 108-9; community partner in research, 3; cultural property, different meanings of, 92-93, 108; house possessions held in trust by chiefs, 101, 111, 104, 108-9; identification of appropriate authority, 16; individual vs. collective possessions, 19-20, 108-9, 111; intellectual property, 97, 98, 100-2, 106-7, 110-11; names, as intangible property, 96-102; nature of law, 96-97; *naxnox* masks, 103-4; oral histories *(adaawk)*, link with ownership of territory/images, 103-4, 105-7, 109-10; ownership, belonging, and identity, 107-8; physical possession of objects vs. right to display, 97, 98-101, 110-11; protection of songs and dances, 96; regalia, 102-4; repatriation of cultural heritage, 20, 93-94, 97, 106, 110-11; role of *adaawk* and feasts, 103-4, 105-7, 109-10; threats to and protection of historical/ceremonial sites, 109, 110. *See also* Gitksan (Gitxsan) First Nation, cultural heritage

Lyackson First Nation, 152, 153

***M**abo* decision (Australia, 1992), 476-77

Macdonald, John A., 136

Manitoba Museum, 376-77

Many Guns, Herman, 279, 280-81, 467

Maori language (Te Reo Maori), 428-29

marriage laws, regarding, 94, 105-6

Marsden, Namaste, 140-41

Marsden, Solomon, 118-19, 123-24
masks, False Face mask (Mohawk), 369-70
masks, *naxnox* (Luuxhon), 103-4
masks (Kwakwa̲ka̲'wakw): inalienable part of whole protocol, 39, 64-65; long-term loan from Museum of Anthropology (UBC), 75-76; rights to, 40; for tourists and collectors, 60; transfers, 20; Transformation Mask, 76
Mathews, Arthur (T'enimgyet), 115-16, 119-20, 122, 142-45
medicine bundles (Kainai/Blood): animate and spiritual nature, 203, 205-7; communal property with individuals as caretakers, 224-27; duty to repatriate, 207; efforts to repatriate, 203-5; inseparability of associated elements, 207, 230-31, 250, 255n51; Long Time Medicine Bundle return, 217-20; and *NAGPRA* definition of sacred, 221; ownership issues with Denver Arts Museum, 216-17, 220-22; protocols re transfer, 19, 206, 225-28, 229-31; requirements for valid transfer, 228-33; *Siikapistaan* process, 226-27; societies responsible for, 207, 233; territorial origins discernible, 232, 234-35; transfer of cultural/spiritual knowledge, 203, 205, 250
medicine bundles (Siksika), 383-84
medicine bundles (Skinnipiikani), 260, 264-65
Menzies, Archibald, 132
methodology. *See* research project; *and under individual First Nations*
Mi'kmaq First Nation, 396
Miller, J.R., 137
Mitchell, Mabel, 159, 171, 186
Mithun, Marianne, 421
Modeste, Ross, 160, 167, 168, 175, 180, 184, 188
Mohawk Bands of Kahnawake, Akwesasne and Kanesatake v. Glenbow, 369-70
Mohawk Nations, 369-70, 418, 430
Mookakin Foundation (Kainai/Blood): aim and mandate, 204-5; community partner in research, 3; development of question sets, 10-11; participation in Alberta repatriation legislation, 5; partnership with Glenbow Museum, 21, 209; successful repatriation efforts, 204-5. *See also* Kainai First Nation (Blood Tribe); research project
Morgan, Guy, 91
Morrison, James, Txawok, 117-18
Mount Newton Crossroads Bowl, *Sddlnewhala,* 382-83
Museum of Anthropology, University of British Columbia, 75-76, 381
Museum of Archaeology and Ethnology, Simon Fraser University, 382-83
Museum of the American Indian (US), 55, 69-70
museums: activities re First Nation collaborations, recording and preserving cultural heritage, 368-69; artifact exhibition in contravention of Hul'qumi'num law, 183-84; attitudes of indigenous peoples toward, role of, 21-22; cultural insensitivity re Skinnipiikani protocols, 298-99; cultural sensitivity training re Blackfoot cultural practice, 214-15; gratitude for preserving cultural heritage, 21, 208, 252-53, 342; Kainai/Blood's building of relationships with, 208-9, 212-17; Ktunaxa/Kinbasket relations with, 342-46; morals and values of greater significance than aboriginal morals and values, 298-99; oral history required for repatriation, 106; ownership concepts vs. Kainai/Blood, 220-21, 224-26; relations with First Nations re repatriation, 21, 27, 367-69 (*see also under* repatriation); repatriation policies, 368-69, 372-80, 407n39; respect necessary for elders and their knowledge, 208-9, 216-17; responsibility to return indigenous items, 74-75; retention of original objects vs. replica, 97, 110-11. *See also* Task Force Report on Museums and First Peoples; *and specific museums, e.g.,* Glenbow Museum
Musqueam First Nation, 394

Na-cho Nyak Dun, First Nation of, 384
names. *See under individual First Nations,* cultural heritage, *e.g.,* Gitksan First Nation, cultural heritage
'Na̲mgis Nation (of the Kwakwa̲ka̲'wakw): banning of potlatches, 35, 449-50; case study methodology, 38-39; children in residential schools, 35; cultural research through U'mista, 3, 36; people and territory, 35-36; research protocols, 38, 77. *See also* potlatch (Kwakwa̲ka̲'wakw); repatriation (Kwakwa̲ka̲'wakw); research project; U'mista Cultural Society
Nanoose First Nation, 189
Nanoose Indian Band v. British Columbia, 179, 196-97
National Museum of Man. *See* Canadian Museum of Civilization

National Museum of the American Indian, 55, 69-70
Native American Graves Protection and Repatriation Act (*NAGPRA,* US), 8, 195; application only to American tribes, 222, 353; First Nations' property rights over ancestral human remains, 195; guidelines on cultural patrimony and repatriation, 220-21; impetus for tribes to enact own policies, 358. *See also under individual First Nations,* cultural heritage, *e.g.,* Kainai First Nation (Blood Tribe), cultural heritage
Native American Languages Act of 1992 (US), 427
Native Title Act (Australia, 1993), 476-77
naxnox (spirit dances), 103-4, 120-22
Newman, Vera, 40, 43, 48-49, 53, 62, 63, 65, 72, 80, 420
Nicholas, John, 326, 331, 335, 337, 339, 343, 480
Nipissing First Nation Land Code, 392
Nisga'a Final Agreement: control by Nisga'a over cultural heritage on Nisga'a lands, 190, 192; Gitanyow court challenge, 104-5; precedence of Canadian laws, 470-72, 485n22; provision re artifacts in museums, 385-86; provisions for protection of cultural heritage, 386-87
Nisga'a First Nation, 106-7, 111, 125-27
Niitsitapiisini: Our Way of Life (museum exhibit), 213
Nitooii (dual understandings, Skinnipiikani), 259-60, 479
Nitsiitapii (Blackfoot) law, 259-61, 301. *See also* laws (Skinnipiikani-Nitsiitapii); Skinnipiikani principles on property and law
Norris, Sally, 159

O*fficial Languages Act* (Canada), 429
Official Languages Act (Northwest Territories), 429
Ojibway Nations, 418. *See also* Poplar Point Ojibway First Nation
Oka, Mary Louise, 206, 207, 208, 211, 217, 220, 225, 226, 232, 235, 240, 248
Old Person, Earl, 371
Oldman River Cultural Centre, 3, 261
oral histories, See *adawx* (or *adaawk*) (Gitksan and Tsimshian oral histories); *and under individual First Nations*
ownership/belonging concept (First Nation): gift exchange system vs. Canadian commodity exchange, 474-75; inalienability and inseparability of cultural heritage, 472-76, 482; "owning as belonging" vs. "owning as property" (Western concept), 4, 5, 6-7, 465-68, 472-76; part of crisis of power with Canada, 472. *See also* ownership/belonging concept *for individual First Nations*
ownership/belonging concept (Gitksan), 19-20, 101, 107-9, 111
ownership/belonging concept (Hul'qumi'num), 158-60, 191-92, 195-96
ownership/belonging concept (Kainai/Blood): breadth of meaning of cultural property, 223; custodial vs. personal/proprietary rights, 225-28; Kainai vs. museums and governments, 220-21, 224-26; private vs. communal ownership, 19, 224-25; property rights in land unknown to Kainai, 223
ownership/belonging concept (Ktunaxa/Kinbasket): *Heritage Act* and lack of enforcement, 337-40, 361; influences on, 327-28; for intangible heritage (names, songs, medicinal knowledge), 328-32; notions of belonging and respect, 328; for tangible heritage (community, family, individual interests), 19, 332-34; traditional territory, sites, and gravesites, 334-37, 361
ownership/belonging concept (Kwakwa̲ka̲'wakw): repatriation and Canadian views of, 73; rights and entitlements, 47, 50-51, 60-61, 62-63, 65; traditions around "belonging," 63-65, 467-68, 473; traditions dynamic and changing, 65-69
ownership/belonging concept (Luuxhon): individual vs. collective possessions, 19-20, 108-9, 111; ownership, belonging, and identity, 107-8; ownership of territory/images, link with oral histories *(adaawk),* 103-4, 105-7, 109-10; physical possession of objects vs. right to display, 97, 98-101, 110-11
ownership/belonging concept (Skinnipiikani): collective keepership of bundles, 264-65; collective vs. personal property, 291; reciprocal nature of *Siikapistaan* vs. Canadian understanding, 295-96; rights to use of lands and resources, 284-86; *Siikapistaan,* 260, 288-89, 292-99, 474; tools of cultural transmission as communal property, 288
ownership concept (Canadian): commodity exchange vs. aboriginal gift exchange system, 474-75; First Nations'

inseparability of cultural heritage, 472-76; "owning as property" vs. First Nations' "owning as belonging," 4, 5, 6-7, 465-68, 472-76; "parallel reciprocal recognition spaces," 466, 478-82; part of crisis of power with First Nations, 472; "recognition space" for aboriginal law and culture, 476-78; severability of things, 467, 474-75; understanding of *Siikapistaan* vs. First Nations', 295-96; view of repatriation of Kwakwa̲ka̲'wakw items, 73; vs. First Nation concept, 20; vs. Kainai concept, 220-21, 224-26

Panel on the Ecological Integrity of Canada's National Parks (2000), 245
Papaschase First Nation, 400
Pard, Allan, 278, 301
Parks Canada, 245-46, 393
Pasco, Juanita, 41-42, 68-69, 72-73, 74
Paterson, Robert K., 10, 372-73
Pauingassi First Nation, 378-80
Pearson, Noel, 476-77
Penelakut Tribe, 152, 153
Peter, Ray, 163, 167, 179, 184, 189
Peters, Ruby, 154-56, 162-63, 177
petroglyphs, 42, 395-96
Pettipas, Katherine, 449-50
Phillip, Nelson, 327
Pierre, Joe, 319, 320, 333, 327, 331, 343, 347, 358
Piikani First Nation, 21, 259, 261. *See also* Skinnipiikani First Nation
Poomaksin (transfer protocol, Skinnipiikani): action, an element of protocol, 267, 271-72, 307; definition, 260; example of *Nitooii* (dual understandings), 479; governing rights to tangible and intangible cultural material, 260; integrated, inalienable elements of transfer protocol (language, venue, song, action), 272-74, 307, 453-54; language, an element of protocol, 267-70, 306-7, 453-54; need for Canadian recognition, 259; reciprocity of, 474; rights pertaining to transfer practices, 260; *Siikapistaan* (reciprocating) as necessary element, 260, 288-89, 292-99, 474; Skinnipiikani principles on, 259, 260, 288-89, 295-96; song, an element of protocol, 267, 272, 307; venue specificity, an element of protocol, 267, 270-71, 307
Poplar Point Ojibway First Nation, 401-4
potlatch (Gitksan), 135-38, 449-50
potlatch (Kwakwa̲ka̲'wakw): Angerman, Sergeant, 53, 54, 56, 84, 85; ban, harms flowing from and traumatic effects, 55-60; ban, impact on continuity of laws, language, culture, 58-60; banning of, 53-55, 58, 449-50; bringing together of community, 52-53, 60; claim for compensation for banning, 37, 84-85; description, 47-49; drama and magic in, 50; as educational and legal system, 50-51, 60; facility to exhibit potlatch items, 36; governance and management of land rights, 60; importance of, 46-53; integral to culture, 34, 40, 46-53, 60-62, 449; link with Kwak'wala language, 25, 43, 61; management of rights and entitlements, 47, 50-51, 60-61; protocols, 48-49; repatriation of potlatch material, 69-76, 86-87; revival of culture and, 34, 47, 60-62, 70-72; sharing of history, 40, 49-50, 60; specific claim (against Canada), 84-87; spiritual and healing aspect, 51-52, 60; tangible and intangible aspects, 34; traditions dynamic and changing, 65-69; transfers of entitlements at, 46-47, 50-51, 65; Village Island potlatch (1921), 54-55. *See also* repatriation (Kwakwa̲ka̲'wakw)
potlatch (Tsimshian), 134-38, 449-50
Povinelli, Elizabeth, 477
Powell, Superintendent, 136, 137
power imbalances: between First Nations and government, 468; precedence of Canadian laws over aboriginal, 249, 297-98, 470-72, 475-76, 477, 485n22; proposal for parallel reciprocal "recognition spaces," 466, 478-82; respect and legal relations, 470-72
Presbyterian Church, 444
Principles and Guidelines for the Protection of the Heritage of Indigenous Peoples (UNESCO), 191
Pritchard, John, 38-39, 53-54, 57, 58, 84, 85
property, concept of. *See* cultural property; *and under individual First Nations, e.g.,* ownership/belonging concept (Gitksan); Gitksan (Gitxsan) First Nation, cultural heritage
Proposed Act Respecting Protection of Archaeological Heritage in Canada, 28n4
protection. *See* cultural heritage, protection
Provincial Museum of Alberta (PMA), 213-14. *See also* Royal Alberta Museum
Provost, Pat, 263-64, 276-77

Quebec and aboriginal language rights, 430-31

Quechua language, 428

Reed, Hayter, 449
repatriation: dealers and private sales, 382-84; evolving relationships between museums and First Nations, 21, 367-69; export laws and, 82-83; funding problems, 21-22; international and US, 216-17, 220-23, 321-22, 352-53, 370-72, 380-81, 382-84 *(see also Cultural Property Export and Import Act; Native American Graves Protection and Repatriation Act)*; land claims and treaty negotiations, 190-94, 320-21, 360, 373, 384-88; litigation (Canada), 369-70; museum policies, 372-77 *(see also individual museums)*; oral material and information, 38-39, 45-46, 77-78; problems with competing claims, 377-80; reasons for repatriation, 18-21; as redress for harm to cultural heritage, 460; sacred ceremonial items, 20; strategies for, 26-27. *See also First Nations Sacred Ceremonial Objects Repatriation Act;* museums; Task Force Report on Museums and First Peoples; *entries for specific museums and individual First Nations; entries under* repatriation
repatriation, ancestral remains: costs, 241-42, 335-36, 352-53; guidelines of Canadian Museums Association, 351-52; guidelines of Task Force, 351-52, 373; Haida (*see* Haida First Nation); Hul'qumi'num (*see* burial customs [Hul'qumi'num]); Kitigan Zibi Anishinabeg First Nation's attempts, 396-97; Ktunaxa/Kinbasket, 335-36, 349-52, 361; Kwaday Dan Ts'inchi, 398-99; protocols regarding human remains (Kainai/Blood), 236, 241-42; reburial (Nanoose), 189; respect for, 22-23, 42; Wikwemikong remains, 397. *See also* Task Force Report on Museums and First Peoples; *individual museums*
repatriation (Gitksan), 93-94, 106. *See also* repatriation (Luuxhon)
repatriation (Hul'qumi'num), 182-84
repatriation (Kainai/Blood): ancestral remains, 236, 241-42; building relationships with museums/governments, 208-9, 212-17, 252; costs of, 212, 252; difficulties with Denver Arts Museum, 216-17, 220-22; elders as educators and negotiators re material culture, 215-17; fears of Kainai/Blood about, 236-38; fears of museums about, 233-35; Kainai/Blood participation in legislative reform, 236-41, 252; legislative intervention, 208-12, 238-41, 252; oral histories as proof of title, 232-33; ownership/belonging concepts of Kainai vs. museums/governments, 220-23, 224-26; priorities to repatriate sacred, ceremonial, 205, 223; from private collections, 240, 256n60; protocols regarding human remains, 236, 241-42; requirements for valid transfer of legal title, 228-33; respect due to elders and spiritual advisors, 208-9, 216-17, 221-22; return of Long Time Medicine Bundle, 217-20. *See also First Nations Sacred Ceremonial Objects Repatriation Act;* Glenbow Museum; Mookakin Foundation (Kainai/Blood); *and entries for* Kainai/Blood *under* laws, medicine bundles, ownership/belonging concepts; *Siikapistaan;* transfers
repatriation (Ktunaxa/Kinbasket): ancestral remains, 335-36, 349-52, 361; determination of ownership, 318, 332-33, 361; development of archives, ecomuseum, cultural resource centre, 324-26; elders' expertise on care and interpretation of material culture, 332-33, 345, 346, 360-61; elders' expertise re material culture, 346; importance to community, 316-17, 341-42, 345, 347, 360; for improved cultural identity and self-esteem, 318-19; international repatriations, 352-53; laws for protection, 356-57, 358-59; letter-writing campaign, 321-22; materials sacred or spiritual in nature, 340-42; moral obligation to return items, 342, 361; museums and, 342-46, 347-49, 361; need to prevent cultural appropriation, 319-20; part of treaty negotiations, 312, 320-21, 360; priority to repatriate sacred, ceremonial, 319; private collectors, 346; protection of archaeological sites, 318; rationale for protection and repatriation, 316-20; Repatriation Advisory Committee, 322; respectful relations needed between natives and non-natives, 356-57. *See also* Ktunaxa/Kinbasket Tribal Council (KKTC), cultural heritage; laws (Ktunaxa/Kinbasket); ownership/belonging concept (Ktunaxa/Kinbasket); transfers (Ktunaxa/Kinbasket)
repatriation (Kwakwaka'wakw): from British Museum, 76, 90n75; from Canadian Museum of Civilization, 55, 69,

73-74; challenges to successful repatriation, 75; determination of ownership, 73-74; export laws and, 82-83; family and community entitlements, 73-74; importance for emotional well-being, 71; importance of confiscated potlatch material, 62, 86-87; information and language, 38-39, 45-46, 77-78; material housed in museum-like facilities, 69, 72, 73, 86, 88n10; from Museum of Anthropology (UBC), 75-76; from National Museum of the American Indian, 69-70; Nowell blanket, 82-83; potlatch material, 62, 69-76, 86-87; rationale for, 70-73, 77-79; as rectification of injustices from potlatch ban, 70-71, 87; role of U'mista, 36-37, 69, 72-73, 74, 76-77; from Royal Ontario Museum, 69, 73; Transformation Mask, 76; of Village Island Potlatch Collection, 69-76. *See also* laws (Kwakwa̲ka̲'wakw); masks (Kwakwa̲ka̲'wakw); ownership/belonging concept (Kwakwa̲ka̲'wakw); potlatch (Kwakwa̲ka̲'wakw); transfers (Kwakwa̲ka̲'wakw)

repatriation (Luuxhon): application of indigenous law, 93-94; challenges, 107; reasons for, 20, 105; replacement of originals by museums, 97, 110-11. *See also* ownership/belonging concept (Gitksan); repatriation (Gitksan)

repatriation (Skinnipiikani): compensation related to *Siikapistaan* principles, 293; full recognition of Nitsiitapii process needed, 258-59; lack of resources, 292-93; need for *Siikapistaan* for proper transfer, 292-94; songs as indicators of rights, 299-300, 309. *See also entries for* Skinnipiikani *under* laws, medicine bundles, ownership/belonging concept, transfers

Report on Industrial Schools for Indians and Half-Breeds (Davin, 1879), 448

research project: authorship and copyright issues, 12-13, 16-18; challenges, 6-7, 14-18; data analysis, 11-12; First Nation partners, xi-iv, 3; identification of appropriate authorities, 15-16; methodology, 9-14; methodology (Hul'qumi'num), 153-54; methodology (Kainai), 205; methodology (Ktunaxa/Kinbasket), 313; methodology (Luuxhon), 92-95; methodology (Northwest Coast *Adawx* Study), 92-95; methodology *(Poomaksin)*, features of report, 261-62; methodology with 'Na̲mgis (Kwakwa̲ka̲'wakw), 38-39; objectives, 2-3; participatory action research (PAR), 9-10; previous research, 1-2; rights of participants, 14-15; sponsors, 2-3; standard question set, 491-92; terminology challenges, 6-7, 14; themes, 3, 18-20, 20-27

residential schools: aboriginal languages forbidden, 43-44, 59, 86, 269-70, 319, 418-19, 451-52; abuse in, 451-52; assimilationist policy of government, 443-44, 445-49, 451-52; church involvement, 443-44, 448; for "civilization" of aboriginal peoples, 444-45, 446-49; enabling legislation, 447-49; legal options for redress, 456-58; loss of cultural knowledge (Ktunaxa/Kinbasket), 316-18, 319, 360; loss of cultural knowledge (Kwakwa̲ka̲'wakw), 4, 43-44, 59, 86

respect: cursory nature of governmental respect, 470; for different practices of ownership (First Nations vs. Canadian), 467-68, 472-76; for diversity of First Nations' cultures, 280-81, 467; Euro-Canadian notions of, 468-69; First Nations' concept of, 469-70; "parallel reciprocal recognition spaces," 466, 478-82; possibility of mutual respect (First Nations and government), 468; power imbalance in Nisga'a Final Agreement, 470-72; "recognition space" for aboriginal law and culture, 476-78; voluntary humbling of oneself, 469. *See also* ownership/property concept *for First Nations and for Canada*

Rockefeller Brothers Fund, 381

Romaine, Suzanne, 427

Roman Catholic Church, 443-44

Royal Alberta Museum: Long Time Medicine Bundle repatriation, 217-20; repatriation of sacred ceremonial items, 238; Scriver Blackfoot Collection, 370-72. *See also* Provincial Museum of Alberta (PMA)

Royal British Columbia Museum: agreement re Nisga'a artifacts, 385-86, 470-71; care of Kwaday Dan Ts'inchi, 398; negotiations for return of Gitanyow artifacts, 107; publication of Gitanyow's legal order, 97; repatriation policies, 352, 375-76; replicas of crest poles removed from Gitanyow, 97, 110

Royal Commission on Aboriginal Peoples (RCAP), 1, 196, 242, 421

Royal Ontario Museum, 55, 73, 369-70, 397

Russell, Donald (Luuxhon), 108, 109-10
Russell, Herb, Ts'iiwa', 104-7, 108, 110
Russell, Victoria, Amsisa'ytxw, 107-9, 110, 111-12

Saanich First Nation, 382-83
Saanich Native Heritage Society, 383
sacred, concept of. *See* spirituality
Salish language, 423
Sanborn, Andrea, 38-40, 51, 58, 60, 71, 73, 76, 81, 467
Sapir, Edward, 421
Sarcee First Nation, 368
Scott, Duncan Campbell, 53, 55, 84
Scriver, Bob, 370-71
Scriver, Thaddeus Emery, 370
Scriver Blackfoot Collection, 370-72
Secwepemctsin (Shuswap) language, 419, 422
Selkirk First Nation Final Agreement, 388
Seymour, Charles, 158, 160, 180, 183, 185, 483
Shovar, Lucille, 337, 338, 355, 357
Shuswap Indian Band. *See* Ktunaxa/Kinbasket Tribal Council
Siikapistaan (reciprocation) (Skinnipiikani): compensation related to *Siikapistaan* principles, 293; creation of perpetual obligation, 295-96; definition of, 260; necessary for *Poomaksin* (rights and transfer protocol), 260, 288-89, 295-96, 474; need for Canadian recognition of, 259; need for in repatriation of material, 292-94; negotiability and deferral of, 296-97; public witnessing of, 294-95; reciprocal "consideration" for rights, 260, 293-94, 295; relative making (securing self-regulated social system), 296-97; *Sikapistaaway* (practice of giving *Siikapistaan),* 260, 288-89; violations of *Siikapistaan* by Canadian government and museums, 258, 298-99
Siikapistaan ("tokens of personal offerings") (Kainai/Blood), 226-27
Sikapistaaway (practice of giving *Siikapistaan)* (Skinnipiikani), 260, 288-89
Siksika First Nation, 383-84
Singleton, Jon, 379-80
Skeetchestn Band, 391
Skeetchestn Band Territorial Heritage Conservation Law, 391
Skidegate Immersion Program (Haida language revitalization), 395
Skinnipiikani First Nation: case study, 258-62, 279-80, 491-92; member of Blackfoot Confederacy, 258; Nitsiitapii (how Blackfoot recognize themselves), 259; Piikani, 21, 259, 261. *See also* Brave Dog Society
Skinnipiikani First Nation, cultural heritage: *ahmitoosiman* (smudge practices), 260-61; Blackfoot language, 205, 246-47; language as element of transfer protocol, 267-70, 306-7, 453-54; medicine bundles, 260, 264-65; medicines, 260, 267, 294; names, 267; ownership concept, 264-65, 284-86, 291; protection, 290-91, 293; repatriation, 258-59, 292-94, 299-300, 309; *Siikapistaan* (reciprocation), 260, 288-89, 293-99, 474; Skinnipiikani language, 267-70, 306-7, 453-54; songs as element of transfer protocol, 267, 272-74, 307, 453; songs as markers of rights, 299-300, 309; stories, 267, 274-75; traditional age-grade societies, 260, 266-68. *See also* Brave Dog Society; cultural heritage, intangible; laws (Skinnipiikani-Nitsiitapii); ownership/belonging concept (Skinnipiikani); *Poomaksin;* repatriation (Skinnipiikani); Skinnipiikani principles on property and law; Skinnipiikani principles on rights and transfer practices; transfers (Skinnipiikani)
Skinnipiikani principles on property and law: adjudication and conflict resolution authority, 301-2, 309; authority of Skinnipiikani law re procedures, 300-1, 309; authority to speak of practices, 290-91, 308; band council vs. ceremonial society authority, 302-4, 309; concept of "Nitsiitapii property," 291, 308; Nitsiitapii authority over property, 290-91; Nitsiitapii law as parallel to Canadian law, 304-5; non-disturbance of sacred places, 283-86, 308; oral claims to rights require transferred rights and practice experience, 289-90, 308; political recognition of diversity of First Nations, 280-81, 308; recognition of Nitsiitapii (Blackfoot) law, 259-61, 300-1; recognition of *Siikapistaan,* 291-99, 308-9; refusal to speak about something to which one has no rights, 282-83, 285-86, 308; rights of relationship to cultural material understood in context of transfer, 287-89, 308; rights to use of lands and resources, 284-86; Skinnipiikani control over research, culture, and heritage, 281-82; songs as markers of rights, 299-300, 309; use of property language, 259. *See also* laws (Skinnipiikani-Nitsiitapii)

Skinnipiikani principles on rights and transfer practices: action as dimension of transfer protocol, 267, 271-72, 307; collective keepership of bundles, 260, 264-65, 306; education of younger generations re transferred rights, 275-78, 307; elders ("grandparents") as advisors and adjudicators, 278-79, 307; integrated, inalienable elements of transfer protocol (language, venue, song, action), 272-74, 307, 453-54; invoking support, 263-64, 306; in Kutoyiis, Blood Clot stories, 275, 307; in Napi (Trickster) creation stories, 274-75, 307; *Poomaksin* (rights and transfer protocol), 259, 260, 288-89, 295-96, 474; song as dimension of transfer protocol, 267, 272, 307; specialized language a dimension of transfer protocol, 267-70, 306-7, 453-54; transfer protocols of "property" (representations of rights), 267, 272, 306; trust and kindness, 265-66, 306; venue specificity as dimension of transfer protocol, 267, 270-71, 307. *See also* transfers (Skinnipiikani)

Sliammon First Nation Crown Lands Referral Tool Box, 393

Smith, Louisa, 380

Sna-naw-as First Nation, 177

Snuneymuxw First Nation, 189, 395-96

Social Sciences and Humanities Research Council of Canada (SSHRC), 10

songs and dances: on acknowledgment of rights through song, 479; association with concept of "belonging," 7; role in ceremonial practice, 25; transfer of, 20

songs and dances (Ktunaxa/Kinbasket), 328-30, 331

songs and dances (Kwakwa̱ka̱'wakw): appropriation and copyright concerns, 42, 83; composers, 63-64; concept and relationships of "belonging," 7, 64-65; entitlements and rights, 49, 60, 62-63, 67-69; inalienable part of whole protocol, 39, 64-65; as intangible cultural property, 39-40; integral part of ceremonies, 46, 49-52, 61, 62-64; as part of family identity, 64; permission needed to borrow, 65-67; transfer of, 46-47, 50-51, 65; as way of reviving Kwak'wala language, 45

songs and dances (Luuxhon), 96

songs (Kainai), 229, 230-31, 247-49

songs *(limx'oy)* and dances (Gitksan), 116, 479

songs (Skinnipiikani): element of transfer protocol, 267, 272-74, 307, 453; as markers of rights, 299-300, 309

South Pender Island development, 177-78, 189

Sparrow, R. v., 429-30

Specific Claims Resolution Act (2003), 85-86

spirit dances. *See naxnox* (spirit dances)

"Spirit Sings" exhibit, 212, 369, 372

spirituality: concern for preservation of, 1; European view vs. First Nation, 5, 133-34. See also *individual First Nations*

Sproat, Gilbert, 136

Stanley, F.G., 445

Statement of Intent: Aboriginal Title Core Territory (Hul'qumi'num Treaty Group), 187

Steinbring, Jack, 378

Stewart, Jane, 442-43

Stó:lō First Nation, 30, 382, 390-91

Stó:lō Nation Heritage Investigation Permit, 390-91

Stó:lō Nation Material Culture Repository, 391

Stone T'xwelatse, 382, 409n100

stories. *See under individual First Nations,* cultural heritage, *e.g.*, Kwakwa̱ka̱'wakw, cultural heritage

Sundance: banning by Canadian government, 449-51, 486n35; of the Kainai First Nation (Blood Tribe), 11, 203, 205, 250; *Siikapistaan's* intercultural dimension, 297; transfer protocols of "property" (representations of rights) (Skinnipiikani), 267

Supreme Court of Canada: *Delgamuukw* case on ownership of traditional lands, 141-42; fiduciary obligation argument of aboriginal peoples, 430; *K.L.B. v. British Columbia* case on fiduciary obligations of government, 457-58; *Sparrow* case on indigenous language rights, 429-30; *Van der Peet* case on distinctness of aboriginal peoples, 415, 477-78; *Wewaykum* case on fiduciary obligations of government, 457

Svanvik, Peggy, 40, 45

Sweden and Haisla Spirit Pole, 380-81

Sylvester, August, 160, 163, 169, 170, 173, 185

Tamilin, Emma, 33, 49, 50-51, 56-57, 66, 70, 71, 73

Tanner-Kaplash, Sonja, 2

Task Force on Aboriginal Languages and Cultures (TFALC), 395, 419-20, 431

Task Force Report on Museums and First

Peoples (1992): establishment, 212, 369, 372; guidelines for repatriation of ancestral remains, 351-52, 373; impact on museums-First Nations relationships, 252, 344, 368; recommendation re repatriation of sacred items, 204; on repatriation of "sacred items" and "cultural patrimony," 372-73; repatriation principles, 322
Tatshenshini-Alsek Park, 398
Teneese, Margaret, 314, 317-18, 323, 325-26, 329, 336, 338, 342, 344, 348, 353, 356
Theodore Last Star Medicine Pipe Bundle, 370-72
Thirst Dance, 449-51
Thomas, Richard, 158, 187, 188
Thorne, Abner, 159, 165, 181, 184, 185, 473
Three Fires Midewiwin Society, 378-80
Tlicho (Dogrib) Agreement, 384-85, 487, 410n122
totem poles, feast poles, crest poles, 97, 105, 106-7, 116-23, 380-81
traditional knowledge. *See* cultural heritage, intangible; cultural knowledge; elder knowledge
transfer protocols (Ktunaxa/Kinbasket), 319-20
transfers and transfer ceremonies (Kainai/Blood): disposition of ritual objects outside the community, 228-33; language's importance in transfer ceremonies, 247-48, 454; protocols re transfers, 19, 206, 225-28, 229-31, 252; requirements for valid transfer, 205, 228-33; songs and their transfer and protection, 248-49; teepee designs, 229-30; transfer of cultural/spiritual knowledge with medicine bundles, 203, 205, 250. *See also* medicine bundles (Kainai/Blood); *Siikapistaan* (reciprocation) (Skinnipiikani)
transfers and transfer ceremonies (Kwakwa̲ka̲'wakw): among families upon marriage, 63; importance of the potlatch in, 46-47, 50-51, 63, 86; regalia for proper performance, 65
transfers and transfer ceremonies (Skinnipiikani): cultural property, 272; definition of, 260; intellectual/intangible property, 272; language as element of protocol, 267-70, 306-7, 453-54; "property" (representations of rights), 267, 474; *Siikapistaan* as necessary element, 260, 288-89, 292-99, 474; songs and as indicators of rights, 272, 299-300, 309; teepee designs, 272. *See also Poomaksin* (transfer protocol, Skinnipiikani); Skinnipiikani principles on rights and transfer practices
Trickster, The: Bobtail of the Monacan, 31, 366; Clown, 31, 366; Nanabush of the Anishinabek, 365-66; rationale for inclusion in this volume, 8; role in indigenous societies, 8-9, 31, 490; Weget (Raven) of the Gitksan, 366, 415; Wisakedjak, 31, 366
Tsimshian First Nation: *adawx* and identity/history, 115-17; banning by Europeans of the potlatch, 135-38; concept of property as identity, 114-15; defence of territory and identity against Europeans, 138-41, 145-46; encounters with Europeans, 129-33; encounters with other foreign groups, 127-28; Hudson's Bay Company and, 133-34; lack of respect for identity, 146; missionaries' attack on indigenous culture, 134-36; *naxnox* ritual before pole-raising feast, 120-22; pole-raising feasts and acknowledgment of territorial rights, 117-23; principle of respect, 115; trade a central part of economy, 128; Tsimshian vs. European worldview, 133. *See also adawx* (or *adaawk*) (Gitksan and Tsimshian oral histories)
Turning the Page: Forging New Partnerships between Museums and First Peoples, 322. *See also* Task Force Report on Museums and First Peoples (1992)
T'xwelatse, 382

u'mista, 36
U'mista Cultural Centre, 36, 62, 69, 72, 88n10
U'mista Cultural Society: case study involvement, 2-3, 10-11, 38-39; claim vs. Canadian government for breaches of fiduciary duty, 37, 84-85; concern with Canada's export and copyright laws, 81-83; on cooperation of museums, 21; language retention/renewal initiatives, 36, 37, 42-46; mandate and objectives, 35-37; museum facility and care of repatriated items, 72-73, 74; recording of traditional songs and oral history, 78-79; repatriation goals, 20, 36-37; repatriation of potlatch items, 69, 73; research protocols, 26, 77; resource centre on Kwakwa̲ka̲'wakw culture, 77-79; strategies for repatriation, 76-77. *See also* Kwakwa̲ka̲'wakw

United Church, 444
United Nations Educational, Scientific and Cultural Organization (UNESCO): Head-Smashed-In Buffalo Jump as world heritage site, 392; principles for protection of First Nations' cultural heritage, 191
United States: legislation on repatriation of religious material, 204; policy of "civilization" of aboriginal peoples (late 1800s), 447-48; repatriation policy of National Museum of the American Indian, 69-70. See also *Native American Graves Protection and Repatriation Act* (US); repatriation, international and US
Universal Declaration of Human Rights (1948), 425
University of Winnipeg Anthropology Museum, 377-80

***V**an der Peet* case, 415, 477-78
Vancouver, George, 132
Vella, Susan M., 457
Victoria Memorial Museum. *See* Canadian Museum of Civilization
Vuntut Gwichin First Nation, 368, 384, 388

Waitangi Treaty and Tribunal, 428-29
Wamiss, Spruce, 42, 43, 45, 61, 66
Wasden, William, Jr., 24, 39, 40, 41-42, 43, 45, 50, 51, 52, 61, 64, 67-68, 72, 78, 79-80
We Are Our Language (Yukon Government), 421
Weasel Head, Frank, 206, 210-11, 219, 225-26, 228, 229, 236-37, 239, 240, 241, 243, 246-47, 249, 436
Weasel Head, Pat (Mookakin), 203-4
Weasel Moccasin, Dan, 212-13
Webster, Gloria Cranmer, 19, 38, 54-55, 70-71, 73-74
Weiner, James, 477
Wewaykum case, 457
Whitefish Lake First Nation, 392-93
Wikwemikong Heritage Organization, 397
Williams, Glen, 95
Williams, Johnson, Gwinu, 99-100
Williams, Robert, 318, 323, 336, 338, 340
Williams, Stanley, Gwisgyen, 117, 118, 120, 123, 142, 482
Winter, Barbara, 382
Wolf Clan, 94
Writing-on-Stone Provincial Park (rock art), 245-46

Xamlaxyeltxw, 125-27

Yukon, 421, 429
Yukon Umbrella Final Agreement, 384, 387-88

Zepeda, Ofelia, 424

Printed and bound in Canada by Friesens

Set in Stone by Robert Kroeger

Copy editor: Joanne Richardson

Proofreader: Lesley Erickson

Indexer: Pat Buchanan